FROMMER'S

BUDGET TRAVEL GUIDE

COSTA RICA, GUATEMALA & BELIZE ON $35 A DAY '91-'92

by Karl Samson

PRENTICE
HALL
PRESS

D1416608

NEW YORK • LONDON • TORONTO • SYDNEY • TOKYO • SINGAPORE

FROMMER BOOKS

Published by Prentice Hall Press
A division of Simon & Schuster Inc.
15 Columbus Circle
New York, NY 10023

PRENTICE HALL PRESS and colophons are registered trademarks of Simon & Schuster Inc.

ISBN 0-13-337130-1
ISSN 1051-6859

Design by Robert Bull Design
Maps by Geografix Inc.

Manufactured in the United States of America

FROMMER'S COSTA RICA, GUATEMALA & BELIZE ON $35 A DAY

Editor-in-Chief: Marilyn Wood
Senior Editors: Judith de Rubini, Pamela Marshall, Amit Shah
Editors: Alice Fellows, Paige Hughes
Assistant Editors: Suzanne Arkin, Ellen Zucker

CONTENTS

LIST OF MAPS viii

PART ONE: COSTA RICA

1 GETTING TO KNOW COSTA RICA 3

1. Geography, History, and Politics 3
2. Some Cultural Background 9
3. Food and Drink 10
4. Recommended Books 13

SPECIAL FEATURES
- What's Special About Costa Rica 4
- Dateline 5
- Did you know . . . ? 9

2 PLANNING A TRIP TO COSTA RICA 14

1. Information, Entry Requirements, and Money 14
2. When to Go—Climate, Events, and Holidays 16
3. Health, Insurance, and Other Concerns 18
4. What to Pack 18
5. Tips for the Disabled, Seniors, Singles, and Students 19
6. Alternative/Adventure Travel 19
7. Getting There 21
8. Suggested Itineraries 22
9. Getting Around 24
10. Accommodations and Dining Notes 26
11. Enjoying Costa Rica on a Budget 26

SPECIAL FEATURES
- What Things Cost in San José 16
- Costa Rica Calendar of Events 17
- Frommer's Favorite Costa Rica Experiences 23
- Fast Facts—Costa Rica 29

3 SAN JOSÉ 31

1. From a Budget Traveler's Point of View 31
2. Orientation and Getting Around 32
3. Where to Stay 38
4. Where to Eat 44
5. Attractions 49
6. Savvy Shopping 54
7. Evening Entertainment 55

SPECIAL FEATURES
- What's Special About San José 33
- Fast Facts—San José 36

8. Easy Excursions 57
9. Moving On—Travel Services 61

4 GUANACASTE AND THE NORTHWEST 62

1. Monteverde 62
2. Liberia 68
3. Playa del Coco 70
4. Playa Hermosa 73
5. Playas Brasilito, Flamingo, Potrero, and Pan de Azucar 74
6. Playa Tamarindo 77

SPECIAL FEATURES
● *What's Special About the
  Northwest 63*

5 THE PACIFIC COAST 81

1. Puntarenas 81
2. Jacó Beach 85
3. Quepos and Manuel Antonio 89
4. Farther South 97

SPECIAL FEATURES
● *What's Special About the
  Pacific Coast 82*

6 THE CARIBBEAN COAST 98

1. Limón and Tortuguero National
  Park 98
2. Cahuita 102
3. Puerto Viejo 107

SPECIAL FEATURES
● *What's Special About the
  Caribbean Coast 99*

PART TWO: GUATEMALA

7 GETTING TO KNOW GUATEMALA 115

1. Geography, History, and Politics 116
2. Art, Architecture, and Literature 119
3. Religion, Myths, and Folklore 122
4. Cultural and Social Life 123
5. Performing Arts and Evening
  Entertainment 123
6. Sports and Recreation 124
7. Food and Drink 124
8. Recommended Books 125

SPECIAL FEATURES
● *Dateline 116*
● *What's Special about
  Guatemala 117*
● *Did you know . . . ? 122*

8 PLANNING A TRIP TO GUATEMALA 126

1. Information, Entry Requirements, and Money 126
2. When to Go—Climate, Events, and Holidays 129
3. Health, Insurance, and Other Concerns 130
4. What to Pack 130
5. Tips for the Disabled, Seniors, Singles, and Students 130
6. Alternative/Adventure Travel 131
7. Getting There 132
8. Suggested Itineraries 135
9. Getting Around 137
10. Where To Stay 139
11. Where to Eat 139
12. Enjoying Guatemala on a Budget 140

SPECIAL FEATURES
- What Things Cost in Guatemala City 128
- Guatamala Calendar of Events 129
- Frommer's Favorite Guatemala Experiences 136
- Fast Facts— Guatemala 142

9 GUATEMALA CITY 145

1. From a Budget Traveler's Point of View 145
2. Orientation and Getting Around 145
3. Where to Stay 152
4. Where to Eat 156
5. Attractions 159
6. Savvy Shopping 166
7. Evening Entertainment 168
8. Moving On—Travel Services 169

SPECIAL FEATURES
- What's Special About Guatemala City 147
- Fast Facts— Guatemala City 150

10 THE GUATEMALAN HIGHLANDS 171

1. Huehuetenango 171
2. Quetzaltenango 175
3. Chichicastenango 182
4. Lake Atitlán and Panajachel 186
5. Antigua 196

SPECIAL FEATURES
- What's Special About the Guatemalan Highlands 172

11 EL PETÉN 211

1. Flores and Santa Elena 211
2. Tikal 219

12 THE ATLANTIC HIGHWAY 225

1. Cobán 225
2. Río Hondo 230
3. Copán (Honduras) 231

SPECIAL FEATURES
- What's Special About the Atlantic Highway 226

4. Esquipulas 233
5. Quiriguá 235
6. Río Dulce and Lake Izabal 237
7. Lívingston and Puerto Barrios 239

13 THE PACIFIC HIGHWAY 243

1. Retalhuleu 243
2. La Democracia 245
3. Lake Amatitlán 246

SPECIAL FEATURES
● What's Special About the Pacific Highway 244

PART THREE: BELIZE

14 GETTING TO KNOW BELIZE 251

1. Geography, History, and Politics 251
2. Some Cultural Notes 254
3. Food and Drink 254
4. Recommended Film and Recordings 255

SPECIAL FEATURES
● What's Special About Belize 252
● Dateline 253

15 PLANNING A TRIP TO BELIZE 256

1. Information, Entry Requirements, and Money 256
2. When to Go—Climate and Holidays 258
3. Health, Insurance, and Other Concerns 258
4. What to Pack 258
5. Tips for the Disabled, Seniors, Singles, and Students 258
6. Alternative/Adventure Travel 259
7. Getting There 259
8. Suggested Itineraries 261
9. Getting Around 265
10. Where to Stay 266
11. Enjoying Belize on a Budget 266

SPECIAL FEATURES
● What Things Cost in Belize 257
● Did you know . . . ? 261
● Fast Facts— Belize 267

16 BELIZE CITY AND THE CAYES 269

1. Belize City 269
2. Ambergris Caye 278
3. Caye Caulker 285

SPECIAL FEATURES
● Fast Facts— Belize City 271

17 ELSEWHERE IN BELIZE 290

1. Belmopan   290
2. Placencia   294
3. San Ignacio and the Cayo District   298
4. Corozal Town and the Northern Highway   305

SPECIAL FEATURES
- *Frommer's Favorite Belize Experiences 291*

APPENDIX 308

A. The Metric System—in a Nutshell   308

INDEX   309

LIST OF MAPS

COSTA RICA:
Costa Rica   6–7
San José   35
Walking Tour—San José   53
GUATEMALA:
Guatemala   120–121
Guatemala City   149
Walking Tour—Downtown
   Guatemala City   165

Walking Tour—The Zona
   Viva   167
Antigua   199
BELIZE:
Belize   262–263
Belize City   273

ABOUT THIS FROMMER GUIDE

What $-A-Day Means The $-A-Day budget is meant to cover accommodations and meals only. Expect to use at least half of the sum on accommodations. Obviously, if two of you are traveling together, it's easier to stay within our budget guidelines.

WHAT THE SYMBOLS MEAN

 FROMMER'S FAVORITES—hotels, restaurants, attractions, and entertainments you shouldn't miss

 SUPER-SPECIAL VALUES—really exceptional values

IN HOTEL AND OTHER LISTINGS

The following symbols refer to the standard amenities available in all rooms:
A/C air conditioning   TEL telephone   TV television
MINIBAR refrigerator stocked with beverages and snacks

The following abbreviations are used for credit cards:
AE American Express   DISC Discover   EU Eurocard
CB Carte Blanche   ER EnRoute   MC MasterCard
DC Diners Club   V VISA

TRIP PLANNING WITH THIS GUIDE

Use the following features:
What Things Cost in . . . to help you plan your daily budget
What's Special About . . . Checklist a summary of each region's highlights—which lets you check off those that appeal most to you
Easy-to-read Maps . . . city and regional sights, neighborhoods, walking tours and city environs
Fast Facts . . . all the essentials at a glance: currency, emergencies, embassies, and more

OTHER SPECIAL FROMMER FEATURES

Cool for Kids—hotels, restaurants, and attractions
Did You Know . . . ?—offbeat, fun facts

INVITATION TO THE READERS

In researching this book, our author has come across many wonderful establishments, the best of which we have included here. We are sure that many of you will also come across wonderful hotels, inns, restaurants, guest houses, shops, and attractions. Please don't keep them to yourself. Share your experiences, especially if you want to comment on places that have been included in this edition that have changed for the worse. You can address your letters to:

Karl Samson
Costa Rica, Guatemala & Belize
Prentice Hall Press
15 Columbus Circle
New York, NY 10023

A DISCLAIMER

Readers are advised that prices fluctuate in the course of time and travel information changes under the impact of the varied and volatile factors that affect the travel industry. Neither the author nor the publisher can be held responsible for the experiences of readers while traveling. Readers are invited to write to the publisher with ideas, comments, and suggestions for future editions.

SAFETY ADVISORY

Whenever you're traveling in an unfamiliar city or country, stay alert. Be aware of your immediate surroundings. Wear a moneybelt and keep a close eye on your possessions. Be particularly careful with cameras, purses, and wallets, all favorite targets for thieves and pickpockets.

PART ONE

COSTA RICA

CHAPTER 1

GETTING TO KNOW COSTA RICA

1. GEOGRAPHY, HISTORY, AND POLITICS

- **WHAT'S SPECIAL ABOUT COSTA RICA**
- **DATELINE**

2. SOME CULTURAL BACKGROUND

- **DID YOU KNOW . . .?**

3. FOOD AND DRINK

4. RECOMMENDED BOOKS

Costa Rica in Spanish means "Rich Coast," which was a misnomer when gold-hungry Spaniards named the country nearly 500 years ago. They found little gold or silver and few Indians to convert and enslave; instead they found a land of rugged volcanic peaks blanketed with dense forests. Costa Rica was ignored for centuries, but today it is beginning to live up to its name. In fact, the country should rightfully be called Costas Ricas since it has two coasts, one on the Pacific and one on the Caribbean Coast. Along these coasts are some of the most beautiful beaches in Central America, and this translates into dollars as resort developments spring up along the shores. The dense forests and rugged mountain ranges that cover much of Costa Rica are also bringing in unexpected revenues. To reduce its national debt, Costa Rica agreed to set aside hundreds of thousands of acres of undisturbed forests as national parks and wildlife preserves. With tropical forests around the world disappearing at an alarming rate, concerned individuals and groups are flocking to Costa Rica to visit and study its pristine wilderness areas.

Costa Rica, bordered by the troubled nations of Nicaragua and Panama, is also a relative sea of tranquility in a region of turmoil. For more than 100 years, the country has enjoyed a stable democracy; in fact, there isn't even a standing army here, which is something that Costa Ricans are very proud of. Former President Oscar Arias Sánchez was awarded the Nobel Peace Prize for his work in implementing a Central American peace plan. With political stability, an educated populace, and vast areas of wilderness, Costa Rica today is a rich coast, indeed.

1. GEOGRAPHY, HISTORY, AND POLITICS

GEOGRAPHY

Bordered on the north by Nicaragua and on the southeast by Panama, Costa Rica (19,530 square miles) is only slightly larger than Vermont and New Hampshire combined. Within this area are more than 750 miles of coastline on both the Caribbean Sea and the Pacific Ocean. Much of the country is mountainous, with three major ranges running from northwest to southeast. Among these mountains are several volcanic peaks, some of which are still active. Between the mountain ranges there are fertile valleys, the largest and most populated of which is the Meseta Central. With the exception of the dry Guanacaste region, much of Costa Rica's

WHAT'S SPECIAL ABOUT COSTA RICA

Beaches
☐ Manuel Antonio National Park, three idyllic beaches with jungle-clad hills behind them
☐ Cahuita National Park on the Caribbean Coast, long deserted beaches and Costa Rica's largest coral reef
☐ Jacó Beach, an inexpensive resort area with many deserted beaches nearby
☐ The beaches of Guanacaste, which receive more sunshine than any of the other beaches in the country

Museums
☐ The Gold Museum in San José, the largest collection of pre-Columbian gold jewelry and ornaments in the Americas
☐ The Jade Museum, also in San José, an equally impressive collection of pre-Columbian jade artifacts and jewelry

Parks/Gardens
☐ Lankester Gardens, near Cartago, hundreds of species of orchids on display
☐ National parks, encompassing 11% of Costa Rica's land
☐ Monteverde Cloud Forest Reserve, a lush jungle that is home to the quetzal, one of the most beautiful birds on earth

Natural Spectacles
☐ Every year, hundreds of thousands of turtles laying their eggs on Costa Rican beaches
☐ Two volcanoes near San José with roads to their rims

Religious Shrines
☐ The basilica in Cartago, with a statue of the Virgin of Los Angeles said to heal the sick
☐ The ruins of a church in Cartago turned into a park

After Dark
☐ San José's National Theater, a stately old opera house with performances almost every night

Ace Attractions
☐ The Jungle Train, winding its way through the jungle as it travels from San José to Limón

Great Adventures
☐ Kayaking and rafting on white-water rivers
☐ Nature-oriented lodges offering rafting, horseback riding, and bird and wildlife spotting

coastal area is hot and humid and covered with dense rain forests. The earliest Spanish settlers found the climate much more amenable in the highlands of the Meseta Central, and to this day most of the population lives in this region.

THE REGIONS

The Meseta Central   The Meseta Central is characterized by rolling green hills between 3,000 and 4,000 feet above sea level, where the climate has been described as "eternal spring." It is Costa Rica's primary agricultural region, with coffee farms making up the majority of landholdings. The rich volcanic soil of this region makes it ideal for growing almost anything. The country's earliest settlements were in this area, and today the Meseta Central is a densely populated area laced with good roads and dotted with small towns.

The Mountains   Surrounding the Meseta Central and extending to Costa Rica's northern and southern borders are three major mountain ranges: the Cordillera Central, the Guanacaste range, and the Talamanca range. Among these mountains are found numerous volcanic peaks, four of which border the Meseta Central. Two of these, Poás and Irazú, are still active and have caused extensive damage during cycles of activity in the past two centuries. Much of the mountainous regions to the north and to the south of the capital of San José have been declared national parks to protect their virgin rain forests from logging.

The Guanacaste Peninsula This northwestern region of Costa Rica is the driest part of the country and has been likened to west Texas. Within this region is one of the last remnants of tropical dry forest left on earth. Because the forest gives way to areas of savannah in Guanacaste, this is Costa Rica's "Wild West," where cattle ranching is the primary occupation.

The Caribbean and the Pacific Coasts On the southern Pacific Coast and the entire Caribbean Coast, there are wide, steamy lowlands, much of which have been converted to banana and oil-palm plantations. Lowland rain-forest vegetation predominates where it has not been cleared, and rainfall reaches more than 200 inches per year.

HISTORY & POLITICS

EARLY HISTORY

Little is known of Costa Rica's history prior to its colonization by Spanish settlers. The pre-Columbian Indians who made their home in this region of Central America never developed the large cities or advanced culture that flowered farther north in what would become Guatemala, Belize, and Mexico. However, from scattered excavations around the country, primarily in the northwest, ancient artifacts have been unearthed that indicate a strong aesthetic. Beautiful gold and jade jewelry, intricately carved grinding stones, and artistically painted terra-cotta ware point toward a highly skilled, if not large, population. The most enigmatic of these ancient relics are carved stone balls, some measuring several yards across and weighing many tons, that have been found along the southern Pacific Coast. The purpose of these stone spheres remains a mystery: Some archeologists say that they may have been boundary markers; others think that they were celestial references.

In 1502, on his last voyage to the New World, Christopher Columbus anchored just offshore from present-day Puerto Limón. Whether it was he who gave the country its name is open to discussion, but it was not long before the inappropriate name took hold. The earliest Spanish settlers found that, unlike the Indians farther north, the native population of Costa Rica was unwilling to submit to slavery. Despite their small numbers and scattered villages, they fought back against the Spanish. However, the superior Spanish firepower and the European diseases that had helped to subjugate the populations farther north conquered the natives. But when the fighting was finished, the settlers in Costa Rica found that there were no more Indians left to oppress into servitude. The settlers were forced to till their own lands, an exercise unheard of in other parts of Central America. Few pioneers headed this way because they could settle in Guatemala, where there was a large native workforce. Costa Rica was nearly forgotten as the Spanish crown looked elsewhere for riches to plunder and souls to convert.

DATELINE

- **13,000 B.C.** Earliest record of human inhabitants in Costa Rica.
- **1,000 B.C.** Olmec people from Mexico arrive in Costa Rica searching for rare blue jade.
- **1,000 B.C.–A.D. 1400** City of Guayabo is inhabited by as many as 10,000 people.
- **300 B.C.–A.D. 700** Mysterious stone spheres are carved by inhabitants of southwest coastal areas.
- **1502** Columbus discovers Costa Rica in September, landing at what is now Puerto Limón.
- **1519–1561** Spanish explore and colonize Costa Rica.
- **1563** City of Cartago is founded in Central Valley.
- **1737** San José is founded.
- **Late 1700s** Coffee is intro-

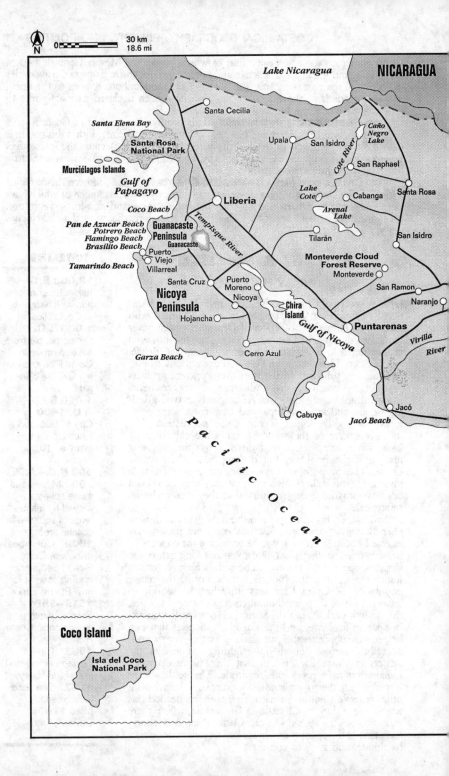

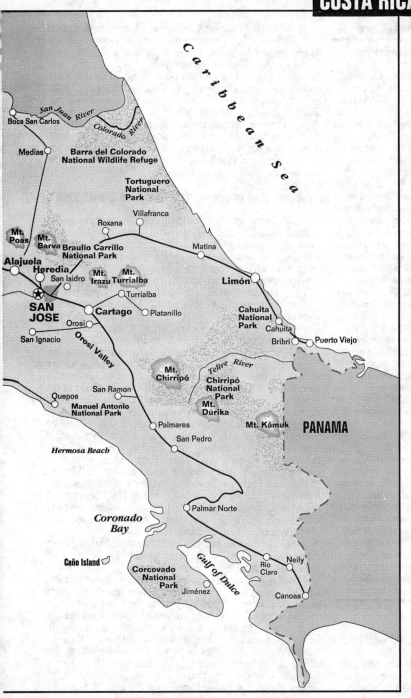

COSTA RICA

Caribbean Sea

San Juan River

Boca San Carlos

Colorado River

Medias

Barra del Colorado National Wildlife Refuge

Tortuguero National Park

Villafranca

Roxana

Matina

Mt. Poas

Mt. Barva

Braulio Carrillo National Park

Alajuela

Heredia

San Isidro

Mt. Irazu

Mt. Turrialba

Limón

SAN JOSE

Orosi

Cartago

Turrialba

Platanillo

Cahuita National Park

Cahuita

San Ignacio

Orosi Valley

Bribri

Puerto Viejo

Telire River

Mt. Chirripó

Chirripó National Park

Quepos

San Ramon

Mt. Dúrika

Manuel Antonio National Park

Palmares

Mt. Kámuk

PANAMA

San Pedro

Hermosa Beach

Coronado Bay

Palmar Norte

Caño Island

Gulf of Dulce

Rio Claro

Neily

Corcovado National Park

Jiménez

Canoas

DATELINE

duced as cash
crop.

- **1821** On September 15, Costa Rica, with the rest of Central America, gains independence from Spain.
- **1823** Capital is moved to San José.
- **1848** Costa Rica is proclaimed an independent republic.
- **1856** Battle of Santa Rosa; Costa Ricans defeat U.S.-backed proslavery advocate William Walker.
- **1870s** First banana plantations are planted.
- **1889** First election is won by an opposition party, establishing democratic process in Costa Rica.
- **1899** The United Fruit Company is founded by railroad builder Minor Keith.
- **1948** After aborted revolution, Costa Rican army is abolished.
- **1987** President Oscar Arias Sánchez is awarded the Nobel Peace Prize for orchestrating the Central American Peace Plan.

It didn't take long for Costa Rica's few Spanish settlers to head for the hills, where they found a climate that was less oppressive than the climate in the lowlands and a rich volcanic soil. Cartago, the colony's first capital, was founded in 1563. It would not be until the 1700s that more cities were founded in this agriculturally rich region. In the late 18th century, the first coffee plants were introduced, and because these plants thrived in the highlands, Costa Rica's fortunes began to turn. The country began to develop its first cash crop. Unfortunately, it was a long and difficult journey transporting the coffee from the highlands to the Caribbean Coast and thence to Europe, where the demand for coffee was growing.

FROM INDEPENDENCE TO THE PRESENT

In 1821, Spain granted independence to its colonies in Central America. Costa Rica joined with its neighbors to form the Central American Federation, but in 1938 it withdrew to form a new nation and pursue its own interests, which differed considerably from those of the other Central American nations. By the mid-1800s, coffee was the country's main export. Land was given free to anyone willing to plant coffee on it, and plantation owners soon grew wealthy and powerful, creating Costa Rica's first elite class. Coffee plantation owners were powerful enough to elect their own representatives to the presidency.

This was a stormy period in Costa Rican history, and in 1856 the country was invaded by William Walker, a soldier of fortune from Tennessee who had grandiose dreams of establishing a slavery state in Central America. Prior to his invasion of Costa Rica, he had invaded Baja, California, declaring himself president of that region, and Nicaragua, where he also set himself up as president. The people of Central America were outraged by the actions of this man, who actually had backing from the U.S. President James Buchanan. The people of Costa Rica, led by their own president, Juan Rafael Mora, marched against Walker and chased him back to Nicaragua. Walker eventually surrendered to a U.S. warship in 1857, but in 1860 he attacked Honduras, claiming to be the president of that country. The Hondurans, who had had enough of Walker's shenanigans, promptly executed him.

Until 1890 coffee growers had been forced to transport their coffee either by ox cart to the Pacific port of Puntarenas or by boat down the Sarapíquí River, which itself was a long way from the main coffee-growing regions, to the Caribbean. In the 1870s a progressive president proposed a railway from San José to the Caribbean Coast to facilitate the transport of coffee to European markets. It took nearly 20 years for this plan to reach fruition. More than 4,000 workers lost their lives constructing the railway, which passed through dense jungles and rugged mountains on its journey from the Meseta Central to the coast. It was under the direction of the project's second chief engineer, Minor Keith, that a momentous deal was made with the government of Costa Rica: In order to continue the financially strapped project, Keith had struck on the idea of using the railway right-of-way (land on either side of the tracks) as banana plantations. The

DID YOU KNOW...?

- Costa Rica has the oldest true democracy in Central America.
- Costa Rica has no army, navy, air force, or marine corps.
- Costa Rica has 10% of the butterflies in the world and more than the entire African continent, as well as more than 1,200 varieties of orchids and more than 800 species of birds.
- San José is farther south than Caracas, Venezuela.
- Costa Rica has a mountain from the top of which you can see both the Caribbean Sea and the Pacific Ocean.
- Isla del Coco, the largest uninhabited island in the world, is in Costa Rica.

export of this crop would help to finance the railway, and in exchange Keith would get a 99-year lease on 800,000 acres of land with a 20-year tax deferment. In 1878 the first bananas were shipped from Costa Rica, and in 1899 Keith and a partner formed the United Fruit Company, a company that would eventually become the largest landholder in Central America and cause political disputes and wars throughout the region.

In 1889 Costa Rica held what is considered the first free election in Central American history. The opposition candidate won the election, and the control of the government passed from the hands of one political party to those of another without bloodshed or hostilities. Thus Costa Rica established itself as the region's only true democracy. In 1948 this democratic process was challenged by a former president (who had been president from 1940 to 1944), Rafael Angel Calderón, who lost a bid at a second term in office by a narrow margin. Calderón, who had the backing of communist labor unions, refused to yield the country's leadership to the rightfully elected president, Otilio Ulate, and a revolution ensued. Calderón was eventually defeated. In the wake of this crisis, a new constitution was drafted; among other changes, it abolished Costa Rica's army so that such a revolution could never happen again.

Peace and democracy have become of tantamount importance to Costa Ricans since the revolution of 1948. When Oscar Arias Sánchez was elected president in 1986, his main goal was to seek a solution to the ongoing war in Nicaragua, and one of his first actions was to close down Contra bases inside Costa Rica and enforce Costa Rica's position of neutrality. In 1987 Sánchez won the Nobel Peace Prize for initiating a Central American peace plan aimed at settling the war in Nicaragua.

Costa Rica's 100 years of nearly uninterrupted democracy has helped make it the most stable economy in Central America. This stability and adherence to the democratic process is a source of great pride to Costa Ricans. They like to think of their country as a "Switzerland of Central America" not only because of its herds of dairy cows but also because of its staunch position of neutrality in a region that has been torn by nearly constant civil wars and revolutions for more than 200 years.

2. SOME CULTURAL BACKGROUND

Art Little is known of Costa Rica's pre-Columbian peoples, but archeological excavations have uncovered a wealth of gold and jade jewelry, elaborately carved grinding stones, and beautiful ceramics.

Since the Spanish conquest, Costa Rica's artists have followed European artistic styles. The Museo de Arte Costarricense exhibits works by the country's better-known artists of the last 400 years. Most artistic movements of those years are represented.

Architecture The pre-Columbian peoples of Costa Rica left few signs of their habitation. The excavations at Guayabo, little more than building foundations and paved streets, are the country's main archeological site. Little colonial architecture remains as well. Numerous earthquakes over the centuries have destroyed most of what the Spanish built. One such earthquake, in 1910, halted the construction of a cathedral in Cartago, the ruins of which are now a peaceful park in the middle of town. The ruins of another church, the oldest in Costa Rica, can be found near the village of Ujarrás in the Orosi Valley. This church was built in 1693 and abandoned in 1833 when the village was flooded. The central plaza in Heredia has a historic church built in 1796, and also on this square is an old fortress tower known as El Fortín.

The People   When the first Spaniards arrived in Costa Rica, the Indian population was not very large. Their numbers were further reduced by wars and disease until they became a minority of the country's total population. Consequently, most of the population of Costa Rica today is of pure Spanish descent, and it is not at all surprising to see blond Costa Ricans. There is still a remnant Indian population on reservations in southeast Costa Rica near the town of Limón. This area also has a substantial population of English-speaking black Creoles who came over from Jamaica to work on the railroad and on the banana plantations. They have never moved far inland, preferring the humid lowlands to the cool Meseta Central. For the most part, these different groups coexist without friction. Literacy is high throughout the country, and nearly 50% of the workforce is women. There is a large, working middle class, and there is not the gross disparity between rich and poor that you see in other Central American countries. Costa Ricans call themselves *Ticos,* a diminutive form of the term *costarricense.*

Famous Costa Ricans   **Oscar Arias Sánchez** (1941–) Former president of Costa Rica. He was awarded the Nobel Peace Prize in 1987 for orchestrating the Central American Peace Plan.

Minor Keith   Engineer who took over construction of the jungle railway that linked San José with Costa Rica's Caribbean Coast. Keith was the co-founder of the United Fruit Company, which played a major role in the turmoil that engulfed Central America for much of the 20th century.

Performing Arts and Evening Entertainment   One of the very first things that Costa Ricans did with their newfound coffee wealth in the mid-19th century was to build an opera house. The elite were upset that opera singers were by-passing their country when they toured the Americas. Today that opera house is known as the National Theater and is as popular as it was 100 years ago. Hardly a night goes by that some performance isn't held in the stately theater.

Mariachi and marimba music have a firm grip on the hearts of all Ticos. In San José there are several 24-hour restaurants where these types of music can be heard live and for free at all hours of the day or night. Discos and casinos are also very popular.

Sports and Recreation   Soccer is the national sport of Costa Rica, but baseball, polo, squash, and handball also are popular. There are currently only three golf courses in Costa Rica: the Cariari Hotel and Country Club in San José, Los Reyes at Guácima in Alajuela, and the Costa Rican Country Club in Escazú. Sportfishing is very popular here, and the waters in and around Costa Rica abound with everything from trout and tarpon to sailfish and marlin. There are fishing tournaments throughout the year and fishing boats for hire on both coasts. You'll need a fishing license (available from your fishing guide).

Surfing is another sport that has caught on in a big way in Costa Rica. There are excellent surfing waves at various points on both coasts, and many hotels offer off-season discounts to surfers.

3. FOOD AND DRINK

Very similar to other Central American cuisines, Costa Rican food is not especially memorable. It relies heavily on rice and beans, which can become very boring when you see it at three meals a day for days on end. Perhaps this is why there is so much international food available throughout the country. However, if you really want to save money, you'll find that Costa Rican food is always the cheapest food available. It is primarily served in sodas, Costa Rica's equivalent of diners.

FOOD

MEALS AND DINING CUSTOMS

Rice and beans are the basis of Costa Rican meals. At breakfast, they're called *gallo pinto* and come with everything from eggs to steak or even to seafood. At lunch or dinner, rice and beans go by the name *casado* (which also means "married"). A casado comes with a cabbage-and-tomato salad, fried plantains (a type of banana), and a meat dish of some sort.

Dining hours in Costa Rica are flexible: Many restaurants in San José are open 24 hours, a sign that Ticos are willing to eat at any time of the night or day. However, expensive restaurants tend to open for lunch between 11am and 2pm and for dinner between 6pm and midnight. In between meals, especially after work and late in the evening, Ticos munch on *bocas* in bars. Bocas are appetizers (usually free) that are served with drinks.

THE CUISINE

Appetizers: As mentioned above, bocas are served with drinks in most bars throughout Costa Rica. Often the bocas are free, but even if they aren't, they're very inexpensive. *Ceviche* (raw seafood marinated in lime juice and chili peppers) is a favorite, usually eaten with crackers. Other popular bocas include *gallos* (stuffed tortillas) and *sopa de mondongo* (tripe soup).

Soups: Black bean soup, *sopa negra,* is a creamy soup with a poached or boiled egg soaking in the broth. It is one of the most popular of Costa Rican soups and shows up on many menus. *Olla de carne* is a delicious soup made with beef and several local vegetables including *chayote, ayote, yuca,* and plantains, all of which have textures and flavors similar to various winter squashes. *Sopa de mondongo* is made with tripe, the stomach of a cow, which some love and others find disgusting. *Picodillo* is a vegetable stew with a little bit of meat in it. It's often served as a side dish with a *casado.*

Sandwiches and snacks: Ticos love to snack, and there are a large variety of tasty little sandwiches and snacks available on the street, at snack bars, and in sodas. *Arreglados* are little meat-filled sandwiches, as are *tortas,* which are served on little rolls with a bit of salad tucked into them. *Gallos* are tortillas stuffed with meat, beans, or cheese. Tacos, tamales, and empanadas also are quite common.

Meat: Costa Rica is a beef country, one of the tropical nations that has converted much of its rainforest land to pastures for raising beef cattle. Consequently, beef is cheap and plentiful, although it may be a bit tougher than you are used to. Spit-roasted chicken is also very popular here, especially when it is roasted over a coffee-wood fire. It is surprisingly tender.

Seafood: Costa Rica has two coasts, and as you would expect, there is plenty of seafood available everywhere in the country. *Corvina* (sea bass) is the most commonly served fish, and it is prepared in innumerable ways, including as ceviche. Surprisingly, although Costa Rica is a major exporter of shrimp and lobster, both are very expensive here. In fact, shrimp is often more expensive than lobster. The reason is that most of the shrimp and lobster are exported, causing them to be very expensive at home.

Vegetables: On the whole, you will find vegetables surprisingly lacking in the meals you are served in Costa Rica. The standard vegetable with any meal is a little pile of shredded cabbage topped with a slice or two of tomato. For a much more satisfying and filling salad, order *palmito* (heart of palm salad). Hearts of palm are considered a delicacy in most places because an entire palm tree (albeit a small one) must be cut down to extract the heart. The heart is a bit like the inner part of an avocado—many leaves layered around one another. These leaves are chopped into large pieces and served with other fresh vegetables, a salad dressing on top. Even here, where the palms are plentiful, *palmito* is relatively expensive. If you want something more than this, you'll have to order a side dish such as *picadillo,* a stew of vegetables with a bit of meat in it. Most people have a hard time thinking of *plátanos* (plantains) as vegetables, but these giant relatives of bananas are sweet and require cooking before they can be eaten. Fried plátanos are one of my favorite dishes. *Yuca* (manioc root) is another starchy staple vegetable of Costa Rica.

One more vegetable worth mentioning is the *pejibaye*, a form of palm fruit that looks like a miniature orange coconut. Boiled pejibayes are frequently sold from carts on the streets of San José. When cut in half, a pejibaye reveals a large seed surrounded by soft, creamy flesh and looks a bit like an avocado. You can eat it like an avocado, too, by just scooping the flesh out.

Fruits: Costa Rica has a wealth of delicious tropical fruits. The most common are mangos (season begins in May); papayas; pineapples; and bananas, which are oddly unavailable on the Atlantic (Caribbean Sea) coast near the banana plantations. Other less well-known fruits include the *marañon*, an orange or yellow fruit with a glossy skin that is the fruit of the cashew tree; the *granadilla* (passion fruit); the *mamón chino*, which Asian travelers will immediately recognize as the rambutan; and the *carmabola* (star fruit). When ordering *ensalada de fruita* in a restaurant, make sure that it is made with fresh fruit and does not come with ice cream and Jell-O. What a shock I had when I first received a bowl of canned fruit covered with Jell-O cubes and three scoops of ice cream!

Desserts: *Queque seco*, which literally translates as "dry cake," is the same as pound cake. *Tres leches* cake is a Nicaraguan cake that is so moist you almost need to eat it with a spoon. *Flan de coco* is a sweet coconut flan. There are many other sweets available, many of which are made with milk and raw sugar (rich and sweet).

GLOSSARY OF COSTA RICAN TERMS
Menu Savvy

Bocas Appetizers
Casado Lunch or dinner meal consisting of rice, beans, a main dish, and fried plantains
Ceviche Marinated seafood salad
Corvina Sea bass
Gallo pinto Breakfast dish consisting of rice, beans, and eggs or meat
Horchata Refresco made with rice flour and cinnamon
Palmito Heart of palm salad
Pinolillo Refresco made with roasted corn flour
Plátanos Plantains, similar to bananas
Refrescos Water- or milk-based drinks made in a blender with fresh fruit
Tortas Small sandwiches

DRINKS
WATER AND SOFT DRINKS

Although water in Costa Rica is said to be safe to drink, I met several people on my last trip who became ill shortly after arriving in Costa Rica. Play it safe and stick to bottled water, which is readily available. *Agua mineral,* or simply *soda,* is sparkling water in Costa Rica. It's inexpensive and refreshing. Most major brands of soft drinks are also available.

Refrescos are a bit like milk shakes and are my favorite drinks in Costa Rica. They are usually made with fresh fruit juice and milk or water. Among the more common fruits used are mangos, papayas, blackberries (*moras*), and pineapples. Carrot juice (*jugo de zanahoria*) is very common, too. Some of the more unusual refrescos are *horchata* (made with rice flour and a lot of cinnamon) and *pinolillo* (made with roasted corn flour). The former is wonderful; the latter requires an open mind. You might also see egg nog on refrescos lists. Order *un refresco de leche sin hiello* if you are trying to avoid untreated water.

BEER, WINE, AND LIQUOR

The German presence in Costa Rica over the years has produced several fine beers, which are fairly inexpensive. Heinekin also is available. Costa Rica distills a wide variety of liquors, and you'll save money by ordering these rather than imported brands. Imported wines are available at reasonable prices in the better restaurants throughout the country. You can save a bit of money by ordering a South American wine rather than a European one. Café Rica and Salicsa are two coffee liqueurs made in Costa Rica; the former is very similar to Kahlua, and the latter is a cream coffee liqueur. Both are delicious.

4. RECOMMENDED BOOKS

GENERAL ECONOMIC, POLITICAL, AND SOCIAL HISTORY

The Costa Ricans (Prentice Hall, 1987) by Richard, Karen, and Mavis Biesanz is a well-written account of the politics and culture of Costa Rica.

To learn more about the life and culture of Costa Rica's Talamanca Coast, an area populated by Afro-Caribbean people whose forebears immigrated from Caribbean islands in the early 19th century, pick up a copy of *What Happen, A Folk-History of Costa Rica's Talamanca Coast* (Ecodesarollos, 1977) by Paula Palmer.

The Costa Rica Reader (Grove Weidenfeld, 1989), edited by Marc Edelman and Joanne Kenen, is a collection of essays on Costa Rican topics. For insight into Costa Rican politics, economics, and culture, this weighty book is invaluable.

FICTION AND TRAVEL

Gabriel Garcia Marquez's *One Hundred Years of Solitude* (Avon, 1976) relates the impact that the United Fruit Company has on a fictitious small town.

The New Key to Costa Rica (Publications in English, 1990) by Beatrice Blake and Anne Becher is a very thorough guide to the country. Everything from Costa Rican Spanish to how to cut a mango is covered.

NATURAL HISTORY

Costa Rica National Parks (Incafo, 1989), by Mario Boza is published in Madrid and available in both hard-bound and soft-cover editions. It is a beautiful picture book of Costa Rica's national parks. Each of the country's national parks is represented by several color photos and a short description of the park in Spanish and English.

Donald Perry's fascinating *Life Above the Jungle Floor* (Simon & Schuster, 1986) is an account of his research into the life amid the tropical rainforest canopy. He built a network of trams through the treetops so that he could study this area of great biological and botanical activity.

CHAPTER 2

PLANNING A TRIP TO COSTA RICA

1. INFORMATION, ENTRY REQUIREMENTS, AND MONEY
- WHAT THINGS COST IN SAN JOSÉ
2. WHEN TO GO— CLIMATE, EVENTS, AND HOLIDAYS
- COSTA RICA CALENDAR OF EVENTS
3. HEALTH, INSURANCE, AND OTHER CONCERNS
4. WHAT TO PACK
5. TIPS FOR THE DISABLED, SENIORS, SINGLES, AND STUDENTS
6. ALTERNATIVE/ ADVENTURE TRAVEL
7. GETTING THERE
8. SUGGESTED ITINERARIES
- FROMMER'S FAVORITE COSTA RICA EXPERIENCES
9. GETTING AROUND
10. ACCOMMODATIONS AND DINING NOTES
11. ENJOYING COSTA RICA ON A BUDGET
- FAST FACTS— COSTA RICA

After you decide to visit Costa Rica, you will likely have quite a few questions. This chapter should tell you everything you need to know about planning your trip—from whether you need a visa to how much of an airport tax you'll have to pay when you head home.

1. INFORMATION, ENTRY REQUIREMENTS, AND MONEY

SOURCES OF INFORMATION

Before you ever leave home, you can get information on Costa Rica by contacting the **Costa Rican National Tourist Bureau.** They have two offices in the United States: 1101 Brickell Avenue, BIV Tower, Suite 801, Miami, FL 33131 (tel. 305/358-2150, or toll free 800/327-7033); and 3540 Wilshire Blvd., Suite 707, Los Angeles, CA 90010 (tel. 213/382-8080).

Once you are in Costa Rica, there are **I.C.T.** (Instituto Costarricense de Turismo) information centers at Juan Santamaría Airport (across from baggage claims and to the left before you go up the stairs after clearing Customs) and beneath the Plaza de la Cultura, Calle 5 between Avenida Central and Avenida 2 (tel. 22-1090). The folks at the downtown office are particularly helpful, and there are photo albums from various lodges around the country so that you can get an idea of what places look like before you decide to go.

ENTRY REQUIREMENTS

Citizens of the United States, Canada, the United Kingdom, Ireland, Australia, and New Zealand do not need a visa to visit Costa Rica if they intend to stay for 30 days or less. All that are necessary to enter the country are a **Tourist Card,** available on arrival, and proof of citizenship and a photo identity card (passport or driver's license and original birth certificate or voter registration card). A passport is not necessary, but without one you cannot extend your 30-day

Tourist Card and must pay $2 for the card. If traveling with a passport and planning to stay for more than 30 days in Costa Rica, you must also purchase, for $2, a special Tourist Card at the airline counter in the country from which you depart. It is much easier to reenter your home country if you have a passport, so I strongly recommend that you acquire one before leaving home.

In the past it has been very difficult and time-consuming to extend a Costa Rican visa. That is easier now, but regulations are still changing. Check with the I.C.T. office in San José to find out what the current regulations are.

MONEY

CASH CURRENCY   The unit of currency in Costa Rica is the colón (¢). There are approximately 85 colónes to the U.S. dollar. The colón is divided into 100 centimos. There are notes in denominations of 1, 2, 5, 10, 50, 100, and 1,000 colónes and coins of 25 and 50 centimos. You might encounter a special issue 5-colón bill that is a popular gift and tourist souvenir. It is valid currency, although it sells for much more than its face value. There are also some older, small-denomination bills and coins floating around.

CURRENCY EXCHANGE CHART

¢	$
1	.01
10	.12
20	.24
30	.35
40	.47
50	.59
60	.71
70	.82
80	.94
90	1.06
100	1.18
200	2.35
300	3.53
400	4.71
500	5.88
600	7.06
700	8.24
800	9.41
900	10.59
1,000	11.76
1,500	17.65
2,000	23.53
2,500	29.41
3,000	35.29
3,500	41.18
4,000	47.06
4,500	52.94
5,000	58.82
10,000	117.65

TRAVELER'S CHECKS   Traveler's checks can be readily changed at banks and hotels. Banks will charge a small commission.

CREDIT CARDS   Major international credit cards accepted readily at hotels throughout Costa Rica include American Express, MasterCard, and VISA. The less expensive hotels tend to take cash only. Many restaurants and stores also accept credit cards. When paying for a hotel room with your credit card, check to see if they charge extra (3 to 5%).

WHAT THINGS COST IN SAN JOSE	U.S. $
Taxi from the airport to the city center	10.00
Local telephone call	.02
Deluxe double (at L'Ambiance)	125.00
Moderate double (at Hotel Don Carlos)	38.40
Budget double (at Petit Hotel)	20.00
Moderate lunch for one (at La Perla)	4.00
Budget lunch for one (at Soda La Casita)	2.50
Deluxe dinner for one, without wine (at El Balcon de Europa)	25.00
Moderate dinner for one, without wine (at La Cocin de Leña)	10.00
Budget dinner for one, without wine (at Restaurante Campesino)	6.00
Bottle of beer	.80
Coca-Cola	.50
Cup of coffee	.50
Roll of ASA 100 Kodacolor film, 24 exposures	8.40
Admission to the Jade Museum	Free
Movie ticket	1.20
Ticket at the National Theater	5.00

2. WHEN TO GO — CLIMATE, EVENTS, AND HOLIDAYS

CLIMATE

Costa Rica is a tropical country and has distinct wet and dry seasons—but some parts are rainy all year, whereas others are very dry and sunny for most of the year. Temperatures vary primarily with elevation not with season. On the coasts it is hot all year, while up in the mountains it can be quite cool at night any time of year.

Generally speaking, the rainy season is from May to November, and the dry season is from December to April. In Guanacaste, the dry northwestern province, the dry season lasts several weeks longer. Even in the rainy season, days often start out sunny, with rain falling in the afternoon and evening. On the Atlantic (Caribbean Sea) Coast, especially south of Puerto Limón, you can count on rain all year round. The best overall time of year to visit is December and January, when everything is still green from the rains, but the sky is clear.

AVERAGE MONTHLY TEMPERATURES AND RAINFALL IN SAN JOSÉ

Month	Temp (°F)	Temp. (°C)	Days of Rain
Jan	66	19	1
Feb	66	19	0
Mar	69	20.5	1
Apr	71	21.5	4
May	71	21.5	17
June	71	21.5	20
July	70	21	18
Aug	70	21	19
Sept	71	21.5	20
Oct	69	20.5	22
Nov	68	20	14
Dec	67	19.5	4

COSTA RICA
CALENDAR OF EVENTS

Because Costa Rica is a Roman Catholic country, most of its holidays and celebrations are church related. The major celebrations of the year are Christmas, New Year's, and Easter, which are celebrated for several days. Keep in mind that Holy Week is the biggest holiday time in Costa Rica, and many families head for the beach (this is the last holiday before school starts). Also, there is no public transportation on Holy Thursday or Good Friday.

MARCH OR APRIL

☐ **Holy Week** (week before Easter), San José and all over the country. Religious processions in the streets.

OCTOBER

☐ **Carnival,** Puerto Limón. For several days leading up to October 12 (Columbus or Discovery of America Day).

DECEMBER

☐ **Carnival,** San José. Last week of December.

HOLIDAYS

Official holidays in Costa Rica include January 1, New Year's Day; March 19, St. Joseph's Day; Thursday and Friday of Holy Week (the week prior to Easter); April 11, Juan Santamaría's Day; May 1, Labor Day; June 29, Saints Peter and Paul Day; July 25, annexation of the province of Guanacaste; August 2, Virgin of Los Angeles's Day; August 15, Mother's Day; September 15, Independence Day; October 12, Discovery of America; December 8, Immaculate Conception of the Virgin Mary; December 25, Christmas Day; December 31, New Year's Eve.

3. HEALTH, INSURANCE, AND OTHER CONCERNS

HEALTH

VACCINATIONS

No vaccinations are required for a visit to Costa Rica, Guatemala, or Belize, unless you are coming from an area where yellow fever exists. However, because sanitation is generally not as good as it is in other developed countries, you may be exposed to diseases for which you may wish to get vaccinations: typhoid, polio, tetanus, and infectious hepatitis (gamma globulin). If you are planning to stay in major cities, you stand little risk of encountering any of these diseases, but if you venture out into remote regions of the country, you stand a higher risk.

Malaria is found in the lowlands on both coasts. Although it is rarely found in urban areas, it is still a problem in remote wooded regions. Malaria prophylaxes are available, but several have side effects and others are of questionable effectiveness. Consult your doctor or your local health board as to what is currently considered the best preventative treatment for malaria.

When you are in El Petén, it is imperative that you sleep in an enclosed room with screens on the windows or beneath a mosquito net. This region is home to vampire bats that frequently carry rabies. The bats are nocturnal, and although they prefer cattle, they have been known to bite humans, especially on the toes and nose. The bite of a vampire bat is entirely painless, but an anticoagulant in the bat's saliva will cause a bite to bleed freely. The greatest risk is not from loss of blood, but from rabies. If not treated immediately, rabies is always fatal. Seek medical attention as soon as possible if you are bitten by a bat or by any mammal for that matter.

INSURANCE

Before leaving on your trip, contact your health insurance company and find out whether your insurance will cover you while you are away. If not, contact a travel agent and ask about travel health insurance policies. A travel agent can also tell you about trip insurance to cover cancellations or loss of baggage. If you have homeowner's or renter's insurance, you may be covered against theft and loss even while you are on vacation. Be sure to check this before taking out additional insurance. Some credit cards provide trip insurance when you charge an airline ticket, but be sure to check with your credit card company. If you decide that your current insurance is inadequate, you can contact your travel agent for information on various types of travel insurance, including insurance against cancellation of a prepaid tour should this become necessary. Or you can contact **International Underwriters/ Brokers, Inc.,** 243 Church St. W., Vienna VA 22180 (tel. 703/281-9500, or toll free 800/237-6615); or **Access America, Inc.,** 600 Third Ave., New York, NY 10116 (tel. 212/490-5345, or toll free 800/284-8300).

If you are driving your car, you will need to get Guatemalan insurance for the time that you are there. It is usually available at border crossings.

4. WHAT TO PACK

CLOTHING

Costa Rica is a tropical country, so to stay comfortable bring lightweight, natural-fiber clothing. In the rainy season an umbrella, not a raincoat (which is too hot), is necessary. Nights at any time of year can be cool in San José and in the mountains, so also bring a sweater or jacket. Good walking shoes are a must if you plan to visit any of the national park trails. Bring something dressy if you plan to attend the National Theater.

OTHER ITEMS

A bathing suit is a must, and a mask and snorkel come in handy. Insect repellent is invaluable. Sunscreen, although available in a few places, is even more expensive than it is in the United States. Bring plenty of film and a spare battery for your camera. I like to carry a little bottle of iodine and a water bottle for purifying questionable water. A small flashlight is handy if you are heading to any of the national parks or the remote beaches.

5. TIPS FOR THE DISABLED, SENIORS, SINGLES, AND STUDENTS

For the Disabled   In general, there are few handicapped-accessible buildings in Costa Rica. In San José, sidewalks are crowded and uneven.

For Seniors   Many airlines now offer senior citizen discounts. Be sure to ask about these when making reservations. Due to its temperate climate, stable political environment, low cost of living, and friendly *pensionado* program, Costa Rica is popular with retirees from North America. There are excellent medical facilities in San José and plenty of community organizations to help retirees feel at home. If you would like to learn more about visiting or retiring in Costa Rica, contact the **Costa Rican National Tourist Board,** 1101 Brickell Ave., Suite 801, BIV Tower, Miami, FL 33131 (tel. 305/358-2150, or toll free 800/327-7033); or the **Costa Rica National Tourist Board,** 3540 Wilshire Blvd., Dept. MS, Suite 707, Los Angeles, CA 90010 (tel. 213/382-8080).

Because of the long dry season, the beaches and resorts of the Nicoya Peninsula are the most popular places with North American seniors.

Elderhostel, 80 Boylston St., Suite 400, Boston, MA 02116 (tel. 617/426-7788), offers very popular study tours for seniors in Costa Rica.

For Singles   You'll pay the same penalty here that you would elsewhere: Rooms are more expensive if you aren't traveling in a pair.

For Students   Costa Rica is the only country in Central America with a network of hostels that are affiliated with the International Youth Hostel Federation. There are hostels in San José, at Lake Arenal, in Rincon de la Vieja National Park, and at Guayabo National Monument. In San José, there is also a student travel agency: **OTEC,** Victoria Building, Avenida 3 between calles 3 and 5 (tel. 22-0866). If you already have an international student identity card, you can use your card to get discounts on hotels, meals, and international flights. If you don't have one, stop by the OTEC office with a passport photo; for a small fee, they'll prepare you one.

Students interested in a working vacation in Costa Rica should contact the **Council on International Educational Exchange (C.I.E.E.),** 205 E. 42nd St., New York, NY 10017 (tel. 212/661-1450). This organization also issues official student identity cards and has offices all over the United States.

6. ALTERNATIVE/ADVENTURE TRAVEL

EDUCATIONAL/STUDY TRAVEL

Many people come to Costa Rica to study Spanish. There are several schools in San José that offer courses of varying durations. Spanish schools can also arrange for homestay, during which you stay with a middle-class Tico family who will help you to speak only Spanish in your daily life. Classes are intensive and often one-on-one. Listed below are some of the larger and more popular Spanish-language schools.

Foreseter Instituto Internacional, Apdo. 6945, 1000 San José (tel. 506/25-3155, 25-0135, or 25-1649; Fax 506/25-9236), is located 75 meters south of the Automercado in the Los Yoses district of San José. The school offers two-, three-, and four-week programs. Classes start the first Monday of every month, and four hours of class are held five days a week. Prices range from $425 for four weeks (language classes only, without homestay) to $1,200 for a four-week language and culture course (including cultural activities and excursions) with homestay.

Centro Lingüístico Conversa, Apdo. 17, Centro Colón, San José (tel. 506/21-7649 or 33-2418; Fax 506/33-2418), provides one of the most attractive environments for studying Spanish at its El Pedregal farm 10 miles west of San José. A four-week course costs $1,450 for one person and $2,700 for married couples. Price includes instruction, text materials, room and board, laundry services, and even airport pickup and dropoff. Courses are offered every month.

Instituto Interamericano de Idiomas Intensa, Apdo. 8110-1000, San José (tel. 506/24-6353 or 25-6009), is on Calle 33 between avenidas 5 and 7 in the Barrios Escalante neighborhood of San José. It offers two- to four-week programs. A four-week program with homestay costs $750.

Instituto Latinoamericano de Idiomas, Apdo. 1001, San Pedro 2050 (tel. 506/25-2495; in the United States, 818/843-1226; in Canada, 416/964-3388), is one block east of the church, then four blocks south and half a block east (no kidding, this really is the street address for the school). Four weeks with homestay here cost $870.

Instituto Universal de Idiomas, Apdo. 751-2150, Moravia (tel. 506/57-0441 or 23-9917), is located on Avenida 3 between calles 3 and 5 on the third floor of the Victoria Building. This is the most conveniently located school, and it charges only $600 for a four-week course (only three hours per day) with homestay.

ECOTOURISM AND ADVENTURE TRAVEL

Ecotourism (from the term "ecological tourism") is the word these days in Costa Rica. With the growing awareness of the value of tropical forests and the interest in visiting rain forests, dozens of lodges and tour companies have sprung up to cater to the tourists interested in enjoying the natural beauties of Costa Rica. These lodges are located in out-of-the-way locations, sometimes deep in the heart of a forest and sometimes on a farm with only a tiny bit of natural forest. However, they all have one thing in common: They cater to environmentally aware people with an interest in nature. Horseback riding, rafting, kayaking, hiking, and birdwatching are among the popular activities offered at these lodges.

Some U.S. tour operators that offer adventure tour packages are the following: **Sobek Expeditions,** Box 1089, Angels Camp, CA 95222 (tel. 209/736-4524, or toll free 800/777-7939); **Wilderness Travel,** 801 Allston Way, Berkeley, CA 94710 (tel. 415/548-0420, or toll free 800/247-6700); **Overseas Adventure Travel,** 349 Broadway, Cambridge, MA 02139 (tel. 617/876-0533, or toll free 800/221-0814); **Costa Rica Connection,** 958 Higuera St., San Luis Obispo, CA 93401 (tel. 805/543-8823, or toll free 800/345-7422); and **International Expeditions,** 1776 Independence Court, Birmingham, AL 35216 (tel. 205/870-5550, or toll free 800/633-4734).

There are also dozens of tour companies in San José that offer nature-related tours from one-day rafting trips to week-long adventures. Since their tours are usually held only when there are enough interested people, it pays to contact a few of the companies and find out what they might be doing when you plan to be in Costa Rica. The following is a list of some of the companies.

Jungle Trails, Apdo. 2413, San José 1000 (tel. 506/55-3486; Fax 506/55-2782), offers tree-planting trips, trekking, volcano trips, and white-water rafting.

Costa Rica Expeditions, Calle Central and Avenida 3, Apdo. 6941, San José (tel. 506/22-0333), offers tours of Monteverde and Tortuguero and white-water rafting.

Tikal Tour Operators, Apdo. 6398-1000, San José (tel. 506/23-2811; Fax 506/23-1916), offers diving and volcano trips and visits to Braulio Carrillo National Park, Ríncon de la Vieja National Park, and Monteverde.

Geotour, Apdo. 469 Y-Griega 1011, San José (tel. 506/34-1867; Fax 506/53-6338), offers tours of Braulio Carrillo National Park, Carara Biological Reserve, and Cahuita National Park.

If your interest is strictly limited to rafting, contact **Rios Tropicales,** Apdo. 472-1200, Pavas (tel. 506/31-6296). This company operates several one- to four-day raft trips.

7. GETTING THERE

BY PLANE

It takes between three and six hours to fly to Costa Rica from most U.S. cities.

Airlines serving Costa Rica from the United States include **American Airlines** (tel. toll free 800/433-7300), **Continental** (tel. toll free 800/231-0856), **Pan Am** (tel. toll free 800/221-1111), **Lacsa-Costa Rican** (tel. toll free 800/225-2272), **Mexicana** (tel. toll free 800/531-7921), **Taca-El Salvadoran** (tel. toll free 800/535-8780), **Tan Sahsa-Honduran** (tel. toll free 800/327-1225), and **Aviateca-Guatemalan** (tel. toll free 800/327-9832).

BEST-FOR-THE-BUDGET FARES

Aeronica (Nicaraguan) and **Sam** (Colombian out of Medellín) are the two lowest-fare airlines for flights between Costa Rica and other Central American nations. The U.S. gateways are Los Angeles, New Orleans, New York, Miami, and Houston.

The cheapest regular fares are **advance purchase excursion** (APEX) fares, which usually must be purchased at least 7 days before departure and limit your visit to 30 days or less. You may also have to pay a penalty if you decide to change dates after purchasing your ticket. At the time of this writing, Continental had a round-trip APEX fare of $470 from New York to San José. Lacsa was charging a few dollars more, and American Airlines was charging around $500.

BUCKET SHOPS

You can shave a little bit off these ticket prices by purchasing your ticket from what is known as a bucket shop. These ticketing agencies sell discounted tickets on major airlines; although the tickets have as many, and sometimes more, restrictions as an APEX ticket they can help you save money. You'll find bucket shop listings—usually just a column of destinations with prices beside them—in the Sunday travel sections of major-city newspapers. You'll almost never get the ticket for the advertised price, but you will probably get it for less than the airline would sell it to you.

REGULAR AIRFARES

A coach-class seat will run you slightly more than $700, and a first-class seat will cost about $1,200.

BY BUS

There is regular bus service between Panama City, Panama, and Managua, Nicaragua. The former is an 18-hour trip; the latter is only 10 hours. Buses leave Panama City at 10pm and leave Managua at 1, 2, 3, 4, 5, and 6am.

BY CAR

Although it is theoretically possible to travel to Costa Rica by car, in practice it is now very difficult, especially for U.S. citizens. The Inter-American Highway (also known as the Panamerican Highway) passes through El Salvador, Honduras, and Nicaragua after leaving Guatemala and before reaching Costa Rica. All three of these countries can be problematic for travelers because of the continuing internal strife. I do not recommend trying to drive to Costa Rica at this time.

PACKAGE TOURS

If you prefer to let someone else make all the arrangements for you and don't mind spending a bit more money, then maybe you should contact one of the following tour operators. They offer a wide variety of tour packages.

MTA International, 1717 N. Highland Ave., Suite 519, Los Angeles, CA 90028 (tel. 213/462-8643, or toll free 800/876-6824).

Sunny Land Tours, 166 Main St., Hackensack, NJ 07061 (tel. 201/487-2150, or toll free 800/631-1992).

Ocean Connection, 16728 El Camino Real, Houston, TX 77062 (tel. 713/486-6993, or toll free 800/331-2458).

Costa Rica Travel, 6001 N. Sauganash, Chicago, IL 60646 (tel. 312/283-3334, or toll free 800/223-7164).

---

8. SUGGESTED ITINERARIES

HIGHLIGHTS

The following are the most important places to visit in Costa Rica:
1. San José
2. Manuel Antonio
3. Monteverde
4. Jacó Beach
5. Cahuita/Puerto Viejo
6. Tortuguero National Park
7. Irazú Volcano
8. Poás Volcano
9. The Nicoya Peninsula
10. Orosi Valley

PLANNING YOUR ITINERARY

IF YOU HAVE ONE WEEK

Day 1: Visit the museums and the National Theater in San José.
Day 2: Make an excursion to the Orosi Valley, Lankester Gardens, and Irazú Volcano.
Days 3 and 4: Travel to Monteverde and spend a day exploring the cloud forest preserve.
Days 5 and 6: Travel to Manuel Antonio National Park and spend a day on the beautiful beaches.
Day 7: Return to San José.

FROMMER'S FAVORITE
COSTA RICA EXPERIENCES

A Day at Manuel Antonio National Park The three tropical beaches in the park are backed by dense jungle-covered hills, and they have few or no people, good snorkeling, waves for surfing or body surfing, a few trails through the jungle, and a freshwater stream pouring across the sand and into the sea. There's no road, so to reach these perfect beaches you have to ford the stream that runs over the beach.

Hiking Through the Monteverde Cloud Forest Preserve Cloud forests are to the mountains what the rain forests are to the lowlands: a dense and diverse forest habitat filled with an amazing variety of plant, insect, and animal life, including more than a dozen species of hummingbirds and possibly the most beautiful bird on earth, the quetzal.

A Night at the San José National Theater Built in the late 19th century with money raised through a tax on coffee exports, this classic opera house is still serving up the best cultural performances in the country.

The Jungle Train The Jungle Train ride from San José to Limón is a journey through remote forests and past tiny villages that are connected to the rest of the country only by this train. Along the miles of lush forest you might see monkeys or rare birds.

A Trip to the Rim of a Volcano Drive to the rim of either Poás or Irazú and gaze down into the sulfurous pits. Poás is lush and green, whereas Irazú is gray and barren, but both offer spectacular views if you arrive before the clouds close in.

IF YOU HAVE TWO WEEKS

Days 1 and 2: Visit the museums and National Theater in San José.
Day 3: Make an excursion to the Orosi Valley, Lankester Gardens, and Irazú Volcano.
Days 4, 5, and 6: Travel to Monteverde and spend two days exploring the cloud forest.
Days 7 through 9: Explore the beaches and trails of Manuel Antonio National Park.
Day 10: Return to San José.
Day 11: Travel by Jungle Train to Puerto Limón.
Days 12 and 13: Travel by canal to Tortuguero National Park and spend a day there.
Day 14: Return to San José.

IF YOU HAVE THREE WEEKS

Follow the outline above for "If You Have Two Weeks." For your third week, explore the many beaches of the Nicoya Peninsula, visit another remote lodge and do a raft trip, or spend part of your time on Jacó Beach on the Pacific Coast and part of your time at Cahuita National Park on the Caribbean Sea Coast.

THEMED CHOICES

The most common choice for a themed vacation in Costa Rica is to make it a **naturalist tour** by visiting as many of the national parks and private nature reserves as you can in the amount of time available. Another possible theme would be to sample as many of the different **beaches** as you can (although I would simply go straight to Manuel Antonio and spend all my time there).

9. GETTING AROUND

BY PLANE

Surprisingly, getting around by air is one of the most economical ways to see Costa Rica. Because the country is quite small, the flights are short and, luckily, inexpensive. **Sansa,** the domestic airline of Costa Rica, has flights Monday through Saturday between San José and Quepos (Manuel Antonio); Monday, Wednesday, and Friday to Tamarindo (Nicoya Peninsula); and Tuesday, Thursday, and Saturday to Barra Colorado (Tortuguero National Park). The airline's offices are at Calle 24 between Avenida Central and Avenida 1 (tel. 21-9414 or 33-5330). These flights last between 20 and 40 minutes. Fares range from $10 to $15 one way. You must check in at the downtown office, from which a free shuttle bus will take you to the airport.

BY TRAIN

Trains in Costa Rica are generally slower than buses and do not go to nearly as many towns. However, the train from San José to Puerto Limón (known as the **Jungle Train**) is one of Costa Rica's major tourist excursions. The only other train you might want to ride is the **electric train** from San José to Puntarenas. Although it is not as picturesque as the Jungle Train and the trip takes longer than using the highway to Puntarenas, the electric train is still an enjoyable trip. See the "Easy Excursions" section of Chapter 3 on San José for details on these two trains.

BY BUS

This is by far the best way to visit most of Costa Rica. Buses are inexpensive, well-maintained, and uncrowded, and they go nearly everywhere. There is no central bus terminal in San José, so you must know which bus line you'll be traveling on. Here is information to help you get from San José to the major tourist destinations:

To Alajuela (Juan Santamaría International Airport) Buses to Alajuela and the airport leave daily from Avenida 2 between calles 12 and 14 every 15 minutes between 5am and midnight. Duration: 20 minutes. Fare: ¢18 (20¢).

To Sarchí Tuasa lines buses leave every 30 minutes daily from the Alajuela station on Avenida 2 between calles 12 and 14. Duration: 1½ hours. Fare: ¢28 (33¢).

To Cahuita and Puerto Viejo Buses to Cahuita leave daily at 6am and 2:30pm from the corner of Avenida 11 and Calle 1. Duration: 4 hours. Fare: ¢300 ($3.50). This bus also stops in Puerto Viejo. Duration: 4½ hours. Fare: Same as above.

To Puntarenas Buses for Puntarenas leave daily every hour between 6am and 6pm from the corner of Calle 12 and Avenida 9. Duration: 2 hours. Fare: ¢100 ($1.18).

To Manuel Antonio National Park Buses leave daily at 6am, noon, and 6pm from the Coca-Cola station on Calle 16 between avenidas 1 and 3. Duration: 3½ hours. Fare: ¢350 ($4.12).

To Jacó Beach Buses for Jacó Beach leave daily at 7am, 3pm, and 3:30pm from Calle 16 between avenidas 1 and 3. Duration: 2½ hours. Fare: ¢160 ($1.88).

To Liberia Buses for Liberia leave daily at 7, 9, and 11:30am and 3, 4, 6, and 8pm from Calle 14 between avenidas 1 and 3. Duration: 4 hours. Fare: ¢160 ($1.88).

To Tamarindo A bus for Tamarindo Beach leaves daily at 3:30pm from the corner of Calle 15 and Avenida 5. Duration: 5 hours. Fare: ¢275 ($3.24).

BY CAR

CAR RENTALS

Avis, Budget, and **Dollar** car-rental agencies all have offices in Costa Rica. You will save a considerable amount on a car rental if you make a reservation in your home country at least one week before you need the car. The least-expensive Budget car available (a Subaru Justy with manual transmission) rents for about $190 per week, plus insurance and tax, in San José, but if you book this same car in advance from the United States, you can get it for $151 per week, plus insurance and tax. Consult your local *Yellow Pages* for the phone numbers of the above agencies.

There are many other car-rental agencies in San José, some with offices at the airport and others with offices downtown. If you didn't make a reservation before you left home or just want to rent a car for a day, try one of the companies listed below. They charge the same rate (around $40 per day, plus insurance and tax, for their lowest-priced car with unlimited mileage).

Elegante Rent A Car, Calle 10 between avenidas 13 and 15 and Paseo Colón at Calle 34 (tel. 21-0136, 21-0284, or 33-8605).

Tico Rent A Car, Calle 10 between avenidas 13 and 15 or Paseo Colón between calles 24 and 26 (tel. 22-8920 or 22-1765).

GASOLINE

Regular gasoline is what is most readily available in Costa Rica. Most rental cars take regular.

DRIVING RULES

To rent a car in Costa Rica, you must be 25 years old and have a passport. A foreign driver's license is valid for the first three months that you are in Costa Rica. Use of seat belts is required for driver and passengers. Motorcyclists must wear a helmet. Highway police use radar, so keep to the speed limit if you don't want to get pulled over.

MAPS

Car-rental agencies and the I.C.T. information centers at the airport and in downtown San José have adequate road maps.

BREAKDOWNS

If your car should break down and you are unable to get it off the road, place a pile of leaves and/or tree branches in the road 100 feet on either side of the car to warn approaching drivers.

BY FERRY

There are two ferries operating across the Gulf of Nicoya between Puntarenas and the Nicoya Peninsula. The car ferry leaves from the north side of the peninsula between calles 33 and 35 and goes to the town of Naranjo. The passenger ferry leaves from behind the market at the north end of Calle 2 and goes to Paquerra. The Paquerra ferry operates only Monday through Saturday.

HITCHHIKING

Although buses go to most places in Costa Rica, they can be infrequent in the remote regions, and consequently local people often hitchhike to get to their destination sooner. If you are driving a car, people will frequently ask you for a ride. If you are hitching yourself, keep in mind that if a bus doesn't go to your destination, there probably aren't too many cars going there either. Good luck.

LOCATING ADDRESSES

There are no street addresses in Costa Rica, at least not often. Addresses are given as a set of coordinates such as "Calle 3 between Avenida Central and Avenida 1." Many addresses include additional information such as the number of meters or *varas* (an old Spanish measurement roughly equal to a yard) from a specified intersection or some other well-known landmark. The Coca-Cola bottling plant that once stood in this area is long gone, but the address descriptions remain. In outlying neighborhoods, addresses can become long directions such as "50 meters south of the old church, then 100 meters east, then 20 meters south." My personal favorite is a rather macabre address using "the spot where the dog burned" as its landmark. Luckily for the visitor, most addresses in downtown San José are straightforward. Good luck.

10. ACCOMMODATIONS AND DINING NOTES

WHERE TO STAY

If you are traveling with several other people, you should definitely look into staying at an **apartotel,** a cross between an apartment and a hotel just as its name implies. You often get two bedrooms or a bedroom and a sofabed, plus a kitchen. Apartotels come fully furnished right down to the pots and pans.

For young travelers, there are a number of **IYHF**-affiliated hostels in Costa Rica.

Although they are not cheap, Costa Rica's many **jungle lodges** are certainly a worthwhile splurge. Birdwatchers, botanists, and anyone interested in nature will be enthralled by the tropical flora and fauna these lodges will help you see.

WHERE TO EAT

Sodas are the cheapest places to eat in Costa Rica, but the country also has a wide variety of restaurants in all price ranges. Choices of international cuisine abound in San José. If you miss McDonald's or Kentucky Fried Chicken, you can eat your fill in San José. Hotel dining rooms are a surprisingly good choice, because, unlike most places, they do not overcharge.

11. ENJOYING COSTA RICA ON A BUDGET

In the past, Mexico was where North Americans headed when they wanted an inexpensive yet exotic holiday. Today many cities in Mexico are nearly as expensive as places back home. Costa Rica, Guatemala, and Belize, on the other hand, are still a travel bargain. They're close to home, and you can still get a bed for $2 a night if that is what you are looking for. If you want to spend more money, there are excellent values to be had throughout the country, especially in old colonial buildings that have been converted to hotels. The aim of this book is to provide you with the information that you'll need to save money on your trip.

THE $25-A-DAY BUDGET

The premise of this book is that you can enjoy Costa Rica, Guatemala, and Belize on a budget of $25 per day per person. You should have absolutely no problem doing so if you don't have a need to stay in a first-class high-rise or resort hotel. Keep in mind that the $25-a-day budget covers only lodging and three meals a day, not transportation costs, museum admissions, cost of souvenirs, and so forth. However, all of these are also quite inexpensive, and if you are willing to stay in the lowest-budget accommodations recommended in this book, you should easily be able to include all your transportation and many other costs in your $25 a day.

This is roughly how I break down daily costs: $18 per person (based on double occupancy) for a room, $3 for breakfast, $5 for lunch, and $9 for dinner. Many young travelers can actually get by on about $10 per day. However, this budget should allow you to live quite well. For those who prefer a bit more luxury, I have included information on hotels and restaurants that are worth the extra bucks. For those who are traveling on a student's or backpacker's budget, there is also plenty of information.

SAVING MONEY ON ACCOMMODATIONS

Best Budget Bets   Your best way to save money on accommodations in Costa Rica is to choose carefully where you want to go. If you are heading to a beach resort that primarily has expensive rooms and you want one of the handful of budget rooms in town, book early (everybody wants those cheap rooms). Cahuita and Puerto Viejo are the backpackers' hangouts in Costa Rica these days.

Seasonal and Other Discounts   During the rainy season, many hotels offer substantial discounts, especially those at the beaches. Surfers and fishermen get discounts at west coast beach hotels (since they tend to come in the rainy season). Some beach hotels also have weekly rates.

Other Money-Saving Strategies   If you want to go to Manuel Antonio on a backpacker's budget, you'll have to stay in Quepos (or put up with less-than-clean accommodations). If you plan on staying for a month or more, look into renting a hotel room.

SAVING MONEY ON MEALS

Best Budget Bets   The cheapest place to eat in Costa Rica will always be a *soda,* the equivalent of a diner in the United States. The food might not be great, but the prices can't be beat. If you like rice and black beans, you can save even more money. Ticos eat rice and beans (with something else on the side) at every meal. At breakfast, rice and beans are called *gallo pinto* and come with everything from eggs to steak or even to seafood. At lunch or dinner, rice and beans go by the name *casado* (which also means "married"). A casado comes with a cabbage-and-tomato salad, fried plantains (a type of banana), and a meat dish of some sort.

Other Money-Saving Strategies   Quite a few hotels in Costa Rica come with kitchenettes, especially those at the beaches. If you visit the local market and fix your own meals, you can save considerably. I try to buy as much and as many different types of tropical fruits as I can when I'm here. You might want to consider buying a little immersion heating coil and a Costa Rican reusable drip-coffee bag. With these two items and a cup, you can make your own fresh coffee every morning, and the coffee here is as fresh as it comes (you have to wait for them to roast it at the market).

SAVING MONEY ON SIGHT-SEEING AND ENTERTAINMENT

Special Discounts/Passes/Free Days   Museum admissions in San José are already so low that there is no need to worry about special discounts (there aren't any). Much of the entertainment in San José is free. Marimba bands play daily outside the National Theater, and it doesn't cost anything to enjoy the bands at La Esmeralda or the Soda Palace. Even the National Theater is quite cheap if you're willing to settle for a balcony seat; even if you're not and want to hobnob with Costa Rica's landed gentry, the price won't break your bank.

Other Money-Saving Strategies   Don't be conned into spending $60 or more for the Jungle Train. A regular ticket costs only about $1.50, and you can easily make the trip on your own without a guide.

SAVING MONEY ON SHOPPING

Costa Rica doesn't have the wide variety of traditional handicrafts that Guatemala has (in fact, many Guatemalan crafts and textiles are sold in Costa Rica), so if you're including Guatemala on your trip to Central America, I suggest that you save your money to spend there. There are a few great buys in Costa Rica, though.

Best Buys   One of Costa Rica's best buys is **coffee.** It's hard to get fresher coffee anywhere. The air for streets around the San José market is redolent with the smell of roasting coffee beans. Stop in at **El Trebol,** Calle 8 between Avenidas Central and 1 (no phone), and you can pick up a pound of beans hot from the roaster for about $1. In tourist shops all over town, this same bag of coffee beans sells for $4 or $5. When buying coffee be sure to buy only bags labeled *100% puro;* otherwise, you will get coffee that has already had sugar added to it (that's the way they like it down here). Also, make sure you buy only whole beans because Costa Rican grinds are too fine for standard drip-filter coffeemakers.

Other good buys in Costa Rica are gold and silver reproductions of pre-Columbian **jewelry,** which you'll find in shops all over San José. You'll probably recognize many of the designs from pieces on display in museums around town. Reproductions of small **carved stone statues** from pre-Columbian times are additional good buys that are surprisingly light and very authentic looking. You'll also find tropical hardwoods carved into all manner of jewelry, bowls, figurines, and knickknacks. Some are quite expensive and others are quite reasonably priced, but all are beautiful.

Although I personally find them to be far too gaudy, brightly painted **miniature ox carts** are a symbol of Costa Rica. Once sugarcane was carried on similar ox carts. Today, even though a few ox carts are still used in various parts of the country, painted ones such as these are strictly tourist items. Sarchí is the ox-cart factory capital and is included on many tours. Large wood-and-leather **rocking chairs** also are manufactured in Sarchí.

Markets   Every town in Costa Rica has a market. It may be open only weekly or may be open daily, but it's there. This is the best place to buy fresh fruits and vegetables. Some markets, such as the one in San José, also sell souvenirs and countless other useful items. Take a look in one of the kitchen utensil stalls; you'll probably find dozens of interesting and inexpensive little gadgets that you can't get at home or for much less than you would pay at home. Be sure to keep close tabs on your money at all times because markets are notorious haunts of pickpockets and purse slashers (thieves who use a razorblade to slice open your purse and then steal the contents).

Bargaining   You should always try to bargain in markets and with street vendors. It's accepted and expected and can save you quite a bit. Tourist prices are always higher, so if you are shopping for souvenirs (especially on the Plaza de Cultura), bargain hard.

SAVING MONEY ON TRANSPORTATION

By Plane   Sansa, Costa Rica's domestic airline, is one of the country's best bargains. For less than $10 and in only 20 minutes, you can fly to Quepos (for Manuel Antonio National Park beaches). Don't forget to take advantage of the free shuttle bus Sansa runs between their downtown offices and the airport.

If you're traveling onward to Guatemala or Panama City by air, check the rates at **Aeronica** (Nicaraguan airlines). They often have special low fares.

By Train   Stay away from tour agencies trying to sell you a Jungle Train excursion. These tours cost about $60 and, although you get to ride in a more comfortable car, you see the same scenery that you would if you paid the normal fare of only ¢130 ($1.53). Be very careful with your belongings because this train suffers from an epidemic of pickpockets and bag slashers. I suggest that you take the train from Cartago to Siquirres and return by bus. This way you can make it a day trip out of San José and don't have to bring all your luggage and money.

By Bus   It is hard to beat the low fares on Costa Rica's intercity buses. The highways are good, so most bus rides are quite comfortable.

By Car   The way to save money on a rental car is to reserve from your home country at least a week before you need the car. You can save $30 to $50 per week this way. Also check to see if your credit card or auto insurance pays your collision damage waiver. You may not have to buy all that insurance if it does.

SAVING MONEY ON SERVICES AND OTHER TRANSACTIONS

Tipping   Tipping is not necessary in restaurants, where a 10% service charge is always added to your bill (along with 10% tax). If service was particularly good, you can leave a little at your own discretion, but it is not mandatory. Porters and bellhops get around ¢50 (59¢) per bag. Taxi fares must be negotiated prior to getting into a taxi, and therefore tips are unnecessary.

Money Changing and Credit Cards   Although it is illegal to change money on the black market (which offers a slightly better rate than the banks do), it is possible to change money in many hotels and avoid the service charge that banks charge. You may even get a better rate at your hotel. By using your credit card, you can lock in that day's official exchange rate and avoid having to pay bank service charges on changing money.

Telephone   The number for the AT&T USA direct operator is 114. You can place collect and calling-card calls through this English-speaking operator at considerable savings over normal Costa Rican telephone rates.

 COSTA RICA

American Express   Costa Rica's only American Express office is in San José, Calle 1 between Avenida Central and Avenida 1 (tel. 33-0044). Open Mon–Fri from 8am–5:30pm.

Business Hours   Banks are open Mon–Fri from 9am–3pm. Bars are open until 1 or 2am. Offices are open Mon–Fri from 8am–5pm (closed for two hours at lunch). Stores are open Mon–Sat from 9am–7pm. Many restaurants stay open 24 hours, while others close between meals.

Camera/Film   Most types of film are available but expensive. Kodachrome is not readily available.

Climate   See "When to Go" in this chapter.

Crime   See *Safety*.

Currency   See "Information, Entry Requirements, and Money" in this chapter.

Customs   You can bring in half a kilo of tobacco products, three liters of liquor, and two cameras duty free.

Documents Required   See "Information, Entry Requirements, and Money" in this chapter.

Driving Rules   See "Getting Around" in this chapter.

Drug Laws   Drug laws in Costa Rica are strict, so stay away from marijuana and cocaine. You'll also need a prescription from a doctor or lab results to have prescriptions filled in Costa Rica.

Drugstores   A drugstore in Costa Rica is a *farmacia*. You'll find at least one in nearly every town.

Electricity   The standard in Costa Rica is the same as in the United States: 110 volts.

Embassies and Consulates   United States Consulate, Avenida 3 and Calle 1, 2nd floor (tel. 22-5566); **Canadian Embassy,** Calle 3 and Avenida Central (tel. 23-0446); **British Embassy,** Paseo Colón between calles 38 and 40 (tel. 21-5566).

Emergencies   For an **ambulance** call 21-5818; to report a **fire** call 118; to contact the **police** call 117, or 127 outside cities.

Etiquette   Ticos tend to dress conservatively and treat everyone very respectfully. Both sexes shake hands.

Hitchhiking   This is permitted. If you're trying to get to remote parks or volcanoes, however, there usually isn't much traffic on such roads. Buses, which are quite inexpensive, go almost everywhere in the country.

Holidays   See "When to Go" in this chapter.

Information   See "Information, Entry Requirements, and Money" in this chapter. Also see individual city chapters for local information offices.

Language   Spanish is the official language of Costa Rica. *Berlitz Latin-American Spanish* (Berlitz Guides, 1989) is probably the best phrasebook to bring with you.

Laundry   For listings of Laundromats, see individual city sections of regional chapters.

Liquor Laws   Alcoholic beverages are sold every day of the week throughout the year, with the exception of two days during Holy Week and the two days before and after a presidential election.

Mail   Mail to the United States takes about one week. A letter to the United States costs ¢18 (21¢), and postcards cost ¢16 (19¢). A post office is called a *correo* in Spanish. You can get stamps either at the post office or at a newsstand.

Maps   The **Costa Rican National Tourist Bureau (I.C.T.)** can provide you with good free maps of both Costa Rica and San José.

Newspapers/Magazines   There are three Spanish-language dailys in Costa Rica and one English-language weekly, *The Tico Times*. In addition, you can get *Time, Newsweek,* and several U.S. newspapers at hotel gift shops and a few of the bookstores in San José.

Passports   See "Information, Entry Requirements, and Money" in this chapter.

Pets   If you want to bring your cat or dog, be sure that it has current vaccinations against rabies and distemper.

Police   The number to call for the **Policia de Transito** is 27-7150 or 27-8030.

Radio/TV   Costa Rica has one English-language television station. In addition, satellite cable TV from the United States is available in most hotels. There are more than 100 radio stations on the AM and FM dials.

Restrooms   These are called *servicios sanitarios* and are marked *damas* for women and *hombres* or *caballeros* for men.

Safety   Although most of Costa Rica is very safe, it is known for its pickpockets. Never carry a wallet in your back pocket. In fact, never carry anything of value in pants pockets. A woman should keep a tight grip on her purse (keep it tucked under your arm). Don't leave valuables in your hotel room. Don't park a car on the street in Costa Rica; there are plenty of public parking lots around San José.

Taxes   All hotels charge 13% tax, and restaurants charge 10% tax and also add on a 10% service charge. There is an airport departure tax of ¢517 ($6.08).

Telephone   Costa Rica has an excellent phone system, with a dial tone similar to that heard in the United States. Phone numbers in Costa Rica have six digits. There is one telephone book for all of Costa Rica. A pay phone costs ¢2 (2¢), and most accept only ¢2 coins. You can get an AT&T operator for making calling-card and collect calls by dialing 114 (pay phones require deposit of coins). The Costa Rican telephone system allows direct international dialing, but it is expensive.

Time   Costa Rica is on Central Standard Time, six hours behind Greenwich Mean Time.

Tipping   See "Saving Money on Services and Transactions" in this chapter.

Tourist Offices   See "Information, Entry Requirements, and Money" in this chapter. Also see specific cities.

Visas   See "Information, Entry Requirements, and Money" in this chapter.

Water   Although the water throughout Costa Rica is said to be safe to drink, many tourists I met on my last trip got sick within a few days of arriving in Costa Rica. Play it safe and stick to bottled drinks as much as possible and avoid ice.

CHAPTER 3

SAN JOSÉ

1. **FROM A BUDGET TRAVELER'S POINT OF VIEW**
2. **ORIENTATION AND GETTING AROUND**
- **WHAT'S SPECIAL ABOUT SAN JOSÉ**
- **FAST FACTS—SAN JOSÉ**
3. **WHERE TO STAY**
4. **WHERE TO EAT**
5. **ATTRACTIONS**
6. **SAVVY SHOPPING**
7. **EVENING ENTERTAINMENT**
8. **EASY EXCURSIONS**
9. **MOVING ON—TRAVEL SERVICES**

In the center of San José is an open-air market where the air smells of roasting coffee. It's near the Coca-Cola. Of course, everyone knows what the Coca-Cola is: the area where once stood the Coca-Cola bottling plant. The address of every business in this neighborhood—stores, restaurants, hotels, and offices—is measured from the Coca-Cola. That's just the way things are in San José. Although it has all the trappings of a modern cosmopolitan city, from an opera house to a McDonald's, there are no street addresses. Everything is "so many *varas*"—an archaic measurement about equal to a yard—"from such-and-such corner" or from the Coca-Cola or from some equally unlikely landmark. Don't worry: If you follow your nose, you'll find the coffee vendor in the market despite the confusing directions.

San José, and modern Costa Rica, was built on coffee. It is one of the country's main exports, along with bananas, and the fortunes that were made shipping coffee to the sleepy souls in Europe helped found San José, which is arguably the most beautiful capital city in Central America. The self-imposed tax on coffee exports helped pay for the National Theater in the latter years of the last century, and coffee revenues provided for the city's university and brought culture to this forgotten backwater of the Spanish empire.

Why does coffee grow so well around San José? The Meseta Central, or Central Valley, in which the city sits, has a perfect climate. At 3,750 feet above sea level, San José enjoys springlike temperatures year round. From nearly any street in the city, you can glance up at lush green mountains planted with coffee. On a clear day, and these are common, the mountains seem close enough to touch. Their patchwork of tiny farms lends San José a small-town feel that lulls visitors into a pleasant sense of familiarity.

1. FROM A BUDGET TRAVELER'S POINT OF VIEW

Budget Bests None of the city's museums charge much in the way of admission; the Jade Museum and the Gold Museum, which are probably the two most impressive museums in Costa Rica, are absolutely free.

Public buses are another of San José's great bargains at only ₡5 (5¢), and taxis are quite inexpensive, although you must agree on a price before you get in (taxi drivers refuse to use their meters).

When it comes to dining, your best bet for saving money is to look for a soda, which serves inexpensive Costa Rican–style meals. No visit to San José would be complete without having at least one meal at the Gran Hotel Costa Rica's patio buffet overlooking the National Theater and all the activity of Plaza de la Cultura.

Discount Opportunities   There aren't many discount opportunities in San José. However, discounts are hardly necessary. Although it is more expensive than other cities in Central America, San José is still inexpensive by North American standards.

What's Worth Paying For   By all means splurge and buy a ticket for a performance at the **National Theater** (Teatro Nacional). Although you can get a seat for as little as $2 or $3, live it up, hobnob with the elite of Costa Rica (but be sure to look the part). At most it might cost you $15 or $20 to hear the national symphony or see a touring opera company.

You're likely to be bombarded with offers to take this tour or that excursion, but most of them can be done just as easily and at a fraction of the cost on public transport. What you should spring for is a trip to **Tortuguero National Park** if you are interested in seeing nesting sea turtles or visiting a remote jungle. If you've never been **white-water rafting,** you won't find a better place to try a one-day excursion than San José, and if you dream of spending a day exploring remote islands surrounded by turquoise waters, take one of the day-long cruises around the **Gulf of Nicoya.**

2. ORIENTATION & GETTING AROUND

ARRIVING

In the following section, I assume that you did not drive through war-torn El Salvador and Nicaragua and did not take the Jungle Train *up* from Puerto Limón.

BY PLANE

Several airlines fly into San José from the United States, Canada, and other Central American countries. You will arrive at the **Juan Santamaría International Airport** near the city of Alajuela, about 20 minutes to downtown San José whether you take a taxi, car, or bus. A taxi into town will cost around ¢850 ($10) and a bus will cost only ¢28 (33¢). The Alajuela–San José buses run frequently and drop you on Avenida 2 between calles 12 and 14, which is very convenient to several of the hotels listed in this chapter. There are several car-rental agencies located at the airport, although if you are planning on spending a few days in San José, a car is a liability. However, if you are planning on heading immediately off to the beaches, it is much easier to pick up your car here than at a downtown office. You'll find the car-rental offices and the bus and taxi stands up the stairs and to the left after you clear Customs.

TOURIST INFORMATION

There is an **I.C.T. (Instituto Costarricense de Turismo)** desk at Juan Santamaría International Airport, where you can pick up maps and brochures before you head into San José. You'll find the desk on the left before you come to the stairs after leaving the Customs inspection counter. The main tourist information center is beneath the Plaza de la Cultura on Calle 5 between Avenida Central and Avenida 2 (tel. 22-1090), beside the entrance to the underground Gold Museum. The people

WHAT'S SPECIAL ABOUT SAN JOSÉ

Museums
- ☐ The Gold Museum, the largest collection of pre-Columbian gold jewelry and ornaments in the Americas
- ☐ The Jade Museum, an equally impressive collection of pre-Columbian jade artifacts and jewelry
- ☐ The National Museum, an excellent collection of pre-Columbian artifacts

Parks/Gardens
- ☐ Lankester Gardens, near Cartago, with hundreds of species of orchids on display

Religious Shrines
- ☐ The basilica in Cartago, with a statue of the Virgin of Los Angeles said to heal the sick
- ☐ The ruins of a church in Cartago turned into a park

Natural Spectacles
- ☐ Two volcanoes near San José with roads to their rims

After Dark
- ☐ San José's National Theater, a stately old opera house with performances almost every night
- ☐ El Pueblo, a shopping, dining, and entertainment complex with nearly a dozen bars, discos, nightclubs, and even a roller-skating rink.

Ace Attractions
- ☐ The Jungle Train, winding its way through the jungle as it travels from San José to Limón

Offbeat Oddities
- ☐ The Serpentarium, a reptilian zoo with dozens of Costa Rica's poisonous snakes on display

Shopping
- ☐ Fresh-roasted Costa Rican coffee, available by the pound for less than $1

here are very helpful, and they even have photo albums of different jungle lodges so that you can have a look at some of your ecotour options. These can be very helpful when you're choosing a lodge to visit. Both offices are open Monday through Saturday from 9am to 5pm.

CITY LAYOUT

MAIN ARTERIES AND STREETS

Downtown San José is laid out on a grid. *Avenidas* (avenues) run east and west, while *calles* (streets) run north and south. The center of the city is at **Avenida Central and Calle Central.** To the north of Avenida Central, the avenidas have odd numbers beginning with Avenida 1; to the south, they have even numbers beginning with Avenida 2. Likewise, calles to the east of Calle Central have odd numbers, and those to the west have even numbers. The main downtown artery is Avenida 2, which merges with Avenida Central on either side of the downtown area. West of downtown, Avenida Central becomes Paseo Colón, which ends at Sabana Park and feeds into the highway to Alajuela, the airport, and the Pacific Coast. Calle 3 will take you out of town to the north and put you on the road to the Caribbean Coast.

FINDING AN ADDRESS

This is one of the most confusing aspects of visiting San José in particular and Costa Rica in general. There are no street addresses, at least not often. Addresses are given as a set of coordinates such as "Calle 3 between Avenida Central and Avenida 1." It is then up to you to locate the building within that block, keeping in mind that the building could be on either side of the street. Many addresses include additional information, such as the number of meters or *varas* (an old Spanish measurement roughly equal to a yard) from a specified intersection or some other well-known landmark. These landmarks are what become truly confusing for visitors to the city because they are often landmarks only if you have lived in the neighborhood all your life. The classic example of this is the Coca-Cola, one of the most common landmarks used in addresses in the blocks surrounding San José's main market. It refers to a Coca-Cola bottling plant that once stood in this area. Unfortunately, the edifice is long gone, but the address descriptions remain. In outlying neighborhoods, addresses can become long directions such as "50 meters south of the old church, then 100 meters east, then 20 meters south." My personal favorite is a rather macabre address using "the spot where the dog burned" as its landmark. Luckily for the visitor, most downtown addresses are straightforward. Good luck. Oh, if you're wondering how mail deliverers manage, you'll be reassured to know that nearly everyone in San José uses a P.O. box. This is called the *apartado* system, abbreviated **Apdo.** on mailing addresses.

NEIGHBORHOODS IN BRIEF

San José is sprawling. Today it is divided into dozens of neighborhoods known as *barrios*. However, because virtually all the listings in this chapter fall within the main downtown area, there is no need to concern yourself with the many outlying neighborhoods.

GETTING AROUND
BY BUS

Buses in San José are cheap, only ¢5 (6¢). The most important buses are those running east and west along Avenida 2 and Avenida 3. The Sabana-Cementerio bus runs from Sabana Park to downtown and is one of the most convenient buses to use. San Pedro buses will take you out of downtown heading east. Unfortunately, taking a bus into town is much easier than taking one out of town, especially if you are trying to catch an outbound Sabana-Cementerio bus. These buses don't run very frequently, and their stops are far apart. Considering this and the congestion on Avenida 3, you'll find that it is generally easier to walk to your destination if it is closer than Sabana Park. Buses are always boarded from the front, and bus drivers can make change. Be especially mindful of your wallet, purse, or other valuables. Pickpockets work the crowded buses. Their favorite trick is to wait at a bus stop until the last person is boarding; then several of them try to crowd on, pushing people onto the bus. In the midst of this melee, wallets often disappear. Never let anyone push you from behind. The Alajuela–San José buses that run in from the airport cost ¢28 (33¢).

BY TAXI

Although taxis in San José have meters (*marías*) the drivers refuse to use them, so you'll have to negotiate the price. The official rate at the time of writing is ¢50 (59¢) for the first kilometer and ¢13 (15¢) for each additional kilometer. If you have a rough idea of how far it is to your destination, you can estimate how much it should cost from these figures. If the first driver gives you a quote that seems way out of line, ask another. You'll find taxis in front of the National Theater (usually at high prices) and around the Parque Central at Avenida Central and Calle Central among other locations.

ON FOOT

Downtown San José is very compact. Nearly everyplace you might want to go is within an area measuring 15 blocks by 4 blocks. Traffic, both vehicular and pedestrian, within this area is heavy. You'll often find it faster to walk than to take a

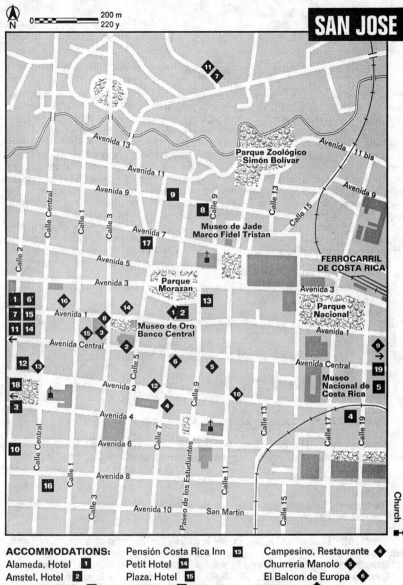

SAN JOSE

ACCOMMODATIONS:
Alameda, Hotel **1**
Amstel, Hotel **2**
Apartotel Castilla **3**
Apartotel San José **4**
Bella Vista, Hotel **5**
Cacts, Hotel **6**
Diplomat, Hotel **7**
Don Carlos, Hotel **8**
Dunn Inn, Hotel **9**
Fortuna, Hotel **10**
Johnson, Hotel **11**
Pensión American **12**

Pensión Costa Rica Inn **13**
Petit Hotel **14**
Plaza, Hotel **15**
Ritz, Hotel **16**
Santo Tomás, Hotel **17**
Talamanca, Hotel **18**
Toruma Youth Hostel **19**

RESTAURANTS:
Amstel Grill Room **1**
Café de Teatro Nacional **2**
Café Parisienne **3**

Campesino, Restaurante **4**
Churreria Manolo **5**
El Balcon de Europa **6**
El Pueblo **7**
Hardee's **8**
Kentucky Fried Chicken **9**
La Casa de Sandwich **10**
La Cocina de Leña **11**
La Esmeralda **12**
La Perla **13**
McDonald's **14**
Nutrisoda **15**
Soda La Casita **16**

bus or taxi. Avenida Central is a pedestrians-only street for several blocks around Calle Central.

BY CAR

If you decide to rent a car for an excursion out of San José, you have two choices: You can pick up your car downtown and then have to deal with downtown traffic, or you can take a bus out to the airport and pick up your car there. Luckily, many of the car-rental offices are on Paseo Colón, a wide boulevard west of downtown.

Avis, Budget, and **Dollar** car-rental agencies all have offices in Costa Rica. You will save a considerable amount on a car rental if you make a reservation in your home country at least one week before you need the car. The least-expensive Budget car available (a Subaru Justy with manual transmission) rents for about $190 per week, plus insurance and tax, in San José, but if you book this same car in advance from the United States, you can get it for $151 per week, plus insurance and tax. Consult your local *Yellow Pages* for the phone numbers of the above agencies.

There are many other car-rental agencies in San José, some with offices at the airport and others with offices downtown. If you didn't make a reservation before you left home or just want to rent a car for a day, try one of the companies listed below. They charge the same rate (around $40 per day), plus insurance and tax, for their lowest-priced car with unlimited mileage).

Elegante Rent A Car, Calle 10 between avenidas 13 and 15 and Paseo Colón at Calle 34 (tel. 21-0136, 21-0284, or 33-8605).

Tico Rent A Car, Calle 10 between avenidas 13 and 15 or Paseo Colón between calles 24 and 26 (tel. 22-8920 or 22-1765).

 FAST FACTS **SAN JOSÉ**

American Express The American Express office is located on Calle 1 between Avenida Central and Avenida 1 (tel. 33-0044). Open Mon–Fri from 8am–5:30pm.

Baby-sitters Your only chance for a baby-sitter in San José is to check with your hotel.

Bookstore The Bookshop, Avenida 1 between calles 1 and 3 (tel. 21-6847), has a wide selection of English-language newspapers, magazines, and books.

Car Rentals See "Getting Around" in this chapter.

Climate See "When to Go" in Chapter 2.

Crime See *Safety*.

Currency Exchange The best thing to do is ask at your hotel. If they can't change money for you, they can direct you to a private bank where you won't have to stand in line for hours.

Dentist If you need a dentist while in San José, your best bet is to call your embassy, which will have a list of recommended dentists.

Doctors Contact your embassy for information on doctors in San José.

Drugstores **Farmacia Fischel,** Avenida 3 and Calle 2, is across from the main post office. Open Mon–Fri from 7:30am–7pm, Sat from 8am–5:30pm.

Embassies and Consulates **United States Consulate,** Avenida 3 and Calle 1, 2nd floor (tel. 22-5566); **Canadian Embassy,** Calle 3 and Avenida Central (tel. 23-0446); **British Embassy,** Paseo Colón between calles 38 and 40 (tel. 21-5566).

Emergencies In case of **fire** dial 118; for the **police** dial 117; for an **ambulance** dial 35-0272 or 21-5818.

Eyeglasses Optica Jiménez, Avenida 2 and Calle 3 (tel. 33-4417 or 22-0233) is open Mon–Sat from 8am–noon and 2–6pm.

Hairdressers/Barbers **El Toque Nuevo,** Avenida 2 between calles 1 and 3 in Edificios Los Arcados (tel. 23-6551), is open Mon–Sat from 9am–7pm. It services both men and women.

Holidays See "When to Go" in Chapter 2.

Hospitals Clinica Biblica, Avenida 14 between Calle Central and Calle 1 (tel. 23-6422), is conveniently located close to downtown and has several English-speaking doctors.

Information See "Tourist Information" in this chapter.

Laundry/Dry Cleaning Sixaola, Avenida 2 between calles 7 and 9, is one of the only places downtown to get clothes cleaned. Unfortunately, their prices are quite high since they charge the same for laundering or dry cleaning. Ask at your hotel—most offer a laundry service.

Libraries The **National Library** is at the corner of Avenida 3 and Calle 15.

Lost Property If you lose something in San José, consider it gone.

Luggage Storage/Lockers Most hotels will store luggage for you while you are traveling around the country.

Newspapers/Magazines The *Tico Times* is Costa Rica's English-language weekly paper serving the expatriate community and tourists. You can also get the *International Herald Tribune, USA Today, Time,* and *Newsweek,* among other English-language publications.

Photographic Needs Film is very expensive in Costa Rica, so bring as much as you will need. If you are caught short, expect to pay ¢725 ($8.53) for a 24-exposure roll of print film. You can buy film and other photographic equipment at **Ilford Dima,** Avenida Central and Calle 5 (tel. 22-3969), open Mon–Fri from 9am–5pm, Sat from 8am–noon. I recommend that you wait to have your film processed when you get home.

Police Dial 117 for the police.

Post Office The main post office (*correo*) is on Calle 2 between avenidas 1 and 3. It's open Mon–Fri from 6am–midnight, Sat from 8am–noon for purchasing stamps. For mailing packages, hours are Mon–Fri 7am–6pm, Sat 7am–noon.

Radio/TV There are six Spanish-language TV channels, one English-language channel, and satellite TV from the United States. There are dozens of AM and FM radio stations in San José.

Religious Services The *Tico Times* has a listing of churches in San José. You can also ask at the tourist office for a list of the city's many churches.

Restrooms These are known as *sanitarios* or *servicios sanitarios.* They are marked *damas* (women) and *hombres* or *caballeros* (men).

Safety Never carry anything of value in your pockets or purse. Pickpockets and purse slashers are rife in San José, especially on public buses and in the markets. The Costa Ricans blame the increase in petty crime on all the refugees from Nicaragua and El Salvador. Leave your passport, money, and other valuables in your hotel safe, and carry only as much as you really need when you go out. If you do carry anything valuable with you, keep it in a moneybelt or special passport bag around your neck. Whichever method you choose, keep things out of sight under your clothes. Also be advised that the Parque Central is not a safe place for a late-night stroll. With these precautions in mind, you should have a safe visit to San José.

Shoe Repairs Al Instante, Avenida 1 between calles 5 and 7 (no phone) is open Mon–Sat from 8am–noon and 1:30–6:30pm. They'll get you back on your feet in an instant.

Taxes All hotel bills have an additional 13.3% tax added on; in restaurants, both a 10% tax and a 10% service charge are added to all bills.

Taxis See "Getting Around" in this chapter.

Telegrams/Telexes You can send telegrams and telexes from the **I.C.E.** office, Avenida 2 between calles 1 and 3. Open daily 7am–10pm.

Telephones Pay phones are not as common in San José as they are in North American cities. When you do find one, whether on the street or in a restaurant or hotel lobby, it may take coins of various denominations or it may take only ¢2 coins. Pay phones are notoriously unreliable, so it is better to make calls from your hotel.

Water The tap water in San José is said to be perfectly fine to drink. Residents of the city will swear to this. However, frequent complaints about intestinal illnesses by tourists make me a bit skeptical about San José's water. I suggest sticking to bottled drinks and *refrescos* with milk as much as possible. *Sin hielo* means "no ice."

3. WHERE TO STAY

Luckily for visitors, there are still a lot of good hotel deals to be had in downtown San José. From high-rise hotels to tiny pensións in colonial-style buildings, you'll find a wide variety of budget choices within walking distance of all the city's major attractions. The following are the best of the budget hotels.

DOUBLE ROOMS FOR LESS THAN ¢1,200 [$14.11]

PENSIÓN AMERICAN, Calle 2 between Avenida Central and Avenida 2, Apdo. 4853, San José. Tel. 506/21-4171 or 21-9799. 34 rms, none with private bath.

$ Rates: ¢339 ($3.98) single; ¢678 ($7.98) double; ¢1,017 ($11.96) triple; ¢1,356 ($15.95) quad. No credit cards.

This is an old favorite with Central American backpack travelers. The prices are about as low as they come in San José, and you don't get much. The rooms are rather dark, the beds vary in quality, and the walls (very thin to begin with) don't go all the way to the ceiling, but the pension stays busy with interesting folks. There's a TV lounge so that you don't have to spend all of your time in your room. The management is friendly and helpful, which is perhaps the reason this place has maintained its good reputation for so many years.

HOTEL BELLA VISTA, Avenida Central between calles 19 and 21, San José. Tel. 506/23-0095 or 33-5477. 30 rms, all with bath.

$ Rates: ¢696.80–¢917.75 ($8.20–$10.80) single; ¢974.40–¢1,835.45 ($11.46–$21.59) double; ¢1,257.60 ($14.80) triple; ¢1,540.90 ($18.13) quad. AE, MC, V.

Close to the National Museum and the train and bus station for the Atlantic Coast, the Bella Vista is still only a 20-minute walk from the Plaza de Cultura. Small rooms open onto a hallway with a few windows, but most of the rooms are quite dark. Cheery carpets and bedspreads and good reading lamps do much to offset the darkness. Tiled bathrooms are one of the bonuses here. Don't miss the wall murals and unusual original artwork throughout the hotel. There is a very popular restaurant out front.

HOTEL JOHNSON, Calle 8 between Avenida Central and Avenida 2a, Apdo. 6638 San José 1000. Tel. 506/23-76-33 or 23-78-27. 57 rms, 3 suites, all with bath.

$ Rates: ¢850 ($10) single; ¢1,050 ($12.35) double; ¢1,730 ($20.35) suite (for five). MC, V.

The lobby of this large, centrally located hotel is on the second floor. You'll find the hotel patronized primarily by Costa Rican businesspeople and families, but it is a good choice for any budget traveler. In the lobby there is a television and several lounge chairs, and on each of the residence floors above there is a sitting area furnished with attractive wicker chairs. On the third floor you'll find one of the most unusual wall decorations I have ever seen in a hotel—a double bass viol. The rooms have tile floors and open onto a narrow air shaft that lets in a bit of light. Bathrooms are relatively clean and roomy. Most rooms come with twin beds (you might want to test a few beds if you're picky about mattresses).

Behind the reception desk there is a breakfast room that serves a limited variety of breakfasts for around ¢180 ($2). Across the lobby is a larger dining room and bar that serves lunch and dinner from an international menu. The special of the day goes for ¢130 ($1.50), while à la carte meals run from ¢240 to ¢400 ($2.82 to $4.70). On Wednesday from 7 to 9pm and Friday from 8 to 10pm there is live music here. During happy hour from 7 to 8pm, you can get two-for-one drinks.

DOUBLE ROOMS FOR LESS THAN ¢2,000 [$23.53]

PETIT HOTEL, Calle 24 between Avenida Central and Avenida 2, Apdo. 7694-1000, San José. Tel. 506/33-0766. 14 rms, 7 with bath.

$ Rates: ¢850 ($10) single without bath, ¢1,275 ($15) single with bath; ¢1,275 ($15) double without bath, ¢1,445–¢1,700 ($17–$20) double with bath; ¢425 ($5) for extra bed. No credit cards.

Despite its location (20-minute walk from the Plaza de Cultura), this is one of my favorite bottom-of-the-budget choices in San José. You'll find all sorts of interesting gringos sitting around the television lounge of this mazelike collection of large and small rooms. The management is very friendly and helpful, and the rooms, although basic, are clean and bright. Some rooms have the same highly polished, beautiful hardwood floor as the lounge. You can use the kitchen here for fixing simple meals, and the refrigerator also is available. There is a pot of free hot coffee on the counter all times of the night or day. The communal toilets could be a bit cleaner, but all in all this is a great place to stay. If you don't want to carry all your luggage with you while you explore the rest of the country and plan to come back to the Petit after your journeys, you can store your excess stuff in a large, locked storage room.

HOTEL CACTS, Avenida 3 bis No. 2845 between calles 28 and 30, Apdo. 379-1005, San José. Tel. 506/21-2928 or 21-6546. Fax 506/21-8616. 13 rms (adding 22 new rooms), 9 with bath.

$ Rates (including Continental breakfast): ¢1,627.75 ($19.15) single without bath, ¢1,921 ($22.60) single with bath; ¢1,627.75 ($19.15) double without bath, ¢1,870 ($22) double with bath; ¢2,465 ($29) triple; ¢2,890 ($34) quad. No credit cards.

This is one of the most interesting and unusual budget hotels I've ever seen, housed in an attractive tropical contemporary home on a business and residential street. You reach the reception area via a flight of outside steps that lead past a small garden area. Once inside, you are in a maze of halls on several levels (the house is built on a slope). My favorite room is the huge bilevel family room with its high beamed ceiling.

HOTEL RITZ, Calle Central between avenidas 8 and 10, San José. Tel. 506/22-4103. 15 rms, 9 with bath.

$ Rates: ¢1,344.70 ($15.82) single; ¢1,728.90 ($20.34) double; ¢1,921 ($22.60) triple; ¢2,185.14 ($25.71) quad. AE.

By far my favorite budget hotel in San José is the Ritz. Robert Brand, the very friendly American owner, will gladly sit with you over a cup of his free Costa Rican coffee and enlighten you about life in the country. He's been running the hotel for nearly two decades, and unfortunately he has plans to retire soon. Hopefully the standards won't decrease and the prices won't increase when the hotel changes hands. Mr. Brand prides himself on having an exceptionally clean hotel, and the many repeat visits and recommendations from North American visitors confirm this. The rooms are a hodgepodge of styles and sizes, so if you don't like the first one you see, try another. There are a lot of books available in the sunny lounge. Large American breakfasts are served.

PENSIÓN COSTA RICA INN, Calle 9 between avenidas 1 and 3, No. 154, Apdo. 10282-1000, San José. Tel. 506/22-5203. Fax 011-506-23-8385. In the United States, P.O. Box 59, Arcadia, LA 71001. Tel. toll

free 800/637-0899; in Canada, 318/263-2059. 34 rms., all with bath.
$ Rates: ¢1,371.82 ($16.14) single; ¢1,735.68 ($20.42) double. No credit cards.
Although the rooms are rather small and dark, this small hotel is popular, especially
with young travelers. If you're a light sleeper, this is definitely *not* the place for you.
The walls are typical of those in old Costa Rican wood buildings—paper thin.
There's a small bar that always seems to have a handful of young foreigners hanging
around as well as a TV lounge with plenty of couches. The rooms are situated off
small courtyards down a maze of narrow hallways. There's no restaurant here, but the
staff will do your laundry for you. Recommended for those who like to stay out late.

DOUBLE ROOMS FOR LESS THAN ¢3,000 [$35.29]

**HOTEL FORTUNA, Avenida 6 between calles 2 and 4, Apdo. 7-1570, San
José. Tel. 506/23-5344.** 30 rms., all with bath. TEL
$ Rates: ¢1,446 ($17) single; ¢2,094 ($24.65) double; ¢3,008 ($35.40) triple;
¢3,471 ($40.85) quad. AE, MC, V.
Located only two blocks from the Parque Central, the Fortuna has a Chinese theme.
Unfortunately, the popular Chinese restaurant in the basement of the hotel was closed
the last time I visited. If it's open when you're here, be sure to check it out. The
second-floor rooms are sunny and warm, and the first-floor rooms are cooler and
darker. Floors are of well-worn tile, but each room has an interesting vanity with a
Chinese-style chair. The brightness of the rooms makes this place feel much more
cheery than other hotels, despite the lack of carpeting.

**HOTEL TALAMANCA, Avenida 2 between calles 8 and 10, Apdo. 449-
1002, San José. Tel. 506/33-5033. Fax 506/33-5420.** 54 rms., all with
bath. TEL
$ Rates: ¢1,897.50 ($22.32) single; ¢2,199.40 ($25.87) double; ¢3,079.15
($36.22) triple. MC, V. **Parking:** small fee.
This hotel has certainly seen better days, but it is conveniently located and economical
and has its own casino that stays open from 2pm to 5am. The rooms will do in a
pinch, and if you want to spend a little extra, you can get a TV in your room. Ask for a
room on one of the upper floors, and you'll get a view of the surrounding mountains.
There is an acceptable restaurant and a disco for those who want to loosen their limbs
after sitting too long at the gambling tables.
   Dining/Entertainment: Casino, discotheque, and restaurant.
   Services: Room service and laundry service.

**HOTEL ALAMEDA, Avenida Central between calles 12 and 14, Apdo.
680, San José. Tel. 506/23-6333 or 21-3045.** 50 rms., all with bath. TEL
$ Rates: ¢1,890 ($22.24) single; ¢2,242–¢2,315 ($26.38–$27.23) double;
¢2,975.40 ($35) triple. MC, V.
This is another of San José's large old hotels. One of its greatest assets is that it is only
a block away from the bus stop for the airport. If your flight arrives after dark and you
don't have a reservation already, this is the first place you should try. Walk around to
the side of the block away from the small park, and you'll see the Alameda across the
street. The rooms are small but carpeted and have clean tiled baths and plenty of
closet space.
   The second-floor restaurant has two walls of windows and commands an excellent
view of the activity on the street. The menu features international and Costa Rican
dishes at prices ranging from about ¢300 ($3.53) to ¢1,000 ($11.76).
   Services: Laundry/dry cleaning, medical service, currency exchange, and
baby-sitting service.

**HOTEL DIPLOMAT, Calle 6 between Avenida Central and Avenida 2,
Apdo. 6606, San José. Tel. 506/21-8133 or 21-8744.** 29 rms., all with
bath.
$ Rates: ¢1,869 ($21.99) single; ¢2,493 ($29.33) double. AE, MC, V.

S It's easy to miss the entrance to this hotel. Watch for it on the east side of the street. The lobby is narrow, and the front door is fairly nondescript. The carpeted rooms are rather small but comfortable nonetheless, and some rooms on the upper floors have nice views of the mountains. The tiled baths are clean, and the water is hot. For $3 extra per night, you can get a TV. If you get too claustrophobic in your room, there is a sitting area on each floor. The Diplomat seems to be popular with North American retirees and businesspeople. The hotel's restaurant is a very attractive dark room with pink tableclothes, flowers on every table, and pastel walls. For those seeking an intimate place for dinner, try one of the tiny booths for two. Prices range from ¢175 ($2.06) for a sandwich to ¢1,500 ($17.65) for a lobster dinner.

HOTEL PLAZA, Avenida Central between calles 2 and 4, Apdo. 2019-1000, San José. Tel. 506/22-5533 or 22-2641. 40 rms., all with bath. TV TEL

$ Rates: ¢1,921 ($22.60) single; ¢2,881.50 ($33.90) double; ¢3,265.70 ($38.42) triple. AE, MC, V. **Parking:** free.

★ ✪ Downtown hotels in San José tend to be rather nondescript from the outside, and the Plaza is no exception. However, when you step through the doors, you enter a very attractive, newly decorated lobby with richly colored plush carpets, sturdy tropical wicker furniture, and unusual hardwood paneling on both the walls and the ceiling. An added attraction of the Plaza is that it is on the pedestrians-only section of Avenida Central, San José's central shopping district.

You'll find the same unusual paneling incorporated into the guest room designs. Recessed lighting, colorful bedspreads, and thick carpets make each room a soothing and relaxing place to return to after a long day of touring. There is even remote control for the TV. Bathrooms (shower only) are small but tiled, and the sinks are outside the bathroom door.

The second-floor restaurant/bar also features a lot of Costa Rican hardwood, including ramadas (Spanish-style covered patios) over the booths even though there is no direct sunshine in the restaurant. The three-course daily special, which might be something as exotic as Spanish beef tongue with cauliflower salad and pastry, goes for only ¢350 ($4.12). An à la carte meal will run from ¢600 to ¢1,200 ($7.06 to $14.12).

Services: Room service and laundry service.

A HOSTEL

TORUMA YOUTH HOSTEL, Avenida Central between calles 29 and 31, San José. Tel. 506/24-4085. 70 beds, all with shared bath.

$ Rates: ¢425 ($5) per person per night with an IYHF card; ¢495 ($5.82) without IYHF card.

S This attractive old building with a long veranda is the largest of Costa Rica's growing system of official youth hostels. Although it is possible to find other accommodations around town in this price range, the atmosphere here is familiar to those who have hosteled in Europe. The large lounge and dining hall in the center of the building has a high ceiling and a great deal of light. The dorms are 16- to 26-bunkbed rooms. Guests have use of the kitchen, but breakfast, lunch, and dinner are served for $2 to $5.

LONG-TERM STAYS

APARTOTEL CASTILLA, Calle 24 between avenidas 2 and 4, Apdo. 944-1007 Centro Colón, San José. Tel. 506/22-2113 or 21-2080. 15 apts., all with bath. TV TEL

$ Rates: ¢2,593.35 ($30.51) single; ¢3,121.63 ($36.73) double; ¢3,649.90 ($42.94) triple; ¢4,067.25 ($47.85) quad. AE, MC, V.

S Housed in the same building as several doctors' offices, this apartotel is convenient to the popular Paseo Colón shopping and restaurant district. The apartments are nothing fancy, but they do have attractive parquet floors, compact kitchens with all utensils, tile bathrooms, and a lot of closet space. If you plan to be in town for an extended period, this would be an excellent choice. You have the convenience of having your own kitchen and rates that are fairly low. You aren't right downtown (it's a 20-minute walk to the Plaza de Cultura), so traffic and noise aren't much of a problem. It is also possible to stay here for only one or two nights, which makes it a good choice if you have rented a car because you can avoid the chaos of downtown streets and be out of San José in a matter of minutes.

APARTOTEL SAN JOSÉ, Avenida 2 between calles 17 and 19, Apdo. 5834-1000, San José. Tel. 506/22-0455 or 21-6684. Fax 506/33-3329. 12 apts., all with bath. TV TEL

$ Rates: ¢3,073.60 ($36.16) single; ¢3,649.90 ($42.94) double; ¢4,034.10 ($47.46) triple; ¢4,514.35 ($53.11) quad. No credit cards accepted. **Parking:** free.

Located almost across the street from the National Museum, this old apartotel has the best location of all those in San José. If you are down here to look into retiring or pursuing a golden business opportunity, this is the place to stay since you can move right in and make yourself at home. Take advantage of the fully equipped kitchen to save money on food bills. The apartments even have daily maid service. The apartotel is tucked away behind another building, so watch closely for the sign and entrance.

Services: Laundry/dry cleaning and safety boxes.

WORTH THE EXTRA BUCKS

HOTEL DON CARLOS, Calle 9 between avenidas 7 and 9, No. 779, Apdo. 1593, San José. Tel. 506/21-6707. Fax 506/55-0828. 10 rms, 5 suites, all with bath.

$ Rates (including Continental breakfast): ¢2,689.40 ($31.64) single; ¢3,265.70 ($38.42) double; ¢3,649.90–¢4,226.20 ($42.94–$49.72) suite. No credit cards accepted.

⭐ If you are looking for a small hotel that is unmistakably tropical and hints at the days of the planters and coffee barons, this is the place for you. Located in an old residential neighborhood only blocks from the business district, the Don Carlos is popular with both honeymooners and businesspeople. A large pre-Columbian reproduction of a carved stone human figure stands outside the front door of this gray hotel, which was a former president's mansion. Inside you'll find many more stone pre-Columbian reproductions, as well as orchids, ferns, palms, and parrots. The wicker furniture in the lounge and the small courtyard leading to a sunny deck with a bubbling fountain tempt guests to relax in the tropical breezes after a day of exploring the capital. There is also an intimate TV lounge with a lending library. Most of the rooms are quite large, and each is a little different from the others. If you are going to be there for a while or plan to return after a few days of exploring, you might want to have a look at several rooms and decide which you like best. My personal favorite is room no. 4, a huge suite with polished hardwood floors, a large table with director's chairs around it, a red-velvet couch and love seat, and some attractive paintings by local artists on the walls. In case you're interested, the paintings throughout the hotel are for sale. This room also has many windows for catching the trade winds.

Only breakfast and light meals are served in the Pre-Columbian Lounge, a small dining room with marble-topped tables. Prices for such things as quiche, tamales, and ceviche range from ¢60 to ¢205 (71¢ to $2.41).

Facilities: TV lounge and gift shop.

HOTEL AMSTEL, Calle 7 and Avenida 1, Apdo. 4192-1000, San José. Tel. 506/22-4622. Fax 506/33-3329. 55 rms., all with bath. A/C TEL

$ Rates: ¢2,805–¢3,266 ($33–$38.42) single; ¢3,554–¢3,938 ($41.81–$46.33) double; ¢3,938–¢4,514 ($46.33–$53.11) triple. AE, MC, V.

S The Amstel has long been one of San José's most popular inexpensive hotels. There's a tour information and car-rental desk in the small lobby. If you've ever been to Amsterdam, you'll recognize much of the wall art and decor here, but why there should be a Hotel Amstel in San José, no one seems to know. There are two types of rooms in the five-story, elevator equipped building: The regular rooms are carpeted and have modern furnishings, but the bathrooms are of an older design; the superior rooms, which cost only slightly more, come with color cable TVs and much larger and more modern bathrooms, each of which includes a tub. Whichever you choose, I'm sure you'll be pleased.

Dining: The restaurant at the Hotel Amstel is legendary in Costa Rica. The menu features traditional Continental and Costa Rican cuisine well prepared and attractively presented. Service is by very proper white-jacketed waiters who will make sure that you want for nothing. The best part of dining here is that it will not blow your budget. The three-course lunch is only ¢400 ($4.70), and an à la carte meal will be between ¢850 and ¢1,800 ($10 and $21.18). There is an attached bar frequented by local businesspeople.

Facilities: TV lounge and gift shop.

Services: Room service and travel agency.

HOTEL DUNN INN, Calle 5 and Avenida 11, San José, Apdo. 1584-1000. Tel. 506/22-3232 or 22-3426. Fax 506/21-4596. 10 rms, 1 suite, all with bath.

$ Rates (including Continental breakfast): ¢3,842 ($45.20) single or double; ¢9,605 ($113) suite. AE, V.

In the same historic neighborhood as the Santo Tomas (below) and the Don Carlos, the Dunn Inn is a noteworthy new small hotel. Housed in a 95-year-old mansion, this hotel offers quiet sophistication at reasonable rates. The courtyard of the old mansion has been partially covered and turned into the dining room. Orchids and bromeliads hang from the brick walls, and a large cage on one side of the room is home to chattering tropical squirrels. A fountain bubbles away beside a huge philodendron vine.

During the restoration, as much of the old hardwood floors was saved as was possible. Consequently, some of the rooms have the original flooring and some are carpeted. All the rooms have overhead fans (air conditioning really isn't necessary in this temperate climate), plenty of windows, and semiorthopedic beds. Although it is quite a bit more expensive than the normal rooms, the one suite is quite luxurious with a whirlpool bath, minibar, hardwood and carpeted floors, potted bromeliads, dual sinks, a lot of sunshine in the bathroom, and paneled walls.

HOTEL SANTO TOMAS, Avenida 7 between calles 3 and 5, San José. Tel. 506/22-3946. Fax 506/22-3950. 20 rms., all with bath.

$ Rates (including Continental breakfast): ¢4,802.50 ($56.50) single; ¢6,243.25 ($73.45) double; lower rates May–Sept. No credit cards. **Parking:** available for small fee.

This is one of the newest little hotels in San José. Even though it is on an otherwise nondescript street, this converted mansion is a real jewel inside. Built around 100 years ago by a coffee baron, the house was recently saved from being bulldozed in order to expand a luxury hotel's parking lot. Under the direction of American Tom Douglas, the old mansion has been restored to its former grandeur. The first thing that you see when you walk through the front door is the beautiful carved desk that serves as the reception area. Throughout the guest rooms you'll find similar pieces of exquisitely crafted antique reproductions made here in Costa Rica from rare hardwoods. The hardwood floors throughout most of the hotel are original and were made from a type of tree that is almost impossible to find today.

The rooms vary in size, but most are extremely large with a small table and chairs. Skylights in the bathrooms help keep the building from being too dark. Electric showerheads provide the hot water here, as they do in so many places in Costa Rica, and can take a bit of instruction in how to coax the most and the hottest water from them. The management is young and ambitious, and there are plans for more expansion and remodeling of the hotel. A casual Continental breakfast is served in the little dining room adjacent to the TV lounge in the lobby.

4. WHERE TO EAT

San José has an amazing variety of restaurants in all price ranges. For a true deal head to a soda, the equivalent of a diner, which serves good and filling Tico food. I have chosen restaurants that are convenient to both hotels and attractions so that you will never have to go too far for a meal. Two of my favorite places to eat are right on the busy Plaza de la Cultura, the heart of San José.

MEALS FOR LESS THAN ¢450 [$5.29]

LA PERLA, Avenida 2 and Calle Central. Tel. 22-7492.
   Cuisine: INTERNATIONAL.
$ **Prices:** ¢85–¢450 ($1–$5.29); 10% extra 10pm–6am. AE, MC, V.
   Open: 24 hours.
It's easy to walk right past this place (I did) the first time that you try to find it. The entrance is on the corner looking across to Parque Central and the restaurant itself is a little bit below street level. La Perla is not long on atmosphere, but the food is good and the portions are huge. The special here is paella, a Spanish rice-and-seafood dish for only ¢325 ($3.82). It is almost impossible to finish the plate that they bring you unless you are absolutely ravenous. You can even get it with extra seafood for ¢395 ($4.65). Another excellent choice is the huevos à la ranchera for ¢200 ($2.35), which is prepared a bit differently than it is in Mexico and makes a filling meal at any time of the night or day. Be sure to try a delicious refresco, made with water or milk and fresh fruit whirred in a blender. *Mora* (blackberry) is my favorite.

LA CASA DE SANDWICH, Avenida 2 and Calle 11. No phone.
   Cuisine: SANDWICHES.
$ **Prices:** ¢100–¢300 ($1.18–$3.52). No credit cards.
   Open: 24 hours.
No matter what time of the night or day hunger strikes you, you can always get a good cheap sandwich at this little hole in the wall. The different types of sandwiches available are scrawled on every possible bit of wall space, and none of them has a price listed. Never fear: There isn't an item on the menu that will break your bank.

CHURRERIA MANOLO, Avenida Central between calles 9 and 11. Tel. 23-4067.
   Cuisine: COSTA RICAN.
$ **Prices:** ¢100–¢300 ($1.18–$3.53). No credit cards.
   Open: Mon–Sat 7am–11pm; Sun 7am–10pm.
You can't miss this popular sandwich spot: Brass footprints embedded in the sidewalk lead right to the front door. There is also a big glass case full of *churros,* a kind of Latin American doughnut that is a long hollow tube. As the name of the restaurant implies, churros are the specialty here, and you can get them with a variety of fillings. However, the menu lists 128 items, including about 60 different sandwiches. There are daily specials and huge ice-cream plates. If you don't understand the Spanish menu, walk over to the case full of premade sandwiches and bocadillos (Costa Rican appetizers) and point to the ones that you want.

RESTAURANTE CAMPESINO, Calle 7 between avenidas 2 and 4. Tel. 22-1170.
   Cuisine: COSTA RICAN.
$ **Prices:** ¢110–¢440 ($1.29–$5.18). No credit cards.

Open: Mon–Sat noon–10pm.

⭐ This intimate little restaurant serves what may be the best chicken that I have ever tasted. This is not at all surprising since chicken is all they serve, and thus they have had time to perfect its cooking. The secret of this delectable dish is in the wood fire over which the chicken is roasted. Owner Jorge Zúñiga uses only coffee root wood, which imparts a delicate flavor that has mouths watering all over the globe at the mere thought of a meal here. Unfortunately, the coffee plantations that provide the roots are switching to a new type of coffee tree that produces smaller roots. Campesino chicken may soon become just a memory if this thoughtless upgrading of coffee plantations continues. Oh, well, get it while it's hot. Depending on how hungry you are, you can get a quarter, half, or full chicken. Don't miss the palmito (heart of palm) salad for ¢300 ($3.53). For ¢350 ($4.12) you can get a half chicken and a quarter bottle of wine. You can't miss this place—watch for the smoking chimney high above the roof, or at street level watch for the window full of chickens rotating over an open fire.

NUTRISODA, Avenida 2 between calles 1 and 3, Edificio las Arcadas. Tel. 55-3959.
   Cuisine: VEGETARIAN.
$ Prices: ¢125–¢220 ($1.47–$2.59). No credit cards.
   Open: Mon–Sat 10am–7pm.
If you've had enough Costa Rican beef or just crave a bit of variety in your dining, stop by for lunch or early dinner at Nutrisoda. This brightly lit dairy-free restaurant is in the basement of the building to the left of the Gran Hotel Costa Rica and serves fresh uncooked meals such as salads and sandwiches. There are also daily special hot meals and excellent soups. Be sure to try some of the unusual homemade nondairy ice cream made with fruit and honey. There is a small notice board where you can find out about local health happenings.

CAFÉ DE TEATRO NACIONAL, Teatro Nacional, Avenida 2 between calles 3 and 5. Tel. 33-4488.
   Cuisine: INTERNATIONAL.
$ Prices: ¢125–¢350 ($1.47–$4.12). No credit cards.
   Open: Mon–Fri 10am–6pm.

⭐ This is absolutely my favorite place to eat in all of San José. Even if there is no show at the Teatro Nacional during your visit, you can enjoy a meal or a cup of coffee here and soak up the neoclassical atmosphere. The theater was built in the 1890s from the designs of European architects and the art nouveau chandeliers, ceiling murals, and marble floors and tables are purely Parisienne. There are even changing art displays by local artists. The menu is limited to a few sandwiches, cakes, special coffees, and an "executive lunch," but the ambience is classic French café. However, the marimba music drifting in through the open window will remind you that you are still in Costa Rica.

SODA LA CASITA, Avenida 1 between Calle Central and Calle 1. Tel. 21-1107.
   Cuisine: COSTA RICAN.
$ Prices: ¢180–¢365 ($2.12–$4.29). AE, MC, V.
   Open: Mon–Sat 8am–8pm.

Ⓢ This is a typical soda. It stays busy with shoppers and working folks from around the neighborhood and does an especially brisk business during lunch. The best deal here is the casado, the Tico lunch special, which includes rice, beans, salad, fried bananas, and a main course. Refrescos and fresh juices are only ¢33 to ¢79 (39¢ to 93¢). The blond-wood booths and ceiling fans give this little soda a cozy feel.

MEALS FOR LESS THAN ¢850 [$10]

LA ESMERALDA, Avenida 2 between calles 5 and 7. Tel. 21-0530.

Cuisine: COSTA RICAN
$ Prices: Entrees ¢140–¢1,400 ($1.65–$16.47). AE, MC, V.
Open: Mon–Sat 24 hours.

No one should visit San José without stopping in at La Esmeralda at least once, the later at night the better. This is much more than just a restaurant serving Tico food: It is the Grand Central Station of Costa Rican mariachi bands. In fact, mariachis and other bands from throughout Central America and Mexico hang out here every night waiting for work. While they wait they often serenade diners in the cavernous open-air dining hall of the restaurant. Friday and Saturday nights are always the busiest, but you'll probably hear a lot of excellent music any night of the week. The food is quite good, classic Tico with heart of palm salad for ¢275 ($3.24), corvina (sea bass) for ¢330 ($3.88), and shrimp for a pricey ¢1,400 ($16.47). The tres leches cake for ¢80 (94¢) just might be the moistest cake on earth. Try it.

CAFÉ PARISIENNE, Gran Hotel Costa Rica, Avenida 2 between calles 1 and 3. Tel. 21-4011.
Cuisine: INTERNATIONAL.
$ Prices: Sandwiches ¢175–¢350 ($2.06–$4.12); starters ¢100–¢1,400 ($1.18–$16.47); entrees ¢350–¢1,800 ($4.12–$21.18). AE, MC, V.
Open: 24 hours.

The Hotel Gran Costa Rica is the grande dame of hotels and as such is considerably outside your budget. However, its picturesque patio café right on the Plaza de la Cultura is a surprisingly inexpensive place to dine (if you stay away from the shrimp and lobster). A wrought-iron railing, white columns, and arches create an old-world atmosphere. There is almost no hour when there isn't something interesting going on in the plaza. Stop by this sophisticated café for the ¢456 ($5.36) breakfast buffet and fill up as the plaza's vendors set up their booths, peruse the *Tico Times* over coffee while you have your shoes polished, or simply bask in the tropical sunshine. For lunch or dinner, you can get steak or corvina for around ¢500 ($5.88). There is also a dinner buffet featuring classic Continental dishes, such as escalopine de milanesa for ¢540 ($6.35). If ordering à la carte, be sure to try the black bean soup with an egg for ¢100 ($1.18).

LA COCINA DE LEÑA, El Pueblo. Tel. 23-3704.
Cuisine: COSTA RICAN.
$ Prices: Entrees ¢400–¢1,600 ($4.71–$18.82). AE, MC, V.
Open: Mon–Thurs 11:30am–11pm; Fri–Sat 11:30am–midnight; Sun 11:30am–10pm.

La Cocina de Leña (The Wood Stove) bills itself as "the best typical restaurant in the country," and I would have a hard time arguing with them on that claim. Although almost every restaurant in Costa Rica offers *tipico* meals, few serve the likes of green banana ceviche or palmito ceviche, ¢150 and ¢200 ($1.76 and $2.35). After such unusual appetizers, you might wonder what could come next. Perhaps oxtail soup served with yuca and platano for ¢400 ($4.70) might appeal to you; if not, there are plenty of steaks and seafood on the menu. If you are an adventurous eater, you will need several trips to this cozy restaurant to try all that appeals to you. I recommend the *chilasuilas,* delicious tortillas filled with fried meat, for ¢400 ($4.70). Black bean soup with an egg is a Costa Rican standard available everywhere, but corn soup with pork for ¢300 ($3.53) is equally satisfying. For dessert there is tres leches cake for ¢100 ($1.18), as well as the more unusual sweetened *chiverre,* which is a type of squash that looks remarkably like a watermelon, for the same price.

Located in the unusual El Pueblo shopping, dining, and entertainment center, La Cocina de Leña has a rustic feel to it with firewood stacked on shelves above the booths, long stalks of bananas hanging from pillars, tables suspended by heavy ropes from the ceiling, and most unusual of all—menus printed on paper bags. Don't miss it.

AMSTEL GRILL ROOM, Avenida 1 and Calle 7. Tel. 22-4622.
Cuisine: INTERNATIONAL.

$ Prices: Menu of the day ¢400–¢450 ($4.70–$5.29); entrees ¢450–¢1,400 ($5.29–$16.47). AE, MC, V.
Open: Daily 6:30–11am, 11:30am–3pm, 6–10pm.

Ask anyone in San José for a restaurant recommendation, and this hotel dining room will always be at the top of the list. For years the Grill Room has maintained its high standards and its atmosphere of quiet sophistication. White-jacketed waiters move unobtrusively between tables, making sure that all the diners are happy. Businesspeople and well-dressed matrons are the primary customers, but tourists in casual attire receive the same careful attention. Lunch here, the most popular meal of the day, is a real bargain. For ¢400 to ¢450 ($4.70 to $5.29), you can order the special of the day or the deluxe special of the day—the only difference between the two is that the deluxe is served with a fish main course. Soup or salad and a dessert round out the meal. Should you choose to order à la carte, try one of the choice steaks of Costa Rican beef or fresh shrimp. In addition to the Continental and American dishes on the menu, there is also a plato tipico that comes with the Tico standby of beans and rice.

LOCAL BUDGET BETS/FAVORITE MEALS

Wherever you go in Costa Rica, the cheapest place to eat is always a place called a soda, which usually serve the Tico standards of rice and beans in different guises. If you can cultivate a taste for this simple meal, you can save a bundle on your food bills. Rice and beans are called gallo pinto when served for breakfast and may come with anything from fried eggs to steak. At lunch and dinner, those very same rice and beans are called casado and served with a salad of cabbage and tomatoes, fried bananas, and a main dish. Gallo pinto might cost ¢100 to ¢150 ($1.18 to $1.76), and a casado might cost ¢150 to ¢250 ($1.76 to $2.94).

Another favorite of Ticos, and tourists, is the refresco. A refresco is a bit like a fresh-fruit milk shake without the ice cream; when made with mangos, papayas, or any of the other delicious tropical fruits of Costa Rica, it is pure ambrosia. Refrescos also are made with water (con agua), but these are not nearly as good as those made with milk (con leche). Despite all the assurances that the water in San José is safe to drink, you're better off avoiding it as much as possible.

SPECIALTY DINING
FAST-FOOD CHAINS

Many of the largest North American fast-food chains have restaurants in San José, with prices that are only slightly lower than those in the United States. Among the chains represented here are **McDonald's,** at Plaza de la Cultura (tel. 57-1112) and also at Calle 4 between Avenida Central and Avenida 1 (tel. 21-3632); and **Hardee's,** Avenida Central and Calle 3 (tel. 23-4646). **Kentucky Fried Chicken** seems to have restaurants all over the city these days (there's one midway down Paseo Colón and another on Avenida Central between Calles 29 and 31). **Pizza Hut** is at Paseo Colón, near Kentucky Fried Chicken (tel. 35-1222).

A DINING COMPLEX

Hop in any taxi and say "El Pueblo," and within a few minutes you'll be dropped at the entrance to a maze of Spanish-style buildings filled with restaurants, bars, nightclubs, discos, and exclusive shops. If you are feeling like a splurge, there are dozens of restaurants here to accommodate you. My favorite is **La Cocina de Leña,** which I described above.

STREET FOOD

On almost every street corner in downtown San José, you'll find a fruit vendor. If you're lucky enough to be in town between April and June, you can sample more varieties of mangoes than you ever knew existed. I like buying them already cut up in a little bag. They cost a little more this way, but you don't get nearly as messy. Be sure to try a green mango with salt and chili peppers. That's the way they seem to like mangoes best in the steamy tropics—guaranteed to wake up your taste buds.

Another common street food that you might be wondering about is called *pejibaye,* a bright-orange palm nut about the size of a small apple. They are boiled in big pots on carts. You eat them in much the same way you would an avocado, and they taste a bit like squash.

LATE NIGHT/24 HOURS

San José has quite a few all-night restaurants—including **La Perla, La Esmeralda, La Casa de Sandwich,** and **Café Parisienne,** all of which are described above. Another popular place, which is almost exclusively for men, is the **Soda Palace** on Avenida 2 and Calle 2 (see the "Evening Entertainment" section in this chapter for more information).

WORTH THE EXTRA BUCKS

EL BALCON DE EUROPA, Avenida Central between calles 7 and 9. Tel. 21-4841.
   Cuisine: CONTINENTAL.
$ Prices: Pastas ¢340–¢395 ($4–$4.65); entrees ¢595–¢1,290 ($7–$15.16). No credit cards.
   Open: Daily noon–10:30pm.

Open since 1908, El Balcon de Europa is one of San José's most popular restaurants. You'll find everyone from Japanese businesspeople to German backpackers in the cramped dining room here, and everyone receives the same personal attention. What attracts people from all walks of life is the outstanding service, gourmet Italian food, and cheese. You may have noticed a lack of cheese in other parts of Costa Rica, but not here. The centerpiece of the restaurant is a table covered with imported European cheeses (at room temperature) and an array of fresh-baked desserts. When you take a seat, a basket of two types of bread and bread sticks immediately arrives, accompanied by a sample plate of cheeses. During the evening, a waiter might even stop by with samples of a new bread the restaurant is serving. (When I visited it was *focaccio,* a delicious pizza-dough bread drizzled with olive oil and sprinkled with herbs.)

On the menu there are 13 different pastas served in a variety of tasty sauces, mostly cream-based. For an entree, try the unusual piccatine al limone, a paper-thin steak cooked in lemon sauce, for ¢595 ($7). There are even a few Costa Rican standards on the menu, such as black bean soup with an egg and beef tongue in tomato sauce. To accompany your meal, there is a limited selection of wines from Europe, California, and South America. Wine prices are very reasonable—around ¢125 ($1.47) for a glass and ¢800 ($9.41) for a bottle.

RESTAURANTS BY CUISINE

COSTA RICAN
Churreria Manolo (p. 44)	B
La Cocina de Leña (p. 46)	M
La Esmeralda (p. 45)	M
Restaurante Campesino (p. 44)	B
Soda La Casita (p. 45)	B

INTERNATIONAL
Amstel Grill Room (p. 46)	M
Café Parisienne (p. 46)	M
Café de Teatro Nacional (p. 45)	B
La Casa de Sandwich (p. 44)	B
La Perla (p. 44)	M

ITALIAN
El Balcon de Europa (*p. 48*)   E

VEGETARIAN
Nutrisoda (*p. 45*)   B

Note: E = Expensive; M = Moderate; B = Budget

---

5. ATTRACTIONS

With its near-perfect climate, compact size, and numerous museums and parks, San José is a delightful city to explore. The museums here are the most modern in Central America and hold a wealth of pre-Columbian artifacts despite the fact that Costa Rica had a very small pre-Columbian Indian population.

SUGGESTED ITINERARIES
IF YOU HAVE ONE DAY

Start your day with breakfast at Café Parisienne on the Plaza de la Cultura. Then visit the **Gold Museum** and see if you can get tickets for a performance that night at the **Teatro Nacional.** From the Plaza de la Cultura, stroll up Avenida Central to the **Museo Nacional.** If you're ready for lunch, try El Balcon de Europa, which is on your way back downtown. After lunch, head over to the **Jade Museum** if you aren't museumed out already. After all this culture, a stroll through the chaos of the **Central Market** is in order. Well worth a stop in this area is the coffee-roasting shop **El Trebol,** where you can pick up freshly roasted coffee for about $1 per pound. Try dinner at Restaurante Campesino before going to the Teatro Nacional. After the performance, you absolutely must swing by **La Esmeralda** for some live mariachi music before calling it a day.

IF YOU HAVE TWO DAYS

Follow the itinerary above. On day two, visit the **Serpentarium** and the **Costa Rican Art Museum** and any sights that you missed the day before.

IF YOU HAVE THREE DAYS

Follow the itinerary for the two days outlined above. On day three, head out to the **Irazú Volcano, Orosi Valley, Lankester Gardens,** and **Cartago.** Start your day at the volcano and work your way back toward San José.

IF YOU HAVE FIVE DAYS

Follow the itinerary for the three days outlined above. Then spend days four and five on other excursions from San José. You can go white-water rafting or horseback riding for a day if you are an active type. If you prefer less strenuous activities, try a cruise around the Gulf of Nicoya.

THE TOP ATTRACTIONS

MUSEO NACIONAL DE COSTA RICA, Calle 17 between Avenida Central and Avenida 2. Tel. 57-1433.

Costa Rica's most important museum is housed in a former army barracks that was the scene of fighting during the civil war of 1948, after which the Costa Rican army was disbanded. You can still see hundreds of bullet holes on the turrets at the corners of the building. Inside this traditional Spanish-style courtyard building, you will find displays on Costa Rican history and culture from pre-Columbian times to the present. In the pre-Columbian rooms, you'll see a 2,500-year-old jade carving that is shaped like a seashell and etched with an image of a hand holding a small animal. Among the most fascinating objects unearthed at Costa Rica's many small archeological sites are many *metates,* or grinding stones. This type of grinding stone is still in use today throughout Central America. However, the ones on display here are more ornately decorated than those that you will see anywhere else. Some of the metates are the size of a small bed and are believed to have been part of funeral rites. A separate vault houses the museum's small collection of pre-Columbian jade jewelry and figurines.

Some of the most celebrated pre-Columbian artifacts in Costa Rica are the almost perfectly spherical carved stone balls that have been found in the southwest part of the country. These spheres can be as large as 9 feet across and weigh 16 tons. No one is sure how they were carved so perfectly or what purpose they served. Several small spheres are on display here.

One room is dedicated to Former President Oscar Arias Sánchez, who won the Nobel Peace Prize for orchestrating the Central American Peace Plan to bring peace to a region that has been continually rocked by revolutions and civil wars for centuries. Another room chronicles the people and history of Costa Rica from the Conquest to the present, utilizing photographs, illustrations, and objects of historical significance.

Admission: ¢20 (24¢).
Open: Tues–Sun 9am–5pm. **Bus:** San Pedro.

MUSEO DE ORO BANCO CENTRAL [GOLD MUSEUM], Calle 5 between Avenida Central and Avenida 2. Tel. 23-0528 or 33-4233, ext. 282.

Located directly beneath the Plaza de la Cultura, this unusual underground museum houses one of the largest collections of pre-Columbian gold in the Americas. On display are more than 20,000 troy ounces of gold in more than 2,000 objects. The sheer number of small gold pieces can be overwhelming in this ultramodern museum; however, the unusual display cases and complex lighting system show off every piece to its utmost. This museum includes a gallery for temporary art exhibits and a numismatic and philatelic museum.

Admission: Free.
Open: Tues–Sun 10am–6pm. **Bus:** Sabana-Cementerio.

MUSEO DE JADE MARCO FIDEL TRISTAN [JADE MUSEUM], Avenida 7 between calles 9 and 9B, 11th floor, INS Building. Tel. 23-5800, ext. 2581.

Among the pre-Columbian cultures of Mexico and Central America, jade was the most valuable commodity, worth more than gold. This modern museum displays a huge collection of jade artifacts from throughout Costa Rica's pre-Columbian archeological sites. Most of the jade pieces are large pendants that were parts of necklaces and are primarily human and animal figures. A fascinating display illustrates how the primitive people of this region carved this extremely hard stone. Of particular interest are the stones that were intricately carved with string saws coated with quartz sand abrasive. Most of the jade pieces date from 330 BC to AD 700.

In addition to the jade collection, there is an extensive collection of pre-Columbian polychromed terra-cotta vases, bowls, and figurines. Some of these pieces are amazingly modern in design and exhibit a surprisingly advanced technique. Particularly fascinating are three vases: one that incorporates real human teeth, one that shows how jade was imbedded in human teeth merely for decorative reasons, and one that resembles a frog-faced human being. Most of the identifying labels and explanations are in Spanish, but there are a few in English.

Admission: Free.
Open: Mon–Fri 9am–3pm.

MUSEO DE ARTE COSTARRICENSE, Calle 42 and Paseo Colón, East Sabana Park. Tel. 22-7155 or 22-7247.

This small museum at the end of Paseo Colón in Sabana Park houses a collection of works in all media by Costa Rica's most celebrated artists. On display are many exceptionally beautiful pieces in a wide range of artistic styles. This exciting collection demonstrates how Costa Rican artists have interpreted the major European artistic movements. In addition to the permanent collection of sculptures, paintings, and prints, there are regular temporary exhibits. On my last visit, there was a fascinating exhibition focusing on animals in Costa Rican art. Included in the exhibit were pre-Columbian stone carvings and wood carvings by Costa Rica's most talented contemporary craftspeople. If the second floor is open during your visit, be sure to go up and have a look at the conference room's unusual bas-relief walls, which chronicle the history of Costa Rica from pre-Columbian times to the present with evocative images of the people.

Admission: ¢40 (48¢); Sun free (suggested donation of ¢30).
Open: Tues–Sun 10am–5pm. **Bus:** Sabana-Cementerio.

MORE ATTRACTIONS

PARQUE ZOOLÓGICO SIMÓN BOLÍVAR, Avenida 11 and Calle 11. No phone.

I don't think that I have ever seen a sadder zoo than this little park tucked away beside the polluted Río Torres. It is a shame that a country that has preserved so much of its land in national parks would ignore its only public zoo. The cages here are only occasionally marked, and many are dirty and small. The collection includes Asian, African, and Costa Rican animals. There are rumors that a new zoo is to be built or that this one is to be renovated. Hopefully something will be done soon about this disgraceful situation.

Admission: ¢20 (24¢).
Open: Wed–Fri 8am–3:30pm; Sat–Sun 9am–4:30pm.

SERPENTARIUM, Avenida 1 between calles 9 and 11. Tel. 55-4210.

The tropics abound in reptiles and amphibians, and this new San José attraction is an excellent introduction to all that slithers and hops through the jungles of Costa Rica. The live snakes, lizards, and frogs are kept in beautiful large terrariums that simulate their natural environments. Poisonous snakes make up a large part of the collection, with the dreaded fer-de-lance pit viper being the star attraction. Also fascinating to see are the tiny, brilliantly colored poison arrow frogs. Iguanas and Jesus Christ lizards are two of the more commonly spotted of Costa Rica's reptiles, and both are represented here. Also on display is an Asian import—a giant reticulate python, which is one of the largest I have ever seen. This little zoological museum is well worth a visit, especially if you plan to go bashing about in the jungles, because it will help you identify the numerous poisonous snakes that you'll want to avoid.

Admission: ¢100 ($1.18).
Open: Daily 10am–7pm.

COOL FOR KIDS

Kids will probably be fascinated by the snakes at the **Serpentarium,** but other than that there isn't a lot for them in San José.

WALKING TOURS —— Downtown San José

Start: Plaza de la Cultura
Finish: Plaza de la Cultura
Time: Allow a full day for this tour, although most of your time will be spent touring the three museums mentioned.
Best Time: Any day except Monday, when museums are closed.

Because San José is so compact, it is possible to visit nearly all of the city's major sites in a single day's walking tour. Begin your tour on the **Plaza de la Cultura,** perhaps after having breakfast at the Gran Hotel Costa Rica.

1. **Teatro Nacional,** which faces the entrance to the Gran Hotel Costa Rica, is a baroque masterpiece. Be sure to take a tour. (See p. 55 for complete information.)

2. **The Gold Museum** is built beneath the Plaza de la Cultura to the left of the Teatro Nacional and houses the largest collection of pre-Columbian gold in Central America. *(See p. 50 for complete information.)*

REFUELING STOP   Undeniably the best lunch in San José is at the **3. Hotel Amstel,** Avenida 1 and Calle 7. White-jacketed waiters attend to your every need.

---

4. **Escuela Metálica,** Avenida 5 and Calle 9, is one of the most unusual buildings in the city. It is made of metal panels that are bolted together and was manufactured in Europe late in the last century. In the park across the street is a beautiful music temple.
5. The **Jade Museum** is one block over on Avenida 7 in the high-rise office building. The cool, dark exhibit halls are filled with jade pendants. *(See p. 50 for complete information.)* Great views of the city!
6. **Casa Amarilla,** across Calle 11 from the Jade Museum, is an interesting building housing the Ministry of Foreign Affairs. It was donated, along with the park across the street, by Andrew Carnegie.
7. **Parque Nacional,** at Avenida 3 and Calle 15, has an impressive monument to the nations that defeated William Walker's attempt to turn Central America into a slave state. Across Avenida 1 is a statue of **Juan Santamaría,** who gave his life to defeat Walker.
8. **Museo Nacional,** Calle 17 between avenidas Central and 2 is housed in a former army barracks that still shows signs of the 1948 revolution. *(See p. 49 for complete information.)*
9. **Café de Teatro Nacional,** Plaza de la Cultura, is without a doubt San José's most elegant place to have a light meal, snack, or coffee and cake.

ORGANIZED TOURS

There are literally dozens of tour companies operating in San José, and the barrage of advertising brochures can be quite intimidating. There really isn't much reason to take a tour of San José since it is so compact—you can easily visit all the major sites on your own. However, if you want to take a city tour, which will run you about ¢1,550 ($18.24), here are some companies that you can contact.

Otec Tours, Edeficio Ferenz, Calle 3 between avenidas 1 and 3, Apdo. 323-1002 (tel. 22-0866).

TAM, Avenida Central and Calle 1, Apdo. 1864-1000 (tel. 23-5111).

Panorama Tours, Calle 9 between Avenida Central and Avenida 1, Apdo. 7323 (tel. 33-3058).

Swiss Travel Service, Hotel Herradura, Apdo. 7-1970 (tel. 32-6742), has several offices around San José. The most convenient is in the Hotel Amstel at Calle 7 and Avenida 1.

SPECIAL/FREE EVENTS

San José is a conservative city and doesn't stage many public festivals or events. Those it does have are strictly religious in nature: The days between Christmas and New Year's and the week prior to Easter are the city's two top periods of celebration. During these times there are parades, dances, and other special events.

SPORTS/RECREATION

Sabana Park, formerly San José's airport, is the city's center for sports and recreation. Here you'll find everything from jogging trails and soccer fields to the National Stadium. For information on horseback riding and white-water rafting trips from San José, see the "Excursions" section in this chapter.

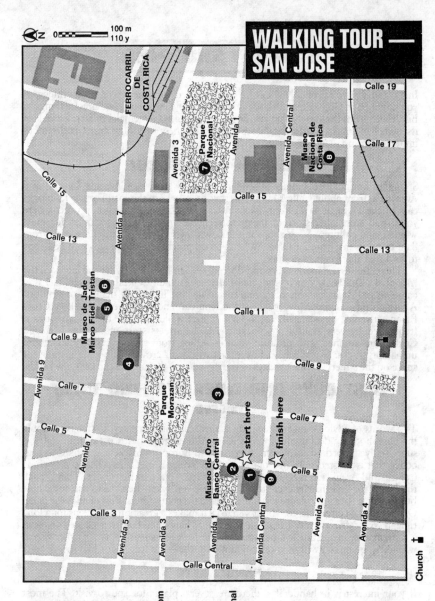

WALKING TOUR — SAN JOSE

N
0 ——— 100 m
          110 y

FERROCARRIL DE COSTA RICA

Calle 19

Calle 17

Calle 15

Avenida Central

Museo Nacional de Costa Rica **8**

Avenida 1

Avenida 3

Parque Nacional **7**

Calle 15

Calle 13

Calle 13

Avenida 7

Calle 11

Museo de Jade Marco Fidel Tristan **5 6**

Calle 9

Calle 9

4

Avenida 9

Calle 7

Parque Morazan

3

Calle 7

Calle 5

Calle 9

Avenida 7

Avenida 9

Museo de Oro Banco Central

2 ☆ start here

1 ☆ finish here

9

Calle 5

Calle 3

Avenida 5

Avenida 3

Avenida 1

Avenida Central

Avenida 2

Avenida 4

Calle Central

Church ✝

SAN JOSE

Walking Tour Area

1 Teatro Nacional
2 Gold Museum
3 Hotel Amstel Grill Room
4 Escuela Metálica
5 Jade Museum
6 Casa Amarilla
7 Parque Nacional
8 Museo Nacional
9 Café de Teatro Nacional

6. SAVVY SHOPPING

In Costa Rica, you probably won't be overwhelmed with the desire to buy things, as you might be in Guatemala. Although there are a few interesting and unique things to buy, there is not the variety that you find everywhere in Guatemala. In fact, for lack of its own handcrafts, Costa Rica does a brisk business of selling crafts and clothes imported from Guatemala.

THE SHOPPING SCENE

Shopping in San José centers around the parallel streets of Avenida Central and Avenida 2, from about Calle 14 in the west and Calle 13 in the east. For several blocks east of the Plaza de la Cultura, Avenida Central is a pedestrians-only street where you'll find store after store of inexpensive made–in–Costa Rica clothes for men, women, and children. Most shops in the downtown shopping district are open from 8am to noon and from 2 to 6pm. When you do purchase something, you'll be happy to find that there is no sales tax.

There are several markets around downtown San José, but by far the largest is the **Mercado Central,** which is located between Avenida Central and Avenida 1 and calles 6 and 8. Inside this dark maze of stalls you'll find all manner of vendors. Although this is primarily a food market, you can find a few vendors selling Costa Rican souvenirs. Be especially careful about your wallet or purse because this area is frequented by very skillful pickpockets. All the streets surrounding the Mercado Central are jammed with produce vendors selling from small carts or loading and unloading trucks. It is always a hive of activity, with crowds of people jostling for space on the streets. In the hot days of the dry season, the aromas can get quite heady.

BEST BUYS AND WHERE TO FIND THEM
COFFEE

Two words of advice—buy coffee. Buy as much as you can carry. Coffee is probably the best shopping deal in all of Costa Rica. Although the best Costa Rican coffee is supposedly shipped off to North American and European markets, it is hard to beat coffee that is roasted right in front of you. **El Trebol,** on Calle 8 between Avenida Central and Avenida 1, is highly recommended as a place to buy coffee. They'll pack the beans for you in whatever size of bag that you want. Be sure to ask for whole beans; Costa Rican grinds are too fine for standard coffee filters. Best of all is the price: One pound of coffee sells for about ¢85 ($1)! It makes a great gift and keeps for a long time in your refrigerator or freezer. If you should happen to buy prepackaged coffee in a supermarket in Costa Rica, be sure that the package is marked *puro;* otherwise, it will likely be mixed with a good amount of sugar—the way Ticos like it.

HANDCRAFTS

If your interest is in handcrafts, there are several places for you to visit. The most appealing artisans market is the daily one on the Plaza de la Cultura. Prices here tend to be high and bargaining is necessary, but there are some very nice items for sale. If you prefer to do your craft shopping in a flea-market atmosphere, head over to **La Casona** on Calle Central between Avenida Central and Avenida 1.

Several other shops around San José sell a wide variety of crafts—from the truly tacky to the divinely inspired. Here are some of the places to look for such items.

MERCADO DE ARTESANOS CANAPI, Calle 11 and Avenida 1. Tel. 21-3342.
Inside you'll find a wide variety of typical Costa Rican handcrafts including large, comfortable woven rope hammocks; reproductions of pre-Columbian gold jewelry and pottery bowls; coffee-wood carvings; and many other wood carvings from rare

Costa Rican hardwoods. The most unusual crafts for sale are the brightly painted miniature oxcarts that are almost the national symbol. These oxcarts are made in the small town of Sarchí, which is mentioned under "Easy Excursions" in this chapter.

Open: Mon–Fri 9am–12:30pm and 1:30–6pm; Sat 9am–12:30pm and 1:30–5pm.

MERCADO NACIONAL DE ARTESANIAS, Calle 11 and Avenida 2. Tel. 23-0122.

Similar crafts at similar prices are available from this shop, which is located only two blocks away from the CANAPI store.

Open: Mon–Sat 8am–noon and 2–6pm.

ANTIC, EDIFICIO LAS ARCADAS, Avenida 2 and Calle 1. Tel. 33-4630.

Located in the building to the left of the Gran Hotel Costa Rica, this tiny shop has—among other things—carved stone reproductions of the pre-Columbian figures on display in the National Museum and Jade Museum. Antic sells crafts from all over Central America, and it is a good place to pick up a *mola*, the appliquéd panels from Panama.

Open: Mon–Sat 9am–noon and 2–6pm.

LA GALERIA, Avenida 1 and Calle 1. Tel. 21-3436.

This small store features some of the best of modern Costa Rican handcrafts. There is a fine selection of wood carvings and gold and silver pre-Columbian jewelry reproductions. The little boxes and bowls of native Costa Rican hardwoods are particularly attractive.

Open: Mon–Fri 8:30am–12:30pm and 1–6pm.

SURASKA, Calle 5 and Avenida 3. Tel. 22-0129.

If you haven't been impressed with the quality of Costa Rican handcrafts found elsewhere, save your money for a visit to this store. Of particular note are the wood carvings by Barry Biesanz and Jay Morrison. These two North American artists turn out exquisite pieces of finely worked hardwood. One of Biesanz's pieces was even given to the Reagans as a gift. Woods used for these works of art include purple heart, rosewood, and lignum vitae, among others. Be forewarned, however, that these pieces sell for hundreds of dollars.

Open: Mon–Sat 9am–noon and 1–6pm.

7. EVENING ENTERTAINMENT

THE ENTERTAINMENT SCENE

To find out about the entertainment scene in San José, pick up a copy of the *Tico Times* (English) and *La Nacion* (Spanish). The former is a good place to find out where local expatriates are hanging out; the latter's "Viva" section has extensive listings of everything from discos to movie theaters to live music.

THE PERFORMING ARTS

TEATRO NACIONAL, Avenida 2 between calles 3 and 5. Tel. 21-1329.

Financed with a self-imposed tax on coffee exports, this grand baroque theater was completed in 1897. Muses representing Music, Fame, and Dance gaze off into the distance from the roof, while statues of Beethoven and Calderón de la Barca flank the entrance. The lobby is simple and elegant. Marble floors, frescoes, and gold-framed Venetian mirrors offer cultured Ticos a grand foyer in which to congregate prior to performances by the National Symphony Orchestra, ballet companies, opera companies, and all the other performers who keep this theater busy almost every night of the year. Within the hall itself, there are three tiers of seating amid an elegant gilt-and-plasterwork decor, and of course the wealthy patrons have their private box seats. Marble staircases are lined with sculptures; the walls are covered with murals and changing art exhibits. The symphony season begins in late April, shortly before the start of the rainy season, and continues on until November. Performances are on Thursday and Friday. In 1990, the National Symphony Orchestra celebrated its 50th anniversary. The Café de Teatro Nacional, just off the lobby, is open daily and is the most elegant café in the city.

Tours: Tuesday through Sunday for ¢100 ($1.18).

Prices: ¢100–¢500 ($1.18–$5.88), purchasers of cheaper tickets must use side entrance. **Bus:** Sabana-Cementerio.

THE CLUB AND MUSIC SCENE

Salsa is the music of young people in San José, and on any weekend you can damage your eardrums at half a dozen or more nightclubs around town. The "Viva" section of *La Nación* newspaper has weekly performance schedules. One of the most popular salsa bands is called Blanco y Negro—watch for them.

The best place to sample San José's nightclub scene is in El Pueblo, a shopping, dining, and entertainment complex done up like an old Spanish village. It's just across the river to the north of town. The easiest way to get here is by taxi; all the drivers know El Pueblo well. Within the alleyways that wind through El Pueblo are a dozen or more bars, clubs, and discos. There is even a roller-skating rink. On my last visit, **Salon Musical Lety** was offering live Latin music nightly, **Cocolocos** was featuring nightly "fiestas," and **Discoteque Infinito** was advertising three different ambiences under one roof. **El Escondite de Morgan** is a piano bar, and the **Tango Bar** is just what its name implies.

THE BAR SCENE

The best part of the varied bar scene in San José is something called a *boca,* the equivalent of a *tapa* in Spain, a little dish of snacks that arrives at your table when you order a drink. In most bars, the bocas are free; but in some, where the dishes are more sophisticated, you'll have to pay for the treats. Also, with the exception of Key Largo, drinks are very reasonably priced at ¢80 to ¢100 (95¢ to $1.20). At the top of the list is a 24-hour restaurant/bar that is a San José institution and so should be a part of anyone's visit.

LA ESMERALDA, Avenida 2 between calles 5 and 7. Tel. 21-0503.

A sort of mariachi Grand Central Station, La Esmeralda is a cavernous open-air restaurant and bar that stays open 24 hours a day. In the evenings, mariachi bands park their vans out front and wait to be hired for a moonlight serenade or perhaps a surprise party. While they wait, they often wander into La Esmeralda and practice their favorite melodies. If you've never been serenaded at your table before, this place is a must.

SODA PALACE, Calle 2 and Avenida 2. Tel. 21-3441.

Strictly for men, this dingy but brightly lit bar hardly lives up to its name. It opens directly onto busy Avenida 2 and is open 24 hours a day. Men of all ages sit at the tables conversing loudly and watching the world pass by. You never know what might happen at the Palace. Mariachis stroll in, linger for a while, then continue on their way. Legend has it that the revolution of 1948 was planned right here.

KEY LARGO, Calle 7 between avenidas 1 and 3. Tel. 21-0277.

Housed in one of the most beautiful old buildings in San José, Key Largo is elegant and expensive. It is worth a visit just to see the interior of the building, but be forewarned—this is known worldwide as San José's number-one prostitute hangout. Any woman who approaches you here is a prostitute.

CHARLESTON, Avenida 4 between calles 7 and 9. No phone.

Jazz lovers will enjoy this relaxed bar with a 1920s theme. Great recorded jazz music plays on the stereo all day and night. There are occasional live bands.

EL CUARTEL DE LA BOCA DEL MONTE, Avenida 1 between calles 21 and 23. Tel. 21-0327.

This very popular bar is reputed to have the best bocas in San José, although you'll have to pay for them. Their cocktails are also famous. Just look around and see what sort of amazing concoctions people are drinking and ask for whichever one strikes your fancy.

NASHVILLE SOUTH, Calle 5 between avenidas 1 and 3. Tel. 33-1988.

As its name implies, this is a country-and-western bar and is very popular with homesick expatriates. It has a friendly atmosphere and fun music.

MORE ENTERTAINMENT
MOVIE THEATERS

Even if you aren't interested in what's playing at one of the downtown theaters, it's worth the ¢130 ($1.53) admission just to gain entrance to one of these old palaces. The screens are huge, and on a weeknight you might have the theater almost to yourself. Check the "Viva" section of *La Nacion* or the *Tico Times* for movie listings and times.

GAMBLING CASINOS

Gambling is legal in Costa Rica, and there are casinos at virtually every major hotel. In most of these hotel casinos, you'll need to get dressed up; but at the casino in the lobby of the Gran Hotel Costa Rica, at Calle 3 between Avenida Central and Avenida 2, on the Plaza de la Cultura, there doesn't seem to be any dress code. Good luck.

8. EASY EXCURSIONS

San José makes an excellent base for exploring the beautiful Meseta Central and the surrounding mountains. Probably the best way to make most of these excursions is by car. Tour companies tend to charge steep rates for their tours, and public transportation to the remote sites, such as the volcanoes, is problematic to nonexistent.

Of all the possible excursions from San José, none is more enjoyable than a visit to Lankester Gardens with a trip up to the top of Irazú Volcano, a stop in Cartago, and a drive through the Orosi Valley.

ORGANIZED TOURS

Rates for various excursion tours from San José are pretty much standardized; if, say, you book a cruise through the Gulf of Nicoya with one company, you will take the same cruise being offered by many other companies. Generally the rates are rather high, with half-day trips costing $25 to $30 and full-day trips costing $65 to $75. At the time of this writing, a day-long tour—whether it was on the Jungle Train, was a gulf cruise, was horseback riding, or was white-water rafting—cost $65. Several companies offer cruises to remote islands in the Gulf of Nicoya, and these excursions include gourmet buffet meals and stops at deserted (until your boat arrives) beaches. Companies offering these trips include **Bay Island Cruises** (tel. 31-2898), **Calypso Island Cruise** (tel. 33-3617), and **Fantasia** (tel. 55-0791).

If you enjoy horseback riding, you have your choice of fascinating locations for day-long trips not far from downtown San José. Contact **Finca Ob-La-Di Ob-La-Da** (tel. 49-1179) for rides in two forest preserves, **L.A. Tours** (tel. 24-5828 or 39-7104) for rides in a cloud forest, or **Finca Los Angeles** (tel. 24-5828) for rides on the beach. Rates are around $65 for a day of riding, including hotel pickup and lunch.

Cascading down from Costa Rica's mountain ranges are dozens of tumultuous rivers, several of which have become very popular for white-water rafting and kayaking. For about $65 you can spend a day rafting through lush tropical forests. Contact **Rios Tropicales** (tel. 31-6296) or one of the tour companies listed under "Organized Tours" in the "Attractions" section.

LANKESTER GARDENS

There are more than 1,200 varieties of orchids in Costa Rica, and no less than 800 species are on display at this botanical garden in Cartago province. Created in the 1940s by English naturalist Charles Lankester, the gardens are now administered by the University of Costa Rica. The primary goal of the gardens is to preserve the local flora, with an emphasis on orchids and bromeliads. The thousands of orchid plants in the garden grow in the diverse habitats that have been created here. Paved trails wander from open sunny gardens into shady forests. In each environment, different species of orchids are in bloom. Be sure to bring lots of color film for your camera. The only disappointment in a visit to Lankester Gardens is that you are allowed to visit for only one hour before you have to leave. There are free guided tours, or you can wander on your own.

Admission is ¢75 (88¢). The gardens are open daily 8:30am–3:30pm with tours every hour on the half hour. To get there take a Cartago bus from San José. In Cartago, cross to the south side of the Central Park and catch a Paraíso bus to Campo Ayala. From this stop, walk 500 yards to the gardens. Alternatively, you can take a taxi from Cartago for between ¢200 and ¢300 ($2.35 and $3.53). If you're driving, take the Paraíso road out of Cartago and watch for a three-foot-tall blue-green cube on the right side of the road.

CARTAGO

Located about 15 miles southeast of San José, Cartago is the former capital of Costa Rica. Founded in 1563, it was Costa Rica's first city—and was in fact its only city for almost 150 years. Irazú Volcano looms up from the edge of town; although it is quiescent these days, it has not always been so peaceful. Earthquakes have damaged Cartago repeatedly over the years, so that today there are few colonial buildings left standing. In the center of the city stand the ruins of a large church that was destroyed in 1910, before it was ever finished. Construction was abandoned after the quake, and today the ruins are a neatly manicured park.

Cartago's most famous building, however, is the **Basílica de Nuestra Señora de Los Ángeles** (the Basilica of Our Lady of the Angels), which is dedicated to the patron saint of Costa Rica and stands on the east side of town. Within the walls of this Byzantine church is a shrine containing the tiny figure of La Negrita, the Black Virgin, which is nearly lost amid its ornate altar. This statue was found at a spring that now bubbles up at the rear of the church on the right side. Miraculous healing powers have been attributed to La Negrita, and over the years thousands of pilgrims have come to the shrine seeking cures for their illnesses and difficulties. The walls of the shrine are covered with a fascinating array of tiny silver images left as thanks for cures affected by La Negrita. Amid the plethora of diminutive arms and legs, there are also hands, feet, hearts, lungs, intestines, kidneys, ears, eyes, torsos, breasts—and, peculiarly, guns, trucks, beds, cars, and planes. There are even dozens of sports trophies that I assume were left in thanks for helping teams win big games. August 2 is the day dedicated to La Negrita. On this day thousands of people walk from San José to Cartago in devotion to this powerful statue.

If you'd like to soak in a warm-water swimming pool, head 2½ miles south of Cartago to Aguas Calientes.

To get there, a bus leaves San José frequently from Avenida Central between calles 13 and 15 and costs ¢22 (26¢). The length of the trip is 45 minutes.

IRAZÚ VOLCANO

Located 20 miles north of Cartago, 11,260-foot-tall Irazú is one of Costa Rica's three active volcanoes (at this time it is dormant). It last erupted on March 19, 1963, on the day that President John F. Kennedy arrived in Costa Rica. The eruption showered ash on the Meseta Central for months after, destroying crops and collapsing roofs but enriching the soil. There is a good paved road right to the rim of the crater. At the top, amid desolate expanses of gray sand, few plants grow. The air smells of sulfur, and clouds descend by noon each day. From the parking area, a short trail leads to the rim of the volcano's two craters, its walls a maze of eroded gullies feeding onto the flat floor far below. If you arrive early enough, before the clouds close in, you may be treated to a view of both the Pacific Ocean and the Caribbean Sea. There are also magnificent views of the fertile Meseta Central and Orosi Valley as you drive up from Cartago. It is officially open only from 8am to 4pm, but there is nothing to stop you from visiting earlier. Don't forget to wear warm clothes. This may be the tropics, but it's cold up at the top. In the busy season, an admission of ¢100 ($1.18) is charged. Plan to arrive at the rim as early as possible, then, on your way down, stop for breakfast at **Restaurant Linda Vista** (tel. 25-5808). It's on the right as you come down the mountain and is open daily from 7:30am to 6pm. At 10,075 feet, it claims to be the highest restaurant in Central America. There are walls of windows looking out over the valley far below, and the walls are plastered with thousands of business cards left by people who have stopped here. They make fascinating reading; if you look long enough you'll probably find a card left by someone you know. A hearty Tico breakfast of gallo pinto with ham will cost about ¢250 ($2.94).

At the time of this writing, there was no longer public bus service to Irazú. Check at the tourist office to see if this situation has changed. The best way to visit is either on a tour from San José (contact one of the tour companies mentioned above) or with a rental car. If you are driving, head northeast out of Cartago toward San Rafael, then continue driving uphill toward the volcano, passing the turnoffs for Cot and Tierra Blanca en route.

OROSI VALLEY

The Orosi Valley, southeast of Cartago, is called the most beautiful valley in Costa Rica. The Reventazón River meanders through this steep-sided valley until it collects in the lake formed by the Cachí Dam. There are scenic overlooks near the towns of Orosi, at the head of the valley, and Ujarrás, on the banks of the lake. Near Ujarrás are the ruins of Costa Rica's oldest church, whose tranquil surrounding gardens are a great place to sit and gaze at the surrounding mountains. Across the lake is a popular recreation center, called Charrarra, where you'll find a picnic area, swimming pool, and hiking trails. In the town of Orosi itself is a colonial church built in 1743. A small museum here displays religious artifacts.

It would be difficult to explore this whole area by public bus, since this is not a densely populated region. However, there are buses from Cartago to Ujarrás as well as buses to the town of Orosi. These buses leave from a spot one block east and one block south of the church ruins in Cartago. A bus that will drop you at the Orosi lookout point leaves from the same vicinity. If you are driving, take the road to Paraíso from Cartago, head toward Ujarrás, continue around the lake, then pass through Cachí and on to Orosi. From Orosi, the road leads back to Paraíso. There are tours of this area from San José.

POÁS VOLCANO

This is another active volcano accessible from San José in a day trip. It is 36 miles from San José on narrow roads that wind through a landscape of fertile farms and dark forests. As at Irazú, there is a paved road right to the top. The volcano stands 8,800 feet tall and is located within a national park, which preserves not only the volcano but also dense stands of virgin forest. Poás's crater is nearly a mile across and is said to be the second-largest crater in the world. Geysers in the crater sometimes spew steam and muddy water 600 feet into the air, making this the largest geyser in the world. There is an information center where you can see a slide show about the volcano, and marked hiking trails through the cloud forest that rings the crater. About 20 minutes from the parking area, along a forest trail, is an overlook onto beautiful Botos Lake, which has formed in one of the volcano's extinct craters. Unfortunately, although this is the most developed and popular national park in Costa Rica, it may not be open when you visit. The volcano seems to have an eruption cycle of 40 to 45 years. It erupted in 1910 and again in 1953, and it may be in the middle of another active period. Be sure to ask at the tourist information center in San José before heading out this way.

There is an excursion bus on Sunday leaving at 8:30am from Calle 12 between avenidas 2 and 4 and returning at 2pm. The fare is ¢200 ($2.35) for the round trip. The bus is always crowded, so arrive early. It is possible to get as far as the town of San Pedro de Poás, but from there you will have to hitchhike or take a taxi ($20 round trip), which makes this alternative as costly as a tour. All the tour companies in San José offer tours to Poás, although they often don't arrive until after the clouds have closed in. If you're traveling by car, head for Alajuela and continue on the main road through town toward Varablanca. Just before reaching Varablanca, turn left toward Poasito and continue to the rim of the volcano.

HEREDIA, ALAJUELA, GRECIA, SARCHÍ, AND ZARCERO

All of these cities and towns are northwest of San José and can be combined into a long day trip, perhaps in conjunction with a visit to Poás Volcano.

Heredia was founded in 1706. On its central park stands a colonial church dedicated in 1763. The stone façade leaves no questions as to the age of the church, but the altar inside is decorated with neon stars and a crescent moon surrounding a statue of the Virgin Mary. In the middle of the palm-shaded park is a music temple, and across the street, beside several tile-roofed municipal buildings, is the tower of an old Spanish fort. Of all the cities in the Meseta Central, this is the only one that has even the slightest colonial feeling to it.

Alajuela is one of Costa Rica's oldest cities, only 12 miles from San José. Although it is an attractive little city filled with parks, there isn't much to see or do here. The **Juan Santamaría Museum**, Calle Central between Avenidas 2 and 3 (tel. 41-4775), commemorates Costa Rica's national hero, who gave his life defending the country against a small army led by William Walker, a U.S. citizen who invaded Costa Rica in 1856 with the goal of setting up a slave state in Central America. Open Tuesday through Sunday 2 to 9pm.

From Alajuela, a narrow, winding road leads to the town of **Grecia,** which is noteworthy for its unusual metal church, painted a deep red with white gingerbread trim. The road to Sarchí is to the right as you go around the church.

Sarchí is Costa Rica's main artisans town. It is here that the colorfully painted miniature ox carts you see all over Costa Rica are made. Ox carts such as these were once used to haul coffee beans to market; today they are entirely decorative and have become a well-known symbol of Costa Rica. Many other carved wooden souvenirs are made here with rare hardwoods from the nation's forests. There are dozens of shops in the town, all of which have similar prices. The other reason to visit Sarchí is to see its unforgettable church. Built between 1950 and 1958, the church is painted pink with aquamarine trim and looks strangely like a children's birthday cake. This outrageously decorated church is the largest pink building I have ever seen. There is even an ox-cart wheel atop one of the church's towers.

Beyond Sarchí, on picturesque roads lined with cedar trees, you will find the town of **Zarcero.** In a small park in the middle of town is a menagerie of topiary sculptures (sculpted shrubs) that includes a monkey on a motorcycle, people and animals dancing, an ox pulling a cart, and a man wearing a top hat. It is well worth the drive to see this park.

The road to Heredia turns north off the highway from San José to the airport. To reach Alajuela from Heredia, take the scenic road that heads west through the town of San Joaquín. To continue on to Sarchí, it is best to return to the highway south of Alajuela and drive west toward Puntarenas. Turn north to Grecia and then west to Sarchí.

THE JUNGLE TRAIN

Although there is now an excellent highway from San José to Limón, the Jungle Train is still one of the most popular excursions in Costa Rica. It takes four times as long to reach Limón via train, but the spectacular scenery is well worth the time. This railway was an engineering marvel when it was constructed late in the 19th century. Prior to this time, the coffee grown around San José had to be either taken by ox cart to a river port in north central Costa Rica and then transported to the Caribbean Coast or taken by ox cart to Puntarenas and shipped around South America. The engineer of the railway, Minor Keith, made a deal with the Costa Rican government for 800,000 acres of land alongside the tracks and planted bananas for export to the United States. Using this land, Keith founded the United Fruit Company, which later came under fire for its massive landholdings throughout Central America. Today tourists ride the rails through the jungles to see the scenery and tiny villages that are connected to the outside world only by way of the railroad. It is a slow ride, with dozens of stops, but vendors get on frequently to sell food and drinks.

There are several ways that you can ride the Jungle Train. You can spend $65 for a tour company excursion in a first-class car that is strictly for tourists. Or, you can pay ¢130 ($1.53) for a regular-class ticket from San José to Limón. The seats aren't as comfortable, but the view is the same. One drawback of riding with the locals is that you become easy prey for the many pickpockets who work on this train. If you choose this way to make the trip, be very careful with your valuables, which really should be left in your hotel safe.

The most interesting part of the journey is between Cartago and Siquirres. If you don't want to waste time riding between less interesting stops, take a bus to Cartago, board the train, get off in Siquirres, and catch a bus back to San José. This is what some of the expensive tours do. Alternatively, you can ride the train to Limón, spend the night there, and continue on the next day to Cahuita or Tortuguero National Park (some tours have Tortuguero tie-ins).

This train leaves San José daily at 10am from the train station on Avenida 3 between calles 21 and 23 and takes 8 hours to reach Limón. If you would rather spend the money for the tourist train, contact **Panorama Tours** (tel. 33-0233 or 33-3058) or one of the other tour operators mentioned under "Organized Tours" in the "Attractions" section.

9. MOVING ON — TRAVEL SERVICES

When it comes time to move on, if you haven't got a return ticket already, stop by the travel agencies of **Super Viajes,** Avenida Central and Calle 1 (tel. 21-6230), or **Servisa Internacional,** Avenida 1 between calles 5 and 7 (tel. 22-2410 or 22-4647).

CHAPTER 4

GUANACASTE AND THE NORTHWEST

1. MONTEVERDE
- WHAT'S SPECIAL ABOUT THE NORTHWEST
2. LIBERIA
3. PLAYA DEL COCO
4. PLAYA HERMOSA
5. PLAYAS BRASILITO, FLAMINGO, POTRERO, AND PAN DE AZUCAR
6. PLAYA TAMARINDO

The northwest of Costa Rica is the country's "Wild West." It is the driest region and toward the end of the dry season resembles west Texas. This resemblance is further accentuated by the presence of large cattle ranches where gigantic, flop-eared white Brahma cattle graze in the fields. The Guanacaste Peninsula, which is divided from the mainland by the Gulf of Nicoya, is where most tourists coming in this direction are headed. Because of its long dry season and relatively dry rainy season (only 65 inches per year), the Guanacaste Peninsula has been targeted for major resort developments. In addition to the towns and beaches mentioned in this chapter, there are many remote beaches, some accessible only by plane, where there are small, but expensive, resorts. Down at the southern tip of the peninsula is an area, Playa Montezuma, that has a few backpacker-type cabinas, but it is very difficult to reach. In upcoming years, all of these beaches should become more accessible; as they do, they will be included in future editions of this book.

1. MONTEVERDE

Distances: 90 miles northwest of San José; 35 miles northwest of Puntarenas.

GETTING THERE By Bus Express buses leave San José Monday through Thursday at 2:30pm and Saturday and Sunday at 6:30am from the corner of Calle 12 and Avenida 5. Duration: 3½ hours. Fare: ¢230 ($2.71). There is also a daily bus from Puntarenas to Santa Elena, which is only a few miles from Monteverde. These buses leave at 2:15pm from the stop across the street from the San José station in Puntarenas. Duration: 2½ hours. Fare: ¢100 ($1.18).

By Car Take the Interamerican Highway toward Puntarenas and follow the signs for Nicaragua. Turn off to the right shortly before Puntarenas and head north. In about 25 miles (41 km), watch for the Rio Lagarto bridge. Just before the bridge is a dirt road to the right. Turn here. From this turnoff, it's another 19 miles (1½ to 2 hours) to Monteverde, but the going is very slow because the road is so bad. Don't try it in the rainy season unless you have four-wheel drive. If you reach the turnoff from the highway before the afternoon bus passes through, you will likely be hailed by people wanting a ride. If your car can handle the additional load, a lift will be greatly appreciated. On remote sections of road throughout Costa Rica, hitchhiking is quite common because buses are often infrequent or nonexistent. One more thing: Be sure you have plenty of gas in the car before starting up to Monteverde. This grueling road eats up fuel, and the one gas station in Monteverde doesn't always have gas.

WHAT'S SPECIAL ABOUT THE NORTHWEST

Beaches
☐ The beaches of Guanacaste, with more sunshine than any of the other beaches in the country

Parks/Gardens
☐ Monteverde Cloud Forest Reserve, a lush jungle that is home to the quetzal, one of the most beautiful birds on earth
☐ Rincón de la Vieja and Santa Rosa national parks, unique habitats including tropical dry forest and a geyser field

Natural Spectacles
☐ Every year, hundreds of thousands of turtles laying their eggs on beaches in Santa Rosa National Park
☐ Arenal Volcano, with a large artificial lake at its base

Activities
☐ Sportfishing for billfish off the northwest coast

DEPARTING The express bus to San José leaves Tuesday, Wednesday, and Thursday at 6:30am, Friday, Saturday, and Sunday at 3pm.

The bus from Santa Elena to Puntarenas leaves daily at 6am.

To get to Manuel Antonio, take the 6am Santa Elena–Puntarenas bus and then catch the 2:30 bus for Quepos. It makes for a long day, but is the only choice you have unless you want to go back to San José and catch the 3pm plane (Tuesday, Thursday, and Saturday only), which will save you only a couple of hours if any.

To reach Liberia, take the Santa Elena-Puntarenas bus at 6am and get off at the Rio Lagarto bridge, where the bus reaches the paved road. You can then flag down a bus bound for Liberia (almost any bus heading north).

ESSENTIALS Orientation Monteverde is not a village in the traditional sense of the word. There is no center of town, only dirt lanes leading off from the main road to various farms. This main road has signs for all the hotels and restaurants mentioned here and deadends at the reserve entrance.

Fast Facts A taxi between Santa Elena and Monteverde costs ¢400 to ¢500 ($4.70 to $5.88).

In the past few years, ecotourism has become big business in Costa Rica, and nowhere is this more apparent than in the tiny village of Monteverde. "Green Mountain" is how the Spanish name translates, and that is exactly what you will find up here at the end of a long, rutted dirt road that passes through mile after mile of pastures. All those pastures were once covered with dense forest, but only a small piece of it now remains. That piece of forest has been preserved as the **Reserva Biologica Bosque Nuboso Monteverde,** the Monteverde Cloud Forest Biological Reserve.

The village of Monteverde was founded in the 1950s by Quakers from the United States. They wished to leave behind the constant fear of war and the obligation to support continued militarism through U.S. taxes. They chose Costa Rica because it was committed to a nonmilitaristic economic path. Since its founding, Monteverde has grown slowly as other people who shared the ideals of the original Quaker founders moved to the area. Although the original founders came here to farm the land, they recognized the need to preserve the rare cloud forest that covers the mountain slopes above their fields.

A cloud forest is much like a rain forest, but much of the moisture comes not from falling rain but from the condensation left by the nearly constant cloud cover that blankets the tops of mountains in many parts of the tropics. Monteverde Reserve covers 4,000 acres of forest, including several different life zones that are characterized by different types of plants and animals. Within this small area are more than 2,000 species of plants, 320 bird species, and 100 different species of mammals. It is no wonder that the reserve has been the site of constant scientific investigations since its founding.

WHAT TO SEE AND DO

Don't expect to see all those plants and animals during your visit because many of them are quite rare or elusive. However, with a guide hired through your hotel or with one of the reserve guides who lead two- to three-hour tours of the reserve, you can see far more than you could on your own. At $12 per person, the tours are expensive, especially after you pay the $5 reserve entrance fee, but I strongly recommend that you go with a guide. I went into the reserve twice in the same morning—once on my own and once with a guide—and with the guide I saw much more and learned much more about cloud forests and their inhabitants. On the other hand, while alone I saw a rare bird, a guan, that I didn't see when walking the trails with a dozen or more other interested visitors. There is much to be said for walking quietly through the forest on your own.

Before venturing into the forest, have a look around the information center. There are several guide books available, as well as posters and postcards of some of the reserve's more famous animal inhabitants. Perhaps the most famous resident of the cloud forests of Costa Rica is the quetzal, a robin-sized bird with iridescent-green wings and a ruby-red breast, which has become extremely rare due to habitat destruction. The male quetzal also has two long tail feathers that make it one of the most spectacular birds on earth. The best time to see quetzals is early to midmorning, with March and April (mating season) being the easiest months to spot these magnificent birds.

Other animals that have been seen in Monteverde include jaguars, ocelots, tapirs, and rare golden toads. This bright-orange toad is known only from a small population here in the reserve. It has been found nowhere else on earth. Unfortunately, three unusually dry years in a row between 1987 and 1990 may have reduced the already small population to extremely low numbers.

Because the vegetation in the cloud forest is so dense, with hundreds of species of epiphytic plants such as orchids and bromeliads hanging from almost every imaginable square inch of tree limb, none of the forest's animal residents is very easy to spot. If you were unsatisfied with your sightings, even with a naturalist guide leading you, you might want to consider getting together a group of people to pay for a slide show of photographs taken in the reserve. The show can be arranged through your hotel or by phoning 61-0952. The cost for a group is $50.

Just outside the entrance to the park is the fascinating **Hummingbird Gallery.** Hanging from trees outside the gallery are several hummingbird feeders that attract more than seven species. At any given moment, there might be several dozen hummingbirds buzzing and chattering around the building. Inside you will, of course, find a lot of beautiful mounted and unmounted color prints of hummingbirds. There are also many other beautiful photos from Monteverde available in prints or postcards. The gallery is open daily from 9:30am to 5pm.

WHERE TO STAY

DOUBLES [MEALS INCLUDED] FOR LESS THAN ¢4,000 [$47.05]

PENSIÓN MONTEVERDE INN, Apdo. 10165-1000 San José. Tel. 506/ 61-2756. 14 rms, 6 with bath.

$ Rates (including three meals per day): ¢1,450 ($17.06) single without bath,

¢1,600 ($18.82) single with bath; ¢2,900 ($34.12) double without bath, ¢3,200 ($37.64) double with bath. No credit cards.

 David Savage and his family are the owners of this simple rustic lodge on a farm between Monteverde and Santa Elena. This is the most economical of the lodges in Monteverde, and although it is a bit of a walk up to the park entrance, this is a good choice for those who have to watch their colónes. The rooms are small and come with two twin beds or a double bed. Hardwood floors keep the rooms from seeming too spartan. You can make a reservation through the Hotel Diplomat in San José (see "Where to Stay" in Chapter 3). The pension's sign and the turn off for the farm are across the street from the Hotel Heliconia.

PENSIÓN FLOR MAR, Apdo. 10165, San José. Tel. 506/61-0909. 13 rms, 3 with bath.

$ Rates: (including three meals per day): ¢1,720 ($20.24) single with bath, ¢1,833 ($21.56) single with bath; ¢3,440 ($40.48) double without bath, ¢3,666 ($43.12) double with bath. No credit cards.

Researchers have been coming to the Monteverde Cloud Forest Reserve since it was created, and for much of that time they have been staying here at the Flor Mar. Obviously, scientists and students are not overly concerned with their accommodations. There are no stunning views, and the rooms are simply furnished. Business is still derived primarily from study groups, and several rooms have bunkbeds. There is even one tiny single room that reminds me of a monk's cell. On your right past the Quetzal (below), this is one of the lodges close to the park entrance. The dining room is large and dark, but there is a much more appealing lounge in the lower of the lodge's two main buildings.

PENSIÓN EL QUETZAL, Apdo. 10165-1000, San José. Tel. 506/61-0955. 10 rms, 7 with bath.

$ Rates (including three meals per day): ¢1,870 ($22) single without bath, ¢2,125 ($25) single with bath; ¢3,740 ($44) double without bath, ¢4,250 ($50) double with bath. No credit cards.

One of the oldest and most popular of Monteverde's rustic lodges, the Quetzal is nearly always full in the busy season (December to May), so be sure to make your reservations well in advance. Staying here is like staying with friends. There are plenty of chairs and lots of reading material around for those who want to brush up on their cloud forest ecology. The rooms are in the main house or in separate buildings, with three or four rooms in each building. Pastures and dark forests surround the buildings. Less than 100 yards away is an informative nature trail operated by the Monteverde Conservation League. If you are coming with a group of four or more, ask for the large room with the sleeping loft. The sign for the Quetzal is on the right not far past the Hotel de Montaña Monteverde (below).

All guests eat together in a small dining room that adjoins the living room.

DOUBLES FOR LESS THAN ¢6,000 [$70.59]

HOTEL FONDA VELA, Monteverde, Puntarenas. Tel. 506/61-2551. 19 rms, 13 with bath.

$ Rates: ¢1,243 ($14.62) single without bath, ¢2,518 ($29.62) single without bath with three meals, ¢2,034 ($23.93) single with bath, ¢3,309 ($38.93) single with bath with three meals; ¢2,034 ($23.93) double without bath, ¢4,584 ($53.93) double without bath with three meals, ¢2,825 ($33.24) double with bath, ¢5,630 ($66.24) double with bath with three meals. V.

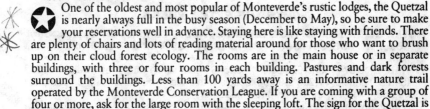 This is one of the newest hotels in Monteverde, and it is closer to the park entrance than most of the others listed here. When I visited, the hotel was only partially completed, and the dining room was a tiny place near the entrance to the farm. By the time you arrive, it should be in full swing with the new dining room and a lot of new rooms that vary in size and style and are housed in four buildings. Some have hardwood floors, and others have flagstone floors. There is abundant wood paneling all around and excellent views from most of the rooms. The buildings are

surrounded by pastures, with the forest only a short walk away. The Fonda Vela is on the right after the sign for the Pensión Quetzal.

HOTEL HELICONIA, Apdo. 10165-1000 San José. Tel. 506/61-1009. 15 rms., all with bath.
$ Rates: ¢2,593.35 ($30.51) single or double; ¢4,174 ($49.11) single with three meals; ¢5,755 ($67.71) double with three meals. No credit cards.
Another new hotel, the Heliconia is back toward Santa Elena, on the left shortly after you pass the turnoff. You don't have the spectacular views here that you have at many of the other lodges in this area, but the rooms are clean and roomy. There is a small collection of mounted moths and butterflies for the amateur lepidopterist in you; if you happen to be musically inclined, there's an organ in the lounge.

SUPER-BUDGET CHOICES

These two extremely spartan places are located in the village of Santa Elena and are down the hill leading toward Monteverde from the bus stop.

EL IMAN, Santa Elena, Puntarenas. Tel. 506/61-1255. 8 rms, 1 with bath.
$ Rates: ¢200 ($2.35) single; ¢400 ($4.71) double. No credit cards.
This extremely basic pension on the outskirts of Santa Elena, which is 3 km from Monteverde, is one of the few choices for those touring Costa Rica on a very limited budget. Rooms here are far from immaculate, but if this is your price category, you haven't got too many choices.

HOTEL TUCAN, Santa Elena, Puntarenas. Tel. 506/61-1007. 7 rms, none with bath.
$ Rates: ¢300 ($3.52) per person per day. No credit cards.
This little hotel is directly across the street from the Iman, but it is slightly cleaner and a touch more appealing. Rooms are tiny and rustic, with wooden floors and walls.
There is a spacious dining area on the first floor where you can get a simple Costa Rican dinner for ¢250 ($2.94).

WORTH THE EXTRA BUCKS

HOTEL DE MONTAÑA MONTEVERDE, Apdo. 70 Plaza G. Víquez, San José. Tel. 506/61-1846 or 33-7078. Fax 506/22-6184. 19 rms., all with bath.
$ Rates: ¢3,074 ($36.16) single, ¢4,636 ($54.54) single with three meals; ¢4,130 ($48.59) double, ¢7,254 ($85.34) double with three meals; ¢5,283 ($62.15) triple, ¢9,969 ($117.28) triple with three meals. AE, MC, V.
This long, low, motel-style building is one of the oldest hotels in Monteverde and is frequently filled with tour groups from San José. The hotel is surrounded by 15 acres of farm and woods that are ideal for quiet strolls or bird watching. There are even horses available for rent. Rooms here are rustic with wood paneling and hardwood floors and come with double or twin; there are even a few rooms with queen-size beds and carpeting. There are plans to add another 16 rooms, a sauna, and a hot tub. The Montaña Monteverde is on the right after the Hotel Heliconia.
The rustic glass-walled dining room offers excellent views. Meals are not mandatory, but a meal plan is available. Attached to the restaurant is a small bar that is always busy in the evening, when people sit around swapping stories of their day's adventures and wildlife sightings.

HOTEL BELMAR, Monteverde, Puntarenas, San José. Tel. 506/61-1001. Fax 506/61-1001. 18 rms., all with bath.
$ Rates: ¢3,362 ($39.55) single, ¢5,096 ($59.55) single with three meals; ¢3,842 ($45.20) double, ¢7,310 ($86) double with three meals; ¢4,418 ($51.98) triple, ¢9,620 ($113.18) triple with three meals. No credit cards.
You'll think that you're in the Alps when you stay at this beautiful Swiss chalet-style hotel. Set at the top of a grassy hill, the Belmar has stunning views all the way to the Gulf of Nicoya and the Pacific Ocean. Afternoons in the

dining room or lounge here are idyllic, with bright sunlight streaming in through a west-facing wall of glass that provides a grandstand seat for spectacular sunsets. Entomologists will be fascinated by the collection of mounted insects in the reading lounge. Most of the guest rooms come with wood paneling, French doors, and little balconies that open onto splendid views. Meals, although not included in the price of a room, are delicious and match the setting. The Belmar is up the road to the left of the gas station as you come into the village of Monteverde.

WHERE TO EAT

This is an easy choice in Monteverde. Many of the hotels require you to take all your meals in their own dining room. If not required to do so, you are strongly encouraged to do so: There are only two restaurants in the area, and if you don't have a car, you will have a long walk between your hotel and the restaurant.

RESTAURANT EL BOSQUE, on the main road through the village before Pensión Quetzal. Tel. 61-1258.
$ Prices: ¢135–¢550 ($1.59–$6.47). No credit cards.
Open: Thurs–Tues noon–9pm.
It looks strangely out of place from the road—a large dining room with three walls of glass hung with suburban curtains—but "The Forest," as its name translates in English, is your only choice around here if you want to go out for a bite to eat. Food is basic—fried chicken, steaks, filet of fish, and Tico standards.

EL SAPO DORADO, Santa Elena. No phone.
$ Prices: ¢250–¢650 ($2.94–$7.65). No credit cards.
Open: Wed–Fri 1–9pm; Sat–Sun 5–11pm.
Watch for the sign to El Sapo Dorado ("The Golden Toad") on your way through Santa Elena. This new bar/restaurant is appealing to the upscale visitors who have begun coming to Monteverde. Every evening at sunset there is classical music, and dinner is served on the veranda. Later in the evening, the atmosphere livens up with loud music and dancing.

SHOPPING

CASEM, on the right just past Restaurant El Bosque, is a crafts cooperative that sells souvenirs made from local hardwoods, embroidered clothing, T-shirts, posters and postcards with photos of the local flora and fauna, hats, and many other items to remind you of your visit to Monteverde.

EXCURSIONS
LAKE ARENAL AND ARENAL VOLCANO

Even though it entails driving over a long, rough dirt road, a visit to these two destinations is possible in a day trip from Monteverde or as a destination after leaving Monteverde. Lake Arenal was created by a hydroelectric project and is becoming known as one of the best sailboarding locations in the world. The constant tradewinds that come sweeping down over the mountains here provide the strong, steady winds that professional sailboarders crave. As yet there are no adequate accommodations for budget travelers right on the lake, but if you are down here with your sailboard, there are a few places to stay within a short drive of the lake.

Arenal Volcano is one of Costa Rica's handful of active volcanoes. It is dangerous to climb the mountain, but it is an amazing sight to watch it erupting from a distance, especially at night, when the glowing molten lava is blasted into the black sky. Even in the day, it is an awesome sight; when viewed from the lake, with the volcano reflected in the water, it is truly enchanting.

Tilarán makes a good base for exploring the lake and the volcano. Try the following hotel for accommodations.

CABINAS EL SUEÑO, Tilarán, Guanacaste. Tel. 506/69-5347. 12 rms.
$ Rates: ¢650 ($7.65) single; ¢1,000 ($11.76) double; ¢1,325 ($15.59) triple; ¢1,650 ($19.41) quad. No credit cards.

Right in the middle of this small town, Cabinas El Sueño is a simple two-story hotel, but it is clean and bright, and the management is friendly. There is parking in back of the hotel and a small courtyard complete with fountain on the second floor of the building. Downstairs there is a restaurant and bar.

---

2. LIBERIA

Distances: 145 miles northwest of San José; 83 miles northwest of Puntarenas.

GETTING THERE By Bus Express buses leave San José from Calle 14 between avenidas 1 and 3 daily at 7, 9, and 11:30am and 3, 4, 6, and 8pm. Duration: 4 hours. Fare: ¢160 ($1.88). From Puntarenas, buses leave at 5:30, 7, and 9:30am and noon. Duration: 2 hours. Fare: ¢90 ($1.06).

By Car Take the Carretera Interamericana from San José. Follow the signs for Nicaragua. Duration: 4 hours without stops.

DEPARTING The Liberia bus station is at the northwest corner of the town's main square, which is about 300 yards from the highway.

The express buses for San José leave at 4:30am, 6am, and 7:30am and 12:30, 2, 4, and 6pm. Duration: 4 hours. Fare: ¢160 ($1.88).

To reach Monteverde take any bus leaving before 1pm for Puntarenas or San José. Get off at the Río Lagarto and catch the Puntarenas-Santa Elena bus around 3:15pm. Buses leave at 6:30 and 9:30am and 3 and 6pm. Duration: 2 hours. Fare: ¢90 ($1.06).

See the specific beach section below for information on how to get to the beach.

ESSENTIALS Orientation The highway passes slightly to the west of town. At the intersection with the main road into town, there are several hotels and gas stations. If you turn east into town, you will come to the central square after less than half a mile.

Liberia itself isn't much of a town. There isn't anything to see here, but there are several fine budget hotels out on the highway at the turnoff for the beaches of the northern Guanacaste Peninsula. Also reachable from Liberia in a day trip are Santa Rosa National Park and Rincón de la Vieja National Park. Accommodations at the beaches range from basic to luxury, with little in between that would fall within your budget. The hotels I have listed here are much better than those charging the same rates right on the beach. If you are more interested in seeing the country than in being on beaches, this is the place for you. Besides, if you want a truly tropical beach experience, I recommend Manuel Antonio National Park to the south.

WHAT TO SEE AND DO

Most people who come up this way are heading to the beaches. Guanacaste is well known as the sunniest and dryest part of Costa Rica, and consequently it is rapidly growing as a tourist resort destination. I prefer the beaches of the southern Pacific Coast and the Caribbean Coast—they are much lusher and have more of that tropical feel that people up north expect of a beach in these latitudes. However, if you can't tolerate the least bit of rain on your holiday in the sun, the beaches up here are where you'll want to be. If you have made it this far north, there are also a couple of national parks that you should not miss.

Santa Rosa National Park is 32km north of Liberia on the Panamerican

Highway. The park, which covers a large peninsula jutting out into the Pacific Ocean, has both historic and environmental significance. Santa Rosa was Costa Rica's first national park. However, it was not founded to preserve the land but to preserve a building, known as La Casona, which has played an important role in Costa Rican independence.

Rincón de la Vieja National Park is an area of geothermal activity similar to Yellowstone National Park in the United States. Fumaroles, geysers, and hot pools cover a small area of this park, creating a bizarre other-worldly landscape. There is a youth hostel near the park for adventurous types who want to explore the area for a few days. Contact the Toruma Youth Hostel, Avenida Central between Calles 29 and 31 (tel. 506/24-4085), in San José for details.

WHERE TO STAY

DOUBLES FOR LESS THAN ¢2,400 [$28.23]

HOTEL BRAMADERO, Carretera Interamericana, Liberia. Tel. 506/66-0371. 25 rms, all with bath, 18 with A/C.

$ **Rates:** ¢1,107 ($13.02) single, ¢1,356 ($15.95) single with A/C; ¢1,469 ($17.28) double, ¢2,034 ($23.93) double with A/C; ¢1,808 ($21.27) triple, ¢2,373 ($27.91) triple with A/C. AE, MC, V.

There isn't much parking at this small, motel-style place, but the rates are good and the rooms are clean if simply furnished. Behind the restaurant is the hotel's small pool, wonderfully cooling in an area that is the hottest, dryest, and dustiest in Costa Rica. Rooms around the pool can be noisy at night, especially on the weekends, when families from San José flee the cool elevations for the warmth of the lowlands.

There is a large open-air restaurant and bar in front of the hotel. Unfortunately, the food here is not worth recommending.

HOTEL LA SIESTA, 350 meters sur de la comandancia, Liberia. Tel. 506/66-0678. 23 rms., all with bath. A/C.

$ **Rates:** ¢1,500 ($17.65) single; ¢2,200 ($25.88) double; ¢2,600 ($30.59) triple. MC, V.

Unlike the other hotels listed here, this one is actually in town. Turn right at the highway crossroads and right again at the Farmacia Lux. Although it is quite small, La Siesta has its own pool, and all its rooms are air-conditioned. The basic rooms are clean and come with either two twin beds or a double and a twin.

Dining: There is a restaurant and bar serving the standard Tico menu of steaks, fried chicken, sea bass, and shrimp. Prices range from ¢300 to ¢500 ($3.53 to $5.88).

DOUBLES FOR LESS THAN ¢3,000 [$35.29]

HOTEL EL SITIO, 75 meters west of the fire station on the road to the beaches, Liberia. Tel. 506/66-1211. 52 rms, all with bath. 18 with A/C.

$ **Rates:** ¢2,091 ($24.60) single, ¢2,500 ($29.41) single with A/C; ¢2,199 ($25.87) double, ¢3,164 ($37.22) double with A/C. AE, MC, V.

This is the newest of Liberia's hotels—and as such is one of the nicest—but all the hotels here seem to follow the same basic Spanish-influenced plans. There are red-tile floors, lots of potted plants, and original paintings of local Guanacaste scenes on the walls. A wagon-wheel chandelier hangs from the high ceiling of the lobby. All the rooms are carpeted and very clean, and you have your choice of twin or double beds. The air conditioners can be noisy, so check before agreeing to a room. The pool area is shady (a welcome relief from the strong Guanacaste sun), and there is even one of those famous pre-Columbian basalt balls by the pool.

NEW HOTEL BOYEROS, Carretera Panamericana, Apdo. 85, Liberia. Tel. 506/66-0995 or 66-0722. 60 rms., all with bath. A/C.

$ **Rates:** ¢1,800 ($21.18) single; ¢2,500 ($29.41) double; ¢2,850 ($33.53) triple; ¢3,200 ($37.65) quad. AE, MC, V.

Arches with turned wooden railings and a red-tile roof give this two-story motel-style building a Spanish feel. Between the reception area and the simple restaurant is a huge convention room. Hopefully your visit won't coincide with that of a rowdy convention. In the courtyard of the hotel are two pools, one for adults and one for children, and a thatch-roofed bar. All the rooms have a private balcony or patio overlooking the pool and gardens. Although the bathrooms are small, there is plenty of closet space. This place is nothing fancy, but all the rooms have air conditioning.

Dining: Meals in the small restaurant, which happens to have a few tables on a terrace under a huge "rubber" tree (actually a type of ficus or fig), serves meals ranging in price from ¢200 to ¢500 ($2.35 to $5.88).

WORTH THE EXTRA BUCKS

HOTEL LAS ESPUELAS, Carretera Interamericana, Apdo. 88, Liberia. Tel. 506/66-0144. 36 rms, 3 suites, all with bath. A/C TEL
$ Rates: ¢3,579 ($42.10) single; ¢4,520 ($53.17) double; ¢5,273 ($62.04) triple. AE, MC, V.

If you're in the mood for a bit of a splurge in Liberia, this is the place for you. Las Espuelas is located about 1km before you reach the Liberia crossroads. Park your car in the shade of the huge old guanacaste tree out front and watch out for iguanas as you cross to the office. Actually these large lizards are very shy of humans and, as adults, eat only fruit. The low-rise hotel is set up around a couple of courtyards with open hallways linking everything. There are reproductions of pre-Columbian statues around the grounds and many open-air lounges. The pool is larger than most around here, and the steady winds rustle the palm trees in the garden. Rooms have tile floors and tiled baths and attractive lamps with basket shades.

Dining: The restaurant and bar have stone walls and a beamed ceiling for that rustic "Wild West" atmosphere that is so much a part of life in Guanacaste. Breakfasts range from ¢150 to ¢225 ($1.76 to $2.65); dinners, mainly steak and seafood, are in the ¢350 to ¢650 range ($4.12 to $7.65).

WHERE TO EAT

You don't have too many choices for dining in Liberia, so your hotel dining room is certainly going to be the most convenient. However, the hotels serve standard fare at best. For meals a cut above what you would expect in this cow town, try the following restaurant.

RESTAURANTE PÓKOPÍ, 75m west of the fire station. Tel. 66-1036.
$ Prices: Entrees ¢315-¢900 ($3.71-$10.59). AE, MC, V.
Open: Sun–Thurs 10am–10pm; Fri–Sat 10am–midnight.

It doesn't look like much from the outside, but this tiny restaurant has a surprising amount of class inside. An even more pleasant surprise is the unusual (for rural Costa Rica) variety of Continental dishes offered on the menu. Order one of the delicious daiquiris from the bar while you peruse the menu, which is on a wooden cutting board. You have your choice of dolphin (the fish not the mammal) prepared five different ways, pizza, chicken cordon bleu, chicken in wine sauce, and other equally delectable dishes. However, for a real surprise, order the chateaubriand for ¢660 ($7.76). It comes to your table with great flare, surrounded by succulent fresh vegetables and a tomato stuffed with peas. Don't miss this treat. Attached to the restaurant there is even a disco that swings into action at 9pm on the weekend, with a ¢200 ($2.35) cover charge. And you thought you were out in the sticks.

3. PLAYA DEL COCO

Distances: 156 miles northwest of San José; 11 miles west of Liberia.

GETTING THERE   By Bus   There is one express bus daily from San José, leaving from Calle 14 between avenidas 1 and 3 at 10am. Duration: 5 hours. Fare: ₡180 ($2.12). From Liberia, buses leave at 5:30am, noon, and 4:30pm.

By Car Follow the directions for getting to Liberia, then turn west at the Liberia intersection for the road to Nicoya and the beaches. Follow the signs.

DEPARTING Buses for Liberia leave at 6 and 9:15am and 2 and 6pm. Duration: 30 minutes. Fare: ₡50 (59¢).

The bus for San José leaves daily at 9:30am. Duration: 5 hours. Fare: ₡180 ($2.12).

ESSENTIALS Orientation Playa del Coco is a tiny village with most of the hotels and restaurants right on the water.

This is one of the most easily accessible of the Guanacaste beaches, with a paved road right down to the water; it has long been a popular destination with middle-class Ticos from San José. Unfortunately, most of the hotels right in town are quite rundown, and the water doesn't look too clean (this is a busy fishing port). The crowds that come here like their music loud and constant, so if you are in search of a quiet retreat, stay away. On the other hand, if your quest is for a cheap place to stay right on the beach, with plenty of cheap food and cheap beer nearby, you'll probably like Playa del Coco.

The water's quite wide at low tide and comes almost to the tree line at high tide. The beach is a grayish brown sand, and trash is a bit of a problem right in town. However, if you walk down the long curving beach to the north of town, you're bound to find a nice clean spot to unfold your blanket.

WHAT TO SEE AND DO

There is not much to do here except lie on the sand, hang out in the sodas, or go to the discos. If you are interested, you might be able to join a soccer match (the soccer field is in the middle of town).

WHERE TO STAY

DOUBLES FOR LESS THAN ₡1,000 [$11.76]

CABINAS EL COCO, Playa del Coco, Guanacaste. Tel. 506/67-0167, 67-0110, or 67-0276. 76 rms., all with bath.

$ Rates: ₡481.50–₡595 ($5.66–$7) single; ₡793–₡963 ($9.33–$11.33) double; ₡1,020–₡1,246 ($12–$14.66) triple; ₡1,246–₡1,530 ($14.66–$18) quad. No credit cards.

If you're a light sleeper, stay away from this super-budget choice. Next door to the hotel is a disco that seems to be in a constant competition with the hotel's restaurant to see who can play louder music. The rooms are pretty dreary, and even the pricier ones with ocean views also have a dirty parking lot right outside their windows. This place is definitely a last resort, and then only for the hardiest of backpackers.

CABINAS LUNA TICA, Playa del Coco, Apdo. 67, Guanacaste. Tel. 506/67-0127 or 67-0279. 37 rms., all with bath, 3 with A/C.

$ Rates: ₡508.50–₡1,300 ($5.98–$15.29) single; ₡875.75–₡1,300 ($10.30–$15.29) double; ₡1,101.75–₡1,875 ($12.96–$22.06) triple; ₡1,400–₡1,875 ($16.47–$22.06) quad. MC, V.

These basic rooms are in two buildings on opposite sides of a street that runs parallel to the beach south of the main square. The annex, across the street from the beach, has newer and slightly nicer rooms, including three with air conditioning. The rooms in the older building are quite dark and set up so that they *don't* catch the nearly constant breezes that blow across the peninsula. It is fairly quiet down at this end of town, and the hotel is right on the beach. If you want to be on the beach and spend as little money as possible, this is the place for you.

DOUBLES FOR LESS THAN ¢2,000 [$23.53]

CABINAS CHALE, Playa del Coco, Guanacaste. Tel. 506/67-0036 or 35-6408. 17 rms., all with bath.
$ Rates: ¢1,246 ($14.66) single; ¢1,586 ($18.66) double; ¢1,926 ($22.66) triple; ¢2,266 ($26.66) quad. No credit cards accepted.

Located down a dirt road to the right as you are coming into town, this small motel is quite a bit better than those right on the beach and also much quieter. Your only company as you stroll down to the beach may be a herd of grazing cattle. The rooms are simply furnished with double beds, overhead fans, and tile floors, and each comes with a Tico clothes-washing sink called a *pila*. There is no sign out front so watch for the wrought-iron and white cinderblock wall.

There is a spartan, screen-walled dining room that is open only during the busy season (November to April). Prices in the restaurant range from ¢175 ($2.06) for breakfast to around ¢300 ($3.53) for dinner.

WORTH THE EXTRA BUCKS

HOTEL RESORT LA FLOR DE ITABO, Apdo. 3332-1000, San José. Tel. 506/33-1109 or 33-1987. Fax 506/67-0003. Or Apdo. 32, Playa del Coco, Guanacaste. Tel. 506/67-0292 or 67-0011. 8 rms, 5 bungalows, all with bath.
$ Rates: ¢3,910 ($46) single; ¢4,335 ($51) double; ¢4,760 ($56) triple; ¢5,185 ($61) quad. AE, MC, V.

If you have a little extra money to spend, this is the place to stay. The grounds are lushly planted, and there are two pools, one for adults and one for kids. Toucans and parrots squawk and talk amid the flowers, adding their own living colors to an already colorful garden. Stone reproductions of pre-Columbian statues add a touch of the mysterious to this quiet retreat. With barely a dozen rooms, service here is intimate. The rooms are spacious (especially the bungalows) and attractively decorated and housed in beautiful two-story houses.

Italian dishes are the specialty of the restaurant, with prices ranging from ¢300 to ¢650 ($3.53 to $7.65) for entrees. The bar is decorated with flags from all over the world, and there is a TV in the lobby for those who want to stay connected to the rest of the world.

WHERE TO EAT

MEALS FOR LESS THAN ¢500 [$5.88]

RESTAURANT-BAR EL OASIS, Calle Principal across from the soccer field. No phone.
$ Prices: ¢150–¢500 ($1.76–$5.88). No credit cards accepted.
Open: Daily 10am–10pm.

On the right as you approach the beach is one of Playa del Coco's better restaurants. In the one large room of the restaurant, you'll find a long table for groups and several other smaller tables. There are traditional Tico-style wrought-iron bars on the windows for a touch of colonial atmosphere; otherwise, this is a very simple place. Meals are all Costa Rican, with an emphasis on seafood and broiled chicken.

RESTAURANT GUAJIRA, on beach opposite the soccer fields. No phone.
$ Prices: ¢250–¢1,000 ($2.94–$11.76). No credit cards.
Open: Wed–Mon 9am–1am.

This breezy family restaurant is right on the beach, so you can watch fishermen bring in the catch while you dine. You know the fish served here is fresh because you can watch them clean it on a picnic table in back of the restaurant. Late at night, the party crowd takes over—and it can get pretty noisy. Be sure to try one or more of the delicious ceviches (raw seafood salads marinated in lime juice and chili peppers, which "cook" the fish). You can order ceviche from oysters, fish, conch, or shrimp. The rest of the menu is your standard Tico seafood fare—corvina (sea bass) prepared in different sauces, lobster or shrimp in garlic and butter, and casados with fried fish.

---

4. PLAYA HERMOSA

Distances: 160 miles northwest of San José; 15 miles west of Liberia.

GETTING THERE   By Bus   Buses leave from Liberia at 11:30am and 5:30pm. Duration: 30 minutes. Fare: ¢50 (59¢).

By Car   Follow the directions for getting to Playa del Coco, but take the right fork (at the dump) as you approach Playa del Coco.

DEPARTING   The bus from Playa Panamá to Liberia leaves at 6am and 4pm, stopping in Playa Hermosa a few minutes later. Ask at your hotel where to catch the bus. Duration: 30 minutes. Fare: ¢50 (59¢).

To reach San José, take the bus to Liberia and then catch one of the many express buses to San José.

ESSENTIALS   Orientation   There is no real town here, just a few houses and hotels on and near the beach.

Playa Hermosa means "Beautiful Beach," an appropriate name. Surrounded by dry rocky hills, this curving gray sand beach is long and wide and rarely crowded, despite the presence of a new luxury condominium development on the hill behind. There are a few Tico-style sodas right on the beach, but little else. Green trees come right down to the edge of the sand, even in the dryest months of the year. At either end of the beach rocky headlands jut out into the surf.

WHAT TO SEE AND DO

At the base of these rocks, you will find tide pools that are fun to explore. **Aqua Sport** (tel. 67-0050 or 67-0158) is the tourist information center and water-sports equipment rental center for Playa Hermosa. Kayaks, sailboards, canoes, bicycles, beach umbrellas, snorkel gear, and parasails are all available for rental at fairly reasonable rates. This is also where you'll find the local post office, public phones, and a restaurant (see "Where to Eat" below).

Beyond Playa Hermosa, where the paved road ends, you'll find one more appealing and even more secluded beach—Playa Panamá. This big bay is lined with dense vegetation now but is scheduled for development in the near future. In fact, the signs are already up announcing the new resorts that will be built. When you visit, you might still be able to find a stretch of beach all to yourself, where you can sit back and watch the pelicans feeding just offshore.

WHERE TO STAY

DOUBLES FOR LESS THAN ¢2,300 [$27.06]

CABINAS PLAYA HERMOSA, Apdo. 112, Liberia, Guanacaste. Tel. 506/67-0136. 20 rms., all with bath.

$ Rates: ¢1,272 ($14.96) single; ¢2,270 ($26.71) double; ¢2,684 ($31.58) triple; ¢3,108 ($36.56) quad. No credit cards.

This little hotel tucked away under shady trees and surrounded by green lawns is run by an American couple who make sure that their guests enjoy the quiet vacation they dreamed about before leaving home. Each large room has a pair of pink Adirondack chairs on its front porch, and the beach is only a few steps away.

Rooms, even though rather dark, are large and have a lot of closet space and double beds. You can also rent snorkeling gear and bicycles here, but you'll find that they are cheaper up the beach at Aqua Sport. There was no sign in front of the hotel when I last visited; just watch for the white archway over the driveway after the curve to the right on the dirt road. The turnoff from the main road is well marked.

The open-air restaurant has a rustic tropical feel to it, with unfinished tree trunks holding up the roof. Seafood and surf and turf are the specialties here. Menu prices range from ¢250 to ¢1,000 ($2.94 to $11.76).

DOUBLES FOR LESS THAN ¢3,200 [$37.65]

LOS CORALES, Apdo. 1158-1002, San José. Tel. 506/67-0255. In San José tel. 57-0259. Fax 506/55-4978. 12 rms., all with bath. A/C.
$ Rates: ¢3,000 ($35.29) 1–6 people; ¢5,000 ($58.82) 7–8 people. No credit cards.
This is one of the newer hotels in Playa Hermosa and does not have any shade. It is in the middle of a large field set back from the beach about 200 yards. If you're down here with your family or a group of friends, you might want to consider staying here. All the accommodations are large two-bedroom apartments that come complete with full kitchen and can sleep up to eight people. There are pools for adults and children, a hot tub, and a volleyball court.

COSTA ALEGRE, Playa del Coco, Guanacaste. Tel. 506/67-0218. In San José tel. 57-1939. 14 rms., all with bath.
$ Rates: ¢3,000 ($35.29) 1–5 people. No credit cards.
About half a mile before the turnoff for Playa Hermosa, you'll see on your left another new hotel that is also popular with Tico families. The apartments here come with full kitchen but sleep only five people. Otherwise, the facilities are very similar— swimming pools, soccer field, volleyball court. The rooms have high ceilings and fans to keep you cool, and there are plans to add air conditioning in the future. A lively (and noisy) atmosphere prevails on the weekends.

Although Costa Alegre is several miles from the beach, it does have a large open-air restaurant and even a barbecue where you can grill any fish you might have caught. Meals in the restaurant average around ¢300 to ¢600 ($3.53 to $7.06).

WHERE TO EAT

AQUA SPORT, on the beach (watch for signs). Tel. 67-0050 or 67-0158.
$ Prices: ¢350–¢1,200 ($4.12–$14.12). MC, V.
Open: Daily 9am–9pm.
Part of the Aqua Sport market and equipment rental shop is a small open-air restaurant with booths of polished hardwood. The beach is only steps away, and the atmosphere is very casual. The food, however, is much better than what you would expect from such a place. The focus is on Continental—with paella for ¢500 ($5.88), lobster provençal for ¢1,200 ($14.12), and shrimp à la diabla for ¢800 ($9.41). You'll also find a variety of crêpes on the menu.

---

5. PLAYAS BRASILITO, FLAMINGO, POTRERO, AND PAN DE AZUCAR

Distances: 165 miles northwest of San José; 35 miles southwest of Liberia.

GETTING THERE   By Air   Even though there are no regularly scheduled flights to the airstrip at Playa Flamingo, it is possible to charter a plane to these beaches.

By Bus   The express bus from San José leaves from the corner of Calle 20 and Avenida 3 daily at 10:30am. Duration: 6 hours. Fare: ¢250 ($2.96). Buses also run from the central park in Santa Cruz, which is south of here on the Nicoya Peninsula.

These buses leave at 4 and 10:30am and 2:30pm (also at 6pm in the dry season). Duration: 2½ hours. Fare: ¢70–¢85 (82¢–$1). If you are coming from Liberia, take a Santa Cruz or Nicoya bus (which run almost hourly) and get off in the village of Belén, which is south of Filadelfia.

By Car Follow the directions for getting to Liberia, then take the road toward Nicoya. After about 24 miles you will see the turnoff for Playa Flamingo and Playa Tamarindo. After another 12 miles take the right fork for Playa Flamingo and Playa Brasilito.

DEPARTING To reach Liberia, buses leave from Potrero village at 5:30am, 12:30 and 5pm. They pass by Playa Potrero, the turnoff for Playa Flamingo, and Brasilito a few minutes later. Ask at your hotel where the best place is for catching the bus. Get off the bus at Belén and wait for a bus going north to Liberia.

To reach San José the express bus leaves from Playa Flamingo daily at 9:30am, stopping in Brasilito at 9:45am. You must buy your ticket in advance (in San José, tel. 21-7202). Duration: 6 hours. Fare: ¢250 ($2.94). You can also take the buses to Liberia and then transfer to an express bus to San José.

ESSENTIALS Orientation These four beaches are strung out over several miles of dirt roads. Hotels are generally well marked, but if you arrive after dark, you'll find it very difficult to find anything.

Almost at the westernmost point of the Nicoya Peninsula are a string of beaches that are rapidly gaining popularity with international sunseekers and North American retirees. The beaches are along two bays separated by a small peninsula, and each has its own very different personality.

WHAT TO SEE AND DO

On **Playa Brasilito** you will find one of the only two real villages in the area. The village of Brasilito will give you some idea of what this entire coast was like not too long ago. The soccer field is the center of the village, and there are a couple of little *pulperias* (general stores). There is a beach, but it is not very appealing—gray sand, with the decrepit village right on the beach—and I can't recommend either of the very basic accommodations here. If you have come this far, you owe it to yourself to stay someplace a little bit more attractive, so read on.

Only a few miles away and at the opposite end of the scale is the luxury resort beach called **Playa Flamingo.** This is one of Costa Rica's top resort beaches, with luxury hotels, a marina, a private airstrip, retirement and vacation homes, and, best of all, one of the only white-sand beaches in the area. In fact, the old name for this beach was Playa Blanca, which made plenty of sense. When the developers moved in, they needed a more romantic name than White Beach, so it became Playa Flamingo, even though there are no flamingos. You probably won't be able to afford any of the hotels here, but you should definitely plan to spend plenty of time on the beautiful beach.

Playa Flamingo is on a long spit of land that forms part of Potrero Bay, or Bahia Flamingo, as the developers wish it to be known. On the ocean side of the peninsula, there is the long white-sand beach, behind which is a dusty road and then a mangrove swamp that is still home to a few caymans (relatives of alligators). If you are not staying on Playa Flamingo, you should know that there are parking spots all along the beach road where you can park your car for the day. There is, however, little shade on the beach, so be sure to use plenty of sunscreen and bring an umbrella if you can. The bay side of the peninsula is where the marina is located.

If you continue along the unpaved road from Brasilito without taking the turn for Playa Flamingo, you will soon come to **Playa Potrero.** The sand here is a brownish gray, but the beach is long, clean, and deserted. You can see the hotels of the Playa Flamingo resort complex across the bay.

Playa Pan de Azucar is the last and prettiest of these beaches. As the name implies it is as white as sugar. The little crescent of sand is surrounded by steep, rugged hills covered with chaparral-type shrubs. In the rocky cove, there is very good snorkeling and swimming. Because the Hotel Sugar Beach takes up the entire cove, you will have to stay here if you want to use this beautiful beach.

WHERE TO STAY

DOUBLES FOR LESS THAN ₵2,500 [$29.41]

CABINAS CRISTINA, Playa Potrero, Santa Cruz, Apdo. 121-Santa Cruz. Tel. 506/68-0997. 3 rms., all with bath.

$ Rates: ₵1,695 ($19.94) single; ₵2,034 ($23.93) double; ₵2,373 ($27.92) triple; ₵2,712 ($31.92) quad. No credit cards.

Although it isn't right on the beach, Cabinas Christina is a great value in this area of high-priced hotels. The rooms are spacious and very clean (and fill up fast) with hot plates, refrigerators, dressers, bars with stools, tiled baths, and double and bunk beds. On the veranda there are large rocking chairs. The friendly owner, Daniel Boldrini, speaks some English. There is a small pool in the middle of a grassy green yard and a thatched-roof palapa. The beach is a five-minute walk away down a dirt road, and Restaurant Las Perlas is only 100 yards away (see "Where to Eat" below).

DOUBLES FOR LESS THAN ₵3,500 [$41.18]

HOTEL SUGAR BEACH, Playa Pan de Azucar, Guanacaste. Tel. 506/68-0959. In the United States, tel. 818/905-5605. 10 rms., all with bath, 9 with A/C.

$ Rates: ₵1,600 ($18.82) single, ₵2,100 single with A/C; ₵2,800 ($32.94) double, ₵3,500 ($41.18) double with A/C; ₵3,950 ($46.47) triple with A/C. No credit cards.

Just as the name implies, the Hotel Sugar Beach is located on a white-sand beach—one of the few in the area and therefore one of the most attractive in my opinion. The beach is on a small cove surrounded by rocky hills. Unfortunately, the hills become very brown and desolate in the dry season (which is when most tourists come to visit), so don't expect the verdant tropics if you come down here in March or April. The hotel itself is perched high above the water on a gentle slope. The managers Julie and Bill Enell have several pet macaws, a few of which are quite gabby and keep the guests entertained. Nature lovers will be thrilled to find wild howler monkeys and iguanas almost on their doorsteps. Snorkelers will also be happy here because the cove here has some of the best snorkeling on the west coast. All but one of the rooms have air conditioning, hot water, and two double beds, and all are spacious and comfortable and have porches in front so that you can sit back and watch birds right from your room. Hammocks under the trees provide a great way to while away a hot afternoon.

The open-air dining room and bar are in a circular building with a panoramic vista of ocean, islands, and hills. The dining room serves up excellent Costa Rican and international meals. The special of the house is jumbo shrimp for ₵1,095 ($12.88), while other meals range from ₵425 to ₵675 ($5 to $7.94).

Facilities: Snorkel trips ($25 per person), sunset cruises ($30 per person), and fishing boat charters ($135).

DOUBLES FOR LESS THAN ₵4,000 [$47.06]

BAHIA FLAMINGO BEACH RESORT, Playa Flamingo, Apdo. 45-5051 Santa Cruz, Guanacaste. Tel. 506/68-0976. 14 rms., all with bath.

$ Rates: ₵2,792 ($32.85) single; ₵3,755 ($44.18) double; ₵4,237 ($49.85) triple; ₵4,718 ($55.51) quad. MC, V.

Despite its name, this little beach hotel is in fact on Playa Potrero. You'll see the resorts of Playa Flamingo across the bay when you stand on the beach. Set in a green garden with a white wooden fence round the property, the Bahia Flamingo feels like a private home in the country. A laid-back atmosphere prevails—with hammocks for dozing, a pool, and miles of nearly deserted beach for strolling and swimming. Most of the rooms have kitchenettes, two double beds, good-sized bathrooms with counter space and hot water, tile floors, and ceiling fans. Fishing and snorkeling trips can be arranged. Watch for the sign pointing down a road to the left a mile or so after you pass the turnoff for Playa Flamingo.

The restaurant here, while nothing fancy, has a nice view of green lawns, white fence, and blue ocean. Meals average ¢450 to ¢1,200 ($5.29 to $14.12).

LONG-TERM STAYS

If you are interested in splurging a bit or have a group of friends or large family, you might want to consider renting a house here. They rent for anywhere between $50 and $300 per day. Fred Schultz is the person to contact (tel. 506/68-0901) for reservation information.

WHERE TO EAT

RESTAURANT LAS PERLAS, Playa Potrero, at the corner near Cabinas Christina. No phone.
$ Prices: ¢150–¢300 ($1.76–$3.53). No credit cards.
Open: Daily 7am–1pm.
On your way through the Playa Potrero area, you can't miss this huge restaurant with the chain-link-fence sides. In the lowlands of Costa Rica, there is little need for walls, but there is a need for security. Chain-link fencing is often the solution. It doesn't look great, but it works. Inside the door, you'll find a huge dance hall–size room with a cement floor. The owner is a retiree from Canada who serves up food just like the food you get back home (breakfast and lunch only). Las Perlas is much more than just a restaurant: It acts as a sort of community center for the resident gringo population. Once a month there are dances here, and across the road they play softball and soccer. Anyone is welcome. The breakfasts are particularly good.

MARIE'S, Playa Flamingo near the Marina Hotel. Tel. 68-0965.
$ Prices: ¢150–¢600 ($1.76–$7.06). No credit cards.
Open: Daily 7am–9pm. Closed Tues May–Sept.
✪ Right in the middle of all the luxury hotels at Playa Flamingo is a great little place for a snack and a swim. This is the only restaurant I have ever visited that had its own swimming pool. Forget what you learned about not swimming after eating; here it's encouraged. Luckily the pool is quite small, so you don't have to worry about drowning from cramps. The menu is primarily sandwiches and other lunch foods, but on the blackboard behind the bar you'll find daily specials such as mahi-mahi (called dorado down here) and, from August to December, lobster and conch. The owners are from Alaska, but they have mastered many Tico favorites, such as heart of palm salad (palmito) and ceviche. Tables in the open-air restaurant are made from slabs of tree trunks. Be sure to try the three-milks cake (a Nicaraguan specialty), which just might be the moistest cake on earth.

---

6. PLAYA TAMARINDO

Distances: 184 miles northwest of San José; 45 miles southwest of Liberia.

GETTING THERE By Air Sansa flies from San José Monday, Wednesday and Friday at 1:10pm. Duration: 30 minutes. Fare: ¢1,700 ($20).

By Bus An express bus leaves San José daily at 3:30pm from the corner of Calle 14 and Avenida 5. Duration: 5 hours. Fare: ¢275 ($3.24). Another express bus leaves from Calle 20 and Avenida 3 (also in San José) at 4pm, but you must buy your ticket in advance. Duration: 5½ hours. Fare: ¢230 ($2.71). From Santa Cruz, there are buses daily at 3pm, with an additional bus at 10am on Saturday and Sunday.

By Car The most direct route is by way of the Tempisque ferry, Nicoya, and Santa

Cruz. The turnoff for the ferry is at La Irma, about midway between Puntarenas and Liberia. Once you're across on the ferry, turn right in Mansión and head north through Nicoya and Santa Cruz to the beach turnoff at Belén.

DEPARTING Monday through Saturday an express bus leaves for San José at 5:45am, on Sunday it leaves at 1:45pm. Duration: 5 hours. Fare: ¢275 ($3.24). The Tralapa express bus (in San José, tel. 21-7202), for which you must buy your ticket in advance, leaves at 7am daily for San José.

ESSENTIALS   Orientation   The unpaved road leading into town runs parallel to the beach and deadends at Cabinas Zully Mar. You'll find virtually all of Tamarindo along this one road.

Fast Facts   There is a public phone with international service at the Fiesta del Mar restaurant (see "Where to Eat" below) at the end of the road. The phone is available from 6am to 9pm.

Tamarindo is a long swath of white sand that curves gently from one rocky headland to another at the far end. Behind the beach are low, dry hills that can be a very dreary brown in the dry season but turn instantly green with the first brief showers of the rainy season. With only one major resort hotel in town, Tamarindo is still a quiet little fishing village. The fishing boats bob at their moorings at the south end of the beach, and brown pelicans fish just outside the breakers. A sandy islet offshore makes a great destination if you are a strong swimmer; if you're not, it makes a great foreground for sunsets.

WHAT TO SEE AND DO

You have to be careful when and where you swim on Tamarindo Beach. There are rocks just offshore in several places, some of which are exposed only at low tide. An encounter with one of these rocks could be nasty, especially if you were body surfing.

Papagayo Excursions (tel. 68-0859 or 68-0652), which has its office at the Hotel Tamarindo Diriá, offers fishermen a chance to go after the big ones that abound in the waters offshore. From here it takes only 20 minutes to reach the edge of the continental shelf and the waters preferred by marlin and sailfish. Although fishing is good all year, the peak season for billfish is between mid-April and August. Rates for up to four people are $250 for a half day and $350 for a full day for the boat. If you aren't an angler, you can arrange to go horseback riding. Rates for horses, with a guide, are ¢1,000 ($11.76) per hour. They also offer two-hour boat tours of the nearby estuary for ¢680 ($18) per person.

Tamarindo Turicentro, which is on the right as you come into town, rents scooters, body boards, beach chairs, and beach umbrellas at reasonable rates. They're open daily but close for siesta.

WHERE TO STAY
DOUBLES FOR LESS THAN ¢2,000 [$23.53]

PENSION DOLY, Playa Tamarindo, Santa Cruz, Guanacaste. Tel. 506/ 68-0174. 12 rms, 6 with bath.
$ Rates: ¢600 ($7.06) single; ¢1,200 ($14.12) double; ¢1,800 ($21.18) triple; ¢2,400 ($28.24) quad. No credit cards.
This is a favorite with backpackers in Tamarindo. It is right on the beach and provides cheap rooms and good food. Other than that, there's not much you can say about this place. Atmosphere is lacking completely. The building is built of cinderblocks and painted wood siding with the rooms on the second floor above an open-air restaurant where the owner of the pension serves up her excellent fish dinners. There are large security gates and a wall around the hotel, so it has a rather industrial feel about it, but you don't have to worry much about leaving things in your room. It's on the right as you are coming into town. If the Doly is full, check directly across the street.

HOTEL POZO AZUL, Playa Tamarindo, Santa Cruz, Guanacaste. Tel. 506/68-0147. 27 rms, 17 with A/C, all with bath.
$ Rates: ¢1,700 ($20) 1–3 people, ¢2,500 ($29.41) 1–3 people, with A/C; ¢3,059 ($35.99) quad with A/C. No credit cards accepted.

This is the first hotel that you'll spot as you drive into Tamarindo. It's on the left side of the road and therefore is not on the beach. There isn't any shade on the grounds, but there are swimming pools for adults and kids. In the rooms with air conditioning, there are also hot plates, refrigerators, tables and chairs, large windows, and pilas for washing clothes. Some rooms have covered parking to keep your car out of the blistering heat. There is no restaurant here, so you'll have to either cook your own meals or travel into town to one of the few restaurants.

CABINAS ZULLY MAR, Tamarindo, Guanacaste. Tel. 506/26-4732. 27 rms, 8 with A/C, all with bath.
$ Rates: ¢1,300 ($15.29) single; ¢1,750 ($20.59) double, ¢2,500 ($29.41) double with A/C. MC, V.

The Zully Mar has long been a favorite of budget travelers staying at Tamarindo Beach, and with the addition of eight new rooms with air conditioning, the hotel has only gotten better. Rates are still reasonable, and there are even plans to add a swimming pool. The new rooms are in a two-story white-stucco building with a wide curving staircase on the outside. The doors to the guest rooms are hand-carved with pre-Columbian motifs. There are high ceilings with fans; tile floors; a long veranda; and large, clean bathrooms. Although there are mango trees out front for shade, there is little other landscaping, and the sandy grounds look a bit unkempt. Don't let this bother you: Miles of beach are just across the street, and even the older rooms are clean and pleasant.

WORTH THE EXTRA BUCKS

HOTEL TAMARINDO DIRIÁ, Playa Tamarindo, Apdo. 21, Santa Cruz, Guanacaste. Tel. 506/33-0530 or 68-0652. 61 rms., all with bath. A/C TEL TV
$ Rates: ¢5,283 ($62.15) single; ¢5,763 ($67.80) double; ¢6,243 ($73.45) triple; ¢6,724 ($79.10) quad. AE, MC, V.

Tamarindo's one luxury resort is wedged into a narrow piece of ground between the town's one dusty road and the beach. Within this tiny strip of land, you'll find all the amenities you would expect in a beach resort. The guest rooms are furnished in heavy wood and colonial-reproduction furnishings, with overhead fans, hot water, and shiny tile bathrooms. Red-tile floors and beamed ceilings add to the colonial atmosphere. The open-air lobby area is built around the swimming pool, where you'll find plenty of lounge chairs and shade (the sun here is very strong). There are reproductions of pre-Columbian stone statues around the lushly planted grounds.

The large dining room continues the colonial theme with oversized dark-wood chairs at the tables, while the adjacent bar utilizes a native design for its conical thatch roof. There are old baskets and carved wooden bread bowls on display in both the restaurant and the bar. Breakfast in the restaurant ranges from ¢125 to ¢300 ($1.47 to $3.53). The lunch and dinner menu focuses on steaks and seafood with prices from ¢300 to ¢1,300 ($3.53 to $15.29). The jalapeño sirloin tips are a favorite with fire-eaters, and the stuffed squid special is another winner.

Facilities: Rentals of surfboards, scuba and snorkeling equipment, sailboards, and horses; trips up the nearby estuary for bird-watching, sea turtle tours, water skiing, and fishing; and game room, gift shop, and conference room.

WHERE TO EAT

On my last visit to Tamarindo, there was a large restaurant almost ready to open. It looked like it would be serving rather pricey meals and will probably be a welcome addition to the limited restaurant possibilities in Tamarindo. At that time, it was going by the name **Restaurant El Milagro** (The Miracle). It's on the left as you come into town.

RESTAURANT EL TERCER MUNDO, at the end of the road. No phone.
$ Prices: Meals ¢150–¢700 ($1.76–$8.24). No credit cards.
Open: Daily 7:30am–10pm.

It's hard to believe that any restaurant would call itself "The Third World," but here it is, right on the beach at the end of the road that leads into Tamarindo. It's a basic Tico-style open-air restaurant, but the food is good, and the view can't be beat. Sit and watch the waves crash over the rocks just offshore while you dine on fresh fish sautéed in garlic for ¢330 ($3.88). The fruit salads here are quite large and delicious and make a wonderful afternoon snack or dessert for ¢135 ($1.59). The bar is a popular hangout with locals and tourists.

FIESTA DEL MAR, at the end of the road. No phone.
$ Prices: ¢250–¢700 ($2.94–$8.24). V.
Open: Mon–Fri 11am–10pm; Sat–Sun 7:30am–10pm.
Across the circle from the Tercer Mundo, the Fiesta del Mar specializes in steak and seafood cooked over a wood fire. Try the grilled steak in garlic sauce for ¢675 ($7.94), and be sure to finish off any meal with the coconut flan for ¢100 ($1.18). After a filling meal, you might want to relax in one of the hammocks the restaurant has strung in the shade for its clients. The open-air dining area is edged with greenery, and there are more of those interesting pre-Columbian stone statue reproductions. This is also where you can find a public phone with international service, available from 6am to 9pm daily.

PICNIC FARE

If you are in the mood for a picnic or are doing your own cooking, be sure to get your bread at **Panaderia Johan,** a Belgian-run bakery on the outskirts of town. There are always fresh-baked goodies here, although what you might find on any given day is never certain. Possibilities include croissants, pizzas, chocolate éclairs, and different types of bread. There are also a couple of tables where you can eat your pizza.

For other picnic essentials, try the **Supermercado** on the right a little farther into town. Watch for the **Tamarindo Turicentro** sign. The market is open Monday to Saturday from 9am to noon and 2 to 5pm, Sunday from 9am to 1pm.

CHAPTER 5

THE PACIFIC COAST

1. PUNTARENAS
- WHAT'S SPECIAL ABOUT THE PACIFIC COAST
2. JACÓ BEACH
3. QUEPOS AND MANUEL ANTONIO
4. FARTHER SOUTH

From the steamy seaport of Puntarenas to the jewel of Manuel Antonio and beyond, the climate of the Pacific coast is humid, and frequently it will be sunny here when it is raining in San José. Greater numbers of tourists gravitate to the Pacific coast than the Caribbean coast, making tourist amenities more available.

1. PUNTARENAS

Distances: 68 miles west of San José; 70 miles south of Liberia; 37 miles north of Jacó Beach; 75 miles north of Manuel Antonio.

GETTING THERE   By Train   The electric train leaves San José daily at 7am and 3pm from the Pacific Train Station on Avenida 20 between calles 2 and 4. Duration: 4 hours. Fare: ¢130 ($1.53).

By Bus   Express buses leave daily every hour on the hour from 6am to 6pm from the corner of Calle 12 and Avenida 9. Duration: 2 hours. Fare: ¢132 ($1.55).

By Car   Head west on Paseo Colón and follow the signs for Alajuela and the airport. These will take you to the Interamerican Highway. After about 50 miles you will see signs for Puntarenas.

By Ferry   The passenger ferry from Paquera, on the Nicoya Peninsula, operates daily at 8am and 5pm. Duration: 1½ hours. Fare: ¢100 ($1.18). The car ferry from Naranjo, also on the Nicoya Peninsula, operates Monday, Tuesday, Wednesday, and Friday at 9am and 6pm; on Thursday, Saturday, and Sunday at 9am and 2 and 6pm. Duration: 1½ hours. Fare: cars, ¢505 ($5.94); adults, ¢70 (82¢); children, ¢35 (41¢).

DEPARTING   The ferry to Paquera leaves daily at 6:15am and 3pm, returning at 8am and 5pm. One-way fare is ¢100 ($1.18). This is a passenger ferry only, but it connects with buses waiting in Paquera to take you to other towns on the Nicoya Peninsula.

The large car ferry to Playa Naranjo leaves Monday through Wednesday and Friday at 7am and 4pm; Thursday, Saturday, and Sunday at 7am, 11am, and 4pm. It returns from Playa Naranjo Monday through Wednesday and Friday at 9am and 6pm; Thursday, Saturday, and Sunday at 9am, 2pm, and 6pm. The trip takes 1½ hours. Fares are ¢35 (41¢) for children, ¢70 (82¢) for adults, and ¢505 ($5.94) for cars.

The bus to San José leaves every hour on the hour between 6am and 7pm. Fare is ¢135 ($1.59). The bus station is a block down from the Hotel Imperial, which is in front of the old main pier.

WHAT'S SPECIAL ABOUT THE PACIFIC COAST

Beaches
- ☐ Manuel Antonio National Park, three idyllic beaches with jungle-clad hills behind them
- ☐ Jacó Beach, an inexpensive resort area with many deserted beaches nearby

Activities
- ☐ Sportfishing out of Puntarenas

- ☐ A day-long cruise around the Gulf of Nicoya

Parks
- ☐ Carara Biological Reserve, a transitional forest between wet and dry regions
- ☐ Corcovado National Park on the Osa Peninsula, one of Costa Rica's most remote national parks

---

The bus to Santa Elena leaves daily at 2:15pm from a stop across the railroad tracks from the San José bus station. Duration: 3¼ hours. Fare: ¢100 ($1.18).

ESSENTIALS Orientation Puntarenas is built on a long, narrow sandspit that stretches 3 miles out into the Gulf of Nicoya. It is only five streets wide at its widest. The ferry docks for the Nicoya Peninsula are near the far end of the town, as are the bus station and market. The north side of town faces an estuary, while the south side faces the mouth of the gulf. The Paseo de los Turistas is on the south side of town, beginning at the pier and extending out to the point.

Puntarenas was once Costa Rica's busiest port, but it was recently replaced by nearby Puerto Caldera. In the manner of all good port towns, it is hot and dirty. Although this is the easiest beach to reach from San José and is popular on weekends with holidaying Ticos, it is not the kind of place that you would want to waste any time in when there are so many other beautiful beaches in the country. The water is polluted, and swimming is not recommended. Thieves work the beach, making it impossible to leave anything unattended. Hopefully these dire warnings will convince you that you don't want to visit Puntarenas. Now the sad part: You may get stuck here against your wishes. Puntarenas is a transfer point for buses going north or south along the coast and is where you catch ferries to the Nicoya Peninsula. You may be forced, due to a missed connection, to spend a night here. I have included enough information to make your stay bearable.

WHAT TO SEE AND DO

Take a walk along the Paseo de los Turistas and notice how similar this side of town is to a few Florida towns 50 years ago. If you want to go swimming, head out to the end of the peninsula to the **Balneario Municipal,** the public pool. It is huge, has a great view (albeit through a cyclone fence), and is surrounded by lawns and gardens. Entrance is only ¢40 (47¢). Open from 9am to 4:30 Tuesday through Sunday.

If you want to get out on the water, there are several options. You can hire a water taxi from **Taximar** (tel. 61-0331 or 61-1143). The taxis charge ¢3,000 ($35.29) per hour and can carry up to six passengers. If you want to do some fishing, contact **Sportfishing Costa Rica** (tel. 55-0791 or 61-0697). The waters off these shores have some of the best sailfish and marlin fishing in the world. Prices are not cheap.

The most popular water excursions from Puntarenas are yacht cruises among the tiny uninhabited islands of the Guayabo, Negritos, and Pájaros Islands Biological Reserve. These cruises include a gourmet seafood buffet and a stop at beautiful and undeveloped Tortuga Island, where you can swim, snorkel, and sun. The water is a clear blue, and the sand is bright white. Several companies offer these excursions, often with round-trip transportation from San José, so you don't even have to spend the night in Puntarenas. **Calypso Tours** (tel. 55-3022 or 61-0585), **Bay Island Cruises** (tel. 31-2898), and **Pacific Islands Adventures** (tel. 55-0791 or 61-0697) offer similar tours and will pick you up at your hotel in San José. The price for one of these trips is a steep ¢5,600 ($65.90). Calypso Tours also offers sunset trips from 5:30 to 7:30pm with music, bocas, and a bar.

WHERE TO STAY

DOUBLES FOR LESS THAN ¢1,500 [$17.65]

HOTEL AYI CON, 50 meters sur del mercado, Apdo. 358, Puntarenas. Tel. 506/61-0164 or 61-1477. 44 rms, 20 with bath.
$ Rates: ¢317.25 ($3.73) single without bath, ¢444.15–¢539.35 ($5.23–$6.35) single with bath; ¢634.5 ($7.46) double without bath, ¢888.30–¢1,078.70 ($10.45–$12.69) double with bath; ¢951.75 ($11.20) triple without bath, ¢1,332.45–¢1,618.05 ($15.68–$19.04) triple with bath; ¢1,269 ($14.93) quad without bath, ¢1,776.60–¢2,157.40 ($20.90–$25.38) quad with bath. No credit cards.

Centrally located near the market and the ferryboat docks, the Ayi Con is your basic low-budget Tico hotel. It's above a row of shops in a very busy shopping district of Puntarenas and is frequented primarily by Costa Ricans; backpackers will find that this is probably the best and the cleanest of the cheap hotels in Puntarenas. If you're just passing through and have to spend a night in town, this place is convenient and acceptable.

HOTEL IMPERIAL, Paseo de los Turistas, frente al Muelle, Apdo. 65, Puntarenas. Tel. 506/61-0579. 28 rms, 10 with bath.
$ Rates: ¢566 ($6.66) single without bath, ¢679 ($7.99) single with bath; ¢1,133 ($13.33) double without bath, ¢1,359 ($15.99) double with bath; ¢1,473 ($17.33) triple without bath, ¢1,699 ($19.99) triple with bath. No credit cards.

Don't be fooled by the grandiose name—this is about as basic a hotel as you'll ever want to stay in. However, I have to include it here because of its amazing atmosphere: It is located directly across the street from the now-little-used main shipping pier for the port of Puntarenas. In its heyday, this long, green wooden building with rusting corrugated-metal roof must have been home to countless sailors and their escorts. The architecture is classic Caribbean, with high ceilings, wide halls, wooden walls that don't go all the way to the ceiling, and bathrooms down the hall. It looks like a huge solid building from the front, but there is actually a narrow courtyard inside (there are even plants growing). It can get noisy, so light sleepers should look elsewhere. However, if you have ever dreamed of stepping onto the set for a play by Tennessee Williams or onto the page of a story by Ernest Hemingway, this is the place.

DOUBLES FOR LESS THAN ¢2,500 [$29.41]

HOTEL TIOGA, Paseo de los Turistas, Apdo. 96. Tel. 506/61-0271. 46 rms., all with bath. A/C
$ Rates (including breakfast): ¢1,812–¢2,719 ($21.32–$31.99) single; ¢2,266–¢3,399 ($26.66–$39.99) double; ¢3,399–¢4,418 ($39.99–$51.98) triple. AE, MC, V.

This 1950s modern-style hotel is on the Paseo de los Turistas, the wide boulevard that runs along Puntarenas's beach. When you walk through the front door, you enter a courtyard with a small pool that has been painted a brilliant shade of blue. There is even a little island with a tree in the middle of the pool. The four-story hotel is built around this pleasant setting. Rooms vary in size, and some come with cold-water showers only, so if you must have hot water (not really necessary in these hot regions), be sure to request it. The larger rooms are very attractive—with huge closets and modern bathrooms. The smaller, less expensive rooms have louvered, frosted-glass windows to let in lots of light and air while maintaining some privacy.

There are a cafeteria and bar on the second floor and a breakfast room and lounge on the fourth floor. You'll be able to look out across the water as you enjoy your complimentary breakfast.

HOTEL LAS BRISAS, Paseo de los Turistas, Puntarenas. Tel. 506/61-2120. 19 rms., all with bath. A/C
$ Rates: ¢2,400 ($28.23) single or double; ¢2,900 ($34.12) triple. No credit cards.

⑤ Out near the end of the Paseo de los Turistas, you'll find a very clean new hotel with large air-conditioned rooms and a small pool out front. All the rooms have tile floors, double or twin beds, and small tables. Large picture windows let in a lot of light. If you're traveling with children, they can stay in your room for free. The owner of the hotel is a friendly Italian man who speaks a bit of Spanish and a bit of English.

You'll find some unusual offerings on the menu of the small open-air dining room in front of the hotel. Smoked pork chops with pineapple, raisins, and wine for ¢450 ($5.29) is just one example. It's worth staying here just to enjoy the food.

WORTH THE EXTRA BUCKS

HOTEL PORTO BELLO, Apdo. 108, Puntarenas. Tel. 506/61-1322 or 61-2122. 35 rms., all with bath. A/C TEL
$ Rates: ¢3,500 ($41.18) single; ¢4,250 ($50) double; ¢5,000 ($58.82) triple. AE, MC, V.

Almost next door to the Colonial (below), the Porto Bello is a slightly more luxurious, although similar, weekend escape resort. The stucco walls of the hotel are almost blindingly white, tempered by the lush, almost overgrown, garden that surrounds the buildings. The modern rooms have high ceilings, red-tile floors, attractive teak-and-cloth headboards, and balconies or patios that are often hidden by the shrubbery. There are pools for adults and kids, with a poolside bar, and even a small beach. You can hire a water taxi for a spin around the bay or book an all-day cruise to some of the remote and picturesque islands out in the gulf.

The open-air restaurant is breezy and cool, with a high ceiling and stucco walls that harken back to local Indian architectural designs. Grilled meats and seafood are the specialties here—with a range of ¢420 to ¢1,350 ($4.94 to $15.88).

CLUB-HOTEL COLONIAL, Apdo. 368, Puntarenas. Tel. 506/61-1833 or 61-1834. 56 rms., all with bath. A/C
$ Rates: ¢3,000 ($35.29) single or double Sun–Wed; ¢3,750 ($44.12) single or double Thurs–Sat; lower rates in off season. AE, MC, V.

⑤ This large hotel on the outskirts of Puntarenas is a popular weekend getaway for wealthy Ticos from San José. The two-story building is surrounded by spacious grounds filled with palms that rustle constantly in the trade winds. Guest rooms are about what you would expect from an interstate motel—carpets, two double beds, medium-sized baths with tubs, and air conditioning—although they also have balconies for enjoying the breezes. Of course, since this is primarily for vacationing families, there is plenty to keep everyone happy: two pools (one for adults, one for children), a tennis court, a game room, and a bar and restaurant (both with TV). If you feel like taking to the water, you can hire a water taxi for a trip around the bay or up an estuary for a bit of bird-watching.

Meals in El Bambu restaurant range from ¢450 to ¢1,350 ($5.29 to $15.88) for primarily seafood dishes. Weekends there is live mariachi music in the evenings. In addition to this restaurant, there is a less formal bar and café.

WHERE TO EAT

Without a doubt, your hotel restaurant is going to be the best place to eat here in Puntarenas. At the **Club-Hotel Colonial,** you can listen to live mariachi music while you dine on fresh seafood. At the **Porto Bello,** the grilled steaks are particularly good. Since you are in a seaport, you should be sure to try the national fish dish of Costa Rica—corvina—at least once.

2. JACÓ BEACH

Distances: 67 miles west of San José; 37 miles south of Puntarenas.

GETTING THERE   By Bus   Buses leave daily at 7:15am and 3:30pm from Calle 16 between avenidas 1 and 3. Duration: 2½ hours. Fare: ¢150 ($1.76).

By Car   Although it is not as direct as taking the bus, you can take the Puntarenas highway from San José and turn south on the Costanera, the coastal road to Puerto Caldera, Jacó, and Manuel Antonio. This is an excellent road. The alternative is to take the narrow and winding old highway, which turns off the Interamerican Highway just west of Alajuela near the town of Atenas.

DEPARTING   To reach Manuel Antonio, you can catch buses that are en route between either San José or Puntarenas and Quepos. They pass by on the highway around 6 and 8am and 2, 2:30, and 8pm. Since schedules can change it is best to ask at your hotel about current times of departures. The best place to catch one of these buses is at El Bosque restaurant at the south end of Jacó near the gas station. Duration: 1½ hours. Fare: ¢50 (59¢).

Two buses a day run between Quepos and Puntarenas at 6am and 4:30pm, with a stop in Jacó. Duration: 1 hour. Fare: ¢100 ($1.18).

The bus for San José leaves daily at 5am and 3pm from the corner of the main street and the road past the airport. Duration: 2½ hours. Fare: ¢150 ($1.76).

ESSENTIALS   Orientation   Jacó Beach is a short distance off the southern highway. One main road runs parallel to the beach, 100 or 200 yards inland from the shore. Off this road branch many narrow, often unpaved, roads leading down to the beach. It is on these side roads that you will find most of the hotels and restaurants. When you stand on the beach here, you are facing almost due south, not west as you might think.

Fast Facts   There is a bank in the middle of town on the main road. Botiquín Garabito, the town's pharmacy, is down the street from the bank. There is a gas station out by El Bosque restaurant at the south end of town. The health center and post office are at the Municipal Center at the south end of town, across from El Naranjal restaurant.

Jacó Beach is currently the most touristy beach in Costa Rica, almost exclusively the turf of Canadian charter tour groups that fly down weekly all winter and occupy most of the higher-priced rooms in town. If you want to stay here, book well in advance. Jacó is on the edge of a wide plain surrounded by high forested hills. The land inshore from the beach is primarily pastures and farms up to the foot of the hills. Despite its discovery by charter tours, Jacó still has a very small-town, undiscovered feel to it. Best of all, it is the first beach on Costa Rica's Pacific Coast that actually feels tropical. Flowers bloom profusely, and tiny streams form pools just behind the beach before they empty into the ocean. At night, the frogs in these pools strike up a tropical symphony.

WHAT TO SEE AND DO

Unfortunately, the water here has a nasty reputation for rip tides, as does most of the water of Costa Rica's Pacific Coast. Even strong swimmers have been known to drown in the powerful rips. Storms far offshore often cause huge waves to pound on the beach, making it impossible to go in the water. You'll have to be content with the hotel pool (if your hotel has one) most of the time. However, if you happen to be a surfer, those same powerful waves and dangerous rip currents spell excitement. This is a popular surfing beach, and there are several even better surfing beaches nearby. Those who want to challenge the waves can rent surfboards for ¢300 ($3.53) an hour and body boards for ¢250 ($2.94) an hour. If you would rather stay out of the surf but still want to get some exercise, you can rent a bike for ¢500 ($5.88) per day or ¢1,000 ($11.76) for a two-seater. Both bikes and boards are available from several places along the main road.

For nature lovers, the nearby Carara Biological Reserve has several miles of trails. There is a loop trail here that takes about an hour and another trail that is open only to tour groups. Among the wildlife you might see here are coatimundis, armadillos, pacas, peccaries, river otters, kinkajous, and, of course, hundreds of species of birds. Admission is ¢100 ($1.18). The reserve is open from 8am to noon and from 1 to 4:30pm daily. No camping is allowed.

WHERE TO STAY

DOUBLES FOR LESS THAN ¢2,400 [$28.23]

CABINAS LAS PALMAS, Playa de Jacó. Tel. 506/64-3005. 23 rms., all with bath.
$ Rates: ¢1,525.50–¢2,260 ($17.95–$26.59) single; ¢1,921–¢2,825 ($22.60–$33.24) double; ¢452 ($5.32) for an extra bed. No credit cards.

Although all the rooms here are acceptable, the newer ones are a bit nicer. Some rooms come with refrigerators, hot plates, kitchen sinks, laundry sinks (pilas), and tables with four chairs so you can set up housekeeping and stay a while. All the rooms have tile floors and very clean bathrooms, and most have two double beds. There are lots of flowers in the garden, and the location down a narrow lane off the main road makes Las Palmas a quiet place. The owner, Leonid Kudriakowsky, is from Canada and speaks English, Russian, German, and Spanish. If you're coming from San José, take the Jacó exit from the Costanera and go straight through the first (and only) intersection you come to. Take a right on the narrow lane just past Cabinas Antonio.

TANGERÍ CHALET, Apdo. 622, Alajuela. Tel. 506/64-3001 or 42-0977. 10 chalets, all with bath.
$ Rates: ¢2,000 ($23.52) 1–4 people; ¢2,500 ($29.41) 5 people; ¢3,000 ($35.29) 6 people. No credit cards.

★ About midway through Jacó on the main road, you'll spot the entrance to this excellent bargain that is popular with families. Each of the ten chalets has three bedrooms, a kitchen, a patio dining area, a breakfast bar, a bathroom, and a private driveway. There are high ceilings and fans in all the rooms to keep the houses cool. Although the chalets are primarily for people planning to stay for a week or more, it is often possible to stay for shorter periods, especially during the off season. On the neatly manicured grounds, you'll find a small pool for adults and another for children, a game room with a pool table, and a snack bar. With a stream on one side and the beach on the other, you'll feel secluded here even though you're in the middle of town. Ask for a chalet away from the road for additional quiet.

CABINAS EL BOHIO, frente al playa, Playa de Jacó. Tel. 506/64-3017. 12 rms., all with bath.
$ Rates: ¢2,260 ($26.59) double or triple; ¢4,520 ($53.18) quad; discounts June–Nov. No credit cards.

Popular with a young crowd, the Bohio has a slightly rundown air about it, but the rooms are quite acceptable. Little care is paid to the garden, and there is almost no shade. There is, however, a small pool and a thatched-roof bar and restaurant that frequently plays very loud rock music. Each room has two double beds, a ceiling fan, a refrigerator, a kitchenette, and a bar. Connecting the 12 rooms is a long porch with comfortable chairs and tables made from tree trunks. Recommended for groups of young people planning to stay here for a while.

DOUBLES FOR LESS THAN ¢3,000 [$35.29]

CABINAS ALICE, 100 meters sur de la Cruz Roja, Playa de Jacó. Tel. 506/64-3061 or 37-1412. 18 rms., all with bath.
$ Rates: ¢2,500 ($29.41) 2–4 people. No credit cards.

S Set beneath the shade of a couple of large old mango trees, this motel-style place is right on the beach. The newer five rooms in back are one of the best deals in Jacó; each comes with a carved wooden headboard and matching nightstand, a tile floor, a large shower, and even potted plants on top of an unusual partial wall that is decorated with glued-on sand trim. The other rooms are pretty basic, with nothing but a double and a single bed in the room. There is even a tiny above-ground pool here. The road down to Cabinas Alice is across from the Red Cross center. Meals are served in a little dining room. You can get a fish filet fried in garlic and butter for under ¢400 ($4.71).

HOTEL ZABAMAR, Playa de Jacó. Tel. 506/64-3174. 8 rms., all with bath.
$ Rates: ¢2,000 ($23.53) single; ¢2,500 ($29.41) double; ¢3,500 ($41.18) triple. No credit cards.

The Zabamar is set back a little from the beach in a barren-looking compound with lots of gravel landscaping. The rooms have red-tile floors, small refrigerators, ceiling fans, and hammocks on their front porches. There are even pilas in little gravel-and-palm gardens (someone must have gotten a good deal on gravel) behind each room. Some rooms even have rustic wooden benches and chairs. There are even three pools here (two for kids). Surfers get a 10% discount and prices for everyone are lower from April 15 to December 15. A little open-air bar/restaurant serves inexpensive seafood.

HOTEL COCAL, Playa de Jacó. Tel. 506/64-3067. 26 rms., all with bath.
$ Rates: ¢2,040–¢2,295 ($24–$27) single; ¢2,890–¢3,315 ($34–$39) double; ¢3,740–¢4,250 ($44–$50) triple. AE, MC, V.

No children are allowed at this hotel right on the beach, so the atmosphere is peaceful. The building is done in colonial style, with arched porticos surrounding the courtyard. In that courtyard you'll find two medium-size pools, a few palapas for shade, and a thatched-roof bar. You can lie on the beach all day reading a book; when you finish that one, swap it for another from the hotel's book swap. Each guest room is well-proportioned with a tile floor, a double and a single bed, a desk, and a porch or balcony. The rooms with ocean views get the best breezes and also cost the most. Because this is one of the hotels used by Canadian charter tours, it fills early. The Cocal is on one of the streets leading down to the beach in about the middle of town. Watch for the sign.

There are two dining rooms (one on each floor) serving three meals a day. The upstairs dining room has a wonderful view of the beach. Service is generally quite good, and so is the food.

Services: Charter fishing boat available for $400 per day.

CAMPING

There are several campgrounds in or near Jacó Beach. **Madrigal,** at the south end of town at the foot of some jungly cliffs, is my favorite. The campground is right on the beach and has a bar/restaurant that is open from 7am to midnight. **El Hicaco,** in town and close to the beach, is right next door to an open-air disco, so don't expect much sleep if you stay here.

WORTH THE EXTRA BUCKS

APARTOTEL GAVIOTAS, 100 metros norte 50 metros este Banco Nacional, Playa de Jacó. Tel. 506/64-3092. 12 apts., all with bath. A/C
$ Rates: ¢5,100 ($60) 1–6 people; ¢2,500 ($29.41) double in off season. AE, MC, V.

★ Although it's on the inland side of the main road and is a bit of a walk from the beach, this is one of the nicest places in town. These little apartments are intended for families or groups who plan to stay for a week or more but are a great bargain even for two people in the off season. Each apartment has a front wall of windows looking onto the little pool, a cathedral ceiling with a clerestory for light, and a fan to keep the room cool. Floors are tile, as are the kitchen counters. The couch in each living room is a bright, cheerful blue, and there are a double bed and a bunk bed. In each bathroom, you'll even find an elegant scalloped sink. There is even a little bar beside the pool. The overall blue-and-white theme here gives it a very cheerful feeling.

APARTAMENTOS EL MAR, Playa de Jacó. Tel. 506/25-7132 or 64-3165. 12 rms., all with bath.
$ Rates: ¢4,500 ($52.94) 2–5 people. MC, V.

At the east end of town, not far from the beach, is a grouping of attractive apartments built in a C shape around a small pool and colorful garden. The apartments are new, clean, and spacious. Each comes with a unique hardwood refrigerator, two couches, a double and a single bed, and a complete kitchen. Overhead fans and high ceilings keep the rooms cool. There is no restaurant since most guests do their own cooking. If you feel like going bicycling, they have a few bikes for rent.

NEARBY AT PLAYA ESTERILLOS

There are two sections of Playa Esterillos, a seven-mile-long nearly deserted beach: Esterillos Oeste and Esterillos Este (Esterillos West and East). It is barely a mile off the highway, but it is very secluded. It makes a good day trip from Jacó if you are looking for someplace with fewer people, or if you want to make yourself at home here, take the Esterillos Este road and check into the following hotel.

HOTEL DELFIN, Apdo. 2260, San José. Tel. 506/71-1640. 15 rms., all with bath.
$ Rates: ¢4,886.06 ($56.50) single; ¢5,374.66 ($55) double; ¢6,351.88 ($65) triple. AE, MC, V.

Secluded and tranquil, this hotel is popular with older North American visitors. There are even a few retirement homes just up the beach from the hotel. With its round-tile-roofed dining room and bright white walls, the Delfin (Spanish for "dolphin") is a real surprise on this remote stretch of dirt road miles from the nearest town. Coconut palms shade the pool, and the beach is literally right outside your room. Rooms have tile floors, balconies overlooking the water, and two double beds.

The wide curving staircase that sweeps down into the dining room from the second floor seems oddly out-of-place—so much grandeur in such a remote spot. However, the meals are well prepared, and the service is good. There is also a bar in the dining area.

Facilities: Pool, table tennis, horse-shoe pitch, shuffleboard, games, bicycles, and lending library.

WHERE TO EAT

Most of the accommodations in Jacó come with kitchenettes, and if you want to save money on meals, I advise shopping at the local *supermercado* and fixing your own. Those hotels that don't have kitchenettes in the rooms usually have small restaurants. One of the best restaurants in town is the dining room at the **Hotel Cocal.** Younger visitors will enjoy the atmosphere at the **Hotel Bohio**'s little restaurant.

MEALS FOR LESS THAN ¢600 [$7.06]

RESTAURANT MARIQUERÍA LOS MANUDOS, Bulevar Jacó. No phone.
Cuisine: INTERNATIONAL.
$ Prices: Entrees ¢300–¢800 ($3.53–$9.41). No credit cards.
Open: Thurs–Tues 10:30am–9pm.

This is a very typical Costa Rican–style beach restaurant. It has chain-link fencing for walls so that the breezes get in but thieves are kept out at night—practical but not very attractive. The large room has a profusion of potted plants, a fish tank, and a few parrots that give it a tropically seedy atmosphere that is not improved by the pool table in back. But don't worry: This is one of Jacó's best restaurants, as evidenced by the wine rack on a table just inside the front door. It is even included on the orientation tour that is given to Canadian charter groups when they first arrive. The best deal here is the whole fish, which is breaded and sautéed in butter and garlic. There are also several types of ceviche. You can even order octopus or squid if you are so inclined. Stay away from the fruit salad; it's one of those monstrosities made with Jell-O and ice cream. You'll find Los Manudos toward the end of the street that leads in past the airport.

EL BOSQUE, 25 meters south of the gas station. Tel. 64-3009.
   Cuisine: INTERNATIONAL.
$ Prices: Entrees ¢350–¢1,000 ($4.12–$11.76). No credit cards.
   Open: Tues–Sun 7am–9pm.

★ Located on the highway leading south to Manuel Antonio, El Bosque (The Forest) is set amid shady mango trees. The dining room itself is a small open-air building with hanging fern baskets and nests of oropendula birds used as decorations. The furnishings are heavy colonial reproductions. Shrimp or lobster is a pricy ¢1,000 ($11.76), but you can get a delicious corvina filet for only ¢350 ($4.12). If you are not in the mood for seafood, you can try a very popular Tico dish—beef tongue in salsa. There is a long list of refrescos to choose from. Besides being a good place to come for breakfast or dinner if you're staying in town, El Bosque makes a great meal stop if you are on your way back from Manuel Antonio.

EVENING ENTERTAINMENT

There are a couple of discos in Jacó that stay busy several nights each week. My favorite is the **Disco La Central** (tel. 64-3067), which is right on the beach at the end of the street opposite Tienda La Flor. The disco is complete with flashing lights and a mirrored ball in a huge open-air hall. A garden bar in a thatched-roof building provides a slightly quieter place to have a drink. **Foxy's** (tel. 64-3002), out on the road to the airport, is another favorite. Both are open Thursday through Sunday with a very low admission and reasonably priced drinks.

EXCURSIONS

It is possible, although expensive, to arrange excursions to almost anywhere in Costa Rica from Jacó. However, for do-it-yourself excursions, you are pretty limited. You might want to visit **Carara Biological Reserve** (mentioned previously in "What to See and Do") or make day trips to other nearby beaches, of which there are many in the vicinity. **Playa Esterillos,** 14 miles southwest of Jacó, is long and wide and almost always nearly deserted (see above). **Playa Hermosa,** 6 miles southeast of Jacó, where sea turtles lay eggs from July to December, is also well known for its great surfing waves. **Playa Herradura,** about 4 miles northwest of Jacó, is ringed by lush hillsides and has a campground and a few very basic cabinas. All of these beaches are beautiful and easily reached by car or possibly by bicycle.

3. QUEPOS AND MANUEL ANTONIO

Distances: 87 miles southwest of San José; 20 miles south of Jacó Beach.

GETTING THERE By Air Flights on Sansa leave from the Juan Santamaría International Airport in San José Tuesday, Thursday, and Saturday at 9:45am and 3pm; and Monday, Wednesday, and Friday at 3:45pm. Duration: 20 minutes. Fare: ¢750 ($8.83).

By Bus Direct buses to Quepos leave San José daily at 6am, noon, and 6pm. Duration: 3½ hours. Fare: ¢330 ($3.88).

By Car Although driving is not as direct as taking a plane or bus, you can take the Puntarenas highway from San José and turn south on the Costanera, the coastal road to Puerto Caldera, Jacó, and Manuel Antonio. This is an excellent road to just beyond Jacó, but then it becomes a rutted and often very muddy washboard road frequented by heavy trucks, making for slow driving. An alternative is to take the narrow and winding old highway, which turns off the Interamerican Highway just west of Alajuela near the town of Atenas and joins the Costanera north of Jacó. You'll still have to drive that miserable road between Jacó and Quepos.

DEPARTING Sansa flights for San José leave Tuesday, Thursday, and Saturday at 10:20am and 3:35pm and Monday, Wednesday, and Friday at 9:45am only. Duration: 20 minutes. Fare: ¢750 ($8.82). Their office is beneath the Hotel Quepos across from the soccer field in Quepos (tel. 71-0161). They're open Monday through Saturday from 7 to 11:30am and 1:30 to 5pm.

Buses leave from the bus station in the market, which is two blocks from the water and one block before the road to Manuel Antonio. Express buses leave at 6am, noon, and 5pm. Duration: 3½ hours. Fare: ¢330 ($3.88). Local buses that take five hours leave at 7 and 10am and 2 and 4pm.

Any bus headed for San José will let you off in Jacó Beach.

Buses for Puntarenas leave daily at 4:30am and 1:30pm. Duration: 2½ hours. Fare ¢150 ($1.76).

ESSENTIALS Orientation Quepos is a small port town at the mouth of the Boca Vieja Estuary. After crossing the bridge into town, follow the road through town and turn left on the road to Manuel Antonio. This road winds through town a bit before starting over the hill to the national park beaches.

Getting Around A taxi between Manuel Antonio and Quepos, or vice versa, costs ¢300 ($3.53). The bus from Quepos to Manuel Antonio takes 15 minutes and departs at 5:40, 8, and 10:30am and 12:30, 3, and 4pm, returning 20 minutes later. Fare: ¢20 (24¢).

Fast Facts There's an English-speaking dentist in town: Dra. Cecilia Quesada (tel. 77-0292); her office is downstairs from the Hotel Quepos. Hours are Monday to Friday from 8 to 11:30am and 2 to 6pm, Saturday from 9am to noon. You'll find a laundry around the corner from the Restaurant Isabel. Open Monday to Friday from 8am to 4pm, Saturday from 8am to noon. They'll even pick up and deliver for ¢220 ($2.59) per kilo. There's a pharmacy called Botíca Quepos on the corner of the main street where you make the turn for Manuel Antonio (tel. 77-0038). Open daily from 7am to 6pm.

Searching for the perfect tropical beach? Manuel Antonio National Park, just over the hill from the small town of Quepos, is a strong contender. If I could go to only one place in Costa Rica, this would be it. It's hot and humid and tends to rain a lot (even in the dry season), but this wouldn't be the tropics if things were otherwise. Imagine lush green mountains covered with dense rain forests, where misty clouds drift slowly down the valleys. Imagine a cool stream flowing over the beach to empty into the bathwater-warm ocean. Imagine a string of beaches connected by trails through forests inhabited by orange-and-purple crabs, three-toed tree sloths hanging from the trees, and chipper squirrel monkeys leaping from branch to branch. Imagine islets just offshore and Technicolor sunsets. Imagine dynamite waves for board surfing and body surfing on one beach and good snorkeling on another only a 10-minute walk away. Sounds idyllic, right? So, what's the catch?

One catch is that more and more people are discovering this gem. It can get crowded on weekends with vacationers from San José. Luckily, the Costa Rican government had the foresight to preserve it as a national park before the developers got hold of it. The other catch is that only two hotels that I know of are right on the beach (and only one is really suitable for anyone but travel-hardened backpackers), so you're going to have to walk or use a vehicle of some sort to get to the beach each day. A small price to pay for such a paradise.

The town of Quepos is just a quiet little port. To the north of town are miles and miles of oil palm plantations. This land was once where Chiquita bananas were grown, but diseases wiped out the banana plantations, and they were replaced by the current palm plantations. Palm oil is said to be one of the unhealthiest oils humans can consume.

WHAT TO SEE AND DO

Manuel Antonio National Park is probably Costa Rica's most popular park and a leading destination for international tourists. It was established in 1972, about 4½ miles south of Quepos. The park is not very large, but within its boundaries are three of the prettiest little beaches I know of. The road from Quepos deadends at the long Playa Espadilla (Espadilla Beach), which is just outside the park. To reach the park itself, you must cross a small stream that is little more than ankle deep at low tide but can be knee or even waist deep at high tide. Just after crossing the stream, you will have to pay the entrance fee of ¢100 ($1.18). Playa Espadilla Sur is the first beach, just inside the park boundaries. You can walk along the beach or follow a trail inside the forest behind the beach. At the far end there is a short connecting trail to Playa Manuel Antonio. A branch trail from this one leads up and around Punta Catedral (Cathedral Point), where there are some spectacular views. If you take this trail, wear good shoes. You're likely to spot monkeys up on the Cathedral Point. From the second beach there is another, slightly longer, trail to the third beach, Puerto Escondido. There is a blowhole on this beach that sends up plumes of spray at high tide. Beyond here, at Punta Serrucho, there are some sea caves. Two other trails wind their way inland from the trail between Playa Manuel Antonio and Puerto Escondido. It's great to spend hours exploring the steamy jungle and then take a refreshing dip in the ocean. The best beach for snorkeling is the second, Playa Manuel Antonio, although the water is often too murky to see much. The park is open daily from 8am to 4pm.

On Playa Espadilla, just a short distance outside the park, there is a little shop on the water that rents surfboards and body boards.

If your tropical fantasy is to ride a horse down the beach with a jungle on one side and the ocean on the other, contact **Punta Quepos Trail Rides** (tel. 77-0566) and ask for Eric. They offer half-day trail rides with lunch on the beach. A multilingual naturalist accompanies every trail ride, pointing out monkeys, sloths, and birds.

If you're into sportfishing and happen to be here between December and April, contact Capt. Rick Miller (tel. 77-0345), who will take you out in his boat *Costa Brava* for $425 per day or $325 per half day. Sailfish, marlin, and tuna are what he goes after most of the time. **Costa Rican Dreams** (tel. 77-0593) has several boats and offers similar prices.

WHERE TO STAY

DOUBLES FOR LESS THAN ¢1,500 [$17.65]

In Quepos

HOTEL CECILIANO, Quepos. Tel. 506/77-0192. 20 rms, 12 with bath.
$ Rates: ¢800 ($9.41) double without bath, ¢1,000 ($11.76) double with bath; ¢1,200 ($14.12) triple without bath, ¢1,500 ($17.65) triple with bath; ¢2,000 ($23.53) quad with bath. No credit cards.

This is an excellent low-budget choice in Quepos. It is run by the mother of the woman who runs the Hotel Quepos (below). Mom must have taught her daughter everything she knows about running a budget hotel because the high standards of cleanliness and friendly service apply here as well. The only drawback is that this newer building is a bit darker than the Quepos. The Ceciliano is about a block before the Hotel Quepos on the same road.

HOTEL MALINCHE, Quepos. Tel. 506/77-0093. 12 rms., all with bath.
$ Rates: ¢500 ($5.88) single; ¢1,000 ($11.76) double. No credit cards.
Another good choice for backpackers, the Hotel Malinche is located on the first street to your left as you come into Quepos. You can't miss the arched brick entrance. Inside you'll find bright rooms with louvered windows but no screens, so be sure to buy

some mosquito coils (mosquito-repelling incense coils, available in drugstores and general stores) before night falls. The rooms are small but have hardwood floors and clean bathrooms.

HOTEL QUEPOS, Apdo. 79, Quepos. Tel. 506/77-0274. 23 rms, 13 with bath.
$ Rates: ¢400 ($4.71) single without bath, ¢600 ($7.06) single with bath; ¢800 ($9.41) double without bath, ¢1,200 ($14.12) double with bath; ¢1,200 ($14.12) triple without bath, ¢1,800 ($21.18) triple with bath. No credit cards.

⑤ If you're traveling on a rock-bottom budget, you'll get a whole lot more for your money by staying here in Quepos and taking the bus to the beaches at Manuel Antonio every day. The rooms here at the Quepos may be small, but they are much cleaner and more appealing than those available in this price category on the other side of the hill. There are hardwood floors, ceiling fans, a large sunny TV lounge, even a parking lot and laundry service. The management is very friendly, and downstairs from the second-floor hotel is the Sansa airlines office, a souvenir shop, a charter fishing office, and an English-speaking dentist. This hotel is across from the soccer field on the way out of town toward Manuel Antonio.

On the Road to Manuel Antonio

CABINAS PEDRO MIGUEL, Manuel Antonio, Quepos. Tel. 506/77-0035. 5 rms., all with bath.
$ Rates: ¢1,000 ($11.76) 1–3 people. No credit cards.
A little way out of town as you climb the hill to Manuel Antonio, this small place offers very basic rooms that are large but could stand a good cleaning. In classic tropical budget style, the floors are cement, and the walls are cinderblock. There are picnic tables on the long veranda that connects the five rooms, and one room has its own kitchen (but no utensils). There is even a tiny swimming pool, but it was empty when I last visited.

Near Manuel Antonio

CABINAS MANUEL ANTONIO, Manuel Antonio, Quepos. Tel. 506/77-0212 or 77-0255. In San José, tel. 53-2103. 18 rms., all with bath.
$ Rates: ¢1,130 ($13.29) 1–4 people; ¢1,350 ($15.88) 5 people. No credit cards.
I don't know how much longer this old cinderblock hotel is going to be around because when I last visited, the waves were lapping at the foundations at high tide. Until it is claimed by the Pacific, it will continue to be popular with the backpacking crowd. Even if it isn't very clean or cheery, it's cheap and right on the beach. How many places in the world will those travelers willing to pay the least amount of money for a room get the prime beachfront location? This is a great place for groups of young people traveling together since many of the rooms are quite large. Be sure to check the fan before you accept a room—not all of them work.

HOTEL MANUEL ANTONIO, Apdo. 88, Manuel Antonio, Quepos. Tel. 506/77-0290. 4 rms., all with bath.
$ Rates: ¢1,356 ($15.95) single or double; ¢1,525.50 ($17.95) triple; ¢1,695 ($19.94) quad. No credit cards.

⑤ Of the three low-budget hotels right by the entrance to the park, this is the nicest. The four rooms are upstairs from a large open-air restaurant, and all are spotlessly clean and have polished hardwood floors, walls, and doors. Large windows keep the rooms bright but also make them a bit warm in the afternoon. The rooms aren't very big, but you'll have to spend quite a bit more to find a room as clean and attractive and close to the beach.

CABINAS RAMIREZ, Manuel Antonio, Quepos. Tel. 506/77-0510. 18 rms., all with bath.
$ Rates: ¢1,850 ($21.76) 1–4 people. No credit cards.
Dark and damp or shady and cool, it's all in the eyes of the beholder. This older low-budget hotel, under the trees just before the road reaches the beach, is popular

with backpackers and surfers. There are fans but no toilet seats. Some of the rooms have metal gates on their porches so that you can leave your surfboard out front and still have it locked up. There are several very unusual and brightly painted cement picnic tables out front and a popular inexpensive restaurant next door. The restaurant is also the local disco and gets pretty noisy at times.

DOUBLES FOR LESS THAN ₡3,000 [$35.29]
Between Quepos and Manuel Antonio

HOTEL PLINIO, Apdo. 71, Quepos. Tel. 506/77-0055. 6 rms., all with bath.
$ Rates (including full breakfast): ₡3,164 ($37.22) double; ₡3,390 ($39.88). AE, MC, V.

⭐ The Plinio has long been a favorite with budget travelers to Manuel Antonio. The hotel is built into the side of a steep hillside, so that it is a steep walk from the parking lot up to the restaurant, which is on the third floor. Once you are up top, though, you'll think you are in a tree house. There are also lots of hanging plants to add to the tree-house feeling. Floors and walls are polished hardwood, and there are even rooms with tree trunk pillars. Take a book off the book exchange shelf and slip into one of the hammocks for a day of relaxing on the veranda. There is a huge map of Costa Rica for you to study before you continue to explore other parts of the country. The view from the open-air dining room is across the treetops. The restaurant (closed Wednesday) serves a variety of good Italian food for ₡400 to ₡550 ($4.71 to $6.47).

By Manuel Antonio

CABINAS VELA-BAR, Apdo. 13, Manuel Antonio, Quepos. Tel. 506/77-0413. 7 rms, 1 apt, 1 house, all with bath.
$ Rates: ₡1,020–₡2,890 ($12–$34) single; ₡1,700–₡4,675 ($20–$55) double; ₡3,400–₡5,100 ($40–$60) triple; ₡3,825–₡5,525 ($45–$65) quad. AE, MC, V.

You have a wide variety of choices in accommodations at this small hotel up a dirt road to the left just before you reach the end of the road to Manuel Antonio. You can choose to stay in a tiny room or a spacious one-bedroom house with tile floors and arched windows. There are double beds and tiled bathrooms in the rooms. The open-air restaurant/bar is deservedly very popular. Although meals are not cheap, they are a welcome change from rice and beans, fried chicken, and steaks. Check the chalkboard for the day's special. Prices range from ₡450 to ₡1,500 ($5.29 to $17.65), with shrimp commanding the highest. A typical day's choices might include fish in sherry sauce or fish in wine sauce. The restaurant is open daily from 7am to 11pm, but does not serve lunch during the low season (June through November).

CABINAS LOS ALMENDROS, Manuel Antonio, Quepos. Tel. 506/77-0225. 16 rms., all with bath.
$ Rates: ₡2,260 ($26.58) double or triple. No credit cards.

⑤ If you continue past the Vela-Bar, you'll come to the best deal among the hotels of Manuel Antonio. The rooms are nothing fancy, but they are clean, roomy, moderately priced, and, best of all, close to the beach. Each room has a fan and either three single beds or a double and twin. Bathrooms are small but tiled, and there are chairs on the front porch of each room. The only drawback here is the lack of circulation, so rooms can get a bit stuffy in the hot season. Looking up from the grassy lawn between the long row of guest rooms and the open-air restaurant, you'll see nothing but jungle-covered hills. The restaurant is one of the better ones around, with prices that are quite reasonable: from ₡325 ($3.82) for pork chops to ₡1,000 ($11.76) for shrimp.

CABINAS ESPADILLA, Manuel Antonio, Quepos. Tel. 506/77-0416. 16 rms, 8 with kitchenette, all with bath.
$ Rates: ₡2,260–₡2,825 ($26.59–$33.24) single; ₡2,825–₡3,390 ($33.23–$39.88) double; ₡3,390–₡3,955 ($39.88–$46.53) triple; ₡3,955–₡4,520 ($46.53–$53.18) quad. No credit cards.

There isn't much shade around these new cabinas, but they are clean and close to the beach. The rooms are spacious even though there isn't much in the way of decor or closet space in any of them. Each sleeps up to four people with a double bed and a bunk bed, with high ceilings and fans to keep each cool. If you plan to stay for a while and want to save some money on meal expenses, you can get a room with a small refrigerator and equipped kitchenette. There are even pilas, local clothes-washing sinks, with each room. Bars on the windows ensure security.

LONG-TERM STAYS

If you decide that you don't want to leave, contact **Blue Marlin** (tel. 77-0295), **La Buena Nota** (tel. 77-0345), or **Manuel Antonio House Rentals** (tel. 77-0560) for information on renting anything from a simple single room to a luxurious house for 12.

WORTH THE EXTRA BUCKS

COSTA VERDE, Apdo. 6944, San José. Tel. 506/77-0584. In Quepos, tel. 77-0560. In San José, tel. 506/23-7946 or 23-1943. Fax 506/ 23-9446. 10 apts., all with bath.
$ Rates: ¢4,250 ($50) double or triple; ¢8,500 ($100) 4–6 people; substantial discounts June–Nov. AE, MC, V.

⑤ There is a fabulous view from the second floor of the main building of this small hotel. Both the floors and the ceilings here are made of polished hardwood, giving every room a warm, tropical feel. The walls are almost completely screen for maximum air flow, even though there are ceiling fans. Each room has a small refrigerator and a hot plate in case you want to fix your own simple meals. Other nice touches are large leather-and-wood rocking chairs and tables made from large slices of tree trunks. When I visited Costa Verde, they had only just opened and had not done any landscaping yet. As quickly as plants grow here in the tropics, they should have that drawback remedied in a hurry. Unfortunately, there is no restaurant here, so you'll need a car to get to a restaurant after the bus stops running.

LA QUINTA, Apdo. 76, Manuel Antonio, Quepos. Tel. 506/77-0434. 7 rms., all with bath.
$ Rates: ¢4,292 ($50.52) single or double; ¢5,198 ($61.15) triple; ¢5,876 ($69.13) quad. No credit cards.
It may be a distance to the beach, but the vistas from the lawns and bungalows of this secluded hilltop hotel are fabulous. All the rooms are spacious and have large blue-and-white-tiled bathrooms with a lot of counter space. Each comes with a small table where you can have breakfast (not included in room rates). The triple and quad rooms are air-conditioned and come with their own refrigerators and hot plates. If you don't feel like going all the way down the hill to the beach, you can get in a little swimming in the tiny pool set into the hillside. There are also hammocks beside the pool for those who want to spend their days swinging in the breeze.

APARTOTEL EL COLIBRI, Apdo. 94, Manuel Antonio, Quepos. Tel. 506/77-0432. 6 rms, 2 apts., all with bath.
$ Rates: ¢3,842 ($45.20) single; ¢4,322.25 ($50.85) double; discount May–Nov. V.

★ If you have dreams of a secluded, tranquil retreat where you can laze in a hammock and watch hummingbirds sipping nectar from crimson flowers, this hotel is for you. The eight elegant rooms are set amid a garden that would have kept Monet or Gauguin happy for years. Narrow paths wind up a hill through lush vegetation that completely hides the rooms from the street. You'll feel as though you have the whole place to yourself in these cozy duplex rooms, each of which has a king-size bed with Guatemalan bedspread, high ceilings with overhead fans, screen-and-cinderblock walls that make the most of the prevailing breezes, red-tile floors, framed posters of Costa Rican wildlife, and French doors leading to a patio. The spacious patios make the rooms seem much larger than they are and come with hammocks, tables and chairs, and barbecues for grilling any fish you might catch. There are even rooms with beautiful kitchenettes that have blue-and-white-tile counters and espresso coffeemakers. True tropical elegance.

KARAHÉ, Apdo. 100-6350, Manuel Antonio, Quepos. Tel. 506/77-0170. 9 rms., all with bath.
$ Rates: ¢5,085 ($59.82) double; ¢6,102 ($71.79) triple. AE, MC, V.
You have to be in good shape to stay at this attractive hotel because the guest rooms are built on a steep hillside and are up a steep flight of steps from the reception area. However, once you've climbed the steps, you might not want to leave your room. The beds, either double or twin, have wicker headboards and floral-print spreads. There are ceiling fans to keep you cool, bathtubs for warm soaks, and refrigerators to cool your drinks. Best of all, most of the rooms have spectacular views over the treetops to the ocean below. The lush gardens are planted with ginger plants, whose red flowers often attract hummingbirds. When you do choose to leave your room, you can go for a swim in the pool or walk down the hill to the beach.

The restaurant is built at treetop level, so your view is of lush tropical vegetation. Wide-plank hardwood floors, unusual ship models in the bar, and tropical flowers on every table give the dining room a casual but sophisticated atmosphere. The specialty of the house is shish-kebabs cooked over an indoor barbecue for ¢650 ($7.65).

HOTEL DIVISAMAR, Apdo. 82, Quepos-6350, Tel. 506/77-0371. Fax 506/77-0525. 20 rms., all with bath. A/C.
$ Rates: ¢5,950 ($70) single or double; ¢6,800 ($80) triple; 25% discount June–Nov. No credit cards.
It can get pretty hot and sticky here at Manuel Antonio, but if you can't handle the heat, you can return to your air-conditioned room. Not many hotels here offer the luxury of air conditioning, so of course the rooms don't come cheap. The hotel is midway between the town of Quepos and the beaches of Manuel Antonio, with a local bus running regularly to the beach. Although you are high on a hill here, you don't get views of the ocean, but you do get a small pool and sunny, neatly manicured grounds. The rooms have tropical tile floors, high ceilings to maintain coolness even when you don't run the air conditioner, colorful floral bedspreads, and unusually artistic towels for wall decorations. The rooms are not very big, but they seem spacious because of the high ceilings.

There are bright floral tablecloths on all the tables in the open-air restaurant. The menu features Costa Rican and international dishes—with prices ranging from ¢300 to ¢850 ($3.53 to $10). Be sure to try the heart of palm omelet.

WHERE TO EAT

Three of the better places to eat in the Manuel Antonio area are the restaurants at **Cabinas Vela-Bar** (good Continental meals), **Hotel Plinio** (Italian), and **Cabinas Los Almendros** (Costa Rican). See the hotel listings above for information about these three restaurants.

MEALS FOR UNDER ¢500 [$5.88]

In Quepos

RESTAURANT ISABEL, frente al mar. Tel. 77-0137.
$ Prices: Sandwiches ¢80–¢140 (94¢–$1.65), full meals ¢260–¢450 ($3.06–$5.29). MC, V.

Open: Daily 7:30am–10pm.

Located on the main street as you come into town from the north, the Isabel is a favorite with budget travelers who are staying in Quepos. The restaurant is a large, sparsely furnished place with lots of tourist information plastered on the walls. The jukebox plays North American oldies, and the TV plays North American cable programming. You can get a variety of steaks, including T-bone with mushrooms; BLTs; seafood soup; and an assortment of breakfasts, from corn flakes to gallo pinto.

Near Manuel Antonio

RESTAURANT MAR Y SOMBRA, Tel. 77-0003.
$ Prices: Full meals ¢300–¢450 ($3.53–$5.29). No credit cards.
Open: Daily 8am–10pm.

⑤ Since there is little need for walls here in the tropics, many restaurants do without. This is a classic example of a traditional Tico restaurant—a cement floor, some tables, and a roof over your head. There are no attempts at style here, but the shady trees and crashing surf a few steps away fill the gap. You can sit at a table on the edge of the room and watch hummingbirds sipping nectar from hibiscus flowers. Despite the lack of decor, this restaurant is very popular, especially on weekends, when the influx of folks from San José make this its headquarters. The food is mostly unmemorable, but there are a few exceptions—such as Spanish-style shrimp, heart of palm salad (always delicious), and fish in salsa. This is also a good place for breakfast. You can take an early stroll down the beach and stop here for gallo pinto or a Spanish omelet. Mar y Sombra is on the right where the road from Quepos reaches the beach at Manuel Antonio.

WORTH THE EXTRA BUCKS

BARBA ROJA, Quepos–Manuel Antonio Road. Tel. 77-0331.
$ Prices: Appetizers ¢250–¢450 ($2.94–$5.29), entrees ¢475–¢1,150 ($5.59–$13.53). No credit cards.
Open: Tues–Sun 7am–midnight.

★ This is the place for an extra-special sunset splurge. Perched high on a hill with stunning views over jungle and ocean, the Barba Roja is the kind of restaurant that you would go back to time and again if you could afford it. The rustic interior is done with local hardwoods that give the dining room a warm glow. Take a seat at the counter, and you can sit for hours gazing out at the view. If you tire of the view, glance around at some of the original art by local artists. There are even a gallery attached to the restaurant and a few tables outside where purple-and-orange crabs scuttle about. Best of all is the food, which is nearly the equal of the view. There are daily specials on the blackboard, such as grilled fish steak served with a salad and baked potato, or you might want to try the chicken breast with herbs and a pasta salad. The restaurant is open for breakfast and serves delicious whole-wheat French toast. For lunch, there are a number of different sandwiches, all of which are served on whole-wheat bread. If you are in the mood to hang out and meet interesting people from all over the world, spend some time at the bar sipping a piña colada or margarita.

EVENING ENTERTAINMENT

You can hang out at the **Vela Bar,** which is up the road to the left just before you reach Manuel Antonio or meet interesting gringos at the **Barba Roja,** which is across from Hotel Divisamar. Other than that, there isn't much to do.

SHOPPING

La Buena Nota, on the left just over the bridge as you enter Quepos (tel. 77-0345), is an informal information center for the area. They also sell beachwear, U.S. newspapers and magazines, and souvenirs. If you'd like to find out about renting a house or chartering a fishing trip, this is the place to ask.

The market (two blocks in from the main road into town) sells lots of delicious fruits. If you are staying a while and doing your own cooking, this is the place to shop. **Super Mas** is a general store on the main street near the corner where you turn to head out to Manuel Antonio.

4. FARTHER SOUTH

Farther south are the undeveloped beaches of **Dominical,** the **Osa Peninsula,** and the port city of **Golfito.** Dominical now has a few very basic pensions suitable for backpackers, but little else. Golfito is being developed as a duty-free port, with lots of stores where Ticos can buy imported goods, but it has no real attractions for tourists. On the Osa Peninsula is the remote **Corcovado National Park** and, just offshore from this, the **Caño Island Biological Reserve.** If you are interested in visiting these remote parks, contact the **Marenco Biological Station,** Apdo. 4025-1000, San José. (tel. 506/21-1594 or 33-9101; Fax 55-1340). This lodge is outside our budget but is really the only acceptable place to stay on the Osa Peninsula.

CHAPTER 6

THE CARIBBEAN COAST

1. LIMÓN AND TORTUGUERO NATIONAL PARK

• **WHAT'S SPECIAL ABOUT THE CARIBBEAN COAST**

2. CAHUITA

3. PUERTO VIEJO

The jungle-covered lowlands of the Caribbean coast seem wilder and more remote than the Pacific coast; a modern highway to the Caribbean did not open until 1987. Many of the people who live on the Caribbean coast are descendants of Jamaicans who came here to work on the banana plantations or to cultivate their own cacao farms. They still celebrate their Afro-Caribbean culture in their festivities and language.

1. LIMÓN AND TORTUGUERO NATIONAL PARK

Distances: 100 miles east of San José (Limón);
156 miles northeast of San José (Tortuguero).

GETTING THERE   By Air   Sansa operates one flight a day on Tuesday, Thursday, and Saturday at 6am to Barra del Colorado. Duration: 40 minutes. Fare: ¢1,000 ($11.76). From Barra you must take a boat to Tortuguero National Park. There are no flights to Limón.

By Train   The Jungle Train from San José to Limón is one of Costa Rica's most popular tourist excursions. It travels through spectacular and remote mountain scenery and departs San José daily at 10am. Duration: 8 hours. Fare: ¢130 ($1.53).

By Bus   Express buses leave every hour on the hour daily from 5am to 7pm from the corner of Calle 21 and Avenida 3 in San José. Duration: 2½ hours. Fare: ¢130 ($1.53). There is no bus service to Tortuguero.

By Car   The Guápiles Highway heads north out of San José before turning east and passing under the Barva Volcano and through Braulio Carillo National Park. This road is as beautiful as the route of the Jungle Train. There are no roads to Tortuguero.

DEPARTING   The bus stop for Cahuita is located one block north of the municipal market. Buses leave daily at 5 and 10am, 1 and 4pm. Duration: 1 hour. Fare: ¢40 (47¢).

The bus stop for San José is one block east and half a block south of the municipal market. Buses leave daily every hour on the hour from 5am to 8pm. Duration: 2½ hours. Fare: ¢130 ($1.53).

ESSENTIALS   Orientation   Nearly all addresses in Limón are measured from the market or from Parque Vargas. The train station is at the west end of town about six blocks from the municipal market. The bus station for buses to San José is on the street between Parque Vargas and the market. The bus stop for Cahuita and Puerto Viejo is a block north of the market. The stop for buses out to Playa Bonita is just around the corner to the north of the Cahuita bus stop. At the east end of town is Parque Vargas, with an old seawall running north.

WHAT'S SPECIAL ABOUT THE CARIBBEAN COAST

Beaches
- [ ] Cahuita National Park, with long, deserted beaches and Costa Rica's largest coral reef
- [ ] Puerto Viejo surfing

Parks
- [ ] Tortuguero National Park, known for the turtles that lay their eggs on the park's beaches

Ace Attractions
- [ ] The Jungle Train, winding its way through the jungle as it travels from San José to Limón

In 1502, on his fourth and last voyage to the New World, Christopher Columbus anchored just offshore from what is now Limón and christened this newfound land Costa Rica ("Rich Coast"). In the 1800s black and Chinese laborers were brought to this area to work on the railroad and the banana plantations. The blacks were of African-Caribbean heritage, accustomed to this hot and humid coastal region, and they stayed on long after the railroad was completed. Laws prevented them from moving into the highlands so here they stayed, creating their own unique Costa Rican culture with more ties to the islands of the eastern Caribbean than to the Spanish culture of Costa Rica's central valleys. Today Limón is a busy port city that ships millions of pounds of bananas northward every year.

There is virtually nothing to see or do in Limón, except during the annual October Carnival. For a week around October 12 (Columbus Day), Limón wakes up, and the citizens don costumes and take to the streets in a nonstop bacchanal orchestrated to the beat of reggae, soca, and calypso music. If you want to experience this carnival, make hotel reservations early.

Should you be stuck here in transit from San José to Tortuguero National Park or to Cahuita, here are a few choices for places to stay. I recommend hopping in a taxi or a local bus and heading out toward Playa Bonita, a small public beach park. Although the water isn't very clean and I don't recommend swimming, the setting is much more attractive than downtown.

WHERE TO STAY AND EAT

DOUBLES FOR LESS THAN ¢1,500 [$17.65]

PARK HOTEL, Avenida 3 between Calles 1 and 3, Apdo. 35, Limón. Tel. 506/58-3476. 25 rms., all with bath.

$ Rates: ¢860–¢1,075 ($10.12–$12.65) single; ¢1,003–¢1,218 ($11.80–$14.33) double; ¢1,147–¢1,290 ($13.49–$15.18) triple. No credit cards.

You can't miss this pink, yellow, and turquoise building across the street from the fire station. It's certainly seen better years, but in Limón there aren't too many choices. Be sure to ask for a room on the ocean side of the hotel because these are brighter, quieter, and cooler than those on the side of the hotel that faces the fire station.

The large sunny dining room off the lobby serves standard Tico fare at very reasonable prices. The daily specials are ¢250 and ¢350 ($2.94 and $4.12).

DOUBLE FOR LESS THAN ¢2,500 [$29.41]

In Town

HOTEL ACON, Avenida 3 and Calle 3, Apdo. 528, Limón. Tel. 506/58-1010. 39 rms., all with bath. A/C TEL

$ Rates: ¢1,160 ($13.65) single; ¢2,100 ($24.70) double; ¢2,560 ($30.12) triple. AE, MC, V.

⑤ This older in-town choice is the best you can do in Limón. The rooms, all of which are air-conditioned (almost a necessity in this muggy climate), are clean and have two twin beds and a large bathroom.

The restaurant on the first floor just off the lobby is a cool, dark haven on steamy afternoons, highly recommended for lunch or as a place to beat the heat. Prices range from ¢500 to ¢1,000 ($5.88 to $11.76). The second-floor discotheque stays open late on weekends, so don't count on a quiet night.

On the Road to Playa Bonita

CABINAS COCORI, Playa Bonita, Limón. Tel. 506/58-2930. 6 apts., all with bath.

$ Rates: ¢2,260–¢2,825 ($26.59–$33.24) single/double; ¢3,955–¢4,520 ($46.53–$53.18) 3–5 people. MC, V.

Located on the water just before you reach Playa Bonita, these apartments command a fine view of the cove and crashing surf. They had only recently opened when I visited, and the grounds were in need of landscaping, but the rooms were quite nice. A two-story white building houses six apartments, each of which has a kitchenette with hot plate and refrigerator and two bedrooms. A long veranda runs along both floors. Staying at this location is far preferable to staying in town. You can get here by bus or taxi.

HOTEL LAS OLAS, Apdo. 701, Limón. Tel. 506/58-1414. Fax 506/58-1678 or Apdo. 440, Cartago. Tel. 506/51-9898. Fax 506/51-7720. 49 rms., 3 suites, all with bath.

$ Rates: ¢1,700–¢2,550 ($20–$30) single; ¢2,550–¢3,400 ($30–$40) double; ¢2,975 ($35) triple; ¢6,375 ($75) suite. AE, MC, V.

⑤ This large older hotel is built directly over a coral reef just offshore, with bridges connecting the building to the parking lot. At high tide, the ocean is directly beneath the hotel, and at times, when the surf is high, it almost seems as if you are looking up at the water. This is as close as you can come to going on a cruise without ever leaving port. Although the hotel has seen a lot of use over the years, the rooms are still quite nice and represent a good value. Each has its own balcony, red-tile floors, exposed brick walls, built-in vanity, large closets, and plenty of counter space in the bathroom. Steps away from the dining room is the pool, which is built directly over the water on a small brick terrace. Across the street is a fascinating little grotto with a statue of the Virgin Mary. Be sure to have a look.

The hotel's restaurant is built on an open-air causeway on the first floor, and it is surprisingly elegant with blue-and-yellow tablecloths, flowers on every table, and elegantly folded napkins. There is a table with wine and fruit in the center of the dining room and a small bar off to one side. Seafood predominates on the menu—with such appetizing offerings as ceviche (marinated fish salad), grilled lobster, sea bass meunière, and jumbo shrimp. Prices range from ¢300 to ¢1,200 ($3.53 to $14.12).

WORTH THE EXTRA BUCKS

HOTEL MATAMA, Apdo. 686, Limón. Tel. 506/58-1123. 15 rms., all with bath. A/C

$ Rates (including breakfast): ¢3,905.80 ($46.48) single; ¢5,153.55 ($60.63) double; ¢6,183.75 ($72.75) triple; ¢7,140 ($84) quad. AE, MC, V.

★ On the same road as Cabinas Cocori and Hotel Las Olas, the Matama is in a class by itself. The hotel consists of several multiplex buildings set amid dense tropical vegetation across the road from the ocean. The strikingly modern design of the buildings, both inside and out, is a welcome surprise in an area of generally unmemorable accommodations. Each room is decorated with attractive matching drapes and bedspreads and has comfortable wicker furniture and, best of all, large bathrooms with solarium gardens that bring the jungle right into your bath. There are even some units with lofts. Splashing around in the small pool, you'll be surrounded by the sounds of the jungle, and if you want to explore nearby jungles further, you can arrange trips here at the hotel.

Seafood is the specialty of the large open-air restaurant, with prices ranging from ¢400 to ¢1,500 ($4.71 to $17.65). The meals are well-prepared and elegantly served, but the service can be a bit slow.

EXCURSIONS

TORTUGUERO NATIONAL PARK

The name refers to the giant Atlantic green sea turtles (tortugas) that come up on the beaches here to lay their eggs every year between June and November.

Located on the remote northeastern coast of Costa Rica, this is one of the country's most popular national parks. Until last year it was fairly easy and inexpensive to reach this remote region, but when the mailboat that used to make regular runs up and down the rivers and canals died, tourists were left with only one feasible choice—take a tour. You will be bombarded with brochures about Tortuguero tours from the moment you set foot in Costa Rica. Tour prices currently range from $125 to $250 per person for a three-day, two-night tour, based on double occupancy. No matter which tour you choose, it is going to cost more than your normal daily budget if you are using this book. However, if it is egg-laying season for sea turtles, this trip might well be worth the splurge. Outside of egg-laying season, I would think long and hard about making this expensive and time-consuming trip, especially if your time is limited. Here is the information that you'll need to make your decision.

Where to Stay

HOTEL ILAN-ILAN, Apdo. 91-1150, San José. Tel. 506/55-2262 or 55-2031. Fax 506/55-1946. 20 rms., all with bath.

$ Rates: ¢10,625 ($125) per person, including meals, for three days and two nights. AE, MC, V.

Currently the best deal on a tour to Tortuguero National Park is offered by this newer lodge. Guest rooms are large, with either a double and a single bed or three singles. Overhead fans will keep you cool in this steamy region. Tico meals are served in the small dining room, and there is a bar where you can meet other adventurers. The tour includes a brief stop at Braulio Carillo National Park en route from San José to Limón by bus, so you actually get two park visits for the price of one. There are bilingual guides to point out wildlife and answer questions.

JUNGLA LODGE, Apdo. 26-1017, San José 2000. Tel. 506/33-0155 or 33-6579. Fax 506/22-0568. 17 rms., all with bath.

$ Rates: ¢10,625 ($125) per person for three days and two nights. AE, MC, V.

Located on the river one kilometer from Tortuguero National Park, this simple lodge is your next best bet. The Jungla Lodge's three-day, two-night tours starting on Tuesdays and Fridays include bus transportation to the coast and the trip up the canals to the park, all meals, bilingual guides, a tour to the park, and a night tour during turtle egg-laying season. The lodge itself is rustic with simply furnished rooms and a spartan dining hall. Guest rooms have wood-paneled walls and come with twin beds. Arranged in long narrow buildings that resemble mobile homes, the rooms share a common porch that has chairs for relaxing after a day of exploring the region's waterways. Dugout canoes with outboards and paddles are available.

TORTUGA LODGE, Avenida 3 and Calle Central, Apdo. 6941, San José 1000. Tel. 506/22-0333 or 23-9975. Fax 506/57-1665. 18 rms., all with bath.

$ Rates: ¢16,915 ($199) per person, including meals, for double occupancy for a one-day, one-night tour; ¢21,165 ($249) per person, including meals, for double occupancy for a three-day, two-night tour; ¢4,675 ($55) per person for extra days, including meals. AE, MC, V.

Though more expensive than the Ilan-Ilan or Jungla Lodge, the Tortuga Lodge offers far more tropical atmosphere, and by that I don't mean that the air is more humid here. The lodge is constructed of tropical hardwoods and thatch with lush flowering plants in the neatly manicured garden. Guest rooms and the dining room/bar are all done in equally rustic, tropical decor. Though motorboats interrupt the quiet occasionally, the solitude and tranquility here are almost palpable. The one-day, one-night tour includes round-trip airfare, and the three-day, two-night tour includes the Jungle Train ride from San José to Limón.

RIO COLORADO LODGE, Apdo. 5094, San José. Tel. 506/32-4063. Fax 506/31-5987. 18 rms., all with bath.

$ Rates (including three meals per day): ¢6,250 ($73.53) single; ¢12,500 ($147.06) double. AE, MC, V.

Though it bills itself as the "world headquarters for tarpon and snook" and is first and foremost a fishing lodge, the Rio Colorado also offers tours to Tortuguero National Park, which is 25 miles to the south. Clinging to the banks of the Rio Colorado, the lodge offers comfortable accommodations with private baths, hot and cold water, and family-style meals in their rustic dining room. A small menagerie here guarantees that you'll see some of the region's fascinating wildlife, even if they elude you in the wild. A recreation room and lounge, complete with satellite TV, provides an excellent environment for socializing in the evenings. There is also daily laundry service here. Fishing boats and guides are included in fishing packages.

---

2. CAHUITA

Distances: 125 miles east of San José; 26 miles south of Limón.

GETTING THERE   By Bus   From San José, there are direct express buses leaving daily at 6am and 2:30pm from the corner of Avenida 11 and Calle 1. Duration: 3½ hours. Fare: ¢300 ($3.53). Or you can take a Limón bus from San José and then catch a Cahuita-bound bus from Limón. San José–Limón buses leave from the corner of Calle 21 and Avenida 3 every hour on the hour daily from 5am to 7pm. Duration: 2½ hours. Fare: ¢130 ($1.53). From Cahuita, buses leave from one block north of the municipal market at 5 and 10am and 1 and 4pm daily. Duration: 1 hour. Fare: ¢40 (47¢).

By Car   Take the Guápiles Highway out of San José bound for Limón. From Limón, head south on the road that runs along the beach and past the airport.

DEPARTING   Buses from Limón stop in Cahuita on their way to Puerto Viejo and Sixaola, which is on the Panamanian border. They stop here around 6 and 11am and 2 and 5pm.

Ask around for the current schedule of Limón-bound buses.

The express buses from Sixaola to San José stop here around 7am and 3:30pm, but check with locals to be sure the schedule hasn't changed. There are rarely any seats left by the time this bus reaches Cahuita. This bus takes 4 hours and costs ¢300 ($3.53). It's probably more comfortable if you take the local bus to Limón and then catch a bus from there to San José. Buses from Limón leave for San José every hour between 5am and 8pm daily.

ESSENTIALS   Orientation   There are only eight sand streets in Cahuita, so you shouldn't get lost. The road in from the highway first reaches a *T* intersection right on the water. To the left are the hotels and cabinas of the Playa Negra area; to the right is Cahuita village itself. The village's main street deadends at the entrance to the national park (a foot bridge over a small stream).

Fast Facts   There is a laundry service, charging ¢350 ($4.12) per load, 50 yards down a path opposite the Cahuita National Park Restaurant. The police station is located where the road from Playa Negra turns into town. The post office is next door to the police station. Open Monday to Friday from 7 to 11am and noon to 4pm.

If you're traveling on a student budget and seeking cut-rate accommodations and a peaceful environment, look no further: You have arrived. Not too many years ago, backpackers in Costa Rica headed to Manuel Antonio, but then that beach was "discovered" and room rates skyrocketed—this is now their destination. Cahuita village traces its roots to Afro-Caribbean fishermen and laborers who settled in the region in the mid-1800s. Today the population is primarily English-speaking blacks whose culture and language set them apart from other Costa Ricans.

The main reason people come to Cahuita, other than for its laid-back atmosphere, are for the miles of pristine beaches that stretch from the south end of town. These beaches, the forest behind them, and the coral reefs beneath the waters offshore are all part of the Cahuita National Park. It is here that you will find Costa Rica's only coral reef (which is not nearly as spectacular as the reefs in Belize).

WHAT TO SEE AND DO

You'll immediately feel the call of the long scimitar of **beach** that stretches south from the edge of town. You can walk on the beach itself or follow the **trail** that runs through the forest just behind the beach. This trail is great for bird watching, and if you're lucky, you might see some monkeys or a sloth. The loud whooping sounds you hear off in the distance are the calls of howler monkeys, who can be heard more than a mile away. Nearer at hand, you are likely to hear crabs scuttling about amid the dry leaves on the forest floor. There are half a dozen or so land crabs living in this region. My favorites are the bright orange-and-purple ones. The trail behind the beach stretches a little more than 4 miles to the southern end of the park at **Puerto Vargas**, where you will find a beautiful white-sand beach, the park headquarters, and a primitive campground with drinking water and outhouses. The reef is off the point just north of Puerto Vargas. There is a small fee for camping, and a ¢100 ($1.18) entrance fee. The national park is open daily from 8am to 5pm.

If you want to find out where the best **diving spots** are (there is even a sunken ship you can visit), I suggest a snorkeling trip by boat. There are two companies running boats out to the reef. **Moray's** (tel. 58-1515, ext. 216), on the road to Playa Negra near the police station and post office, charges ¢1,000 ($11.76), plus another ¢500 ($5.88) for snorkeling gear. **Cahuita Tours & Rentals** (tel. 58-1515, ext. 232), around the corner on the village's main street, charges the same for a 3½-hour glass-bottom boat ride and only ¢300 ($3.53) for snorkel gear. If you want just to rent snorkeling equipment here, it will cost ¢500 ($5.88). You can also rent horses, bicycles, and binoculars. Sportfishing and tours by Jeep also are available. Moray's arranges river trips and boat trips to Tortuguero if you have enough people. **Brigitte** (watch for the sign on Playa Negra) rents horses for ¢300 ($3.53) per hour or ¢500 ($5.88) per day. The best places for swimming are on Playa Negra, behind Letty Grant's in the little cove, and beyond the mouth of the Peresoso River inside the national park.

Please keep an eye out for poisonous snakes around here. I was almost bitten by one on a path on Playa Negra. If you aren't a herpetologist, assume that all snakes here are poisonous and thus give them a wide berth.

WHERE TO STAY

DOUBLES FOR LESS THAN ¢1,200 [$14.12]

HOTEL CAHUITA, Cahuita. Tel. 506/58-1515, ext. 201. 23 rms., 11 with bath.
$ Rates: ¢339 ($3.99) single without bath, ¢791 ($9.31) single with bath; ¢565

($6.65) double without bath, ¢1,096 ($12.90) double with bath; ¢847 ($9.95) triple without bath, ¢1,469 ($17.30) triple with bath; ¢1,130 ($13.30) quad without bath, ¢1,841 ($21.65) quad with bath. AE, MC, V.

Across the street from Cabinas Vaz, the Cahuita looks quite rundown from the street, but it is not nearly as bad once you get inside. The better rooms, those in the new building, have private baths, abundant light, and good ventilation. Still, they're none too special. Those in the older section of the hotel are rather gloomy. Ask for one of the rooms with a private bath.

CABINAS PALMER, Apdo. 865, Limón. Tel. 506/58-1515, ext. 243. Or Apdo. 1445-1002, P. Estudiantes, San José. Tel. 506/27-0927. 22 rms., 8 with bath.

$ Rates: ¢700 ($8.24) single/double without bath, ¢900 ($10.59) single/double with bath, ¢1,200 ($14.12) single/double with kitchen; ¢100 ($1.20) per extra person. No credit cards.

Down the street from the bus stop, toward the water, is another good choice for backpackers and other ultra-low-budget travelers. The management at Cabinas Palmer is very friendly and helpful and dedicated to providing folks with decent inexpensive accommodations. For those who are really pinching pennies, I recommend the "boarding house"—an old-fashioned Caribbean-style wood building that has been split into several small rooms, none of which has a private bath. However, the shared toilets and showers out back are very clean. If you're willing to spend a bit more, try one of the rooms in the newer cinderblock building. These are larger and have bathrooms shared with one other room; some even have kitchenettes. All of these rooms have back doors that open onto a sunny garden where you can sunbathe in privacy. Look for the pretty blue-and-yellow building with the red roof on the right as you walk toward the water from the bus stop.

SURF SIDE CABINS, Apdo. 360, Limón. Tel. 506/58-1515, ext. 246-203. 19 rms., 4 with bath.

$ Rates: ¢565 ($6.65) single without bath, ¢1,017 ($11.96) single/double with bath; ¢678 ($7.98) double without bath; ¢879.50 ($10.35) triple, ¢1,253 ($14.74) triple with bath; ¢937.90 ($11.03) quad, ¢1,469 ($17.28) quad with bath. No credit cards.

Despite its name, this hotel is not right on the water; however, it is one of the nicer places here in Cahuita. All the rooms are clean and have been recently painted. Louvered windows let in a lot of light and air. There are rooms with double beds, twin beds, and even bunk beds.

The restaurant is popular with locals, who sit and play dominoes for hours, and it can get noisy at times. Prices for Tico meals range from ¢175 to ¢900 ($2.06 to $10.59). While I was eating here one night, a large sloth crawled into the open-air restaurant from an adjacent tree. With entertainment like that, it's hard not to recommend this place.

CABINAS VAZ, Cahuita. Tel. 506/58-1515, ext. 218. 14 rms., all with bath.

$ Rates: ¢963 ($11.33) single; ¢1,190 ($14) double; ¢1,446 ($17.01) triple; ¢1,643 ($19.45) quad; ¢1,869 ($21.99) quint. No credit cards.

Only steps from the park entrance, Cabinas Vaz is one of the more popular places in town, especially with folks from San José, which means that it can get pretty noisy on the weekends. The rooms are in an L-shaped building behind the Restaurant Vaz, with a few located directly above. I recommend asking for a room as far from the restaurant as possible because the tape player stays on loud from dawn until long after dark. Rooms are simple but clean, and they have fans and large wardrobes.

DOUBLES FOR LESS THAN ¢1,600 [$18.82]

CABINAS SOL Y MAR, Cahuita. Tel. 506/58-1515, ext. 37. 8 rms., all with bath.

$ Rates: ¢1,236–¢1,545 ($14.54–$18.18) single/double; ¢1,545–¢2,060 ($18.18–$24.24) triple; ¢2,060–¢2,472 ($24.24–$29.08) quad. No credit cards.

The more expensive rooms here are the ones upstairs, which have more light and catch more of the breezes, an important factor in these hot, humid, and cloudy climes. However, all the rooms are large and quite clean and have fans. There isn't much decor, but you're only steps from the park entrance and the beach. Because of the nearby restaurants, it can be a little noisy here at night.

CABINAS BLACK BEACH, Cahuita. Tel. 506/58-1515, ext. 251. 4 rms., all with bath.

$ Rates: ₡730 ($8.59) single; ₡1,356 ($15.95) double; ₡1,692 ($19.90) triple. No credit cards.

Although there are only four rooms here, this is the nicest hotel in Cahuita. The four rooms are in two two-story cabins with stone foundation walls and polished hardwood walls above. The downstairs rooms are cool and dark, and the upper rooms have balconies. Lattice-and-screen walls help let in every little breeze. The cabinas are across a dirt road from a black-sand beach, as their name implies, with a long green lawn between. It's a long walk back into town, but because it is, this place is quiet at night.

The restaurant, which specializes in Italian food, is tiny, with hardwood floors, no walls, and tables with built-in checkerboards.

CABINAS ATLANTIDA, Cahuita. Tel. 506/58-1515, ext. 213. 10 rms., all with bath.

$ Rates: ₡1,500 ($17.65) single/double; ₡1,900 ($22.35) triple. MC, V.

Run by a French Canadian, the Atlantida is one of the few hotels in Cahuita that is more than basic, and soon it will be the only hotel in town with hot water—if current plans are carried out. Set amid a large lawn with a grove of fruit trees behind, this comfortable hotel is about a mile out of town on the black-sand beach. There are hammocks hanging from trees, and a resident sloth occasionally comes down from its strangler fig to hang from the front gate. It's worth staying here just for the chance of seeing this shy, slow-moving creature. The rooms have cement floors and two double beds, shutters on the windows for security, and overhead fans. Bathrooms are tiled and very clean. In the off-season, the restaurant is not open, but guests are allowed to use the kitchen for light cooking.

During the busy season, three meals a day are served, with the emphasis on Continental cuisine.

LONG-TERM STAYS

CHALET HIBISCUS, Playa Negra Road, Cahuita. No phone. 1 house with bath.

$ Rates: ₡3,000 ($35.29) per week; ₡10,000 ($117.65) per month. No credit cards.

If you're planning a long stay in Cahuita, I advise checking into this beautiful chalet. Although it is about 2 miles from town on the road along Black Beach, it is well worth the journey. The house has two bedrooms that sleep up to six people, with hardwood paneling all around, a full kitchen, hot water, red-tile floors, a pila for doing your laundry, and even a garage. A spiral staircase leads to the second floor, where you'll find ornate Nicaraguan rocking chairs and hammocks on the balcony, which looks over a green lawn to the ocean. If you ever wanted to be marooned on the Mosquito Coast, this is the place to live out the fantasy. The chalet is both simple and elegant, with truly tropical styling. The setting is serene and beautiful. If you're staying down the beach and decide to check this place out, be sure to ring the bell outside the gate—there are guard dogs on the grounds.

WHERE TO EAT

RESTAURANTE TIPICO CAHUITA. Tel. 58-1515, ext. 204.

$ Prices: ₡200–₡1,200 ($2.35–$14.12). No credit cards.
Open: Daily 7am–10pm.

⭐ The restaurants in Cahuita are not exactly memorable places, but this one has an upscale feel to it. There is actually some semblance of interior decor: A surfboard and a few original oil paintings hang on the walls, and a large seashell mobile lamp hangs from the ceiling. On the tables there are fresh flowers and lamps with basket shades for moody lighting. Only a screen wall stands between you and the great outdoors. As the name of this place implies, the food is typical Costa Rican. Rice and beans seem to come with every meal, but there is everything from steaks to lobster to accompany them. You'll also find some unusual refrescos on the menu, including *horchata* (a drink made from rice and almonds), *tamarindo* (a sour black fruit drink that is as refreshing as lemonade), black cows, and egg nog. There are dozens of choices for breakfast and a tempting assortment of desserts.

RESTAURANT VAZ. Tel. 58-1515, ext. 218.
$ Prices: ¢200–¢1,600 ($2.35–$18.82). No credit cards.
Open: Daily 7am–10pm.
If you don't mind loud music while you eat, you might enjoy having a meal here. The menu is basically the standard Cahuita seafood and casados menu, but if you can get five people together and give the restaurant 24-hours notice, they'll prepare a meal of local specialties for you. The pancake with fresh fruit makes a delicious and filling breakfast for ¢169 ($1.88). They also have an interesting assortment of refrescos. If you have had enough fried food lately, try the baked redfish. There's not much atmosphere in this basic Tico restaurant.

RESTAURANT EDITH, by the police station. No phone.
$ Prices: About ¢250 ($2.94). No credit cards.
Open: Sat–Thurs 7am–9pm. (No breakfast on Sunday.)
💲 If you eat at only one place while you are in Cahuita, make it this unusual establishment. Everyone was talking about it when I last visited. Miss Edith is a local lady who decided to start serving up home-cooked meals to all the hungry tourists hanging about in Cahuita, and her young daughters take the orders while Mom cooks up a storm out back. You enter the dining room itself through a screen door, which is a bit of an anomaly since the dining room has no walls. There are only a handful of tables, and the day's choices are written on a chalkboard. Never interrupt one of the girls when she is reciting the refrescos available—she might have to start all over from the beginning in her sing-song voice. The menu usually lists casados, chop suey, and spaghetti with a variety of meats and fish. Don't expect fast service. To find Miss Edith's, head down to the opposite end of the road that ends at the park entrance and turn right. It's a few steps down on the left.

RESTAURANT CAHUITA NATIONAL PARK. Tel. 58-1515, ext. 244.
$ Prices: ¢250–¢1,000 ($2.94–$11.76). No credit cards.
Open: Daily 8am–10pm.
If you're out on the park beach and hunger suddenly strikes, this is the closest place to get a meal. The tables are underneath a high thatch roof surrounded by shady trees, so it always stays cool in here. Some of the tables are painted with backgammon boards so that guests can while away an afternoon. If you are tired of the great outdoors, you can retire to the indoor bar and watch cable TV. Seafood is the specialty here, although steaks, pork chops, and pasta also are available.

SNACKS

There is a tiny bakery and gift shop on the left side of the main road as you head toward the park entrance, just before you reach the little park that serves as bus stop. The coconut pie, brownies, ginger snaps, banana bread, and corn pudding are all delicious. Prices range from ¢25 to ¢75 (30¢ to 90¢).

EVENING ENTERTAINMENT

Watch a sloth or play dominoes at the Surf Side or go to sleep early—those are the most popular choices with visitors here. However, if you're adventurous, you can visit the town's one nameless saloon, a ramshackle place across the street from the village park. There is even a disco, complete with mirrored ball and flashing lights, in the back of this bar on weekends.

SHOPPING

As you might have guessed, Cahuita is not exactly a shopper's paradise. However, there is one interesting shop that you should be sure to visit while in town. **Tienda de Artesania,** in a small yellow house on the road to Playa Negra, is a women's craft cooperative headed by Letty Grant. She and her group of five or so women paint T-shirts and make coconut jewelry. The store is open Monday through Friday from 8am to 5pm. Miss Letty also rents out a few rooms, so if you're planning on staying a while, you might want to ask her about these.

At Restaurant Vaz and a couple of other places around the village, you can pick up a copy of Paula Palmer's *What Happen, A Folk-History of Costa Rica's Talamanca Coast* (Ecodesarollos, 1977). The book is a history of the region based on interviews with many of the area's oldest residents. Much of it is in the traditional Creole language, from which the title is taken. It makes fun and interesting reading, and you just might bump into someone mentioned in the book.

EXCURSIONS

You might want to get a group together and organize a trip from here to Tortuguero. See the folks at **Moray's** (tel. 58-1515, ext. 216) to arrange things. They can also arrange other types of tours here and at **Cahuita Tours and Rentals,** around the corner.

---

3. PUERTO VIEJO

Distances: 135 miles east of San José; 34 miles south of Limón.

GETTING THERE   By Bus   You can get off the Sixaola-bound express bus from San José out on the highway at El Cruce (the crossroad) and walk into town, but it is a 3-mile hike. If you call José Luis Ferández at the Hotel Maritza (tel. 58-3844) or Johnny León at the Pulpería Manuel León (tel. 58-0854) two days in advance and tell him which bus you will be on, he will have a taxi meet you at El Cruce. This bus leaves from the corner of Avenida 11 and Calle 1. Duration: 4½ hours. Fare: ¢300 ($3.53). If you take one of the hourly buses from San José to Limón, which leave from Calle 21 and Avenida 3 every hour between 5am and 7pm, and then transfer in Limón to a Puerto Viejo–bound bus, you will get dropped right in the village. These buses leave Limón from the block north of the municipal market at 5 and 10am and 1 and 4pm. Duration: 1½ hours.

By Car   To reach Puerto Viejo, continue south from Cahuita for another 10 miles. Watch for a gravel road that forks to the left from the paved highway. This road will take you into the village after another 3 miles.

DEPARTING   The local bus from Puerto Viejo to Limón leaves daily at 6:30, 9:30, and 11:30am and 4:30pm, but check to make sure that the schedule hasn't changed.

The direct bus to San José leaves El Cruce (the highway crossroad) at 6:30, 9:30, and 11:30am and 4pm. Duration: 4 hours. Fare: ¢300 ($3.53). Alternatively, you can take a local bus to Limón and then transfer to a San José bus.

ESSENTIALS   Orientation   The dirt road in from the highway runs parallel to Playa Negra just before entering the village of Puerto Viejo. There are about six dirt streets. The sea will be on your left and forested hills on your right as you come into town.

Fast Facts   Public phones are located at Hotel Maritza and Pulpería Manuel

León. The nearest bank is in Bribri, about 6 miles away. There is a Guardia Rural police post near the park on the beach.

Even smaller than Cahuita, Puerto Viejo is where you go if you think that Cahuita has been spoiled and is too crowded with tourists. Accommodations here are even more spartan than those in Cahuita (with one or two exceptions). The road into town from the highway leads through old cacao plantations, which have been all but abandoned due to a blight that has killed off most of the trees.

WHAT TO SEE AND DO

Most people who show up in this remote village have only one thing on their mind—surfing. Just offshore from the village park is a shallow reef where powerful storm-generated waves sometimes reach 20 feet. These waves, known locally as *salsa brava,* are the biggest and most powerful on the Atlantic Coast. Even when the waves are small, this spot is recommended only for very experienced surfers because of the danger of the reef. For swimming, head out to **Playa Negra,** along the road into town, where the surf is much more managable.

If you aren't a surfer, there isn't much else for you to do here. The same activities that prevail in Cahuita are the norm here as well. Read a book, take a nap, or walk on the beach. However, if you have more energy, you can rent a bicycle (ask for Aldo Figuerola or Jacobo Bent) or a horse (from Antonio at Tropical Paradise) and head down the beach toward Punta Uva, which is a little less than 5 miles down a dirt road.

If you have an interest in medicinal plants, ask around for Miss Dolly, a local expert who enjoys sharing her knowledge with interested visitors.

WHERE TO STAY

DOUBLES [WITHOUT BATH] FOR LESS THAN ¢1,000 [$11.76]

HOTEL MARITZA, Puerto Viejo, Limón. Tel. 506/58-3844. 18 rms., 6 with bath.
$ Rates: ¢300 ($3.53) single without bath; ¢515 ($6.06) double without bath, ¢1,500 ($17.65) double with bath. AE, MC, V.
This is another very basic hotel upstairs from a popular restaurant, which also happens to have one of the only public phones in town. The rooms are just what you would expect from such a place: Not overly clean, rather small, and dark. But if you're here for the surf or want your money to last as long as possible, there's not much to complain about. The jukebox in the restaurant downstairs gets played a lot at night and is a very important factor when you consider whether you want to stay here.

HOTEL PUERTO VIEJO, Puerto Viejo, Talamanca. No phone. 20 rms., all with shared bath.
$ Rates: ¢350 ($4.12) single; ¢700 ($8.24) double; ¢1,050 ($12.36) triple; ¢1,400 ($16.48) quad. No credit cards.
Although it is managed by locals, this backpackers' hotel is owned by an avid surfer from California; consequently, the hotel is frequented by like-minded young people. The rooms are extremely basic (there aren't even fans) with nothing but beds and a light in them, but the communal toilets and showers are fairly clean. When surf is all you can think about, where you sleep is rarely of any concern. The new two-story building is an eclectic blend of Caribbean traditional wood and modern tropical concrete block.

CABINAS BLACK SANDS, Puerto Viejo, Talamanca. No phone. 4 rms., none with bath.
$ Rates: ¢450 ($5.29) single; ¢750 ($8.82) double; ¢2,000 ($23.53) 6 people. No credit cards.

⭐ The owners of these rustic beachside thatch huts are refugees from chilly Wisconsin. They offer basic accommodations in a secluded spot on a long black-sand beach. Three of the rooms are in one building, which has a communal kitchen and dining room table. If there are six of you, you can rent the entire house. If you don't have the whole place to yourself, remember that the folks next door can hear everything you say because the walls don't go all the way to the ceiling. It's wonderfully tranquil out here, but it's a long walk to the nearest restaurant; it's better if you plan to do your own cooking.

CABINAS CHIMURI, Ken Kurst, Cabinas Black Sands, Lista de Correos, Puerto Viejo de Limón, Talamanca. Tel. 58-3844 and leave a message with Ana or José. 4 cabins, none with bath.
$ Rates: ¢850 ($10) double; ¢1,700 ($20) quad. No credit cards.

⭐ If you don't mind being a 15-minute walk from the beach, I'm sure that you'll enjoy this rustic lodge. It is built in traditional Bribri Indian–style with thatched-roof A-frame cabins in a forest setting. In fact, it is a short stroll down a trail from the parking lot to the lodge buildings, and there are other trails on the property as well. This lodge is definitely for nature lovers who are used to roughing it: Accommodations are very basic, but meals are served. The lodge also runs several different hiking and horseback trips into the rain forest and the adjacent Bribri Indian Kékoldi Reserve. Trips range from one day of horseback riding to three days of hiking. If you're interested in the longer hiking trip, be sure to make reservations at least two months in advance since they make this trip only four times between March and October.

CABINAS JACARANDA, Cahuita. No phone. 5 rms., 1 with bath.
$ Rates: ¢500 ($5.88) single; ¢1,000 ($11.76) double; ¢1,500 ($17.65) triple; ¢2,000 ($23.53) quad. No credit cards.

Ⓢ This basic backpackers' special has a few nice touches that set it apart from the others. The floors are cement, but there are mats, with Japanese paper lanterns covering the lights and mosquito nets hanging over the beds. Since the Coral Restaurant moved down the street, the Jacaranda has been adding more rooms.

DOUBLES FOR LESS THAN ¢2,000 [$23.53]

CABINAS PLAYA NEGRA, Puerto Viejo, Limón. Tel. 506/56-1132 or 56-6396. 5 rms., none with bath.
$ Rates: ¢2,000 ($23.53) 1–4 people. No credit cards.
These colorfully painted two-story buildings, on a side road as you come into Puerto Viejo, have a very Caribbean flavor. Each duplex shares one bathroom; the rooms are large and sunny. Screened porches with rocking chairs are a pleasant place to spend an afternoon if it isn't too hot, which it often is in the hot season. The beach is about 200 yards down a narrow dirt road.

WORTH THE EXTRA BUCKS

EL PIZOTE, Puerto Viejo, Talamanca. Tel. 506/22-4547. Fax 506/21-3011. 8 rms without bath, 6 bungalows.
$ Rates: ¢1,700 ($20) single without bath, ¢4,250 ($50) single with bath; ¢2,550 ($30) double without bath, ¢4,250 ($50) double with bath; ¢3,400 ($40) triple without bath, ¢5,100 ($60) triple with bath; ¢3,825 ($45) quad without bath, ¢5,525 ($65) quad with bath. No credit cards.

⭐ Although it bills itself as a surf resort, this comfortably rustic little resort would be ideal for anyone who simply wants to get away from it all. Located about a half mile outside of town, El Pizote is set back from the black-sand beach that runs beside the dirt road into town. The name El Pizote is Spanish for "coatimundi," a raccoonlike creature that is common in Costa Rica. They even have a few in a cage near the restaurant.

The rooms are in two beautiful, unpainted wooden buildings that are completely hidden from the road or even from the parking lot. You have to walk through a dense grove of dracaena plants, which you might recognize as a common houseplant. The rooms are cool—with polished wood walls, double beds, and absolutely beautiful bathrooms that have wood slat floors in the showers and huge screen windows looking out on dense jungle. There are unusual burlap-and-bamboo window shades, ceiling fans, and reading lamps. You'll feel like a tropical planter when you check in here. For activity, there are hiking trails into the forest, the beach, and the volleyball court.

The restaurant serves breakfast ($6) and dinner ($11), but drinks are available all day. There is a set menu each evening, which might be lobster with broccoli or an equally delectable fish plate.

WHERE TO EAT

SODA TAMARA, one block from the end of the road into town, no phone. **$ Prices:** ¢175–¢325 ($2.06–$3.82). No credit cards.
Open: Wed–Mon 6:30am–9:30pm.

This little Tico-style restaurant has become a popular spot with budget-conscious travelers and has begun upgrading its image to appeal further to tourists. There is now a small patio dining area in addition to the dark dining room. The white picket fence in front gives the restaurant a very homey feel. At the counter inside, you'll find homemade cocoa candies and unsweetened cocoa biscuits. These are made by several ladies in town, but unfortunately, for several years, the cocoa trees in this area have been dying from some type of blight.

SNACKS

To really sample the local cuisine, you need to look up a few local ladies. Ask around for Miss Dolly and see if she has anything cooking. Her specialties are bread (especially banana) and ginger biscuits, but she will also fix a special Caribbean meal for you if you ask a day in advance and she has time. Miss Sam makes pineapple rolls, plantain tarts, and bread. Miss Daisy makes pan bon, ginger cakes, paties (meat-filled turnovers), and coconut oil (for tanning). Julia and Mateo bake whole-wheat bread. Just ask around for these folks and someone will direct you to them.

SHOPPING

Souvenirs Denise, across the street from Soda Tamara, sells hand-painted T-shirts and coconut shell jewelry. There are also a couple of *pulperías* (general stores) in the village.

EXCURSIONS

The most interesting excursion from Puerto Viejo is a horseback trip to the nearby **Kékoldi Indian Reservation** (tel. 58-3844). These trips are led by Mauricio Salazar, who also runs Cabinas Chimuri. On these one-day trips, you ride through virgin forest where you are likely to see dozens of species of birds and perhaps a sloth or two or some monkeys. Keep a watch out for the magnificent keel-billed toucans that frequent this region. Mauricio will tell you about the customs of the Bribri and Cabécár people who inhabit the reservation. Although the native peoples have adopted western dress, they still maintain their religious beliefs and closeness to nature. The trips cost about ¢1,800 ($21.18) for a day of riding. If you are interested in heading deeper into the forest, longer trips also can be arranged.

You should be able to arrange for someone in town to take you out fishing or snorkeling for a reasonable price.

If you continue south on the coast road from Puerto Viejo, you will come to a couple of even smaller villages. **Punta Uva** is 5 miles away, and **Manzanillo** is just over 9 miles away. There is the trail along the beach from Barra Cocles to Manzanillo, a distance of about 6 miles. Another enjoyable hike is from Monkey Point to Manzanillo (about 3½ miles). There is a reef offshore from Manzanillo that is good for snorkeling. In Manzanillo, ask for Willie Burton, who rents snorkeling equipment and will take you out in his boat to different locations.

Still farther south is the **Manzanillo-Gandoca Wildlife Refuge,** which extends all the way to the Panamanian border. Within the boundaries of the reserve live manatees and crocodiles and more than 350 species of birds. The reserve also includes the coral reef offshore. On one 5½-mile-long beach within the reserve, four species of sea turtles nest from March to July.

PART TWO

GUATEMALA

CHAPTER 7

GETTING TO KNOW GUATEMALA

1. **GEOGRAPHY, HISTORY, AND POLITICS**
- **DATELINE**
- **WHAT'S SPECIAL ABOUT GUATEMALA**
2. **ART, ARCHITECTURE, AND LITERATURE**
- **DID YOU KNOW . . . ?**
3. **RELIGION, MYTHS, AND FOLKLORE**
4. **CULTURAL AND SOCIAL LIFE**
5. **PERFORMING ARTS AND EVENING ENTERTAINMENT**
6. **SPORTS AND RECREATION**
7. **FOOD AND DRINK**
8. **RECOMMENDED BOOKS**

Guatemala: The very name seems exotic as it rolls off the tongue. Even though it is possible to drive there by way of Mexico, Guatemala seems worlds away. The name conjures up images of lost cities in the steamy jungle and colorfully clothed Mayan Indians. These are here, yes, but there is more. Guatemala is also a country rich in Spanish history, the history of the Conquest. Colonial architecture—with its arches, porticos, stucco walls, and cobblestone streets—has been preserved in the city of Antigua, once the capital of all Central America. Ruins of churches, monasteries, and universities have become parks, giving the late 20th century a glimpse of the greatness of Central America in earlier times.

With nearly 50% of the population claiming Indian ancestry and clinging to ancient customs and costumes, Guatemala is culturally fascinating. Spanish is the official language, but ancient Indian languages such as Quiché and Mam are still spoken in the highlands. Primitive rituals and masked dances are the last vestiges of the once-great Mayan culture.

Guatemala has been called "the land of eternal spring" because of the nearly perfect weather that the highlands enjoy throughout the year. It was this gentle climate that first attracted Spanish settlers, and today it is this same climate (and the stunning setting) that attracts tourists from all over the world to Lake Atitlán, which is encircled by volcanoes and which many people claim is the most beautiful lake in the world.

Why, then, has Guatemala not become overrun with tourists? Politics. Central America in the last 20 years became a terra incognita for citizens of the United States. Nicaragua and El Salvador have given the entire region a bad name. Civil wars, revolutions, death squads, and communist guerrillas throughout the narrow strip of land connecting North and South America made the headlines and stopped the once-growing flow of tourists to the region. Guatemala, suffering plenty of its own internal strife, became one of those places that only soldiers of fortune and journalists wanted to visit.

But things have changed in Guatemala, and things remain the same. Ancient cultures that have their roots in the mysterious Mayan civilization of more than 1,000 years ago survive, although these Indian peoples continue to struggle for land reform and a better standard of living. There is still occasional guerrilla activity in remote regions of Guatemala, but these are generally far from anyplace to which a tourist would likely venture. Every year, more tourists discover the ancient Mayan ceremonial center of Tikal; Antigua, once the capital of Central America; the stunning vistas of Lake Atitlán; and the fascinating Indian cultures and crafts of the Guatemalan highlands. From the jungled plains of El Petén to the volcanoes of the Sierra Madre, Guatemala offers a diversity of natural and artificial beauty unrivaled anywhere in Central America.

1. GEOGRAPHY, HISTORY, AND POLITICS

GEOGRAPHY

Guatemala is the northernmost country of Central America, bordered on the north and west by Mexico; on the south by the Pacific Ocean, El Salvador, and Honduras; and on the east by the Caribbean Sea and Belize. Covering 42,000 square miles, Guatemala is roughly the size of the state of Tennessee. Stretching from northwest to southeast are several volcanic mountain ranges that form the backbone of the country.

THE REGIONS

To the south of the mountains lies the Costa Sur, the South Coast, a narrow strip of plains. To the northeast is El Petén, a vast, high, jungle-covered rolling plain. This is the most remote and least developed region of Guatemala and was at one time the heart of the Mayan culture.

DATELINE

- **200 B.C.** Earliest record of inhabitants at Mayan city of Tikal.
- **A.D. 600–A.D. 900** Mayan civilization reaches its zenith.
- **1523** Pedro de Alvarado, under command from Hernán Cortés, marches into Guatemala with an army of Spanish and Indian troops.
- **1524** Iximché becomes the first Spanish capital of Guatemala and renamed Santiago (St. James).
- **1527** The capital is moved to the Valley of Almolonga at the *(continues)*

HISTORY

The earliest Mayan culture dates back to the Formative Period (in Mesoamerican civilizations) from 300 B.C. to A.D. 100, but it did not fully flower until the Classic Period (A.D. 200 to 925). By A.D. 600 the Mayas were the most important culture in Mesoamerica. The advanced culture of Teotihuacan was declining, while the Mayas were rising intellectually and artistically to a height never before reached by the natives of the New World. In Guatemala and the Yucatan peninsula, the Mayas built magnificent ceremonial centers; carved intricate hieroglyphic stelae; and developed superior astronomical, calendrical, and mathematical systems.

Then in the Late Classic Period, around A.D. 790, the Mayan civilization began to decline. Over the next 40 to 100 years, one village after another was abandoned, until by the end of the 9th century, the last chapter of this brilliant civilization was closed. Why? No one is certain. Was it the population explosion? The misuse of land? The northern barbarians who were roaming Mesoamerica? Whatever the reason, the Postclassic Period, from A.D. 900 up to the Spanish Conquest, shows the loss of splendor and the beginning of a polity of class systems (priests, merchants, and serfs), government regulation and taxation, trade guilds, and a primitive but productive agriculture.

In 1519 Hernan Cortes conquered Mexico, and in 1523 he sent his chief lieutenant, Pedro de Alvarado, to explore the region of Guatemala. Alvarado led an expedition

WHAT'S SPECIAL ABOUT GUATEMALA

Great Towns/Villages

- ☐ Antigua, one of Guatemala's colonial capitals, with beautiful architecture, atmosphere, and many ruins
- ☐ Chichicastenango, famous for great shopping and rituals performed by local Indians

Mayan Ruins

- ☐ Tikal, the largest Mayan city yet excavated
- ☐ Copán (actually in Honduras), nearly as impressive as Tikal
- ☐ Quiriguá, known for its intricately carved stelae (record-keeping stones)

Natural Spectacles

- ☐ Lake Atitlán, said to be the most beautiful lake in the world
- ☐ Volcanoes, live or dormant, that you can climb
- ☐ Semuc Champey cataracts and the quetzal preserve near Cobán

Museums

- ☐ The Museum of Archeology and Ethnology in Guatemala City, Central America's finest collection of pre-Columbian artifacts
- ☐ The Ixchell Museum in Guatemala City, dedicated to the indigenous clothing of Guatemala
- ☐ The Popol Vuh Museum in Guatemala City, small but contains many beautiful terra-cotta artifacts

Events/Festivals

- ☐ Holy Week (the week before Easter) in Antigua, celebrated with daily processions through the streets
- ☐ Ancient Indian dances performed in towns and cities around the country

Religious Shrines

- ☐ The basilica in Esquipulas, with a statue of Christ that is the object of a massive pilgrimage every year
- ☐ The Church of San Francisco, with the remains of Hermano Pedro, who is said to heal the sick

Architectural Highlights

- ☐ Ruins of colonial churches, monasteries, convents, universities, and government buildings all over the town of Antigua

Shopping

- ☐ The Chichicastenango market on Sunday and Thursday, flooded with vendors selling beautiful Guatemalan textiles at the best prices in the country
- ☐ Panajachel's Calle Santander, lined on both sides with vendors selling "gringo" fashions in Guatemalan fabric

---

against the Quiché people (then the most powerful and wealthy tribe in Guatemala). In the words of a 16th-century Spanish historian, Alvarado was "reckless, merciless and impetuous, lacking in veracity if not common honesty, but zealous and courageous." It wasn't long before Alvarado had conquered the indigenous peoples and was named representative of the sovereign power of Spain. He set about establishing a typical Spanish colonial empire, founding cities and towns throughout Central America, and converting the Indians to Catholicism. But unlike Mexico, Central America did not yield vast amounts of gold and silver for the conquerors and was thus somewhat of a disappointment. Many of the Spaniards stayed on, however,

DATELINE

foot of Agua Volcano and given the name of Santiago.

- **1541** Pedro de Alvarado dies from injuries sustained when a horse falls on him. His second wife, Doña Beatriz, proclaims herself Captain General,

(continues)

DATELINE

becoming the first woman head of a government in the Americas. The second Santiago (today's Ciudad Viejo) is destroyed by a flood.

- **1542** The capital is moved to the site of present-day Antigua.
- **1696** Tikal is discovered by a Franciscan friar seeking to convert Indians to Christianity.
- **1773** Antigua is destroyed by a series of earthquakes.
- **1775** The capital is moved again, this time to the Valley of Ermita (the hermitage), site of today's Guatemala City.
- **1821** Guatemala, along with the rest of Central America, gains independence from Spain.
- **1847** Guatemala becomes an independent nation separate from the other Central American nations.
- **1870s** Coffee becomes the main export of Guatemala.
- **1944** Period known as "10 years of spring" begins, and the country experiences fair elections and peace.
- **1952** Land re-
(continues)

to carve out large coffee plantations using the Indians as laborers.

Early in the 19th century, Guatemalan and other Central American leaders followed the lead of other Latin American states and declared their independence from Spain. The captain-general of Guatemala became the chief executive. But in Mexico the empire of Agustín Iturbide had been formed, and conservative Guatemalan leaders voted for annexation to the empire. This political arrangement didn't last. A republican Federation of Central American States was formed in 1823. The federation lasted some 15 years but was continually torn by internecine battles, both political and military. By 1840 Central America had taken the political form it has today, and political struggles were confined to the large towns. As a result, except for Guatemala City and the provincial capitals, "progress" is a stranger to much of the country, leaving it untouched and incredibly beautiful.

POLITICS

Throughout its history, Guatemala has been subjected to tumultuous political upheavals. Even before the Spanish Conquest, the various Indian tribes of the highlands had been constantly at war. When Pedro de Alvarado marched into the country with his armies, he utilized these feuds to his advantage, playing one tribe against the other and eventually conquering the entire country. During the colonial period, priests from various Catholic sects were busy converting (and virtually enslaving) the Indian population that remained after the wars and European diseases had taken their toll (between 75 and 90% of the native population was lost after the Conquest). The Church and the wealthy Spanish landowners thus had a ready, if unwilling, workforce at their command. They used this conscripted workforce to make themselves wealthy.

Pure Spanish blood is rare in Guatemala today, but the Ladino population, which is descended from marriages of Indians and Spaniards, are firmly in control of the government. Those of Indian ancestry (generally defined as anyone who wears traditional attire and farms on subsistence plots) have almost no power. Although Guatemala is ostensibly a democracy (with elections held every four years), the military wields a great deal of power. Throughout the past 100 years, the military has often taken control of government, suspending the constitution as necessary to maintain its power. There is a great disparity between the rich and the poor. Wealthy landowners own nearly all of the land in the country, with peasants forced to farm small plots on the least productive land. This disparity has led to constant conflicts for nearly 200 years as the liberal parties have tried to wrest power from the wealthy and the Church.

Today there is still guerrilla activity throughout much of Guatemala, but on a relatively small scale. The guerrillas, primarily poor, rural Indians from the highlands, continue to demand land reform.

2. ART, ARCHITECTURE, AND LITERATURE

ART

The Mayas, who reached a cultural peak around A.D. 600, have left an amazing legacy of intricately beautiful works of art. Stone carvings, pottery, and gold and jade jewelry give us some idea of the high level of artistic ability reached by this ancient culture. The stylized figures depicted on many works of Mayan art are actually historical records. Through these images, archeologists have been able to deduce a great deal about Mayan culture. The Museum of Archeology and Ethnology in Guatemala City has the most outstanding collection of pre-Columbian art in all of Central America, and the Popul Vuh Museum, also in Guatemala City, has a smaller but equally interesting collection.

DATELINE

form policies cause United Fruit Company, a foreign-owned company and the largest landowner in Guatemala, to lose much of its land.

• **1954** CIA-backed Guatemalan exiles invade Guatemala from Honduras and overthrow government.

• **1950s–Present** Scattered guerrilla activity continues.

ARCHITECTURE

As long ago as 2000 B.C., the Mayas were building at Tikal, an ancient religious center in the remote Petén region of Guatemala. Today the hundreds of pyramids, temples, and palaces that have been excavated make this one of the great archeological finds of the New World. Using limestone, the Mayas at Tikal erected one pyramid after another, often building directly on top of previously existing structures. Many of these buildings incorporated what has come to be known as the Mayan, or corbelled, arch. Although not a true arch (a keystone is not used), the Mayan arch allowed ancient architects to build structures entirely of stone, structures that have withstood the ravages of time and today are a testament to the architectural skills of Mesoamerica's greatest civilization. In 1979, Tikal was declared a "World Cultural and Natural Monument" by UNESCO.

With the Spanish Conquest came an entirely new form of architecture: Moorish influences, interpreted by Spanish architects, were incorporated into the many colonial cities erected by the Spanish throughout Guatemala. Unfortunately, Guatemala is a land of volcanic activity and is subject to earthquakes of devastating magnitude, so much of the country's colonial architecture has been destroyed over the years. However, the city of Antigua, once the capital of all Central America, was destroyed several times by earthquakes and floods, but still it preserves its colonial heritage. It was named a "Heritage of Humanity" by UNESCO in 1979. At one time, the city was the grandest in all the Americas, but after the devastating earthquake of 1773, many of the most grandiose churches, universities, and convents were destroyed. Today the ruins of these buildings have been turned into parks and museums, giving Antigua much of its charm. Regulations prohibiting obtrusive signs and advertising help the city retain its 17th-century atmosphere. There are literally dozens of colonial and colonial-style buildings of architectural interest here.

Guatemala City, on the other hand, has few historical buildings. It was to this location that the capital was moved, after Antigua was destroyed, in the mistaken belief that the new city would be safe from natural disasters. Over the years, the city's colonial buildings were destroyed by earthquakes. Guatemala City's most architectur-

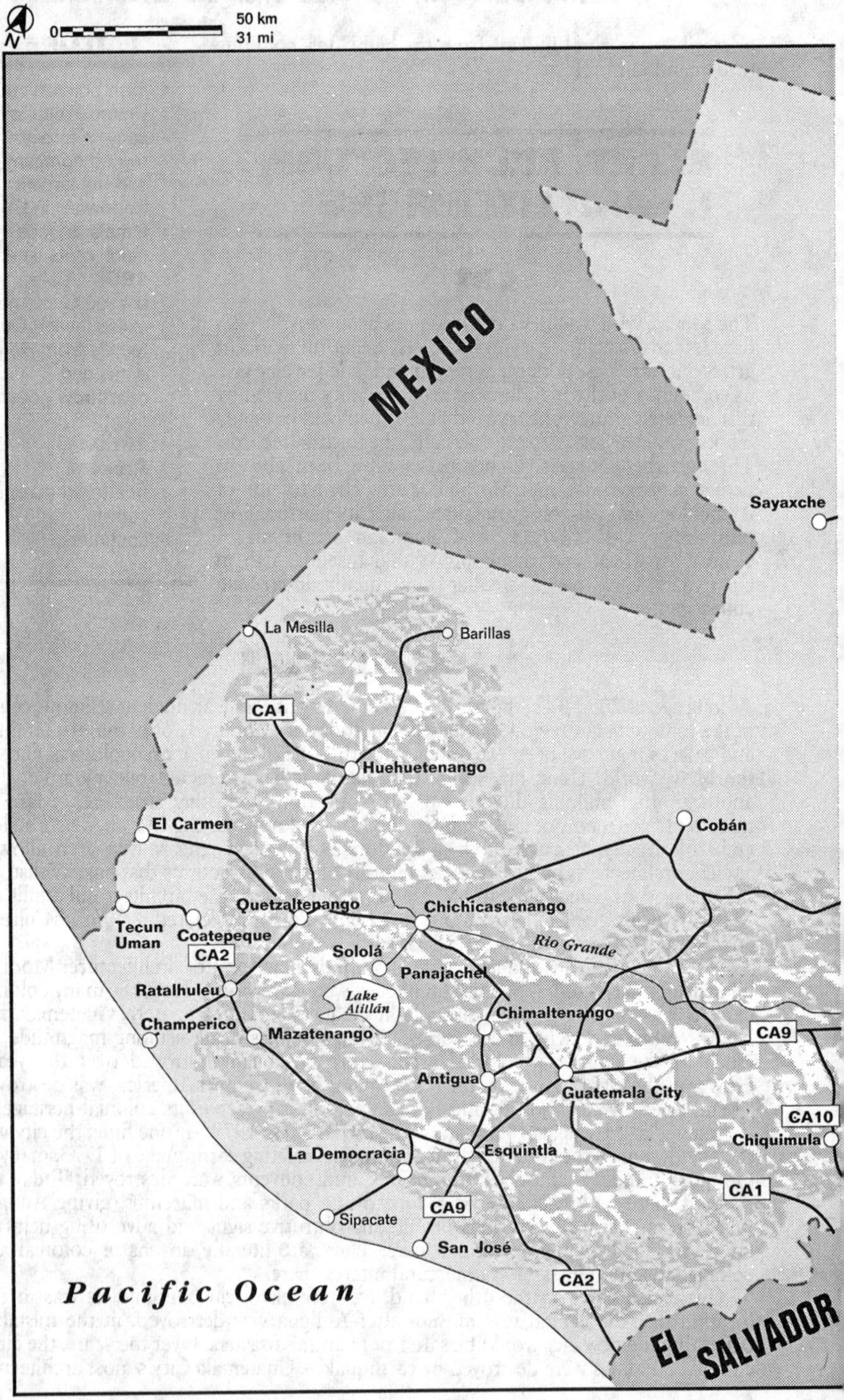

N
0
50 km
31 mi
MEXICO
Sayaxche
La Mesilla
Barillas
CA1
Huehuetenango
El Carmen
Cobán
Quetzaltenango
Chichicastenango
Tecun
Uman
Coatepeque
Rio Grande
CA2
Sololá
Panajachel
Ratalhuleu
Lake
Atitlán
Chimaltenango
Champerico
Mazatenango
CA9
Antigua
Guatemala City
CA10
Chiquimula
La Democracia
Esquintla
CA1
CA9
Sipacate
San José
Pacific Ocean
CA2
EL SALVADOR

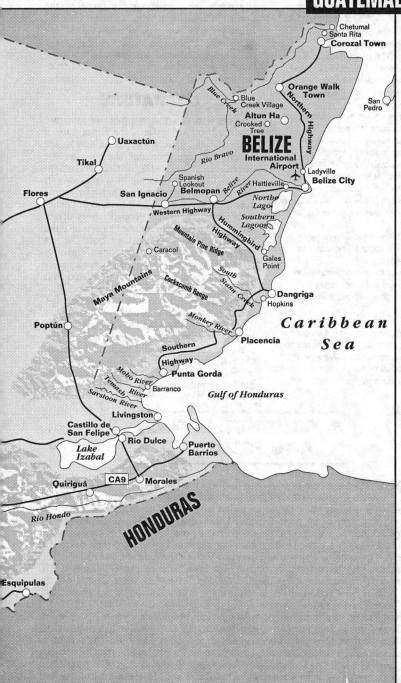

GUATEMALA

❓ DID YOU KNOW . . . ?

- Tikal is the largest excavated Mayan ruin.
- Nearly 50% of the Guatemalan population is Indian, descended from the ancient Mayas.
- Antigua was once the capital of all of Central America.
- There is a town on the Caribbean Coast where the people are predominantly black, with English as their mother tongue.
- The quetzal, described as the most beautiful bird in the world, is the national bird of Guatemala.
- Manatees live in the Río Dulce, a river that drains into the Caribbean Sea.
- The United Fruit Company was once the largest landholder in Guatemala.
- The Indians of the Guatemalan highlands still practice rituals passed down from the ancient Mayas.
- Lake Atitlán was formed by the crater of a giant extinct volcano.
- Guatemala City is the fourth capital of Guatemala; the others were destroyed by earthquakes, volcanic eruptions, and floods.

ally noteworthy buildings are those of the Centro Cívico and the Centro Cultural Miguel Angel Asturias, constructed in the 1950s and 1960s. The façades of the former buildings are covered with murals, while the latter is designed to resemble the superstructure of a luxury cruise ship.

LITERATURE

The single most significant piece of literature produced in Guatemala is the *Popol Vuh*, a history of the Quiché people written in the Mayan language sometime shortly after the Conquest. Although the original accordian-pleated codex is housed in a museum in Dresden, Germany, there is a beautiful reproduction in the Popol Vuh Museum in Guatemala City. It is an exact copy in every detail, down to the type of tree used to produce the paper. The book consists of both Mayan glyphs and small, colorful paintings. The original was discovered in the early 18th century in Chichicastenango and was translated into Spanish. Numerous editions of the Popol Vuh are now available in both Spanish and English and offer fascinating reading.

Nobel laureate Miguel Angel Asturias is known and loved for his novels and translations into Spanish of ancient Indian legends. Otto René Castillo is a revolutionary poet whose works are unavailable in Guatemala but are popular outside the country.

3. RELIGION, MYTHS, AND FOLKLORE

The melding of ancient Mayan traditions and religious beliefs with Roman Catholicism has created a singular form of Catholicism that is filled with obscure rituals and the worship of Mayan gods thinly disguised as saints. The Mayan religion was pantheistic, and many of the gods demanded human sacrifices. When Spanish priests arrived preaching the worship of yet another god, the Mayas of Guatemala were amenable and readily accepted Catholicism but continued to worship their old gods. Over the years, the old gods became associated with Catholic saints, and today every village and town has its patron saint, whose feast day is cause for great celebration. An important part of many fiestas is masked dancing. Several of these dances depict historical events. See "Performing Arts and Evening Entertainment" in this chapter for more information on masked dances.

In several towns in the highlands, a strange cult holds sway over the people. In these villages, the Indians turn to a god known as Maximón, or San Simón, for intervention in their lives. Maximón, although he looks like little more than a mannequin wearing a hat, is a very real god to these people, and he may be derived from the ancient Mayan god Mam. The people come to him to solve their problems, to protect them, to find them a wife or husband, and to bring them wealth. It is the way in which they worship Maximón that is the strangest: Cigar smoke is blown into his face, and liquor is poured into the mouth of the mask that serves as his face. There are Maximóns in Santiago Atitlán and Zunil, among other places. Should you go looking for Maximón, be sure to bring a gift—money is probably the safest offering.

Guatemalans as a rule are extremely devout, and nowhere is this devotion to the Catholic Church more evident than in Antigua during Semana Santa (Holy Week), the week prior to Easter Sunday. During this week, solemn processions march through the streets of the city. Intricate "carpets" made of colored sawdust, flowers, and pine needles are constructed in the streets, only to be trampled by men and women who march through the city carrying massive wooden floats atop which stand sculptures of Christ, the Virgin Mary, and various saints. Men dressed as Roman soldiers and mourners in black or purple robes commemorate the death and resurrection of Christ amid clouds of incense and doleful music played by marching bands. The pageantry of these processions is unsurpassed anywhere in Latin America, and the devout march through the streets from morning until late at night. Even though the processions in Antigua are the largest and draw immense crowds of spectators, nearly every town and village in Guatemala has similar processions during Holy Week.

4. CULTURAL AND SOCIAL LIFE

Guatemalan cultural life is decidedly stratified. The population of the country is almost evenly divided between the indigenous peoples (Indians) and the *ladinos* (those who can trace their ancestry to Spain). However, these are becoming very loose terms. Today an Indian who moves to the city and gives up his or her traditional dress in favor of North American or European fashions becomes a ladino; an Indian who becomes wealthy and gives up farming also may be labeled a ladino, as may any Indian who is educated. The term *indigeno* has come to refer almost exclusively to the poor peasants who cling to their traditional ways and still farm the rugged mountains of the Guatemalan highlands.

Down on the Caribbean Coast is yet a third culture, that of the English-speaking blacks who migrated from Jamaica in the 18th century. These people have nothing in common with the rest of Guatemala's population and maintain their isolation in the small town of Lívingston, which can be reached only by boat. Here in Lívingston, the sound of the marimba band, which is ubiquitous in the rest of the country, is replaced by reggae music from the Caribbean islands and, increasingly, by rap music from the United States.

5. PERFORMING ARTS AND EVENING ENTERTAINMENT

The sound of the marimba, a large wooden xylophone played with rubber mallets, permeates Guatemala just as mariachi music does in Mexico. The instrument is often so large that it takes several people to play it. The rhythms that are produced are complex and hypnotic. You'll find marimba bands performing at nearly all celebrations, in restaurants, and on the radio (there are all-marimba radio stations).

Celebrations in Guatemala often include masked dances that have their basis in ancient Mayan customs. The most popular dance is the dance of the conquistadors, in which dancers dressed as Pedro de Alvarado and Tecún Umán symbolically re-enact the battle that brought about the downfall of the Quiché people and the eventual conquest of Guatemala. By far the most famous "dance," if it can be called that, is the *palo volador* (the flying pole). In this breathtaking acrobatic display, two men climb to the top of a 60-foot pole, attach ropes to their ankles, and "fly" to the ground as the rope unwinds from the top of the pole. This ancient ritual is staged several times a year in different parts of the country, including Guatemala City and Chichicastenango.

Evening entertainment in Guatemala is pretty much restricted to going to the movies (U.S. movies dubbed in Spanish), hanging out in bars (a male-dominated activity), and going to discos (mostly in the capital only).

6. SPORTS AND RECREATION

The national sport of Guatemala is soccer (here known as *futbol*). In 1990 the national team even made it to the World Cup playoffs in Italy, an event that caused much talk and elicited great pride from the team's fans. Bicycle racing is also a very popular sport, and cyclists are frequently seen, especially on Sunday, puffing up the hill on the highway between Guatemala City and Antigua. Keep an eye out for cyclists when driving, especially if you are still on the road after dark, because some races go far into the night, and the roads are not lit.

One favorite recreational activity among Guatemalans and tourists alike is volcano climbing. There are several volcanoes in the country that can easily be climbed in a day, and the views from the tops of these peaks can be spectacular if the weather is clear. Perhaps the most popular climb is up Pacaya Volcano, near Lake Amatitlán. It is possible to climb within about 100 yards of the cone of this active volcano (on a separate cone) and watch it erupt every few minutes.

7. FOOD AND DRINK

FOOD
MEALS AND DINING CUSTOMS
The Cuisine

Traditional Guatemalan cuisine is very similar to Mexican food in many ways. The staples are beans (here they are black beans) and corn in the form of tortillas. To this are added rice and perhaps a bit of stewed chicken. Such meals are not often found in restaurants, except in the simplest of *comedores* (basic food stalls most often found in or near markets). Restaurants throughout Guatemala lean heavily toward international food—with everything from chow mein to spaghetti showing up at nearly every meal.

There are a few exceptions to the generally lackluster Guatemalan cuisine. In El Petén, wild game, including venison and turkey, is readily available. Because the country has two coasts, it is not surprising that throughout Guatemala, seafood is readily available, good, and inexpensive. However, I suggest that you stay clear of any freshwater fish, which tend to have a muddy flavor and may come from very polluted rivers and lakes.

Pepian is the de facto national dish of Guatemala. It is a thick, often grainy, stew made with chicken, vegetables, and toasted pumpkin seeds. *Cak ik* is a specialty of Cobán, a stew made with turkey or chicken, plantains (similar to bananas), and vegetables.

DRINKS
WATER AND SOFT DRINKS

Tap water in Guatemala is generally not safe to drink unless you treat it yourself. Hotels and restaurants often have large bottles of purified water on hand, from which they fill pitchers for their guests. If you have doubts about the water, it is best to avoid it. Tikal is one place where the water is notorious for making people sick. Bottled water, although relatively expensive, is readily available throughout the country, as is *agua mineral,* which is club soda. All major brands of soft drinks also are available. However, while in Guatemala you should take advantage of the delicious fresh juices and *licuados* (fruit juice blended with ice and water or milk), which are wonderful and very cheap. You can get a tall glass of fresh-squeezed orange juice for 25¢ in some places. Some of my favorite licuados are those made with milk and papaya or mango. It is usually a good idea to get your licuado with milk and no ice to avoid consuming the water.

BEER, WINE, AND LIQUOR

Several brands of locally brewed beer are available at very reasonable prices throughout Guatemala. Virtually all the wines are imported and consequently are expensive; those imported from South America are the cheapest and often are quite good. All types of hard liquor are manufactured in Guatemala, with rum being the most popular.

8. RECOMMENDED BOOKS

The *Popol Vuh* (Simon & Schuster, 1986) is one of the only records we have of Mayan life before the Conquest. It provides fascinating insights into the history, culture, and religion of these pre-Columbian people.

If you can find any English translations, or if you read Spanish, the novels and Indian legends translated into Spanish by Miguel Angel Asturias offer insight into Guatemalan life. Asturias won the Nobel Prize for Literature in 1967.

To learn more about the history of Central America, try *A Brief History of Central America* (University of California Press, 1989) by Hector Perez-Brignali, who is himself a Central American. If you want to gain a better understanding of the plight of Guatemalan Indians, *A Cry from the Heart* (Health Institutes Press, 1990) by V. David Schwantes will certainly enlighten you.

CHAPTER 8

PLANNING A TRIP TO GUATEMALA

1. **INFORMATION, ENTRY REQUIREMENTS, AND MONEY**

2. **WHEN TO GO—CLIMATE, EVENTS, AND HOLIDAYS**

- **WHAT THINGS COST IN GUATEMALA CITY**

- **GUATEMALA CALENDAR OF EVENTS**

3. **HEALTH, INSURANCE, AND OTHER CONCERNS**

4. **WHAT TO PACK**

5. **TIPS FOR THE DISABLED, SENIORS, SINGLES, AND STUDENTS**

6. **ALTERNATIVE/ ADVENTURE TRAVEL**

7. **GETTING THERE**

8. **SUGGESTED ITINERARIES**

- **FROMMER'S FAVORITE GUATEMALA EXPERIENCES**

9. **GETTING AROUND**

10. **WHERE TO STAY**

11. **WHERE TO EAT**

12. **ENJOYING GUATEMALA ON A BUDGET**

- **FAST FACTS— GUATEMALA**

Once that you have decided to visit Guatemala, you'll be likely to have a lot of questions: How much is it going to cost? When should I go? Where in Guatemala should I plan to go? How do I get there? How do I get around once I get there? Will I be able to communicate with people there? These are some of the many questions that this chapter will answer for you. In addition, you'll find information on health precautions that you should take before and during your visit, saving money on flights to Guatemala, studying Spanish in Guatemala, arranging alternative vacations, and finding more information before you leave home and after you arrive. In short, you'll find all the information that you'll need to make your visit as easy and enjoyable as you dreamed it would be.

1. INFORMATION, ENTRY REQUIREMENTS, AND MONEY

SOURCES OF INFORMATION

For information on Guatemala before you leave home, you can contact the **Guatemalan Tourist Commission,** P.O. Box 144351, Coral Gables, FL 33114-4351 (tel. 305/854-1544; Fax 305/854-4589). Within Guatemala, you will find **INGUAT** (Guatemalan Tourist Commission) offices or desks in Guatemala City (downtown and at the airport), Antigua, El Petén (Santa Elena Airport), Panajachel, and Quetzaltenango. See the appropriate chapters for details.

ENTRY REQUIREMENTS

To enter Guatemala, you will need a passport and either a visa or a Tourist Card, which is available on entering the country; a visa must be arranged at a Guatemalan embassy or consulate. The Tourist Card costs $5, and the visa costs $10. Both are issued for 30 days, so the Tourist Card, if you can use one, is the better deal. However, even if you don't need a visa but plan to cross into Guatemala at the La Mesilla–El Carmen border crossing, you should get one. The border officials here have been known to refuse Tourist Cards to people.

British, Canadian, Irish, and Australian citizens *must* have a Guatemalan visa, available at any Guatemalan consulate. Visas cost $10, and you'll need to submit a passport photograph along with your application. Be sure that you have yours when you hit the border.

MONEY
CASH CURRENCY

The unit of currency in Guatemala is the quetzal (Q). It's named after Guatemala's national symbol, the freedom-loving quetzal bird, which was revered by the ancient Mayas. One quetzal is divided into 100 centavos. There are 1-, 5-, 10-, and 25-centavo coins and bills in denominations of 50 centavos and 1, 5, 10, 20, 50, and 100 quetzals. At this writing, $1 U.S. will buy you Q4, so each quetzal is worth about 25¢, and one centavo is worth less than a quarter of a penny.

American dollars can be exchanged for Guatemalan quetzals ("quetzal*es*" in Spanish) easily and legally in many shops, hotels, and restaurants, as well as at banks. If a bank isn't open, ask at a shop. Sometimes shops give a better exchange rate than the banks, sometimes not. You will get better rates of exchange the closer you are to Guatemala City. Ask around. The dollar-to-quetzal exchange rate began climbing late in 1989 and has been variable since, although from one week to the next there are only slight changes. It is a good idea not to change too much at one time just in case the rate changes to your benefit.

If you need to exchange other foreign currency (Canadian dollars, German marks, English pounds, and so forth), you'll probably find it most convenient to exchange it at a bank. Banks are found nearly everywhere that you are likely to go, except at Tikal; if you are staying at one of the three Tikal hotels, you can change traveler's checks or dollars at the hotel.

By the way, in Guatemalan villages you may hear the Maya words *pisto* for money (quetzals) and *leng* for centavos.

It's good to have $25 or so in U.S. dollars of small denominations with you at all times for emergencies (most places will take them if you don't have the proper local currency).

CURRENCY EXCHANGE CHART

Q	$
1	.25
2	.50
3	.75
4	1.00
5	1.25
6	1.50
7	1.75
8	2.00
9	2.25
10	2.50
15	3.75
20	5.00
25	6.25
30	7.50
35	8.75
40	10.00
45	11.25
50	12.50
75	18.75
100	25.00
150	37.50
200	50.00

250	62.50
300	75.00
350	87.50
400	100.00
450	112.50
500	125.00
550	137.50
600	150.00
650	162.50
700	175.00
750	187.50
800	200.00
850	212.50
900	225.00
950	237.50
1,000	250.00
2,000	500.00
3,000	750.00
4,000	1,000.00

TRAVELER'S CHECKS

Traveler's checks drawn in U.S. dollars are only slightly more difficult to change than cash dollars. You can change them at banks, hotels, restaurants, and even shops all over Guatemala, although hotel rates are usually not very good. Even bank rates vary considerably, so it is a good idea to shop around. It can take quite a while to change traveler's checks at a bank, so go as early in the day as possible, when the lines are shorter.

WHAT THINGS COST IN GUATEMALA CITY	U.S. $
Taxi from the airport to the city center	6.25
Local telephone call	.03
Double at Westin Camino Real Hotel (deluxe)	120.00
Double at Hotel Pan American (moderate)	58.50
Double at Chalet Suizo (budget)	8.00
Lunch for one at Los Antojitos (moderate)	4.00
Lunch for one at Cafetería el Roble (budget)	2.00
Dinner for one, without wine at Estro Armonico (deluxe)	15.00
Dinner for one, without wine at El Gran Pavo (moderate)	10.00
Dinner for one, without wine at Restaurant Ruby (budget)	4.00
Bottle of beer	1.00
Coca-Cola	.25
Cup of coffee	.30
Roll of ASA 100 Kodacolor film, 36 exposures	6.00
Admission to the Popul Vuh Museum	.75
Movie ticket	.75
Theater ticket to the National Theater	2.50

CREDIT CARDS

The major international credit cards most widely accepted in Guatemala are MasterCard, VISA, Diners Club, and American Express. Very low-budget hotels and restaurants rarely accept credit cards, but moderate or expensive ones usually do. There are some exceptions. As in most places, it is very difficult to rent a car without a major credit card.

2. WHEN TO GO — CLIMATE, EVENTS, AND HOLIDAYS

CLIMATE

The conditions in Guatemala are similar to those in Mexico, with basically two seasons: The rainy season, from May to October, is called *invierno* (winter), and the dry season, from November to April, is called *verano* (summer). In the rainy season, it rains virtually every day, sometimes all day but sometimes only in the afternoon. It will also be chillier in the highlands and muggier in the lowlands during these months. During the dry season, the sun shines nearly every day, and there is almost never any rain. Days, even high in the mountains, are warm, but nights can be quite cold.

Average annual temperatures in Guatemala's highlands are 64° to 68°F; in Guatemala City, 68° to 72°F; in El Petén and along the Atlantic Highway, 77° to 86°F.

AVERAGE MONTHLY TEMPERATURES AND RAINFALL IN GUATEMALA CITY

Month	Temp. (°F)	Days of Rain
Jan	63	2
Feb	65	2
Mar	69	2
Apr	69	5
May	73	8
June	71	20
July	70	17
Aug	70	16
Sept	70	17
Oct	67	13
Nov	65	6
Dec	64	2

GUATEMALA CALENDAR OF EVENTS

MARCH OR APRIL *average temp. 65°F or 69°F, rainy days 2*

✪ *Semana Santa (Holy Week) processions.* Devout Roman Catholics, many dressed in robes, carry huge floats through the streets of the city. Streets are decorated with "carpets" made from flowers, colored sawdust, and pine needles.
Where: Antigua. *When:* The week leading up to Easter. *How:* Make hotel reservations months in advance and reconfirm often.

NOVEMBER average temp. 65°F, rainy days 6

☐ **All Saints' Day,** Santiago Sacatepequez. Giant kites are flown from the graveyard. November 1.
☐ **All Saints' Day,** Todos Santos Cuchamatán. Horse races and the dance of the Conquest. November 1.

HOLIDAYS

Official holidays in Guatemala include January 1, New Year's Day; Good Friday; May 1, May Day; June 30, Army Day; August 15, Assumption of the Virgin Mary; September 15, Independence Day; October 20, Revolution Day; November 1, All Saint's Day; December 25, Christmas; December 31, Last Year's Day

3. HEALTH, INSURANCE, AND OTHER CONCERNS

See Chapter 2, "Planning a Trip to Costa Rica," for information.

4. WHAT TO PACK

CLOTHING

Bring extra-warm clothes for the mountain towns, which can get quite cold at night at any time of year. Good walking shoes are an absolute necessity here, because even sidewalks in Guatemala City can be rough and uneven; in smaller towns, the streets are often cobblestone, which is hard on the feet no matter what kind of shoes you are wearing. Last, a good pair of walking shoes is essential to enjoying the Mayan ruins of Tikal. You want good traction when climbing steep pyramids. An umbrella in the rainy season is much more useful than a raincoat, which will cause you to sweat in the heat. You'll end up just as wet as if you hadn't worn the raincoat at all.

OTHER ITEMS

Plenty of insect repellent for the lowland towns will help keep mosquitoes off you at night—very important, since malaria is still found in many parts of Guatemala. Sunscreen for your nose is necessary if you plan to spend a lot of time outdoors in the mountains, where the sun is much stronger. I like to carry a little bottle of iodine and a water bottle so that I can sterilize tap water wherever I go. Although the water is supposedly safe to drink here, I prefer not to take chances, especially in remote areas.

A few other items that have proven invaluable through countless trips all over the world are a Swiss army knife, a collapsible umbrella (great for rain or to keep off the tropical sun), a small flashlight, and a travel alarm clock or a watch with an alarm. In addition, I always wear a watch with a tiny built-in calculator, which can cost as little as $30 and is great for making quick exchange-rate calculations.

5. TIPS FOR THE DISABLED, SENIORS, SINGLES, AND STUDENTS

For the Disabled Guatemala is not an easy country for the disabled to get around. The streets are often narrow, with broken or nonexistent sidewalks, and in some cases they are even of cobblestone. Public transit is overcrowded, so a private vehicle is an absolute necessity. Few if any hotels or public buildings are accessible to the handicapped. However, don't be put off if you have your heart set on visiting Guatemala. I once met a man in a wheelchair on the remote Río Dulce. He had hired a boat to take him from Lívingston on the coast to the old Spanish fort of San Felipe, three hours up river.

For Seniors   You won't find senior citizen discounts in Guatemala, but the prices are so low that they really aren't necessary.

For Singles   Though single travelers are discriminated against in hotel pricing just as they are in so many other places, if you are traveling on a budget, you will find that room rates are surprisingly low.

For Students   Students may want to look into studying Spanish for a while in Antigua or Quetzaltenango. The courses are quite inexpensive and you can save more by staying with a local family.

6. ALTERNATIVE/ADVENTURE TRAVEL

EDUCATIONAL/STUDY TRAVEL

Every year, thousands of people come to Guatemala from Europe and North America to study Spanish in Antigua. There are literally dozens of schools offering courses and one-on-one tutoring at very reasonable prices. Some people make Antigua their first stop in Latin America so that they can learn some Spanish before traveling on to other countries. Listed below are some of the better schools in Antigua. When choosing a Spanish school, you should make sure how many hours of study you will receive each day, whether this is one-on-one or group instruction, clarify whether you want to study grammar or conversation, take a look at the textbooks that will be used to see if they seem well written, and find out whether the price includes meals and accommodations with a local family. In addition to the schools listed below, there are others in Quetzaltenango and Huehuetenango, but Antigua is such a beautiful town that I strongly recommend you attend classes there.

   Proyecto Linguistico Francisco Marroquin, Apdo. 237, 4a Av. Sur No. 4, Antigua (tel. 320-406), is one of the oldest and most respected of the Spanish schools. It offers four-week intensive courses (six hours of study daily) for Q2000 ($500), which includes room and board. A $125 nonrefundable deposit is required, but this money is then applied toward your tuition. This is the only school in Antigua that is certified in Washington, D.C., to administer the Foreign Service Institute's examination for fluency in Spanish.

   Centro Linguistico Maya, 5a Calle Poniente No. 20, Antigua (tel. 320-656). Weekly rates, including room and board, start at Q340 ($85) for four hours of study five days a week.

   Centro Linguistico Antigua, 6a Av. Norte No. 25, Antigua (no phone). Weekly rates, including room and board, start at Q280 ($70) for four hours of study five days a week.

   Tecún Umán Linguistic School, 6a Calle Poniente No. 34, Apdo. 68, Antigua (no phone). Rates, including room and board, start at Q280 ($70) for four hours of study five days a week.

   Professional Spanish Language School, 7a Av. Norte No. 82, Antigua (tel. 320-161), is affiliated with the Shawcross Aid Programme for Highland Indians. Profits from the school go to this program, which is providing teachers, potable water systems, clothing, medicine, and food to Indians in remote villages. Its rates are competitive.

RIVER TRIPS

The ancient Mayas of El Petén had a far-flung empire that was connected by river routes, the old Mayan trade route, that cross El Petén and extend into Mexico. Trips on these rivers include days of river travel by outboard-powered boats through jungles, with stops at several remote Mayan ruins. **Tropical Tours,** 4a Calle 2-50 "A", Zona 10 (tel. 323-748, 345-893, or 345-894), offers eight-day rafting trips down the Usumacinta and La Pasión rivers. **Expedicion Panamundo,** 3a Av. 16-52, Zona 10 (tel. 681-315 or 683-010), offers a similar trip of nine days if there are enough people interested. The trip can be scheduled for as few as 5 people or as many as 15. The cost is around $1,000 per person, including all transfers within Guatemala.

---

7. GETTING THERE

BY PLANE

Guatemala is easily accessible by air from the United States, Canada, Mexico, Europe, and South America. The country now has two international airports, with most international flights arriving at La Aurora Airport in Guatemala City. It's served from New York by **Lacsa Costa Rican Airlines, Pan American,** and **Continental;** from Los Angeles by **Lacsa Costa Rican Airlines, TACA International,** and **Pan American;** from Mexico City and San José, Costa Rica, by **Mexicana** and **Lacsa;** from Miami by **Pan American, Aviateca,** and **TACA International;** from Houston by **Continental** and **TACA International;** from New Orleans by **Aviateca** and **TACA International;** and from Cancún, Mexico, by **Aeroquetzal.** Most other flights to Guatemala connect through one of these airports.

There are now daily flights between Belize City and Santa Elena, Petén. These flights are primarily meant to allow people vacationing in Belize to fly to Tikal without having to go to Guatemala City first. However, the flights continue on to Guatemala City. At no extra cost, you can stay several days in Flores and Tikal before continuing on to the capital.

BEST FOR THE BUDGET

Among the best values for fares and service is **Lacsa Costa Rican Airlines,** which comes as a surprise to many people. Although you may not know it, Lacsa is in fact Central America's major airline—with convenient flights; good cabin service; and a wide range of special fares, packages, and tours. San José, Costa Rica, is Lacsa's home base, but this airline has the distinction of flying the only nonstops between New York (JFK) and Guatemala City. Be sure to check with Lacsa for current schedules and fares (or ask your travel agent to do so) because they may end up saving you a good deal of time, money, and inconvenience.

Even though it can be inconvenient due to bad flight schedules, **Aeronica,** the Nicaraguan national airline, is by far the cheapest for flights from Guatemala City to Nicaragua, Costa Rica, and Panama. Special deals frequently are available through the airline's Antigua office.

BUCKET SHOPS

In my opinion, there is almost no reason to pay the regular full airfare for any international ticket. In nearly every major city in the United States and Britain, there are now discount ticket agencies known as bucket shops. These companies sell airline tickets on major carriers at a substantial discount over what you would pay the airline for the same ticket. In many cases, low-cost tickets that would be nonrefundable through an airline are refundable with a $100 penalty through a bucket shop. You'll find bucket shops advertising in major newspapers (which are often available at your local library, even if you live in a small town), ads that are usually just columns of destinations accompanied by prices. These ads often are misleading because the price listed may be available only to students and does not include taxes; but even when all the additional charges are included, you almost always save money at a bucket shop.

APEX FARES

At the time of writing, APEX fares, which are the lowest regular fares, but which have restrictions such as when you must fly and when you must pay for your ticket, range from $430 on Continental to $475 on Lacsa (from New York City).

REGULAR AIRFARES

Regular, full-price, airfares to Guatemala from New York City ranged from $491 in coach and $1,206 in first class on Continental to $611 for a coach seat on Lacsa (no first class) or Pan Am (first class on Pan Am is about the same).

BY BUS

There are three bus routes into Guatemala, two from Mexico, and one from Belize. Buses leave San Cristobal de las Casas, Mexico, for the border station at Ciudad Cuauhtemoc, in the mountains. After border formalities, passengers board a Guatemalan bus for the rest of the journey. This bus leaves the Guatemalan border station at La Mesilla and heads for Huehuetenango and Guatemala City. The bus from the border will drop you at transfer points for Chichicastenango or Quetzaltenango if you wish. Other buses go to Huehuetenango. Take your pick. If you are coming from Tapachula, Mexico, you can take a bus from the downtown bus station or catch a minibus to the border crossing at Talisman. As in La Mesilla, there will be buses waiting on the Guatemalan side of the border. These buses are bound for Guatemala City or the nearby town of Tecún Umán with a connection to Quetzaltenango if desired. From Belize, you can catch a bus bound for the border town of Benque Viejo, Belize, in either Belize City or San Ignacio. Depending on which bus you catch, you may be taken all the way to the border station or may be dropped at the bus station in Benque Viejo, in which case you will need to take a taxi (inexpensive) the rest of the way. This route is favored by those wishing to visit the impressive Mayan ruins at Tikal. After border formalities, cross the bridge and walk up to the intersection, where a bus will likely be waiting. You then continue, down a very rough dirt road, in a Guatemalan bus to the city of Flores. If you leave early enough in the morning, it is possible to get off this bus at El Cruce and catch a connecting bus directly to Tikal. You will be approached by money changers at all of these border stations; although these changers don't give very favorable rates (unless you have dollars or traveler's checks), they often are the only choice you have.

You can shorten procedures at the border a bit by getting your Tourist Card or visa in advance at a Guatemalan consulate, but don't spend a day doing it. If you're near a consulate (hours are usually 9am to 2pm weekdays) it's a good plan; if not, you can always get one at the border. The best place to get a Tourist Card or visa in advance is the Guatemalan Embassy in Mexico City or Belize City or the Guatemalan Consulate in Tapachula. If at all possible, try to get a visa before you reach the border, especially if you plan to cross at Tapachula, where the officials often refuse to issue Tourist Cards. Tourist cards now cost $5.

BY CAR

The same routes that apply to buses also are available to cars. However, keep in mind that if you're driving from Belize, you're going to travel some of the worst roads that you have ever seen between the Guatemalan border and El Cruce 65 miles away. Even after you reach the city of Flores, you have an equally bad road to take to get to the rest of Guatemala. This route is nearly impassable in the rainy season and very difficult during the rest of the year. Only try it if your car has high clearance and, preferably, four-wheel drive. From Tehuantepec, Mexico, you can head either to Tapachula and the Pacific Slope road to Guatemala City or to Tuxtla Gutierrez and San Cristobal de las Casas for the high mountain road to Guatemala City. The low road along the Pacific Slope goes through lush tropical country and a few pretty towns. Straighter and faster than the high road, it still has several disadvantages: It's heavily trafficked (especially when the sugarcane harvest is on) and hot and muggy all the time; the border officials at Tapachula-Talisman have a reputation for unpleasantness and extortion; and, except for the lushness, there's not much to stop and see along the road. The high road, by contrast, is reached by going through San Cristobal, one of the prettiest places in Mexico; the border officials are somewhat better (although not efficient); there is virtually no traffic for the first 100 miles into Guatemala; the mountain scenery is breathtaking; and interesting towns and villages abound all along the road. Perhaps you can see that I prefer the high road, despite its disadvantages: some landslides in the rainy season (late May to October), even though they are cleared away pretty quickly by road crews, and a curvy (but very good and safe) 40-mph mountain road.

Should you change your mind once you've entered Guatemala, you can switch roads by taking the paved road between Retalhuleu and Quetzaltenango.

The border-crossing procedures are the same at both posts (although, as mentioned, there are more hassles at Tapachula-El Carmen on the low road). See the preceding section, "By Bus," for information on shortening border procedures.

The road from San Cristobal de las Casas, Mexico, is fairly fast. It's slightly over 100 miles from San Cristobal to Ciudad Cuauhtemoc, the border station, and you should be able to cover it in about 2½ hours. After winding through the mountains east of San Cristobal, you descend to a plain before heading into the mountains that mark the border. The first Customs post you'll come to is where you hand in your car papers and Tourist Card (you fill out a new one when you return from Guatemala). Go on to the border proper, about a mile down the road, and pass the barrier into Guatemala.

You must get a Guatemalan Tourist Card ($5) right across the border, if you don't already have one. After getting your card (have your passport or birth certificate ready), drive on for a mile or so to the Customs inspection station, where you'll get your car papers, usually after a fairly serious look at the car and its contents. You may have to open a few bags, but it's wise just to follow the inspector around and do exactly and only what he or she asks. You may also be asked to take a bag or two into the station for a quick inspection.

While you're getting your car papers, someone will wash your tires with a disinfectant solution. This fumigation is required and costs a dollar or so—a bothersome but fairly minor nuisance. The entire border crossing takes about an hour. The officials are businesslike, sometimes even friendly (especially if you show an interest in Guatemala), and the whole procedure is quite painless. The Guatemalan border stations keep regular business hours: 8am to noon and 2 to 6pm Monday through Friday, 8am to noon on Saturday. You can cross at other hours and on Sunday, but you'll end up paying a little extra.

Note that Mexican auto insurance is not valid in Guatemala. Buy Guatemalan insurance through your agent at home, or through the AAA, or within Guatemala. It is usually available at border crossings.

PACKAGE TOURS

Clark Tours, 9 Boston St., Suite 10, Lynn, MA 09104 (tel. 617/581-0844, or toll free 800/223-6764), has been organizing tours to Guatemala since 1929. **Sobek**

Expeditions, Box 1089, Angels Camp, CA 95222 (tel. 209/736-4524, or toll free 800/777-7939), is known primarily for its adventure tours, but it also has excellent cultural tours of Guatemala. For information on other companies offering organized tours to Guatemala, contact a travel agent.

8. SUGGESTED ITINERARIES

HIGHLIGHTS

The following are Guatemala's top tourist destinations.
1. Antigua
2. Chichicastenango
3. Panajachel
4. Quetzaltenango
5. Tikal
6. Guatemala City

PLANNING YOUR ITINERARY
IF YOU HAVE ONE WEEK

Day 1: Spend one day in Guatemala City visiting the museums.
Days 2 and 3: Settle into Antigua and explore this beautiful little colonial town for two days.
Day 4: Visit Chichicastenango if it is market day and spend the night there. If it is not market day, arrange your schedule accordingly.
Day 5: Return by way of Panajachel and beautiful Lake Atitlán, spending a day there.
Days 6 and 7: Spend your last two days visiting the Mayan ruins in Tikal. This is a rushed itinerary, but you will get an overview of Guatemala, its people, its history, and its landscape.

IF YOU HAVE TWO WEEKS

With two weeks, you can spend more time in some of Guatemala's many beautiful locations.

Days 1 and 2: So that you won't have to carry your purchases around with you, head first to Tikal for two days. Don't buy anything here because prices are much lower in Chichicastenango and Panajachel.
Days 3 through 6: Make Antigua your base of operations for the next four days. Spend three days enjoying colonial Antigua, with perhaps a trip to climb a volcano or a visit to a nearby village. Take a day trip to Guatemala City to see the museums.
Day 7: From Antigua, head to Chichicastenango for market day and spend the night there.
Days 8 through 10: Continue on to Quetzaltenango, the heart of the highlands, the next day. Spend three days exploring the Indian villages near Quetzaltenango.
Days 11 through 14: By now you should be ready for a rest, so head to Panajachel and relax on the beach of this volcanic lake for four days, taking ferries to the little villages that ring the lake.

IF YOU HAVE THREE WEEKS

Days 1 and 2: Head first to Tikal for two days.
Days 3 and 4: After returning to Guatemala City, take a bus to Cobán for two days

and visit the quetzal preserve and other natural wonders of this mountainous region.

Days 5 through 8: Continue toward the Caribbean Coast, but turn north to Río Dulce and take a boat down the river to Lívingston. You will probably have to spend the night in Río Dulce. Spend a couple of days in Lívingston or Puerto Barrios.

Day 9: Head back toward Guatemala City, with a stop at the ruins of Quiriguá.

Day 10: Spend a day visiting the museums of Guatemala City, then head for Antigua.

Days 11 through 13: Spend three days exploring Antigua.

Day 14: Go to Chichicastenango for market day and spend the night.

Days 15 through 17: Continue on to Quetzaltenango. Spend three days there visiting small villages on their market days.

Days 18 through 21: Head to Panajachel and Lake Atitlán for four days of rest and recreation.

THEMED CHOICES

Archeology buffs will want to take in Guatemala's many Mayan ruins, which include Tikal and several smaller and more remote sites in the Petén region. You might end up spending a week or more in this area. After flying back to Guatemala, you should head

FROMMER'S FAVORITE
GUATEMALA EXPERIENCES

A Boat Ride Down the Río Dulce   Long narrow boats with outboard motors carry passengers between Río Dulce and Lívingston, stopping at a manatee preserve en route. Forested mountains rise up on either side of the river, and along its banks are the huts of fishermen for whom the river is the only link to the outside world.

Chichicastenango on Market Day   Guatemalan textiles are some of the most beautiful in the world, and Chichicastenango is the place to buy them. The local Indians wear colorful traditional costumes, and age-old rituals based on Mayan rites are performed in front of the town's main church and on a hillside just outside of town. There are great deals here late in the afternoon, when vendors are packing up their goods.

Antigua During Semana Santa   During the week prior to Easter, Antigua's cobblestone streets are the scene of religious processions in which thousands of people participate, carrying heavy religious floats on their shoulders as they march slowly through incense-filled streets.

Dawn and Dusk in Tikal   At the opening and close of each steamy day, the ruins come alive with the roar of howler monkeys, the chatter of spider monkeys, the squawking of parrots and toucans, and the songs of countless species of other birds. If you're lucky, you might even see a "herd" of coatimundis.

Climbing Pacaya Volcano   This is one of the few active volcanoes in the world that you can hike to the top of while it's exploding and spewing out molten rock, but hiking to the top of Pacaya is not for the faint of heart. The last bit of climbing to reach the peak of the volcano's quiet cone (it has two cones) can be extremely difficult when the winds are strong.

next for the ruins in Copán, Honduras, just over the border from Guatemala. This will probably take you another two or three days. Two much less impressive sites are Iximché near Lake Atitlán and Zaculeu outside Huehuetenango. The huge carved-stone heads in La Democracia also are worth an excursion.

9. GETTING AROUND

BY PLANE

Tikal is probably the only place in Guatemala that you will want to reach by air. Airfare between Guatemala City and Flores (the closest city to the Tikal ruins) is about $50 each way. There are several flights a day on three airlines: Aeroquetzal, Aerovias, and Tapsa. If you are a very serious student of archeology, you may want to charter a plane to reach some of the remote Mayan sites. Such a charter flight, in a small plane, can work out to be fairly inexpensive if you have enough people to fill the plane.

BY BUS

Every town of any size in Guatemala has several bus companies that operate to surrounding towns and to the capital; minibus services connect the smaller villages or run the very frequent services between towns a short distance apart.

BY CAR

The main roads in Guatemala are better than the main roads in Mexico—with smoother, harder surfaces; gentler curves; and better maintenance.

CAR RENTALS

Car rentals are available in Guatemala City, Antigua, and Flores/Santa Elena.

GASOLINE

Unleaded gasoline is rarely available in Guatemala. Rental cars use regular gasoline. Prices on my last visit were not much higher than those in the United States. However, the country was running out of foreign hard currency with which to buy fuel, and the government was beginning to raise gasoline prices to reduce consumption and therefore reduce the need for foreign currency with which to buy more fuel. Expect gasoline to cost slightly more than you are used to paying.

DRIVING RULES

The most important driving rule here is to stop for police and military checkpoints and blockades, which you will encounter frequently. Present the officer with your driver's license (international driver's licenses are best but not necessary), your vehicle registration papers, and perhaps your rental agreement. You should get everything back within a minute and be on your way. *Remember:* Never drive without your passport. Occasionally, it is not the police, but leftist guerrillas, who have barricaded the road. Should you encounter one of these barricades, do as you are instructed and you will likely be sent on your way unharmed. Otherwise, driving rules in Guatemala are basically the same as they are in the United States, except that you must be 18 years old to drive. Also keep in mind that if you see a pile of leaves, grass, or branches from a tree or bush piled in the road, it is a signal that there is a vehicle stopped on the road ahead.

MAPS

Ask for a map when you rent a car. These maps are about the best that are available. If you want to get a map before you arrive, contact the nearest INGUAT (Guatemalan Tourist Commission) office. See "Information, Entry Requirements, and Money" in this chapter for addresses and phone numbers.

BREAKDOWNS

If you should have a breakdown, immediately pile some branches in the road at least 100 feet on either side of your car. Wait for help from the national police.

BY RV

There are almost no facilities for recreational vehicles in Guatemala. I know of only two small RV campgrounds, both of which are near Guatemala City. If you come down here with your RV, you'll have to make do. Try asking at hotels if you can park in their parking lots or stopping by the local police station and asking where it would be best to park.

BY FERRY

There are a few ferries in Guatemala that you should know about. It is possible to enter the country from Belize on a ferry that plies between Punta Gorda, Belize, and Puerto Barrios, Guatemala. The ferry makes the trip a couple of times a week. Another ferry also runs between Puerto Barrios and Lívingston, across the mouth of the Río Dulce. There is a mail boat that makes a regular run between Lívingston and the town of Río Dulce, which is several hours up the river. There are also several ferries that operate on Lake Atitlán, providing service between Panajachel and several small villages on the shore of the lake. See the pertinent chapters for details on these ferries.

HITCHHIKING

Because buses in Guatemala are so cheap and go nearly everywhere in the country, you should not need to hitchhike. However, if you're driving a car, you will often notice hitchhikers. It is very common for hitchhikers to wait at toll booths and highway police check points. Often you will be asked by an officer if you can give someone a ride.

FINDING AN ADDRESS

The street-numbering system in Guatemala is logical, easy to use, and found in every town. In fact, the system is so good that there's almost no excuse for getting lost anywhere but in Guatemala City! Once you get the hang of it, you'll be on your way to the exact location of any hotel or restaurant. Here's how it works: Every town is planned on a grid with avenidas running roughly north to south and calles running east to west. Addresses are given in the following form: 2a. Av. 4-17, which means that the place you're after is on 2nd Avenida, at 4th Calle, number 17 (2a is "Spanish" for 2nd, 3a for 3rd, and so on). You can even tell what side of the street the building will be on. If the street number is even, it'll be on the right side; if the number is odd, it'll be on the left—as you walk along the avenida toward higher-numbered calles. You can guess, then, that 3a. Av. 5-78 will be on 3rd Avenida between 5th and 6th calles (closer to 6th, as the house number is a high one), on the right side. Once you get the hang of it, you'll see that it's a marvelous system.

The only exceptions are in Antigua and Guatemala City. In Antigua, avenidas and calles are also designated Norte, Sur, Oriente, and Poniente, the central point being the main square. If, say, the address you're looking for is 5a. Av. Norte 9, all you need to do is make sure that you're not on the Sur, or southern, half of 5th Avenue. In Guatemala City, the system works in the downtown section, but the city sprawls beyond the practical limits of the plan, so you'll find within the downtown area an address such as 14 av. "A" 2-31, 14—"A" being a short street or alley between, and parallel to, 14th and 15th Avenues. Outside the downtown area of the capital, you'll also run into diagonales, rutas, vias, and other designations.

One last note: Each town is also divided into zones, but in the small towns (everywhere but Guatemala City), almost every important place is in Zona 1. If a zone number does not appear as a part of any address given in this book, you can assume that the place you're looking for is in Zona 1.

10. WHERE TO STAY

The division between luxury and squalor that used to reign throughout Guatemala's hostelries has been modified in most towns, so that now wherever you go you'll find a selection of hotels in all price categories—from Q20 ($5) or less to Q120 ($30) or more for doubles. At Christmas, New Year's, and especially Holy Week (the week before Easter), most hotels are fully booked weeks in advance, so plan accordingly.

In the higher-priced hotels, expect pretty good service, a comfortable and sometimes wonderfully quaint and picturesque accommodation, a private bath, a fairly good restaurant, and extras such as 24-hour hot water and a garage or parking lot. In the inexpensive places, you usually get only a very small room, one light bulb, two beds, a small nightstand, and a plastic pitcher of drinking water. But there's always a shower nearby, often with hot water. Most of these little places have a *comedor,* or dining room, where the señora's home-cooked meals are served for something like Q8 ($2). By our reckoning, the most expensive places, although often charming, are slightly too expensive for what you get, while the low-priced places are sensational (if spartan) bargains.

By the way, taxi drivers in some Guatemalan towns may receive commissions from certain hotels for bringing new customers. If your taxi driver suggests strongly that your chosen hotel is "bad" or "too expensive" and wants to take you to another, think twice. Have him go to your chosen hotel first, so that you can at least get a price and inspect a room.

11. WHERE TO EAT

Guatemala has a wide range of restaurants—from tables set up in local markets to gourmet French establishments. In most of the places you will likely be visiting, you will find at least two or three decent restaurants where you can get a filling meal for $5 or less. The least expensive place to eat is called a comedor. These very basic eateries may offer only one set meal each day. You'll eat with locals when you eat at a comedor, and you'll enjoy locals' prices. A *cafetería* derives its name from café (coffee) and is someplace to sit and drink coffee and maybe have a pastry.

12. ENJOYING GUATEMALA ON A BUDGET

THE $25-A-DAY BUDGET

See the corresponding heading in Chapter 2, "Planning a Trip to Costa Rica."

SAVING MONEY ON ACCOMMODATIONS

Best Budget Bets The cheapest accommodations in Guatemala are usually called *pensiones. Albergue* and *posada* are other titles often attached to budget lodgings in the place of the word "hotel." In Antigua, a very popular tourist town, there are a few apartment hotels that represent an excellent value since each apartment comes with a kitchenette that allows you to do your own cooking.

Seasonal Discounts Keep in mind that nearly everyone in Guatemala goes on holiday during the Semana Santa (Holy Week), the week prior to Easter. Not only are rooms difficult to find, but also room rates nearly double. Rates are also higher at Christmas and New Year's.

Other Money-Saving Strategies Although our budget in Guatemala allows us the luxury of a private bath, if you're willing to forsake this and walk down the hall, you will save considerably on your hotel bills. Rooms with air conditioning are also much more expensive and rarely necessary. If there are two of you traveling together, getting one double room instead of two singles will usually save you money. Getting a *cama matrimonial* (double bed), instead of two twin beds, will also save you money in many cases. If there is a view from the hotel, you will pay for it; take a room without the view to save even more money.

SAVING MONEY ON MEALS

The *menu del dia* is the way to save money in Guatemala. This lunch special is usually a large three-course meal for much less than you would pay for just an entree at regular prices. These meals are served until the pot is empty. Breakfasts are usually surprisingly expensive, but if you stop by the market and buy some fruit and pick up some bread at a *panaderia,* you will need only a cup of tea or coffee to put together a tasty breakfast.

SAVING MONEY ON SIGHT-SEEING AND ENTERTAINMENT

You won't find any special discount days at museums, and there aren't discount tickets to theaters. However, because the prices are so low in Guatemala already, it hardly matters.

SAVING MONEY ON SHOPPING

Best Buys Guatemala's best buy is in textiles. Most visitors come here because they have become fascinated by the colorful cotton textiles woven by the highland Indians. Brilliant colors in bold stripes are the norm. These beautiful fabrics are sewn into a wide variety of traditional and modern fashions and are considerably less expensive than they are back home. The best place to buy textiles is always in the villages where they are manufactured. There are several villages near Quetzaltenango that are known for different textiles. You can make trips to the different villages on their respective market days and bargain for beautiful pieces of cloth. For ready-made fashions, the best places to shop are in Chichicastenango and Panajachel. The stores in Antigua tend to be expensive, although they sell contemporary designs.

Another good buy is jade, which was highly valued by the Mayas. Their jade quarries were lost for hundreds of years but were rediscovered a few years ago. Beautiful jade jewelry is available at several shops in Antigua. The prices are high, but the jade is of the highest quality.

Stay away from any pre-Columbian artifacts that are offered to you as being *originales*. It is against the law to buy, sell, or export original pre-Columbian art. It is also very doubtful whether anything offered to you truly is an original. High-quality fakes are common, and many people have been taken when they "got a great deal" on a piece of ancient Mayan pottery.

Markets Every town and village in Guatemala has its market day. Once or twice a week, people from all over the region will come into town to buy and sell their wares. The most famous market in the country, and now a major tourist destination, is the one at Chichicastenango. It takes place on both Thursday and Sunday; the Sunday market is larger and more colorful. You will always get a better deal in a market than you will in a tourist shop, and often they have the same items for sale. The market in Antigua is a prime example of this, so be sure to visit this market before making any purchases in Antigua. Calle Santander in Panajachel isn't really a market, but it is lined with vendors' stalls that offer those beautiful Guatemalan textiles at some of the best prices in the country.

Bargaining When making purchases in markets, especially when buying tourist items, be sure to bargain hard. The prices can be inflated several hundred percent if you look like you have the money to pay. Try to avoid looking "rich" and you'll save money; if you're wearing expensive jewelry and watches, you'll automatically be charged a high price. Bargaining is much easier late in the day when the vendors are packing up and will often lower their prices far below midday quotes. If you ask the price of something, you have expressed an interest in buying it and will be expected to negotiate for the item. This can be very frustrating if you're trying to do a little comparison shopping. If you ask the price and don't buy, you'll have to learn to live with the intimidating stares. It is much harder to bargain in shops, but it is possible, especially if you are buying several items. More and more shops are displaying "Fixed Prices" signs.

SAVING MONEY ON TRANSPORTATION

By Plane There is only one domestic flight of concern to visitors to Guatemala—the flight between Guatemala City and Flores, El Petén. All three airlines offering this flight charge about $50 each way. The flights are often booked up by large tour groups, so try to reserve in advance. See Chapter 11 on El Petén for details.

By Bus Although cleaner and more comfortable, first-class buses are more expensive and run less often than the second-class buses known to travelers as "chicken buses." Whether this name derives from the livestock carried among the passengers or the disquieting passing habits of the drivers is a matter for speculation. Chicken buses almost always leave from the market of a town and are for those seeking adventure.

By Car To save money on a rental car, reserve at least one week ahead with a company in your home country. Once in Guatemala, the best way to save money on car rentals is to drive one with a stick shift and forsake air conditioning, which isn't really necessary in most of the country. Be sure to ask for a free road map when you pick up your car. When filling up the gas tank, ask for regular. *Lleno* means "full."

SAVING MONEY ON SERVICES AND OTHER TRANSACTIONS

Tipping Bellhops: Q1 to Q2 (25¢ to 50¢) per bag. Waiters/waitresses: 10 to 15%. Taxi drivers: not necessary. Porters: Q1 (25¢) per bag.

Money Changing and Credit Cards Currency exchange rates vary from bank to bank in Guatemala, so it pays to check with a few banks before changing money. *Prensa Libre*, the daily newspaper, publishes a list of exchange rates at various Guatemala City banks. Although hotels will often change money, they tend to give very low rates. By using your credit card to pay hotel and restaurant bills, you will be locking in the bank exchange rate for the day the bill is submitted to a bank. This can work to your advantage and save you money if the value of the quetzal is falling rapidly against the dollar (that is, you're getting more quetzals for your dollar each day). However, make sure that you aren't charged a higher rate for using your credit card.

Telephones You'll save money on local phone calls by going to a phone booth rather than by calling from your hotel; budget hotels in Guatemala rarely have phones in the rooms anyway. For international calls, I suggest using AT&T USA Direct. By dialing 190, you will reach an English-speaking AT&T operator. However, only calling-card and collect calls can be made this way. You'll save time, money, and aggravation by making your call to the United States this way.

FAST GUATEMALA

American Express The only office is in Guatemala City at Avenida La Reforma 9-00, Zona 9 (tel. 311-311).

Business Hours Banks are generally open Monday to Friday from 9am to 3pm, with *ventanillas especialles* (special windows) open longer hours. Bars generally stay open until 2am, except on Sunday, when they close at midnight. Office hours are Monday to Friday from 8am to 4:30pm. Less expensive restaurants tend to be open all day, while more expensive ones tend to close for a couple of hours between meals. Shops are generally open Monday to Friday from 9am to 12:30pm and 3 to 7pm, Saturday from 9am to noon. Shops catering primarily to tourists usually have longer hours and stay open on weekends.

Camera/Film Color print and Ektachrome film are readily available, but more expensive than in the United States. It's best to bring your own. If your camera requires odd-size batteries, be sure to bring some spare ones with you. You can get a camera repaired in Guatemala City, but I can't vouch for the quality of service.

City Code If dialing Guatemala City phone numbers from outside Guatemala, it is necessary to dial "2" after the country code (502).

Climate See "When to Go" in this chapter.

Crime See *Safety*.

Currency See "Information, Entry Requirements, and Money" in this chapter.

Customs When you enter Guatemala, Customs may or may not search your bags. You can legally bring in two bottles of liquor, two cartons of cigarettes, one still camera plus six rolls of film (rarely if ever enforced), and one movie camera.

Documents Required See "Information, Entry Requirements, and Money" in this chapter.

Driving Rules See "Getting Around" in this chapter.

Drug Laws Although marijuana and cocaine are readily available, the drug laws are strict, and there is nothing your embassy can do to get you out of jail. If you take prescription drugs, play it safe and bring your prescription with you. Most prescription drugs are actually available over the counter in Guatemala.

Drugstores Drugstores here are called *farmacias*.

Electricity The current is 110 volts.

Embassies and Consulates Canada: Embassy and consulate, 7a Avenida 11-59, Zona 9, Edificio Galerías España (tel. 321-411 or 321-413). United Kingdom:

Embassy and consulate, 7a Avenida 5-10, Edificio Centro Financiero, Torre 11, Nivel 7, Zona 4 (tel. 32-1601).

United States: Embassy and consulate, Avenida La Reforma 7-01, Zona 10 (tel. 311-541 to 311-555).

Emergencies Emergency phone numbers are different in each city. Check the appropriate chapter.

Hitchhiking Buses are so cheap here that hitchhiking generally isn't necessary, unless you are trying to get someplace really remote. Local people frequently hitchhike, and if you're driving you will probably be asked for rides quite regularly.

Holidays See "When to Go" in this chapter.

Information See "Information, Entry Requirements, and Money" in this chapter. Also see individual city chapters for local information offices.

Language Spanish is the national language; many different Indian dialects derived from ancient Mayan languages also are spoken, primarily in the mountains. A good phrasebook to take with you is the *Berlitz Latin-American Spanish for Travelers* (Berlitz Guides, 1989).

Laundry For listings of Laundromats, see individual city chapters.

Liquor Laws Officially you must be 18 years old to buy alcoholic beverages in Guatemala.

Mail Mail to the United States takes anywhere from one to two weeks. A postcard to the United States costs 40 centavos; a letter costs 20 centavos for the first 5 grams, 10 centavos for each additional gram. Stamps often are available at hotel desks; otherwise, you'll have to go to a post office. It is always a good idea to make sure that the stamps on your letter get canceled. If you want to ship a package home, it is best to use one of the shipping companies in Antigua or Panajachel; otherwise, you must go to the Central Post Office in Guatemala City. Don't close the package until after it has been inspected. Surface mail can be very slow (a month or more). Air mail is much faster.

Maps Road and city maps are available from INGUAT offices and car-rental agencies (if you're renting one of their cars). You can also buy very detailed maps at the Instituto Geográfico Militar, Avenida Las Americas 5-76, Zona 13, but this is not very convenient.

Newspapers/Magazines You'll find several U.S. newspapers and magazines available at major hotels throughout the country, although these newspapers may be a day or two old and are expensive. *Prensa Libre* is Guatemala's most popular daily paper.

Passports See "Information, Entry Requirements, and Money" in this chapter.

Pets Rabies is common in Guatemala, so it is best to leave your pet at home. If you must bring it, your dog must have vaccinations for rabies, distemper, leptospirosis, hepatitis, and parvovirosis, while your cat must have vaccinations against rabies, distemper, and hepatitis. Please do not buy any parrots that you are offered. These beautiful birds are disappearing in the wild due to hunting for the live bird trade.

Police The phone number for the Policia Nacional is different in every town. You will find it in the phone book at the beginning of the section for each town or city. In Guatemala City dial 120; in Antigua, dial 320-251; in Panajachel, dial 621-120.

Radio/TV There are plenty of AM and FM radio stations throughout the country. You're never far from a marimba music station. Most expensive hotels have satellite cable TV either in the rooms or in a TV lounge, so you can keep in touch with U.S. programming. A TV schedule is published daily in the newspaper *Prensa Libre.*

Restrooms These are known as *servicios* or *servicios sanitarios.* Public toilets, rarely clean, are usually free. However, you will have to buy your own toilet paper from the restroom attendant at a table outside the door.

Safety The government of Guatemala continues to wage a small-scale war against rebel guerrillas in the highlands. You will see gun-carrying soldiers almost anywhere you go in the country, but the main tourist areas are kept free of fighting; if I didn't tell you, you probably would not know that there was any fighting going on here at all.

Of greater importance is protecting yourself against pickpockets. I suggest getting a money pouch that you can wear under your clothes, either around your neck or around your waist. Be cautious with your bags when traveling by bus. Bags have been known to disappear from the roofs of buses, so try to keep your bag inside the bus with you.

Taxes   The Guatemalan government levies a 17% room tax on each night you spend in a hotel. When a hotel receptionist quotes you the room price, the tax may or not be included in the quotation. Ask to make sure. In this book I will quote room prices with the tax included, so that you'll know the total charge you will have to pay for a room.

Telephone   The dial tone in Guatemala is a long, low tone similar to that heard in the United States. Telephone numbers vary in the number of digits that they have—usually four, five, or six digits. There is only one telephone book for all of Guatemala. You'll find several copies available at Guatel (the national telephone company) offices.

A pay phone in Guatemala is called a *telefono monedero,* but it is not very common. A three-minute local call will cost you 10 centavos (2.5¢). Machines accept various coins but do not give change.

The best way to make a long-distance call is to call collect or to use an AT&T calling card by dialing 190. This number connects you directly to an English-speaking AT&T operator and is much faster than trying to make a call through a Guatel office. If you must pay for the call yourself, you will need to go to a Guatel office and wait in line or pay a premium and call from your hotel. Calls have a tendency to go through better early in the morning. Sometimes it is impossible to place international calls through Guatel, especially in Antigua.

Time   Guatemala is 6 hours behind Greenwich Mean Time, which is the same as Central Standard Time.

Tipping   See "Saving Money on Services and Transactions" in this chapter.

Tourist Offices   See "Information, Entry Requirements, and Money" in this chapter. Also see specific cities.

Visas   Guatemalan visas are available but not necessary. On entering the country, you can pick up a Tourist Card ($5), which is good for 30 days—after which time you must go to the Immigration office to request an extension.

Water   Consider all tap water unfit for drinking. I always carry a little bottle of iodine, a water bottle, and an eye dropper for fixing my own drinking water. Bottled water, although expensive, is also readily available.

CHAPTER 9

GUATEMALA CITY

1. FROM A BUDGET TRAVELER'S POINT OF VIEW
2. ORIENTATION AND GETTING AROUND
- WHAT'S SPECIAL ABOUT GUATEMALA CITY
- FAST FACTS— GUATEMALA CITY
3. WHERE TO STAY
4. WHERE TO EAT
5. ATTRACTIONS
6. SAVVY SHOPPING
7. EVENING ENTERTAINMENT
8. MOVING ON— TRAVEL SERVICES

The Guatemalan capital is a city of over two million souls. It's the biggest and most modern city in the country—indeed, in all Central America—and is the headquarters for companies, airlines, and government. However, it is not a major point of attraction for anyone who visits Guatemala for pleasure rather than for business. After the spectacular beauty of the countryside, the clean air and relative quiet of the provincial towns, the capital almost puts you off: The decibel level and pollution index go up almost as soon as you leave Antigua and start on the Guatemala City road.

But since all roads lead to the capital, it's the transportation hub of the nation, and chances are you'll find occasion to pass through. Here's the information that you'll need to make a short visit pleasant.

1. FROM A BUDGET TRAVELER'S POINT OF VIEW

Budget Bests Luxury hotels in Guatemala City are no longer the great deal that they once were, but there are still plenty of less luxurious hotels offering good value at moderate prices. Restaurant prices are still quite low. You can confidently walk into almost any restaurant in the city without having to worry about how much you are spending—and that includes major hotel restaurants. Taxis are about what you would expect to pay for them in other major cities around the world, but public buses are a super deal at only 30 centavos (7.5¢).

Discount Opportunities The only people who get any sort of discounts in Guatemala City are students and children, who get a reduction on museum admissions. However, admission fees are already so low that these discounts hardly matter.

What's Worth Paying For The only thing that I can really say is worth paying for in Guatemala City is a plane ticket to Flores in El Petén, which is where the famous Mayan ruins of Tikal are located. The one-hour flight costs only $50 and saves up to 18 hours of grueling bus travel over one of the worst roads I have ever traveled.

2. ORIENTATION AND GETTING AROUND

Guatemala City can be a confusing place, but with a little information, getting there and getting around can be quite painless and inexpensive.

ARRIVING
BY PLANE

If you fly to Guatemala, you will arrive at the capital's La Aurora International Airport, in the southern part of the city only about 15 or 20 minutes from the center by taxi. La Aurora is small but modern and pleasant, equipped with a bank, dozens of interesting craft and clothing shops, several small cafeterias, and snack bars. Before you pass through Customs and Immigration, you will come to an INGUAT Tourism Information Desk staffed by an English-speaking agent. Guatemalan Tourist Cards can be obtained here, at the cost of $5. Also available are brochures and a schedule for the minibus service to Antigua and Panajachel operated by **Buses Inter-Hotel y Turismo** (tel. 320-011 to 320-015).

If the Banco de Guatemala in the arrivals hall is closed when you arrive, ask at the souvenir shops to find someone who will change U.S. dollars into Guatemalan quetzals for you.

Outside the lower level of the terminal building are car-rental booths and taxi ranks. Taxi fare from the airport to Zona 9 or 10 is Q16 ($4); to Zona 4 is Q20 ($5); and to Zona 1, the very center, is Q25 ($6.25). A small tip is appreciated but not required. You should have chosen your desired hotel by this time; examine the address and find its zone number so that you'll know what the taxi fare will be.

It is also possible to get into town on a public bus for only 30 centavos (7.5¢). There is a bus stop on the near side of the road directly in front of the terminal. The black no. 5 (as opposed to the red no. 5, which runs a similar route but does not go all the way to the airport) "Aeropuerto" bus comes by frequently. The trip downtown will take about 30 minutes.

For those going directly from the airport to Antigua or Panajachel, there is another option. You can take a minibus operated by Buses Inter-Hotel y Turismo, which makes two runs daily from the airport to Antigua and continues on once a day to Panajachel. Because their schedule is constantly changing, be sure to ask for a current schedule at the information desk inside the terminal. The trip takes two hours, due to numerous stops at Guatemala City hotels. In Antigua, the minibus drops passengers at several of the top hotels. The fare of Q50 ($12.50) to Antigua is considerably more than that of a local bus leaving from downtown (see below), but it is only about half to a quarter of the taxi fare to Antigua. If there are even as few as two of you, you might want to look into hiring a taxi. Be prepared to bargain for the fare, which can be as low as Q100 ($25).

BY BUS

Unfortunately, because intercity bus routes are handled by dozens of bus companies, there is no single terminal where you will arrive. You have to know which company you are traveling with to know where you will be arriving. The list of bus companies, routes, and times at the end of this chapter should help you to figure out where you are when you arrive. Then you can walk to your destination (fairly easy in most cases if you're not carrying too much luggage and can find an intersection with both street names posted), catch a local bus (difficult because buses must use streets outside the main hotel and restaurant district), or hail a taxi (easiest). In the general chaos and disorientation of your first arrival in Guatemala, I suggest that you take a cab, even if you're on the tightest of budgets. It will save you much frustration and aggravation. Be sure to agree on a fare before getting into the cab. I have found that most taxi drivers in Guatemala City are pretty honest about their fares. Tipping is not necessary.

BY CAR

If you're driving into Guatemala City, you'll probably come in on the Carretera al Atlántico or the Pan American Highway. There are few signs when you come into town on the former: You suddenly find yourself no longer on a highway and surrounded by traffic. The heart of the city is to the south (left). Your best bet is to

WHAT'S SPECIAL ABOUT GUATEMALA CITY

Museums
- ☐ The Museum of Archeology and Ethnology, Central America's finest collection of pre-Columbian artifacts
- ☐ The Ixchell Museum, dedicated to the indigenous clothing of Guatemala
- ☐ The Popol Vuh Museum, small but containing many beautiful terra-cotta artifacts

Events/Festivals
- ☐ The ancient Indian dances performed several times a year.

Architectural Highlights
- ☐ The Centro Cultural Miguel Angel Asturias, which resembles a luxury cruise ship

- ☐ The Centro Cívico, with high-rise buildings covered with murals

Churches
- ☐ The Yurrita Chapel, a fascinating mixture of architectural styles

Offbeat Oddities
- ☐ The Mapa en Relieve, a huge relief map of Guatemala

Ancient Ruins
- ☐ Kaminal Juyú ruins on the outskirts of the city

---

take 8a Avenida into downtown. If you're coming in on the Pan American Highway, just continue straight into town, following the signs, and you'll find yourself on 5a Avenida. There is also a ring road (Anillo Periférico) that will help you avoid downtown if you just want to get around the city. To connect between the Carretera al Atlántico and Pan American Highway, take the ring road around the north side of the city.

Most of Guatemala is easy to drive in, with good, uncrowded roads and fairly courteous drivers. All that changes in the capital, where cars whirl around you and whiz by at warp speed. The most important thing to know is that they turn off many of the traffic lights at 8pm! There is presently a movement to discontinue this practice, which is equivalent to rolling up the sidewalks and is very odd to find in a capital city of this size. But if the signals are out when you drive here at night, be aware that traffic on avenidas has priority over the traffic on calles—but don't trust anybody.

TOURIST INFORMATION

Contact **INGUAT,** the **Instituto Guatemalteco de Turismo** (Guatemalan Tourist Commission), 7a Av. 1-17, Zona 4 (tel. 311-333 or 311-337), in the Centro Cívico (Civic Center) complex. The entrance to the INGUAT building, marked by a blue-and-white sign bearing the letter *i,* is just south of the railroad viaduct on 7a Avenida. It's open weekdays from 8am to 4:30pm, on Saturday from 8am to 1pm; closed Sunday.

MAPS

The tourist office and car rental agencies have free maps of Guatemala City.

CITY LAYOUT
MAIN ARTERIES AND STREETS

Although Guatemala City is the largest city in all Central America, most visitors need to familiarize themselves with only a small portion of it. Plaza Mayor, between 5a and 7a avenidas and 6a and 8a calles, is the heart of the city. From here south on 6a

Avenida, you'll find the city's greatest concentration of stores. The sidewalks are always jammed with pedestrians and vendors. Most of the buses you will want to use run on 7a and 10a avenidas. Avenida La Reforma, which is the most attractive avenue in the city, is a southern extension of 10a Avenida and divides Zona 9 and Zona 10.

FINDING AN ADDRESS

The street-numbering system in Guatemala City, at least within the downtown area, is logical and easy to use. Once you get the hang of it, you'll be on your way to the exact location of any hotel or restaurant. Avenidas run roughly north to south, and calles run east to west. Addresses are given in the following form: 2a Av. 4-17, which means that the place you're after is on 2nd Avenue, at 4th Calle, number 17 (2a is "Spanish" for 2nd, 3a for 3rd; however, after 10, numbers are simply written 11, 12, and so on). You can even tell what side of the street the building will be on. If the street number is even, it'll be on the right side; if the number is odd, it'll be on the left—as you walk along the avenida toward higher-numbered calles. You can guess, then, that 3a Av. 5-78 will be on 3rd Avenue between 5th and 6th calles (closer to 6th, as the house number is a high one) on the right side. Once you get the hang of it, you'll find that it's a marvelous system. Unfortunately, the city sprawls beyond the practical limits of the plan, so you find within the downtown area an address such as 14 Av. "A" 2-31, 14—"A" being a short street or alley between, and parallel to, 14th and 15th avenidas Outside the downtown area of the capital, you'll also run into diagonales, rutas, vias, and other designations.

In an attempt to remedy this situation, all addresses in Guatemala City also have a "zona" designation. A zona is a section of the city. Most of downtown is within Zona 1. The system works well here, but when you cross into another zona, you may find that the numbering system has started all over again. Such is the case in Zona 10. Here you may find the address 4a Av. 16-27, Zona 10, but there may also be a 4a Av. 16-27, Zona 1. Always be sure that you are in the right zona.

NEIGHBORHOODS IN BRIEF

Zona 1 is the downtown shopping, hotel, and restaurant district. Starting at the Plaza Mayor in the north, Zona 1 extends to the Centro Cívico in the south.

Zonas 9 and 10 are the prettiest residential neighborhoods and flank Guatemala City's **Zona Viva,** the upscale hotel, restaurant, nightlife, and boutique district. The Zona Viva centers around the wide Avenida la Reforma, the capital's most attractive avenue and actually the southern continuation of 10a Avenida. Avenida la Reforma divides zonas 9 and 10, with Zona 9 to the west and Zona 10 to the east. It's here that you'll find most of the city's well-to-do residents, as well as the best hotels, the most important embassies, various corporate headquarters, and also several of the city's finest museums.

Zona 13, in the southern part of the city, is where you'll find the large Parque Aurora, just west of the airport. The park holds Guatemala City's museums of modern art, archeology, and natural history, as well as its zoo, hippodrome (racetrack), and a government crafts market. There's also an amusement park amid towering, shady trees. It's a pleasant place.

GETTING AROUND

BY BUS

Public buses in Guatemala City are incredibly cheap—only 30 centavos (7.5¢). However, city buses are rolling wrecks, often without windows and desperately in need of paint, muffler work, seat cushions, and the like. At busy times they can be wall-to-wall in human flesh. Bus stops are not well marked. But outside of peak times, for all their discomforts and unsightliness, these buses do provide very cheap and quite convenient transportation up and down the long north-to-south avenidas.

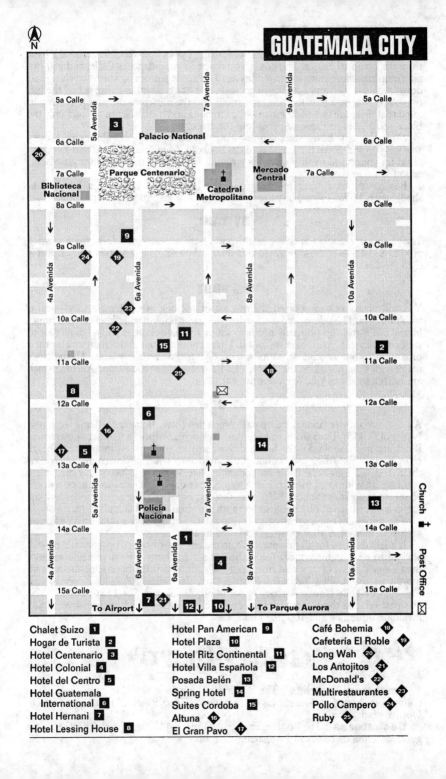

GUATEMALA CITY

N

Church ✝
Post Office ⊠

Chalet Suizo **1**
Hogar de Turista **2**
Hotel Centenario **3**
Hotel Colonial **4**
Hotel del Centro **5**
Hotel Guatemala
    International **6**
Hotel Hernani **7**
Hotel Lessing House **8**

Hotel Pan American **9**
Hotel Plaza **10**
Hotel Ritz Continental **11**
Hotel Villa Española **12**
Posada Belén **13**
Spring Hotel **14**
Suites Cordoba **15**
Altuna **16**
El Gran Pavo **17**

Café Bohemia **18**
Cafetería El Roble **19**
Long Wah **20**
Los Antojitos **21**
McDonald's **22**
Multirestaurantes **23**
Pollo Campero **24**
Ruby **25**

To reach Parque Aurora, take bus no. 6, which leaves from 8a Calle across the park from the National Palace. The bus travels down 8a Avenida to 18 Calle, and you can pick it up anywhere along its route. Bus no. 5 ("Parque Aurora"), which travels up and down avenidas 5, 7, and 8, will also get you there. It's a 20-minute trip; get off the bus two stops after you pass the zoo, and you'll find the museums on your left. Keep in mind that there are two no. 5 buses—the red no. 5 and the black no. 5—and only the black no. 5 goes to Parque Aurora and the airport.

After the city buses stop running (late in the evening), minibuses take over, zooming up and down the major avenidas between Zona 1 and Zona 9 and Zona 10. Hold up your hand to stop one. They run all night, until the city buses growl into action again in the morning.

Bus routes are subject to change, so the best course is to ask a hotel clerk, shopkeeper, police officer, or passerby which bus to take to your destination.

BY TAXI

Taxis are surprisingly expensive in this city, with an average ride in town costing around $3 or $4—almost the same as in a large American city. A taxi to the airport is Q25 ($6.25).

ON FOOT

You will probably find yourself doing a lot of walking in Guatemala City—and it won't be easy. The sidewalks are crowded, the traffic is loud, and diesel exhaust fumes fill the air. Buses run primarily north to south and vice versa; if you're going east to west or vice versa, you'll have to hoof it. I have chosen hotels and restaurants for their proximity to one another so as to minimize your time on the streets. All the city's major sights are out along the Avenida La Reforma and in the Parque Aurora, which are both a long bus ride from downtown.

BY CAR

All the major international car-rental companies (Avis, Budget, Dollar, Hertz, and National/Tilden/Eurocar) have booths at La Aurora Airport and offices downtown. Rates are high: about $50 or $60 a day when you add in fees, insurance, mileage charges, and gas. Also, you cannot get insurance to cover all losses by collision or theft. You will usually be liable for something like $600 to $1,500 on any car, unless you take an additional insurance at about $2 per day. This extra insurance reduces your responsibilities to about $250. This is scary, but if you take precautions (park the car in a safe space at night and so forth) things should work out all right.

The minimum age for renting a car is usually 25 years; have a valid driver's license with you, as well as your passport and credit card.

It is not unusual for all the rental cars in the city to be booked up, so you'd be well advised to reserve in advance. You'll also get a much better rate if you reserve more than a week ahead of time and from your own country. If the big companies have no more cars, try calling **Tabarini Rent-a-Car,** 2a Calle "A" 7-30, Zona 10 (tel. 316-108), or **Tally Renta Autos,** 7a Av. 14-60, Zona 1 (tel. 514-113 or 23-327). The cheapest vehicles these companies offer are pickup trucks, which rent for around $35 including insurance and 100 free kilometers.

 GUATEMALA CITY

American Express The American Express office (the only one in the country) is located at Avenida La Reforma 9-00, Zona 9 (tel. 311-311 or 347-463). Open weekdays only.

Bookstores The Book Exchange, 12 Calle 6-14, Zona 9 (tel. 319-923), has a good selection of books in English and Spanish.

Car Rentals See "Getting Around" in this chapter.

Climate See "When to Go" in Chapter 8.

Crime See *Safety.*

Currency Exchange Bank hours are usually weekdays from 8:30am to 2pm (to 2:30pm on Friday), closed weekends; some banks have *ventanillas especiales* (special teller windows) that are open at other times. The Banco del Quetzal, also called Banquetzal, has an office at 10a Calle 6-28, Zona 1 (tel. 512-153 or 512-055), near the Hotel Ritz Continental—open Monday to Friday from 8:30am to 8pm, Saturday from 9am to 1pm.

Dentist Contact your embassy for a list of English-speaking dentists in Guatemala City.

Doctors Contact your embassy for a list of English-speaking doctors in Guatemala City.

Drugstores Guatemala City uses a duty-pharmacy (*farmacia de turno*) system. Ask for directions to the nearest pharmacy, then look in the window for the address and telephone number of the nearby pharmacy that is open that day or night. Two conveniently located drugstores are the Pharmacia Klee, 6a Avenida and 12 Calle, Zona 1 (tel. 23-905 or 20-060); and the one at 6a Avenida and 14 Calle, Zona 1 (tel. 23-906).

Embassies and Consulates Canada: Embassy and consulate, 7a Av. 11-59, Zona 9, Edificio Galerías España (tel. 321-411 or 321-413). United Kingdom: Embassy and consulate, 7a Av. 5-10, Edificio Centro Financiero, Torre 11, Nivel 7, Zona 4 (tel. 32-1601).

United States: Embassy and consulate, Avenida La Reforma 7-01, Zona 10 (tel. 311-541 or 311-555).

Emergencies For fire department call 123; for the national police call 120; for an ambulance call 128.

Eyeglasses Get your glasses repaired or replaced at Nacional Optica, 6a Av. 14-55, Zona 1.

Hairdressers/Barbers Salon Ramiro, 5a Av. 140-02, Zona 1, is a conveniently located hairdresser.

Holidays See "When to Go" in Chapter 8.

Hospitals Two good private hospitals are the Centro Medico, 6a Av. 3-47, Zona 10 (tel. 323-555), and Hospital Herrera Llerandi, 6a Av. 8-71, Zona 10 (tel. 36-771 or 36-775). For the names and addresses of others, consult your embassy or consulate or the *Yellow Pages* of the telephone directory under "Hospitales."

Information See "Tourist Information" in this chapter.

Laundry/Dry Cleaning First check with your hotel—most offer laundry service and can tell you where the nearest dry cleaner (*lavanderia seca*) is located. If you still need to find someplace, try these two: Lavanderia Cisne, Ruta 7, 7-34, Zona 4 (tel. 316-756), is open weekdays from 8am to 7pm and Saturday from 8am to 6pm; Centro, 9a Calle 6-65, Zona 1 (tel. 24-641), is open weekdays from 8am to 1pm and 3 to 7pm, Saturday from 8am to 2pm.

Libraries Biblioteca Nacional, 4a Avenida and 8a Calle, doesn't have much of interest unless you're a student who wants to do research. It's an incredibly large building. The student library is on the 5a Avenida side off 8a Calle, and as you enter you'll notice a controversial, high-relief sculpture done by artist Efrain Recinos. To the right is Centenario Park, where the Declaration of Independence was signed.

Lost Property You can contact the police or tourist office, but neither is really set up to handle lost and found.

Luggage Storage Your only choice if you want to leave a bag is to ask at your hotel; if you need to leave the bag for only a few hours, ask at the INGUAT (Tourist Information Center), 7a Av. 1-17, Zona 4.

Newspapers/Magazines Try the lobbies of major hotels for current editions of U.S. newspapers and magazines. They usually have *USA Today, The International Herald Tribune, The New York Times, Time,* and *Newsweek.* Guatemala's most popular daily newspaper is *Prensa Libre,* in which you'll find information on cultural events around town.

Photographic Needs   There are 1-hour to 24-hour film processing centers all over downtown these days, but I still recommend waiting until you get home to have your processing done. Film is expensive.

Police   See *Emergencies.*

Post Office   The central post office is at the corner of 12 Calle and 7a Avenida in Zona 1—open weekdays from 8am to 7pm, Saturday from 8am to 3pm; closed Sunday. It has no sign to identify it. Look for the men selling postcards in large racks—that's the front door. Other post offices are generally open weekdays from 7:30am to 12:30pm and 1 to 2:30pm, Saturday from 8 to 11am.

Radio/TV   Marimba is the national music and is heard on many radio stations. Many hotels now have satellites and offer U.S. programming.

Religious Services   Guatemala is a Roman Catholic country, in which there are dozens of Catholic churches, many of them old and beautiful. Some conveniently located churches include Catedral Metropolitana, 7a Avenida between 6a and 8a calles, Zona 1; Capuchinas, 10a Avenida and 10a Calle, Zona 1; and Nuestra Señora de la Merced, 11 Avenida and 5a Calle, Zona 1.

Restrooms   In Guatemala, public restrooms are called *servicios* or *servicios sanitarios.* Men are *caballeros* and women are *damas.* There aren't many public toilets around, but you will find them in restaurants and the lobbies of large hotels.

Safety   Guatemala City is very urban, with all the problems you would expect in a densely populated area. Take extra precautions with your money, credit cards, traveler's checks, and passport whenever you are out, especially if you are in a market or a crowded bus or on a busy sidewalk. It is best to wear a moneybelt large enough to hold your money and passport under your clothes. I like the type that you wear around your neck; they're easier to get at when you need them. Carry only as much cash as you think you'll need when venturing out of your hotel and try to keep it in a buttoned pocket so you don't have to pull your moneybelt out in public. The areas around 7a Avenida and 18 Calle and 18 Calle between 4a Avenida and 8a Avenida are well known as haunts of pickpockets, so try to avoid these areas. If you are driving a car, never park it on the street. There are plenty of public parking lots available for only a few cents an hour. Look for signs reading *estacionamentos.*

Taxes   The 17% hotel tax is included in hotel room rates quoted in this book.

Taxis   See "Getting Around" in this chapter.

Telegrams   To send a telegram dial 127. International telegrams are handled by the Guatel, the Guatemalan telephone company. The main office is at 7a Avenida 12-39, Zona 1 (tel. 80-598). All other telegrams are handled by post offices.

Telephones   Most telephone numbers in Guatemala City have six digits, but a few old ones have only five. Special information and emergency numbers have only three digits. For intercity long-distance calls, dial 121; for international calls, dial 171. Directory assistance is 124; the correct time is 126. A pay phone in Guatemala is called a *telefono monedero.*

Water   Although the tap water in the capital is chlorinated and presumably safe, it's probably a good idea to stick to bottled mineral water, soft drinks, wine, beer, and the like.

3. WHERE TO STAY

Just as you would expect in a large cosmopolitan city, Guatemala City has a wide variety of hotels in various price categories. Those at the low end of the budget tend to be concentrated in the area within a few blocks of 6a Avenida between 6a Calle and 16 Calle in Zona 1. You'll find a couple at the top end of your budget in Zona 4, but nearly all of the city's luxury hotels are in zonas 9 and 10. It is relatively safe, but Zona 1 is hardly what you might call an attractive neighborhood, and there is little of interest to see or do. Most visitors to Guatemala spend as little time as possible in the capital, and I suggest you follow suit. However, if you're forced to spend a night here, try these suggestions.

DOUBLES FOR LESS THAN Q50 ($12.50)

CHALET SUIZO, 14 Calle 6-82, Zona 1, Guatemala City. Tel. 502/513-786. 45 rms., 20 with private bath.

$ Rates: Q12–Q23.50 ($3–$5.88) single; Q20–Q32 ($5–$8) double; Q28–Q40 ($7–$10) triple; higher prices are for rooms with baths. No credit cards.

This is a homey place with a lot of plants in the courtyard and several Swiss travel posters to give authenticity to the name. The rooms are clean and quite presentable, although some are darker and more claustrophobic than others. As in most budget establishments, you should look before you sign in. The hotel underwent an extensive remodeling and expansion in 1990, and the new rooms are very attractive and are still an excellent bargain.

There is a tiny restaurant two doors away that is frequented almost exclusively by folks staying here. Meals are very reasonably priced ($2 to $3).

HOTEL LESSING HOUSE, 12 Calle 4-35, Zona 1, Guatemala City. Tel. 502/513-891. 8 rms., all with bath.

$ Rates: Q14.75 ($3.70) single; Q23.40 ($5.85) double. No credit cards.

This place is managed by an efficient and genial señora who will invite you in and show you her eight rooms, which feature craft decorations and some pretensions to style. Each room has two or three beds and a private bath (shower) with hot water. The hotel is located in a good area and has been a trustworthy refuge for travelers for many years.

SPRING HOTEL, 8a Av. 12-65, Zona 1, Guatemala City. Tel. 502/26-637, 514-207, or 514-876. 28 rms., 10 with bath.

$ Rates: Q12.29 ($3.07) single without bath, Q15.21 ($3.80) single with bath; Q19.21 ($4.80) double without bath, Q23.99 ($6) double with bath. DC.

A fairly good location, decent rooms in an old-style building converted for use as a hotel, and a sunny little courtyard make this another acceptable rock-bottom choice. The rooms are not fancy and might have a bit of peeling paint, but they are large and at a good price.

HOTEL HERNANI, 15 Calle 6-56, Zona 1, Guatemala City. Tel. 502/22-839. 20 rms.

$ Rates: Q17.55 ($4.38) single; Q29.25 ($7.31) double; Q38.60 ($9.65) triple. No credit cards.

This dignified small hotel in a fairly good location is another fine choice for those watching every penny. Many rooms here have private bathrooms, but the baths are separate from the rooms—the bathroom down the hall is yours only, but it's not connected to your room.

HOGAR DEL TURISTA, 11 Calle 10-43, Zona 1, Guatemala City. Tel. 502/25-522. 10 rms., all with bath.

$ Rates: Q40 ($10) single; Q50 ($12.50) double. No credit cards accepted. **Parking:** Free.

The street may look rather depressing and industrial, but once inside the hotel you'll forget the outside world. A simple converted city house, the Hogar del Turista is very popular with the backpacking crowd. Two narrow courtyards provide light and sun, and two bright, pleasant local ladies keep everything clean. Native blankets cover the beds, and Guatemalan crafts decorate the walls. Most rooms have windows opening onto the courtyards to provide light, but there are a few dolorous rooms without any windows at all. Breakfast can be had for Q6 ($1.50).

DOUBLES FOR LESS THAN Q100 [$25]

HOTEL COLONIAL, 7a Av. 14-19, Zona 1, Guatemala City. Tel. 502/26-722, 22-955, or 81-208. 42 rms., all with bath.

$ Rates: Q45 ($11.25) single; Q60 ($15) double; Q75 ($18.75) triple. No credit cards.

S If you'd like to stay in a grand old mansion converted into a hotel, try the Colonial. The pleasant interior court has been covered over with translucent plastic panels to let the sun in but to keep the rain out; the walls are of frighteningly tactile stucco; and the parlor is furnished in ponderous neocolonial pieces. The guest rooms gleam and shine—there is nothing tattered or worn here. Carved bedsteads and huge old wardrobes, although not antique, are properly colonial. All rooms have baths, but some rooms are more luxurious than others, so examine several before taking your pick.

HOTEL CENTENARIO, 6a Calle 5-33, Zona 1, Guatemala City. Tel. 502/80-381 to 80-383. 43 rms., all with bath.

$ Rates: Q49.84–Q62.31 ($12.46–$15.58) single; Q66.46–Q78.92 ($16.62–$19.73) double; Q83.07–Q95.54 ($20.77–$23.89) triple; Q99.68–Q112.15 ($24.92–$28.04) quad; higher rates are for rooms with TV. AE, DC, MC, V.

Want to stay right near the National Palace? This old-fashioned hotel is right on the main square, almost next door to the National Palace. The façade of the hotel is quite plain and unprepossessing, but it's painted a bright blue that you can't miss. Built at least 50 years ago, the Centenario has been well maintained and recently redecorated. It's a modest place, but the staff is particularly helpful, providing carafes of drinking water, free ice, maps of the city, and pocket calendars. The rooms are simple but nice enough, many with good beds (often there's a double and a single bed in a room). The private baths have showers that are well worn but tidy.

SUITES CORDOBA, 6a Av. "A" 10-52, Zona 1, Guatemala City. Tel. 502/22-602. 9 suites, all with bath. TV TEL

$ Rates: Q87.75 ($21.94) single; Q99.45 ($24.86) double; Q111.15 ($27.79) triple; 10% discount for weekly stays. DC, MC, V.

Directly across the street from the Ritz Continental is another good downtown choice, especially for those planning a long stay in Guatemala City. All the suites come complete with kitchenettes, living rooms, and bedrooms with two double beds. The decor and furnishings, rather spartan, are nevertheless modern and comfortable. A built-in vanity and Formica-topped bar provide convenience without taking up space. The suites are only four years old and are reached by elevator from a small reception area. This is an excellent choice for businesspeople or families on a tight budget.

DOUBLES FOR LESS THAN Q150 [$37.50]

HOTEL GUATEMALA INTERNATIONAL, 6a Av. 12-21, Zona 1, Guatemala City. Tel. 502/84-441 to 81-445. 33 apartments, all with bath.

$ Rates: Q70.20 ($17.55) single; Q111.15 ($27.79) double; Q128.70 ($32.18) triple. DC, MC, V.

This is an excellent value for those who covet space and a central location. In this convenient location in the midst of the commercial district, you'll find a very plain lobby and two elevators that will take you up to 33 furnished apartments. Each of these modern accommodations has one double bed and one single; a small living room with a day bed; a table and chairs for dining or working; a tiled bathroom with tub and shower with glass doors; and a kitchen with a full-size refrigerator/freezer, four-burner range, sink, and an assortment of pots, pans, tableware, and utensils. It's a popular spot with well-informed gringos.

POSADA BELEN, 13 Calle "A" 10-30, Zona 1, Guatemala City. Tel. 502/29-226, 534-530, or 513-478. 10 rms., all with bath.

$ Rates: Q102.96 ($25.74) single; Q121.68 ($30.42) double; Q140.40 ($35.10) triple; lower rates in May and September. AE, DC, MC, V.

⭐ This small family-run pension has long enjoyed an excellent reputation. Since the Belen is on a little downtown side street, its rooms are quiet, and the quiet is further encouraged by a policy of discouraging guests with children under 5 years of age. The pension has a charming, sunny courtyard with tropical plants; parrots; a fountain; much wrought-iron decoration; many fine examples of local textiles, including weavings and native blankets; a cozy breakfast room; and a rack of used books for exchange. The price is a bit high, but the Belen is certainly a unique place. The rooms are attractively appointed with lots of local arts and crafts. There are even skylights in the bathrooms. Francesca Sanchinelli, your hostess, speaks excellent English.

Breakfast and lunch are served; if you let them know in advance, dinner also is served. Prices range from Q8 ($2) for a Continental breakfast to Q64 ($8) for a full dinner.

HOTEL DEL CENTRO, 13 Calle 4-55, Zona 1, Guatemala City. Tel. 502/81-281 or 81-282. Fax 502/22-705. 60 rms., all with bath. TV
$ Rates: Q122.85 ($30.71) single; Q140.40 ($35.10) double; Q157.95 ($39.49) triple. AE, DC, MC, V.

Ⓢ This is perhaps the all-around best place to stay when considering its location, services, comforts, and price. A five-story building with colonial-inspired modern decor, the Del Centro has all the comforts and conveniences—from thick carpets and plush furniture to large, light, and airy guest rooms with two double beds, separate seating areas, big color TVs, and small but new and very clean tile bathrooms. Although there is a bit of street noise, this hotel offers the best value in the city and has been doing so dependably for several decades.

In the Del Centro's second-floor restaurant, a typical daily special meal might be soup, shrimp cooked in a beer batter, potatoes and fresh vegetables, dessert, and coffee for Q14 ($3.50), plus drink, tax, and tip.

HOTEL VILLA ESPAÑOLA, 2a Calle 7-51, Zona 9, Guatemala City. Tel. 502/365-417, 365-611, 365-515, 323-362, 323-381, or 318-503. 67 rms., 3 suites, all with bath. TEL
$ Rates: Q117 ($29.25) single; Q140.40 ($35.10) double. AE, DC, MC, V.
Parking: free.
This Spanish colonial–style motel, just south of downtown in Zona 4, could easily have been transported here from a Texas interstate. All the expected amenities are here, except the swimming pool. Rooms are carpeted and have one or two double beds. For a little bit extra, you get a TV in your room. You'll even find a tub in the bathroom, not just a shower.

Down in the bright basement of the hotel, you'll find a large dining room decorated with colonial reproductions. The menu, which features both Guatemalan and international cuisine, is varied and reasonably priced—with meals ranging from about Q20 ($5) to Q40 ($10). There is also a small bar down here.
Service: Laundry service.

WORTH THE EXTRA BUCKS

Besides the top-rated choices above, the Guatemalan capital has several hotels that, while technically outside your budget, will undoubtedly appeal to readers willing to spend just a little more.

HOTEL PLAZA, Via 7, 6-16, Zona 4, Guatemala City. Tel. 502/363-173, 316-337, or 310-396. 64 rms., all with bath. 6 suites.
$ Rates: Q140.40 ($35.10) single; Q163.80 ($40.95) double; Q163.80 ($40.95) single suite; Q187.20 ($46.80) double suite. AE, DC, MC, V.

Ⓢ The Plaza is not downtown, but in Zona 4, south of the Civic Center. It's located just off busy 7a Avenida, but most of the rooms are quiet. This pleasant hostelry might best be described as a Spanish Bauhaus motel, with echoes of old Spain coming through the clean lines and curves of the Bauhaus idiom—you'll see what I mean. Two motel-style floors are arranged facing the enclosed parking lot or the courtyard's heated swimming pool. The guest rooms are comfy and well-kept, with good baths. The Plaza is within walking distance of the Zona 4 bus terminal if your bags are light; you will have to ask your way frequently to get through the maze of streets. Ask for Septima Avenida, and once you get to that major avenue, the Plaza isn't far away. There's a nice restaurant and bar where a meal will run around Q20 ($5).

HOTEL RITZ CONTINENTAL, 6a Av. "A" 10-13, Zona 1, Guatemala City. Tel. 502/21-085, 80-889, 81-671 to 81-675 or 818-71 to 81-875. Fax 502/24-659. 202 rms., all with bath. TV TEL

$ Rates: Q128.70 ($32.18) single; Q163.80 ($40.95) double; Q181.35 ($45.34) triple. AE, DC, MC, V. **Parking:** free.

This hotel was one of the city's premier luxury hotels several decades ago, and its marble-paved lobby still bustles with activity. In a glass case here you'll see a stuffed quetzal, the iridescent-green national bird of Guatemala. Its swimming pool is still a good refresher. The 202 guest rooms have been well maintained and now have cable color TV sets, parquet floors, and marble-accented bathrooms. Doors and cabinets are intricately carved, and a candle on the bathroom counter lends an air of romance. Most rooms are quiet, which is a blessing after walking the noisy streets of this city. The location is excellent, and the prices are reasonable.

The restaurant and bar (with live entertainment) are popular with guests and local people alike. A table d'hôte lunch in the Ritz's dining room will cost about Q12.75 ($3.20). In La Taberna bar, you'll find live Spanish easy-listening music Monday through Saturday at 6pm.

HOTEL PAN AMERICAN, 9a Calle 5-63, Zona 1, Guatemala City. Tel. 502/26-807, 26-808, or 26-809, or toll free 800/223-6764. Fax 502/26-402. 60 rms., all with bath. TV TEL

$ Rates: Q205.92 ($51.48) single; Q234 ($58.50) double; Q290.16 ($72.54) triple. AE, DC, MC, V. **Parking:** Q3 (75¢).

★ This is a colonial-style hotel in the very midst of Zona 1. The spacious interior courtyard is now covered, equipped with a fountain, decorated with framed huipiles, and set with tables and chairs to serve as a dining area. Waiters and waitresses are in traditional country garb. With the soothing sound of water from the fountain, it's a very enjoyable place for lunch. In keeping with the 1930s decor, there is one elevator, manned by an operator, to take you upstairs. The rooms seem not to have changed much since the hotel's heyday and, although quite clean and tidy, are still furnished the same way. If you're an art deco aficionado, you'll be in heaven. The clean private bathrooms have tubs and showers, and each room has a large cable color TV. Rooms facing the street can be noisy, but those overlooking the courtyard are quiet.

Even if you don't plan to stay here, come by for the set-price lunch, which might be a Guatemalan plate of chuchitos (tamales à la Chichicastenango), black beans, and fried bananas; a tropical fruit plate; or a beef pot roast. The portions are huge, and the prices are a reasonable Q8 ($2) to Q20 ($5), plus drink, tax, and tip.

4. WHERE TO EAT

For the best food at the best price in the most pleasant surroundings, the thing to do in Guatemala City is to dine at one of the better hotels. The Hotel Del Centro, Hotel Pan American, and Hotel Ritz Continental all have good dining rooms serving tasty food in large portions at surprisingly reasonable prices, usually around Q20 ($5) to Q30 ($7.50) for an entire meal. Refer to the descriptions of those hotels given above for details. For more reasonably priced meals, you might try the following.

MEALS FOR LESS THAN Q20 [$5]

RESTAURANT LONG WAH, 6a Calle 3-70, Zona 1. Tel. 26-611.
   Cuisine: CHINESE.
$ Prices: Main dishes Q6–Q9 ($1.50–$2.25). No credit cards.
   Open: Daily 11am–11pm.
This noisy restaurant is in the midst of Guatemala City's tiny Chinatown district, a few blocks west of the Parque Central on 6a Calle at 4a Avenida, along with several other Chinese restaurants bearing names such as Felicidades and Palacio Real and China Hilton. The five rooms at the Long Wah, done in the predictable gold lanterns, red booths, and black wainscoting, are often bustling with diners out for a change of pace. Adapt the Spanish transliterations on the menu slightly, and you'll see that "chaw mein" is chow mein, "wantan" is wonton, and so forth. The most expensive dishes are those with shrimp for Q16 ($4). Beer is served.

RESTAURANT RUBY, 11 Calle 6-56, Zona 1. Tel. 26-438.
   Cuisine: CHINESE.
$ Prices: Main dishes Q6–Q10 ($1.50–$2.50). No credit cards.
   Open: Daily noon–8:45pm.
For Chinese food closer to the Hotel Ritz Continental, try Ruby. The menu is suitably bewildering, running to 133 items, but the special plates (large or small) give you samplers of the best items. Ruby is one high-ceilinged corridor, a lunch counter, and several rear dining rooms that are always busy. The menu is in Chinese, Spanish, and English, and a number of new-world dishes make it into the list.

RESTAURANT BOLOGNA, 10a Calle 6-20, Zona 1. Tel. 51-1167.
   Cuisine: ITALIAN.
$ Prices: Main dishes Q7–Q13 ($1.75–$3.25). No credit cards.
   Open: Wed–Mon 10am–10pm.
Around the corner from the Hotel Ritz Continental is a tiny storefront place serving lunches and dinners Italian style—with pizzas, spaghetti, ravioli, and lasagna and even some fancier dishes, such as grilled meats and rabbit (*conejo*) alla bolognese. It's a good choice if you're in the mood for Italian.

MEALS FOR LESS THAN Q30 [$7.50]

LOS ANTOJITOS, 15 Calle 6-28, Zona 1. Tel. 27-804.
   Cuisine: GUATEMALAN.
$ Prices: Appetizers Q2–Q8 (50¢–$2); main dishes Q8–Q20 ($2–$5). AE, DC, MC, V.
   Open: Daily 11am–11pm.
If you have just spent the day walking all over the city, you owe it to yourself to spend the evening at Los Antojitos. You enter past a señora who is slapping out tortillas and cooking them over hot coals by the door. Take a seat in one of the many dining rooms, preferably one near the front, where you get a window. Let the marimba band serenade you while you indulge in plate after plate of delectable *antojitos* (appetizers). My approach to the menu each time I visit is to order a few antojitos I've never tried before. After several visits, I still haven't come close to tasting all the tempting dishes. If you're absolutely famished, you might even want to try ordering both an antojito and a main course, but be forewarned that either one is a meal in itself. El banquete is just that—a banquet for one—and the típico nacional and típico especial are both excellent introductions to the meat-heavy but tasty foods of Guatemala. The best chile relleno I've ever had came out of this kitchen, and the creamy, spicy salsa is out of this world.

RESTAURANT ALTUNA, 5a 12-31, Zona 1. Tel. 20-669.
   Cuisine: SPANISH.

$ Prices: Main dishes Q10–Q24 ($2.50–$6). AE, DC, MC, V.
Open: Daily 12:30–11pm.

Just a few steps north of the Hotel Del Centro is a big restaurant with lots of dining rooms done in European style—with dark-wood furniture, white tablecloths, and formal but pleasant and unobtrusive decor. The service is smooth and polished, and the specialties are Spanish cuisine and seafood, with fish and squid, shrimp, steaks, chicken, and even doves cooked in sherry on the menu. A full meal here, all included, will come to about Q30 ($7.50) per person. Popular with local businesspeople at lunch.

EL GRAN PAVO ["The Big Turkey"], 13 Calle 4-41, Zona 1. Tel. 510-933 or 29-912. Also at 12 Calle 6-54, Zona 9. Tel. 325-693 or 313-976.
Cuisine: MEXICAN.
$ Prices: Main dishes Q14–Q28 ($3.50–$7). DC, MC, V.
Open: Daily 9am–1am.

Plain but clean and cheerful, El Gran Pavo adjoins the Hotel Del Centro and is fairly large, with several dining rooms. A long menu tries admirably to cover every variety of Mexican cuisine, from Veracruz seafood and mole poblano through panuchos yucatecos to cabrito al horno. The antojito (appetizer) menu alone is enough to keep adventurous diners busy for weeks. The range of prices is as wide as that of the menu selections. A big Mexican combination plate, drink, tax, and tip will cost about Q24 ($6). That unusual beribboned umbrella just inside the door is actually a design based on a Guatemalan kite.

LOCAL BUDGET BET

CAFETERÍA EL ROBLE, 9a Calle 5-46, Zona 1. No phone.
Cuisine: GUATEMALAN.
$ Prices: Q3–Q4 (75¢–$1). No credit cards.
Open: Daily 7am–9pm.

If your budget is really low, take a look at the little place across from the entrance to the Hotel Pan American. A cafetería in Guatemala is not a place where you stand in line with a tray while a surly foodservice worker ladles unidentifiable stuff onto your plate. There are cafeterías all over town; they're where local office workers go when they're tired of fried chicken and burgers. This clean little café is nothing fancy, but you can get breakfast here for less than a dollar and lunch for only slightly more, any day of the week.

SPECIALTY DINING
FAST-FOOD CHAINS

MCDONALD'S, at 10a Calle 5-30, Zona 1. Tel. 519-862.
Cuisine: BURGERS.
$ Prices: Q2–Q6 (50¢–$1.50). No credit cards.
Open: Daily 6:30am–10pm.

Guatemalans go for burgers in a big way, and McDonald's clones are springing up all over. For a taste of home, stop in and order a "queso burguesa" and a soft drink, or go all out and have a Big Mac, papas fritas, and a drink for less than Q7 ($1.75). They serve breakfast scrambled eggs and pancakes here as well. By the way, a "quarto de libra" is a Quarter-Pounder.

POLLO CAMPERO, 9a Calle and 5a Avenida, Zona 1. Also at 6a Avenida and 15 Calle, Zona 1. Also at 8a Calle 9-29, Zona 1. No phone.
Cuisine: CHICKEN.
$ Prices: Full meal Q4–Q8 ($1–$2). No credit cards.
Open: Daily 7:30am–10:30pm.

Imitations of Colonel Sanders' eateries have sprung up all over Guatemala in recent years. For a taste of fried chicken Guatemalan-style, seek out a branch of Pollo

Campero, which is bright and cheery with orange-and-yellow tables and burnt-orange floor tiles. You'll feel as though you're back home at your favorite chicken restaurant. A lunch consisting of two pieces of chicken, french fries, and a soft drink or coffee costs Q6 ($1.50); supper, with one more piece of chicken plus salad, costs just slightly more.

A DINING COMPLEX

MULTIRESTAURANTES, 10a Calle and 6a Avenida, Zona 1. No phone.
  Cuisine: INTERNATIONAL.
  $ Prices: Q2–Q8 (50¢–$2). No credit cards.
  Open: Daily 7am–9pm.
This city has its own version of those North American multi-eateries where several fast-food stands share a common seating area. It's a spacious hall with a covered courtyard, nice tile floors, a fountain, and fancy wooden picnic tables inside a five-story shopping mall. Available cuisines include Guatemalan, North American, Chinese, and Italian.

FOR PASTRY

CAFÉ BOHEMIA, 11 Calle 8-48. Tel. 82-474.
  Cuisine: PASTRIES.
  $ Prices: 60 centavos–Q2 (15¢–50¢). No credit cards.
  Open: Mon–Sat 9am–7pm.
When you're hungry for cakes and pastries, seek out this little café where Central European country furniture and aproned waitresses put you in the mood for the selection of bakery treats in the display cases. Coffee and pastry should cost less than a dollar; if you're a bit hungrier, you can get a ham-and-cheese sandwich, a filled croissant, or a whole cake.

RESTAURANTS BY CUISINE
Price Category

CHINESE	
Restaurant Long Wah (p. 157)	B
Restaurant Ruby (p. 157)	B
GUATEMALAN	
Los Antojitos (p. 157)	M
Cafetería El Roble (p. 158)	B
ITALIAN	
Restaurant Bologna (p. 157)	B
MEXICAN	
El Gran Pavo (p. 158)	M
SPANISH	
Restaurant Altuna (p. 157)	M

Note: B = Budget and M = Moderate.

5. ATTRACTIONS

This, the largest city in Central America, spreads across a narrow plateau cut by deep ravines. The old downtown section of the city, Zona 1, is centered on the Palacio Nacional (National Palace), the Catedral Metropolitana (Metropolitan Cathedral), and the Biblioteca Nacional (National Archives and Library), all of which face the Parque Central. Start your tour here, then work your way south to see the city's other sights, all the way to the Parque Aurora, near the airport at the southern end of town in Zona 13.

SIGHT-SEEING STRATEGIES

IF YOU HAVE ONE DAY

Head first to the Museum of Archeology out near the airport. Then head over to the Paseo de la Reforma area to visit the Popol Vuh Museum and the Ixchel Museum. These three museums should just about fill your day.

IF YOU HAVE TWO DAYS

On your second day, visit the Mapa en Relieve and the Parque Central, where you will find the Metropolitan Cathedral and the National Palace. After lunch, stroll down 6a Avenida for a bit of shopping. You might also hop a bus and visit the Yurrita Chapel.

IF YOU HAVE THREE DAYS

Visit the ruins of Kaminal Juyú on the outskirts of the city and perhaps the Museo de Artes e Industrias Populares.

IF YOU HAVE FIVE DAYS

If you have this much time, you should spend at least two days in Antigua, which is much more interesting than Guatemala City and is only an hour away.

THE TOP ATTRACTIONS

MUSEO DE ARQUEOLOGÍA Y ETNOLOGÍA, Building No. 5, Parque La Aurora. Tel. 720-489.

The beautiful stark-white Moorish building in Parque La Aurora is the Archeological and Ethnological Museum, which boasts the largest and most spectacular collection of Mayan carvings in the world. One of the more famous pieces now on display is the throne from Piedras Negras, which you should not miss. The throne had been in storage for a decade while the museum was being renovated.

As you wander through the archeological section of the museum, you'll see beautiful black ceramic vessels from excavations in Zaculeu (Preclassic Period, A.D. 200); an outstanding collection of clay masks (Postclassic Period, A.D. 925 to 1200), and artifacts of shell, alabaster, obsidian, and flint (Classic Period, A.D. 200 to 925).

There is also an ethnological section in the museum, with a textile room in which are displayed 150 native costumes. Moving through the other ethnological rooms, you'll see a glass rotunda exhibiting the types of dwellings the Indians used, exhibits of nutrition (foods that originated in America), and industry (baskets, ceramics, weaving, and so on).

Admission: Q1 (25¢).

Open: Tues–Fri 9am–4pm; Sat–Sun 9am–noon and 2–4pm. **Bus:** Black no. 5.

MUSEO POPOL VUH, EDIFICIO GALERIA REFORMA, 6th floor, Avenida La Reforma 8-60, Zona 9. Tel. 847-121.

In 1977 Jorge and Ella Castillo donated their personal collection of Mayan art to the Universidad Francisco Marroquin, which now cares for it in the Museo Popol Vuh, named for the sacred "painted book" of the Quiché Mayans, now known as the Dresden Codex. There is a copy of this unique book on display in the museum.

The immense collection of Mayan art is arranged by region and period, as is a smaller collection of colonial religious and secular art. Some of the Mayan pieces are simply gorgeous: polychrome vases, huge burial urns, incense burners, and ceramic figurines. The religious art, mostly of the 16th to 18th centuries, includes some handsome altars in wood with silver trim. You'll find folk art here as well: face masks, which are still made and used in many regions, and mannequins wearing regional costumes. This collection is perhaps the finest in the city.

There's a good museum shop here, with an excellent bookstore and a nice crafts collection. On the ground floor in the same building is the Café Reforma, good for a light lunch, snack, or pick-me-up beverage.

Admission: Q3 (75¢) adults; Q1 (25¢) college students; 50 centavos (13¢) secondary-school students; 25 centavos (6¢) children under 12; Q5 ($1.25) to take photos.

Open: Mon–Sat 9am–5:30pm. **Bus:** Any Avenida la Reforma bus.

MUSEO IXCHEL DE TRAJE INDÍGENA (Ixchel Native Dress Museum), 4a Avenida 16-27, Zona 10. Tel. 680-713.

Ixchel, wife of the Mayan sky god, Itzamna, was goddess of the moon and protectress of women in childbirth. The museum bearing her name is dedicated to the woven art of Guatemala's Mayan women and to their village life-style. It's a private, nonprofit museum established in a large house in this luxury neighborhood, walking distance from the Museo Popol Vuh. From the Popol Vuh, walk south on Avenida La Reforma about seven blocks, past the Westin Camino Real Hotel, and turn left (east) onto 16 Calle. Go a few blocks along 16 Calle to 4a Avenida and turn right (south), and the museum will be on your left; you'll see a group of Guatemalan village women gorgeously dressed in their own handwork waiting near the museum gate to offer you textiles to buy.

The two floors of the house are filled with exquisite examples of Guatemalan traditional weaving from the various sections of the country. Artful use of mannequins has created lifelike situations that work well to give you a feeling for the creative, hard-working indigenous people of Guatemala. Several figures represent members of the cofradías, the traditional village socioreligious groups whose duties and beliefs bridge the gap between traditional Mayan and Roman Catholic religion. Other exhibits demonstrate the weaving process through the use of looms, diagrams, and photographs. There are also exhibits showing tie-dying, which is done in Huehuetenango and some other towns. Signs on the exhibits are in English as well as in Spanish.

On the ground floor, the museum has a nice shop selling books, crafts, and textiles.

Admission: Q2.50 (63¢) adults; Q1 (25¢) college students; 50 centavos (13¢) secondary-school students; 25 centavos (6¢) children under 12.

Open: Mon–Fri 9am–5:30pm. **Bus:** Any Avenida la Reforma bus.

PALACIO NACIONAL, Plaza Mayor, 6a Calle between 6a and 7a avenidas. No phone.

The heart of Guatemala's governmental power is here in the Palacio Nacional (National Palace), built at a cost of Q2,800,000—when that amount had a much higher exchange rate than today—by Gen. José Ubico, president from 1939 to 1943. The palace has three entrances you can use; the fourth, on the back, is for VIPs, whose darkened, bulletproof cars bristling with radio antennas wait in readiness there. The main entrance facing the Parque Central is the site of exhibits that change from time to time; it's the two side entrances that will take you inside the palace. You will catch the mood of the palace as you climb the brass-and-wood stairways up through three levels of beautiful wood-beamed ceilings, hand-carved stone-and-wood columns, frescoed arches, large wrought-iron-and-glass lanterns, tile floors, and numerous murals by Alfredo Galvez Suarez. It's fascinating, with all the interest of a museum yet not so overpowering as to be an unlivable place. There's a sense of harmony about the palace that you don't often find in government buildings. The two side entrances lead up to symmetrical floors, both of which overlook separate courtyards on the ground floor.

Admission: Free.

Open: Mon–Fri 9am–5pm; Sat 10am–noon. **Bus:** Any bus that stops at Plaza Mayor.

MAPA EN RELIEVE, Parque Minerva, 11 Calle and 6a Avenida at the end of Avenida Simeon Cañas, Zona 2. No phone.

Perhaps you've heard of Guatemala's famous Relief Map, a scale model of the entire country. It's 40 by 80 yards, with a depth of 2 yards; the proportions of the mountains (especially the volcanoes) have been exaggerated so that the topography of the country is readily apparent. You can observe the map from ground level or climb up one of the observation platforms for a look at Guatemala from the air. The major towns and features are marked by labels and little pennants. It's nice that Guatemala is small and distinct enough that such a map could be built. Francisco Vela, the engineer who created the map, had to traverse the country by donkey to collect all the information necessary to construct the map in 1904. The map is several dozen blocks to the north of the National Palace. To reach it, follow 7a Avenida north to its very end, where it joins Avenida Simeon Cañas near the Parque Minerva.

Admission: Free.
Open: Daily 9am–5pm. **Bus:** Nos. 1 and 18.

MORE ATTRACTIONS

RUINS OF KAMINAL JUYÚ, Zona 7. Tel. 516-224.

Kaminal Juyú was a very early Mayan city (300 B.C. to A.D. 900), flourishing before the classic Mayan cities of Tikal and Palenque. The earliest people (the Miraflores) planted crops and made excellent ceramics and carved jade. They seem to have been dominated by the priestly class that held all the power. By A.D. 300 Kaminal Juyú had been conquered by the people of Teotihuacan (near Mexico City), but the rulers who came from Mexico were "Mayanized" over the years. The remains of the Intermediate Period (the Esperanza Period), before the peoples were completely assimilated, show a strange mixture of Mayan and Teotihuacan art and culture.

The Spanish conquerors who came in the 1500s make no mention of Kaminal Juyú, probably because the city had been burned and destroyed when it was abandoned in A.D. 900. It wasn't until the late 18th century that mounds were discovered, and only in 1899 did Maudslay begin the first excavations. About 200 mounds have been found here—some from the Miraflores' time, when structures were built of adobe and pumice, others from the later Esperanza Period, when the inhabitants built pyramids and temples of limestone. Archeologists have found traces of Teotihuacan influence, such as stepped temple platforms called *tablero y talud* covered in red stucco, slit-eyed figurines, and three-legged pottery cylinders, and also of influence from Monte Alban (Tlaloc figures with large headdresses). In the tombs here were the finest jade objects found in all Guatemala, and in fact these people valued jade more than they did gold. The objects found in the tombs, which include precious stones, pottery, terra-cotta figurines, and incense burners, are in the Archeological Museum and the Museo Popol Vuh, as are the stelae carved with hieroglyphs, earlier than any stelae found in the Petén (before A.D. 290).

Urban development has covered or destroyed much of the ancient city, and what you see today are substructures of buildings from various periods, built mostly of ordinary clay and rubble. There are a few of limestone covered in a lime wash, which is not too impressive a sight.

Admission: 50 centavos (13¢).
Open: Daily 8am–6pm. **Bus:** Take bus BC, "Kaminal Juyú," to the intersection of Diagonal 24 and 24a Avenida; the entrance is just west of Diagonal 24.

CATEDRAL METROPOLITANA, Plaza Mayor, 7a Avenida between 6a and 8a calles. No phone.

Despite its look of antiquity, the Metropolitan Cathedral, on the east side of the Parque Central, was built between 1782 and 1815. The wrought-iron gates into the cathedral precincts are locked every day between 1 and 3pm (the caretaker's lunch, I suppose). Don't enter with expectations of seeing a gorgeous symphony of gleaming gold and flowery decoration. As with many Guatemalan churches, this national symbol is quite plain, even severe, inside. The Archbishop's Palace is next to the cathedral.

Admission: Free.
Open: Daily 8am–7pm. **Bus:** Any bus that stops at Plaza Mayor.

CAPILLA YURRITA, Ruta 6 8-52, Zona 4. Tel. 363-514.

Located in a newer section of town, amid car dealers and offices, it is one of the most architecturally unusual churches in Guatemala City. If you have been through this part of town already, you may have noticed the tall steeple and wondered what it was. The chapel, built in 1928, is a bizarre structure worthy of Bavaria's mad King Ludwig. It draws on numerous architectural styles, including Gothic and Russian Orthodox church architecture. Notice the work lavished on the front doors. This is a privately owned family chapel, but the public is welcome to visit.

Admission: Free.

Open: Tues–Sat 8am–noon and 3:30–6pm; Sun 8am–1pm and 4–7pm. **Bus:** Red or black no. 5.

MUSEO DE ARTES E INDUSTRIAS POPULARES, 10a Calle 10-72, Zona 1. Tel. 80-334.

This small downtown museum is housed in an old colonial-style house. The collection includes naïve art paintings of processions and dances by Guatemalan artists. There are also examples of indigenous handcrafts, including carved and painted gourds, tin candle holders, and masks for the dances of the highland villages. There is also a large collection of antique musical instruments.

Admission: 25 centavos (6¢).

Open: Tues–Fri 9am–4pm; Sat–Sun 9am–noon and 2–4pm.

MUSEO DE HISTORIA, 9a Calle 9-70, Zona 1. Tel. 536-149.

To learn more about the history of Guatemala, stop by this museum. It has been undergoing renovation in recent years and is slowly taking on a modern appearance inside, although the exterior still looks quite decayed. The collection covers Guatemalan history from pre-history through the discovery, conquest, and colonization by Spain. Exhibits are more extensive for the period beginning after the country's independence in 1821. In these rooms you'll learn how the economic, social, and cultural life of the nation was shaped.

Admission: Free.

Open: Tues–Sun 8am–4pm.

MUSEO NACIONAL DE ARTE MODERNA, Building No. 6, Parque La Aurora. Tel. 720-467.

This small museum is located directly across the street from the Archeological Museum. The interior of the building is striking, with a high wooden rosette ceiling and white plaster walls. The museum was founded in 1934 and contains paintings and sculpture from the late 18th century up to the present. Some well-known Guatemalan painters, such as Carlos Merida and Garavito, are represented here. The historical section is smaller, the exhibit of greatest interest here being a collection of coins from the colonial period. There are sometimes temporary exhibits here that cause the permanent collection to be closed off. Call first.

Admission: Q1 (25¢).

Open: Tues–Fri 9am–4pm; Sat–Sun 9am–noon and 2–4pm. **Bus:** Black no. 5.

CENTRO CÍVICO, 21 Calle between 6a and 7a avenidas, Zona 1.

The central part of the city holds the Centro Cívico and Ciudad Olímpica, important complexes of buildings dedicated to city and national government and to sports. This is the pride of Guatemala City because of its modern architecture. The city fathers claim that it is "the most advanced architecture in Latin America." The center includes the well-known (and always hopelessly crowded) Bank of Guatemala, the Social Security Building (IGSS), and Olympic City. Much of the exterior relief sculpture is the work of artists Efrain Recinos and Carlos Merida. As you enter the complex (at the intersection of 6a Avenida and Diagonal 2), you'll see a statue of a wolf with Romulus and Remus underneath; the statue is inscribed "From Eternal Rome to Immortal Guatemala." To the right as you face the statue is City Hall and directly ahead of you in the distance is the Bank of Guatemala, constructed from 1962 to 1966. The high-relief murals in concrete are by Dagoberto Vasquez and depict the history of Guatemala. The Social Security Building behind City Hall was designed by

Roberto Aycinena and Jorge Montes; the enormous mosaic, completed in 1959, is by Carlos Merida. On the hill behind you is the Fortress of San José and the National Theater, which looks a lot like a blue-and-white ocean liner. Olympic City, farther to the east, is an enormous building that houses the Mateo Flores Stadium (named after the athlete who won the Boston Marathon in 1952), the National Gymnasium, a swimming pool, tennis courts, and a Boxing Palace.

COOL FOR KIDS

If you have your kids with you, then you should definitely plan on spending a lot of time at Parque la Aurora. The kids will definitely enjoy the amusement park and zoo and maybe even the Museum of Archeology.

WALKING TOUR — DOWNTOWN

Start: Plaza Mayor

Finish: Centro Cívico

Time: 3 hours

Best time: Mon–Fri 8am–6pm
Begin your tour on the Plaza Mayor, Guatemala City's central square.

1. **Palacio Nacional,** the seat of government in Guatemala, is on the north side of the square.
2. **Catedral Metropolitana** is on the east side.
3. **Biblioteca Nacional** is on the west.
4. **Mercado Central,** most of which is beneath a small open square, is in the block behind the Catedral Metropolitana. After you have visited these sites, stroll down busy 6a Avenida, the city's main shopping street. Take your time, stop and shop, and have a bite to eat.

REFUELING STOP　About halfway down 6a Avenida is my favorite Guatemala City restaurant, **5. Los Antojitos,** at 15 Calle 6-28.

---

6. **Centro Cultural Miguel Angel Asturias,** one of the most unusual buildings I've ever seen, is at the southern end of 6a Avenida. From the east and west, it resembles the superstructure of an ultramodern ocean liner. The cultural center houses three theaters.
7. **Centro Cívico and Ciudad Olímpico,** which both feature equally interesting architecture, are a block to the east.

WALKING TOUR — THE ZONA VIVA

Start: Museo Popol Vuh

Finish: Parque Aurora zoo

Time: All day
The Zona Viva is where the wealthy of Guatemala eat, shop, and live. It is also home to the city's most interesting museums.

1. **Museo Popol Vuh,** on Avenida La Reforma, is one of the city's best museums, with an excellent collection of pre-Columbian art. (*See listing on p. 160 for complete information.*) From here head south to 16 Calle, where you should turn left. It is a rather long walk, but the avenue is shady and there are plenty of

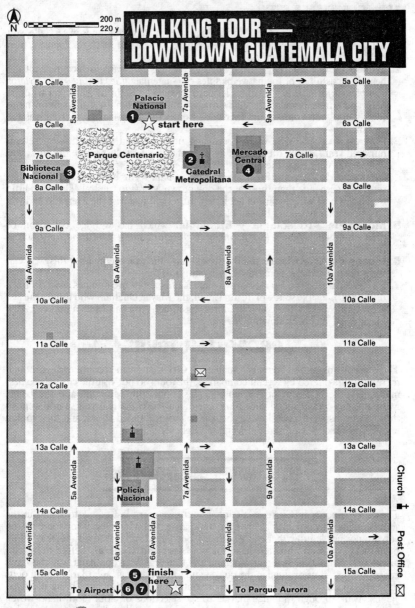

200 m
220 y
N

5a Calle
5a Avenida
7a Avenida
9a Avenida
5a Calle

6a Calle
Palacio
National
① ☆ start here
6a Calle

7a Calle
Parque Centenario
Mercado
Central
④
7a Calle

Biblioteca
Nacional ③
② †
Catedral
Metropolitana
8a Calle

8a Calle

9a Calle
9a Calle

4a Avenida
6a Avenida
8a Avenida
10a Avenida

10a Calle
10a Calle

11a Calle
11a Calle

✉

12a Calle
12a Calle

†

13a Calle
13a Calle

†

5a Avenida
7a Avenida
9a Avenida

Policía
Nacional

14a Calle
14a Calle

4a Avenida
6a Avenida
6a Avenida A
8a Avenida
10a Avenida

⑤ finish
here →
15a Calle
15a Calle

To Airport ↓ ⑥ ⑦ ↓ ☆   ↓ To Parque Aurora

Church ■†

Post Office ✉

GUATEMALA
CITY

Downtown

① Palacio Nacional
② Catedral Metropolitana
③ Biblioteca Nacional
④ Mercado Central
⑤ Los Antojitos
⑥ Centro Cultural Miguel Angel Asturias
⑦ Centro Cívico and Ciudad Olímpica

restaurants and shops to visit. Walking past the walled compounds of 16 Calle, you will get an idea of how the wealthy live here. When you reach 4a Avenida, turn right. A few houses down on the left is the—

2. **Museo Ixchel de Traje Indígena,** where you can learn to recognize all the beautiful costumes of the native peoples of Guatemala. *(See listing on p. 161 for complete information.)* Head back out to Avenida La Reforma when you are done here and carefully cross the busy road. Continue down 14 Calle several more blocks until you come to another wide boulevard, Diagonal 12. Across it is the entrance to—

3. **Parque Aurora.** You will be crossing under an old aqueduct built several hundred years ago by the Spanish as you enter the park. Just inside the park, you will see on your right the—

4. **Mercado de Artesanía,** where the prices tend to be high and the handcrafts seem less authentic than those at the downtown Mercado Central. There is a little restaurant here where you can get lunch. Turn right just past the Mercado and you will be within two long blocks of the—

5. **Museo de Arqueología y Etnología,** which has a huge collection of pre-Columbian artifacts. *(See listing on p. 160 for complete information.)* Across from this museum is the—

6. **Museo de Arte Moderno.** If you still have time or energy after this, you can walk north on the Avenida del Observatorio to the—

7. **Parque Zoológico La Aurora,** which is only about five minutes away. In front of the zoo is a large statue of Tecun Uman, the Mayan chieftain who fought the last great battle against the conquistadores. From here you can catch a taxi or take a black no. 5 bus back downtown.

ORGANIZED TOURS

There are no organized tours of Guatemala City that I can recommend. Although there are tours offered by several companies, the tours do not visit the city's three best museums—the Museum of Archeology, the Popol Vuh Museum, and the Ixchel Museum. You would spend your time here much more wisely if you simply went to these museums, perhaps following the walking tour outlined above, and then took a taxi to the Plaza Mayor and the Mapa en Relieve.

6. SAVVY SHOPPING

The savvy shopper in Guatemala City should save every last penny to spend in the shopper's heavens of Chichicastenango and Panajachel. However, if for some reason you are not headed to either of these places but would still like to buy some of those beautiful Guatemalan textiles, head for the **Mercado Central.** Before the earthquake of 1976, the area directly behind the Catedral Metropolitana was the city's central market. It was ruined in the quake, and a new one was built that has most of its shopping space below street level (they're not going to let a quake "bring it down" again!). Walk through the huge market to see selections of cloth (both hand-woven and machine-made), leather goods, woodcarvings, metalwork, baskets, and other handcrafts. It's worth at least a stroll through. All of the streets near the market are devoted to shopping as well. Be especially careful with your valuables: Pickpockets and purse slashers make a very good living here. Open Mon–Sat 9am–6pm, Sun 9am–noon.

The **Mercado de Artesanía** (Handcrafts Market), located in Parque Aurora, is an outdoor area with vendors' stalls, a small courtyard, and a modern restaurant. The products on sale represent a good portion of Guatemala, and the prices are not bad. They have leather goods, woven cloth, huipiles (blouses), ceramics, baskets, and hand-painted terra-cotta figurines. If you're traveling extensively throughout Guate-

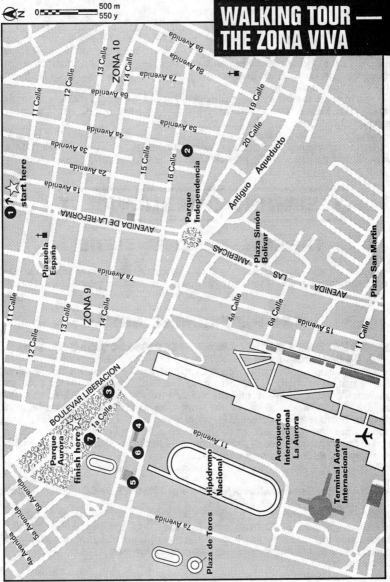

WALKING TOUR — THE ZONA VIVA

ZONA 10

13 Calle
14 Calle
12 Calle
11 Calle

9a Avenida
8a Avenida
7a Avenida
6a Avenida
5a Avenida
4a Avenida
3a Avenida
2a Avenida
1a Avenida

start here

15 Calle
16 Calle

19 Calle
20 Calle

Antiguo Aqueducto

② Parque Independencia

AVENIDA DE LA REFORMA

Plaziela España

Parque Independencia

LAS AMERICAS

Plaza Simón Bolívar

AVENIDA

Plaza San Martín

7a Avenida

ZONA 9

13 Calle
14 Calle

11 Calle
12 Calle

4a Calle

6a Calle

15 Avenida

11 Calle

BOULEVAR LIBERACION

③

1a Calle

④

⑥

⑤

⑦

Parque Aurora

finish here

6a Avenida

5a Avenida

4a Avenida

7a Avenida

11 Avenida

Hipódromo Nacional

Aeropuerto Internacional La Aurora

Terminal Aérea Internacional

Plaza de Toros

✈ Airport

✝ Church ■

0 ⸻ 500 m / 550 y

GUATEMALA CITY

The Zona Viva

① Museo Popol Vuh
② Museo Ixchel de Traje Indígena
③ Parque Aurora
④ Mercado de Artesanía
⑤ Museo de Arqueología y Etnología
⑥ Museo de Arte Moderno
⑦ Parque Zoológico La Aurora

mala, you'll find these products elsewhere, but it's probably worth a trip to see what they have here. Although prices are a little higher here than at the shops in Mercado Central, this is a very pleasant place, and you may even be entertained by a marimba band. As for the quality of the merchandise, it's good—with the exception of woven goods, especially huipiles, which are of higher quality in the villages. Open Mon–Sat 9am–6pm, Sun 9am–1pm.

If you're in the market for low-quality clothing and low-priced shoes, head for 6a Avenida. For higher quality and correspondingly higher prices, visit the many boutiques in the Zona Viva along Avenida La Reforma.

If you're buying large quantities and want to ship things home, your best bet is to use one of the shipping companies in Antigua or Panajachel. This will save you the aggravation of dealing with the post office and all its paperwork.

7. EVENING ENTERTAINMENT

THE ENTERTAINMENT SCENE

Although it is the largest in Central America, Guatemala City has very little in the way of an entertainment scene. If you crave cultural programs or lively nightlife, you're out of luck here.

THE PERFORMING ARTS

CENTRO CULTURAL MIGUEL ANGEL ASTURIAS, 24 Calle 3-81, Zona 1. Tel. 24-041 or 24-044.
Perched high atop a hill overlooking the Centro Cívico is a dramatic blue-and-white building that looks strangely like a luxury cruise ship. Don't worry—the polar ice caps haven't melted; this is the city cultural center, home to three theaters. Inaugurated in 1978, the building is the work of Guatemalan artist Efraín Recinos. The Gran Teatro seats more than 2,000 people. The much smaller Teatro de Cámara is for chamber music concerts, while the Teatro al Aire Libre, an open-air theater, stages everything from music to dance to drama. Check *Prensa Libre*, the city's daily newspaper, for information on performances.
Prices: Q10–Q60 ($2.50–$15), depending on performance and seat.

IGA (Instituto Guatemalteco-Americano), Ruta 1, 4-05, Zona 4. Tel. 310-022, 310-589, or 347-218.
This is the cultural heart of the English-speaking community in Guatemala City. Its small theater is near the Centro Cultural. When I was last in town, the month's programming included a performance of the play *K2*, a visit by the Lar Lubovitch Dance Company, and a video showing of the opera *Carmen*.
Prices: Free–Q60 ($15).

THE BAR, CLUB, AND MUSIC SCENE

The best place to look for active nightlife is in the Zona Viva, the area along Avenida La Reforma in Zona 9 and Zona 10. Here you will find the city's greatest concentration of expensive restaurants, bars, discos, and nightclubs. Probably your best bet will be to head to one of the major hotels in this area. Both the Hotel Conquistador Sheraton and the Westin Camino Real Hotel have popular discos frequented by locals and tourists. The **Manhattan,** 7a 14-44, Zona 9 in La Galería, and **Kahlua,** 1a 13-29, Zona 10, are two more popular discos. If you want to listen to live marimba music while you dine, have dinner at **Los Antojitos,** 15 Calle 6-28, Zona 1.

8. MOVING ON — TRAVEL SERVICES

If you don't already have a ticket out of the country, you can contact **Viajes Internacionales Paco Sandoval,** 6a Av. 9-62, Zona 1 (tel. 510-522 or 533-477), or **Clark Tours,** 7a Av. 6-53, Zona 4 (tel. 310-213), both of which are conveniently located.

BY PLANE

When the time comes for your flight out, take a taxi or the black no. 5 "Aeropuerto" bus out to the airport, leaving an hour or more for check-in, Customs, and immigration. There are a few duty-free shops past the immigration desks, but the shops in the main check-in are much more interesting.

Here are some of the most-used airlines serving the country; all have offices and counters at La Aurora Airport, and some have ticket offices downtown as well.

Aeronica, 10a Calle 6-20, Zona 9 (tel. 316-759 or 325-541).

Aeroquetzal, Avenida Hincapié and 18 Calle, Zona 13, Hangar no. 8 (tel. 365-214).

Aerovias, Avenida Hincapié and 18 Calle, Zona 13, at La Aurora Airport (tel. 347-935 or 325-686).

Aviateca, Avenida Hincapié, Zona 13 (tel. 318-222 or 318-227).

Continental, La Aurora Airport (tel. 312-051).

Iberia, Avenida La Reforma 8-60, Zona 9 (tel. 373-911).

Lacsa, 7a 14-44, Zona 9, Edificio La Galería (tel. 373-905, 307-906, or 307-907).

Mexicana, 12 Calle 4-55, Zona 1 (tel. 518-824 or 518-834).

Pan American, 6a 11-43, Zona 1 (tel. 22-144 or 22-146).

Sahsa, 12 Calle 1-25, Zona 10, Edificio Geminis 10, Local 208 (tel. 321-071, 321-072, 321-073).

Taca, 7a 14-35, Zona 9 (tel. 322-360).

BY BUS

Since the best way to explore the rest of Guatemala is by bus, you will want to know about bus companies.

Antigua: Transportes Unidos, 15 Calle 3-65, Zona 1 (tel. 24-949). Departures: Every 30 minutes from 7am to 8pm. Duration: 1 hour. Fare: Q1.20 (30¢).

Chichicastenango: Veloz Quichelense, Terminal de Buses, Zona 4. Departures: Every 30 minutes from 5am to 6pm. Duration: 4 hours. Fare: Q5 ($1.25).

Cobán and the Biotopo del Quetzal: Escobar Monja Blanca, 8a Calle 15-16, Zona 1 (tel. 511-878). Departures: 5, 7, 8, 9, and 10am, noon, and 2, 2:30, 4, and 4:30pm. Duration: 4 hours. Fare: Q4.75 or Q6.35 ($1.19 or $1.59).

El Carmen, Guatemala/Talisman, Mexico: Galgos, 7a Calle 19-44, Zona 1 (tel. 23-661 or 534-868). Departures: 5:45 and 10am, noon, and 3:30 and 5:30pm. Duration: 5 hours. Fare: Q7.50 ($1.88).

Esquipulas: Rutas Orientales, 19 Calle 8-18, Zona 1 (tel. 537-282 or 512-160). Departures: Every 30 minutes from 4am to 6pm, with stops at El Rancho, Río Hondo, Zacapa, and Chiquimula. Duration: 4 hours. Fare: Q4.75 or Q6.60 ($1.19 or $1.65).

Flores, Petén (Tikal): Fuentes del Norte, 17 Calle 8-46, Zona 1 (tel. 513-817). Departures: 1, 2, 3, and 7am and 11pm. Duration: 14 hours, with stops at El Rancho, Morales, Río Dulce, San Luis, and Poptún. Fare: Q15 or Q32 ($3.75 or $8).

Huehuetenango: Los Falcones, 7a Calle 15-27, Zona 1 (tel. 81-979). Departures: 7am and 2pm. Duration: 5 hours, with stops at Chimaltenango, Los Encuentros, and San Cristóbal Totonicapán (for Quetzaltenango). Fare: Q7.50 ($1.88).

La Democracia: Chatia Gomerana, Muelle Central (Central Dock), Terminal de Buses, Zona 4. Departures: Every 30 minutes from 6am to 4:30pm, with a stop at Escuintla. Duration: 2 hours. Fare: Q2.25 (56¢).

La Mesilla (to Mexico): El Condor, 19 Calle 2-01, Zona 1 (tel. 28-504). Departures: 4, 8, and 10am and 1 and 5pm. Duration: 7 hours. Fare: Q7.50 ($1.88).

Puerto Barrios: Litegua line, 15 Calle 10-42, Zona 1 (tel. 27-578). Departures: Every hour from 6am to 5pm (buses at 10am and 5pm are express). Duration: 6 hours. Fare: Q9 normal or Q11 express ($2.25 or $2.75).

Panajachel: Rebuli, 3a 2-36, Zona 1 (tel. 516-505). Departures: Every hour from 6:45am to 4pm. Duration: 3 hours. Fare: Q4.25 ($1.06).

San Salvador (El Salvador): Melva Internacional, 4a Calle 1-20, Zona 9 (tel. 367-248). Departures: 6, 7:30, 9, 10, and 11am, noon, and 1pm. Fare: Q7.50 ($1.88). Duration: 5 hours.

Quetzaltenango: Transportes Galgos, 7a Calle 19-44, Zona 1 (tel. 23-661). Departures: 5:30, 8:30, and 11am and 2:30, 5, 7, and 9pm. Duration: 4 hours. Fare: Q6 ($1.50).

CHAPTER 10
THE GUATEMALAN HIGHLANDS

1. **HUEHUETENANGO**
- **WHAT'S SPECIAL ABOUT THE GUATEMALAN HIGHLANDS**
2. **QUETZALTENANGO**
3. **CHICHICASTENANGO**
4. **LAKE ATITLÁN AND PANAJACHEL**
5. **ANTIGUA**

The Guatemalan highlands are a convoluted quilt of cultivated hillsides. The land has been turned on its side, but the tenacious Indians cling to the steep mountains and plant their corn as they have for thousands of years. Narrow roads wind through the mountains, and around nearly every bend is another breathtaking vista. Picture-perfect volcanic peaks, some sitting in silent grandeur, others providing explosive reminders of their presence, rise up above the surrounding mountains. However, it is the people of these mountains that capture the heart and imagination of the visitor to this country. Descended from the ancient Mayas, the indigenous people of the Guatemalan highlands pursue a way of life entirely separate from the life of the *ladinos*, the more Spanish inhabitants of this country's cities and towns. The Indians cling to their age-old traditions, many of which have been incorporated into Roman Catholic rituals. Most of the men and women of this region also continue to wear their very colorful traditional attire. In this often dry and dusty landscape, their skirts and huipiles (blouses), pants and jackets are bold splashes of unlikely colors—lime green and cherry red, indigo and purple, and magenta and fuchsia. Every village has its own styles and colors, so that when people leave their village, they can be recognized wherever they go. Nowhere is this more apparent than around the banks of Lake Atitlán, which many people claim is the most beautiful lake in the world. Every village around the lake has a slightly different fashion, which makes excursions around the lake particularly interesting.

Nestled at the base of these rugged mountains, in the shadow of a perfectly shaped volcano, is Antigua, the colonial capital of Guatemala. Amid the ruins of Spanish churches, monasteries, and convents, this city goes about its quiet life, attracting people from all over the world to enjoy its cobblestone streets and stucco walls.

---

1. HUEHUETENANGO

Distances: 160 miles northwest of Guatemala City;
52 miles southeast of La Mesilla (Mexican border);
51 miles north of Quetzaltenango.

GETTING THERE **By Bus** Buses from Guatemala City to Huehuetenango leave from 7a Avenida 15-27 daily at 7am and 2pm. Duration: 5 hours. Fare: Q7 ($1.75). If you're coming from the border, there'll be a bus there to meet your Mexican bus.

By Car From the Mexican border, it is a fairly easy 52 miles. Watch for the turnoff for Huehuetenango, which is about 4 miles off the highway. If you're coming from Guatemala City, continue going straight through the intersection known as Cuatro Caminos (Four Roads), which is the turnoff for Quetzaltenango. Watch for the Huehuetenango turnoff from the highway.

DEPARTING You can catch a bus to Quetzaltenango either near the market

WHAT'S SPECIAL ABOUT THE GUATEMALAN HIGHLANDS

Great Towns/Villages
- ☐ Antigua, one of Guatemala's colonial capitals, with beautiful architecture, atmosphere, and many ruins
- ☐ Chichicastenango, famous for its shopping and rituals performed by local Indians.

Natural Spectacles
- ☐ Lake Atitlán, said to be the most beautiful lake in the world
- ☐ Volcanoes, live or dormant, that you can climb

Events/Festivals
- ☐ Holy Week (the week before Easter) in Antigua, celebrated with daily processions through the streets
- ☐ Ancient Indian dances performed in towns and cities around the country

Religious Shrines
- ☐ The Church of San Francisco, with the remains of Hermano Pedro, who is said to heal the sick

Architectural Highlights
- ☐ Ruins of colonial churches, monasteries, convents, universities, and government buildings all over the town of Antigua

Shopping
- ☐ The Chichicastenango market on Sunday and Thursday, flooded with vendors selling beautiful Guatemalan textiles at the best prices in the country
- ☐ Panajachel's Calle Santander, lined on both sides with vendors selling "gringo" fashions in Guatemalan fabric
- ☐ Villages around Quetzaltenango with colorful markets on different days of the week

---

downtown or at the bus terminal, which is a mile or so outside town on the road to Quetzaltenango. Duration: 1 hour. Fare: Q1.50 (38¢).

Buses for Guatemala City leave throughout the day from the bus terminal on the road to Quetzaltenango. Duration: 5 hours. Fare: Q7 ($1.75).

ESSENTIALS Orientation Huehuetenango's main square, reference point for everything in town, is bounded by 2a and 3a calles and by 4a and 5a avenidas.

Fast Facts Market day is every day. Feast days are July 12 to 18.

Huehuetenango, although it is miles from the Mexican border, has the feel of a border town. It is the first major settlement on the road into Guatemala from Mexico and is the provincial capital of Huehuetenango (alt. 6,240 feet; pop. 37,000). There isn't much to keep you here, but the ruins of Zaculeu are only a few miles from town, and there's an assortment of hotels and restaurants, all within your price range. If you've taken a car or a bus from San Cristóbal, Mexico, this is the logical place to spend the night.

This town might be your first glimpse of Guatemalan culture, and you'll be pleasantly surprised the farther you go into the country. The costumes seem to get more and more colorful and unusual as you head southeast through the highlands. Notice that throughout this region, it's traditional for women to wear aprons all the time—they come in all sizes, shapes, and colors. No matter what sort of apron she has, every woman must have one.

On the road from Huehuetenango, the vistas continue: old men, young boys, teenage girls—literally everyone is on foot and carrying something. The men use a "tump line" (a rope or strap from the backpack load to the forehead) to distribute the weight of the huge bundles they carry, or they put their packs in a large piece of cloth, tying the ends so that they can loop it over their forehead and carry the load on their back. It's a constant reminder that horses were not found in this hemisphere before the Conquest and that the Indian civilizations knew nothing about the wheel. It also shows how little Indian culture has changed from that day to this.

WHAT TO SEE AND DO

First, there's the **market,** a nice one that's busy every day. It's located at 3a Avenida and 4a Calle, and its four great walls hold a busy collection of fruit stands, candle sellers, cloth shops, basket sellers, dried chile sellers, and even a bottle shop where you can purchase an old instant-coffee jar (nothing goes to waste in this town!). The sturdy shopping basket you paid $10 for in Oaxaca can be bought here, with a minimum of bargaining, for $3. Shopkeepers are very obliging—most are friendly, all are curious—and they expect you to bargain for their merchandise.

Besides the market, you'll want to take a look at the **ruins of Zaculeu.** Avoid self-appointed "guides" and take one of the very battered minibuses that depart from in front of the Hotel Maya and the Rico MacPolo at the corner of 3a Avenida and 4a Calle, near the entrance to La Plaza market. The bus fare is only 35 centavos (9¢). Alternatively, you can take a taxi for around Q15 ($3.75) for the round trip. You can also walk—it's a pleasant hike of about 45 minutes—and chances are better than not that someone will stop to give you a lift.

If you drive, head out of town on 9a Avenida and keep following the signs on this 2½-mile ride, even though they seem to be leading you on a wild goose chase. You may have to ask directions a few times despite the signs. The ruins at Zaculeu date from the Postclassic Period just before the Spanish Conquest. The Postclassic Period began in A.D. 900, when the Mayan civilization began to fade out and become absorbed by the Mexican tribes that were moving down from the north. Out of this assimilation of Mexican and Mayan cultures arose three powerful nations, one of which was the Mam, who settled in the area around Huehuetenango and made their capital at Zaculeu. The Mayan culture had been greatly diffused by this time, so you will see very little similarity between the Mayan ruins of Yucatan and Petén and those at Zaculeu.

This site was restored in 1940 by the United Fruit Company "as a contribution to Guatemalan culture." The site is small, however, and there are several mounds that have not been uncovered; at present there are no plans for further excavation. The restoration was so complete, down to the coat of mortar that covered the temples, that it appears as a reconstruction rather than a restoration: "perfect temples" down to the manicured lawns. The surroundings are beautiful, and the ruins are worth a visit. There is a small but interesting museum on the premises. Entrance is free to the ruins and museum, courtesy of the United Fruit Company.

Then you can always take a walk around town. No doubt a local boy will appoint himself your guide and expect a quarter for pointing out the obvious. He'll be very friendly, but you can ignore him politely if you wish.

WHERE TO STAY

DOUBLES FOR LESS THAN Q40 [$10]

AUTO HOTEL VASQUEZ, 2a Calle 6-67, Huehuetenango. Tel. 502/641-338. 20 rms, 15 with bath.

$ Rates: Q8 ($2) single without bath, Q12 ($3) single with bath; Q16 ($4) double without bath, Q20 ($5) double with bath. No credit cards.

Small but modern, the Hotel Vasquez is two blocks from the main plaza. If you happen to arrive when they are drying the laundry in the parking lot, it may not seem too appealing, but never fear—the rooms, although small, are not bad. It's not the place to stretch out, since the tiny rooms here are almost completely filled by their furnishings of beds and bathroom.

HOTEL MARY, 2a Calle 3-52. Huehuetenango. Tel. 502/641-569. 25 rms, 11 with bath.

$ Rates: Q14 ($3.50) single without bath; Q20 ($5) double without bath, Q24 ($6) double with bath; Q32 ($8) triple with bath. No credit cards.

⑤ Newer than the Hotel Vasquez, the Hotel Mary is a small hotel only a block from the main plaza and directly across the street from Guatel and the post office. The rooms are on four floors (no elevator), with open-air hallways that run the length of the building. It's very basic, but clean. You'll find a bit of off-street parking underneath the hotel by the reception desk.

There is a small restaurant on the second floor, where meals average Q8 ($2).

DOUBLES FOR LESS THAN Q80 [$20]

HOTEL ZACULEU, 5a Av. 1-14, Zona 1, Huehuetenango. Tel. 502/641-086 or 641-575. 36 rms, all with bath.

$ Rates: Q30–Q75 ($7.50–$18.75) single; Q40–Q110 ($10–$27.50) double. No credit cards.

★ The long-time favorite of travelers passing through Huehuetenango is a colonial-style hotel a block away from the town's main plaza. Many of the rooms are decorated with local handcrafts—hand-woven cloth, tin candlesticks, and clay water pitchers. Some rooms are truly charming, others are not. The older rooms at the front of the hotel open onto a beautiful courtyard filled with flowers and bordered by a colonial arcade. Although these rooms have more of a Guatemalan flavor to them, they are also closer to the street and therefore are noisier than the rooms in back. The new rooms, built in 1990, are done in a modern Spanish style—with bright bathrooms, carpets, and TVs. The higher prices are for these new rooms. Additional facilities include a private parking lot and the best restaurant in town. Huehuetenango gets a lot of travelers coming from or going to the border, and many stay at the Zaculeu, lending it an oldtime roadhouse character. It's a good place to strike up a conversation and gather information for the trip ahead.

HOTEL PINO MONTANO, Huehuetenango. Tel. 502/641-637. In Guatemala City, tel. 502/531-394. 20 rms., all with bath.

$ Rates: Q40 ($10) single; Q70 ($17.50) double. AE, DC, MC, V.

If you're driving a car and prefer to be out where the air smells good and the nights are quiet, head 3 miles out of town to the Pino Montano. It's on the La Mesilla road, which branches off from the road to Guatemala City. This comfy little countryside motel is a collection of small bungalows in a nice setting. There is a small pool if you happen to be here when the weather is warm.

The restaurant/bar provides sustenance and a place to relax after a day on the road.

OTHER SUPER-BUDGET CHOICES

Besides these modest hostelries, Huehuetenango has half a dozen even more modest places where the price for a bed is about Q8 ($2) per person. They're respectable, with the bare necessities.

WHERE TO EAT

Your best bet for a meal in Huehuetenango will likely be your hotel. If you should want to try someplace else, this restaurant is convenient.

EBONY RESTAURANT, 2a Calle 5-11. No phone.
   Cuisine: GUATEMALAN/INTERNATIONAL.
$ Prices: Q4–Q6 ($1–$1.50). No credit cards.
   Open: Daily 6am–11pm.
Around the corner from the main plaza you'll find a small, dark restaurant popular

with the young generation in Huehuetenango. The walls and ceiling are made of split bamboo, and there are wicker baskets for lampshades. The overall effect is that of a tropical beach hangout, even though you're a long way from the ocean. On the menu are chicken, pork chops, steaks, and chorizo, all for Q4 ($1), and a variety of breakfasts for the same price. Delicious fresh fruit licuados are only Q1.50 (38¢).

EVENING ENTERTAINMENT

In the evening everybody gathers in the main square, especially the young, to see and be seen. One of the main features of this plaza is a relief map of Guatemala, a miniature version of the famous relief map in Guatemala City. There are occasional band performances here, with the musicians taking up their positions in a bandshell on top of the municipal building across the street from the plaza. If there are no festivities the night you're here, the next best attraction at night is the movie theater on 5a Calle, half a block out of the square.

---

2. QUETZALTENANGO

Distances: 49 miles south of Huehuetenango; 161 miles northwest of Guatemala City; 96 miles northwest of Panajachel.

GETTING THERE By Bus Keep in mind that almost all buses use an abbreviation of Quetzaltenango's Indian name. Look for the word Xela or Xelaju on the windshield. Buses from Guatemala City leave from 7a Av. 19-44, Zona 1 (tel. 23-661) daily at 5:30, 8:30, and 11am and 2:30, 5, 7, and 9pm. Duration: 4 hours. Fare: Q5.70 ($1.43). From Chichi or Panajachel, take a bus to Los Encuentros crossroad and flag down a Quetzaltenango bus. Coming from Antigua, you must first take a bus to Chimaltenango and then flag down a Quetzaltenango bus.

By Car If you're coming from the Pacific Highway, take the Quetzaltenango toll road turnoff just past Mazatenango. Coming from Huehuetenango or Guatemala City, turn south at Cuatro Caminos, the intersection just north of Quetzaltenango.

DEPARTING At the main bus terminal on 13a Avenida and 4a Calle, Zona 3 (near Parque Minerva), there are second-class buses leaving regularly for cities all over Guatemala. These buses usually leave when they are full and are always very crowded. However, they leave much more frequently than the first-class buses of the companies mentioned above. Ticket prices are also slightly less. There are buses out here from the main plaza, or you can take a taxi for Q5 ($2).

To reach Chichicastenango, take a second-class bus from the Zona 3 bus terminal.

There are no direct buses to Panajachel. Take any bus headed toward Guatemala City and get off at Los Encuentros. From here you can get a bus down to Panajachel.

Rutas Lima, 11 Av. 4-07, Zona 1 (tel. 061-4134, 061-2033, or 061-4139), with another office next to the Pension Bonifaz at 2a Calle 1-07, Zona 1, has several buses daily to Guatemala City.

Transportes Galgos, 2a Calle 5-66, Zona 2, and Autobuses Americas, 2a Calle 3-33, are both about a mile northeast of the Parque Centro America, and inconvenient to reach except by taxi. They have daily service to Guatemala City.

Transportes Higueros, 12a Avenida and 7a Calle, Zona 1 (tel. 061/2233), is beneath the tourist office in the Casa de la Cultura building (facing the building, go around to the right-hand side).

All of these buses take about 4 hours and charge Q8 ($2).

Any bus headed to the Mexican border will stop in Huehuetenango. Duration: 1 hour. Fare: Q1.30 (33¢). You can also get second-class buses to Huehuetenango from the Zona 3 bus terminal.

ESSENTIALS Orientation The Parque Centro America is the center of town; most of the principal buildings face it, including the new municipal market, the Tourism Office and town hall, the church, the museum, and several hotels and restaurants. The streets are not well marked in this town, so keep track of where you're going.

Fast Facts   Many of the city's banks face the Parque Centro America. Normal hours of operation are Monday to Friday from 8:30am to 2:30pm. The Banco Industrial, on the Parque in the Palacio Municipal, at 11a Avenida and 5a Calle (tel. 061-2258 or 061-2288), is open on weekdays until 3pm; it has a *ventanilla especial,* or special teller, on duty weekdays from 3 to 6pm and Saturday from 8:30am to 12:30pm.

Take your laundry to the **Lavanderia Mini-Max,** 14a Avenida C-47, at 1a Calle, facing the plaza with the classical Teatro Municipal, and next to the Taberna de Don Rodrigo.

The **Tourist Office** (tel. 061-4931) is in the Casa de la Cultura (also called the Museo de Historia Natural) at the lower end of the Parque Centro America—open Monday to Friday from 8am to noon and 2 to 6pm, Saturday from 8am to noon; closed Sunday.

Market day is every day. Feast days September 12 to 18.

Named by the Aztecs for what is now the national bird, Quetzaltenango is the country's second-largest town (alt. 7,800 feet; pop. 73,000). It was built on the site of the Quiché Maya Indian ancient capital of Xelaju, and the Indians still call it by this name. Quetzaltenango is a booming, growing city—but the countryside surrounding it is marvelously beautiful. In the marketplace, men and women wear traditional costumes of heavily embroidered cloth. These are not costumes in the sense that they're put on for special occasions, but rather they're the normal, everyday clothing in this traditional rural culture. The Indian garb contrasts strikingly with the Italianate columns and monuments in the main square, the Parque Centro America.

Heading east to Guatemala City, you will see more sights along the road. The local costumes here include kilts for the men, held up by large leather belts. Herds of black sheep and boys hawking good-luck charms made of straw turn up at intervals along the way.

WHAT TO SEE AND DO

Quetzaltenango is not really a sight-seer's town, but rather a way station on the highway, at least as far as tourists are concerned. While you're here, though, take a look in the **Museo de Historia Natural,** with a collection of exhibits that might most kindly be termed "eclectic." Also have a look in the **cathedral** and the **Palacio Municipal** (city hall). All three of these prominent buildings are on the Parque Centro America.

Walk north on 14a Avenida to la Calle, and you'll come face-to-face with the city's impressive neoclassical **Teatro Municipal.** If there's a performance, rehearsal, or meeting in progress when you visit, you'll have to be content with the view from the outside. Inside, however, are three tiers of seating, the lower two of which have private boxes for theatergoers. The boxes were rented by prominent families by the season or the year; each is equipped with a vanity for women.

There is a small **market** to the left of the museum, at the southeastern corner of the Parque Centro America. Although you'll find a few food stalls and shops selling everyday items on the lower level, much of the space here is tourist-oriented. Guatemalan fabrics have been used to make dresses and other garments according to North American styles. It's worth a walk through.

The city's large market is the **Mercado La Democracia,** in Zona 3, about ten blocks northwest of the Parque Centro America. To get there, walk along 14a Avenida to 1a Calle. Turn left, walk to 16a Avenida, then turn right. Walk along 16a Avenida, cross Calle Rodolfo Robles (the first major cross-street you encounter), and the market will be on your right. It extends for about two blocks.

La Democracia is the people's market, with fruits, vegetables, tortillas, beans, chickens (live and killed), shoes, children's clothing, and fabrics for sale. The selection of fabrics is not large, but the prices are fairly good. As of this writing, the local merchants do not actively solicit your business just because you're a foreigner. Their best customers are local people, not tourists.

Less than a mile west of the Parque Centro America is the **Parque Minerva,** and its neoclassical **Templo de Minerva,** built to honor the classical goddess of education and to inspire Guatemalan youth to new heights of learning.

WHERE TO STAY

DOUBLES FOR LESS THAN Q60 [$15]

CASA SUIZA, 14a Avenida "A" 2-36, Zona 1, Quetzaltenango. Tel. 502/061-4350. 18 rms., 12 with bath.

$ Rates: Q15.20 ($3.80) single without bath, Q23.40 ($5.85) single with bath; Q23.40 ($5.85) double without bath, Q35.10 ($8.80) double with bath; Q32.80 ($8.20) triple without bath, Q41 ($10.25) triple with bath. No credit cards.

Swiss in name only, this very basic pension is located across the street from the Hotel Modelo (below). Walk through the streetside doors, and you'll find yourself in a colorfully painted courtyard. All the rooms here have high ceilings that make them seem very spacious. The bathrooms, which were obviously added on long after the building was constructed, are housed within glass-and-metal cabinets in the corner of the rooms. This place has loads of character but little charm. However, the señorita who runs the pension is very friendly. A fixed-price menu is served in the dining room—Q6 ($1.50) for breakfast and Q8 ($2) for lunch.

HOTEL RÍO AZUL, 2a Calle 12-15, Zona 1, Quetzaltenango. No phone. 20 rms., all with bath.

$ Rates: Q29.25 ($7.32) single; Q35.10 ($8.80) double; Q46.80 ($11.70) triple. No credit cards. **Parking:** Q3 (75¢).

⑤ A new choice in town, the Río Azul is conveniently located close to the Parque Centro America and many good restaurants. The owner of the hotel, who speaks little English, is nevertheless a wealth of information about the area and can help you organize your tour of Guatemala. The rooms are simple, but the red-tile floors give them a rustic appeal. Some rooms have nice views, and all have very clean bathrooms. Security is tight here, so you don't have to worry much about your belongings.

HOTEL KIKTEM-JA, Edificio "Fuentes," 13a Avenida 7-18, Zona 1, Quetzaltenango. Tel. 502/061-4304. 20 rms., all with bath.

$ Rates: Q46.80 ($11.70) single; Q58.50 ($14.63) double; Q70.20 ($17.55) triple. No credit cards.

✪ Only a block or so off the Parque Centro America, the Kiktem-Ja is a gloomy favorite of mine. The guest rooms are arranged around a courtyard (where you can park your car) that you enter through a large gate set into the outside wall of the building. The building is done in colonial style, with arched doors and windows and stone walls. There are some nice little touches, such as locally made blankets enblazoned with the hotel's name and fireplaces in 10 rooms, but there are also conspicuous lacks, such as toilet seats. Still, the hotel is pretty good by local standards.

DOUBLES FOR LESS THAN Q90 [$22.50]

GRAN HOTEL AMERICANO, 14a Avenida 3-47, Zona 1, Quetzaltenango. Tel. 502/061-8118 or 061-8219. 12 rms., all with bath.

$ Rates: Q52.65 ($13.16) single; Q64.35 ($16.10) double; Q70.20 ($17.55) triple. No credit cards.

⑤ In the middle of the restaurant district of Quetzaltenango, you'll probably hear the computerized cacophony of a video arcade. Don't rush by: Upstairs you'll find one of the better hotel deals in town. Luckily, the video games are shut off by 11pm, and upstairs you can barely hear them even when they are going full blast. All the rooms are carpeted, although few have windows. The bathrooms are tiny but adequate, and the beds are comfortable. Generally, this is a convenient place to get a good night's sleep before moving on. Downstairs there is a restaurant that serves excellent breakfasts.

HOTEL DEL CAMPO, Km 224, Camino a Cantel, Quetzaltenango. Tel. 502/061-2064 or 061-8082. 108 rms., all with bath.
$ Rates: Q88 ($22) double; Q112 ($28) triple. DC, MC, V.

Although it is a bit out of the way, on a side road off of the Pan American Highway, the del Campo is Quetzaltenango's largest, most modern, and most comfortable place to stay. Constructed in the 1970s, it has a decor that features natural wood and red brick. The guest rooms have private baths (showers) done in linoleum (not tile) and are generally bright and nice. Avoid the bottom-floor rooms because they can be dark; ask for a room numbered in the 50s. Some rooms have TVs, but these cost a bit more.

There are two restaurants here done in a rustic mountain decor, with large windows letting in lots of light. The prices are very reasonable, averaging Q9 to Q12 ($2.25 to $3). A small bar provides a comfortable gathering spot.

Facilities: Heated indoor swimming pool and game room.

HOTEL MODELO, 14a Avenida "A" 2-31, Zona 1, Quetzaltenango. Tel. 502/061-2715 or 061-2529. 24 rms., all with bath.
$ Rates: Q70 ($17.50) single; Q88 ($22) double; Q105 ($26.25) triple. MC, V.

This solid, dependable, moderate-price leader is located on a narrow, short street between 14a and 15a avenidas. An obliging family operates the hotel, and they will welcome you in the high-ceilinged lobby with its big fireplace. When they show you one of the guest rooms, you'll find it decorated with solid-color bedspreads, gaily colored Guatemalan huipiles (blouses) drawn on frames, and contemporary paintings. The rooms have hardwood floors and are equipped with small private bathrooms with tiled showers. Some rooms also have small black-and-white TVs.

There's a small but good restaurant located off the lobby serving breakfast (7:30 to 9:30am), lunch (1 to 4pm), and dinner (7 to 9pm) daily. Breakfast will cost around Q8 ($2), and lunch and dinner may be had for Q16 ($4). You'll also find a small bar just off the lobby.

HOTEL CENTROAMERICANA INN, 4a Calle and 14a Avenida, Zona 3, Quetzaltenango. Tel. 502/061-4901. 14 rms., all with bath. TV TEL
$ Rates: Q40 ($10) single; Q80 ($20) double; Q120 ($30) triple; Q160 ($40) quad. DC, MC, V.

Although not as far out of town as the Hotel del Campo, this lodging is somewhat out of the center, near the city's main market, La Democracia. It's not all that convenient, but it does have large rooms with hardwood floors and huge bathrooms with hot running water. The hallways are rather gloomy, but the large restaurant is bright and sunny. The large lobby and restaurant seem to belong to a much larger hotel. In fact, there were more rooms here in the past, but with a recent remodeling, many of the old rooms were converted to other uses. There is a parking lot in back of the building.

SUPER-BUDGET CHOICES

Everything else in town is a good deal simpler and more basic than the preceding lodging places. If you like your comforts, you'd better find a room in one of the choices above. However, if you're out to save money, read on!

CASA KAEHLER, 13a Avenida 3-33, Zona 1, Quetzaltenango. Tel. 502/061-2091. 7 rms., 1 with bath.
$ Rates: Q15 ($3.75) single without bath, Q20 ($5) single with bath; Q20 ($5) double without bath, Q25 ($6.25) double with bath; Q26 ($6.50) triple without bath; Q32 ($8) quad without bath. No credit cards.

Before World War II, most of the coffee fincas on Guatemala's Pacific Slope were run by Germans, hence the German flavor of this city. It's very apparent in the name of this little place, which resembles a modest, old-fashioned

European family pension. The guest rooms are very simple and plain but clean and quite cheap. For a bit more comfort, request room no. 7 (*cuarto numero siete*), which has a private bathroom and a double bed. Regardless of which room you stay in, you can make use of the beautiful sitting room with its rocking chairs and stained-glass windows. It's very homey and quiet at this place that's popular with young people studying Spanish here in Quetzaltenango.

HOTEL CAPRI, 8a Calle 11-39, Zona 1, Quetzaltenango. Tel. 502/061-4111. 20 rms., all with bath.

$ Rates: Q12 ($3) single; Q24 ($6) double; Q36 ($9) triple; Q48 ($12) quad. No credit cards.

Very similar to the Kiktem-Ja, only more gloomy, the Capri is a block off the Parque Centro America behind the Museo (Casa de la Cultura). This is recommended only for those accustomed to traveling rough. Numerous other modest pensions in this neighborhood offer similar rates.

WORTH THE EXTRA BUCKS

HOTEL PENSION BONIFAZ, 4a Calle 10-50, Zona 1, Quetzaltenango. Tel. 502/061-4241 or 061-2959. 63 rms., 2 suites, all with bath. TV

$ Rates: Q125 ($31.25) single; Q140 ($35) double; Q180 ($45) suite. AE, DC, MC, V.

The Bonifaz, the city's long-running favorite, is at the upper end of the Parque Centro America. This is the most comfortable place downtown, within walking distance of almost everything. Half of the rooms here (and these are preferable) are in the older, original building. They have french doors leading onto small balconies overlooking the street and are quite spacious. The furnishings are fairly new, and the bathrooms are quite large. The rest of the rooms are in a modernized addition with wood paneling and Danish modern furniture. Not really fancy, the rooms are large, the bathrooms are done in tile (some with only showers), and a number of rooms have two double beds. The second-floor lounge has a beautiful view of the mountains and the city, and there is also a small, but very pleasant garden in the back of the hotel.

Dining/Entertainment: The hotel has three dining rooms, all of which serve the same excellent food. El Patio is a covered courtyard filled with potted plants and chrome furniture. The light here during the day is beautiful. El Restaurante and Los Balcones are the two formal dining rooms, both done in colonial decor, with wrought-iron chandeliers and a fireplace in one of them. The waitresses are dressed in traditional highland costumes. The service is efficient and very pleasant, and the restaurants are generally very quiet. The food here is primarily Continental, with such offerings as stroganoff, filet mignon, spaghetti, and breaded shrimp. Prices are in the Q15 to Q20 ($3.75 to $5) range for entrees. Don't miss the tempting pastry cart. There's a small selection of wines to accompany your meal. Just inside the front door is a sedate but cheery bar.

Facilities: Gift shop, Mexican consulate, and parking lot.

WHERE TO EAT

The best place to dine is in the dining room of the Pension Bonifaz, where you can start with a fruit cocktail or a bowl of savory black-bean soup; go on to filet mignon, smoked pork chops, or roast chicken; and finish up with cake or pie—for about Q40 ($10) per person, including tax, tip, and a beverage. Lighter fare, including a very substantial club sandwich, can be had, with a drink, for only half that much.

The dining room in the Hotel Modelo is also worth your consideration at mealtime. For a stroll past many of this city's eligible eateries, make your way to the corner of 14a Avenida and 3a Calle, then walk uphill along 14a Avenida.

PASTELERÍA BOMBONIER, 14a Avenida 2-20, Zona 1. Tel. 6225.
Cuisine: SANDWICHES.
$ Prices: Q3–Q5 (75¢–$1.25). No credit cards.

Open: Daily 9am–9pm.

This is a tiny family-run snack place with only a handful of tables—but with hamburgers priced at less than a dollar, it's a real bargain for a light meal.

TABERNA DE DON RODRIGO, 14a Avenida C-45. No phone.
   Cuisine: SANDWICHES.
$ Prices: Q4–Q6 ($1–$1.50). No credit cards.
   Open: Daily 10am–10pm.

Across the street from the plaza with the impressive Teatro Municipal you will find a place where local young people like to gather, chat and consume hamburgers, cheeseburgers, hot dogs, cakes, Cokes, lemonade, coffee, and draft beer. To the local people it's a stylish place, but a light meal here will not cost more than a dollar or two. The specialty is a giant sandwich called the Don Rodrigo super sandwich. Order one of these and a beer for a total bill of less than Q10 ($2.50), and you've got a very filling and very cheap meal.

POLLO FRITO ALBUMAR, 4a Calle 14-16, Zona 1 and 4a Calle 13-84, Zona 3. No phones.
   Cuisine: GUATEMALAN/INTERNATIONAL.
$ Prices: Q4–Q12 ($1–$3). No credit cards.
   Open: Daily 7am–10:30pm.

⑤ Primarily fried-chicken restaurants, these two family fast-food places also serve a variety of other meals, including filet mignon and some delicious tipico favorites. And you can't beat the prices—even a steak will cost you only Q12 ($3). The one in Zona 3 is more family-oriented than the one downtown. At the former, you'll find a huge slide to keep your kids entertained while you enjoy your meal. Meals are served either in a large dining room or on tables outside by the slide. The downtown restaurant is very conveniently located a block away from Parque Centro America.

RESTAURANT SHANGHAI, 4a Calle 12-22, Zona 1. Tel. 4154.
   Cuisine: CHINESE.
$ Prices: Main dishes Q6–Q10 ($1.50–$2.50). No credit cards.
   Open: Daily 8am–10pm.

Chinese restaurants are common throughout Guatemala, and whenever you get tired of rice and beans and meat, you can always head to one for a big plate of steaming vegetables. The food is far from authentic and the staff seems to be 100% Maya (not Chinese), but the restaurant does add variety to your dining. The combination plates are priced even less than most main dishes. And in very un-Chinese fashion, there is a tempting array of cakes displayed in the front of the restaurant, including Guatemalan-style cheesecake.

CAFETERÍA EL KOPETIN, 14a Avenida 3-31, Zona 1. Tel. 2401.
   Cuisine: GUATEMALAN/INTERNATIONAL.
$ Prices: Main dishes Q7–Q14 ($1.75–$3.50). DC, MC, V.
   Open: Daily 11am–10pm.

★ In this dark, modern, family-run place with red tablecloths and natural wood, the specialty is outstanding appetizers. A person could make a meal on just an assortment of some of these delicious starters. Try the *quesos fundidos* (melted cheese) or one of the spicy *chorizo* sausage appetizers, both under Q5 ($1.25). The *parillada* for Q14 ($3.50) is a carnivore's delight that includes five different meats, potatoes, and vegetables. The menu also lists everything from shrimp and fish to filet mignon, all priced around Q10 ($2.50), but there are burgers and sandwiches for much less. El Kopetin is only two blocks off the Parque Centro America.

PIZZA RICCA, 14a Avenida 2-52, Zona 1. Tel. 8162.
   Cuisine: PIZZA.
$ Prices: Pizzas Q8–Q20 ($2–$5). No credit cards.

Open: Daily 11am–9:30pm.

This is a tidy little place with cozy booths and a busy wood-fired oven filled with pizzas bubbling and baking. The white-uniformed staff tends the fires and the pies. Order your pizza small, medium, or large; have a beer or soft drink; and the bill will come to about Q8 ($2) per person.

EVENING ENTERTAINMENT

As you might have guessed, Quetzaltenango doesn't exactly turn on at night. The evenings here are usually cool if not downright chilly. You can drop in at the Pension Bonifaz and have a drink in the bar or sneak into their TV lounge. Or you can seek out a film in English at one of the city's several cinemas located not far off the Parque Centro America. If your hotel room has a fireplace, search for firewood. Say "Quiero comprar lena" ("I want to buy firewood"), and people will point the way to a nearby supplier. Then you'll need kindling, tinder, and matches, perhaps a glass of something, a comfortable chair, and a good book.

If you speak French, you might want to drop by the **Alianza Francesa,** which has been serving the city's cultural needs since 1951. It's at the corner of 14a Avenida "A" and 1a Calle, facing the Teatro Municipal. A few steps up the street from it is the big **Teatro (Cinema) Roma.**

EXCURSIONS

There are dozens of Indian villages in the vicinity of Quetzaltenango, all of which have markets one or more days a week. These markets are excellent places to shop for local crafts and to see Indians in their colorful attire. The following is a list of nearby villages with their market and festival days. On festival days you may get to see the traditional dances, such as the Dance of the Conquest, the Dance of the Moors, and the **palo volador** (flying pole).

Salcaja: Market day is Tuesday; festival is August 25.

San Cristóbal Totonicapan: Market day is Sunday; festival is July 26.

Totonicopan: Market days are Tuesday and Saturday; festival is the last week of September.

Almolonga: Market days are Wednesday and Saturday; festival is July 27.

Cantel: Market day is Sunday; festival is August 15.

Zunil: Market day is Monday; festival is November 25.

San Juan Ostuncalco: Market days are Thursday and Sunday; festival is from January 29 to February 3.

San Pedro Sacatepequez: Market days are Tuesday, Thursday, and Sunday; festival is June 24 to 30.

San Marcos: Market days are Tuesday and Friday; festival is April 22 to 27.

Olintepeque: Market day is Tuesday; festival is June 24.

SAN FRANCISCO EL ALTO AND MOMOSTENANGO

Quetzaltenango is high in the mountains, but you can go even higher (660 feet higher, to be exact) to visit the small town of San Francisco El Alto, famous for its Friday market featuring hand-woven wool blankets. The town is only a mile off the Pan American Highway over a paved road (or 2 miles over a dirt road, the back way). Buses run from Quetzaltenango three or four times a day. The view from the large, cobblestone municipal plaza where the market is held is fabulous (if you get a clear day). The town itself is very quiet, with virtually no action and very few people in evidence, except on Friday.

Past San Francisco El Alto, 10 miles from the Pan American Highway, is the small town of Momostenango (market day is Sunday), famous throughout Guatemala for its chamarras (woolen blankets). Buses from Quetzaltenango chug and bash over the rough dirt road daily, winding up through the forests and down through the valleys.

The road may be impassable during parts of the rainy season. On the way into town, the road passes little shops advertising blankets and woolen goods for sale, retail and wholesale.

For meals there are several modest cafés, one attached to the Casa de Huespedes Paclom. There is little to do here but interact awkwardly with the citizenry and buy blankets. Chamarras, serapes, and other fine things all are made by hand here, and the local people in this high-altitude place know what warm blankets mean at night. Look for comely designs and fine-quality wool.

For buses to San Francisco El Alto and Totonicapan, look behind the market next to the Casa de la Cultura. At 10a Avenida and 8a Calle, there is a parking lot with buses and minibuses to these destinations.

ZUNIL AND FUENTES GEORGINA

For sheer eye-popping brilliance, no other traditional attire in Guatemala is as colorful as that worn by the women of Zunil. This small village is only a few miles south of Quetzaltenango on the road down to Retalhuleu, but it seems a world away. Built on a steep hillside above a little river, Zunil is almost always cool and damp. To stay warm and dry, the women of the village cover themselves with cloaks of shocking pink, magenta, violet, and lavender. As they hurry down the cobblestone streets with their cloaks swaying behind them, they are like apparitions of a long-forgotten civilization.

Zunil is also home to one of the Maximón effigies that are found in a few villages here in the highlands. Maximón (also known as San Simón), is a thinly disguised Mayan god, Mam. He is revered by the local population for his powers to answer prayers and heal the sick. Maximón, who lives in a small house up the hill behind the church, consists of a mannequin wearing a mask, jacket and pants, hat, and dozens of scarves. He sits in state on a large chair, where he meets with those seeking his favors. The traditional way to worship Maximón is to blow cigar smoke in his face and pour liquor into his mouth. The Indians believe devoutly in Maximón, and if you should wish to meet with him, be sure to take him an offering (a few quetzales is acceptable).

Just past Zunil on the left is an alternate route into Quetzaltenango. If you turn up this road and then turn right on the first dirt road, you'll be heading for Fuentes Georginas, one of the most enchanting places in Guatemala. Several miles up this rough and muddy dirt road, at the head of a valley that begins on the flanks of Zunil Mountain, is a hot springs complex that feels at times like the most remote spot on earth. Clouds of steam rise from the pale-blue sulfurous waters and drift up a steep hillside that is draped with fronds of giant ferns. Beside the pool is a bar and tiny restaurant where you can order simple meals. There are a few basic cabins here, with tubs that can be filled with water from the hot springs. If you're looking for the ultimate low-budget spa, this is it. Cabins rent for less than $10 per night.

3. CHICHICASTENANGO

Distances: 75 miles northwest of Guatemala City;
50 miles northeast of Quetzaltenango; 25 miles north of Panajachel.

GETTING THERE By Car If you're coming from Guatemala City or Quetzaltenango, the turnoff from the highway you'll take is called Los Encuentros. There's a small open market where people from the surrounding hills sell vegetables and other produce, and entrepreneurs from the towns sell locally made clothes. There's also a gas station and a postal and telephone office.

The road to Chichicastenango is scenic, even dramatic, diving down into a deep ravine and then climbing the other side steeply. Along the way are the inevitable cornfields and local women weaving beautiful clothes near their modest homes.

DEPARTING Buses arrive and leave from various points around the market;

several lines are based near the Hotel Santo Tomas. Just say the name of your destination to any bus driver or policeman, and you'll be directed to the proper corner. There are direct buses to Quetzaltenango, and to Panajachel for Q4 ($1), as well as to Guatemala City. If you can't find a direct bus that's headed in your direction, catch any bus out to Los Encuentros, and wait there for a passing bus along the Pan American Highway that's going to the right place.

ESSENTIALS Orientation The center of town is, of course, the central square, where the market is held. Coming into town from Los Encuentros, you must turn left at the Hotel Santo Tomas and go down a few blocks. The square will then be two blocks or so over to your left.

Fast Facts The post office (correos) is at 7a Avenida 8-47, two blocks northwest of the Hotel Santo Tomas on the road into town. Very near it is the Guatel telephone office, at 7a Avenida 8-21, on the corner of 8a Calle. Market days are Sunday and Thursday. Feast days are December 18 to 21 and Holy Week.

Once a sleepy Indian village, Santo Tomas Chichicastenango (alt. 6,650 feet; pop. 6,500) is today one of Guatemala's most popular tourist destinations. They come for the same reason that Indians have come here for centuries—to shop at the market. Although the market is still where local women buy the necessities of life and local farmers sell their produce, it is also where foreigners come to get the best deals on Guatemalan textiles. Every Sunday and Thursday, the town's central square becomes a maze of stalls selling both traditional and modern textiles, machine- and hand-made.

Facing the market square is the Santo Tomas church, which figures prominently in the religion, both pagan and Christian, of the region. On the circular stone steps of the church, women sell flowers in the morning; throughout the day, Indians approach the massive doors of the church swinging censers made from old coffee cans. The fragrant incense smoke rises in clouds and drifts over the heads of the shoppers pushing their way among the stalls. Amid the chatter of vendors and shoppers, you can hear the chanting of a petitioner at the doors. The ritual is centuries old; the language is Quiché.

Don't expect to be the only gringo witnessing these rituals. Tour companies have discovered this town, and on market days huge buses roar in to deliver several hundred curious cloth buyers. You can avoid the crowds and still see the local weaving by coming on a nonmarket day, when a few stands are always open and the whole town is a lot quieter. Signs are in English: "Bar and Steak House," "Handwoven Indian Costumes," and "Typical Souvenirs." It's mostly for the day-trippers, though; it must be, for there are only four hotels in town. I am fascinated by this town and its bustling market.

Note that Chichicastenango is a small town, with few street signs or numbers, so you have to ask around to find everything.

WHAT TO SEE AND DO

Chichicastenango certainly isn't what you'd call an exciting place, except on market days, and that's its very fascination. Unless you're an anthropologist or a textile expert, you won't spend more than an afternoon looking over the marvelous hand-woven and embroidered cloths for which the district is famous. Chichicastenango's other claim to fame, its much-vaunted paganism, involves things that you can't look for, although you may happen on them: On a rainy night, a young man swings a censer swiftly back and forth before the locked doors of the Santo Tomas church, barking admonitions and chants at a woman kneeling in prayer on the bare stones. The symbols, paraphernalia, and words are Christian, but the inspiration is clearly pagan.

On Sunday, the service in the Church of Santo Tomas presents a fascinating vignette of life: Within the church, Christian mass is in progress, while behind the church, pagan rites are being held. The church dates from the mid-1500s. Its significance and power are not those of the Catholic Church so much as of the local male groups known as **cofradías.** Each of these associations pays homage to its own patron saint and has religious and civic duties. In effect, the cofradías are as important as the local Catholic and municipal authorities; among the local people, they're more important. If you're in Chichicastenango on a major church holiday or on one of the cofradías' saints' days, you may see a cofradia procession, led by its alcalde (chief) and a ragtag band, winding through the town and the market.

For a look at more of this town's pre-Christian culture, take a short hike to the Shrine of Pascual Abaj, on the outskirts of town. Facing the Santo Tomas church, turn right, walk down the hill on 5a Avenida to 9a Calle, and turn right. Go down the hill on 9a Calle (a dirt road), around the bend to the left; when the road turns sharply to the right, bear left and follow a path through the cornfields, keeping the ditch on your left-hand side. First, you come to a collection of buildings that include a farmhouse and a storehouse for costumes used in festival processions. If you greet the farmer or his wife, and if the children are around, chances are that you'll be invited to see the children perform a local dance in full costume. Do this: Greet the family as you pass through toward the shrine (you literally walk across their porch). By the time you return, the children will be costumed and ready to begin. After the dance, a tip is in order.

To get to the shrine, proceed up the hill behind the farmhouse, along the dirt path to the top of the hill covered in fragrant pines. At the very top is a clearing, and in it is the primitive carved-stone head of the idol, surrounded by little fireplace altars. Chances are good that a local man or woman will be chanting and praying at one or more of the altars and burning pungent incense. You can observe the rites without disturbing them.

Chichicastenango has a museum facing the main square, the **Museo Regional.** Admission is free, although the museum never seems to be open when I am in town. The two large exhibit rooms have plain glass-fronted cabinets in best 19th-century museum style. In the left room are objects, figurines, and necklaces of jade, as well as clay incense burners, effigy pots and plainer vessels, metates (grindstones for corn), flint and obsidian arrowheads and spearheads, clay figurines, and copper ax-heads. In the right room are polychrome pots and those with reliefwork on them. Some of these are particularly nice.

WHERE TO STAY

DOUBLES FOR LESS THAN Q80 [$20]

PENSIÓN CHUGUILÁ, Santo Tomás Chichicastenango. Tel. 502/056-1134. 21 rms., 16 with bath.

$ Rates: Q20 ($5) single without bath, Q40 ($10) single with bath; Q25 ($6.25) double without bath, Q45 ($11.25) double with bath; Q30 ($7.50) triple without bath, Q54 ($13.50) triple with bath. No credit cards.

The budget traveler's version of the Mayan Inn is a charming old place a few blocks off the square. You enter from the cobbled street to find a cobbled courtyard (partly filled with parked cars) and a very pleasant portico paved in tiles and furnished with easy chairs, coffee tables, and tropical plants. The simple but pleasant dining room is to the left as you approach the reception desk. Most of the guest rooms have private baths, and some have fireplaces; there are even a few two-room suites that each have a bedroom and sitting room with fireplace. Furnishings are colonial in style, with accents of local cloth.

Breakfast in the dining room costs Q8 ($2). Lunch and dinner go for Q16 ($4).

MAYA LODGE, Santo Tomás Chichicastenango. Tel. 502/056-1167. 10 rms., 7 with bath.

$ Rates: Q30–Q35 ($7.50–$8.75) single; Q60–Q70 ($15–$17.50) double. No credit cards.

If you'd like to be right in the thick of things on market day, this is the place for you. It's right on the main square where the market is held, and you'll have to weave your way through the maze of vendors to get in or out of the hotel. The rates are reasonable, and the accommodations are fairly comfortable. Try to get one of the cozy rooms with a fireplace (*chimenea*). Although rather bare compared to the town's other hostelries and perhaps a bit dark, this hotel is still a far cry from basic. The clean, presentable rooms have their own tables and chairs in the long narrow courtyard.

Breakfast in the simple little comedor costs Q8 ($2). Lunch and dinner go for Q12 ($3).

WORTH THE EXTRA BUCKS

Chichicastenango is an excellent place to let go of your budget and indulge yourself, because a little more money buys such an unforgettably beautiful experience.

HOTEL SANTO TOMAS, Santo Tomás Chichicastenango. Tel. 502/056-1061 or 056-1316. Fax 502/056-1306. 43 rms., all with bath.

$ Rates: Q187.20 ($46.80) single; Q238.70 ($59.70) double; Q290.20 ($72.54) triple. DC, MC, V.

The most modern hotel in town, the Santo Tomas has become very popular with tour groups and is now even trying to lure conferences to Chichicastenango. You can't miss it as you come into town on the main road, but ask anyone to direct you if you have trouble. Colonial in style, it's modern in facilities and thus a favorite with bus-tour operators. The Santo Tomas's rooms are arranged on two levels around two courtyards, each with its own fountain, gardens, and menagerie of parrots. Many of the rooms are filled by tour group participants, and the hotel is often abustle with guests arriving, leaving, heading out on shopping excursions, or returning from the same. If you want to stay here, you must reserve as far ahead as possible. The large, cheery rooms are decorated with local cloths and blankets and have private bathrooms and fireplaces. Most have twin beds. Pet parrots and macaws squawk and talk in the courtyard all day, and throughout the hotel are pieces of local upper-class art—fancy robes, church statuary, antique altars, and so forth.

Dining/Entertainment: There are a large, attractive colonial-style dining room and also some tables set out under the arcade for courtyard dining. A table d'hôte breakfast here is priced at Q12 ($3.00), and lunch and dinner cost Q30 ($7.50), with drinks, tax, and tip included. The hotel's nice bar has two rooms. A marimba band plays at lunch.

Facilities: Solar-heated swimming pool, Jacuzzi, sauna, and exercise room on the terrace out back.

MAYAN INN, 8a Calle and 3a Avenida, Santo Tomás Chichicastenango. Tel. 502/056-1176. In Guatemala City, tel. 502/310-213 or 310-316. 30 rms., all with bath.

$ Rates: Q224.64 ($56.16) single; Q262.08 ($65.52) double; Q299.52 ($74.88) triple. AE, DC, MC, V.

The best in town, and perhaps the most enjoyable hotel in Guatemala, is this lovely old hotel on a quiet side street a few blocks from the bustling main market square. The inn was started in 1932 by Alfred S. Clark (of Clark Tours fame); it's composed of several colonial buildings, and the guest rooms are arranged under red-tile porticos around courtyards planted with beautiful tropical gardens and lush grass. Parrots squawk and whistle here and there, and in the afternoons a local marimba band provides pleasant entertainment. The guest rooms are simple but absolutely charming, with antique furnishings, including carved-wood bedsteads, headboards painted with country scenes, heavily carved armoires, and rough-hewn tables, many of which were found by Mr. Clark himself. Each room has a little fireplace, with split logs laid ready to burn and a few sticks of *ocote* (fatwood) with which to kindle. Everywhere throughout the hotel are those gorgeous local textiles: window curtains, bedspreads, even shower curtains! Private bathrooms are tiled and, if a bit old-fashioned, also spacious and decently kept up; many have tubs.

I must mention that virtually all the staff at the Mayan Inn are dressed in local costumes, including colorful headdress, sash, black tunic with colored embroidery, half-length trousers, and squeaky leather *caites* (sandals). The costume is not purely Mayan, but a Spanish farmer's costume brought over by the conquistadores and adapted by the Guatemalans to their own culture. Although a stay at the Mayan Inn is technically out of your budget range, I urge you to stay here if at all possible—and it may not be possible for you to get reservations. But try.

Dining: The hotel has its own cozy colonial bar with fireplace (of course), and two dining rooms with simple pale-yellow walls, beamed ceilings, red-tile floors, stocky colonial-style tables and chairs, and more local cloth. You can order à la carte, but it makes the most sense to have the daily table d'hôte meals, which cost Q12.84 to Q16.38 ($3.21 to $4.10) at breakfast, Q35.20 ($8.80) at lunch, and Q44.50 ($11.12) dinner, plus tip and drinks. A typical dinner might be cream of tomato soup; roast lamb, broiled beef, or beef tongue in a savory sauce; followed by salad; and rhum baba or ice cream for dessert.

WHERE TO EAT

Meal possibilities are best in the above hotels, but if you're out for adventure and want to save money, take a look at the little comedors in the market and near the post office and Guatel office on the road into town (7a Avenida). There are also several restaurants around town that cater almost exclusively to the tour-bus trade. Their menus are primarily international, with a few Guatemalan favorites thrown in for good measure.

RESTAURANTE EL TORITO, Comercial Giron, 2nd floor. No phone.
$ Prices: Complete meal Q8–Q16 ($2–$4). No credit cards.
   Open: Mon–Wed and Fri–Sat 8am–9pm; Thurs and Sun 7am–9pm.
"The Little Bull," as its name implies, is primarily a steak house; however, you can also get chicken, fish, shrimp, chorizo, and pork chops. All the meals come with soup, potatoes, rice, and bread or tortillas. It is on the second floor of a new shopping arcade and has a few tables on the balcony overlooking the courtyard. The restaurant's main room is huge, obviously designed to accommodate busloads of diners. Light streams in through a wall of windows at dinner.

EXCURSIONS
A SIDE TRIP TO SANTA CRUZ DEL QUICHÉ AND NEBAJ

Called simply Quiché by the natives, the provincial capital is only 20 miles farther along the road from Chichicastenango. A day trip will hold no great thrills, but you can take a look at its famous church, watch the local women weave straw hats as they walk (distances here are measured in hat-making time!), or have a shave and a haircut in the barbershop by the market. There are some ruins 2 miles from town at Ciudad Gumarcaan (no public transportation), once the royal city of King Quiché. Nothing's been excavated or rebuilt, and the grass-covered stone mounds give you the eerie feeling that you're walking in a dead city.

You can continue past Quiché by bus over a bumpy and dusty (or muddy) road for a good number of miles to Nebaj, a more-or-less remote village in which your arrival will be the day's big event. The few *norteamericanos* who venture into Nebaj come to see the exquisitely beautiful costumes and headdresses of the Nebaj women, said by crafts experts to be the most beautiful in all of Guatemala. The trip is a fairly long one.

---

4. LAKE ATITLÁN AND PANAJACHEL

Distances: 75 miles west of Guatemala City;
50 miles southeast of Quetzaltenango; 25 miles south of Chichicastenango.

GETTING THERE   By Bus   Rebuli buses from Guatemala City leave from 3a

Avenida 2-36, Zona 9 (tel. 516-505) daily every hour from 6:45am to 4pm. Duration: 3 hours. Fare: Q4 ($1). From Quetzaltenango or Chichicastenango, take a bus to Los Encuentros, then change to a bus for Panajachel (you may have to change buses in Sololá).

By Car   Lake Atitlán can be reached from either the north or the south, although the southern route is not recommended due to frequent rebel activity in that area. Coming from Guatemala City, take the Patzún turnoff and continue down to Panajachel. Coming from Quetzaltenango, take the Sololá road. If you're coming from Chichicastenango, you must first turn west onto the highway before turning south a few miles later for Sololá and Panajachel.

DEPARTING   The town's main bus stop is at the very center, where Calle Principal intersects Calle Santander, across from the Hotel Mayan Palace and the Banco Agricola, but buses leave from other parts of the town as well. All these buses operate several times per day.

If you're headed to Antigua, you may have to take a bus to Chimaltenango and change there for a minibus to Antigua. The ride to Chimaltenango takes about 2½ hours; that from Chimaltenango to Antigua, 30 minutes.

Buses of the Rebuli and Higueros lines head off for Guatemala City several times daily.

Mendoza, Princesita Utatlan, Quiroga, and Trans-Occidente buses go to Chichicastenango.

Higueros and Morales buses go to Quetzaltenango.

ESSENTIALS Orientation   Panajachel lies on the northern shore of Lake Atitlán, at the foot of the mountains. Coming into town from Sololá, you descend the mountainside along a serpentine road; you might like to stop at the scenic overlook. Near the bottom of the hill, you pass the turnoff on the right for the deluxe Hotel Atitlán, then for the Hotel Tzanjuyu, and next for the Cacique Inn, before continuing into town along the Calle Principal, the main street. There's a grocery store on the right, then a Texaco service station. Finally you come to the heart of town: the intersection of the Calle Principal and the Calle Santander, where you will see the INGUAT tourist office, the Banco Agricola, and the Hotel Mayan Palace. Calle Santander, on the right, goes down to the beach and the Hotel Monterrey.

Farther along, the Calle Principal holds several more hotels, restaurants, and shops and also the post and telegraph offices and the church. By the church are the town hall, the police station, and the marketplace, busiest on Sunday, but with some activity on weekdays from 9am to noon.

Parallel to the Calle Santander, going from the center of town to the beach at the Hotel del Lago, is the Calle Rancho Grande.

Fast Facts   The INGUAT Tourism Office is in the center of town on the Calle Principal near the Hotel Maya Palace. It's open Wednesday to Sunday from 8am to noon and 2 to 6pm, Monday from 8am to noon; closed Tuesday.

Near the Circus Bar on Calle Santander is the Gallery Bookstore, where you can find new and used books in English, Spanish, and other languages. It also has maps of Guatemala, local art, and Guatemalan coffee. If you've bought more stuff than you can carry, you can use the shipping service here to send your purchases home.

The town's handiest bank is the Banco Agricola, on Calle Principal in the center of town—open Monday to Friday from 9am to 3pm (to 3:30pm on Friday), but note that currency-exchange hours are 9am to noon only! If the bank is closed, see if you can change money at your hotel or at some other hotel.

Bicycle rentals ($1 per hour) are available from a shop on Calle Santander just around the corner from Calle Principal heading away from the beach.

Market day is Sunday. Feast days are October 2 to 6.

The road from the main highway winds through the mountains and then descends to the lake through the provincial capital of Sololá (alt. 6,825 feet; pop. 9,000). Before you reach this town, however, you get glimpses of one of the most beautiful lakes in the world, a clear-blue mirror more than a mile above sea level, ringed by near-perfect-shaped volcanoes. The lake is not heavily settled or developed, so that much of its natural beauty remains in its pristine state. Fishing, swimming, boating (some waterskiing), and hiking along the shore keep most lake visitors busy, and there are some restaurants and even a nightspot or two (they open and fold every two weeks, it seems) to keep people from going to bed too early. A good selection of hotels in all price ranges completes the picture.

Sololá has been here a long time, since 1547 to be exact. Even earlier than that, it was a Mayan town. Stop to inspect the ornate cathedral façade (Sololá has a bishop) and for the fabulous market (on Tuesday and Friday). The most exciting day of the year in Sololá is August 15, date of the annual festival. If you're anywhere nearby on that date, don't miss it.

From Sololá, head down the hill for Panajachel (that's "Pahn-ah-ha-chell"—alt. 5,150 feet; pop. 5,000), the resort town on the lakeshore. This is where you'll want to make your headquarters, not in Sololá. Market day in Panajachel is Sunday.

WHAT TO SEE AND DO

It's only a 10- or 15-minute walk to the beach from any of the hotels mentioned below, and the beach is hardly ever crowded, perhaps because the water's a little chilly. There are beach cubicles for changing clothes, and several little eateries and soft-drink stands serve up snacks advertised on signboard menus. The one indispensable activity in Panajachel is sitting at one of the picnic tables along the beach, sipping a cool drink, and looking out over the water to the clouds scraping the tops of the volcanoes—you'll never forget the scene.

One of the main activities in Panajachel is shopping for clothes made from Guatemalan fabrics. All along Calle Santander, from Calle Principal to the beach, are vendors' stalls. After a while the riot of colors becomes overwhelming, so be sure to buy early in your stay before you get burned out on all the tipico clothing. Remember: Back home this stuff is still unique.

WHERE TO STAY

Because Panajachel is one of Guatemala's major tourist destinations and is, in fact, the country's top beach resort, there is a wide selection of accommodations available.

DOUBLES FOR LESS THAN Q60 [$15]

HOTEL MAYA KANEK, Calle Principal, Panajachel, Sololá. Tel. 502/062-1104. 26 rms., all with bath.
$ Rates: Q17.55–Q23.40 ($4.40–$5.85) single; Q29.25–Q35.10 ($7.30–$8.80) double; Q40.95 ($10.25) triple. No credit cards.
Among this town's cheaper hotels is the Maya Kanek, just down from the church. It's a motel-style arrangement, with simple, fairly well-used quarters facing a cobbled court with a small garden. Twin beds, small showers, toilets without seats, and dim light bulbs make this a fairly basic place to put up. One advantage is that you can park your car in the safety of the courtyard. Although you hear more noise in the rooms upstairs from the reception desk, these are relatively new.

HOTEL FONDA DEL SOL, Calle Principal, Panajachel, Sololá. Tel. 502/062-1162. 20 rms., 10 with bath.
$ Rates: Q19.90 ($4.97) single without bath, Q26.91 ($6.73) single with bath; Q29.25 ($7.31) double without bath, Q35.10 ($8.78) double with bath; Q38.61 ($9.65) triple without bath, Q47.97 ($11.99) triple with bath. AE, DC, MC, V.
Just as you are coming to Panajachel's main intersection on the road from Sololá, you'll see on your right this two-story hotel. The ground floor is a cheap restaurant, while the upper floor is reserved for simple guest rooms that are fairly worn but low priced. The hotel has a parking lot.
Service: Laundry service.

HOTEL GALINDO, Calle Principal, Panajachel, Sololá. Tel. 502/062-1168. 18 rms., all with bath.

$ Rates: Q18–Q25 ($4.50–$6.25) single; Q38 ($9.50) double; Q56 ($14) triple. AE, DC, MC, V.

In the center of town, the Galindo is now under new management, and the rooms have been redecorated. There is also a children's swimming pool now, but you'll have to hunt for it among dense foliage. On the sides of the garden, the guest rooms are small, with even tinier private bathrooms (showers only). At the back of the garden are several roomier suites, each with bedroom, small sitting room with fireplace, and veranda. For my money, the suites are the better deal, but if the new management keeps the prices this low, this may become the best deal in town.

There is a large and airy restaurant at streetside, and behind it is a surprisingly lush jungle of a garden courtyard set with wrought-iron café tables and chairs, furnished with a gazebo.

Service: Laundry service.

HOTEL PRIMAVERA, Calle Santander, Panajachel, Sololá. Tel. 502/062-1157. 8 rms., all with bath.

$ Rates: Q40.95 ($10.24) single; Q58.50 ($14.62) double. AE, DC, MC, V.

One of Panajachel's newest little budget hotels is a German-owned place at the end of Calle Santander farthest from the beach. The two-story hotel has a pretty little garden in the courtyard out back. The rooms are simple but clean and very appealing because they are new. The bathrooms in some of the rooms have skylights. Run with German efficiency, this is an excellent choice.

Meals in the first-floor German restaurant range from Q12 to Q30 ($3 to $7.50).

DOUBLES FOR LESS THAN Q120 [$30]

HOTEL MAYA PALACE, Calle Principal, Panajachel, Sololá. Tel. 502/062-1028. 24 rms., all with bath.

$ Rates: Q58.50 ($14.63) single; Q76.05 ($19) double; Q93.60 ($23.40) triple. AE, DC, MC, V.

On the intersection of Calle Principal and Calle Santander at the heart of Panajachel you'll find a good choice in the bottom end of this price category. The rooms are fairly clean and were recently remodeled. They all have large windows looking out onto the open hallway that runs the length of the hotel. You'll have a nice view of the hills behind town from here, and you can watch the action in the street below. Several rooms even have color TVs. The office is in the antique store directly opposite the hotel.

HOTEL MONTERREY, Panajachel, Sololá. Tel. 502/062-1126. 30 rms., all with bath.

$ Rates: Q100 ($25) single; Q112 ($28) double; Q125 ($31.25) triple. No credit cards.

Hidden away on a dirt lane a few hundred yards off Calle Santander is a rather stark blue-and-white, two-story motel-style establishment. Don't be put off by the dry and dusty parking lot. Facing the lake across its own lawns, which extend down to the beach, the Monterrey offers you clean and cheerful accommodations in pleasant surroundings.

The simple restaurant serves three meals a day, with prices ranging from Q8 ($2) for breakfast to Q16 ($4) for lunch and dinner.

HOTEL PLAYA LINDA, Calle Rancho Grande, Panajachel, Sololá. Tel. 502/062-1159. 19 rms., all with bath.

$ Rates: Q93.60–Q140.40 ($23.40–$35.10) single; Q117–Q163.80 ($29.25–$40.95) double. AE, DC, MC, V.

If you want to be as close to the lakeshore as possible, take a look at this hotel. A modernish building of brick, stone, white stucco, and dark wood, it has a small lawn, an aviary, lots of bougainvillea, and an assortment of guest rooms priced according to what sort of view they have. Rooms 1 through 5 are the best, on the second floor facing the lake; rooms 6 through 14 have no views but are a bit cheaper; rooms 1B through 4B are suites, and 5B is a large family suite. The one drawback here is that the area in front of the hotel becomes a dusty, noisy parking lot on weekends and holidays, spoiling the wonderful views. Meals in the open-air restaurant, with a fabulous view, range from Q12 to Q15 ($3 to $3.25).

HOTEL TZANJUYU, Panajachel, Sololá. Tel. 502/062-1318. In Guatemala City, tel. 502/310-764. 32 rms., all with bath.

$ Rates: Q96 ($24) single; Q120 ($30) double; Q135 ($33.75) triple. No credit cards.

Located at the western end of town off Calle Principal, the Tzanjuyu was Panajachel's prime place to stay several decades ago, and it still has an old-fashioned air about it. If other hotels are full, you can get a passable, tidy room here with private tiled bath and a view of the lake. The lawns here are not kept up as well as those at some of the other, more expensive hotels, and there is little shade. There is, however, a nice little pool.

In the large restaurant/bar, the waiters wear jackets and ties. A meal will run you less than Q25 ($6.25).

DOUBLES FOR LESS THAN Q150 [$37.50]

HOTEL REGIS, Calle Santander, Panajachel, Sololá. Tel. 502/062-1149. 19 rms., all with bath.

$ Rates: Q108 ($27) single; Q128 ($32) double; Q144 ($36) triple. MC, V.

Opposite the Guatel office on Calle Santander, which is the road from the center of town to the beach, stands a pretty hotel. The small, colonial-style complex is set back from the street across a lush lawn shaded by palms and equipped with a children's swimming pool and a small playground (swings and slide). The reception area and dining room are decorated with lots of local crafts. The guest rooms are in long, low buildings and separate bungalows, each with a nice veranda facing the lawn. There are also two rooms that have kitchenettes if you plan to be staying a while and want to save money by doing some of your own cooking. TVs are available for Q20 ($5) extra per night. María Mercedes Weymann, who manages the hotel, speaks excellent English and is a wealth of information. She has a small gift shop in the hotel lobby.

RANCHO GRANDE INN, Calle Rancho Grande, Panajachel, Sololá. Tel. 502/062-1554. In Guatemala City, tel. 502/764-768. 7 rms., all with bath.

$ Rates (including breakfast): Q112.32 ($28.08) single; Q131.04 ($32.76) double; Q149.76 ($37.44) triple. DC, MC, V.

Founded several decades ago by Milly Schlesier, the Rancho Grande was conceived as an inn of German country-style architecture in a tropical Guatemalan setting. Since 1975 the inn has been owned by Marlita Hannstein, who has preserved the lovely white-stucco cottages with red-tile or thatched roofs and small sitting porches, all set in emerald lawns beneath towering palm trees. It's a quiet place, equally convenient to town and to the beach, where you'll receive a warm welcome. The bungalows can hold as many as five people, which makes them an excellent choice for families. However, the rooms tend to be in great demand. Highly recommended.

SUPER-BUDGET CHOICES

Besides these hotels, Panajachel abounds in very simple, extremely cheap family pensions. You'll see them all along the Calle Santander and in other parts of town. Bath facilities may consist of a cold-water tap and primitive shower, but the price per person is usually only Q6 ($1.50), which is about as cheap as you can find anywhere in the world these days.

HOSPEDAJE CABANA COUNTRY CLUB, Calle Rancho Grande, Panajachel, Sololá. No phone. 22 rms, none with bath.
$ Rates: Q5 ($1.25) single without bath; Q10 ($2.50) double without bath. No credit cards.

🅢 Near the Rancho Grande Inn you'll find the most unusual of this type of rock-bottom pension. Despite its name, the Hospedaje Cabana is a low-budget accommodation. The rooms are arranged along a central courtyard parking area and are built to resemble log cabins. Each is just large enough to hold two twin beds. Sheets and blankets are included in the price.

HOSPEDAJE SANTA ELENA ANNEXO, Panajachel, Sololá. No phone. 12 rms., none with bath.
$ Rates: Q8 ($2) single; Q16 ($4) double. No credit cards.
Here you get a bed, one sheet, no blankets, a light, and a small table—period. But the señora keeps it all tidy; there are little tables in the modest courtyard (which you share with banana plants and parrots), and you get the use of a cold-water shower and toilet. The Annexo is off Calle Santander on the road to the Hotel Monterrey. The original Hospedaje Santa Elena is closer to the center of town, on the path up to the lookout.

WORTH THE EXTRA BUCKS

HOTEL VISION AZUL, Panajachel, Sololá. Tel. 502/062-1426 or 062-1419). In Guatemala City, 41a Calle 18-67, Zona 12, Guatemala City. Tel. 502/761-483. 24 rms, 8 bungalows, all with bath.
$ Rates: Q140.40 ($35.10) single; Q168.50 ($42.12) double; Q196.60 ($49.14) triple or bungalow. AE, DC, MC, V.

⭐ A short distance outside of town on the road to the Hotel Atitlán, you'll find this very attractive white-stucco hotel with brick arches and volcanic stone accents. It is built into the hillside with a view across grassy lawns and through a grove of trees to the lake. Set in the midst of those lawns is a sunny swimming pool. Unfortunately, between you and the lawns and lake is a dusty dirt road that gets a lot of traffic on the weekends. Otherwise, the location is quiet. There is little to disturb you in one of the main building's big, bright guest rooms with a spacious terrace. The bungalows are small and located on the road so that they are not really a very good deal. Verdure is everywhere: bougainvillea, bananas, and ivy. The chirp of the birds is the loudest noise, except for the rumble of passing cars going to the Hotel Atitlán.

The Vision Azul has a decent restaurant, where meals range from Q10 to Q20 ($2.50 to $5).

CACIQUE INN, Calle Embarcadero, Panajachel, Sololá. Tel. 502/062-1205. 33 rms., all with bath.
$ Rates: Q206 ($51.50) single; Q234 ($58.50) double; Q262 ($65.50) triple. No credit cards.
Another excellent, quiet choice, this hotel is off Calle Principal at the western edge of town. A *cacique* is a native chieftain, and the inn has been hosting notables—both native and foreign—for many decades. In its own walled compound not far from the lakeshore, the inn has a spacious court planted with tropical shrubs and trees and green lawns and furnished with a tidy little swimming pool. The guest rooms, dining room, bar, souvenir shop, and reception desk are in low, rustic-inspired buildings facing the court. Lots of rounded stone, tree trunks, and other country touches were used in construction. The rooms are large, each with a fireplace (with wood laid, ready to light), two double beds with locally made blankets, and odd sliding glass-and-wrought-iron doors that take some getting used to. It's a welcoming place, obviously with a history all its own.

Lunch or dinner in the simple but light and airy dining room can be ordered à la carte; the table d'hôte dinner is about Q20 ($5).

HOTEL ATITLÁN, Panajachel, Sololá. Tel. 502/062-1416, 062-1441, or 062-1429. 42 rms., all with bath.
$ Rates: Q308 ($77) single; Q304 ($85) double; Q372 ($93) triple. AE, DC, MC, V.

About 1½ miles (a 15- or 20-minute walk or a $2 taxi ride) from the center of town is Panajachel's most expensive hotel. This is a fairly lavish Guatemalan-style establishment—with spacious grounds; various tropical gardens filled with bougainvillea, ivy, and geraniums; and spaces for sun and spaces for shade. The rambling three-story colonial-style hotel has gleaming tiled floors, antique woodcarvings, and exquisite local craft pieces as decoration, as well as an experienced and obliging staff. The guest rooms have nice private baths, twin beds, local craft decorations, and shady balconies from which to enjoy the view of the grounds and the lake. In case you're curious about the looming high-rise monstrosity next door, it is a deluxe hotel project that ran out of money several years ago and has yet to be completed. It is nothing but a massive eyesore on the banks of one of the most beautiful lakes in the world.

Dining/Entertainment: A good restaurant with a long wall of glass providing a stunning view of lake and volcanoes and a nice open-air patio looking across the swimming pools to the lake are great places for a meal, whatever the weather might be. In the cool months, a fire burns in a large fireplace in the dining room. In the evening, the cozy bar is a good place for a drink before heading off to the dining room and a table by the fireplace. Meals are in the Q20 to Q30 ($5 to $7.50) range.

Facilities: Swimming pool and private beach.

HOTEL DEL LAGO, Calle Rancho Grande, Panajachel, Sololá. Tel. 502/ 062-1555 to 062-1560. Fax 502/962-1562. In Guatemala City, Edificio Real Reforma 1-M, Avenida La Reforma 13-70, Zona 9, Guatemala City 01009. Tel. 502/348-016 or 316-941. Fax 502/234-8016. 100 rms., all with bath.

$ Rates: Q360 ($90) single; Q400 ($100) double. AE, DC, MC, V.

The largest hotel in town, a favorite with groups, is right on the beach near where the ferries leave for various villages around the lake. This six-story structure is as close as Panajachel comes to an operating high-rise, and its 100 modern guest rooms provide almost half the town's luxury lodging. Guest quarters have two double beds, beautiful bathrooms with tub/shower combinations and lots of marble, plus marble dressing tables and vanities. Every room has a balcony with that fabulous lake view. The grounds are planted with colorful tropical flowers that seem to bloom year round.

Dining: The large semicircular dining room behind the lobby offers spectacular views of the garden, pool, lake, and volcanoes. The service is good, and the meals, primarily Continental, are well prepared. A dinner here will cost around Q20 to Q30 ($5 to $7.50). The bar, adjacent to the dining room, features a curving stone wall covered with plants—a very comfortable place for a drink.

Facilities: Two swimming pools (one for children), rental bicycles, and game room.

WHERE TO EAT

The best dining is in the fancy hotels. For more modest meals, Panajachel has numerous places to offer, many of which are run by foreigners looking for a way to stay in Panajachel. These restaurants often go out of business within a year of opening. Often some other foreigner moves in, renames the restaurant, changes the menu, and tries to make a go of it. Consequently, you might find that a restaurant recommended here no longer exists but another restaurant occupies the same location. Give it a try as long as you're there—it may be the next "in" restaurant, and you'll have helped discover it.

MEALS FOR LESS THAN Q20 [$5]

LA HAMBURGUESA GIGANTE, Calle Santander. No phone.
   Cuisine: BURGERS/GUATEMALAN.
$ Prices: Q6–Q12 ($1.50–$3). No credit cards.
   Open: Daily 8am–10pm.
This is a long-time favorite in Panajachel, a congenial place with dependably tasty

food at moderate prices. Try the carne asada, or grilled chicken, for about Q12 ($3). Breakfast is served here as well.

RANCHÓN TÍPICA ATITLÁN, Calle Santander. No phone.
Cuisine: GUATEMALAN.
$ Prices: Main dishes Q8–Q12 ($2–$3). No credit cards.
Open: Daily 8am–11pm.

Another currently popular place is opposite the Hotel Regis. The walls are of rough-hewn logs, and the floor is of cobblestone. The specialty here is fish fresh from the lake for Q12 ($3). Although the service can be slow, you're likely to be entertained by young vendors who wander into the restaurant every few minutes. You can also order roast chicken for the same price as the fish. The restaurant is open from breakfast until late in the evening.

MEALS FOR LESS THAN Q30 [$7.50]

LA LAGUNA RESTAURANT, Calle Principal. Tel. 62-1231.
Cuisine: GUATEMALAN/INTERNATIONAL.
$ Prices: Main dishes Q8–Q20 ($2–$5). DC, MC, V.
Open: Daily noon–9:30pm.

Set back from the road in a large grassy garden is a little Spanish-style house that has been converted into a simple-but-chic restaurant (by Panajachel standards). Within the dark dining room are several unusual lamps and sculptures made from old automobile parts. There are also a few tables on the veranda and out in the garden, where you can watch a pet parrot preening. This is the only restaurant I've ever been to that actually kept its rats on display (pet white rats in a cage). The menu includes *pepian de pollo,* the Guatemalan national dish, a stew with a thick dark gravy. There are plenty of seafood entrees and a few dishes made with black bass from the lake. Be sure to try the papaya mousse for desert.

TOCOYAL, Calle Rancho Grande. Tel. 62-1555.
Cuisine: GUATEMALAN/INTERNATIONAL.
$ Prices: Main dishes Q10–Q25 ($2.50–$6.25). DC, MC, V.
Open: Daily 7am–9pm.

Down at the end of Calle Rancho Grande, right on the beach, is this restaurant with one of the best views in the world. Take a seat on one of the restaurant's two terraces or inside the thatched-roof dining room with sliding glass walls and gaze across the lake at the volcanoes. It would be a crime not to have at least one sunset dinner here during your stay—in fact, you might want to eat here every evening. With views like these, it doesn't really matter what the food is like, but luckily meals here are tasty, and the service is good. The menu includes fresh lake fish and seafood, international pasta dishes, sandwiches, and that Guatemalan carnivore's delight, the *parrillada.* There is live music here on Saturday evening.

EL PATIO, Calle Santander. No phone.
Cuisine: INTERNATIONAL/GUATEMALAN.
$ Prices: Breakfast Q5–Q10 ($1.25–$2.50); lunch and dinner Q12–Q22 ($3–$5.50). DC, MC, V.
Open: Sun–Fri 7am–9pm; Sat 7:30am–10pm.

As its name implies, this popular restaurant does indeed have a streetside patio for dining, plus a bright and attractive interior room. Quiet music soothes your spirit as you order from the menu, which includes a good assortment of sandwiches and *platos fuertes* (main courses) such as pepian de pollo (Guatemala's national dish), Szechuan chicken, cassoulet, roast pork, Virginia-style ham, chicken à la king, and filet mignon. Drinks are served.

AL CHISME "TO THE GOSSIP," Calle Los Arboles. No phone.
Cuisine: INTERNATIONAL.
$ Prices: Breakfast Q6–Q12 ($1.50–$3); main dishes Q15–Q20 ($3.75–$5). No credit cards.

Open: Thurs–Tues 7am–10pm.

With an excellent assortment of salads and pastries, it is no wonder this restaurant was an instant hit in Panajachel. The meal includes all manner of European and American favorites, such as crêpes, pastas, salads, shrimp scampi, lamb chops in mint sauce, and chicken Cordon Bleu. The music on the stereo is what you would expect if this restaurant were in Seattle or Miami. The narrow patio out front has a nice view of the steep hills outside town. You'll really get a sense of being inside a volcano when you gaze up at those walls.

MEALS FOR LESS THAN Q40 [$10]

LA POSADA DEL PINTOR AND THE CIRCUS BAR, Calle Los Arboles. No phone.
   Cuisine: INTERNATIONAL.
$ Prices: Pizzas Q10–Q20 ($2.50–$5); full meals Q15–Q35 ($3.75–$8.75). No credit cards.
   Open: Daily noon–midnight.

Perhaps the most interesting place in the center of town is on the section of Calle Santander across Calle Principal (that is, in the direction away from the beach). It's a rustic bar with stools, plus dining tables spread with blue-and-white-checked cloths. The walls are covered in old circus posters, and quiet jazz issues from speakers here and there, filling the dining rooms and the small courtyard. In addition to pizzas, there are many more interesting dishes on the menu, including shrimp thermidor, potato salad, steaks, pastas, and desserts. If you drop by for just a drink, expect to pay Q3 ($1.20) for a straight drink and Q5 ($1.25) to Q10 ($2.50) for a cocktail. There's live entertainment in the bar some evenings.

CASABLANCA, Calle Principal. No phone.
   Cuisine: INTERNATIONAL.
$ Prices: Sandwiches Q10–Q20 ($2.50–$5); entrees Q18–Q44 ($4.50–$11). DC, MC, V.
   Open: Daily 6–10pm (sometimes later).

With the opening of this classy restaurant/bar, Panajachel emerged into the world of upscale resort towns. Mellow jazz music plays on the stereo, and on the weekend this place has live jazz, Latino, reggae, and salsa. Contemporary art hangs from the walls, sunshine filters through skylights, and diners on two floors gaze out at pedestrians through the large windows. Young and hip waiters in bow ties hurry between the kitchen and the tables. And, of course, it couldn't be called Casablanca without a few ceiling fans. If your German is good, you can grab a German magazine off a table here and spend the evening brushing up on world events. Daily specials for about Q14 ($3.50) are the best deal here, but if you're in the mood for a splurge, you can dine on steak or lobster. Try the shrimp-stuffed avocado salad for a starter. If you aren't in the mood for a big meal, you can get a sandwich (I'd stay away from the steak tartare sandwich because the beef here is not inspected).

SAVVY SHOPPING

Panajachel is one of Guatemala's main towns for shopping. Calle Santander is a virtual gamut of small shops and vendors' stalls where great deals can be had if you are a shrewd bargainer. Guatemalan textiles made into very casual international fashions are the main draw here.

EXCURSIONS

There are regularly scheduled boats to many of the villages that perch on the shores of Lake Atitlán, but by far my favorite is the following.

SANTIAGO ATITLÁN

The village of Santiago Atitlán, across the lake from Panajachel on the southern shore, provides the destination for a nice cruise on the lake. The attractions of the town are its traditional life-style, its huipiles embroidered with brilliantly colored flocks of birds, and its unusual history.

To get to Santiago, catch the daily boat at 9am from the special dock near the Hotel Tzanjuyu, at the western edge of town. The return trip departs from Santiago at about 11:30am. A round-trip ticket costs Q9 ($2.25). Another boat, charging about the same price, departs from the public beach near the Hotel del Lago, at the end of Calle Rancho Grande, at 8:45 and 9am and 4pm, departing on the return trip from Santiago at 11:45am and 1pm. The outbound trip across the lake by either boat takes about 1¼ hours; you get about 1¼ hours to visit Santiago; and the return trip takes 1¼ to 1½ hours, depending on the wind.

While cruising across the lake, admire the perfect volcanoes and consider that Lake Atitlán is a caldera, formed by the tremendous eruption of an enormous volcano that eons ago literally blew its top off, creating the lake basin. The boat soon enters the bay at Santiago.

At the wharf, children from the town will greet you, selling souvenirs such as little embroidered strips of cloth and penny whistles of clay. Leave the boat, turn left, and walk until you come to a town street paved in stone blocks.

Up the street on the right, is a sign that says "Visite la casa de la escultura y pintura, visit the house of sculpture and paintings." If you follow the sign's admonition, you will see the works of Diego Chavez and his two sons, Diego and Nicolas, the village's self-trained artists. Besides the paintings, there are wood carvings: figurines and bas-reliefs. In the courtyard, the grandmother spins her distaff while the mother weaves the local design into cloth.

Along this street, which is strolled by every tourist coming up from the docks, are most of the town's shops, which sell huipiles and other craft items. The cloth is truly gorgeous, with days of beautiful and painstaking handwork invested in each piece. You may well fall in love with the fanciful designs (as I did) and begin to haggle over a particular item.

Up the hill a bit farther is the town square, the town office, and the huge old church. Within the stark, echoing church are some surprising sights. Along the walls are wooden statues of the saints, each of whom gets a new shawl embroidered by local women every year. On the carved wooden pulpit, note the figures of corn (from which man was formed, according to Mayan religion); of a quetzel bird reading a book; and of Yum-Kax, the Mayan god of corn. There is similar carving on the back of the priest's chair. The walls of the church bear paintings, now covered by a thin layer of plaster. A memorial plaque at the back of the church commemorates Fr. Stanley Francis Rother, a missionary priest from Oklahoma who was beloved by the local people but despised by ultrarightist elements, who murdered him right here in the church during the troubled year of 1981.

Where to Stay

PENSIÓN ROSITA, Santiago Atitlán. No phone. 10 rms., none with bath.
$ Rates: Q8 ($2) single; Q16 ($4) double. No credit cards.
Located to the right of the school and behind the basketball court off the main plaza, this very basic pensión has very stark, bare rooms. The toilet and shower facilities here are extremely basic. Only for those accustomed to primitive conditions.

HOTEL CHI-NIM-YA, Santiago Atitlán. No phone. 12 rms., 1 with bath.
$ Rates: Q10 ($2.50) single; Q20 ($5) double. No credit cards.
This is perhaps a better bet than the Pensión Rosita. The rooms are a little bit larger and cleaner but still extremely basic. Even the plumbing is slightly better. The best room in the house, with private facilities and a lake view, costs Q20 ($5). The best

view in the place is from room 106, which is large and airy, with windows all around. The hotel is connected to a modest food shop in which you can get snacks, some basic supplies, and cold drinks. The hotel is up from the boat dock on a street to the left.

Where to Eat

RESTAURANT EL GRAN SOL, near the Hotel Chi-Nim-Ya. No phone.
$ Prices: Breakfast Q5–Q6 ($1.25–$1.50), main dishes Q8 ($2).
There is a great view over the lake from the palapa-shaded terrace of this restaurant, the nicest in Santiago Atitlán. Bamboo and thatch provide the proper tropical atmosphere to accompany the splendid view. Signs in both English and Spanish announce that no beer is sold here.

IXIMCHE

A short distance east of the Los Encuentros crossroads on the Pan American Highway, on the way toward Chimaltenango, there is a turnoff for the town of Tecpan and signs pointing the way through the town to the ancient Mayan city of Iximche. If you have a car, make the detour to see this beautiful archeological site.

As you enter the site, you pass a small building, the museo, on your right. Then you enter the city itself, past some grass-covered mounds and into the main complex of plazas. On many of the pyramids here, the outer coating of plaster is visible in places. When you come to the first uncovered buildings, look for traces of painting on the low structure to the left.

Iximche was selected as the site for the capital city of the Cakchiquel Maya partly because of its natural defenses, as it is on a promontory surrounded on three sides by ravines. It was the Cakchiquel capital when the conquistadores came in the early 1500s, having been founded only a half-century before. The Cakchiquels formed an alliance with the Spaniards, who founded Tecpan nearby and who used Tecpan as their center of operations for the conquest and government of Guatemala. But later these two warlike peoples had a falling out; in the ensuing battles, the Cakchiquels lost to the Spaniards. Still, the Cakchiquel capital city escaped massive destruction and stands today as a fascinating monument to that people.

5. ANTIGUA

Distances: 28 miles southwest of Guatemala City;
62 miles east of Panajachel.

GETTING THERE   By Bus   Buses leave Guatemala City from 15 Calle 3-65, Zona 1, every 30 minutes between 7am and 7pm. Duration: 1 hour. Fare: Q1.50 (38¢).

By Car   The road to Antigua heads northwest out of Guatemala. The junction for Antigua is in San Lucas Sacatepequez, which is a short distance over the hill that the road climbs as it leaves Guatemala City.

DEPARTING   Buses run very frequently between Antigua and Guatemala City, and minibuses shuttle between Antigua and Chimaltenango, on the Pan American Highway all day long. Buses trundling along the Pan Am Highway will stop in Chimaltenango and take you on to your final destination, whether it be the capital or the Mexican border.

If you're headed for Guatemala City, the problem with the bus is that it lands you at the central bus station, which is not really a bus station at all, but a chaos of market stalls, double-parked streets, crowds, noise, heat, and confusion. Many foreign visitors used to avoid this inconvenience by taking a taxi between Antigua and Guatemala City, but this luxury cost as much as $40 or $45 per carload, one way. Now, however, there is a better way. Buses Inter-Hotel y Turismo (tel. 320-011 to 320-015 in Guatemala City) runs comfortable scheduled minibuses on a circular route past many of Guatemala City's luxury hotels (El Dorado, Conquistador Sheraton, Cortijo Reforma, Fiesta, Camino Real), and La Aurora airport, then out Bulevar Tecun Uman to Antigua, stopping at various spots in town and terminating at the Ramada hotel. The return run from Antigua to Guatemala City starts at the Hostal Tetuan, goes to the Ramada, the Hotel Antigua, the Posada de Don Rodrigo, the Restaurant Doña Luisa, and the Hotel Aurora, before heading out of town to the airport and the capital. Schedules are set up to get you to the airport in time for a flight to Tikal or a flight home. Cost for a one-way ticket is Q20 ($8), more than for the normal bus but substantially less than for a taxi. Check at any of the aforementioned establishments for the latest fares and schedules.

Antigua's bus station is located in the market.

Buses for Guatemala City leave every 30 minutes between 7am and 7pm. Duration: 1 hour. Fare: Q1.50 (38¢).

To get to Panajachel by bus, you must first catch one of the frequent buses to Chimaltenango. In Chimaltenango, you can flag down one of the hourly Guatemala-Panajachel buses. Duration: 3 hours. Fare: Q4 ($1).

To reach Chichicastenango, first catch a bus to Chimaltenango, then flag down one of the half-hourly buses that make the run from Guatemala City to Chichicastenango. Duration: 3½ hours. Fare: Q5 ($1.25).

To reach Quetzaltenango again, you must first catch a bus to Chimaltenango, then flag down a bus from Guatemala City. They pass by around 6:30 and 9:30am, noon, and 3:30, 6, 8, and 10pm. Duration: 4 hours. Fare: Q6 ($1.50).

ESSENTIALS Orientation Unlike most Guatemalan towns, Antigua has a street numbering system that includes compass designations; the central point for the plan is the city's main plaza, called the Parque Central. Calles run east to west, and so 4a Calle west of the Parque Central is 4a Calle Poniente; avenidas run north to south, and thus 3a Avenida north of the Parque Central is 3a Avenida Norte. Remember your directions here: norte (north), sur (south), oriente (east), poniente (west).

Most intercity buses arrive and depart from the area of the market, four blocks west of the Parque Central. Although this is not an official bus station, just an empty lot, I'll call it the bus station for the sake of convenience.

Fast Facts Antigua's tourist office is in the Palacio de Gobierno, at the southeast corner of the Parque Central, next to the intersection of 4a Avenida Sur and 5a Calle Oriente. Go here for answers to questions and for information about guided hikes and climbs on the volcanoes.

Banks tend to be open Monday to Friday from 9am to 2pm (to 2:30pm on Friday), but the Banco del Agro, on the north side of the Parque Central, has a ventanilla especial (special teller) open longer hours and also on Saturday.

The post office (Correos)—open Monday to Saturday from 8am to noon and 2 to 8pm (closed Sunday)—is at 4a Calle Poniente and the Alameda de Santa Lucia, west of the Parque Central near the market.

The Guatel telephone office is just off the southwest corner of the Parque Central, at the intersection of 5a Calle Poniente and 5a Avenida Sur.

For books in English and Spanish, look for the shop called Un Poco de Todo, on the Parque Central at the northwest corner—open Monday to Friday from 9:30am to 1pm and 3 to 6pm. Another shop, selling Spanish books, postcards, maps, and photocopies, is Casa Andinista, at 4a Calle Oriente no. 5, just a few steps off the Parque Central.

Market is daily. Feast day is first Friday of Lent.

Officially called Antigua Guatemala, this well-preserved colonial city (alt. 5,020 feet; pop. 27,000) was the capital of the country from 1543 to 1773. Even before it was the capital, however, it was on the way to becoming the cultural and religious center of the country. Pedro de Alvarado encouraged the Dominican, Mercedarian, and Franciscan friars to come and teach here, and the church spent a great deal of money in subsequent centuries to make this the most impressive city in Central America.

As the capital of the Captaincy-General of Guatemala, Antigua's official name was La muy Noble y muy Leal Ciudad de Santiago de los Caballeros de Goathemala, or

Santiago for short, and from here orders went out to all parts of the region (which included the present-day states of Guatemala, Belize, Honduras, El Salvador, and Costa Rica). The city's population peaked at 55,000, and the citizens could boast that they lived in the third-oldest Spanish city in America (founded in 1542) and that they had the first Pontifical University in the hemisphere (founded in 1675). It remains impressive to this day, still beautiful and much-visited by tourists, even though the ravages of the earthquakes of 1773 and 1976 are plain to see, along with the effects of 14 smaller quakes, fires, and floods that damaged the city between 1540 and 1717. Some buildings have been in ruins since the quake of 1773; in the quake of 1976, some of the finest churches were badly damaged, but reconstruction efforts are now complete. The San Francisco church, virtually ruined in earlier quakes, was barely touched in the recent one. If you look at the photographs of the reconstruction work on display in the church, you'll see why: Modern construction methods using steel reinforcing rods kept everything in place.

Coming down into the valley of Antigua from Guatemala City, you'll see Antigua's impressive situation, surrounded by three magnificent volcanoes named Agua, Fuego, and Acatenango—Agua is the grand one to the south, visible throughout the town; Fuego is the middle one, which is always smoking.

Antigua is packed full on Good Friday because of its unique pageantry during Holy Week, so if you plan to be here at that time be sure to reserve your room weeks (even months) in advance. At other times of year, Antigua is one of the most delightful towns to make your base, greatly preferable in all ways to Guatemala City. I highly recommend that you settle in at Antigua and make day trips to the capital, rather than vice versa.

WHAT TO SEE AND DO

Antigua is one of the most pleasant towns to stroll around in: It's quiet because there are few cars, and the buses are routed outside the main area; the air is clean (no exhaust fumes), with an occasional smell of wood smoke; and there are beautiful colonial buildings around every corner. You can see some 35 churches and monasteries in Antigua. The best thing is to meander through the lovely cobbled streets and see what you discover. The following are the high points.

While you're on the main square (Parque Central), take a look at the **Palacio de Gobierno,** officially named the Palace of the Royal Audiencia and the Captaincy-General of Guatemala. Construction was begun in 1543, but earthquakes and the ravages of time destroyed almost everything but the façade on the park. Most of what you see was rebuilt about 100 years ago. The façade bears the insignia of the Bourbons and the name of the monarch reigning at the time, Charles III.

Also on the plaza, on the north side at 4a Calle Oriente, is the **Museo de Santiago,** which was set up a few years ago to preserve some of Guatemala's history. On display in the 16th-century building, which once was the palace of the Council of the Realm of Guatemala, are cannons, guns, swords, religious articles, and an old Quiché marimba. Not terribly exciting, but certainly worth the 25¢ admission. Note the barred rooms that were used as cells when the palace was converted to a prison in the 19th century. Admission is free on Sunday and holidays. It's open daily from 9am to 1pm and 2 to 6pm.

Of the other notable buildings, the **University of San Carlos** comes next. The university was founded in 1676 and was the third university (after those in Mexico and Lima) in Spanish America. Much of the building you'll see was built around 1763 after the previous structure was damaged by the inevitable earthquake. Today the university building serves as the Colonial Museum, open daily from 9am to noon and 2 to 6pm.

As you enter the university, you can almost feel a change in time period. You come first to a beautiful open courtyard with a fountain, peaceful except for the sound of running water. Off to the right is the first of nine salons decorated in 17th- and 18th-century style, hung with paintings and dotted with the statuary of the period. One of the foremost painters of the time, Thomas de Meilo (1694–1739), is well

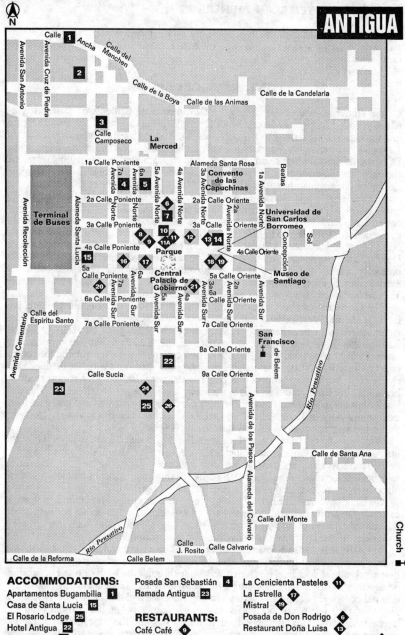

ANTIGUA

ACCOMMODATIONS:

Apartamentos Bugambilia **1**
Casa de Santa Lucia **15**
El Rosario Lodge **25**
Hotel Antigua **22**
Hotel Aurora **14**
Hotel "El Descanso" **10**
Hotel Placido **3**
Hotel Posada de Don Rodrigo **7**
Hotel Sol-Mor **2**
Pension El Arco **5**
Posada San Sebastián **4**
Ramada Antigua **23**

RESTAURANTS:

Café Café **9**
Café Flor **21**
Casa de Café Ana **24**
Doña Maria Gordillo
  Dulces Típicos **18**
El Sereno **20**
Fonda de la Calle Real **11A**
La Cenicienta Pasteles **11**
La Estrella **17**
Mistral **19**
Posada de Don Rodrigo **6**
Restaurant Doña Luisa **13**
Restaurant Italiano "El Capuchino" **16**
Restaurant Katok **12**
Restaurant Mesón Panza Verde **26**
Restaurante Pizzeria
  Italiana Martedino **8**

represented, and although the museum is not slick, or even well run, the atmosphere succeeds in giving you a taste of old Antigua. The last of the rooms is the library (*biblioteca*).

ANTIGUA'S CHURCHES

Of the churches, one of the best is the **Convent and Church of Our Lady of Mercy,** called simply La Merced by local people. It's at the end of 5a Avenida Norte, and the façade is something to behold—you'll see what I mean. Legend has it that the 12 sprays in the church's foundation are symbolic of the Apostles, which makes sense. La Merced is much more of an attraction than the cathedral on the main square, but the latter has the distinction of being the church in which were buried such illustrious figures of Guatemalan history as Pedro de Alvarado, discoverer of the country, and one of his wives; and Bernal Díaz de Castillo, whose day-to-day account of the conquest of Mexico and Guatemala has become a classic (it's available in Penguin paperback). Back in the 16th century, some 180,000 gold pieces went toward the construction of this cathedral. Inside are 68 vaulted arches carved with angels and coats-of-arms. The dome is 70 feet high; the altar is decorated with gold and lacquer. Unfortunately, very little remains intact of this once-opulent cathedral, but it is presently under reconstruction to repair the sections that collapsed with the earthquakes. Since the quake of 1976, entrance to the cathedral has been limited to Tuesday to Sunday from 8am to noon; closed Monday.

The **Convent of the Capuchinas,** 2a Avenida Norte and 2a Calle Oriente, was built by the monastic order for the sisterhood of the Capuchins in 1736. The nuns were invited to come here from Madrid by the bishop of Santiago (Antigua). Earthquakes have destroyed a good part of the building, but what remains is fascinating. As you enter, you'll find a plan of the convent to your right and the central court to your left. Notice the unusual pillars, rather squat and wider at the base than at the top. At the west end of the court is the bath and laundry room, made of beautiful pink stone, and next to it is a stairway leading down into the crypt. There's a small museum, on the right as you enter, in which you can see tiles and ceramics from excavations done in 1974 and 1975 on several churches in Antigua; some of the relics found in these excavations date as far back as 400 B.C.

When leaving the museum, turn right and walk through a small patio and take the first left, to where a large white tunnel leads to a lower-level room that must be seen to be believed: It is ring-shaped, with a large concave pillar in the middle. Any sound reverberates for a long time. Although I'd like to think some sort of religious rite took place here, it seems that this was a *bodega* (wine cellar).

Go back upstairs and turn right to the central courtyard, turn left, and go upstairs to get to the monastic cells, complete with a mockup of a nun saying her vespers. In the central courtyard, two stairways lead to an upper level from which you can get a good idea of the layout of the convent and the surrounding area.

The **Church of San Francisco,** at 7a Calle Oriente and 2a Avenida Sur, was once a very beautiful building and is still fine, but earthquakes destroyed a lot of the best work on the façade. The church was built through the wish of one Fray Toribio de Benavente Motolinia, a Franciscan friar who arrived in Guatemala in 1544. Of the original church about all that survives is a single chapel, and that houses the remains of Hermano Pedro de Betancourt, a Franciscan who came to Antigua in about 1650 and later established a hospital where he cared for the sick and the poor for 15 years. He is remembered as an unselfish and saintly man, and people still come to solicit his help for cures. The walls around his resting place hold the most fantastic array of testimonial plaques, letters, photos, and memorabilia. You may see someone quietly praying before his crypt, gently knocking on it to let Hermano Pedro know that he's needed.

The church was restored in 1961 using modern methods, and this helped it to survive the 1976 quake; only rubble remains of the convent of the Franciscans to the south of the church.

THE MARKET AREA

The market is located between Alameda de Santa Lucia and Alameda de la Recoleccion. It is a busy market selling everything from vegetables and baskets to huipiles (Guatemalan hand-woven, embroidered blouses) and beautiful cloth. The village women file in early every day (except Sunday, when the market is closed) with their wares of jackets, huipiles, and rugs. On Sunday there is a tourist-oriented market all around the Parque Central.

The only better place to shop for handsome Guatemalan clothes is in the village of San Antonio, 5 miles south of town. Principal market days here are Monday, Thursday, and Saturday. You can get there easily by taking any of the numerous buses outside the market going to San Antonio; the trip takes 15 minutes.

As you wind down into that town, you'll see a number of stands hung with bright-colored items. The prices for the women's handwork have gone up considerably in the past years—frankly, it's about time. The prices they used to ask were just not fair compensation for the work involved. Anyway, someone got smart, and there now seems to be a type of cooperative among the village women, for all the prices seem to be pretty much fixed.

To buy local silverwork, you must go to the nearby village of San Felipe, where there's a silver factory. Catch a bus near the market in Antigua for the 1¼-mile ride, and when you get to the village, ask for the factory—there are no street signs.

Also out here near the market, at the western end of 5a Calle Poniente, is the Monumento a Landívar, a set of five colonial-style arches set in a little park next to the bus station. Rafael Landívar, a Jesuit priest and poet, lived and worked in Guatemala during the mid-1700s. After the Jesuits were expelled from New Spain, he returned to Italy, where he wrote the works that Guatemalans continue to value as the best poetry of the colonial period. The house in which Landívar lived while in Antigua (then the capital of Guatemala, of course) was nearby on 5a Calle Poniente.

HOLY WEEK

From Palm Sunday until Easter, Antigua celebrates—and celebrates in style! This is perhaps one of the best pageantries of Holy Week anywhere in Central America, and they claim it's "comparable to the one held in Seville." There are large processions on Palm Sunday, Holy Thursday, and Good Friday, each involving hundreds of men and boys dressed in deep-purple robes (*cucuruchos*), rhythmically swaying under the heavy load of the 40-foot wooden casketlike platform topped with a statue of Christ carrying the cross. It is a most awesome sight, accompanied by incense and rhythmic silence that pervades the procession that lasts all day long and often into the night. On Good Friday, not to be missed, are the numerous *alfombras* (sawdust rugs) made by each neighborhood that line the processional streets. They are made with colored sawdust, pine needles, *coroso* (2- to 3-foot-tall slender yellow flowerlike seeds), and flowers in beautiful patterns and scenes.

This festival is very popular and packed with Guatemalans and foreigners who have come to enjoy the ceremonies. *You'll need hotel reservations well in advance.*

A brochure listing the events during Holy Week can be obtained through the Tourism Office, but here is a quick rundown on the processional times: **Palm Sunday** (3 to 10pm), leaves from La Merced; **Holy Thursday** (4 to 9:30pm), leaves from the Church of San Francisco; and **Good Friday** (8am to 3pm), leaves from La Merced; (4:30 to 11:30pm) leaves from Escuela de Cristo.

WHERE TO STAY

DOUBLES FOR LESS THAN Q50 [$12.50]

EL ROSARIO LODGE, 5a Avenida Sur 36, Antigua Guatemala. Tel. 502/032-0336. 10 rms., all with bath.
$ Rates: Q29.25–Q35.10 ($7.31–$8.78) single/double. No credit cards.
Antigua is not a very noisy town, but the quietest of the quiet places is five blocks

south of the Parque Central, down 5a Avenida Sur. El Rosario is just about at the end of the paving, on the right side. Although it's a short walk from the plaza, the pleasant setting amid shady trees makes it worthwhile. The rooms come in a variety of shapes and sizes and have many extras, such as native blankets and craftwork decorations; some rooms have terraces and fireplaces. Furnishings have a Teutonic accent because the ownership here was German for many years.

CASA DE SANTA LUCIA, Alameda de Santa Lucia 5, Antigua Guatemala.
No phone. 12 rms., all with bath.
$ Rates: Q33 ($8.25) double. No credit cards.

The Casa de Santa Lucia is located in Antigua's busiest street, only two blocks from the bus station, but most of the rooms are quiet enough for sleeping and studying. The decor here is modern colonial with a lot of dark wood, much of it shaped on the lathe, creating a good atmosphere in the public rooms even though this is a very inexpensive pension. The guest rooms are quite plain and simple and have seen some wear, but the tiled showers always seem to have hot water.

HOTEL "EL DESCANSO," 5a Avenida Norte no. 9., Antigua Guatemala.
Tel. 502/032-0142. 4 rms., 2 with bath.
$ Rates: Q35.10 ($8.78) double; Q40.95 ($10.24) triple; Q52.65 ($13.16) quad. No credit cards.

Waiting for you only a half block north of the Parque Central, in the building facing the restaurant called Café Café (see "Where to Eat" below), is a little pension with only four rooms. This place is nothing fancy, just a place to rest, as the name implies. The rooms vary in size and the amount of light they get, but they are all fairly comfortable. This is a sort of Guatemalan homestay, and you'll feel like part of the family by the end of your visit.

DOUBLES FOR LESS THAN Q100 [$25]

APARTAMENTOS BUGAMBILIA, Calle ancha de los Herreros No. 27, Antigua Guatemala. Tel. (in Guatemala City) 502/25-125 or 83-715. 10 apts., all with bath. TV
$ Rates: Q58.50 ($14.63) per day 1–4 people; Q292.50 ($73.13) per week 1–4 people. No credit cards.

If you're planning to spend a week or more in town to study Spanish or simply because you like it here and would rather have a place of your own than stay with a local family, this is the place for you. Although these small apartments are expensive by local standards, they're a great deal by anybody else's. You're a 15-minute walk from the action around the Parque Central, but if you're fixing your own meals this shouldn't matter much. Knock on the nondescript front door, and you'll be ushered into a sunny courtyard full of flowering plants and squawking parrots. Each apartment has a complete kitchen, two double beds, and a cable TV. The bathrooms are walled with either tile or marble, and the ceilings are either beamed or have translucent panels that produce a soft light. Each apartment is different. My favorite is room 9, which has a banquette with cherubs above it built into one wall. If you plan to be here during Semana Santa (Holy Week), you'll have the added bonus of getting to watch the processions pass by your door.

HOTEL SOL-MOR, Avenida El Desengaño no. 26, Antigua Guatemala.
Tel. (in Guatemala City) 502/920-809. 5 rms., all with bath.
$ Rates: Q80 ($20) single; Q100 ($25) double; Q120 ($30) triple. No credit cards.

A 10-minute walk from the Parque Central, the Sol-Mor is directly across the street from another pretty little park filled with tall palm trees. The Sol-Mor is housed in a 160-year-old building, and many interesting architectural touches from that period remain. In the breakfast room, there are old laundry tanks the likes of which you can still see women using around town. This one has been turned into a planter and fountain. The rooms are built around a courtyard and a back garden. In the first courtyard, you'll find the hotel's name spelled out in living red-leafed plants in the grass. The back garden has a tiny pool, a parking area, and a few white wrought-iron tables and chairs for relaxing on sunny days. On the roof there is a terrace where you can enjoy the views and the sunshine. There are plans to turn this terrace into a little bar. All five rooms have carpeting, but the furnishings are simple. The twin beds are covered with shocking-pink chenille spreads that are hardly in keeping with the general motif of the hotel, but you can't have everything. Still, this is one of my favorite hotels in Antigua.

POSADA SAN SEBASTIÁN, 7a Avenida Norte No. 67 (Calle San Sebastián), Antigua Guatemala. Tel. 502/032-0465. 7 rms., all with bath.
$ Rates: Q45 ($11.25) single; Q90 ($22.50) double. No credit cards.

On a quiet street about 10 minutes from the Parque Central you'll find a tranquil little hotel. Luis Mendez Rodriguez, the English-speaking owner, takes pride in his accommodations—and it shows. All the rooms have two double beds, some with Momostenango blankets on them, and the bathrooms are modern and clean. The floors are of highly polished tile that squeaks when you walk across it. The grassy courtyard also serves as a parking area, and there's an old orange grove in back of the house and a community room with a fireplace and a TV.

There's a breakfast room where breakfast will cost you Q12 ($3).
Service: Laundry service.

DOUBLES FOR LESS THAN Q150 ($37.50)

HOTEL AURORA, 4a Calle Oriente 16, Antigua Guatemala. Tel. 502/ 032-0217. 16 rms., all with bath.
$ Rates: Q100–Q120 ($25–$30) single; Q120–Q140 ($30–$35) double; Q160 ($40) triple. No credit cards.

An old favorite in the moderate range, even though it has become considerably more expensive in recent years, the Aurora is housed in a traditional colonial building. A grassy courtyard decorated with flowers and graced by a fountain is surrounded by a portico set with wicker furniture and paved in shiny tiles. For cool evenings, there's a snug parlor with a fireplace. The guest rooms are lofty and airy but a bit dark (as befits their colonial style), with odd bits of furniture both antique and not. All is in good condition. Meals are taken in a grand old-fashioned dining room.

SUPER-BUDGET CHOICES

Antigua has many little family pensions where tourists (often students learning Spanish) can stay for rock-bottom rates. The tourist office has information on how to get in touch with willing families. However, for a similar experience, try this popular pension; although it always seems to be full, you might get lucky.

PENSION EL ARCO, 5a Avenida Norte no. 32, Antigua Guatemala. No phone. 10 rms., none with bath.
$ Rates: Q10 ($2.50) single; Q18 ($4.50) double. No credit cards.
Just north of the arch, this old colonial building has been divided up, and a smiling señora rents very plain rooms without baths. Some of the rooms are sort of claustrophobic, with no windows, so it's a good idea to look at your room before you rent it.

HOTEL PLACIDO, Avenida el Desengaño no. 25, Antigua Guatemala. No phone. 15 rms., 4 with bath.
$ Rates: Q8 ($2) single without bath, Q10 ($2.50) single with bath; Q16 ($4) double without bath, Q20 ($5) double with bath; Q24 ($6) triple without bath, Q30 ($7.50) triple with bath. No credit cards.
Spartan and dark but probably acceptable to hardy young travelers here to study Spanish on a limited budget, the Placido is on a busy street. Take a room at the back and the buses on the street out front shouldn't disturb you too much. There's a tiny

religious grotto under the stairs leading to the second floor and colorful framed Guatemalan towels decorating the walls. The rooms with baths are the better deal. Try to get a room with a window.

WORTH THE EXTRA BUCKS

You can splurge and have an unforgettable time in Antigua by staying at one of its several fine hotels.

HOTEL POSADA DE DON RODRIGO, 5a Avenida Norte no. 17., Antigua Guatemala. Tel. 502/032-0291 or 032-0387. 33 rms., all with bath.
$ Rates: Q175.50 ($43.88) single; Q198.90 ($49.73) double; Q222.30 ($55.58) triple. AE, DC, MC, V.

Guests here can easily conjure up the life-style of the Captains-General of Guatemala. The hotel is arranged around two courtyards, both very beautiful, the hind court having a tinkling fountain to entertain diners in the hotel's restaurant. The guest rooms have period furnishings: brass or carved-wood bedsteads, beamed ceilings, woven floor mats, and other antique or "antiqued" furnishings. All the rooms have private baths and 24-hour hot water that sometimes is little more than a warm trickle. Aside from this one drawback, the hotel is a rough-cut jewel. Rates are occasionally lower than those listed above, so be sure to ask for their best rates.

The main dining room and the bar of the open-air patio restaurant keep up the theme of colonial opulence, and marimba music entertains guests each afternoon.

HOTEL ANTIGUA, 8a Calle Poniente no. 1, Antigua Guatemala. Tel. 502/032-0331 or 032-0288. In Guatemala City, tel. 502/532-490 or 27-575. 60 rms., all with bath.
$ Rates: Q234 ($58.50) single; Q280.80 ($70.20) double; Q318.24 ($79.56) triple. AE, DC, MC, V.

This hotel, most favored by Guatemala's wealthy residents, is an expansive place only two blocks from the Parque Central. The hotel takes up an entire city block between 5a Avenida Sur and 4a Avenida Sur, and the block north of it serves as its parking lot. As you enter the colonial portal between two lion's-head fountains, you'll find what might best be termed a Spanish colonial country club, with beautiful lawns and a large heated swimming pool, patios with café tables, a children's playground, sun decks, and red-tile porticos over the low buildings surrounding the courtyard. These buildings hold the guest rooms, each with private bath and fireplace and many with two double beds. From the grounds, you get surprising views of the ruined colonial church of San José, across 5a Avenida to the west. Keep in mind that prices are nearly double during Semana Santa.

The dining room is suitably large and elegantly colonial, and the loungelike Conquistador Bar is woody and masculine. You might want to come for a drink in the bar even if you can't afford to splurge on a room.

RAMADA ANTIGUA, 9a Calle Poniente, Antigua Guatemala. Tel. 502/032-0011. 119 rms., 35 suites, all with bath.
$ Rates: Q280.80 ($70.20) single; Q327.60 ($81.90) double. AE, DC, MC, V.

The other deluxe hotel in town is a modern establishment (member of the international Ramada chain) with colonial-inspired decor. The hotel's architects have successfully blended the efficiency of a large, modern luxury hotel with the spirit of colonial Antigua. The very spacious rooms have balconies, fireplaces (firewood supplied, of course), modern tile bathrooms with tubs and showers, color TVs—in short, all the conveniences. The Ramada is a short distance out of town, to the southwest on the Carretera a Ciudad Vieja. Remember that prices here are substantially higher during Semana Santa.

The hotel's restaurant surrounds a huge fireplace kept blazing on any chilly evening.

WHERE TO EAT

Antigua is an excellent place in which to look for a meal. Although elegant dining is to be had only at the three top hotels and a couple of the "Worth the Extra Bucks" restaurants (described below), there's plenty of good food—and good value—here. By and large, restaurants don't have telephones in this town, and there's little need for them in any case.

MEALS FOR LESS THAN Q20 [$5]

RESTAURANT DOÑA LUISA, 4a Calle Oriente no. 12. No phone.
   Cuisine: INTERNATIONAL.
$ Prices: Breakfast Q3–Q6 (75¢–$1.50); sandwiches Q5–Q8 ($1.25–$2). No credit cards.
   Open: Daily 7am–11pm.
This busy two-story café is the town's traditional and very popular meeting place, and it is not far off the main square. Enter the building, and you'll see a small central courtyard set with dining tables, but there are more dining rooms and porticos on the upper level. Doña Luisa's is frequented almost exclusively by gringos; the newsy bulletin board bears messages in both Spanish and English, with a few notices in French and German thrown in for good measure. The menu is eclectic—with sandwiches of many varieties (made on good bread baked right here), yogurt, chili, cakes and pies, and also more substantial fare. Alcohol is served, as is excellent Antigua coffee.

LA ESTRELLA, 5a Calle Poniente no. 6. Tel. 320-480.
   Cuisine: CHINESE.
$ Prices: Main dishes Q5–Q20 ($1.25–$5). No credit cards.
   Open: Daily 11am–9pm.
There are 102 items on the menu here, not including the extensive cocktail menu, so if you can't find something that strikes your fancy, you just aren't trying. The most enjoyable part of eating here, or at any Chinese restaurant in Guatemala, for that matter, is translating the menu. *Tacos chinos* are egg rolls; anything *agridulce* is sweet and sour; and *salsa de soya* is soy sauce. You get the picture. There is little in the decor to lead you to believe that this is a Chinese restaurant, but the food, if not inspired, is recognizably Chinese. The bowls of soup here are huge, and the meal portions also are generous. Most dishes, including 18 shrimp entrees, are Q8 to Q10 ($2 to $2.50).

CASA DE CAFÉ ANA, 5a Avenida Sur no. 36. No phone.
   Cuisine: GUATEMALAN/INTERNATIONAL.
$ Prices: Main dishes Q6–Q9 ($1.50–$2.25). DC, MC, V.
   Open: Daily 8am–9pm.
Located at the corner of El Rosario Lodge, the Casa de Café Ana is a quiet place serving very inexpensive meals. For Q9 ($2.25), you can get a complete lunch or dinner that includes soup, meat, pasta, vegetables, dessert, and coffee or tea. This is a deal that is hard to beat, even in Guatemala. There also are sandwiches and omelets on the menu. Rough-hewn log and bamboo-mat walls give the restaurant a rustic feel.

MISTRAL, 4a Calle Oriente no. 7. No phone.
   Cuisine: GUATEMALAN/INTERNATIONAL.
$ Prices: Licuados Q2.50–Q5 (63¢–$1.25); main dishes Q6–Q16 ($1.50–$4). AE, DC, MC, V.
   Open: Daily 8am–11pm.
For the best licuados in Guatemala, stop in here at any time of day. Mistral specializes in freshly prepared juices of fruits and vegetables, many of which are served in huge glasses known as *globos*. Watermelon and strawberry with milk

is my favorite. They also have a complete menu that includes sandwiches and crêpes. The room in front is a noisy TV lounge and bar, but there are also a nice partially covered courtyard and several small dining rooms in the back.

CAFÉ FLOR, 4a Avenida Sur no. 1. No phone.
   Cuisine: MEXICAN.
   $ Prices: Main dishes Q7–Q9 ($1.75–$2.25). No credit cards.
   Open: Daily 9:30am–10pm.
It is difficult to think of Mexican food as exotic and foreign when you are this far south of the border, but that is exactly what it is in Guatemala. Locals and tourists alike put away plates of tacos, burritos, and enchiladas. You can have yours made with beef, chicken, pork, or tofu. The restaurant is on two levels, with a couple of window tables that are sunny spots for lunch. There is occasional live music here, with local musicians coming in to play the restaurant's baby grand piano and their own instruments.

RESTAURANTE PIZZERIA ITALIANA MARTEDINO, 4a Calle Poniente no. 18. Tel. 320-514.
   Cuisine: ITALIAN.
   $ Prices: Main dishes Q8–Q20 ($2–$5). DC, MC, V.
   Open: Daily 9am–11pm.
Heading away from the Parque Central toward the bus station, you'll run across a long, brightly lit restaurant on the right. It's packed every night with hungry Spanish students and locals out for an inexpensive Italian meal. It looks small from the street, but there are three dining rooms that you can't see until you go inside. Stop by for dinner, and you might be serenaded by an accordionist. A big window on the kitchen lets you observe all the bustling about that goes on back there.

FONDA DE LA CALLE REAL, 5a Avenida Norte no. 5. No phone.
   Cuisine: GUATEMALAN/INTERNATIONAL.
   $ Prices: Full meal Q10–Q17 ($2.50–$4.25).
   Open: Daily 11am–10pm.
Popular as a hangout and meeting place for Spanish students, the Fonda is known for its delicious *caldo real*—a delicious chicken soup that comes with tortillas and a condiment tray of oregano, cilantro, lime slices, chopped onions, and ground chili pepper—for Q6 ($1.50). Although the restaurant doesn't look like much at street level, upstairs there are 30 tables where you can sit comfortably and order roast chicken, fondues, steaks, and chops prepared by several busy señoras working hard in the downstairs kitchen. Steaks are the most expensive items.

CAFÉ CAFÉ, 5a Avenida Norte no. 14. No phone.
   Cuisine: GUATEMALAN/INTERNATIONAL.
   $ Prices: Complete meal Q12–Q20 ($3–$5). MC, V.
   Open: Daily 11am–10pm.
Inside La Casa de las Gárgolas shopping center, a courtyard surrounded by a dozen or so shops and travel agencies, is this pleasant restaurant. Tables and potted palms nearly fill the small courtyard, leaving little room for shoppers to move around. The courtyard dining room is covered, so that you don't have to worry about rain. The menu includes a full fixed-price lunch *(almuerzo)* or dinner *(cena)* of local dishes, such as stuffed green peppers and rice and beans. A short wine list includes French, Spanish, Italian, Argentine, and Chilean wines. This is a great place to stop for lunch if you're busy shopping on "Fifth Avenue."

MEALS FOR LESS THAN Q30 ($7.50)

RESTAURANT ITALIANO "EL CAPUCHINO," 6a Avenida Norte no. 8. Tel. 320-613.
   Cuisine: ITALIAN.
   $ Prices: Main dishes Q8–Q32 ($2–$8). No credit cards.
   Open: Daily 10am–10pm.

Between 4a and 5a calles Poniente, 1½ blocks from the Parque Central, you'll find one of Antigua's popular Italian restaurants. The façade of the restaurant doesn't look like much, but there are a covered interior court and arcade, with simple dining tables set out. Homey rather than fancy, the restaurant features a long menu of Italian food: pizzas, chicken cacciatore, lasagna, ravioli, spaghetti bolognese, and some gringo favorites, such as roast beef and mashed potatoes. Most meals here will not run over Q25 ($7.50). In the evening, mariachi bands often stop by the restaurant; for a small tip, they will serenade you.

RESTAURANT KATOK, 4a Avenida no. 7. No phone.
　Cuisine: GUATEMALAN/INTERNATIONAL.
$　**Prices:** Main dishes Q10–Q25 ($2.50–$6.25). DC, MC, V.
　Open: Daily 11am–11pm.

⭐　Antigua is full of delightful little restaurants, and this is one of my favorites, located a block away from the Parque Central in a colonial building. You can dine in one of several dining rooms or out on the portico beside a lush little garden. There are beautiful old black-and-white photos of Antigua on the walls (they're even for sale if you're interested). Fresh flowers grace every table, and waiters in black jackets make sure that everything is to your satisfaction. The plato típico especial Katok is a bounteous platter that includes two types of sausage, steak, ham, beans, cheese, fried bananas, salad, potatoes, and fried green onion—all for Q16 ($4). The parrillada Katok is similar but feeds two or three people for Q40 ($10). Soups here are excellent and can be enough for a light meal. There's even a children's menu on Sunday. Also, there's a wide assortment of cocktails, beer, and wine.

POSADA DE DON RODRIGO, 5a Avenida Norte no. 17. Tel. 320-613.
　Cuisine: GUATEMALAN/INTERNATIONAL.
$　**Prices:** Main dishes Q12–Q20 ($3–$5). AE, DC, MC, V.
　Open: Daily 11am–2pm and 6–9:30pm.

S　Although this is a splurge hotel, you can enjoy lunch here even if you're on a tight budget. You can order a filling platillo chapín (plate of Guatemalan specialties), including carne asada (grilled beef), guacamole, and frijoles refritos with rice and cheese, for Q18 ($4.50); with a drink, tax, and service, the bill may come to Q24 ($6). The menu also features a vegetarian plate, fish filets, chicken, pork, and tenderloin of beef *(lomito)*. Even a full à la carte meal will cost only Q30 ($7.50). The situation is pleasant, and the staff (dressed in traditional costumes) is accommodating and helpful.

SWEETS AND PASTRIES

DOÑA MARÍA GORDILLO DULCES TÍPICOS, 4a Calle Oriente no. 11. No phone.
　Cuisine: SWEETS.
$　**Prices:** Q1–Q2 (25¢–50¢). No credit cards.
　Open: Mon–Sat 9am–6pm.

Located across the street from the Hotel Aurora, this shop—filled with all sorts of sweets, desserts, and confections made from milk, fruit, eggs, marzipan, chocolate, and sugar—brings a bit of heaven to earth. Some local crafts are on sale as well. There is always a crowd of loyal customers filling the shop. Note that the treats here are for take-out only—there's no place to sit and munch. Since few if any of these sweets will be familiar to you, your best bet is to try a little of whatever looks good until you find the one that you can't live without.

LA CENICIENTA PASTELES, 5a Avenida Norte no. 7. No phone.
　Cuisine: PASTRIES.
$　**Prices:** Cake Q1–Q2 (25¢–50¢) per slice. No credit cards.
　Open: Daily 10am–9:30pm.

With beautiful local textiles on the walls and a display case full of delectable cakes and pastries, Cenicienta is always jammed with young students indulging themselves. The daily menu includes quiche Lorraine and quiche chapín (Guatemalan style), yogurt and fruit, New York cheesecake, and numerous licuados. Don't be discouraged by the crowd in the front room; there is another dining area in the courtyard out back. You also can get anything to go.

WORTH THE EXTRA BUCKS

RESTAURANT MESÓN PANZA VERDE, 5a Avenida Sur no. 19. No phone.
  Cuisine: CONTINENTAL.
$ Prices: Main dishes Q24–Q30 ($6–$7.50). No credit cards.
  Open: Tues–Sat 7:30am–9am, noon–3pm, and 6:30–10pm; Sun 7:30–9am and noon–4pm.

If you want to be pampered and surround yourself with elegance, head out 5a Avenida Sur to one of Antigua's classiest little restaurants. The European owner knows how to make his guests happy. You might start your meal with six snails for Q13 ($3.25), then order a perfectly done steak with béarnaise, wine, or chile sauce for Q25 ($6.25). Top it off with chocolate mousse or peach melba for Q8 ($2). There are also daily specials that include such tempting courses as tortellini consommé, avocado stuffed with seafood, and shrimp in garlic. Your bill might come to Q40 or Q60 ($10 or $15), which is a fraction of what you would pay for this same meal back home.

EL SERENO, 6a Calle Poniente no. 30. Tel. 0320-073.
  Cuisine: INTERNATIONAL.
  Reservations: Recommended, especially at dinner.
$ Prices: Appetizers Q6–Q16 ($1.50–$4); main dishes Q28–Q40 ($7–$10). AE, MC, V.
  Open: Wed–Sun noon–3pm and 6:30–9:30pm.

Between the Alameda de Santa Lucia and 7a Avenida Sur, next door to the Tecun Uman School of Spanish, is one of Antigua's finest restaurants. Within this colonial house are several small dining rooms. There are corner fireplaces, original oil paintings (many for sale), a small open-air portico, and carefully tended plants here and there. A doorman will welcome you, and a barman awaits your order in the small old-fashioned bar. The service is as refined as the cuisine. You might start with potage au pistou and go on to smoked beef tongue in a provençal sauce, ham in a sauce of crème de cassis and mustard, or filet mignon with mushrooms. Desserts in this land of German and Austrian influence are rich and delicious. The menu changes weekly, with new items being added all the time. With a glass of house wine, a full dinner might cost as little as Q45 ($11.25) per person—but it could be as high as Q80 ($20) per person, or perhaps even a bit higher, depending on your wine selection. Whatever you pay, you won't soon forget your meal here.

EVENING ENTERTAINMENT

Because most people in Antigua are here studying Spanish, this is generally an early-to-bed, early-to-rise town. There are, however, several bars that are popular with both Spanish students and their instructors. Spending time in the bars is almost a requirement for some students who actually learn most of their Spanish in that less structured environment.

PICASSO CAFÉ, 7a Avenida Norte No. 3. No phone.
This quiet café caters to games players. There are boards for chess, backgammon, and darts. There are also cards available and occasionally live music in the evenings. Open daily until 11pm.

BIANCO'S, 6a Avenida Norte No. 17. Tel. 320-727.
Tuesday through Saturday evenings from 9 to midnight there is live music, primarily reggae and rock. Happy hour is Tuesday through Thursday from 5 to 7pm with two-for-one drinks. Open until midnight.

EL CABILDO BAR, 6a Avenida Sur No. 21. No phone.
There is live music here every Saturday night, and the daily happy hour from 5 to 7pm is also popular. Each night of the week features a different theme: Thursdays are

Ladies' Nights and Sundays feature salsa, merengue, soca, and samba music. Open 5pm to 1am daily.

MOSCAS Y MIEL, 5a Calle Poniente No. 5A. No phone.
This little bar bills itself as a "disco bar." If you feel like dancing and don't mind being the only one gyrating beneath the flashing lights, check it out. Open 5pm to 3am daily.

SHOPPING

Antigua has recently become a very reputable jade center: An ancient Mayan quarry near Nejar was rediscovered in 1958 and has been reopened. Jade from this quarry was sent to the Smithsonian Institution, which verified that the stones are jadeite, the highest quality of jade and equal to Chinese jade. Buying jade is a tricky business, for unless you're an expert, you may end up buying low-quality stones pawned off as the real thing. Jadeite is characterized by its hardness (6.5 to 7), which differs from many other stones and can easily be distinguished from softer stones. If a stone can be scratched with a pocketknife, then it isn't jadeite.

The quality of jade is also differentiated as gemstones and carving stones. The gemstones are the most ·valuable and are rated according to their purity and the intensity of their color and translucency. A good gemstone jade can be more valuable than a diamond, and because of its hardness, it can take a jade carver half a day to carve just one simple pendant. Therefore, know that if you go looking at the real things, you'll be looking at price tags in the $100-and-up bracket.

Two dealers in jade with good reputations and experience, not to mention beautiful collections, are **La Casa de Jade** (that's pronounced "ha-deh" not "jayd"), 4a Calle Oriente 3; and **Jades** ("ha-dess"), 4a Calle Oriente 34.

EXCURSIONS
CIUDAD VIEJA

You also can visit Ciudad Vieja, which is actually midway along the route to San Antonio. Although there's not much to see here now, only an old church, this was once the capital of Guatemala. A flood destroyed it in 1541, and the city was moved to a new site, which is today Antigua. Buses to Ciudad Vieja leave the market (Alameda de Santa Lucía and 5a Calle Poniente) for the ten-minute ride.

VIEWS OF THE CITY

You can get a fine panorama of the city of Antigua by walking along la Avenida Norte northward to the outskirts of town. Pretty soon you'll come to a path leading uphill to a small park and a cross mounted on a pedestal. The walk takes only 20 to 30 minutes and is well worth it for the view. Go around to the back of the hill and see Ciudad Vieja, the town that was the forerunner of Antigua. Women should *never* make this trip without one or more large male escorts. In fact, it is questionable whether anyone should venture up here anymore. Rapes and robberies on this deserted hill have become far too commonplace. Before heading up here, ask around or check the bulletin board at Casa Andinista for recent reports.

Ambitious mountaineers can climb up Agua, the impressive volcano that seems to be on the outskirts of town. Start by taking the bus from behind the Antigua market to Santa María de Jesús. After a 20-minute ride, the bus will drop you in the main square of the village of that name; from the square, a road leads out of town and up the volcano. It's a fairly easy hike (not a climb) to the top for someone who's used to hiking. The free bonuses are everywhere: lovely wildflowers, good smells, lots of forest, and more mist the higher up you get. You can reach the top in four hours if you push it, five hours if you don't. *Remember:* The air's thinner here than at sea level. When you reach the top, you'll see the crater and a magnificent view (if it's a clear day and the clouds don't shut you off).

If you've ever wanted to climb an active volcano, this is the place to do it. A 2½-hour drive from Antigua is Pacaya, a live volcano that can easily be climbed by anyone in good health. Every few minutes the volcano erupts, spewing red-hot rocks into the air. A nearby dormant cone serves as a perfect vantage point for observing the eruptions. Many adventurous types camp out near the peak to watch the eruptions at night; others simply make the hike a day trip. **Agencia de Viajes Tivoli Antigua,** located at Galería Un Poco de Todo on the northwest corner of the Parque Central (tel. 320-892), offers overnight trips for Q80 ($32). For day trips, check the bulletin boards around town. There are often enterprising folks organizing trips for around Q40 ($16).

CHAPTER 11

EL PETÉN

1. FLORES AND SANTA ELENA

2. TIKAL

El Petén is Guatemala's vast, wild, low-lying jungle province—a land of dirt roads and four-wheel-drive vehicles, of mammoth Mayan ceremonial centers and towering temples. In its dense jungle cover you'll hear the squawk of parrots, the chatter of monkeys, and the rustling of strange animals moving through the bush. The landscape here is as different from Guatemala's highlands as night is from day.

There are three reasons to penetrate El Petén. First and foremost is to visit Tikal, the greatest Mayan religious center yet uncovered (Caracol in Belize is said to be much larger but has not yet been excavated) and perhaps also to see Uaxactún, another great city even deeper in the jungle. The second is birds: The jungles of Petén are home to a wondrous variety of exotic birds, including the rare, shy quetzal, and some birdwatchers go to Tikal just to fill up their life lists. The third reason to go into El Petén is to see a different Guatemala, one of small farming villages and hamlets, without paved roads or colonial architecture, but with the same smiling inhabitants that you no doubt encountered in the highlands.

---

1. FLORES AND SANTA ELENA

Distances: 280 miles northeast of Guatemala City;
84 miles west of the Belizean border.

GETTING THERE   By Air   Going by plane is easy and exciting but expensive. Although it is possible to visit Tikal on a one-day excursion by plane from Guatemala City, I encourage you to stay over at least one night in Flores or even at Tikal itself, for there is a great deal to see and to experience and a day trip simply cannot do it justice.

The following three small airlines fly daily between Guatemala City's La Aurora Airport and Flores. In addition, Aerovias now flies between Flores and Belize City.

Aerovias, La Aurora Airport, Gate 9, 2nd floor (tel. 325-686 and 345-386 to 345-390).

TAPSA, Avenida Hincapié and 18 Calle, Zona 13 (tel. 314-860), now has a ticket office in the main terminal.

AeroQuetzal, Avenida Hincapié and 18 Calle, Zona 13 (tel. 311-173, 347-685, or 347-689) also has a desk at the airport in the main terminal.

The one-way fare is around Q210 ($52.50). You can buy your ticket from a travel agency in Guatemala City or Antigua or directly from the airlines. If you plan to buy your ticket at the airport, note that the ticket counters are attended only when flights are leaving or arriving, which means at breakfast time and late afternoon. Because these flights are so popular with tourists, they are often booked weeks or even months in advance during the busy dry season—so it is advisable that you make your reservation as early as possible. Schedules are liable to frequent change, but generally there are flights out in the morning, with return flights in the afternoon. At the Flores Airport, minibuses, taxis, and tour buses will meet your flight, ready to whisk you out to Tikal, about an hour's drive away. When you arrive at the airport in Flores, you may be subject to a cursory Customs and Immigration check because this is a special Customs and Immigration district. Flying to El Petén is highly recommended.

By Bus   Going by bus is very cheap compared to going by plane, but it is extremely tiring, time-consuming, and unpleasant. However, if your money is low and your stamina is high, you can get there from Guatemala City by bus. Certainly, you'll never forget the ride. Keep in mind that if you want to get on the Flores-bound bus in Río Dulce, you may not get a seat. In fact, you may even have to ride on the roof (not recommended). The bus trip from Guatemala City to Flores takes 14 hours when the road is in good condition and costs Q15 ($3.75) or Q32 ($8) for a comfortable deluxe bus. Contact **Fuentes del Norte,** 17a Calle 8-46, Zona 1 (tel. 513-817) in Guatemala City. The journey from Guatemala City to the Río Dulce bridge is fine, over a fairly well-maintained paved highway. But for the last 126 miles or so (six or eight hours), from Río Dulce to Flores, the road is a battlefield of potholes and ruts, especially during the rainy season (May through October). Be prepared for an awful lot of jostling, banging, and bone-crunching after the bus reaches the end of the paved road north of Río Dulce.

From Belize, it is slightly less difficult and time-consuming, although the road is just as bad for several hours of the trip. The schedules change, but there is presently a bus leaving for Flores from Melchor de Mencos on the Guatemala side of the border daily at 1pm. Thus you should plan to be at the border as early as possible in the morning and allow an hour or two for border formalities. If you leave Belize City for San Ignacio or Benque Viejo by 8 or 9am, you should reach the border in time to catch that 1pm bus.

If you're in a rush to get to Tikal, you can get off the bus at El Cruce (Ixlu), where a road turns right for Tikal, and hope to flag down a passing minibus. However, these minibuses tend to be heading back to Flores in the afternoon and not to Tikal, so it is probably best just to head straight to Flores.

By Car   There is no Pan American Highway crossing El Petén. Going by private car is not as bad as going by the bus, but it is almost as bad. The trip from Guatemala City or Belize is over the same roads the bus takes, but you have the luxury of stopping along the way. For the trip from Guatemala City, I'd recommend spending the night at the Hotel Izabal Tropical near the Río Dulce bridge (see Chapter 12) and starting for Flores bright and early. An alternative is to make it along the bad road as far as Poptún and camp at the Finca Ixobel, where there are some services, including showers and meals.

The journey from the Belizean-Guatemalan border point at Benque Viejo (Belize) and Melchor de Mencos (Guatemala) to Flores takes about three hours by car. The road has lots of potholes and ruts from Melchor to El Cruce, and the average speed is probably 20 miles per hour. It's a rough trip, worse in the rainy season, but it doesn't last all that long—at least not compared to the gruelling ride from Guatemala City to Flores. After El Cruce (Ixlu), the road is paved and fast all the way to Tikal or Flores.

It is also possible to talk with a travel agent or taxi driver in Belize City or San Ignacio and hire a taxi or minibus and driver to take you to Flores and/or Tikal. This will be quite expensive, but if you find others with whom to split the cost, it might be worth it.

By Boat and Bus   A newly developing route is the overland one from Palenque in Chiapas, Mexico, to Flores by bus and boat. It's an adventurous route for the hardy only, because you will have to endure long hours in beat-up buses on bad roads and spend the night in a jungle village short on services. I have not yet taken this route. The following information was gleaned from travelers on the road.

Start out from Palenque by taking a 9am bus to Emiliano Zapata, then another bus from Zapata to Tenosique. At Tenosique, catch a 1pm bus to La Palma, where a boat will be waiting. Pack yourself and your belongings into the little boat and hope that the engine doesn't die. The boat will head down the Río San Pedro to El Naranjo, which is within Guatemala. There is one small, utterly basic hotel in El Naranjo where you can try to grab a little sleep—if there are beds available. As it is the only place in town, it gets away with charging Q20 ($5) for a double. There may be little bedding provided and it can get cold here, so have some camping gear or warm clothes. A bus departs from El Naranjo for Flores at 3am, and this, too, can be a very chilly journey (believe it or not). The entire trip from Palenque to Flores can be done for under $20 per person, including your sleep break at the El Naranjo Hilton.

If you take this route, please drop me a note and provide more information so that I can pass it on to other travelers.

ORIENTATION
CITY LAYOUT

The town of Flores, capital of El Petén, is on an island in Lake Petén Itzá, connected to the shore by a causeway. It's only a 10- or 15-minute walk from Santa Elena or San Benito across the causeway to Flores, and, in fact, the three towns actually form one settlement. You can find all the essential services here, although this is certainly no cosmopolitan center.

Santa Elena is a village really, a place of potholed dirt streets with dogs sleeping in the sun and men chatting quietly beneath the shade of a tree. But Santa Elena is the place nearest to the airport, which is out of town a half mile or so, and Santa Elena has the best selection of moderately priced hotels in the area.

GETTING AROUND
BY CAR

Rental cars, some of them four-wheel-drive Suzukis, are offered by several businesses in town, including some hotels. The place to find all the car-rental companies is in the arrivals hall at Flores Airport. Two companies there are **Koka** (tel. 081-1233 or 081-1526) and **Los Jades** (tel. 081-1741 or 081-1734). They will rent you a car, minibus, four-wheel-drive vehicle, or pickup truck or will arrange for a taxi tour to Tikal or anywhere else. Basic rates for a four-wheel-drive car are about Q220 ($55) per day, including free mileage. The Hotel Maya Internacional will rent its guests a Suzuki four-wheel-drive vehicle for about the same price.

FAST FACTS

There is a bank in Flores proper, open Monday to Friday from 8:30am to 2:30pm (to 3:30pm on Friday). You may be able to change money at your hotel.

There is a post office in Santa Elena. It's just down the street from the Hotel San Juan and is open Monday to Friday from 8am to 4:30pm.

Although the town of Flores is built on a small island in Lake Petén Itzá and is connected to the mainland by a rock-and-dirt causeway, it is a hot and dusty town with nothing to recommend it. If it weren't for the nearby ruins at Tikal, this would be a forgotten little village surrounded by jungle. However, there are some nice views of Flores from the mainland town of Santa Elena, which is even less appealing than Flores. For some strange reason, the paved road that leads to Tikal stops the moment it reaches the town limits of Santa Elena. A fine gray limestone powder covers the trees, grass, and houses here. It is all too easy to imagine the dust coating you if you stay too long in town. It's best to head out to Tikal immediately and avoid spending any more time here than necessary.

Unfortunately, there is not much potable water at Tikal, and the Guatemalan government wisely wants to limit development within the national park itself, so the plan is to develop Flores as the tourism center of El Petén, with sightseers going to Tikal by day. The recent construction of comfortable hotels in town has done nothing to make Flores or Santa Elena more appealing, but the hotels do make these towns slightly less dreary for tourists.

WHAT TO DO

If you're stuck in town for some reason, you can hire a boat and boatman to take you around this section of the large lake. Included in your boat tour will be stops at La Guitarra, an island with a small zoo and a tourist center, and La Mirador, a point from which you can view a nearby Mayan ruin. On the causeway is a shop that rents kayaks and sailboards. For a more traditional form of water transport, ask around about renting a dugout canoe and paddle yourself around the lake. Be careful, though: Winds pick up in the afternoon and can whip up the waters.

WHERE TO STAY

Lodging possibilities are rapidly improving here, but so is the tourist traffic, so you may find rooms in short supply. If you want to stay at one of the comfortable hotels, it'd be a good idea to try and reserve a room in advance or at least to call ahead to see how busy the hotel is.

DOUBLES FOR LESS THAN Q40 ($10)

In Santa Elena

HOTEL SAN JUAN, Santa Elena, Petén. Tel. 502/081-1562. 60 rms., 35 with bath.
$ Rates: Q20 ($5) single/double without bath; Q32 ($8) double with bath; Q40 ($10) triple with bath. AE, DC, MC, V.

This modest hotel near the causeway to Flores has plain, clean, large rooms with two or three beds, largish bathrooms with tile showers, cold water (hot on occasion), perhaps toilet seats, and—of all things—TVs! The two-story building is undistinguished but utilitarian. The owner has recently added 18 rooms with air conditioning. Keep in mind that the San Juan acts as a bus stop for buses to various other towns in El Petén, so buses begin leaving (with much shouting, revving of engines, and blowing of horns) around 5am. It's almost impossible to sleep through this cacophony, so you need to be a heavy sleeper to stay here (or you can plan to take an early bus yourself). There's a comedor off the courtyard parking lot, and in the lobby you'll find all sorts of information on getting around El Petén. This is also the place to book tickets on express minibuses to the Belize border and Mexico.

HOTEL MONJA BLANCA, Santa Elena, Petén, Tel. 502/081-1340 or 081-285. 29 rms., none with bath.
$ Rates: Q12 ($3) single; Q24 ($6) double; Q36 ($9) triple; Q40 ($10) quad. No credit cards.

The Monja Blanca is among the oldest hotels in Santa Elena and once catered to the archeologists who came to excavate Tikal. It's a family-run place that has seen better days, particularly those when the old, small in-town airport was right next door and there was only one plane a day. Still, it will do in an emergency if everything else is full. The small rooms with baths are well used and not especially congenial. There are overgrown gardens and a small eatery and bar. The hotel is on a street to the right as you come into town from the airport.

In Flores

POSADA EL TUCAN, Calle Centroamericana no. 45, Flores, Petén. No phone. 5 rms., none with bath.
$ Rates: Q16 ($4) single; Q35 ($8.75) double; Q45 ($11.25) triple. No credit cards.

This backpackers' delight opened early in 1990 and was an instant success. It's built on the water, with a pleasant garden and two little piers for sunning or swimming. There are several tables in the garden where you can relax over a cold beer and a good book. The rooms are spacious with double or twin beds, all sharing a single large bathroom that has hot water (something places in this price range rarely offer). If you're traveling on a shoestring budget, this should be your first choice. The hotel is behind a very attractive little restaurant with a bar in one corner. The decor is tropical jungle, and the meals are international and Guatemalan standards.

DOUBLES FOR LESS THAN Q80 [$20]

In Santa Elena

COSTA DEL SOL, Santa Elena, Petén. Tel. 502/081-1336. 17 rms., all with bath.
$ Rates: Q50 ($12.50) double; Q60 ($15) triple; Q70 ($17.50) quad. No credit cards.

About a block away from the market and bus park is the Costa del Sol, one of Santa Elena's better choices in the budget category. You don't have a lake view, but you do get a swimming pool and you're close to the bus station, which is a plus if you arrive after dark on the bus from Guatemala City. Several of the rooms here have air conditioning, and the large family rooms come with small refrigerators. Let them know in advance, and they'll pick you up at the airport. Family-run, the Costa del Sol seems to cater primarily to vacationing Guatemalan families.

The restaurant is a spacious and simple affair with a stuffed jaguar at one end. Meals here range from Q8 ($2) to Q16 ($4).

In Flores

HOTEL YUM KAX, Flores, Petén. Tel. 502/081-1686. 42 rms., all with bath.
$ Rates: Q40-Q60 ($10-$15) single; Q55-Q75 ($13.75-$18.75) double; Q65-Q85 ($16.25-$21.25) triple; Q80-Q110 ($20-$27.50) quad. DC.

The name is pronounced "Yum Kash," and the hotel is to the left as you cross the causeway. Don't worry—it looks better inside than it does from the causeway vantage point. The guest rooms are bare but not bad—with fans, good cross-ventilation to catch breezes on the lake, twin beds, toilet seats, and tile showers. The higher prices are for rooms with air conditioning. Yum Kax, by the way, is the Mayan god of corn. The hotel seems to be under perpetual expansion, so don't be surprised if there is construction work going on when you visit.

The hotel has a restaurant with a nice view of the water, and there are several others nearby.

HOTEL PETÉN, Flores, Petén. Tel. 502/081-1692. Fax 502/081-1662.
In Guatemala City, tel. 502/83-095. 21 rms., 14 with bath.
$ Rates: Q80 ($20) double; Q90 ($22.50) triple. AE, DC, MC, V.

From the street, this hotel looks like a very modest Caribbean town dwelling; enter the doorway, and you'll find a small courtyard with tropical plants and a nice brick-and-stucco building of several floors. The friendly manager will show you a comfy if plain room with a fan and an electric hot water showerhead in the bathroom and perhaps a balcony overlooking the water. Most of the rooms here have been recently remodeled, but try to get a room on the top floor (nos. 33, 34, and so on) with a view of the lake. If you can't, be aware that the hotel's roof is actually a terrace that enjoys that same view. The hotel also offers some very basic rooms in another building, a ramshackle wooden structure a short stroll away, for Q30 ($7.50) double without private bath. These rooms can be very hot and are prone to mosquitoes, so look somewhere else before accepting one of these rooms. There are big plans afoot to completely remodel the Petén, and hopefully the hotel will stay open during the remodeling.

There's a restaurant on the ground floor.

DOUBLES FOR LESS THAN Q150 [$37.50]

In Santa Elena

HOTEL MAYA INTERNACIONAL, Santa Elena, Petén. Tel./Fax 502/081-1276. In Guatemala City, 2a Avenida 7-78, Zona 10, Guatemala City.

Tel. 502/363-909, 346-235, or 246-236. Fax 502/346-237. 20 rms., all with bath.

$ Rates: Q120 ($30) single; Q140 ($35) double; Q160 ($40) triple. AE, DC, MC, V.

⭐ This is Santa Elena's old standard, where a number of thatched wooden bungalows have been built on stilts, partly on land and partly over the lake. The bunglows form a sort of bay in which water lilies flower and water birds hunt for food. You can sit on your porch and watch as sudden squalls sweep dramatically across the lake. The rooms, two to a bungalow, are quite basic, with twin beds and well-used bathrooms with showers, but they're comfortable enough. The only hot water is from the showerhead, which has an electric heater on it that "heats" the water up to lukewarm. *Warning:* The occupants of the other guest room in your bungalow can hear every word you say, so be discreet.

The hotel dining room is in a separate, larger thatched structure at the end of a short causeway out in the lake. All three meals are served, rough and ready but tasty enough. Breakfast is around Q10 ($2.50), and dinner is about Q25 ($6.25).

In Flores

SAVANNA HOTEL, Flores, Petén. Tel. 502/081-1248. In Guatemala City, tel. 502/768-775. 23 rms., all with bath. AC.

$ Rates: Q80 ($20) single; Q110 ($27.50) double; Q130 ($32.50) triple; Q145 ($36.25) quad. No credit cards.

⑤ One of the nicest hotels in Flores is located on the side of the island farthest from the causeway and on the same road as the Hotel Petén. Built right on the water, this four-story hotel boasts a tiny island with sunning decks just offshore. Ask for a room at the back that overlooks the water; these rooms have windows on three sides and great views, especially when the frequent rainstorms whip the lake into whitecaps. The Savanna is often filled up by groups, so plan ahead.

The Savanna has a two-story open-air restaurant where a meal will cost you about Q20 ($5).

WORTH THE EXTRA BUCKS

In Santa Elena

HOTEL DEL PATIO-TIKAL, Santa Elena, Petén. Tel. 502/081-1229). In Guatemala City, 4a Calle 5-16, Zona 9, Guatemala City. Tel. 502/323-365. 20 rms., all with bath. TV

$ Rates: Q200 ($50) single/double. AE, DC, MC, V.

⭐ Located across the street from the Hotel Maya Internacional, The Del Patio-Tikal is one of the newest hotels in town and consequently is very clean and modern. The building is built in colonial Spanish style around a grassy central courtyard with a fountain in the middle. Lounge chairs here in the garden are a great place to relax after an exhausting day of hiking from one ruin to the next. Each of the rooms has large closets, a color TV, a ceiling fan, tile floors, and an immaculate tiled bathroom.

The restaurant/bar serves international and típico Guatemalan meals in the Q15 to Q40 ($3.75 to $10) range. For Q20 ($5), they'll also fix you a box lunch for you to take on your day's outing to the ruins at Tikal. It's hard to beat a box picnic atop a Mayan pyramid. The box lunch saves you the hassle of walking all the way out to the little comedores near the parking lot at the ruins.

Service: Laundry service.

HOTEL TZIQUINAHA, Santa Elena, Petén. Tel. 502/081-1359. In Guatemala City, tel. 502/20-528. 36 rms., all with bath. A/C TV

$ Rates: Q200 ($50) single; Q220 ($55) double; Q240 ($60) triple. AE, DC, MC, V.

On the outskirts of Santa Elena, on the road to the airport and Tikal, is this moderately priced hotel, with modern concrete-and-stucco buildings arranged on landscaped lawns. There's also a swimming pool at the center of the complex, although the water is not always clean. There are some rough edges here, because

Santa Elena is not exactly cosmopolitan, but basically the staff is willing and the rooms are comfortable and carpeted, if a bit musty from the damp jungle air. Each room has a tile bath (shower), one double and one twin bed, a minirefrigerator, and air conditioning. The hotel caters mostly to tour groups and tends to fill up quickly, so try to make reservations as far in advance as possible.

The restaurant/bar serves all three meals with prices ranging from Q8 ($2) for breakfast to Q20 ($5) for lunch and dinner. There is a TV in the bar that plays American cable stations.

Facilities: Swimming pool, tennis court, car-rental office, and gift shop.

NEARBY PLACES TO STAY

EL GRINGO PERDIDO, "THE LOST GRINGO," Flores, Petén. Tel. (in Guatemala City) 502/20-605 or 25-811. 40 beds, none with bath.
$ Rates: Q40–Q56 ($10–$14) per person per night. No credit cards.

Two miles off the Tikal highway, along a rough dirt road from the hamlet of El Remate (which is north of El Cruce-Ixlu on the Tikal road, 22 miles from Flores), you'll find one of Guatemala's only jungle lodges. It's a little offbeat paradise arranged along the lakeshore, with shady, rustic hillside gardens, a little restaurant, a bucolic camping area, and simple but pleasant guest quarters. A bungalow has four beds (two sets of bunks), a shower, a toilet, and a patio with palapa cover and hammock. A camarote is a smaller room with a toilet and washbasin and two sets of bunks; it's a little cheaper than the bungalow. Beds in the dormitory (eight beds to a room) are cheaper still. The place calls itself a Parador Ecologico (Ecological Inn), which it is. The very friendly staff will welcome you. El Gringo Perdido offers good swimming in the lake, 3 kilometers of nature trails, quiet times, and tranquility. The Biotopo Cerro Cahui, a preserve for the endangered Petén turkey, is just across the road, and down the road a short walk are several swampy areas where you might see a few caymans (a Central American relative of the alligator). Access is by taxi from Santa Elena or the airport; once you're here, you'll be here for a while, unless you have your own wheels.

A little bit beyond El Gringo Perdido, on the same road, is the construction site of the Hotel Camino Real Tikal, a luxury resort hotel that will have comforts never before seen in Petén. The first phase of 56 rooms should be completed sometime in 1991; a total of 128 rooms is planned. For information, contact Hoteles Camino Real in Guatemala City; Westin Hotels, which works with Camino Real, may also have information.

WHERE TO EAT

All the restaurants in Flores and Santa Elena tend to be fairly simple and open all the time. Beer, drinks, and sometimes even wine are served. In Santa Elena, you can drop by the restaurant at the Hotel Maya Internacional and have a full meal for about Q30 ($7.50) while enjoying the view across the lake.

In Santa Elena

VENTANAS DEL LAGO, Santa Elena. No phone.
Cuisine: INTERNATIONAL.
$ Prices: Q9–Q25 ($2.25–$6.25). DC, V.
Open: Daily 11am–10:30pm.
As is often the case with budget restaurants in Guatemala, the location is far better than the food. Ventanas del Lago has a fabulous location right on the water, just steps from the causeway in Santa Elena. Light jazz music plays on the stereo, and the large windows provide an uninterrupted view of Flores and the lake. Sunset is an especially fine time to sit at one of the window tables. In the center of the dining room is a column covered with bromeliads and orchids, and ceiling fans turn slowly overhead. Oil paintings of traditional Guatemalan life decorate the pale-blue walls; louvered windows let in the breezes off the lake. The food is unexceptional. There is a lot of seafood on the menu, even though the sea is a long way off. I'd stick to the

chicken and steaks, both of which are prepared in a half dozen or so ways. Soups are the standard instant powdered kind that you find in almost every restaurant in Guatemala.

In Flores

RESTAURANT LA JUNGLA, Calle Centroamerica. No phone.
Cuisine: GUATEMALAN/INTERNATIONAL.
$ Prices: Entrees Q8–Q14 ($2–$3.50). No credit cards.
Open: Daily 10am–11pm.

You have to fight your way through the dense wall of hanging plants in the doorway to enter this aptly named restaurant. Animal skins, including jungle cats, snakes, birds, turtles, and alligators, cover the walls here. There is even an out-of-place painting of a moose done on deerskin and a few dried giant mushrooms to complete the motif. Also included are a tiny streetside terrace with two tables, tablecloths woven with the restaurant's name, and a standard Petén burgers/spaghetti/venison menu.

RESTAURANT LA MESA DE LOS MAYAS, Santa Elena. Tel. 811-240.
Cuisine: GUATEMALAN/INTERNATIONAL.
$ Prices: Q8–Q20 ($2–$5). DC, MC, V.
Open: Daily 7:30am–11pm.

This restaurant, on the street with the post office (Correos), is a popular place with two dining areas and plenty of tables—simple but pleasant enough here in the jungle. The menu is similar to those in the other restaurants, but it also includes wild turkey, venison, and tepezquintle (a jungle rodent the size of a rabbit). When I last visited, there was an entertaining pet toucan hopping from table to table.

RESTAURANT GRAN JAGUAR, Calle Centroamerica. No phone.
Cuisine: GUATEMALAN/INTERNATIONAL
$ Prices: Entrees Q12–Q20 ($3–$5). No credit cards.
Open: Mon–Sat 11am–10pm.

Not far from the Hotel Petén, this is an unusual restaurant with a bold jungle decor. The walls are made from rough-hewn slabs of wood with the bark still on them, and there are abundant plants, both real and artificial. On your table you'll find a bowl of salt and a basket of napkins made from Guatemalan fabric. In one corner is a bar with some pre-Columbian reproductions and a huge basket above it. Baskets have also been used for lamps. The interesting menu lists a brochette of venado (venison), the most expensive item on the menu at Q20 ($5). Otherwise there are hamburgers, fish, steaks, spaghetti, and lots of drinks. This may be the most expensive place on the island.

Important Warning: Reports of guerrilla activity near the Tikal National Park continue. From what I have heard, on the Flores-Tikal road there is an incident every now and then in which armed men stop a tourist bus, lecture the tourists on the rightness of the rebel cause, and release them unharmed. There have been no reports of physical harm and only one unconfirmed report of robbery (as this report had it, holders of American passports were singled out). Most visitors to Tikal do not look on this as a significant danger. If you're an American citizen staying in Flores or Santa Elena, it might be a good idea to entrust your valuables to the management of your hotel before setting out on the road to Tikal.

These incidents may well have ceased by the time you read this. If you have doubts, you can call the **U.S. Department of State's Citizens' Emergency Service** (tel. 202/647-5225) in Washington, D.C., on weekdays from 8:15am to 10pm, for an up-to-date report. Or if you're already in Guatemala when you read this, inquire at your embassy in Guatemala City or ask the locals in Flores for news on the current situation.

2. TIKAL

Distances: 338 miles northeast of Guatemala City; 40 miles north of Flores.

GETTING THERE By Car The ride from Flores to Tikal along a good paved road takes less than an hour by private car. Head north out of Santa Elena, past the airport, and keep going straight. This road deadends at Tikal. Watch out for pedestrians and animals (both domestic and wild) on the roadway.

By Minibus A much faster and more pleasant way to go is by minibus. Minibuses from Flores and Santa Elena, and from the airport, leave at 6, 8, and 10am and return at 2, 4, and 5pm. You can get a minibus at almost any hotel. If your hotel doesn't offer one, go to the Hotel San Juan in Santa Elena. Duration: 1 hour. Fare: Q20 ($5) per person, one way.

By Bus If you want to take the bus, go to the Hotel San Juan in Santa Elena the night before you want to travel, buy your ticket, and be on the spot the next day at 7am or 1pm, which is when the buses leave. Duration: 2 to 3 hours. Fare: Q5 ($1.25).

By Taxi A taxi from the town or the airport to Tikal costs Q120 ($30) or Q140 ($35) total, round trip, for up to three people.

DEPARTING If you go out to Tikal one day, stay overnight, and want to return to Flores another day, the best plan is to talk to the minibus and taxi drivers at Tikal after they arrive from their morning runs from Flores. They'll arrange a place for you.

By air is by far the preferable way to continue to Guatemala City. Aerovias, AeroQuetzal, and TAPSA all depart Santa Elena airport at 4pm for Guatemala City. Duration: 1 hour. Fare: Q210 ($52.50).

Fuentes del Norte buses leave from the market for Guatemala City daily at 1, 5, 9, and 11am, 3, 10, and 11pm. Duration: 14 hours. Fare: Q14 ($3.50).

To reach Belize, Aerovias now flies from Santa Elena to Belize City.

Buses for Melchor de Mencos, on the Belize border, leave from the market, with a stop at Hotel San Juan, at 5, 8, and 10am and 2pm. Duration: 3½ hours. Fare: Q6 ($1.50). From the border there are buses onward to various destinations in Belize. If you want to be sure of getting a seat, get the bus at the market, not at the Hotel San Juan.

A minibus to Melchor de Mencos leaves from Hotel San Juan at 5am. Duration: 2 hours. Fare: Q20 ($5). At the border you can connect with a Belizean bus to Belize City and from there, at 1pm, to Chetumal, if you want to be in Mexico in one day.

ESSENTIALS Orientation The road from Flores ends in the parking lot of Tikal National Park. There are two museums, three hotels, and three little comedores here. The ruins are a 20- to 30-minute walk through the forest from the parking lot.

Fast Facts There is a post office and telegraph office on the left as you arrive at the parking area.

The most spectacular of the many Mayan ceremonial centers is at Tikal. Over 3,000 buildings have been located and mapped in the immediate area of the famous Great Plaza, and there must be thousands more in the rest of the 200-square-mile Parque Nacional Tikal. Almost as impressive as the ruins is the jungle setting of Tikal, filled with exotic birds, spider monkeys, howler monkeys, ocelots, and other wildlife. Tikal is a "must" for visitors to Guatemala.

In a few years, the installations at Parque Nacional Tikal will be completed, and you'll find a spanking-new cafeteria, a museum, an administration building, rental bungalows, and so forth.

Be sure to have enough quetzals for your stay. There are no banks here, and the hotels, although they take traveler's checks as payment for a room, won't change traveler's checks for you. Have quetzals, or at least U.S. dollars. Otherwise, you'll have to bus down to Flores, 40 miles away, to cash a check.

Another thing you should bring with you to Tikal is insect repellent. All year round, but especially in the rainy season (May to October), you'll need the stuff. Don't come without it.

Because all of Tikal is a national park, you will have to pay a Q5 ($1.25) entry fee on the road into the park. The ticket is normally good for one 24-hour overnight stay.

WHAT TO SEE AND DO
THE RUINS AT TIKAL

Tikal is the largest of the Mayan ceremonial centers. So far, archeologists have mapped about 3,000 constructions, 10,000 earlier foundations beneath surviving structures, 250 stone monuments (stelae and altars), and thousands of art objects found in tombs and cached offerings. There is evidence of continuous construction at Tikal from 200 B.C. through the 9th century A.D., with some suggestion of occupation as early as 600 B.C. The Maya reached their zenith in art and architecture during the Classic Period, which began about A.D. 250 and ended abruptly about A.D. 900, when for some reason Tikal was abandoned. Most of the visible structures at Tikal date from the Late Classic Period, A.D. 600 to 900.

No one's sure just what role Tikal played in the history of the Maya: was it mostly a ceremonial center for priests, artisans, and the elite? Or was it a city of industry and commerce as well? In the 6 square miles of Tikal that have been mapped and excavated, only a few of the buildings found have been domestic structures; most are temples, palaces, ceremonial platforms, and shrines. Workers are now beginning to excavate the innumerable mounds on the periphery of the mapped area, and they have been finding modest houses of stone and plaster with thatched roofs. Just how far these settlements extended beyond the ceremonial center and how many people lived within the domain of Tikal is still to be determined. At its height, Tikal may have covered as much as 25 square miles.

Tikal is such an immense site that you will need several days to see it thoroughly, but you can visit many of the greatest temples and palaces in one day. To do it properly, you should have a copy of the excellent guidebook to the ruins—*Tikal,* by William Coe, written under the auspices of the University Museum of the University of Pennsylvania. Archeologists from Penn, working in conjunction with Guatemalan officials, did most of the excellent excavation work at Tikal from 1956 to 1969. Write to the museum in Philadelphia for a copy of the guide or pick one up in Flores or at Tikal ($16). One of the best features of the guide, and a real necessity given the size of the Tikal complex, is a very detailed map of the area. Don't take a chance on getting lost from site to site.

The best time to visit the ruins is early in the morning if you can manage it. The ruins open at 6am, and from then until 11am they're uncrowded. The ruins close at 5:30pm, but you can get a special pass at the park headquarters building to visit the temples when they're bathed in moonlight—an unforgettable vision.

Walking along the road that goes west from the museum toward the ruins, turn right at the first intersection to get to Twin Complexes Q and R. Seven of these twin complexes are known at Tikal, but their exact purpose is still a mystery. Each complex has two pyramids facing east and west; at the north is an unroofed enclosure entered by a vaulted doorway and containing a single stela and altar; at the south is a small palacelike structure. Of the two pyramids here, one has been restored and one has been left as it was found, and the latter will give you an idea of just how overgrown and ensconced in the jungle these structures had become.

At the end of the Twin Complexes is a wide road called the Maler Causeway. Turn right (north) onto this causeway to get to Group P, another twin complex, a 15-minute walk; turn left (south) onto the causeway to get to the Great Plaza.

Some restoration has been done at Complex P, but the most interesting points are the stela (no. 20) and altar (no. 8) in the north enclosure. Look for the beautiful glyphs next to the carving of a warrior on the stela, all in very good condition. The altar shows a captive bound to a carved-stone altar, his hands tied behind his back—a common scene in carvings at Tikal. Both these monuments date from about A.D. 751. As for Temple IV, it's said to be the tallest structure surviving from the pre-Columbian era, standing 212 feet from the base of its platform to the top. The first glimpse you get of the temple from the Maudslay Causeway is awesome, for the temple has not been restored, and all but the temple proper (the enclosure) and its roof comb are covered in foliage. The stairway is occluded by earth and roots, but if you're adept at scrambling, you can make your way to the top of the temple from its northeast corner. Do it if you can: The view of the setting and layout of Tikal—and all of the Great Plaza—is magnificent. From the platform of the temple, you can see in all directions and get an idea of the extent of the Petén jungle, an ocean of lush greenery. Temple III is in the foreground to the east; Temples I and II are farther on at the Great Plaza. To the right of these is the South Acropolis and Temple V. The courageous and nonacrophobic can get even a better view by clambering up a metal ladder on the south side of the temple to the base of the roof comb.

Temple IV, and all the other temples at Tikal, are built on this plan: A pyramid is built first, and on top of it is built a platform; the temple proper rests on this platform and is composed of one to three rooms, usually long and narrow and not for habitation but rather for priestly rites. Most temples have beautifully carved wooden lintels above the doorways, but the one from Temple IV is now in a museum in Basel, Switzerland. The temple is thought to date from about A.D. 741. Ladders allow you to climb to the top of this one.

From Temple IV, walk east along the Tozzer Causeway to get to the Great Plaza, about a ten-minute walk. Along the way you'll pass the twin-pyramid Complex N, the Bat Palace, and Temple III. Take a look at the altar and stela in the complex's northern enclosure—two of the finest monuments at Tikal—and also the altar in front of Temple III, showing the head of a deity resting on a plate. By the way, the criss-cross pattern shown here represents a woven mat, a symbol of authority to the Mayas.

THE GREAT PLAZA

Entering the Great Plaza from the Tozzer Causeway, you'll be struck by the towering stone structure that is Temple II, seen from the back. It measures 125 feet tall now, although it is thought to have been 140 feet high when the roof comb was intact. Also called the Temple of the Masks, from a large face carved in the roof comb, the temple dates from about A.D. 700.

Temple I, the most striking structure in Tikal, reaches 145 feet above the plaza floor. The temple proper has three narrow rooms with high corbeled vaults (the Mayan "arch") and carved wooden lintels made of zapote wood, which is rot-resistant. One of the lintels has been removed for preservation in a museum. The whole structure is made of limestone, as are most others at Tikal. It was within this pyramid that one of the richest tombs in Tikal was discovered, containing some 180 pieces of jade, 90 bone artifacts carved with hieroglyphic inscriptions, numerous pearls, and objects in alabaster and shell.

The North Acropolis (north side of the Great Plaza) is a maze of structures from various periods covering an area of 21 acres. Standing today 30 feet above the limestone bedrock, it contains vestiges of more than a hundred different constructions dating from 200 B.C. to A.D. 800. At the front-center of the acropolis (at the top of the stairs up from the Great Plaza) is a temple numbered 5D-33. Although much of the 8th-century temple was destroyed during the excavations to get to the Early Classic Period temple (A.D. 300) underneath, it's still a fascinating building. Toward the rear of it is a tunnel leading to the stairway of the Early Classic temple, embellished with two 10-foot-high plaster polychrome masks of a god—don't miss these.

Directly across the plaza from the North Acropolis is the Central Acropolis, which covers about 4 acres. It's a maze of courtyards and palaces on several levels, all connected by an intricate system of passageways. Some of the palaces had five floors, connected by exterior stairways, and each floor had as many as nine rooms arranged like a maze. Look for the graffiti on some of the palace walls.

Before you leave the Great Plaza, be sure to examine some of the 70 beautiful stelae and altars right in the plaza. You can see the full development of Mayan art in them, for they date from the Early Classic Period right through to the Late Classic. There are three major stylistic groups: the stelae with wrap-around carving, on the front and sides with a text on the back; those with a figure carved on the front and a text in glyphs on the back; and those with a simple carved figure on the front, a text in hieroglyphs on the sides, and a plain back. The oldest stela is no. 29 (now in the Tikal museum), dating from A.D. 292; the most recent is no. 11 in the Great Plaza, dating from A.D. 879.

THE MUSEUM

The museum contains a good collection of pottery, mosaic masks, incense burners, etched bone, and stelae that is chronologically displayed—beginning with the Pre-Classic objects on up to the Late Classic ones. Of note are the delicate 3- to 5-inch mosaic masks made of jade, turquoise, shell, and stucco. There is a beautiful cylindrical jar from about A.D. 700 depicting a male and female seated in a typical Maya pose. The drawing is of fine quality, and the slip colors are red, brown, and black. Also on exhibit are a number of jade pendants, beads, and earplugs as well as the famous stela no. 31, which has all four sides carved. On the two sides are spear throwers, each wearing a large feathered headdress and carrying a shield in his left hand; on the front is a complicated carving of an individual carrying a head in his left arm and a chair in his right. It is a most amazing stela from the Early Classic Period, considered one of the finest. Admission to the museum is 50 centavos (20¢).

WHERE TO STAY

There are only three lodging places at Tikal in the national park. Rooms are often difficult to get, and making reservations is not easy. However, if you really want to stay at Tikal (an unforgettable experience), here are your choices.

JAGUAR INN, Tikal, Petén. No phone. 2 bungalows (with bath), 3 tents.
$ Rates: Q48 ($12) double in bungalows, Q24 ($6) double in tents. No credit cards.
The Jaguar Inn is a tiny place on the other side of the old museum. It offers the lowest rates of any of the hotels here at the ruins and has only two airy thatched cottages with wood and native-cloth furnishings and simple bathrooms and three large tents, each of which has two beds. The management here is English. To reserve a room, send a telegram, then follow it with a deposit when you get a confirmation. Meals can be had in the quiet screen-walled dining room for Q10 ($2.50) for breakfast, Q14 to Q18 ($3.50 to $4.50) for lunch, and Q18 ($4.50) for dinner. You may order à la carte as well. The restaurant hours are 7am to 8:30pm.

JUNGLE LODGE, 29a Calle 18-01, Zona 12, Guatemala City. Tel. 502/760-294. 32 rms., all with bath.
$ Rates: Q120 ($30) single; Q160 ($40) double; Q200 ($50) triple; Q240 ($60) quad. No credit cards.
Parts of the complex here were built to house the archeological teams working at Tikal, but with the recent remodeling, all the vestiges of these old and rustic accommodations are gone. It's the biggest establishment here at the ruins. You'll stay either in one of the tin-roofed bungalows or in the thatched and half-timbered main building, which also houses the dining room, bar, and reception desk. The bungalow rooms are the better choice because they are very spacious, with large bathrooms, hot water, skylights, high ceilings, and two double beds. Each comes with its own little porch and lounge chairs. Unfortunately, despite the louvered windows, these rooms have little air flow and can get hot in the day. Try for a room here first, even though it may be filled by a tour group.
Three meals a day in the dining room will run you about Q50 ($12.50).

HOTEL TIKAL INN, Tikal, Petén. No phone. 15 rms., all with bath.
$ Rates (including breakfast and dinner): Q120–Q140 ($30–$35) single; Q240–Q280 ($60–$70) double. No credit cards.

★ This is the most pleasant of the three hotels at the ruins. Set back amid the trees, it's the farthest from the museum as you walk down the old airstrip. Several large thatched-roof huts, a swimming pool, and a somewhat dramatic main building make this place look a little grand for the jungle setting. The accommodations are quite simple but clean. The bungalows have hardwood floors and are very nicely decorated with típico fabrics. To facilitate airflow, the walls of these rooms don't go all the way to the ceiling, and consequently these rooms don't have much conversational privacy. The smaller rooms in the main building have cement floors but the same attention to decor. All the rooms are airy and cool. To make a reservation, write or send a telegram.

CAMPING

There is one more lodging possibility: camping. Just off the parking lot at the end of the road and the airstrip is a nice lawn with some trees for shade, marked and designated as the camping area. It has simple plumbing and cooking facilities and charges Q10 ($2.50) for use of the showers. If you have the gear, this is the place for you. You can also rent hammocks and pitch them under palapas for an additional Q10 ($2.50). Keep in mind, however, that in this area there are vampire bats, even though they don't often bite humans. Be sure to use a tent or mosquito net to keep the bats off while you sleep.

WHERE TO EAT

Besides the hotels above, there are several little eateries (comedores) between the main open area and the gate at the beginning of the road to Flores. As you arrive at Tikal from Flores, you'll see them on the right side: **Comedor Imperio Maya, Comedor Corazon de Jesus,** and **Comedor Tikal & Tienda Angelita.** All are similar in comfort and style (there are none), all are rustic and pleasant, all are run by local women, and all serve huge plates of fairly tasty food at low prices. I had a huge piece of roast chicken, with rice, beans, melon, and a soft drink for Q8 ($2). You may get little choice; what's cooking that day (usually chicken) is what there is. If you have a friend with you, be sure to order a fruit plate for Q7 ($1.75), the largest and most delicious fruit plate I've ever encountered.

Another choice is the **snack bar** behind the new Stelae Museum, the big building on the left as you pull into the parking area. It is in a large covered area with several tables and is open daily from 7am to 8pm. A steak and salad here will run you around Q26 ($6.50).

Within the area of the ruins there are picnic tables beneath shelters and itinerant soft-drink peddlars, but no snack stands. If you want to spend all day at the ruins without having to walk back to the settlement for lunch, take sandwiches.

EXCURSIONS
UAXACTÚN

About 16 miles from Tikal (40 miles from Flores) into the jungle stands the Mayan ceremonial city of Uaxactún ("Wah-shahk-toon"). Few tourists penetrate the jungle to see Uaxactún because the road is terrible, and in the rainy season (May through October) it may be completely impassable.

You won't see anything at Uaxactún as impressive as what is at Tikal, but if you want to see another Mayan city, rent a four-wheel-drive vehicle, be sure you know how to place it in four-wheel drive, fill the gas tank (in Flores), and set out from Tikal on the journey, which should take an hour or less.

The road, really a Jeep track, winds through the jungle, up and down hills and through sloughs of mud where you'll need that four-wheel drive. You may encounter one or two other vehicles on this road, in which case you must do some fancy maneuvering.

When you arrive at Uaxactún, check in and sign your name at the guard's hut, then turn right to see a vast swath of grass—the former airstrip, no longer in use. About halfway down the airstrip (now a favorite pasture for cattle), roads go off to the left and to the right to the ruins.

You can get soft drinks and snacks in the village here. No doubt some budding entrepreneur will open a tiny eatery when the tourist traffic increases, but for now you should bring your own food and drink.

The pyramids at Uaxactún were uncovered and put in a "stabilized" condition so that no further deterioration would result; they were not restored. White mortar is the mark of the archeologists, who patched cracks in the stone to prevent water and roots from entering.

Up to the right from the airstrip, about a 10- or 15-minute walk, are Grupo E and Grupo H. To the left off the runway, about a 20-minute walk, are Grupo A and Grupo B. At Grupo A, early excavators sponsored by Andrew Carnegie simply cut into the sides of the temples indiscriminately, looking for graves. This unfortunate work destroyed many of the temples, which are now in the process of being reconstructed.

EL CEIBAL AND OTHER MORE REMOTE RUINS

If your life's passion is Mayan ruins or you simply crave more adventure than you have had so far on your visit to El Petén, maybe you should plan to visit some of the more remote ruins of this region. In addition to exploring seldom-visited Mayan ruins, you'll be traveling by river through uninhabited jungles where you'll likely encounter a great deal of wildlife, which might include coatimundis, howler monkeys, anteaters, tapirs, and possibly even jaguars.

El Ceibal is the most accessible of these other ruins. To reach El Ceibal, first take a bus the 40 miles from Flores to Sayaxche, which is a good-sized town for El Petén (it even has a few basic hotels). From Sayaxche, you must hire a boat to carry you 11 miles up the Río de la Pasión. El Ceibal is a Late Classic ruin (A.D. 600 to 900) known for having the only circular temple in all of El Petén. There are also several well-preserved stelae arranged around one small temple structure on the central plaza. Many of the designs at El Ceibal indicate that the city had extensive contact with cities in the Yucatán, but whether this contact was due to trade or to warfare is unclear.

In order to visit ruins such as **Yaxchilan, Piedras Negras,** and **Altar de los Sacrificios,** you'll have to spend days camping on remote rivers. The best way to visit these would be on an organized trip; this way you would not have to leave anything to chance. Contact **Tropical Tours,** 4a Calle 2-50 "A," Zona 10, Guatemala City (tel. 502/323-748, 345-893, or 345-894), or **Expedicion Panamundo,** 3a Av. 16-52, Zone 10 (tel. 502/681-315 or 683-010) for information on organized river trips through this region. If you try it on your own, you'll have to rely on someone's recommendation to find a reliable boatman, arrange for several days' meals, bring your own tent, and make sure there is enough fuel to get you there and back. In short, you'll have to mount your own small-scale river expedition into the jungle. However, it can be done, and if you set out to try it, you'll certainly meet other like-minded adventurers with whom to share the costs.

CHAPTER 12

THE ATLANTIC HIGHWAY

1. COBÁN
• WHAT'S SPECIAL
  ABOUT THE
  ATLANTIC HIGHWAY
2. RÍO HONDO
3. COPÁN (HONDURAS)
4. ESQUIPULAS
5. QUIRIGUÁ
6. RÍO DULCE AND
  LAKE IZABAL
7. LÍVINGSTON AND
  PUERTO BARRIOS

H eading east from Guatemala City, you'll leave the cool highlands and descend first into dry rolling hills and as you approach the coast, then into lush tropical vegetation. The branch roads off this highway tend to be in excellent shape. The Carretera al Atlántico (Atlantic Highway), which has been undergoing much-needed major repairs in the past few years, opens up several interesting destinations, including the mountainous state of Alta Verapaz and its capital, Cobán; the Mayan ruins at Copán, Honduras; the great pilgrimage church at Esquipulas, famous throughout Central America; the marvelous Mayan stelae and zoomorphs at Quiriguá; the Río Dulce and Lake Izabal, on the road to Tikal; and Guatemala's Caribbean port and laid-back hideaway, Puerto Barrios and Lívingston.

When leaving Guatemala City by private car, be prepared to pay a few small tolls at points along the Atlantic Highway. The tolls (for which you get a receipt) are only a few cents each—more of a bother than an expense.

1. COBÁN

Distances: 132 miles northeast of Guatemala City;
214 miles west of Puerto Barrios.

GETTING THERE **By Bus** Buses from Guatemala City leave from 8a Av. 15-16, Zona 1 (tel. 511-878), daily at 4, 5, 6, 7, 8, 9, 10, and 11:30am, noon, and 12:30, 1, 1:30, 2, 2:30, 3:30, 4, 4:30, and 5pm. Duration: 4 hours. Fare: Q4.75 or Q6.35 ($1.19 or $1.59).

By Car Take the Carretera al Atlántico to El Rancho, then turn left for Cobán.

DEPARTING Buses leave frequently throughout the day for Guatemala City. Duration: 4 hours. Fare: Q4.75 or Q6.35 ($1.19 or $1.59).

To reach Puerto Barrios first take a bus to the junction with the Atlantic Highway at El Rancho and then catch one of the frequent buses bound for Puerto Barrios.

ESSENTIALS **Orientation** If you're driving, watch out for a fork in the road as you approach Cobán. The road becomes one way at this point, so be sure you take the right fork. This road leads to the city's central plaza, on which stands the cathedral. Most of the hotels and restaurants listed here are within a few blocks of the plaza.

Fast Facts The Banco del Agro, where you can change money and traveler's checks, is two blocks from La Posada on the road leading to Guatemala City. The

WHAT'S SPECIAL ABOUT THE ATLANTIC HIGHWAY

Mayan Ruins
- ☐ Copán (actually in Honduras), nearly as impressive as Tikal
- ☐ Quiriguá, known for its intricately carved stelae (record-keeping stones)

Natural Spectacles
- ☐ Semuc Champey cataracts and the quetzal preserve near Cobán

Religious Shrines
- ☐ The basilica in Esquipulas, with a statue of Christ that is the object of a massive pilgrimage every year

---

Guatel office is on the main plaza. Feast days are Holy Week and August 4.

Although the road east from Guatemala City rapidly carries you down to hot dusty lowlands where cactus and other desert plants abound, a side trip north to the department of Alta Verapaz will take you into the most beautiful region of the country. High in these cloud-shrouded mountains, iridescent birds flit among trees draped with orchids, bromeliads, and ferns. The valleys are given over to pastures, and the lower mountain slopes are covered with coffee plantations (once owned by Germans) and farms that grow decorative tropical plants for export as houseplants to colder climes. These tropical-plant farms are often hidden under acres of canvas, which protects the plants from the burning rays of the tropical sun. It is shocking to see entire hillsides hidden beneath these sheets.

Even though Cobán (alt. 4,290 feet; pop. 15,000) has a long history, dating back to colonial times, it is the countryside surrounding the city that is the main attraction here. Alta Verapaz abounds in natural wonders, and Cobán is an excellent base for exploring the rest of the region. There are several excellent and very inexpensive hotels, which offer the best values in all of Guatemala.

WHAT TO SEE AND DO

In Cobán itself there is very little to do. Activity focuses on the central plaza and the market behind the cathedral. The Catedral de Santo Domingo, founded in 1687, is rather spartan both inside and out. The cracked bell just inside the front door is not a Guatemalan Liberty Bell but a church bell that fell and cracked when the bell tower was struck by lightning. Also facing the central plaza are the art deco Palacio Municipal and another government office building with a two-story façade of long porticos in the colonial style. In the plaza itself is a very modern-looking band shell that is the site of evening concerts in the dry season.

If you head out of town on the road to Guatemala City for a few blocks, you'll see a church high on a hill to your right. This is El Calvario, a small church in the middle of an old cemetery. The church is reached by a long flight of steps that lead up the hill. As you climb, you'll see little alcoves where offerings are made by the devout. At the top there are beautiful views of the surrounding valley and mountains.

Near the village of Tactic, about 20 miles before you reach Cobán, is an unusual natural phenomenon: the Pozo Vivo (Living Well), a pool of water formed by a spring that bubbles up from the ground in the middle of a beautiful green pasture. It derives its name from the way the sand at the bottom of the pool dances while the surface remains smooth as glass. It would hardly be worth stopping for, but it offers a chance to take a short stroll through this beautiful valley. There is an attractive colonial church in the town of Tactic itself, and excellent silver and gold jewelry is made and sold here. From the peak of Chi-Ixim hill, just outside of town, there is an excellent view of the town and its surrounding fields.

Nearby San Pedro Carchá, which is about 8 miles from Cobán, is another town famous for its silver filigree work. Situated atop a hill, the town has a large colonial church. During the town's feast days (June 24 to 29), masked dances are performed in the streets. If you're a member of the Polar Bear Club and enjoy swimming in ice-cold waters, you'll want to pay a visit to Las Islas, a nearby waterfall with a large pool at its base.

Both Tactic and San Pedro Carchá can be reached by frequent bus or minibus service from the market in Cobán. Several interesting excursions (details below) also are possible from Cobán.

WHERE TO STAY

DOUBLES FOR LESS THAN Q40 [$10]

HOTEL COBÁN IMPERIAL, 6a Avenida 1-12, Zona 1, Cobán, Alta Verapaz. Tel. 502/0511-131. 7 rms., all with bath.
$ Rates: Q19.89 ($4.97) single; Q23.40–Q35.10 ($5.85–$8.78) double. No credit cards.

This rather nondescript hotel is simple but clean and conveniently located close to the Parque Central and El Calvario on the corner of 1a Calle. I would make this a last-choice accommodation.

There is a small restaurant serving very inexpensive meals just off the lobby.

HOTEL MANSION ARMENIA, 7a Avenida 2-18, Zona 1, Cobán, Alta Verapaz. Tel. 502/051-2284. 22 rms., all with bath.
$ Rates: Q23.40 ($5.85) single; Q35.10 ($8.78) double; Q46.80 ($11.70) triple. No credit cards accepted.

On the street leading to the base of El Calvario (The Calvary), Cobán's little chapel and cemetery, is this two-story neocolonial motel, which offers an excellent value. All the small rooms have arched windows facing onto a parking lot that is locked up at night. The tile floors are squeaky clean, and there are double beds, tables, and wardrobes in most of the rooms. Because of its location off the main street, it's a very quiet place for a good night's sleep.

There is a small restaurant at the back of hotel that serves three meals a day.

DOUBLES FOR LESS THAN Q60 [$15]

HOTEL LA POSADA, 1a Calle 4-12, Zona 2, Cobán, Alta Verapaz. Tel. 502/051-1495. 14 rms., all with bath.
$ Rates: Q35.10 ($8.78) single; Q52.65 ($13.16) double; Q70.20 ($17.55) triple. No credit cards. **Parking:** Free.

⭐ This rustic colonial hotel may be the best deal in all of Guatemala, perhaps because gringos as a whole have not yet discovered this beautiful region. Although the hotel is wedged between the two busiest streets in town and is consequently noisy, it still manages to maintain a rural atmosphere. You enter the hotel through a large gate and find yourself in a well-tended garden. Along the portico to the left is the office, where you can play table tennis if you like. The floors throughout are wood, and antique wooden benches line the portico. Traditional masks hang from the walls; and *santos*, little statues of saints, are seemingly everywhere. There is a TV lounge with wide-plank floors and shocking-pink furniture. The guest rooms have beamed ceilings, old or antique furniture, and private baths with hot water. You'll spot signs for La Posada on your left just as you approach the Parque Central.

There is a cozy restaurant with a fireplace.

HOTEL RABIN AJAU, Calzada Minerva 5-37, Zona 1, Cobán, Alta Verapaz. Tel. 502/512-296. 11 rms., all with bath.

$ **Rates:** Q46.80 ($11.70) single; Q58.50 ($14.63) double; Q70.20 ($17.55) triple. No credit cards. **Parking:** Free.

With two restaurants and a disco, this basic hotel is the closest Cobán has to a resort, which it definitely is not. In Guatemalan terminology, it is a *turicentro*, just down the street from La Posada as you head out of town on the road to Guatemala City. Wood paneling throughout the hotel gives it a rustic, mountain-lodge appeal. Oil paintings by a local artist hang in the small lobby. The service is nothing exceptional here, but then you aren't paying much either.

One of the restaurants is a pizzeria, and the other serves typical Guatemalan meals. Prices range from Q6 to Q16 ($1.50 to $4).

WHERE TO EAT

CAFÉ EL TIROL, 1a Calle 3-13. No phone.
  Cuisine: COFFEE/SANDWICHES.
$ **Prices:** Coffee Q1–Q4 (25¢–$1); sandwiches Q4 ($1). No credit cards.
  Open: Daily 11am–9pm.

★ Directly across the street from the fountain at the south end of the Parque Central is a new café that is a showcase for Guatemalan coffees. Cobán is coffee-growing country, and you probably saw a great deal of it on your way up here. Don't miss the opportunity to tap into it at its source. If you're a coffeeholic, you'll find the assortment here absolutely mouthwatering: coffee "as black as midnight"; café americano; coffee with cocoa and whipped cream; espresso with cardamom; espresso with chocolate, sweet cream, and cinnamon; and even an assortment of coffees with different liquors. Tea and cocoa drinkers are not shunned either. To accompany your coffee, there are delicious pastries and some simple sandwiches. This is a great place for a late-night cup and cake or a light lunch. Have your repast on the portico surrounded by brilliantly colored bougainvillea vines.

EL GANADERO, 1a Calle across from La Posada. No phone.
  Cuisine: STEAKS/GUATEMALAN.
$ **Prices:** Main dishes Q8–Q18 ($2–$4.50). DC, MC, V.
  Open: Daily noon–10pm.

This newly opened branch of a popular Guatemala City restaurant serves up excellent steaks in a thatched-roof building set back from the street. It is actually in the courtyard of an older building and is reached by a short hallway hung with contemporary local art. There are more interesting paintings hanging behind the bar in this brightly lit restaurant. Waiters in black vests and bow ties take your order and make sure that all is as it should be during your meal. Try the steak with three sauces—it's delicious. And absolutely do not miss the garlic bread—I had to order two baskets of it.

EXCURSIONS

MARIO DARY RIVERA BIOTOPO

Located at kilometer 163 on the road leading to Cobán, this nature reserve is one of the last places in the country where Guatemala's national bird, the resplendent quetzal, is still found. In pre-Columbian times, the most expensive garments, those worn by kings and princes, were often made from thousands of bird feathers. The most highly prized feathers of all were those of the quetzal, a pigeon-sized bird of the Central American cloud forests. Both the male and the female quetzal sport iridescent green and brilliant red feathers. This beautiful coloring alone would be enough to label them the most beautiful birds in the world, but to add to this display of color, the male of the species also has two willowy tail feathers that can reach almost a yard in length—the most highly prized feathers in pre-Columbian times.

The male quetzal's tail feathers resemble the fronds of epiphytic ferns that cling to the branches of trees in its cloud forest habitat. Cloud forests, which form only at high elevations, are similar to lowland rain forests. They are perpetually damp, but the moisture here is not generally in the form of rain. The warm tradewinds that pick up moisture as they cross the Caribbean Sea are forced up into colder elevations by Guatemala's mountain ranges. As the moist air cools, it forms dense clouds that blanket the mountains for most of the year, keeping the forests damp. Thousands of species of plants have evolved to make the most of this damp environment. Branches of trees are covered with orchids, ferns, bromeliads, and other epiphytic plants. A stroll along the trails of this nature reserve is certain to elicit gasps from those unfamiliar with the dense tangle of vegetation that comprises a cloud forest. Among the most interesting plants are the tree ferns, which can grow up to twenty feet tall with huge feathery crowns. Many plants that are sold as houseplants in the north grow wild here.

Hundreds of species of birds call this forest home, and a sharp-eyed birdwatcher can easily spot several dozen, perhaps even a quetzal, in a hike through the reserve. Because of the density of the forest, the mammals that inhabit the reserve are much more difficult to spot. Among those that you might see are monkeys and ocelots.

Where to Stay and Eat

HOSPEDAJE EL RANCHITO DEL QUETZAL, Km 163, Baja Verapaz. No phone. 16 beds, none with bath.

$ Rates: Q10 ($2.50) single; Q20 ($5) double. No credit cards.

For those who would like to be as close to the *biotopo* as possible and don't have much money to spend, this is your only choice. There are two very rustic cabins here, each with eight beds. It's just a step above camping, but the log cabins beneath tall trees are picturesque. Bring your own food or buy meals at the comedor right here.

POSADA MONTAÑA DEL QUETZAL, Km 156 Ruta a Cobán, Baja Verapaz. In Guatemala City, 23 Calle "B" 34-42, Zona 5, Colonia Vivibien, Guatemala City. Tel. 502/31-41-81. 8 rms., 10 bungalows, all with bath.

$ Rates: Q35.10–Q40.95 ($8.78–$10.24) single; Q46.80–Q87.75 ($11.70–$21.94) double; Q64.35–Q93.60 ($16.09–$23.40) triple; Q102.96–Q120.50 ($25.74–$30.13) quad; higher rates are for weekends. DC, MC, V.

Located within 4 kilometers of the quetzal preserve, this is the most luxurious hotel in the entire region. The hotel, situated on manicured grounds surrounded by forests, is a popular weekend destination for wealthy citizens of Guatemala City who come for the cool, clean country atmosphere. There are trails through the nearby forests, where you might even spot a quetzal, and exotic plants, such as tree ferns, are abundant on the grounds themselves. The bungalows are considerably larger than the rooms and are a particularly good deal. Each comes with two bedrooms, a separate living room, and a fireplace, which keeps the rooms very cozy on cold nights. A great place for a long relaxing stay. Highly recommended.

Dining: There are two restaurants and an open-air thatched-roof bar. One restaurant looks onto the parking lot and is a good place to stop for breakfast or lunch if you're just passing through. The other restaurant has a wall of windows looking onto the swimming pool. Breakfast is served from 7 to 10am, lunch from noon to 3pm, and dinner from 6 to 9pm. Meal prices range from Q4 ($1) for breakfast up to Q20 ($5) for dinner. You have a choice of numerous dishes, primarily Guatemalan and international cuisine, at every meal.

Facilities: Swimming pool, children's pool, playground, fishing pond, and hiking trails.

LANQUÍN CAVES AND SEMUC CHAMPEY

Northeast of Cobán 42 miles on a rough dirt road is the village of Lanquín and its nearby caves. The drive to this area is difficult and time-consuming, so leave early in the morning. Don't even think about trying it in the rainy season. Even in the dry season, you'll need a four-wheel-drive vehicle if you want to go as far as Semuc Champey. You might be able to hire a taxi in Cobán to bring you out here.

The mountains throughout this region are limestone and consequently are laced with caverns and sinkholes. Of the caves in the region, those at Lanquín are the most famous, extending for several miles into a mountain, with the Lanquín River running through immense halls. You can find a guide in the village who will turn on the lights in the caves and lead you through. The going is often slippery, so be sure to wear shoes with good traction. It's also a good idea to carry a couple of flashlights in case the power should go off.

Another 6 miles beyond Lanquín is Semuc Champey, a startlingly beautiful ravine that is also a result of the limestone of this region. Pools of icy water collect in bowls carved out of the limestone by torrents of water. Amazingly, each pool is a different shade of turquoise. All around are steep cliffs and lush vegetation. However, these jewel-like pools are only part of the magic of Semuc Champey. Just upstream from the pools, the Cahabón River cascades through a narrow gorge and suddenly disappears into a sinkhole. Further downstream, after passing under a natural bridge on top of which are several turquoise pools, the river re-emerges. After the difficult journey to reach this remote and rugged area, you'll certainly want to stay far longer than you had originally planned. If you have camping gear with you, there is a place here to pitch a tent; otherwise, the nearest lodging is in Lanquín, but it is very basic.

2. RÍO HONDO

Distances: 77 miles east of Guatemala City; 96 miles west of Puerto Barrios.

GETTING THERE   By Bus   Any bus headed for Esquipulas, Puerto Barrios, or Flores will stop at Río Hondo. From Guatemala City, these buses leave from 19a Calle 8-18, Zona 1 (tel. 537-282) or 15a Calle 10-42, Zona 1 (tel. 27-578).

By Car   The Atlantic Highway passes south of Río Hondo.

DEPARTING   The buses for Puerto Barrios pass right in front of all three of the hotels. Just step out and flag one down. The same applies to buses bound for Guatemala City.

The town of Río Hondo is just north off of the Atlantic Highway, where Highway CA 10 turns south to Chiquimula and Esquipulas. But on the highway, near this important intersection, is a collection of establishments that serve travelers: service stations, shops, and motels.

WHERE TO STAY AND EAT

Although there are several small hotels in Chiquimula and a few other very modest places near Quiriguá, by far your best opportunity for accommodations in this entire region is here at Río Hondo. You won't find other places this comfortable until you get to Lake Izabal.

HOTEL NUEVO PASABIEN, Km 126, Carretera al Atlántico, Santa Cruz Teculután, Zacapa. Tel. 502/0417-201. 29 rms., all with bath.
$ Rates: Q15–Q35 ($3.75–$8.75) single; Q27–Q47 ($6.75–$11.75) double; Q12 ($3) per extra bed. No credit cards.
Across the highway from the two motels listed below is this slightly more "rustic" hotel, with some guest rooms in an older two-story wood building and others in the familiar bungalow units. The pool here is just as nice as those at the other two motels and includes both a high and a low diving board. The newer bungalows are much nicer than the older rooms and well worth the few extra dollars they cost. There's one restaurant facing the highway and another open-air one behind it.

HOTEL EL ATLÁNTICO, Km 126, Carretera al Atlántico, Santa Cruz Río Hondo, Zacapa. Tel. 502/0417-160. 24 rms., all with bath.
$ Rates: Q30 ($7.50) single; Q50 ($12.50) double; Q60 ($15) triple; Q75 ($18.75) quad. No credit cards.

★ This hotel is next door to the Longarone (below). For a description, read that of the Motel Longarone, as the Atlántico is a virtual clone of that hotel. It's newer and a bit cheaper, an indisputable—even fantastic—bargain.

Prices for a complete meal here are in the Q10 to Q24 ($2.50 to $6) range.

MOTEL LONGARONE, Km 126, Carretera al Atlántico, Río Hondo, Zacapa. Tel. 502/0417-126. 74 rms., all with bath.

$ Rates: Q70–Q95 ($17.50–$23.75) single; Q95–Q140 ($23.75–$35) double; Q185 ($46.25) 3–5 people. DC, MC, V.

★ The old standby here, and still the best in my opinion, is the Longarone, which you will find by looking for its large sign. Behind the dining room is a lovely Olympic-size swimming pool complete with diving board, poolside arbor patio, and umbrella-topped tables with lounge chairs and café service sheltered by palm trees and brightened by bougainvillea and other tropical flowering plants. It's a heavenly little oasis, so much so that the motel often fills up with weekend vacationers from the capital—not something you'd expect to happen in a roadside motel. The guest rooms are built in a bungalow arrangement, with two accommodations per bungalow. The rooms have high ceilings, tile baths, fans, air conditioners, and simple but suitable decor. The more expensive rooms come with TVs. The problem with the Longarone is that once you bed down here or get a sample of the poolside life, you hardly want to travel on.

The motel has a spacious, airy dining room set back from the highway. Above the bar in the dining room are two photographs of the Italian town of Longarone—one before it was swept from the face of the earth by a great landslide, one afterward. The food in the restaurant is tasty, and the service is pleasant. A full, standard menu of Guatemalan and American favorites, with a sprinkling of Italian dishes, is offered. Expect to spend about Q24 to Q32 ($6 to $8) for a full meal here, less for a light lunch or snack.

---

3. COPÁN (HONDURAS)

Distances: 112 miles east of Guatemala City; 68 miles south of Río Hondo.

GETTING THERE By Bus You take a bus first to Chiquimula, then take another to the border at El Florido. Chiquimula-bound buses leave Guatemala City from 19a Calle 8-18, Zona 1 (tel. 537-282), every 30 minutes from 4am to 6pm. From Chiquimula, there are buses to the border at 6 and 11am. If you leave Guatemala City at 7am or earlier, you can make the 11am bus and be at the Honduran border by 3:30pm (unfortunately the ruins close at 4pm). You can take a minibus or hire a taxi or motorcycle to take you the remaining 9 miles to the ruins. Alternatively, you can hire a taxi in Chiquimula for the 40-mile ride to the ruins. This might be the best bet if there are four of you. By hiring a taxi, you can go over and back in a day with plenty of time to explore the ruins. A taxi for this trip should cost about Q48 ($12) each way.

By Car If you're driving, it'll take you four or five hours to reach Copán from Guatemala City. Turn off the Atlantic Highway at Río Hondo and take CA 12 south past Zacapa and Chiquimula. Just south of Chiquimula is a small sign pointing to a dirt road on the left. Take it—it may be a bad road, but it's all you've got. The distance to the border is 40 miles, over mountains, through streams and villages.

DEPARTING There are frequent buses daily from Esquipulas to Guatemala City. These buses will drop you in Chiquimula for the bus to the Honduran border and Copán ruins or at Río Hondo for buses to Puerto Barrios or El Petén.

ESSENTIALS You'll have to go through a good deal of formality (and cash) on both sides of the border before you are finally allowed to proceed, and I recommend that only those with a rather intense interest in Mayan ruins attempt it. The charge for a car and driver—all costs included—can be as much as $10 before you're actually in the ruins (the $1 charge for admission to the ruins is included in this figure). If you're game, here's the gamut: Guatemalan Immigration, police, Customs, Hacienda (Finance Ministry), guards (at three separate stations); Honduran Immigration, fumigation, and Customs (two stations), then the ruins. (The Honduran lempira, by the way, is worth 50¢ U.S.) On your way back through, it's easier (and cheaper). Pick up your Guatemalan Tourist Card at the immigration office, and the exit stamp will be canceled. It is possible to get a temporary exit permit that lets you avoid getting a new Tourist Card and thus save the $5 charge. Be sure to ask about it. *Important:* If you need a visa to get into Guatemala, try to get a multiple-entry visa so that your visit to Copán will not necessitate you getting a new visa in Honduras.

The Mayan ruins at Copán, just across the border in Honduras, are among the most impressive in this region. However, at this writing it is very difficult to get there and back in a day by public transportation and tedious to travel by private car. Tours run from Guatemala City to Copán and back in a day (one long day), and if your time is short, you should probably plan to visit Copán this way. If time is no problem, plan to go by bus or by car and to find a bed in one of the modest hostelries in the village near the ruins.

WHAT TO SEE AND DO
THE RUINS AT COPÁN

Copán is in a valley about 2,000 feet high, right on the Copán River. The area is lush and fertile, good for growing tobacco but cooler than most Mayan sites (which are in sea-level jungle). As with most early cities, Copán has had several locations in its 1,500 years of existence. The first settlement (Early Classic, about A.D. 400) was where the village of Copán is today. By the Late Classic Period (about A.D. 700), most of the area in the Copán valley had been occupied at one time or another. But the Main Structure, about a mile east of Copán village, did not become the religious and governmental center until the middle of the 8th century A.D.; and not until this time did the Mayan artisans of Copán reach their highest level of achievement.

As you enter the village, you'll see signs to the parking lot and a bit farther on a booth where you buy a ticket for the ruins and museum. The museum is on the main plaza in town and has the standard collection of stelae, sculptures, a tomb complete with skulls, and many small jade and stone objects. You can purchase a guidebook to the ruins, which is not really worth it, but the area is so large that a guide is almost a necessity.

From the museum it's about a half-hour walk to the Main Structure, a mile east, and you'll need at least a full day to see these ruins. Plan to spend another day if you want to dig around the other sites: Copán cemetery, quarry beds, and the stone buildings outside Santa Rita. There are vestiges of settlements everywhere in the valley.

The Main Structure is in the center of the valley, north of the Copán River, and covers 62 acres: five plazas surrounded by temples, pyramids, and platforms, all built at different times between A.D. 730 and 850. The largest complex, 130 feet high from the plaza floor, is at the southern end. Called the Acropolis, it was the center for religious life in the city. On the Acropolis's northeast corner (left as you face it from the plaza) is the famous Hieroglyphic Stairway, decorated with some 2,500 glyphs on the 63 stairs that lead up to Temple 26. (The stairs have been restored—a landslide in the 19th century toppled all but 15 of them.) Unfortunately, they won't let you get close enough to the stairs to have a good look at the glyphs.

The stairs on the north side of the Acropolis lead to the Eastern and Western Courts. Archeologists think the Eastern Court was the most sacred spot at Copán because it contains Temple 22 (north side of the court), the most magnificent structure in Copán. Much of the work on the façade has been destroyed, but you can tell from the vestiges of mosaic and sculpture how grand it was. Note the two giant death's-heads intermeshed with squatting figures and grotesque monsters over the door to the sanctuary. The Western Court is less impressive, although Temple 16, a stepped-platform type, is impressive enough. When Maudslay began excavations in 1885, he found fragments of sculpture that had once decorated this temple strewn all over the Western Court.

The Great Plaza at the northern end of the Main Structure is similar in layout to the Great Plaza at Tikal. From dates on the 20 stelae and 14 altars found here, archeologists think that the Great Plaza was the first complex built in the Main Structure. The center of life may have shifted to the Acropolis area once that part was finished.

Be sure to notice the special artistry that Copán's sculptors exhibited in carving the glyphs here, for Copán's glyphs are the finest examples of this Maya "writing." Also, the unusual sculptures, unique in Mayan art, owe a lot of their beauty to the greenish volcanic stone found only at Copán.

WHERE TO STAY AND EAT

Copán is primarily a day-trip excursion and few people choose to stay here. The village near the ruins does, however, have a handful of absolutely basic hotels where you can get a room for Q8 to Q40 ($2 to $10). There are also a couple of basic little restaurants in the village.

4. ESQUIPULAS

Distances: 138 miles southeast of Guatemala City;
59 miles south of Río Hondo.

GETTING THERE By Bus Buses leave Guatemala City from 19a Calle 8-18, Zona 1 (tel. 537-282), every 30 minutes from 4am to 6pm. Duration: 4 hours. Fare: Q4.75 or Q6.60 ($1.19 or $1.65).

By Car From the Atlantic Highway, take the Esquipulas turnoff at Río Hondo.

ESSENTIALS Orientation Esquipulas centers around its famous basilica and its adjacent park. There is a lookout above town on the road from Río Hondo that will give you an excellent view of the town.

The scenery is beautiful on the CA 12 highway down from Chiquimula, and the town of Esquipulas with its church comes into view while you're still high above it. The church, famous as a place of pilgrimage, looks altogether too big for such a small town.

WHAT TO SEE AND DO

Esquipulas is not much different from any other Guatemalan town, except for its basilica—but the basilica is very special, indeed. Called by some the "Basilica of all Central America," it was ordered built by the first archbishop of Guatemala, Pedro Pardo de Figueroa, in 1759. The archbishop wanted such a grand place to house the sacred statue of Christ Crucified that had been made in 1594 by Quirio Cantano. The statue had had a long history of miraculous events connected with it even before the church was built: In 1740 it was said to have perspired profusely, a miracle authenticated by the then-bishop of Guatemala.

Devout Catholics visit the basilica throughout the year, but the rites during Holy Week attract a larger-than-average crowd, as does the Festival of the Holy Name of Jesus (January 6 to 15). At times such as these, it's possible for visitors to file past the statue and even to kiss it, although the lines are unbelievably long.

Besides the statue, which is quite small and housed in the glass case above the altar, the church boasts the largest bell in Central America, installed in 1946. And the building itself is impressive, simple (for the style of the time) but harmonious, with four tall corner towers and beautiful grounds.

The market just outside the church is especially active during the two festivals mentioned; in fact, it takes on a carnival atmosphere: stalls selling snacks, such as fried banana slices; games of skill and chance; and the normal market activities of selling hand-woven blankets and—here in Esquipulas—religious articles and trinkets. There are even fireworks displays during the festivals.

WHERE TO STAY

The hotel situation in Esquipulas has improved tremendously in recent years. Most of the town's hotels are very near the great church. Enterprising hoteliers realized that pilgrimages were big business and that wealthy Central Americans, as well as the poor, came to see the Black Christ. Consequently, there are now several very comfortable hotels in town catering primarily to religious pilgrims but providing amenities such as swimming pools and fine restaurants.

DOUBLES FOR LESS THAN Q60 [$15]

HOTEL LOS ANGELES, 2a Avenida 11-94, Zona 1, Esquipulas, Chiquimula. Tel. 502/0421-254. 35 rms., 22 with bath.
$ Rates: Q15 ($3.75) single without bath, Q22 ($5.50) single with bath; Q30 ($7.50) double without bath, Q44 ($11) double with bath. V.

If you want a double room with private bath, this is the cheapest place in town. Costing somewhat less than the Payaqui next door (below), the Los Angeles enjoys the same proximity to the basilica. The guest rooms, basic but fairly clean, are around a small courtyard that is almost completely filled by the hotel's restaurant; consequently, first-floor rooms don't get much light. The Los Angeles shares the same parking lot with the Payaqui; it's around behind the two hotels.

In the restaurant, you can get a typical Guatemalan meal for Q8 to Q10 ($2 to $2.50) and listen to marimba bands during fiestas.

HOTEL POSADA DEL CRISTO NEGRO, Barrio Las Crusitas, Esquipulas, Chiquimula. Tel. 502/0431-482. 32 rms., all with bath. TV TEL
$ Rates: Q40 ($10) single; Q60 ($15) double; Q80 ($20) triple; Q120 ($30) quad. DC, MC, V.

If you continue 1 kilometer on the highway to Honduras, past the turnoff for downtown, you'll come to one of Esquipulas's better bargains. It is located on the outskirts of town and therefore quieter than the downtown choices. Every room has its own covered parking area and rocking chairs in front. Inside you'll find carpeting, double or twin beds, minirefrigerators, fans, and clean rooms. Unfortunately, even with all these comforts, the rooms are far from being attractive; despite the location in the country, an excess of cement gives the hotel a very urban feel. However, this feeling is tempered by tall pine trees and a swimming pool. There is a large conference hall.

In the restaurant, a meal will run between Q15 and Q20 ($3.75 and $5).

DOUBLES FOR LESS THAN Q100 [$25]

HOTEL MONTECRISTO, 3a Avenida 9-12, Zona 1. Esquipulas, Chiquimula. Tel. 502/0431-453 or 0431-256. 30 rms., 12 with bath.
$ Rates: Q14 ($3.50) single without bath, Q40 ($10) single with bath; Q28 ($7) double without bath, Q64 ($16) double with bath; Q81 ($20.25) triple; Q100 ($25) quad. MC.

Another downtown choice—a bit simpler and slightly more expensive than the Los Angeles for rooms with private baths—the Montecristo is a short walk down a busy shopping street from the basilica.

There is a very attractive covered courtyard here with a dining area in the middle of it.

HOTEL PAYAQUI, 2a Avenida 11-56, Zona 1, Esquipulas, Chiquimula. Tel. 502/0431-143 or 0431-371. 40 rms., all with bath.

$ Rates: Q60 ($15) single; Q90 ($22.50) double; Q110 ($27.50) triple; Q130 ($32.50) quad. DC, MC, V.

The best place right downtown—and it's nothing exciting—is the Payaqui, which has decent rooms, a tiny swimming pool, and a private parking lot. It's located right across the street from the basilica and consequently very popular with pilgrims. There are even postings of hours of church services in the lobby. The family rooms are quite large, and some of them have large windows. The carpets throughout are a bit old and faded, but overall this hotel is a good choice.

WORTH THE EXTRA BUCKS

HOTEL EL GRAN CHORTI, Km 222, Esquipulas, Chiquimula. Tel. 502/ 0431-371 or 0431-143. In Guatemala City, Avenida La Reforma 8-60, Zona 9, Edificio Galería Reforma, Of. 124, Guatemala City. Fax 502/317-149. 20 rms., all with bath. A/C TV TEL

$ Rates: Q165 ($41.25) single; Q200 ($50) double; Q300 ($75) triple or quad; Q355 ($88.75) 5–6 people. AE, DC, MC, V.

⭐ Unexpected luxury at very reasonable prices is what you'll find at this modern hotel, situated high on a hill overlooking Esquipulas and the basilica, with sweeping views across mountains and valleys. Swing off the highway onto the hotel's cobblestone driveway, and you'll know immediately that no expenses were spared in building this grand hotel. A fountain bubbles away in the middle of the green-marble lobby, while bright sunshine streams in through a skylight. Outside, the grounds are beautifully landscaped, with shocking-pink bougainvillea everywhere. The hotel is even reforesting the hillsides surrounding its property.

All the rooms are large and come with small refrigerators, two double beds, beautiful tile-and-marble bathrooms with tubs, carpeting, very modern furnishings, and bougainvillea-framed balconies. The suites, an exceptional deal if you're traveling in a group, also have desks, tables, large closets, and lockers for your bags.

Dining/Entertainment: You'll be immediately confronted by a cart full of luscious-looking pastries when you enter the restaurant, which is just off the lobby. The service is excellent, and the large windows let in plenty of light. There are daily specials, such as lobster thermidor, for Q40 ($10), and on the weekend there's a breakfast buffet for Q15 ($3.75). The menu features a wide variety of international dishes with an emphasis on steaks and seafood. Prices range from Q20 to Q30 ($5 to $7.50). Another, simpler restaurant serves less expensive meals. On the weekend there's also an open-air disco beside the pool. At other times you will also find a poolside bar.

Facilities: Large swimming pool with slide and water-polo facilities, children's pool, trampoline, gift shop, and small convention hall.

WHERE TO EAT

As for food, your best bet is to stick to the hotel dining rooms listed above. The Hotel Payaqui has the best food downtown, for what that distinction is worth, but if you're looking for a truly delicious meal, head out to El Gran Chorti. Their daily special is an exceptionally good deal, and they even have a breakfast buffet. The restaurant at El Gran Chorti makes a great lunch stop if you have just come down here for the day. There are also lots of cheap eateries and snack places around town where you can get a typical meal for Q5 ($1.25).

5. QUIRIGUÁ

Distances: 136 miles east of Guatemala City; 67 miles west of Puerto Barrios; 56 miles south of Río Dulce.

GETTING THERE   By Bus   Any bus headed to Puerto Barrios will drop you off at the junction with the road to the ruins or in the village of Quiriguá. From here it is possible to walk or hire a motorcycle to take you the remaining 2½ miles to the ruins.

By Car   The ruins of Quiriguá are 2½ miles south of the Atlantic Highway at kilometer 205 on a dirt road that leads through a banana plantation.

DEPARTING   Buses for Puerto Barrios and Guatemala City pass by on the highway frequently throughout the day. If you are heading to El Petén, you can catch a bus as far as the turnoff for Río Dulce or wait for one of the direct buses.

The stelae in a beautiful jungle park at Quiriguá are among the most impressive Mayan relics and well worth a visit. With a car, you can visit Quiriguá using Río Hondo as a base. But if you're traveling by bus, you may have to stay in the village of Quiriguá, which is quite a walk from the ruins.

WHAT TO SEE AND DO
THE RUINS

Quiriguá is a Late Classic Mayan city, dating from A.D. 692 to 900. It was a dependency of Copán, and it was here that the Mayan methods of quarrying and carving great pieces of stone reached the height of excellence. The area around Quiriguá was once-dense forest of ceiba, mahogany, and palm, but at the turn of this century, the trees and bush were cleared to make way for the farms and plantations of the United Fruit Company. All that remains of the forest is the 75-acre park in which the ruins are set, about a mile south of the highway through the banana plantation.

The ruins were discovered in 1840, and Maudslay took an interest in them later (1881–1894); after the turn of the century, several teams came and excavated at Quiriguá. The site has been restored by the University of Pennsylvania, sponsored by the National Geographic Society.

Quiriguá has three sites, but only the one most lately occupied (A.D. 751–900) is of interest. This is the one in the excellent park, reached by crossing the railroad tracks, going through the parking lot, and then walking along a path to the southwest. From the great plaza (about 1,500 feet long, north to south), it's an awesome sight: a lofty, lush grove with a gigantic ceiba tree in the middle. A yellow-billed ticu may poke its head out of a hole in a dead tree, or you may see a 2-foot-long brilliant-green iguana moving slowly in the grass.

At the southern end of the plaza is the largest of the complexes, a temple plaza raised above ground level and surrounded by six temple-palace structures built at different times between A.D. 750 and 810. Take a look at the structure on the east side, which has two altars, designated Q and R by archeologists, in front of the west doorway. Both these altars represent human figures seated cross-legged. Also look at the 9-foot-high mosaic head over the doorway in the north façade of "Structure 2," on the southwest corner of the plaza. Another sculpted mask with huge teeth is on the southwest corner of the same structure. And on Structure 1, at the far southern end of the plaza, look at the beautiful hieroglyphic inscriptions around the doors.

To me, Quiriguá is synonymous with the grand stelae the Mayas did so well. As you enter the park, you'll pass several of these, carved from brown sandstone, 13 to 35 feet tall. The most famous is 35-foot Stela "E," the tallest stone shaft in Mesoamerica, which is about one-fourth of the way down the plaza as you walk south. (There are two stelae side by side here; facing south, "E" is the one on your right.) Both the front and the back are carved with a man standing on a platform and holding in his right hand a manikin scepter (a Mayan ceremonial wand depicting a long-nosed god). The northern face is the best preserved. On the sides are glyphs that archeologists have used to date this stela at A.D. 771. Most of the other stelae here have similar figures, many having beards that seemed to come into fashion with the Maya for a 30-year period. Stela "D," at the far north end of the plaza, has a figure with a beard; some of the glyphs on the sides have been deciphered, indicating that this figure is "Two-armed Sky," a ruler of Quiriguá in A.D. 766, a native of Copán.

Look also at the "zoomorphs," huge boulders carved into monsters. Zoomorph "B," behind Stela "E," is one such monster who has a human torso and head protruding from (or, rather, disappearing into) his mouth. Another good one is at the far southern end of the plaza, on the east side: A crouched man is covered by a shield (looking like a human turtle); the shield, seen from the top, is clearly the face of a deity with two large earplugs, and the crouched figure has a face at each end. There are several more of these zoomorphs; to see them well you have to take your time and look at them from every possible angle.

A note on the sandstone used here: The Mayas were lucky in that the beds of this stone in the nearby River Motagua had cleavage planes good for cutting large pieces and that the stone, when freshly cut, was very soft and hardened only after some exposure to the air. No wonder the highly skilled Mayan craftsmen picked Quiriguá for their most impressive sculpture.

WHERE TO STAY AND EAT

HOTEL DOÑA MARÍA, Km 181, Carretera al Atlántico at Doña María Bridge. No phone. 22 rms., all with bath.
$ Rates: Q10 ($2.50) single; Q18 ($4.50) double; Q25 ($6.25) triple. No credit cards.
It looks quite forlorn from the front, but behind the façade of this hotel is an airy dining and sitting area with a fine view of the river and the emerald-green grass and tall palm trees that line its banks. A small dam creates a swimming area where children and adults from Guatemala City splash on the weekend. The rooms here are a bit musty, dark, and claustrophobic, but if you spend all of your waking hours swimming in the river, hiking in the mountains, and touring Quiriguá, it might be worth it.

HOTEL ROYAL, Quiriguá. No phone. 15 rms., 2 with bath.
$ Rates: Q7 ($1.75) per person without bath, Q15 ($3.75) per person with bath. No credit cards.
The only place to stay in this little dirt-street hamlet several miles from the ruins is a short drive off the highway. It's a Caribbean-style wood structure with numerous large, high-ceilinged, well-ventilated rooms. Each room has a concrete floor on which are arranged four or five beds, a cold-water washbasin and, if you're lucky, a shower and a toilet, perhaps with a seat. The walls are painted green. You'll find numerous coat hooks for clothing storage and perhaps a small table. If business is slow, you may be able to rent one of the large bathless rooms entirely for yourself. Although severely plain, the rooms are clean, and the family who runs the place is friendly enough.
Dining: A little comedor here is the only place for basic meals.

HOTEL SANTA MONICA, Km 200, Carretera al Atlántico, Los Amates, Izabal. No phone. 8 rms., all with bath.
$ Rates: Q15 ($3.75) single; Q30 ($7.50) double. No credit cards.
$ Although it is located behind a Texaco gas station and a 24-hour convenience store, this small, new hotel is very clean and comfortable. The rooms are large, carpeted, and come with two beds each.
There is a restaurant next door to the hotel where you can get inexpensive Guatemalan meals.

---

6. RÍO DULCE AND LAKE IZABAL

Distances: 180 miles east of Guatemala City; 62 miles northwest of Puerto Barrios; 56 miles north of Quiriguá.

GETTING THERE   By Bus   Buses bound for Flores leave Guatemala City from

17a Calle 8-46, Zona 1 (tel. 513-817), at 1, 2, 3, and 7am and 11pm, stopping in Río Dulce about 5 hours later.

By Car   The turnoff for Río Dulce is just past the town of Morales.

DEPARTING   Warning: If you plan to proceed from Río Dulce to Flores by bus, be aware that you are very unlikely to get a seat on the bus when it arrives in Río Dulce. In fact many people (usually backpacking travelers) end up riding on the roof because there isn't any standing room on the bus. The road from Río Dulce to Flores is one of the worst in the country, and the trip is very uncomfortable even if you have a seat. If you want to be sure of getting a seat on the bus, you may have to go back to Guatemala City.

ESSENTIALS Orientation   The town of Río Dulce is little more than a cluster of market stalls and shops, located at the foot of the toll bridge over the river at the mouth of Lake Izabal. The road to Castillo de San Felipe is a narrow muddy lane to the left after you cross the bridge. Boats for Lívingston can be hired at the docks to the right after you cross the bridge.

Thirty miles northwest of the Atlantic Highway lie Lake Izabal and the Río Dulce, which connects the lake with the Gulf of Honduras and the Caribbean Sea. The lake and its jungle-and-forest setting are quite beautiful, but swimming is not recommended in the beaches near the road because the water's not very clean. It's very good for powerboating, however, and on weekends the wealthy citizens of the capital come to the lake and exercise the glittering craft stored on the shore. The lake was famous as a refuge for pirates in days gone by, and its entrance was protected by the picturesque fortress called the Castillo de San Felipe, on the northern shore, a 4-kilometer walk from the bridge. Today, most people who come to the lake, if not out for the boating, are on their way to Tikal by road.

WHAT TO SEE AND DO

CASTILLO DE SAN FELIPE

Ask down at the docks to find a boatman who's willing to ferry you to the Castillo de San Felipe. The minimum for a trip is two fares, and the boatman will rarely rush you to get through the castle. Plan to spend about a half hour there, about two hours for the entire trip.

The castle was built in the 1600s by the Spaniards to keep pirates out of Lake Izabal, which was being used as a shipping point for gold that had been collected by the conquistadores. Restored in the 1950s, the fort is the only one of its kind in Guatemala. It is in a beautiful, tranquil setting on the banks of the lake, with palm trees waving in the breezes and clouds billowing overhead. You're likely to be the only visitors to the fort and can play at fighting off marauding pirates as you wander through the maze of damp chambers that comprise the fort.

A TRIP DOWN THE RÍO DULCE

Another boat trip that you can make is down the Río Dulce to Lívingston or Puerto Barrios. The trip will take between two and three hours. You first travel past luxurious vacation homes on the shores of El Golfete, another large lake that begins at the bridge. Then, as you travel farther from the bridge, the houses disappear, and all you see are distant forested mountains. At the far end of El Golfete, the river narrows and passes between steep cliffs. Here and there along this section of the river are tiny huts that are the homes of local families who fish the river by night. The river is still their only link with the outside world, and you have a sense of being far from civilization as you motor past their simple huts.

An added bonus of going downriver is a chance to visit the Chocon Machacas

Manatee Preserve. You aren't likely to see any manatees because of the motor on the boat, but there is a short trail through the forest where you are likely to see leaf-cutter ants, pacas (small rabbitlike rodents), and lots of birds.

Every Tuesday and Friday at 6am, a mail boat leaves Río Dulce for Lívingston. The cost is only Q36 ($9). If you want to hire a boat to take you down to Lívingston, expect to pay around Q100 to Q125 ($25 to $31.25) for the boat, which will carry four to six people. The mail boat returns from Lívingston on Tuesday and Friday at 11am. It's best to be on hand at least half an hour early to be sure that you get a seat. In Río Dulce the mail boat leaves from the north side of the bridge. The mail boat may stop at the manatee preserve for an extra Q4 ($1). If you hire a boat, be sure to say that you want to stop at the preserve.

WHERE TO STAY AND EAT

Although there are a couple of small hotels near the bridge, your best low-budget choice in the area is out by the Castillo. You can hire a boat to take you there, or you can walk or drive the 4-kilometer road.

HOTEL DON HUMBERTO, Río Dulce. No phone. 11 rms., all with bath.
$ Rates: Q11 ($2.75) single; Q15 ($3.75) double; Q19 ($4.75) triple. No credit cards.

A five-minute walk down a quiet path from the Castillo de San Felipe is this tranquil little budget hotel. This neighborhood was once the haunt of pirates, but today it is primarily given over to vacation homes for the wealthy of Guatemala City. The location is very quiet, and the park surrounding the Castillo is very pretty. If you want to get away from it all and not spend much money, this would be a great place to do it. The rooms are very basic but have private baths (showers). The hotel even has its own little dock down on the lake shore, which is only about 100 yards away.

The open-air restaurant serves meals from 7am to 8pm.

WORTH THE EXTRA BUCKS

HOTEL IZABAL TROPICAL, Costado, Castillo de San Felipe, Lago de Izabal. Tel. 502/0478-401. In Guatemala City, tel. 502/357-902. 12 rms., all with bath.
$ Rates: Q100–Q160 ($25–$40) single; Q120–Q168 ($30–$42) double; Q136–Q188 ($34–$47) triple; Q160–Q208 ($40–$52) quad. AE, DC, MC, V.

A former Peace Corps volunteer clued me in to this great deal, located very close to the Hotel Don Humberto and reached by taking the dirt road to the left shortly after you cross the bridge over the Río Dulce. Follow the signs even though they lead you down an increasingly rugged road. Eventually, after about 2½ miles, you will reach the hotel. It's built on the edge of the lake and is very popular with boaters. Thatch bungalows with bamboo walls look out over the water. The grounds are neatly manicured, with colorful tropical flowers in bloom year round. By the two swimming pools (one for adults, one for children), there are thatched sunshades to save your skin from getting too burned. Beside the piers is a circular thatched-roof bar where rock music blares and young people gather.

Slightly higher than the bar is a circular open-air dining room that is much more sedate. You can enjoy spectacular views across the lake to the mountains in the distance while savoring delicious international meals at prices that range from Q15 to Q30 ($3.75 to $7.50).

7. LÍVINGSTON AND PUERTO BARRIOS

Distances: 185 miles east of Guatemala City; 67 miles
east of Quiriguá; 62 miles southeast of Río Dulce.

GETTING THERE   By Bus   Buses leave Guatemala City from 15a Calle 10-42,

Zona 1 (tel. 27-578), every hour on the hour from 6am to 5pm. Duration: 6 hours. Fare: Q9 ($2.25) regular or Q11 ($2.75) express.

By Car   Puerto Barrios is at the end of the Atlantic Highway. From here, it is necessary to take a boat to Lívingston.

By Boat   The only way to get to Lívingston is by boat, either from Puerto Barrios or from Río Dulce. From Puerto Barrios, the ferry takes about 1½ hours, leaving daily at 10am and 5pm and returning daily at 5am and 2pm. The one-way fare is Q4 ($1). For Q8 to Q10 ($2 to $2.50), you can take a fast launch that will get you there in about half the time. These small boats leave only when they are full, so you might have to wait for a while. If you don't feel like waiting or have a group, you can simply charter one of these boats for a little more than you would otherwise pay. This is also a good way to get back from Lívingston. Since boatmen who live in Puerto Barrios often have to head home without passengers, they're much more willing to carry you for your price. Bargain hard.

See the Río Dulce section for information on boats between Lívingston and Río Dulce.

DEPARTING   The ferry from Lívingston to Puerto Barrios leaves at 5am and 2pm daily. Duration: 1½ hours. Fare: Q4 ($1).

Buses for Guatemala leave hourly from 6a Avenida between 9a and 10a Calles. Duration: 6 hours. Fare: Q9 ($2.25) regular or Q11 ($2.75) express.

A passenger ferry leaves on Tuesday and Friday at 8:30am for Punta Gorda in southern Belize. Duration: 3 hours. Fare: Q20 ($5). Be sure to get your passport stamped with an exit stamp before getting on the boat. You can get tickets and your exit stamp at the end of Calle 9 near the ferry docks in Puerto Barrios. This boat also stops in Lívingston before continuing on to Belize, though only a limited number of tickets are sold for the Lívingston to Punta Gorda leg of the voyage.

The mail boat leaves Lívingston every Tuesday and Friday at 11am. Duration: 3 hours. Fare: Q36 ($9). You can also hire a boat to take you up river. The going rate is around Q100 to Q125 ($25 to $31.25).

ESSENTIALS   Orientation   Puerto Barrios is laid out in a grid similar to those used throughout Guatemala. Calles run toward the water, with the ferry to Lívingston located at the end of 12a Calle. The post office is at the corner of 3a Avenida and 7a Calle. The Guatel office is at 10a Calle and 8a Avenida.

On the Bahía de Amatique, at the end of the Atlantic Highway, are several towns and settlements that are mostly devoted to shipping bananas and entertaining the workmen, navvies, and sailors who do the shipping. Puerto Barrios and Santo Tomas de Castilla (also called Matias de Galvez) are port towns next door to one another—Barrios being the original town and Santo Tomas the new planned port. There's not much to do here unless you're into studying the shipment of bananas, but across the mouth of the Río Dulce is a different sort of place.

Lívingston, on the easternmost tip of the Río Dulce's northern bank, is a world unto itself, somewhat difficult to reach, primitive, and quiet. Like parts of neighboring Belize, it is friendly and informal to the utmost degree, very Caribbean, and, well, just very comfortable, although it has few of the "modern" comforts. There is little to "do" in Lívingston except swim, sunbathe, explore the tropical surroundings by boat or on foot, read, talk, and get to know the people. Somehow these activities will quickly become all you'll want to do, and every day will be deliciously half-full of activity and half-full of just taking it easy.

WHERE TO STAY AND EAT

There aren't too many recommendable places to stay in Lívingston. In fact, I don't care for Lívingston at all, even though there are many young travelers who think that it's great. I suggest that you stay in Puerto Barrios and visit Lívingston as a day trip.

PUERTO BARRIOS
Doubles for Less Than Q40 [$10]

HOTEL DEL NORTE, 7a Calle and 1a Avenida, Puerto Barrios. Tel. 502/048-0087. 29 rms.

$ Rates: Q12–Q24 ($3–$6) single; Q20–Q36 ($5–$9) double; Q28–Q50 ($7–$12.50) triple; Q60 ($15) quad. No credit cards.

My favorite place to stay in Puerto Barrios is this Caribbean classic, which will transport you into a Hemingway frame of mind. The huge cream-colored wooden building with green trim is right on the water, and long wide verandas stretch the length of the building on both floors. You can sit out here and sip a beer and watch the banana boats sail away for northern ports. Inside, the high ceilings and the wide hallways help to keep the old building cool in the summer. The rooms, however, are small, with twin beds, but the high ceilings make them seem much larger than they really are.

The dining room has a very old-fashioned air about it, with a huge old sideboard taking up most of one wall. Here you'll find a variety of seafoods, including lobster for Q25 ($6.25) per pound. Other seafood meals range from Q12 to Q20 ($3 to $5). There's also a bar where you can relax in a leather chair and sip a tropical cocktail.

HOTEL EL REFORMADOR, 16a Calle and 7a Avenida no. 159, Puerto Barrios, Izabal. Tel. 502/048-0533 or 048-1531. 36 rms., all with bath.

$ Rates: Q20–Q45 ($5–$11.25) single; Q40 ($10) double; Q55 ($13.75) triple; Q80 ($20) quad. No credit cards.

In a very modern building near the center of town, the Reformador is just off the main road as you come into town from Guatemala City. The guest rooms are built around two small, sunny courtyards full of potted plants. There are rooms with air conditioning, but the showers have cold water only, so you're better off sticking to a fan and saving some money. Some of the rooms even have TVs (you have your choice of black-and-white or color, but either one costs extra).

The small restaurant on the second floor gets a lot of sunlight and serves meals that range from Q6 to Q12 ($1.50 to $3).

DOUBLES FOR LESS THAN Q100 [$25]

HOTEL HENRY BERRISFORD, 9a Avenida and 17a Calle, Puerto Barrios, Izabal. Tel. 502/048-1557 or 048-1030. In Guatemala City, Avenida La Reforma 1-64, Zona 9, Guatemala City. Tel. 502/317-866 or 317-858. 32 rms., all with bath. A/C TV

$ Rates: Q60 ($15) single; Q80 ($20) double; Q100 ($25) triple; Q130 ($32.50) quad. No credit cards.

About a block away from the Reformador is this slightly nicer hotel that is still very reasonably priced. The three-story cement building is not very attractive, even though a balcony surrounds most of the second and third floors. However, in back of the main building, you'll find an unusual covered recreation area that includes two pools, a bar, arcade games, and, of all things to find in this sweltering climate, a hot tub. The rooms here are comfortable, and most have large windows so that they get plenty of sunlight. If you want a hot shower (rarely necessary around here), you'll have to ask for one of the rooms with hot water.

The hotel's restaurant serves international, Guatemalan, and Caribbean meals at reasonable prices.

LÍVINGSTON
Doubles for Less Than Q20 [$5]

HOTEL CARIBE, Lívingston, Izabal. Tel. 502/048-1073. 27 rms., none with bath.

$ Rates: Q6 ($1.50) single; Q12 ($3) double; Q18 ($4.50) triple; Q24 ($6) quad. No credit cards.

One of the better budget choices in Lívingston, the Caribe is up the street to the left when you get off the ferry from Puerto Barrios. The two-story building is set into a shady hillside on the water, and if you get a room at the back, you can listen to the waves lapping on the beach. The rooms are very basic, with twin beds. The bathrooms (cold water only) are down the hall and are kept tolerably clean.

HOTEL RÍO DULCE, Calle Central just up the hill from the main dock, Lívingston. Tel. 502/481-059. 13 rms., none with bath.

$ Rates: Q10 ($2.50) single; Q20 ($5) double. No credit cards.

This hotel's building is a classic example of Caribbean architecture—a pale-blue wood-frame house with a white picket fence and a big front porch. Around back are some thatch-roofed huts to further the tropical ambience. Hammocks under the palm trees and hibiscuses blooming in the yard complete the scene. This is a backpackers' favorite in Lívingston, even though the rooms are small and very basic, with shared cold-water showers—just as you'd expect.

Worth the Extra Bucks

HOTEL TUCAN DUGU, Lívingston, Izabal. In Guatemala City, 11a Calle 2-72, Zona 9, Guatemala City. Tel. 502/318-681, 314-279, or 322-813. 36 rms., 5 suites, 4 bungalows, all with bath.

$ Rates: Q160 ($40) single; Q175 ($43.75) double; Q250 ($62.50) triple; Q300 ($75) quad. DC, MC, V.

Although most accommodations in Lívingston are what you might anticipate based on the Caribbean life-style, the Tucan Dugu is quite different. This is Guatemala's only resort on the Caribbean Coast. Modern but still definitely Caribbean in style, it has many conveniences and comforts, including a swimming pool and two restaurants. You'll see the hotel on a low hill beside the ferry dock as your boat pulls into town. The two-story white building has a thatch-covered roof to give it a properly rustic appeal. The Tucan Dugu offers three types of rooms: standard, suite, and bungalow. My favorites are the bungalows, even though these are the only rooms that don't have hot water. They are built into the hillside below the main building and are reached by wooden stairs and elevated walkways. You can sit on your porch or balcony no matter which type of room you choose and gaze off across the Gulf of Honduras.

Dining: There are two restaurants here, one serving deluxe breakfasts and elegant seafood dinners. This circular dining room has a high thatched roof and louvered windows that leave no doubt that you are in the tropics. The other restaurant is less expensive and more casual, located in the bar adjacent to the swimming pool.

Services: Scuba diving, water skiing, sailboarding, sailing, boating, and sportfishing in both fresh water and salt water.

Facility: Swimming pool.

CHAPTER 13

THE PACIFIC HIGHWAY

1. RETALHULEU
- **WHAT'S SPECIAL ABOUT THE PACIFIC HIGHWAY**

2. LA DEMOCRACIA

3. LAKE AMATITLÁN

The Pacific Highway (Carretera al Pacífico) will be of little interest to you unless you're en route to or from Mexico by car or bus. The towns of the region are primarily agricultural and industrial centers, but they make good rest stops if you're driving. In fact, many of the hotels along this route have swimming pools and cater to middle-class Guatemalans from the cool highlands, who come down to this sweltering coastal region to soak up a little warmth. If you're passing through on a weekend, don't be surprised if all the rooms are taken.

Few people head straight for Guatemala City; instead they head up into the mountains as soon as possible to Quetzaltenango, Lake Atitlán, or Antigua. There are several roads up from the lowlands to these mountain towns, although the main route is the road up to Quetzaltenango.

---

1. RETALHULEU

Distances: 113 miles west of Guatemala City; 32 miles south of Quetzaltenango; 75 miles east of Tapachula, Mexico.

GETTING THERE   By Bus   A bus from the Mexican border into town takes about an hour and will cost about Q1 (25¢). Buses bound from Guatemala City to the Mexican border at either Tecun Umán or El Carmen stop at Retalhuleu en route. Galgos, 7a Avenida 19-44, Zona 1 (tel. 23-661), has departures at 5:45 and 10am, noon, and 3:30 and 5:30pm. Duration: 4 hours. Fare: Q6 ($1.50). Fortaleza, 19 Calle 8-70, Zona 1 (tel. 717-994), has departures at 5:30 and 9:30am for about the same price.

By Car   You can cross the border at either El Carmen or Tecun Umán. From Tecun Umán it is about 50 miles on the highway; from El Carmen it is about 19 miles to the intersection with the highway from Tecun Umán, where you turn left for Retalhuleu.

DEPARTING   There are several buses a day from Retalhuleu to Guatemala City. The Pacific Highway itself bears right at the Quetzaltenango junction and heads out to Mazatenango, a bustling farm and industrial town right astride the highway with lots of activity. From there the highway goes up hill and down through sugarcane fields and by little fincas (farms or plantations). Every now and then an exceptionally beautiful ceiba tree will catch your eye, huge and of fine proportion, its blade-like buttress roots standing as much as 20 feet high at the base.

Buses for the border leave regularly throughout the day.

ESSENTIALS   Orientation   The town of Retalhuleu is a couple of miles off the highway, but there are two hotels right on the highway that are better than those in town.

WHAT'S SPECIAL ABOUT THE PACIFIC HIGHWAY

Natural Spectacles

☐ Lake Amatitlán, almost as beautiful as the larger Lake Atitlán.

Monuments

☐ The town of La Democracia, with several huge carved-stone heads that predate the Mayas

---

Retalhuleu is a quiet small town with little to recommend it other than a number of acceptable hotels that are the best for some miles around. The three downtown hotel choices are close to the pretty main square in front of the church.

WHAT TO SEE AND DO

Just 3 miles out of town is the junction with the toll road to Quetzaltenango, an exciting drive that winds up 2 miles in altitude in only an hour's time. The road is good, and the scenery is exceptional: Four of the highest volcanoes in Guatemala flank the macadam strip, two on either side. At the cloth-weaving town of Zunil, there's a turnoff to the famous hot springs at Georgina, which are up the side of a volcano on a rough dirt road (see the Quetzaltenango section for details).

You can catch either a direct Retalhuleu-Quetzaltenango bus or an eastbound bus to the Quetzaltenango junction and wait there for a bus up into the mountains.

WHERE TO STAY AND EAT

If you've just driven in from Mexico, Retalhuleu is a good introduction to the types of accommodations available throughout Guatemala. Prices on the whole are lower here than in Mexico, and you tend to get more for your money. If you don't want to drive into Retalhuleu proper, you can stay at a motel on the highway. Otherwise, there are three choices downtown. Unfortunately, both of the highway hotels were full when I discovered them, so I cannot vouch for the cleanliness of the rooms. However, their surroundings were very nice, and they're certainly worth a look if you're in the area.

HOTEL SIBONEY, Cuatro Caminos, San Sebastián, Retalhuleu. Tel. 502/071-0149. 24 rms., all with bath. A/C TV TEL

$ Rates: Q58.20–Q76.05 ($14.55–$19) double away from pool; Q70.20–Q87.75 ($17.55–$24.95) double overlooking pool. AE, DC, MC, V.

This is the first hotel that you'll come to near Retalhuleu, on the left at the intersection leading into town. Large trees shade the parking area. The rooms come with two double beds and color cable TVs so that you can watch all your favorite shows.

There's a huge restaurant with screen walls that let in every least tropical breeze. Steaks and seafood are the specialties.

HOTEL "LA COLONIA," Km 178 Carretera al Pacífico, San Sebastián, Retalhuleu. Tel. 502/071-0038 or 071-0054). 46 rms., all with bath.

$ Rates: Q40.95 ($23.40) single; Q58.50 ($14.60) double; Q76.05 ($19) triple; Q93.60 ($23.40) quad. DC, MC, V.

Most of the rooms at this motel-style accommodation have air conditioning to help you beat the heat if the two pools aren't enough to cool you off.

The restaurant, which leans heavily toward steak and seafood, is open from 6am to 10pm.

HOTEL ASTOR, 5a Calle 4-60, Zona 1, Retalhuleu. Tel. 502/071-0475). 6 rms., 4 with bath.

$ Rates: Q28.10 ($7.03) double without bath, Q32 ($8) double with bath. No credit cards accepted.

This hotel is an old mansion in which the grand rooms have been split down the middle to make bedrooms for guests. Even so, the spaces are larger than those in most modern luxury hotels. The rooms are entered from a verdant courtyard surrounded by a colonnade.

A small dining room looks onto the courtyard, and meals here are very substantial. Breakfast is served from 7 to 9am; lunch is served from noon to 2pm; dinner is served from 7 to 9pm. A typical dinner might be delicious black beans, potatoes, filet steak smothered in onions and tomatoes, plus fried bananas and mangoes (from the tree out back) for dessert, for only Q18 ($4.50) per person.

HOTEL MODELO, 5a Calle 4-53, Zona 1, Retalhuleu. Tel. 071/0256. 7 rms., all with bath. TEL
$ Rates: Q15.20 ($3.80) single; Q30.40 ($7.60) double; Q45.60 ($11.40) triple; Q60.80 ($15.20) quad. No credit cards.

This small hotel is directly across the street from the Astor, and although it is not as atmospheric, it is still a good choice. All the rooms have private baths, and fans to help you sleep through the steamy nights. The rooms are set around a flowered courtyard, and all have hardwood floors and high ceilings. You might even find a small black-and-white TV in the room. Throughout the hotel there are framed huipiles (colorful blouses worn by Indian women) and contemporary paintings by local artists.

The small restaurant and bar are just off the tile-floored lobby. Offerings and prices are comparable to those at the Astor.

POSADA DE DON JOSÉ, 5a Calle 3-67, Zona 1, Retalhuleu. Tel. 502/ 071-0180 or 071-0841. 30 rms., all with bath. A/C, TEL.
$ Rates: Q36.27 ($9) single; Q58.50 ($14.60) double; Q74.88 ($18.70) triple; Q87.75 ($21.95) quad. AE, DC, V. **Parking:** Free.

A modern and luxurious downtown choice, the Don José is only a few blocks away from the Astor. This is the most comfortable downtown hotel, and you may feel that you owe it to yourself, after the arduous border crossing, to sit back and enjoy the air conditioning or the swimming pool. Try to get a room on the second floor overlooking the plaza. These rooms are quite large, and the view is pleasant.

2. LA DEMOCRACIA

Distances: 57 miles southwest of Guatemala City; 69 miles east of Retalhuleu; 45 miles southwest of Lake Amatitlán.

GETTING THERE By Bus In Guatemala City, Chatia Gomerana, Muelle Central, Terminal de Buses, Zona 4, has buses every 30 minutes from 6am to 6:30pm. Duration: 1½ hours. Fare: Q1.50 (38¢). You can also take a bus to Siquinalá and then get a local bus to La Democracia.

By Car If you're coming from the west on the Pacific Highway, turn right in Siquinalá. From Guatemala City, take the Carretera al Pacífico to Siquinalá and turn left.

DEPARTING You can catch a bus to Siquinalá and then transfer to a Guatemala City bus, or catch one of the less frequent buses that stop in La Democracia on their run from Sipacate to Guatemala City.

ESSENTIALS Orientation La Democracia is a tiny town. The road into town forks to the left off of the highway.

About 125 miles along this road from the border is the small town of Siquinalá. By its main plaza is a paved road that heads south to the coastal town of Sipacate, but long before you reach the coast—in fact, only 5 miles from Siquinalá—is the town of

La Democracia, famous for some strange boulder-sized Pre-Classic Mayan (sometimes called pre-Olmec) statues and artifacts found at a nearby farm, Finca Monte Alto. When you get to La Democracia, follow the signs for "El Museo." The museum is on the town's main square (two blocks east of the main road). The plaza is simple but has a pleasant cement gazebo built around a large ceiba tree, and several of the large stone sculptures decorate the square.

WHAT TO SEE AND DO

La Democracia Museum was built in 1967 to house the numerous objects found during excavations at Finca Monte Alto and the smaller fincas of Río Seco, La Gomera, and Ora Blanca. The museum (open Tuesday to Sunday from 9am to noon and 2 to 5pm; closed Monday and holidays) is not large, so you should be able to see everything in an hour or so. Unfortunately, organization and classification are not the museum's high points, so you'll see primitive pottery and terra-cotta figurines (mostly female); obsidian blades, spears, and knives; and curious zoomorphic jars all mixed together, the primitive with the sophisticated. Some of the figurines have elaborate headdresses similar to those found in Zapotec Monte Alban (Mexico). There are several stone "yokes" and stone replicas of mushrooms, which immediately suggest that hallucinogenic mushrooms and their replicas were used in ceremonies by these people.

Outside the museum, in front of it and in the plaza, are the great Buddha-like stone figures and heads carved from boulders—11 of these have been found to date. Just what they represent is a mystery: Similar crude carvings have been found in El Salvador and as far north as Chiapas in Mexico—but are they deities, chiefs, or local dignitaries? Professor Edwin Shook, who headed the excavations here from 1968 to 1970 under the auspices of the National Geographic Society and Harvard's Peabody Museum, says that they were made during the period from 300 B.C. to the birth of Christ. He maintains that they were carved by a Mayan people, not "pre-Olmecs" as many others thought; the Olmecs carved much more sophisticated heads, complete with headbands and ornaments, while these are really very crude images chipped out of the sides of boulders. His theory is that they were carved by a Pre-Classic Mayan people who settled at Monte Alto about 1000 B.C., reached the peak of their civilization from 300 B.C. to A.D. 1, and then declined by about A.D. 300. If this is so, these people would be very early Mayas, earlier than the people who settled at Tikal and Palenque, but so far no Mayan glyphs—which would be proof of their race—have been found at Monte Alto. Perhaps some will turn up, for found at Kaminal Juyú (in Guatemala City) were glyphs that predate those found at Tikal; therefore it's thought that Mayan hieroglyphic writing may have started here on the Pacific Slope and then progressed north and east to the Petén and Yucatán.

The town of La Democracia itself is not what I'd call wildly interesting, unless you're an anthropologist who loves sticky heat, so plan on a quick visit to the museum and the plaza and then a quick retreat to the mountains.

From Siquinalá it's only about 45 miles up into the mountains to Guatemala City. On the way you go through Esquintla, a largish town (flat, hot, and humid) with virtually nothing to recommend it, and later you pass near Lake Amatitlán, a popular haven with weekenders from the capital.

3. LAKE AMATITLÁN

Distances: 17 miles south of Guatemala City;
45 miles northeast of La Democracia.

GETTING THERE By Bus There are buses every 30 minutes from the Terminal de Buses in Zona 4 in Guatemala City. Duration: 30 minutes. Fare: Q1 (25¢).

By Car Take the Carretera al Pacífico south and watch for the turnoff to Lake Amatitlán.

DEPARTING Catch a bus from the public beach back into Guatemala City. They run every 30 minutes throughout the day.

ESSENTIALS Orientation The lake is 7½ by 2½ miles, with villas and vacation homes surrounding it. At the northwest end of the lake, near the highway, is one of the only public beaches on the lake.

Don't confuse this small lake with Lake Atitlán to the northwest; the latter is a spectacular sight, whereas this one, Lake Amatitlán, is not all that interesting. After exiting from the highway, bear left at the gas station, then left again at the *T*, then right down the wide, straight street to the lakefront.

WHAT TO SEE AND DO

The government has built a park here on the shore with little stone thatch-roofed changing cubicles, picnic tables, and the like. The swimming at this beach is not great because the water tends to be dirty, so your best bet for a dip would be either to walk along the road to the left past the villas and cottages to a rock outcrop or to rent a rowboat for an hour, row out a short distance, and swim. Near the entry road where you came in are various little restaurants and soft-drink stands that will do nicely for lunch. As for a hotel, the one that's here is more on the order of a thermal spa, not really suitable for one-night stays. As I said, the lake is mostly a place for denizens of the capital to cool off in for a day. Don't plan an extended stay.

You may notice several *balnearios* (warm spring swimming pools) in the area. This is an area of much geothermal activity. There are hot springs at various places around the edges of the lake, and even the bottom of the lake itself is filled with hot springs. Perhaps this is why the ancient Mayas of this region used the lake for making offerings to the gods. The soft, hot mud of the lake bottom has preserved most of these offerings, and divers continue to recover amazing terra-cotta pots and urns, many of which are on display at the Popol Vuh Museum in Guatemala City.

Warning: In recent years, pollution from Guatemala City has been contaminating this small lake. It is questionable whether you should swim here at all. Definitely do not eat any fish that was taken from the lake.

GLOSSARY OF GUATEMALAN TERMS
Archeological

Corbeled arch False arch used in construction of Mayan buildings
Stela(e) Stone with carved figures (usually of warriors, princes, or kings) and glyphs, erected as a record of a historic event
Pre-Classic Period Mayan period from 300 B.C. to A.D. 300
Early Classic Period Mayan period from A.D. 300 to 600
Late Classic Period Mayan period from A.D. 600 to 900
Post-Classic Period Mayan period from A.D. 900 to the Conquest

Music and Dance

Marimba Instrument related to the xylophone and also the music performed on this instrument—the most popular music in Guatemala
Palo Volador "Flying pole," an acrobatic performance that has been popular in Guatemala since Mayan times; men spin from ropes tied to their ankles as they descend from a tall pole

Religious

Anda Float carried in Holy Week processions
Cofrade Member of a cofradía
Cofradías Indian religious organizations that oversee various rituals in villages around the country.
Maximón Mayan god who is found in several towns around the highlands, dressed in

jacket, pants, and hat with a wooden mask for a face; Indians believe he answers their prayers

Pascual Abaj Another Mayan god whose shrine is on a hill near Chichicastenango

Menu Savvy

Cak ik Mayan stew made with turkey or chicken, plantains, and vegetables
Licuado Milk- or water-based drink made in a blender with fresh fruit
Pepian Thick stew made with chicken, vegetables, and pumpkin seeds
Plátanos Plantains, similar to bananas

PART THREE

BELIZE

CHAPTER 14

GETTING TO KNOW BELIZE

1. GEOGRAPHY, HISTORY, AND POLITICS

• WHAT'S SPECIAL ABOUT BELIZE

2. SOME CULTURAL NOTES

• DATELINE

3. FOOD AND DRINK

4. RECOMMENDED FILM AND RECORDINGS

If you learned your geography before 1973, you may never have even heard of this tiny country. Before that, Belize was known as British Honduras, a colony whose sole purpose was to supply hardwoods and other wood products throughout the British empire. Consequently, Belize is a Central American anomaly: It is an English-speaking nation surrounded by Spanish-speaking neighbors. With a population of only about 200,000 people, it is also the least-populated country in all Central America. The importance of this statistic is only now becoming significant as environmentalists discover the vast undisturbed wilderness of Belize, where jaguars still roam the jungle in search of tapirs and macaws still screech in the treetops. Add to this the dozens of tiny islands, known as cayes, set amid the world's second-longest barrier reef (which offers excellent diving and fishing opportunities) and a population that is more than 60% black Creoles and Garifunas (people of black and Indian ancestry), and you have what is ostensibly a Caribbean island nation on the Central American mainland. The most important British legacy left to Belize, however, is a stable political environment in a region of constant turmoil. To understand Belize, you have to go see it for yourself because, as the Belizeans say, "Seeing is Belizing!"

1. GEOGRAPHY, HISTORY, AND POLITICS

GEOGRAPHY

Belize is a narrow strip of land on the Caribbean Coast of Central America, located due south of Mexico's Yucatán Peninsula. It covers an area of 9,000 square miles, about the same size as the state of Massachusetts, and is bordered on the west and south by Guatemala and on the east by the Caribbean. Offshore from mainland Belize are hundreds of tiny islands, known as cayes (pronounced "keys"), that rise up from the world's second-longest barrier reef, which extends for more than 180 miles along the Belizean coast. From the wide, flat coastal plains, Belize rises up to mountain peaks of more than 3,000 feet, the source of the many rivers that wind through the country, which were for years the only means of transport within Belize.

THE REGIONS

THE CAYES Belize's offshore islands lie between the coast of the mainland and the protection of the 180-mile-long Barrier Reef. The reef, easily visible from many of the

WHAT'S SPECIAL ABOUT BELIZE

Beaches
- [ ] Placencia, the longest and best beach in Belize

Natural Spectacles
- [ ] The barrier reef off the coast of Belize, the second longest in the world
- [ ] The Blue Hole on the Hummingbird Highway, a sinkhole filled with clear water
- [ ] Mountain Pine Ridge, a forest reserve with waterfalls and caves

Zoo
- [ ] The Belize Zoo, small but with an extremely well-treated menagerie

Ancient Ruins
- [ ] Xunantunich, a Mayan pyramid that is still the tallest building in Belize
- [ ] Caracol, although not yet excavated, thought to be the largest Mayan city ever discovered

- [ ] Altun Ha Mayan ruins, with several excavated temples

Islands
- [ ] Dozens of small islands, known as cayes, off the coast of Belize, including Caye Caulker and Ambergris Caye, which have small hotels

Parks
- [ ] The Cockscomb Basin Wildlife Preserve, the only jaguar preserve in the world
- [ ] The Community Baboon Sanctuary, an unusual program in which local farmers help protect baboons

Activities
- [ ] Canoeing and horseback riding in the Cayo District
- [ ] Birdwatching anywhere in the country
- [ ] Scuba diving on the barrier reef

cayes, offers some of the world's most exciting snorkeling, diving (visibility is up to 200 feet), and fishing. The more developed cayes offer various day and overnight trips to explore this lively underwater world.

For those whose main sport is catching rays, not fish, it should be mentioned that the cayes, and Belize in general, lack wide, sandy beaches. Although the water is as warm and clear blue as it's touted to be, most of your sunbathing will be on docks or on deck chairs at a hotel's swimming pool.

Ambergris and Caulker are the most easily accessible cayes, but it is possible, for a price, to arrange visits to others: Caye Chapel, an exclusive resort with one luxury hotel; Half Moon Caye, whose beautiful beach (yes, a real beach) and lagoon appear on many of Belize's travel promotion posters; and St. George's Caye, site of the decisive 1798 battle between the British settlers and a Spanish invasion force.

You'll get more for your money on Caulker than on Ambergris, but if nightlife is what you're looking for, you won't find it on Caulker. Caulker is very laid-back, to say the least. It makes Ambergris Caye's San Pedro look like a teeming metropolis.

CAYO DISTRICT   This mountainous district near the Guatemalan border is rapidly becoming Belize's second most-popular destination. Here you'll find some of Belize's most beautiful countryside and most fascinating natural and artificial sights. The limestone mountains of this region have produced numerous caves, sinkholes, jagged peaks, and waterfalls. There are clear flowing rivers that are excellent for canoeing as well as mile after mile of unexplored forest full of wild animals. This was also the site of several major Mayan settlements more than 1,000 years ago. Caracol is said to be the largest Mayan city known, but it has not yet been fully excavated. Xunantunich is a smaller, but still impressive pyramid-and-temple complex not far from the town of San Ignacio.

HISTORY

Before the arrival of the first Europeans (shipwrecked English sailors), this was the land of the enigmatic Mayas. Although most people think of Mexico's Mayan cities in the Yucatán and Guatemala's Tikal when they hear the word "Mayas," recent discoveries suggest that what is today known as Belize was once the center of the Mayan empire. River and coastal trade routes connected dozens of cities and small towns throughout this region to the now better known and more frequently visited cities of Mexico and Guatemala. Caracol, a recently discovered city in the Cayo District of western Belize, is said to be the largest Mayan city yet discovered. Unfortunately, very little of this amazing discovery has been excavated or is likely to be excavated. The funding for massive restorations, such as those done at Tikal and Chichén Itzá, simply are not available.

Corozal Town, in northern Belize, is built on the site of the last Mayan city still occupied when this area was discovered by a Spanish expeditionary force in the 1530s. By the time those first unlucky sailors washed ashore, the Mayan civilization was a mere remnant of its former glory.

Belize likes to play up the fact that it was founded by pirates and buccaneers, and, indeed, these unsavory characters were some of the first to make this region their base of operations, but they were hardly a civilizing influence. By the mid-17th century, British loggers were settling along the coast and making their way up the rivers and streams in search of mahogany for shipbuilding and other types of wood for making dyes. When it formally became the colony of British Honduras in 1862, it was firmly established as a major source of wood for the still-expanding British empire. The forests were exploited, but agriculture was never encouraged. The British needed their colony to remain dependent on the mother country, so virtually all the necessities of life were imported. Few roads were built, and the country remained unexplored and undeveloped with a tiny population, mostly clustered along the coast.

During the 18th and 19th centuries, African slaves were brought to British Honduras, and black Caribs also migrated here from the Caribbean Islands. They established their own villages and culture along the coast. In the mid-19th century, many Mexican and Guatemalan refugees fled across the borders into British Honduras and founded such towns as Corozal Town and Benque Viejo.

In the early 1960s, groundwork was laid for granting British Honduras independence. However, based on 16th-century Spanish claims to all Central America, Guatemala claimed that the territory belonged to them. Fearful of an invasion by Guatemalan forces, the British delayed granting independence until an agreement could be reached with Guatemala. Although the 1964 constitution granted self-government to the British colony, it was not until September 21, 1981, that Belize, which had changed its name in

DATELINE

- **2000 B.C.–A.D. 1000** Mayan civilization flourishes.
- **1638** Shipwrecked English sailors establish the first European settlement.
- **1783** English settlement rights are recognized.
- **1786** Settlements become self-governing. British superintendent takes up residence.
- **1798** The last Spanish attack is beaten off by the British.
- **1859** The border between Guatemala and British Honduras is established.
- **1862** The area officially becomes the colony of British Honduras.
- **1931** Hurricane destroys Belize City.
- **1948** Guatemala, laying claim to British Honduras, closes border.
- **1957** First Mennonite farmers arrive from Mexico.
- **1964** The new constitution provides for self-government, but Guatemalan claims to the country delays independence.
- **1973** British Honduras renamed Belize.
- **1981** Belize becomes an independent.

1973, actually gained its independence. Due to continuing hostility between Guatemala and Belize, the British maintain a protective force in Belize. Fortunately, the mere threat of having to do battle with the British has deterred Guatemala from acting on its claim. Thus Belize is Central America's newest nation.

POLITICS

The British legacy in Belize is a stable government with a parliamentary system with regular elections that are contested by two major parties and several smaller parties. The country's small newspapers are mouthpieces for the various parties and frequently filled with stories disparaging the actions of the other parties. They make fun reading.

2. SOME CULTURAL NOTES

Art and Architecture Belize was set up as a colony to provide wood and wood products to the British empire. With its tiny population and isolation from the outside world, it did not develop any outstanding artists, writers, or architects. There are only one or two tiny natural history museums in the country and the same number of colonial buildings of any interest in Belize City. Clapboard houses built on stilts were typical and quite a few of these buildings, often painted in the pastel colors that are so popular throughout the Caribbean, remain in small towns. There are, however, a number of excavated Mayan ruins scattered around the countryside. Xunantunich, near the town of San Ignacio, is a pyramid that is still the tallest artificial structure in the country.

People Modern Belize (pop. 200,000) is a very unlikely mixture of peoples and cultures: Although the descendants of the Maya still populate the western and southern jungle areas, the majority of Belizeans are black Caribs or Creoles, descendants of slaves shipwrecked in transit from Africa, who established their own African-type culture in the Caribbean. The first Europeans to settle in Belize were pirates turned loggers, but today they have been joined by Britons and North Americans, Chinese, Lebanese, and the adherents of a German Protestant sect, called Mennonites. All these people live in apparent harmony and mutual respect, divided by no great differences in wealth or power. English is the official language of the country, but Indian languages, Spanish, German, Arabic, Chinese, and Creole patois also are spoken depending on the district.

Nightlife Evening entertainment is limited. There are only a handful of movie theaters in the country. Bars, which occasionally have live bands are about the extent of the nightlife scene in Belize.

Sports and Recreation Soccer is the national sport, but the two most popular recreational activities are scuba diving and sportfishing. Belize has the best of both. The offshore coral reef is the second-longest barrier reef in the world, while the waters, both offshore and inland, teem with such popular gamefish as tarpon, snook, bonefish, barracuda, and snapper. Many companies in Belize offer fishing and diving trips.

3. FOOD AND DRINK

FOOD

Don't expect gourmet food during your visit to Belize. Even the most basic meals in restaurants are much more expensive than they would be in Guatemala or Mexico. Belize has little in the way of its own cuisine, so you'll find burgers, pizzas, fried fish, and Chinese food—and, if you look hard, even a little local food. Because Belize only recently began to grow its own beef and crops, the country relied for a long time on wild game. A favorite is gibnut, a large forest rodent that looks like a cross between a rat and a deer. Another popular wild animal found prepared in restaurants is the sea turtle, endangered all over the world, including in Belize. It's not yet illegal to sell sea turtle within Belize, but international agreements prohibit its export. Please don't order gibnut, turtle steak, or other wild game. Belize is struggling to preserve its natural environment, and as long as people order wild game, it will show up on menus.

Belize has also been a major exporter of lobster for many years, but overfishing has caused the population to decline. It is still available and quite inexpensive, but there is a season on lobster. Please do not order lobster between March 15 and July 15.

DRINKS
WATER AND SOFT DRINKS

Much of the drinking water in Belize is rainwater. People use the roof of their house to collect water in a cistern which supplies them for the year. Always ask for drinking water at your hotel. Tap water generally is not considered safe to drink. Most major brands of soft drinks are available. Also popular in Belize are fresh lime juice and fresh orange juice.

BEER, WINE, AND LIQUOR

Belikin beer and Belikin stout are local beers, but a few other imported brands also are available. Several commercially bottled fruit wines are produced in Belize using native fruits. These wines are very sweet and are more a novelty than anything else. In remote parts of the country, you'll find homemade fruit wines that are a bit like hard cider. Most restaurants serve mixed drinks, with a variety of domestic and imported liquors available.

4. RECOMMENDED FILM AND RECORDINGS

Although it didn't do very well at the box office, you might want to watch a video of *The Mosquito Coast,* which was filmed in Belize. If you're taken by the pounding beat of soca music (a Caribbean music akin to calypso) and Belize's own punta rock (a kind of reggae-rock fusion), you can pick up cassette tapes in Belize City.

CHAPTER 15

PLANNING A TRIP TO BELIZE

1. INFORMATION, ENTRY REQUIREMENTS, AND MONEY

- **WHAT THINGS COST IN BELIZE**

2. WHEN TO GO—CLIMATE AND HOLIDAYS

3. HEALTH, INSURANCE, AND OTHER CONCERNS

4. WHAT TO PACK

5. TIPS FOR THE DISABLED, SENIORS, SINGLES, AND STUDENTS

6. ALTERNATIVE/ ADVENTURE TRAVEL

7. GETTING THERE

- **DID YOU KNOW . . . ?**

8. SUGGESTED ITINERARIES

9. GETTING AROUND

10. WHERE TO STAY

11. ENJOYING BELIZE ON A BUDGET

- **FAST FACTS— BELIZE**

More and more intrepid explorers are discovering Belize's natural and historic wonders: bird, monkey, and jaguar sanctuaries; Mayan ruins; mahogany forests; and huge limestone caves. The interior does not give itself up easily, though, and that's why it has remained so special and undeveloped. However, most people who visit Belize are still headed to the cayes (islands) off the coast for deep-sea fishing or scuba diving (marvelous but very expensive). Belize is probably the most expensive country in Central America, but there are still bargains to be had. There are no sprawling resort hotels that you find in other places in the Caribbean; instead, you'll find small hotels (some with as few as five or ten rooms). Unfortunately, many of these small hotels are overpriced for what you get. In the past few years, the tourist influx to Belize has outstripped the availability of accommodations— consequently prices have risen. This book will help you to find the best deals in Belize, whether they are on rooms, meals, car rentals, or tours.

1. INFORMATION, ENTRY REQUIREMENTS, AND MONEY

SOURCES OF INFORMATION

The **Belize Tourist Board,** 15 Penn Plaza, 415 Seventh Ave., 18th floor, New York, NY 10001 (tel. 212/268-8798, or toll free 800/624-0686; Fax 212/695-3018) will send you a package of information about the country. You can also contact the **Belize Tourist Bureau,** 53 Regent St., P.O. Box 325, Belize City (tel. 501/02-77213)—open Monday to Friday from 8am to noon and 1 to 5pm. Whether your interest is pirate lore or bird identification, you'll find books of interest in the shops on Ambergris Caye.

ENTRY REQUIREMENTS

You need a valid passport to enter Belize. No visa is required for U.S. or Commonwealth citizens. When entering, you will be asked how long you plan to stay. Whatever you say is what gets stamped in your passport. Be sure to say that you're staying longer than you actually plan, just in case you want to.

MONEY

The unit of currency in Belize is the Belizean dollar, abbreviated B$. Denominations of B$1, B$5, B$10, B$20, B$50, and B$100 are available. Coins come in 1B¢, 5B¢, 10B¢, and 25B¢ denominations. On the black market, $1 U.S. equals B$2. The B$–Mexican peso rate fluctuates greatly, and those with pesos are always at a disadvantage. Although it is officially illegal, the black market is where everyone changes money because the banks charge a 2% commission. Never change money with someone who approaches you on the street. Always ask at your hotel where you can change money. If they can't make the transaction themselves, they'll tell you who will.

CURRENCY EXCHANGE CHART

B$	$
1	.50
2	1.00
3	1.50
4	2.00
5	2.50
6	3.00
7	3.50
8	4.00
9	4.50
10	5.00
50	25.00
100	50.00

WHAT THINGS COST IN BELIZE   U.S. $

Taxi from the airport to the city center	12.50
Local telephone call	0.50
Double at Ramon's Reef Hotel (deluxe)	100.00
Double at Barrier Reef Hotel (moderate)	60.00
Double at Rubie's Hotel (budget)	20.00
Lunch for one at Elvi's Kitchen (moderate)	6.00
Lunch for one at The Pizza Place (budget)	4.00
Dinner for one, without wine at Paradise Hotel (deluxe)	30.00
Dinner for one, without wine at Lily's (moderate)	12.50
Dinner for one, without wine at Marino's (budget)	7.00
Bottle of beer	1.00
Coca-Cola	0.50
Cup of coffee	0.75
Roll of ASA 100 Kodacolor film, 36 exposures	8.50
Admission to the Xunantunich ruins	1.50

2. WHEN TO GO — CLIMATE AND HOLIDAYS

CLIMATE

The climate of Belize is very similar to that of southern Florida. In the summer months, it is very hot (temperatures in the shade approach 100°F), with rain almost daily from June to December. The amount of rainfall varies considerably with the regions. In the south, there may be more than 150 inches per year, while in the north there is rarely more than 50 inches per year. The dry season extends from January to May, with temperatures dipping down as low as 40°F in the mountains of the Cayo District. There is also a brief dry period in August. Although temperatures on the coast can climb quite high in the summer, the constant tradewinds offer a bit of relief.

HOLIDAYS

Official holidays in Belize include January 1, New Year's Day; March 9, Baron Bliss Day; Good Friday, Holy Saturday, Easter Monday; May 1, Labor Day; May 24, Commonwealth Day; September 10, St. George's Caye Day; September 21, Independence Day; October 12, Columbus Day; November 19, Garifuna Settlement Day; December 25, Christmas; December 26, Boxing Day; December 31, New Year's Eve.

3. HEALTH, INSURANCE, AND OTHER CONCERNS

See Chapter 2, "Planning a Trip to Costa Rica," for information.

4. WHAT TO PACK

See Chapter 2, "Planning a Trip to Costa Rica," for information on what to pack. In addition, bring a bathing suit and plenty of sunscreen. If you have your own snorkeling or scuba-diving equipment, you should bring this as well.

5. TIPS FOR THE DISABLED, SENIORS, SINGLES, AND STUDENTS

For the Disabled Few streets in Belize have sidewalks, and on the cayes there are really no streets at all, only sandy lanes and paths. Consequently, disabled visitors to Belize have a difficult time.

For Seniors Don't expect to find senior-citizen discounts here. The tourism industry is still a fledgling in Belize, and seniors are treated the same as anyone else. But you may be able to save 10% on your airline ticket; Continental was offering a senior-citizen discount at the time of this writing. If you don't think you have the energy required for a visit to a jungle lodge, think again. The jungle lodges of Belize offer a wide variety of activities that people of all ages will find enjoyable. You're never too old to explore the jungles!

For Singles   As in most places, the single traveler is at a disadvantage in Belize. Single-room rates are usually higher than what each person would pay in a double room. Some hotels do have single rooms, though. These usually do not have private baths and are generally quite small, but if you don't plan to spend much time in your room, you can save money with one of these. In San Ignacio, Eva's Restaurant serves as a meeting ground for lone travelers seeking other adventurers to help cut the cost of taxis, canoe rentals, and tour rates. Tell Bob behind the counter what you're interested in doing, and he'll do his best to find you some like-minded folks willing to split the cost.

For Students   Check with the airlines when purchasing a ticket; there are sometimes special fares for students.

6. ALTERNATIVE/ADVENTURE TRAVEL

NATURAL HISTORY TOURS

Much of Belize is still unspoiled forest inhabited by hundreds of species of birds and rare animals, including the world's largest population of jaguars. There are several tour companies that operate natural history tours to Belize. These trips usually include visits to wildlife preserves, hikes in the jungle, bird-watching visits to Mayan ruins, and, just to balance things out, spending a few days on the beach. **Great Trips,** 1616 W. 139th St., Burnsville, MN 55337 (tel. 612/890-4405, or toll free 800/552-3419; Fax 612/894-9862), offers several different tours. **International Expeditions,** 1776 Independence Court, Birmingham, AL 35216 (tel. 205/870-5550, or toll free 800/633-4734), and **Sea & Explore,** 1809 Carol Sue Ave., Suite E, Gretna, LA 70056 (tel. 504/366-9985, or toll free 800/345-9786; Fax 504/366-9986), also operate similar nature tours to Belize.

If you're a member of the Sierra Club, Smithsonian Institution, or Audubon Society, you might look into their programs—all three offer annual trips to Belize.

7. GETTING THERE

BY PLANE

Even though it is only two hours by air from Miami, Belize is expensive to reach—one reason it has not yet been overdeveloped. Daily flights to Belize City run from New York, Los Angeles, Miami, Houston, and New Orleans, with additional flights from Mexico City, Cancún, Guatemala City, and Tikal. Carriers flying from the United States include **TACA** (tel. toll free 800/535-8780), **Tan Sahsa** (tel. toll free 800/327-1225), **Continental** (tel. toll free 800/231-0856), and **American** (tel. toll free 800/433-7300). **Aerovias** (tel. 305/883-1345), a small Guatemalan airline, has flights from Guatemala City or Tikal. **Tropic Air** (in Belize, tel. 501/26-2012) and **Aerocaribe** (in Cancún, tel. 988-42133), two Belizean airlines operating small planes, now offer service from Cancún to Belize City.

BEST FOR THE BUDGET

The lowest scheduled airfare is advance purchase or APEX, which carries restrictions on day of departure, length of stay, date of purchase, and penalties for changed schedules. At the time of this writing, Continental and American Airlines were offering the lowest fares to Belize—round-trip APEX fares, for maximum 30-day stays at around $530. Since bucket shops, selling discounted air tickets, have not yet begun selling Belize tickets, these prices are about the lowest you'll find. Remember: If you're a senior citizen, check to see if you can get a discount.

The other low-cost option is to fly to Cancún and then travel by bus or air (two Belizean airlines now fly between Belize City and Cancún) to Belize.

REGULAR AIRFARES

At the time of this writing, the regular airfares, which have no restrictions, on Continental Airlines (for example) were $712 in coach and $1,200 in first class.

BY BUS

There are only two land routes into Belize—from Chetumal, Mexico, and from Santa Elena, Guatemala. Both routes offer daily service, although the road from Guatemala can become impassable in the rainy season. Buses from Mexico cross the border and proceed into Corozal Town. From Corozal Town, you can catch a bus to Belize City or fly to San Pedro on Ambergris Caye.

Buses from Guatemala drop passengers in Melchor de Mencos at the bridge that separates Guatemala and Belize. You must then cross the bridge and catch a Belizean bus or take a taxi. The first town in Belize is Benque Viejo, which has few services or accommodations and is less than a mile from the border. Your best bet is to continue another 8 miles into San Ignacio by either bus or taxi. If you arrive early in the day, you can share a taxi for only B$4 ($2); otherwise, you'll have to pay about B$30 to hire a taxi to San Ignacio. The bus from the border to San Ignacio is B$1 (50¢). From San Ignacio, you can catch a bus to Belize City.

See "By Car" below for details on crossing the border.

BY CAR

If you're driving from Chetumal, you must hand in your Mexican Tourist Card (and/or car papers, if you have them) at the Mexican border station. You'll be issued new ones if you re-enter Mexico. The official may ask you to pay an "exit tax." There is no such tax—he's ripping you off, so ignore him. If you have Mexican auto insurance, get the policy stamped by an official so that you can get a rebate for the days you're outside Mexican territory. You'll buy Belizean insurance across the river. Cross the bridge over the Río Hondo, and you're in Belize.

Both Mexican and Belizean border stations seem to be open during daylight hours all week, with no breaks for lunch.

Your entry permit is the rubber stamp put on your passport (other forms of identification are not accepted), and it will show how long you're allowed to stay. You won't be allowed into the country unless you have enough money to support yourself for the length of your stay. Ask for a couple of weeks, and you'll probably get it. To be on the safe side, ask for a few more days than you think you'll need; the cayes can be very enticing.

Be sure to get a Temporary Import Permit for your car, even if no one tells you a thing about it. Ask for the Customs official if he's not there and get the permit, or you'll be held up at the border when you leave the country. Also required is auto insurance, which you can buy in the restaurant across the road from the border station.

After they've stamped your passport, issued your auto permit, and inspected your car (a process that ranges from a glance through the window to a good search), and

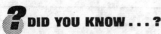

DID YOU KNOW . . . ?

- Belize has the second-longest barrier reef in the world.
- Belize is the newest nation in Central America. It gained its independence from the United Kingdom in 1981.
- Nearly 65% of Belize is uninhabited wilderness.
- Belize has the world's first and only jaguar preserve.
- English is the official language of this Central American nation.
- Belize has a sizable population of Mennonite farmers who speak an archaic form of German.
- Belize City has been destroyed by hurricanes several times.
- Belize was first settled by pirates.
- Belize has some of the best scuba diving in the world.

after you've bought auto insurance, you're on your way. The money changers at the border will give the standard two-to-one for your U.S. dollars. However, don't change pesos here because you'll lose a tremendous amount. There are banks in Corozal Town (open Monday to Friday from 8am to noon, Saturday from 8 to 11am) 7 miles down the road, where you'll get a better rate on pesos but a worse rate on dollars.

BY SHIP

For adventurous travelers, there's a ferry from Puerto Barrios, Guatemala, to Punta Gorda, Belize, on Tuesday and Friday at 7:30am. The one-way fare for the 3-hour trip is Q8 ($2). You can buy your ticket at the Immigration Office on 9a Calle, where you should be sure to get your passport stamped before leaving. Secure a ticket the day before your departure. After arriving in Punta Gorda, take the bus north (along a rough dirt road) or fly to Belize City.

PACKAGE TOURS AND CRUISES

U.S. companies specializing in package tours to Belize are **Great Trips,** 1616 W. 139th St., Burnsville, MN 55337 (tel. 612/890-4405, or toll free 800/552-3419; Fax 612/894-9862); **International Expeditions,** 1776 Independence Court, Birmingham, AL 35216 (tel. 205/870-5550, or toll free 800/633-4734); and **Sea & Explore,** 1809 Carol Sue Ave., Suite E, Gretna, LA 70056 (tel. 504/366-9985, or toll free 800/345-9786; Fax 504/366-9986).

Small cruise ships, primarily geared for scuba divers, have also begun plying the turquoise waters of Belize and, if you're a diver this may be the best way to see the country's underwater wonders. **American Canadian Caribbean Line, Inc.** (tel. toll free 800/556-7450) offers 12-day cruises for as little as $99 per day. **Ocean Quest,** 512 S. Peter St., New Orleans, LA 70130 (tel. toll free 800/338-3483), also offers dive-oriented cruises. **Coral Bay Cruises,** 17 Fort Royale Isle, Fort Lauderdale, FL 33308 (tel. 305/563-1711, or toll free 800/433-7262), has week-long cruises with unlimited diving starting at $1,750.

8. SUGGESTED ITINERARIES

HIGHLIGHTS

The following are Belize's most important destinations.

1. Ambergris Caye
2. Caye Caulker
3. Placencia
4. Cayo District

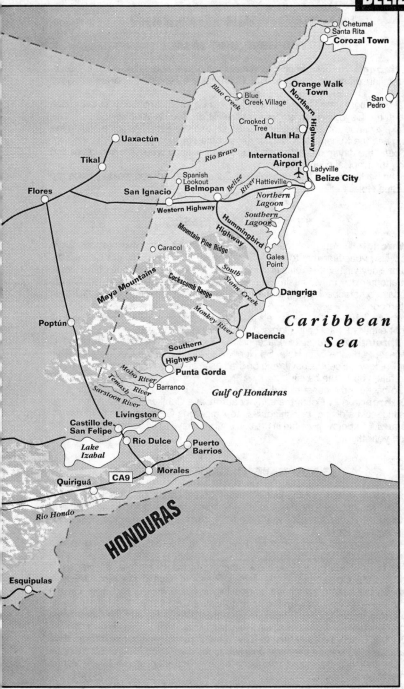

BELIZE

PLANNING YOUR ITINERARY

IF YOU HAVE ONE WEEK

Days 1 through 3: Fly directly to Ambergris Caye and relax on the beach, go snorkeling or scuba diving at Hol Chan Marine Reserve, and sail to Caye Caulker.

Day 4: Take the boat from Caye Caulker to Belize City and continue west to the San Ignacio in the Cayo District, stopping at the Belize Zoo on your way.

Day 5: Take a canoe trip on the Macal River, visiting the Panti Medicine Trail in the morning and the Xunantunich Mayan ruins in the afternoon.

Day 6: Spend the day in the Mountain Pine Ridge, visiting waterfalls and caves and enjoying the tropical scenery.

Day 7: Head back to Belize City, stopping at Guanacaste Park and making a side trip to the Blue Hole.

IF YOU HAVE TWO WEEKS

Days 1 through 4: Your first four days should be spent in the mountainous Cayo District. Use your first day to reach San Ignacio, with a stop at the Belize Zoo. Spend one day visiting the ruins at Xunantunich and canoeing on one of the rivers. Spend another day in Mountain Pine Ridge visiting waterfalls and caves. On the fourth day go horseback riding in the morning and visit the Panti Medicine Trail in the afternoon.

Days 5 and 6: Journey into Guatemala to visit the impressive ruins of Tikal, spending the night either at Tikal or in Flores.

Days 7 through 8: Travel to Placencia on the southern coast, with stops at Guanacaste Park, the Blue Hole, St. Herman's Caves, and the Cockscomb Basin Jaguar Preserve. Spend a day lazing on the beach and snorkeling, perhaps hiring a boat to take you to the cayes.

Day 9: Go back up the coast to Belize City.

Days 10 through 12: Catch the early boat to Caye Caulker. Hang out and/or go snorkeling, scuba diving, or fishing. Sail to Ambergris Caye on your third day.

Days 13 and 14: Enjoy more fun in the sun until you have to fly back to the mainland to catch your flight.

IF YOU HAVE THREE WEEKS

Days 1 through 4: Explore the jungle by foot, horse, canoe, or Jeep. During your time here, you should visit the Xunantunich ruins, the Panti Medicine Trail, and Mountain Pine Ridge. On your way here from Belize City, stop at the Belize Zoo and Guanacaste Park.

Days 5–7: Spend two days exploring Tikal ruins in Guatemala, returning to San Ignacio on your third day.

Days 8–11: Continue on to Placencia, stopping at the Blue Hole, St. Herman's Caves, and the Cockscomb Basin Jaguar Preserve. Spend the next two days relaxing on the beach, swimming, snorkeling, scuba diving, and fishing. On the eleventh day, proceed back up the coast to Belize City.

Day 12: Using Belize City as a base, make a trip to Altun Ha and the Community Baboon Sanctuary.

Days 13–16: Catch the early boat to Caye Caulker and spend the next three days enjoying the laid-back atmosphere. Snorkel, scuba dive, or go fishing. Read a good book. On your last day, sail to Ambergris Caye and stop at Hol Chan Marine Reserve to go snorkeling.

Days 17–21: Relax in the sun. If you didn't visit the Altun-Ha ruins already, you can do so by boat from here. Try an excursion to the Mexican Rocks for snorkeling or rent a sailboard. Fly back to Belize City to catch your flight home.

THEMED CHOICES

Although many people see Belize as just another Caribbean resort, it has much more to offer, especially to naturalists and birders. A trip focusing on the natural parks would include stops at the Cockscomb Basin Jaguar Preserve, the Community Baboon Sanctuary, the Crooked Tree Wildlife Sanctuary, Mountain Pine Ridge, Guanacaste Park, the Hol Chan Marine Reserve, and the Belize Zoo.

9. GETTING AROUND

BY PLANE

Because of the lack of decent roads in most of Belize, flying is recommended as a means of getting around. There are flights between Corozal Town and San Pedro and between Belize City and Corozal Town, San Pedro, Dangriga, Big Creek, and Punta Gorda. The flights are not cheap, but they will save you many hours of travel over very bad roads.

BY BUS

Buses run between all the main towns in Belize, with Belize City acting as the hub for most routes. However, the bus service is not always frequent. The fares are low, and the buses are generally in good condition.

BY CAR

Most roads in Belize are not paved, and so you must have a very sturdy vehicle, preferably with four-wheel drive (especially in the rainy season). There are really only two paved highways—the Northern Highway and the Western Highway. The Hummingbird, or Southern, Highway was partially paved at one time, but now it is a battlefield of potholes. You'll be thankful for plain old dirt after driving this road. If you're driving your own car, install heavy-duty shocks. Also keep your eyes peeled for "sleeping policemen"—speed bumps (usually unmarked)—that can be found as you enter any populated area.

BY RV

There are a few campgrounds scattered around Belize. You can also camp at the Cockscomb Basin Jaguar Preserve. You'll need an overnight permit, available at the preserve headquarters.

BY FERRY

Boats make regular runs to Caye Caulker and Ambergris Caye from Belize City; others operate between Big Creek and Placencia, which is not an island but a long spit of land.

HITCHHIKING

You can hitchhike in Belize, but the buses are better and quite cheap. The only time you might wish to hitchhike is if you're trying to get to some of the remote parks and preserves without taking a tour or hiring a car. Remember there is little traffic on Belize's back roads.

10. WHERE TO STAY

If you can afford only one splurge during your visit to Belize, I highly recommend that you stay two or three nights at one of the many jungle lodges. Several are located in the beautiful Cayo District near the town of San Ignacio. Although you may spend double your normal budget, it's worth it. I've met people here who dearly regretted that they'd spent so much time in the cayes and couldn't stay longer in the Cayo District.

11. ENJOYING BELIZE ON A BUDGET

THE $25-A-DAY BUDGET

See Chapter 2, "Planning a Trip to Costa Rica," for details.

SAVING MONEY ON ACCOMMODATIONS

The same tactics for saving money in Costa Rica and Guatemala apply here.

SAVING MONEY ON MEALS

There are few daily specials here in Belize, but seafood is plentiful and usually inexpensive compared with other dishes. The cheapest courses on most menus are rice and beans accompanied by some form of meat or seafood.

SAVING MONEY ON SIGHT-SEEING AND ENTERTAINMENT

The major sights in Belize are its beaches, forests, and national parks. There are no discounts. The only entertainment in the country is the occasional live band in a bar.

SAVING MONEY ON SHOPPING

Belize doesn't really produce much of anything. The only things of real interest are works of art by local artists—and these are rarely cheap. Avoid buying anything in a hotel lobby because the prices are always higher there.

SAVING MONEY ON TRANSPORTATION

Taxis, especially those in the Cayo District, are ridiculously expensive. Likewise, the rental cars here are the most expensive that I have encountered anywhere in the world. A 15-year-old gas-guzzling Detroit tank rents for almost $100 per day. Add to this gasoline at $2 per gallon. Save money by taking very inexpensive local buses, or, if you absolutely must hire a taxi, try to get together with several other people and share the expense. Eva's Restaurant in San Ignacio is a good place to meet people with whom to share a cab to some of the more interesting sites in the area. Just tell Bob at the counter what you're interested in doing.

SAVING MONEY ON SERVICES AND OTHER TRANSACTIONS

Tipping   Bell hops: B$1 per bag. Waiters/waitresses: 10 to 15%, but only in better restaurants. Taxi drivers: none. Porters: B$1 per bag.

Money Changing and Credit Cards   Although it is officially illegal, changing money on the black market (at a hotel or with someone recommended by your hotel manager) will save you the 2% bank service charge. Credit cards are not widely accepted at restaurants, but they are accepted at hotels. Using your credit cards will get you the official two-to-one rate without having to pay a service charge.

Telephone Calls   There are direct-dial AT&T phones at the Belize International Airport and at the main phone office in downtown Belize City.

 BELIZE

American Express   Belize's only American Express office is in Belize City, upstairs from Belize Global Travel Services, 41 Albert St. (tel. 2-77363). Open Mon–Fri 8am–noon and 1–4:30pm, Sat 8am–noon.

Business Hours   Banks are open Mon, Tues, and Thur 8am–noon, Wed 8am–1pm, and Fri 3–6pm. Offices are open from 8am to noon and 1 to 5pm. Restaurants generally open daily 11am–2pm and again 6–10pm. Stores are open daily 8am–noon, 1–4pm, and 7–9pm (many are only open in the morning on Wednesday).

Camera/Film   Film is available in Belize, but it's very expensive. Bring plenty from home. Remember to bring spare camera batteries also.

Climate   See "When to Go" in this chapter.

Country Code   The country code when dialing Belize is 501.

Crime   See *Safety*.

Currency   See "Information, Entry Requirements, and Money" in this chapter.

Documents Required   See "Information, Entry Requirements, and Money" in this chapter.

Driving Rules   See "Getting Around" in this chapter.

Drug Laws   Although marijuana is grown in Belize, it's illegal, and the penalties for its possession are stiff. The same goes for cocaine. Be sure to bring along copies of any prescription medicine that you might need because this can save you problems with Customs officials and help you get prescriptions filled while you're here.

Drugstores   You'll find licensed pharmacies in most towns in Belize.

Electricity   Current is 110 volts.

Embassies and Consulates   United States Embassy, 20 Gabourel Lane, Belize City (tel. 02-7161 or 02-3886); Canada Consulate, 29 Southern Foreshore, Belize City (tel. 02-3084); British High Commission, Embassy Square, Belmopan (tel. 08-2146 or 08-2147). Keep in mind that there is no Guatemalan embassy or consulate in Belize. If you need a Guatemalan visa (citizens of Canada, Ireland, the United Kingdom, and Australia need them), the nearest consulate is in Chetumal, Mexico.

Emergencies   Fire and ambulance, dial 90; for the police, dial 22-222 in Belize City or Belmopan, 2022 in San Ignacio, Benque Viejo or San Pedro, 23129 in Placencia, 2120 in Caye Caulker, 22-022 in Dangriga, Orange Walk, or Corozal Town.

Hitchhiking   It's possible, but not many people do it because the buses are so inexpensive.

Holidays   See "When to Go" in this chapter.

Information   See "Information, Entry Requirements, and Money" in this chapter. Also see individual city chapters for local information offices.

Language   English is the official language, although Spanish, several Indian dialects, and Creole also are spoken.

Laundry   For listings of Laundromats, see individual town and island chapters.

Liquor Laws   You must be 18 years old to purchase alcoholic beverages in Belize.

Mail   Letters take about a week to reach the United States. A postcard to the United States costs 30B¢ (15¢) and a letter costs 60B¢ (30¢). You can usually buy stamps at your hotel and in stores selling postcards as well as at the post office. Post offices are open from Mon–Thur 8am–5pm, Fri from 8am–4:30pm. It is best to ship parcels from the Parcel Post Office, 1 Church St., in Belize City. Open Mon–Thur 8am–noon and 1–4:30pm, Fri 8am–noon and 1–4pm.

Maps   The Belize Tourist Authority information center in Belize City has several different maps—some free, others for a few dollars. If you plan to drive, I recommend the *Driver's Guide to Beautiful Belize,* a small book that takes you mile by mile down every road with many small maps. It's available at Tropical Books, 9 Regent St., Belize City.

Newspapers/Magazines   The *Miami Herald* is the most readily available international newspaper in Belize at larger hotels throughout the country. The Belizean newspapers are profoundly lacking in hard news, being primarily mouthpieces for the many political parties in the country.

Passports   See "Information, Entry Requirements, and Money" in this chapter.

Pets   If you want to bring your pet along, you must have a recent veterinarian's certificate of good health and inoculation against rabies.

Police   See *Emergencies.*

Radio/TV   Radio stations in Belize play mostly reggae and soca music. Satellite TV is available at most hotels.

Restrooms   In hotels and restaurants only.

Safety   Belize City has a reputation for being a dangerous place. Whenever you're traveling in an unfamiliar city or country, stay alert. Be aware of your immediate surroundings. Wear a moneybelt and keep a close eye on your possessions. Be particularly careful with cameras, purses, and wallets—all favorite targets of thieves and pickpockets.

Taxes   There is a B$20 ($10) departure tax when you leave the country by air and a B$1 (50¢) departure tax when you leave it overland. The hotel room tax is 5%, which I have included in the rates listed in this book.

Telephone   Pay phones can be found on the street. They accept coins of different denominations but do not give change. The dial tone is similar to that in the United States. If you make a call from a pay phone and nothing happens, try dialing 8 and then the number. Phone numbers in Belize differ in the number of digits that they have. However, whenever dialing within Belize, you must always dial a zero first; when calling from outside Belize, you don't use the zero. Each town or region has its own prefix, starting with zero. There's only one phone book for all of Belize. The main telephone office in Belize City is on Bishop Street, just around the corner from Albert Street. You'll find direct-dial AT&T phones here.

Time   Belize is on Central Standard Time, or six hours behind Greenwich Mean Time.

Tipping   See "Saving Money on Services and Other Transactions" in this chapter.

Tourist Offices   See "Information, Entry Requirements, and Money" in this chapter. Also see individual city chapters.

Visas   A visa is not necessary to visit Belize.

Water   Avoid tapwater, which is often from shallow wells or rivers, except in Belize City, where it is considered safe to drink. Throughout the country people rely on cisterns to collect rainwater for drinking. At your hotel, ask for a pitcher of drinking water; otherwise, bottled water is available.

CHAPTER 16

BELIZE CITY AND THE CAYES

1. BELIZE CITY
- **FAST FACTS— BELIZE CITY**
2. AMBERGRIS CAYE
3. CAYE CAULKER

Although it is a small country, Belize can be difficult to get around. There are few paved roads, so the best way to get from one place to another is by small plane or boat, which makes for adventure. Even if you are looking only to improve your tan, you will have to travel a lot before you can hit the beach. Many people come here specifically because there are still adventures to be had in the wilds of the interior. Whether you are out to spot a jaguar or just hoping to see a toucan in the wild, Belize can fulfill your dream.

---

1. BELIZE CITY

Distances: 103 miles S of the Mexican border;
82 miles E of the Guatemalan border.

GETTING THERE By Air Continental, American, TACA, Tan Sahsa, Aerovias, and several local airlines serve Belize City's two airports. See Chapter 15, "Planning a Trip to Belize," for details.

By Bus Belize City is well served by about half a dozen different bus lines that run to all corners of the country that have roads. See Chapter 15, "Planning a Trip to Belize," for more details.

By Car There are only two highways into Belize City—the Northern Highway, which leads to the Mexican border, and the Western Highway, which leads to the Guatemalan border.

By Boat The *Andrea* and *Andrea II* make the run between San Pedro, Ambergris Caye, and Belize City Monday to Saturday. There also are boats that run between Caye Caulker and Belize City daily.

DEPARTING Belize City's bus stations are about ten blocks from the Swing Bridge. From Albert Street between the Swing Bridge and the Central Park, walk up Orange Street, cross a canal, continue to the far side of the next canal and turn left for Novelos, located on West Collet Canal (tel. 02-7372); Batty Bros., on East Collet Canal (tel. 02-2025), is to the right before you cross the canal. Transportes del Carmen doesn't really have a terminal, but their buses are parked on West Collet Canal across from Batty Bros. The last two companies, Venus (tel. 02-3354) and Z-Line (tel. 02-3937), are farther away, off Orange Street; turn right onto Magazine Road to find them.

Batty Bros. runs four buses a day to San Ignacio: at 6:30 (this is the only one that goes to Melchor de Mencos, Guatemala), 8, 9, and 10am. The trip takes 1½ hours to Belmopan, where there's a brief stop, then another 1½ hours to San Ignacio. Novelos buses leave for San Ignacio every hour on the hour from 11am through 6pm. The schedule is pared down a bit on Sunday. Transportes del Carmen also runs a few buses out to San Ignacio. Venus and Z-Line serve Dangriga, Mango Creek, Placencia, and Punta Gorda. Batty Bros. and Venus split the northern route to Chetumal; between the two of them, a bus runs every hour.

"The stereo speakers are as big as houses" exclaimed a recent visitor to Belize City (pop. 50,000), and even though that is a bit of an exaggeration, Belize City does rock to a Caribbean beat. Maybe all the rocking is due to the city's shaky foundations. Legend has it that the city was founded 300 years ago by pirates and built out of the marshes on a foundation of empty rum bottles. Whether that is true or not, Belize City is surrounded on three sides by water, and at high tide it is nearly swamped. Several hurricanes have inundated the city over the years, causing extensive damage each time and affecting the creation of two other towns—Belmopan and Hattieville. Belmopan, at the geographical center of the country, may be the capital of Belize, but Belize City is the cultural and commercial center. It's a strange, fascinating warren of narrow streets and canals (the latter being little more than open sewers and pretty pungent in hot weather), modern stores, dilapidated shacks, and quaint wooden mansions. It's not the kind of place that you want to hang around any longer than necessary, but if you happen to be stuck here for a day or two, explore a bit—you might be surprised by what you find.

ORIENTATION

ARRIVING

If you arrive by plane from outside Belize, you'll land at the Philip S. W. Goldson International Airport, which is located 10 miles northwest of the city on the Northern Highway. A taxi into town will cost B$25 ($12.50). If you fly in from somewhere else in Belize, you'll land at the Municipal Airport, which is on the edge of town. A taxi from here should be no more than B$6 ($3).

If you arrive in town by bus, you'll be somewhere on the west side of town, depending on where you came from and which bus line you used. All the bus stations are within 10 blocks of Albert Street, which is an easy walk in the day, but it is not recommended after dark. A taxi from the bus station to any hotel in town will cost B$3 ($1.50) for one person or B$2 ($1) per person for two or more people.

If you arrive by car from Mexico, keep on the road into town, paying close attention to one-way streets, and you'll end up at the Swing Bridge. If you're arriving on the Western Highway, stay on it after it becomes Cemetery Road, and you'll end up at the intersection with Albert Street, a block away from the Swing Bridge.

INFORMATION

The **Belize Tourist Board,** 53 Regent St. (tel. 02-7213), next to the Hotel Mopan, is open Monday to Thursday from 8am to noon and 1 to 5pm, to 4:30pm on Friday; closed on weekends. There's a lot of information here, but come with some idea of what you want to know or they won't know what to do with you. Travel agencies are another good source of information.

CITY LAYOUT

Belize City is surrounded on three sides by water, with the murky waters of the Haulover Creek dividing the city in two. The Swing Bridge, near the mouth of Haulover Creek, is the main route between the two halves of the city. At the south end of the bridge is the market and the start of Regent Street and Albert Street, where you'll find most of Belize City's shops and offices. To the east of these two major roads is a grid of smaller roads lined with dilapidated wooden houses. On the north side of the bridge and to the right, you'll find a pleasant neighborhood of old mansions. This is where you'll find the U.S. embassy, a couple of guest houses, and several expensive hotels. Cemetery Road heads out of town to the west and becomes the Western Highway, and Freetown Road becomes the Northern Highway.

GETTING AROUND

The only way to get around town is on foot or by taxi, unless you have your own car.

BY TAXI

A taxi is B$3 ($1.50) for one person between any two points in town and B$2 ($1) per person for two or more people. You'll find taxis waiting on the Market Square near the Swing Bridge, or you can call **Caribbean Taxi Garage** (tel. 2-72888) or **Cinderella Taxi** (tel. 2-45240).

BY CAR

Car Rentals

I don't know of anyplace in the world where it is more expensive to rent a car. It seems that anyone who can get a couple of old Detroit eight-cylinder bombs down here from Texas can open up a car-rental agency. You can count on these cars guzzling expensive gas and breaking down at some point (not my idea of a fun way to spend my vacation). Avis and National are currently the only international car-rental agencies with offices in Belize. **Avis** has just relocated in the new airport terminal (tel. 2-31987). Its rate for a Suzuki 4X4 with unlimited mileage is around B$200 ($100) a day, including insurance; by the week, the rate drops about B$20 ($10) per day. **National,** 126 Freetown Rd. (tel. 2-31586 or 2-31587) has similar rates. The **Belize Guest House,** 2 Hutson St. (tel. 2-77569) also rents Suzuki 4X4s (primarily to guests of the hotel) and charges only B$160 ($80) per day, including insurance.

To rent a car cheaper than this, you'll have to put up with a gas-guzzling Detroit V-8, which, since gasoline is so expensive in Belize, can actually end up costing more than one of the above-mentioned cars. **Crystal Auto Rentals,** 1½ miles on Northern Highway (tel. 2-31600), is one such agency. A big old bomb rents for B$140 ($70) per day, including insurance. There are several other companies listed in the phone book, but all of them are of doubtful reliability because of the age of the cars they rent.

 BELIZE CITY

American Express   The office is located upstairs from Belize Global Travel Services, 41 Albert St. (tel. 2-77363). Open Mon–Fri 8am–noon and 1–4:30pm, Sat 8am–noon.

Bookstores   The Book Center, 144 North Front St. (tel. 2-77457), sells magazines and classic books and is open Mon–Fri 8am–noon, 1–5pm, and 7–9pm, Sat 8am–noon, 1–4:30pm, and 7–9pm. The Belize Bookshop, Regent and Rectory streets (tel. 2-72054), sells books, magazines, and local and U.S. newspapers and is open Mon, Tues, and Thurs 8am–noon and 1:30–5pm, Wed 8am–noon, and Sat 8am–noon and 1:30–3pm.

Car Rentals   See "Getting Around" in this chapter.

Climate   See "When to Go" in Chapter 15.

Crime   See *Safety*.

Currency Exchange   All banks are around the Central Park, though few people use banks for changing money because they charge a commission. Ask your hotel manager about changing money. If the hotel can't help you, they can point you in the right direction.

Dentist   Contact your embassy for the name of a reliable dentist.

Doctors   Contact your embassy for the name of a reliable doctor.

Drugstores   Brodie's Pharmacy, Regent Street at Market Square (tel. 2-77-76, ext 26), is open Mon, Tues, Thurs, and Sat 8:30am–7pm, Wed 8:30am–12:30pm, Fri 8:30am–9pm, and Sun 9am–12:30pm.

Embassies and Consulates   United States Embassy, 29 Gabourel Lane (tel. 02-77161); Canada Consulate, 120 A New Rd. (tel. 02-31060); Mexico Embassy, 20 North Park St. All are open Mon–Fri 9–11am for Tourist Cards.

Emergencies   Fire and ambulance call 90; police call 72210.

Eyeglasses   The Belize Vision Center, 9 Daly St. (tel. 2-45038), can repair or replace your glasses. Open Mon–Fri 8am–noon and 4–7pm, Sat 8am–noon.

Holidays   See "When to Go" in Chapter 15.

Hospitals   St. Francis Hospital and Diagnostic Center, 28 Albert St. (tel. 2-77068 or 2-75658), has a 24-hour emergency room.

Information   See "Information" in Chapter 15.

Laundry/Dry Cleaning   The Belize Laundromat, 7 Craig St. (tel. 2-31117), charges B$10 ($5) for one large load of laundry, washed and dried. Open Mon–Sat 8am–5pm.

Luggage Storage/Lockers   Ask at your hotel; otherwise, there's no place to leave luggage in Belize City.

Lost Property   The best you can do is contact the police.

Newspapers/Magazines   The *Miami Herald, Time,* and *Newsweek* are available at the bookstores mentioned above.

Photographic Needs   Venus Photo, corner of Albert and Bishop Streets (tel. 2-73596), sells film (expensive). Open Mon–Sat 8am–5pm and 7–9pm. A 36-exposure roll of ASA 100 print film costs B$10 ($5).

Police   See *Emergencies*.

Post Office   The main post office is on Front Street at the north end of the Swing Bridge (tel. 2-72201). Open Mon–Thurs 8am–5pm, and Fri 8am–4:30pm. The parcel post office is located at 1 Church St., next door to the Belize Telecommunications Ltd. office. Open Mon–Thurs 8am–noon and 1–4:30pm, Fri 8am–noon and 1–4pm.

Radio/TV   Local radio stations primarily play reggae, soca, and rap music. Satellite cable TV is what most people here watch.

Religious Services   Among the denominations with churches in Belize City are Anglican, Baptist, Presbyterian, Jehovah's Witness, and Seventh Day Adventist.

Restrooms   You'll find them in restaurants and hotels, but that's about it.

Safety   Like any big city, Belize City has its share of criminals and dangers, although with a bit of caution and common sense, you shouldn't have any problems. You'll hear that you shouldn't go out alone at night in Belize City, but there's nothing that should prevent you from walking from a restaurant to your hotel in pairs, down well-lit main streets. Look like you know where you're going and don't flash money. If someone tries to engage you in conversation not to your liking, excuse yourself politely. Invariably, people who get ripped-off are participating in illicit exchanges. You certainly won't have any problems on the cayes, where life never exceeds a snail's pace.

Taxes   There is a 5% tax on hotel rooms.

Taxis   See "Getting Around" in this chapter.

Telephone   For all your long-distance needs, head to the Belize Telecommunications Ltd. office at 1 Church St. Open Mon–Sat 8am–9pm, Sun 8am–6pm. There are two AT&T USA direct phones here.

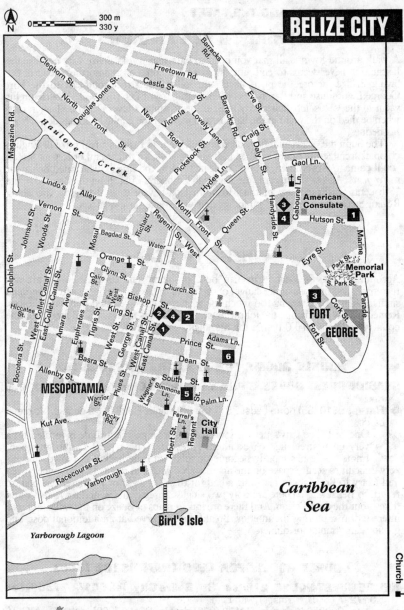

BELIZE CITY

N

0 — 300 m
330 y

Barracks Rd.

Cleghorn St.

Freetown Rd.

Castle St.

North Front St.

Douglas Jones St.

New Road

Victoria St.

Lovely Lane

Barracks Rd.

Eve St.

Craig St.

Daly St.

Gaol Ln.

Magazine Rd.

Haulover Creek

Lindo's Alley

Vernon St.

Johnson St.

Woods St.

Mosul St.

Bagdad St.

Richard St.

Regent St. West

Water Ln.

Pickstock St.

Hydes Ln.

North Front St.

Queen St.

Gabourel Ln.

Handyside St.

American Consulate

Hutson St.

Marine Parade

1

3

4

Hiccatee St.

Dolphin St.

West Collet Canal St.

East Collet Canal St.

Amara Ave.

Tigris St.

Euphrates Ave.

Cairo St.

Far West St.

Orange St.

Glynn St.

Bishop St.

King St.

West St.

George St.

West Canal St.

East Canal St.

Church St.

Prince St.

Adams Ln.

Eyre St.

N. Park St.
S. Park St.

Memorial Park

FORT

Cork St.

Fort St.

GEORGE

3

2 **4** **2**
1

6

Bocotora St.

Basra St.

Allenby St.

Plues St.

Warrior's Lane

Simmons St.

Dean St.

South St.

Palm Ln.

5

MESOPOTAMIA

Warrior St.

Rocky Rd.

Kut Ave.

Ferrel's Ln.

Albert St.

Regent St.

City Hall

Racecourse St.

Yarborough

Bird's Isle

Yarborough Lagoon

Caribbean Sea

Church ✝

Belize City

BELIZE

ACCOMMODATIONS:

Belize Guest House **1**
El Centro **2**
Fort Street Guest House **3**
Mom's Triangle Inn **4**
Mopan **5**
Seaside Guest House **6**

RESTAURANTS:

Dit's **1**
Macy's **2**
Mom's **3**
Pizza House **4**

WHAT TO SEE AND DO

A walk around town is all that you need to entertain you in Belize City because the fascination never seems to end. Turn right as you come off the northeast end of the Swing Bridge, before the post office, and follow the street southeast to the Fort George Lighthouse and Baron Bliss Memorial. Baron Bliss, who visited Belize on his yacht in the 1920s, left Belize City most of his fortune (a few million dollars, in fact) when he died on the yacht in the harbor, and many of the public buildings derive from his bequest.

The Supreme Court building, off the small Central Park, is a real prize of English colonial architecture (à la Caribbean). If you walk down to the end of Regent Street, you'll come to Government House, built in 1814 by the British, who ruled Belize for many years. Across the street is the Anglican Cathedral of St. John the Baptist. In the 19th century, three kings of the Mosquito Coast were crowned here. Also along Regent Street are several old buildings that were once slave quarters.

WHERE TO STAY

Accommodations in Belize City can be a problem: The cheapest hotels are not recommended because of the danger of theft, and the expensive hotels often commit a similar offense by charging too much for what you get. I've listed only safe choices. Remember: When dialing the following phone numbers from within Belize, drop the country code and dial 0 before the first digit.

DOUBLE ROOMS FOR LESS THAN B$30 [$15]

SEASIDE GUEST HOUSE, 3 Prince St., Belize City. Tel. 501/2-78339. 6 rms.

$ Rates: B$10 ($5) dorm beds; B$17 ($8.50) single; B$28 ($14) double. No credit cards.

One of Belize City's newest low-budget lodgings, the Seaside is located on a very quiet street just off Southern Foreshore. This typical Caribbean wood-frame house has rapidly become popular with the backpack crowd, and it's very difficult to secure space on the first day that you're in town. Talk to owners Fred and Mary Jo Prost about reserving a bed for the next night or whenever you plan to return to Belize City. There are only two singles, three doubles, and a five-bed dorm here—but they're all clean. And there are lots of maps of Belize on the walls for those interested in exploring the interior. Breakfasts are served at an additional cost, and groups can arrange for dinners.

DOUBLE ROOMS FOR LESS THAN B$100 [$50]

BELIZE GUEST HOUSE, 2 Hutson St., Belize City. Tel. 501/2-77569. Fax 501/2-77569. 7 rms., 1 with bath.

$ Rates: B$80 ($40) single; B$100 ($50) double; B$120 ($60) triple. AE, MC, V.

This guest house is in my favorite Belize City neighborhood, in which the shady streets are lined with stately old homes that once housed the British officials who governed Belize. Today, the neighborhood is home to embassies, doctors, and lawyers. Although this is not one of the more attractive homes in the neighborhood, it is the closest to the water. In fact, the Belize Guest House claims that it is only 5 feet from the water, and when they complete their eight new rooms, they'll be even closer. The rooms here are large but not luxuriously furnished. Some have air conditioning, while others have only fans. However, if you get too hot, you can always step out on the veranda, which looks directly over the Caribbean and catches the nearly constant tradewinds. You can arrange to rent a Suzuki four-wheel-drive vehicle here at rates lower than at other rental agencies in town. There is no restaurant here, but complimentary coffee and drinks are available. A large lounge with dark wood-paneled walls is a great place to relax and read one of the books from the guest house's library. Laundry service and air ticketing available.

MOM'S TRIANGLE INN, 11 Handyside St., Belize City. Tel. 501/2-45073 or 2-45523. 6 rms., all with bath.

$ Rates: B$63 ($31.50) single, B$84 ($42) single with A/C; B$73.50 ($36.75) double, B$94.50 ($47.25) double with A/C; B$12.50 ($6.25) per extra person; kids under 12 free. MC, V.

This is perhaps the best all-around choice in Belize City. All the rooms are fairly spacious and have private baths and carpeting. There's a comfortable lounge for socializing. After the first day, you'll have access to the refrigerator. Lockers can be rented for $1 a day. Mom's is renowned for its commitment to travelers. Mom also has plans to open a medium-size luxury hotel on the outskirts of town within the next few years. Be sure to ask if the new hotel has opened yet when you make your reservations.

Service: Laundry service.

HOTEL MOPAN, 55 Regent St., Belize City. Tel. 501/2-77351 or 2-73356. Fax 501/2-75383. 12 rms., all with bath.

$ Rates: B$70 ($35) single, B$95 ($47.50) single with A/C; B$95 ($47.50) double, B$135 ($67.50) double with A/C; B$115 ($57.50) triple, B$145 ($72.50) triple with A/C; B$145 ($72.50) quad. MC, V (add 3% to bill).

The rooms here are rather basic and quite expensive for what you get, which seems to be pretty much the norm in Belize. What you're paying for is a private bathroom and security. Although the front part of the hotel is in an interesting old Caribbean-style building, the guest rooms are in back in a new concrete building. The lower rooms are very dark and have air conditioning, while the rooms on the top floor have only fans but get plenty of light and breeze. Some of Belize City's most interesting folks swap stories at the bar, which is open from 11am to 10pm. Owners Jean and Tom Shaw offer a wealth of information.

WORTH THE EXTRA BUCKS

FORT STREET GUEST RESTAURANT & GUESTHOUSE, 4 Fort St., P.O. Box 3, Belize City. Tel. 501/2-45638. Fax 501/2-78808. 5 rms., with bath.

$ Rates (including full breakfast): B$88 ($44) single; B$108 ($54) double. MC, V.

⭐ There aren't too many old homes left in Belize City—repeated hurricanes have made sure of that—so it is a special treat to stay in one of the city's old gems, such as the Fort Street Guesthouse. Even though all the rooms here share one bathroom (a definite drawback), you won't find accommodations like these anywhere else in town. Situated on a triangular corner lot with a grassy front yard, the lovely, restored 1928 house has a long flight of steps leading up to the first floor, where you'll find a gift shop selling many Guatemalan típicos. The guest rooms are located on the second floor, where you'll also find two wicker sitting areas. The table settings of crystal goblets and linen cloths set a very romantic mood here in the first-floor dining room. The woodwork is dark and rich; it's right out of an old New England village with a dash of Caribbean thrown in. Breakfast comes with the room, and you place your breakfast order the night before by leaving a note in a bottle outside the door of your room. Lunch, served from 11am to 2pm, is a good value at B$7 ($3.50) to B$13 ($6.50). Dinner is pricy for your budget at B$25 ($12.50).

HOTEL EL CENTRO, 4 Bishop St., P.O. Box 122, Belize City. Tel. 501/2-72413, 2-77739, or 2-78101. Fax 501/2-74553. 12 rms., all with bath. A/C TEL TV

$ Rates: B$70–B$90 ($35–$45) single; B$120–B$170 ($60–$85) double. AE, MC, V.

This is a bit of a splurge, but the rooms are new, clean, and air-conditioned—with private baths, phones, and TVs, so you can have all the amenities and still be right in the heart of the business and shopping district. At street level is an air-conditioned restaurant where a breakfast of two eggs, two pieces of toast, two pieces of bacon, coffee, and juice will cost B$7 ($3.50). They also serve lunch and dinner, with prices ranging from B$5 ($2.50) for sandwiches to B$22 ($11) for a steak or seafood combination dinner. Fried lobster is only B$16 ($8).

WHERE TO EAT

Unless you're a hard-core adventurer or keep missing boat connections, you probably won't need more than a couple of meals here.

MACY'S, 18 Bishop St. Tel. 02-73419.
  Cuisine: BELIZEAN.
$ Prices: B$8–B$10 ($4–$5). No credit cards.
  Open: Mon–Sat 11:30am–10pm.

⭐ For authentic Belizean cooking, try this tiny local place. The food is consistent, the service is friendly, and the dining room is cool and cozy. Order a fish filet with rice and beans for B$8 ($4), or be more daring and try one of their daily chalkboard specials, such as deer or gibnut (a small forest-dwelling rodent the size of a rabbit and the de facto national dish of Belize). A tall glass of cold, fresh-squeezed orange juice is a bargain in the Belizean heat at B$2 ($1).

MOM'S, 11 Handyside St. Tel. 02-45073 or 02-45523.
  Cuisine: AMERICAN/CREOLE/MEXICAN.
$ Prices: Sandwiches B$3–B$8 ($1.50–$4); main meals B$10–B$20 ($5–$10). MC, V.
  Open: Sun–Fri 6am–10pm.

Mom's still reigns supreme as the gathering place for travelers, despite the slow service. The bulletin boards are jammed with information and messages, and the glass door is constantly sliding open and closed as hungry folks wander in and out throughout the day. With 15 tables, Mom's can accommodate quite a few people. Don't be deceived by the run-down appearance of Handyside Street. Mom's has been here for many years and continues its high standards of quality. Due to popular demand, Mom has just added a number of Mexican dinners to the menu.

THE PIZZA HOUSE, 11 King St. Tel. 02-73966.
  Cuisine: PIZZA.
$ Prices: Whole pizza B$20 ($10).
  Open: Daily 10am–10pm.

Take a seat at the counter to wait for your hefty veggie or meat combo. A whole pizza can feed three or four hungry people. A cold glass of fresh lime juice is refreshing— the ideal accompaniment to a hot pizza here.

DIT'S, 50 King St. Tel. 02-73330.
  Cuisine: CAKES.
$ Prices: Slice of cake B$1 (50¢); meals B$4.50 ($2.25).
  Open: Daily 7am–9pm.

When a cake craving strikes you in Belize City, search out this little place. A tempting assortment of cakes and pies are displayed in a glass case at the counter, with many Central American specialties that you may never have encountered before—such as cow pie, raisin pie, three-milks cake, and coconut tarts. Dit's also serves simple meals and, on Friday and Saturday, cows-foot soup.

EVENING ENTERTAINMENT

The numerous bars in Belize City can be rough places and are not recommended unless you have a local guide to take you to places he knows. If you just want to relax over a drink, try the second-floor bar at the **Bellevue Hotel** on Southern Foreshore. It looks over the water and occasionally has live bands on the weekends.

The **Baron Bliss Institute, 1 Bliss Promenade. Tel. 02-77267,** named for and financed by Belize City's benefactor, is the city's cultural center, where you'll find a public library, three Mayan stelae, and occasional cultural performances, including the annual Festival of the Arts.

EXCURSIONS
ALTUN HA RUINS

About 30 miles north of Belize City on the Old Northern Highway are the ruins of Altun Ha, an ancient Mayan city thought to have existed here since about A.D. 250. Watch for the turnoff to the right just past Sand Hill. Once you're on the Old Northern Highway, watch for a small and rather inconspicuous sign for the Maruba Resort on the right side of the road. From the highway, it's a bumpy 2¼ miles to the ruins. About 1½ miles in, the road forks—take the right fork.

Altun Ha flourished during the Classic Period of Mayan civilization, up to the 800s. It was an important trading center linking the coastal and interior settlements. Only a few of the most imposing temples, tombs, and pyramids have been uncovered and rebuilt; hundreds more lie under the jungle foliage. The unique jade-head sculpture of Kinich Ahau (the Mayan sun god), the largest well-carved jade from the Mayan era, was discovered here. Today, it's kept in a bank vault in Belize City out of public view. The site was named after the village in which it's situated—Rockstone Pond, the literal Mayan translation meaning "stone water." The archeological work was done principally by the Royal Ontario Museum beginning in 1964 and although restoration has resulted in some anachronistic juxtapositions, it's a beautiful ruined city, well worth the visit.

A soft-drink stand and picnic area are available.

Don't go too far off the beaten track in this area. (You wouldn't want to stumble on someone's private marijuana plantation.) If you're an intrepid explorer of lost ruins, get a guide.

There is no public transport to Altun Ha, so you'll need to take a tour, a taxi, or your own wheels.

Admission: B$3 ($1.50), children under 12 free.
Open: Daily 8am–5pm.

Where to Stay and Eat

There's only one place to stay anywhere near the Altun Ha ruins, and it's a major splurge. However, it's one of the nicest and most interesting small lodges I found in Belize.

MARUBA RESORT, 40½ Old Northern Highway, Maskall Village. Tel. 501/03-22199. P.O. Box 300703, Houston, Texas 77230. Tel. 713/799-2031. Fax 713/795-8573. 10 rms., 1 suite all with bath.

$ Rates: B$132–B$180 ($61–$90) single; B$180–B$218 ($90–$109) double; various meal plans additional. AE, MC, V.

You'd hardly expect to find a luxury resort while driving down this potholed stretch of the Old Northern Highway, but that is just what you'll encounter tucked away on an old farm. Perhaps you'll feel like being pampered after several very hard days on the road—how about a soak in the hot tub, a massage, and a manicure or pedicure? Every room is unique, with such unusual design touches as Guatemalan blankets on the beds, animal skins on the walls, "modern art" doors, four pillows on the beds, and Chinese sandalwood soap in the bathrooms. There is a very attractive little swimming pool with its own waterfall, and around the grounds you'll find many caged wild animals. The only drawback to this otherwise idyllic retreat are the numerous biting insects that appear at different times of year—be sure to bring some insect repellent.

The dining room/bar is equally a work of art. In the lounge, a long built-in sofa has a screen of potted plants separating it from the dining area. The bar itself is made of stone and rough logs with a dugout canoe full of business cards hanging above it.

Tables in the dining room are set with porcelain and crystal. Meals here are expensive, but you'll rarely find better in Belize. Breakfast is B$20 ($10), lunch is B$25 ($12.50), and dinner is B$45 ($22.50).

---

2. AMBERGRIS CAYE

Distance: 36 miles N of Belize City; 40 miles SE of Corozal Town.

GETTING THERE By Plane There are more than 20 flights a day from Belize City Municipal Airport. Duration: 15 minutes. Fare: B$33 ($16.50) one way and B$66 ($33) round trip on Island Air; B$39 ($19.50) one way and B$70 ($35) round trip on Tropic Air. Fares on Maya Airways are similar.

There are two flights a day to Corozal Town. Duration: 20 minutes. Fare: B$54 ($27) one way and B$104 ($52) round trip on Maya Air.

By Boat The *Andrea* and *Andrea II* make the trip Mon–Sat once a day. They depart from Belize City at 4pm. They depart from San Pedro for the return trip Monday to Friday at 7am, Saturday at 8am. Duration: 75 minutes. Fare: B$20 ($10) one way, B$38 ($19) round trip.

The other option is to take one of the private boats that dock behind the Esso station near the Swing Bridge. If you decide to go with one of these, don't pay until you're out of the boat at your destination. Too many people get stung this way—use good judgment.

The *Banana Boat* makes two runs a day from Caye Caulker on Mon, Wed, Fri, Sat, and Sun. (trip time: 30 minutes). It departs from Caye Caulker at 9:30am and 4pm and from San Pedro at 9am and 3:30pm. Duration: 30 minutes. Fare: B$20 ($10) one way, B$35 ($17.50) round trip.

Cesario Rivera (tel. 026-2217) makes runs from Caye Caulker in his boat *Thunderbolt* Monday to Saturday around 9am. The return trip to Caye Caulker is at 7:15am. Duration: 30 minutes. Fare: B$20 ($10) one way. Both the *Banana Boat* and *Thunderbolt* arrive at the Lagoonside Marina off Angel Coral Street.

You can also come over on one of the sailboats that make trips to the Hol Chan Marine Reserve and then stop for a few hours in San Pedro. Bob's *Island Girl* and Amado's *Miss Conduct* are two reliable choices. Departures are between 10 and 11am. Fare: B$25 ($12.50), including drinks.

ESSENTIALS Orientation San Pedro is only three streets wide. Formerly called simply Front, Middle, and Back streets, they acquired new names in 1990. They are now (in the same order) Barrier Reef Drive, Pescador Drive, and Angel Coral Street.

Fast Facts Belize Bank, across from the Spindrift Hotel on Barrier Reef Drive is open Mon–Fri 9am–3pm, and Sat 9am–noon. Lopez Drugs below the Spindrift Hotel on Barrier Reef Drive is the island's drugstore—open Mon–Thurs 8am–noon and 5:30–9pm, Fri 8am–2pm, Sat–Sun 7am–9pm. Emergency numbers: police 2022; fire 2372; medical 90. There is a laundry service located across from Vanessa's Jewelry Shop on Barrier Reef Drive. The post office is located below the Spindrift Hotel—open Mon–Thurs 8am–noon and 1–5pm, Fri 8am–noon and 1–4:30pm. For a taxi, call 026-2089 or 026-2038.

For most sun seekers, scuba divers, and anglers, Belize means only one thing—Ambergris Caye. Although it's the largest of Belize's cayes (pronounced "keys" just like in Florida), Ambergris Caye still has only one small town, San Pedro. Most of the island's 2,500 permanent residents live in this once-quiet fishing village, which is now the country's most developed tourist haunt. Many visitors to San Pedro liken it to the Florida Keys 40 or 50 years ago—slow paced, uncrowded, with wooden houses and sand streets. In the past few years, however, much of the land has been sold to developers, and there are now hundreds of foreign-owned vacation homes tucked away on small lots all over the island. Still, a traffic jam in San Pedro is when one of the island's golf carts, which are used to shuttle guests between the hotels and restaurants, has to stop for a hermit crab crossing Barrier Reef Drive.

The island is 25 miles long and ½ mile wide (at its widest), dotted throughout by marshy lagoons. San Pedro's west side faces a lagoon, and its east side faces the Barrier Reef, only a quarter of a mile away. (From town, you can hear and see the waves crashing over it.) You can walk from one end of the town to the other, from the airport to Paradise Resort Hotel, in about ten minutes.

Whether you arrive by plane at the southern end of town or by boat at one of the east docks, you'll soon be acquainted with San Pedro's three sandy streets: Barrier Reef Drive, Pescador Drive, and Angel Coral Street (formerly known as Front, Middle, and Back streets). Most tourist hotels and services are on Barrier Reef Drive, or "the beach" (the waterfront strip of sand that is reached by taking any right turn off Barrier Reef Drive as you head north). Pescador Drive has small grocery stores and private residences; there isn't much of interest to tourists on Angel Coral Street. Along with an airport, a bank, a post office and several restaurants, gift shops, and tourist agencies, San Pedro has accommodations ranging from first-class to budget digs. Even so, it's difficult to find a good value in lodging here.

WHAT TO SEE AND DO

This is a beach resort, so you can expect to find most of the standard activities (on a limited scale). There are no submarine rides, but you can rent a sailboard; there are no sunset dine-and-dance cruises, but you do get a rum punch when you go out on a glass-bottomed boat. Sorry golfers: There are no golf courses here—yet.

First, you should be aware that there really isn't any beach to speak of on Ambergris Caye: There is a narrow strip of sand where the land meets the sea, but even at low tide it isn't wide enough for you to unroll a beach towel in most places. The widest section of sand happens to be right in the middle of town, where all the boats dock (not a pleasant place to hang out). Try walking north or south from town along the water to find a more secluded spot where you can sit and stare out to sea. Otherwise, the beachfront (read "expensive") hotels create their own beaches by building retaining walls and filling them in with sand.

Likewise, swimming is not what you might expect. For a 100 yards or more out from shore, the bottom is covered with seagrass. Beneath the grass is a layer of spongy roots and organic matter topped with a thin layer of white sand. Walking on this spongy sand is most unnerving, and it's easy to trip and stumble. Swimming is best off the pier at the Paradise Resort Hotel, where the management has created a sort of swimming pool in the sea by scooping out a deep spot and clearing away all the grass. All the beaches on the caye are public, and you can probably use the hotel's lounge chairs if it's a slow day. *Beware:* The ladder into the water at the end of the dock is very slippery. The best swimming is from boats anchored out in the turquoise waters between the shore and the reef.

So why do people bother to come here if there is no beach and you can't go swimming right off the shore? They come for the turquoise waters and the coral reef. Less than a quarter mile offshore is the longest coral reef in the western hemisphere. Only Australia's Barrier Reef is longer than this one. There are a number of reputable places to get diving and snorkeling equipment and instruction. **The Coral Beach Dive Club** (tel. 026-2013) offers a full range of rentals and expensive overnight tours. The **Bottom-Time Dive Shop,** on the south end of Front Street, is for serious and would-be diving enthusiasts. If you're a diver, you know how expensive it will be. There's a diving school at Ramon's Reef Hotel, where you can practice in the pool before going out. Snorkeling equipment is available at several locations in town for about B$10 ($5). If you're an independent type, just rent your own snorkeling gear and hop off one of the docks. However, you really need to go out to the reef to see much of anything other than sand and sea grass.

The best snorkeling is at the **Hol Chan Marine Reserve,** which is about 4 miles southeast of San Pedro. *Hol chan* is a Mayan term meaning "little channel," which is exactly what you'll find here—a narrow channel cutting through the shallow coral reef. The walls of the channel are popular with divers, and the shallower areas are frequented by snorkelers. Some of the exciting residents of the area are several large green moray eels (friendly but dangerous), stingrays (don't touch), and nurse sharks (harmless). The reserve covers 5 square miles and is divided into three zones: the reef, the seagrass beds, and the mangroves. There's also a small "blue hole," which is a deep well formed by a collapsed cavern. A much larger, deeper, and more famous blue hole is far to the south of here. Don't confuse the two—this is not the blue hole that Jacques Cousteau explored. Nor is it the blue hole on the Hummingbird Highway. There is a B$3 ($1.50) charge for diving at Hol Chan, which is usually not included in the price of the boat excursion.

There are several boats offering trips out here. The *Reef Seeker Glass-Bottom Boat* tour for B$20 ($10) includes a one-hour trip, an hour of snorkeling, and a complimentary rum punch. If there are enough people, two trips depart daily at 9:15am and 2pm. *The Coral Jungle* makes three stops: one at a sunken boat, one at the blue hole, and one at Hol Chan. It leaves at 9am and 2pm on 2½-hour trips and charges the same price as the *Reef Seeker*. Make reservations at the Barrier Reef Hotel. Most of the native fishermen are trustworthy for boat excursions. Decide what you want to do, then check out the people who could take you.

Make arrangements at **Amigo Travel** (tel. 026-2180) on Barrier Reef Drive for a full day on Shirley Smith's catamaran, *Me Too,* which is docked at Ramon's Reef. For B$35 ($17.50), you get snorkeling equipment and instruction, a guide, drinks, and bathroom facilities.

Stop by **Island Rentals** in Fido's Courtyard, behind The Pizza Place (tel. 26-2471), for all your rental needs—from houses to bicycles to underwater cameras. The helpful folks here also rent motorboats, sailboats, sea kayaks, jet skis, scooters, golf carts, and videos, and will also arrange tours of Belize's interior. They'll book your trip on *Me Too,* too.

The local windsurfing school is housed at Sun Breeze Beach Resort. Rental rates are high.

Sportfishing is also very popular on the island. The two travel and tour agencies mentioned above can arrange fishing trips for you for between B$400 and B$500 ($200 and $250). You can also contact **Abel Guerrero** directly (tel. 026-2043) to arrange any sort of fishing trip. Abel has 25 years of experience and knows all the best spots. He also does snorkeling trips and trips to the mainland.

WHERE TO STAY

Wherever you stay, you'll never be more than a minute's walk from the water. Although there are affordable places to stay here, the choices are small establishments, few in number, and not particularly good values.

DOUBLES FOR LESS THAN B$40 ($20)

MILO'S, P.O. Box 21, San Pedro, Ambergris Caye. Tel. 501/26-2033. 9 rms, none with bath.
$ Rates: B$20 ($10) single; B$25 ($12.50) double; B$30 ($15) triple. No credit cards.
Milo's are the cheapest rooms on the island for a few reasons: You'll share a bathroom with someone else, the rooms are rather dark, and there's no atmosphere to speak of. Some people swear by Milo's, though. The question you must answer for yourself is: How much time will I be spending in my room? At least the shared bathrooms here are clean. You can find out about rooms here in the general store downstairs. Milo's is just before the Paradise Hotel on Front Street.

RUBIE'S HOTEL, Front Street, San Pedro, Ambergris Caye. Tel. 501/26-2063. 9 rms, 5 with bath.
$ Rates: B$20 ($10) double without bath, B$40 ($20) double with bath. No credit cards.

Down at the airport end of town, you'll find a place called Rubie's. Of the nine rooms here, five have private bath and about half look onto the water. In fact, this may be the only place in town that doesn't charge more for a water view, and it's definitely the cheapest place on the island with a water view. The floors are wooden, the rooms are simply furnished with a couple of beds and little else, and the cement showers are generally clean.

DOUBLES FOR LESS THAN B$60 ($30)

HOTEL SAN PEDRANO, Front Street, San Pedro, Ambergris Caye. Tel. 501/26-2054 or 026-2093. 7 rms, 1 apt., all with bath.
$ Rates: B$50 ($25) single; B$60 ($30) double; B$70 ($35) triple; B$85 ($42.50) quad; B$375 ($187.50) apt. per week. AE, MC, V.
Although few of the rooms here have ocean views, they do have nice wooden floors and well-maintained blue patio furniture. There are a single and a double bed in every room and clean baths with tubs. What views you do have from the wide veranda are over the rooftops of adjacent buildings. The hotel is upstairs from a small gift shop toward the northern end of Front Street.

TOMAS HOTEL, Front Street, San Pedro, Ambergris Caye. Tel. 501/26-2061. 8 rms., all with bath.
$ Rates: B$60 ($30) single or double, B$84 ($42) single or double with A/C; B$80 ($40) triple, B$104 ($52) triple with A/C. No credit cards.
Toward the north end of Front Street, directly across the street from an old wooden house painted blue with flower designs on it, you'll spot the sign for the Tomas Hotel. The modern cement building is one of the better budget hotels on the island. All the rooms were recently renovated and have tile floors, very clean bathrooms, and fans. There's a deck on the second floor where you can get a bit of sun.

DOUBLES FOR LESS THAN B$90 ($45)

MARTHA'S, Middle Street, San Pedro, Ambergris Caye. Tel. 501/26-2053. 16 rms.
$ Rates: B$60 ($30) single; B$90 ($45) double; B$120 ($60) triple; B$140 ($70) quad. MC, V.
It's hard to believe that a hotel located upstairs from a grocery store could be so expensive, but here in San Pedro, nothing is cheap. At least the new rooms here are larger than those at most other hotels. There are reading lights over the two double beds, ceiling fans, and big verandas at either end of the building so that you can watch the sunrise or sunset. You'll find Martha's about halfway down Middle Street.

LILY'S, on the beach, San Pedro, Ambergris Caye. Tel. 501/26-2059. 10 rms.
$ Rates: B$80 ($40) double; lower rates in off-season. No credit cards.
If you want a private bath and a water view, you'll have to pay for it. Lily's is on the beach, right behind the Tomas Hotel, which is toward the north end of Front Street. The rooms are large and have ceiling and table fans, wood paneling, and typical fluorescent lighting. Get your money's worth by watching the sun rise every morning and listening to the waves lap at your doorstep after the sun sets. There are a seating area on the front veranda and lounge chairs on the beach for the guests' use. Don't forget your mosquito repellent. Not all of the rooms here have a water view—be sure to ask.

WORTH THE EXTRA BUCKS

BARRIER REEF HOTEL, San Pedro, Ambergris Caye. Tel. 501/26-2075. 12 rms., all with bath.
$ Rates: B$120 ($60) single or double; B$140 ($70) triple or quad. MC, V.

⭐ This pricy little hotel is my favorite building in San Pedro. Directly across the street from the town square, the Barrier Reef is a blindingly white building designed to resemble a traditional Caribbean wooden house. On the second floor is a long veranda, and on the third floor is a small balcony. Three gables extend seaward from the roof to complete the picture. Each room has a double and a single bed with a built-in headboard, tile floors, a fan or air conditioning. The nicest rooms are those facing the water, for the view and for access to the nicest section of veranda. On the first floor, the Navigator restaurant and bar is a very casual place serving pizzas for B$15 to B$40 ($7.50 to $20). Daily specials include such fare as shrimp scampi and fish filet in lemon sauce.

LONG-TERM STAYS

San Pedro is Belize's number-one tourist destination, and it has more vacation and retirement homes than anywhere else in the country. Consequently, there are quite a few houses available for rent on a daily, weekly, or monthly basis. Check with the place below or with one of the realtors or travel agencies in San Pedro when you arrive.

FIDO BADILLO, San Pedro, Ambergris Caye. Tel. 501/26-2286, 2 cabañas, both with bath.
$ Rates: B$120 ($60). MC, V.
A seven-minute walk up the beach north of town, each of these two cabañas comes complete with a stove, a small refrigerator, a bar, and hot water. The larger of the two has two double beds and a single, and the other has a double bed and a day bed. Both are right on the beach and are very quiet. The Fido (pronounced "Feedo") is well known on Ambergris Caye and runs boat trips up the rivers on the mainland.

S&L TRAVEL SERVICE, P.O. Box 700, Belize City. Tel. 501/2-77593. Fax 501/2-73200. All with bath.
This company has several efficiency suites available with maid service, color TVs, and transportation to and from the San Pedro airport. Write or call for current rates.

WHERE TO EAT

Seafood is, of course, the most popular food on the island, and there's plenty of it around all year. However, please keep in mind that there are seasons for lobster, conch, shrimp, and sea turtles (sea turtles are endangered, and turtle steaks should never be ordered). Lobster is available from July 15 to May 15; conch is available from October 1 to June 29; and shrimp is available from August 15 to April 14. When lobster is in season, it's the best deal on the island, and you can order it for three meals a day and not go bankrupt. However, it is rock lobster and is not as flavorful as northern, cold-water lobster.

MEALS FOR LESS THAN B$15 ($7.50)

TAI-PEI CHINESE RESTAURANT, toward the north end of Front Street. Tel. 026-2460.
   Cuisine: CHINESE.
$ Prices: B$6–B$15 ($3–$7.50). No credit cards.
   Open: Daily 11:30am–3pm and 5pm–midnight.
You can't miss the Tai-Pei—it's the building with the flashing Christmas lights toward the north end of Front Street. It's a kind of cross between Caribbean and Chinese, with ceiling fans and hanging lanterns. You check off the dishes you want on an order sheet and then wait for the waiter to bring your food to you. The full gamut of standard Chinese meals is available here: chop suey, chow mein, hot-and-sour soup, egg-drop soup, wontons, and so on. However, there are also a few unusual items on the menu, such as conch chow mein and fried tofu with mushrooms and beef.

THE PIZZA PLACE, Front Street. No phone.
   Cuisine: PIZZA.
$ Prices: Whole pizza B$26–B$34 ($13–$17); per slice B$2.50–B$4.25 ($1.25–$2.13). No credit cards.

Open: Sun–Thurs 6:30–9pm; Fri–Sat 6:30–10pm.

For a light snack any day of the week, try this walk-up window. Sit at bar stools under a palapa hut, or take your meal away. If you want a combo selection, the minimum order is two pieces. Juices and shakes are B$2.50 ($1.25) but aren't very big. A large pizza here is plenty for four people. Don't confuse the seating area with San Pedro's Grill, which is fine for a drink but overpriced for the food served.

NAVIGATOR, Barrier Reef Hotel, Front Street. Tel. 026-2075.
  Cuisine: SEAFOOD/PIZZA.
$ Prices: Dinners B$12–B$20 ($6–$10); pizzas B$15–B$38 ($7.50–$19). MC, V.
  Open: Sun–Thurs 7am–midnight; Fri–Sat 7am–2am.

As the name implies, the motif here is nautical. Glass Japanese fishing floats hang from the ceiling, the stern of a small boat juts out from a wall à la the Hard Rock Café, there's a ship's wheel, and trophy fish hang on the walls. Aside from these decorations, the restaurant is rather plain, with cement floors and wooden booths. However, the Navigator serves some of the tastiest and most unusual pizzas I've ever had. Try a taco pizza, a seafood special with lobster, or perhaps the shrimp BLT pizza. You can also get sandwiches and daily seafood specials, such as shrimp scampi and fish filet in lemon-butter sauce. The salads here are also quite good.

MEALS FOR LESS THAN B$20 [$10]

ELVI'S KITCHEN, halfway down Middle Street. Tel. 026-2176.
  Cuisine: SEAFOOD/INTERNATIONAL.
$ Prices: Seafood dinners B$10–B$25 ($5–$12.50). AE, MC, V.
  Open: Breakfast 7–9:30am; lunch 11:30am–2pm; dinner 6–10pm.

Elvi's is the most popular restaurant on Ambergris Caye, and it may be the only restaurant in all of Belize that ever has a waiting line. Even after they enlarged the dining room, they still couldn't handle the dinner crowds who came for the substantial servings, good prices, and food cooked to order. The restaurant is a thatched, screened-in hut with picnic tables, a tree growing up through the roof, and a floor of crushed shells and sand—very tropical. Fans cool the place nicely. A typical dinner here might include squid, scallops, and shrimps in red sauce with spaghetti, okra, and cream of vegetable soup. Be sure to have a fruit shake while you're here.

MARINO'S, one block south of Elvi's on Middle Street. Tel. 026-2184.
  Cuisine: SEAFOOD/BELIZEAN.
$ Prices: B$6–B$26 ($3–$13). No credit cards.
  Open: Daily 11:30am–2:30pm and 6–10pm.

While tourists flock to Elvi's, locals go to Marino's. There isn't as much atmosphere, but the prices are a bit lower and you won't have to stand in line to get a table. The restaurant is quite spartan, but there are some works by local artists hanging on the walls. The best deal in the house is the rice and beans with fried fish and potato salad for B$6 ($3). If you're especially hungry, start your meal with conch fritters or fish fingers for B$6 ($3). The grilled dinners also are good and come with steamed vegetables and a choice of french fries, baked potato, or rice.

WORTH THE EXTRA BUCKS

LILY'S, on the beach in the middle of town. Tel. 026-2059.
  Cuisine: SEAFOOD.
$ Prices: B$25 ($12.50). MC, V.
  Open: Breakfast 7–10am; dinner 6–9pm; lunch by request.

Lily's Hotel, on the waterfront, is also home to one of the best restaurants in San Pedro. You don't get much choice here, but if you like seafood, you'll love this place. A fish, lobster, conch, or fish/shrimp combo dinner costs B$25 and is served family style so that you can eat your fill. The delicious food is cooked to order and comes with french fries, cole slaw, and a vegetable. The restaurant itself is brightly lit, but there are candles on the tables and wicker chairs for atmosphere.

COCO PALMS RESTAURANT, Sun Breeze Resort at the south end of Front Street. Tel. 026-2191.
Cuisine: SEAFOOD/MEXICAN.
$ Prices: Sandwiches B$4–B$12 ($2–$6); complete meals B$12–B$35 ($6–$17.50). AE, MC, V.
Open: Daily 6am–10pm.

⑤ For an elegant and delicious splurge meal, head down to the southern end of Front Street to the elegant tropical restaurant behind the Sunbreeze Resort. Comfortable wicker chairs, ceiling fans, and coral-pink and seafoam-green linen set the mood. The service and food are both excellent. On a hot sunny day, the large windows and air conditioning make this the ideal place for relaxing and enjoying the sight of palm trees. Start your meal with ceviche or a salad, then move on to something like the seafood platter (the most expensive item on the menu, but it comes with generous portions of shrimp, lobster, conch, and fish) or something less pricy, such as Caribbean fish broiled with mayonnaise, lime juice, bell peppers, onions, and tomatoes for B$22 ($11). Mexican and Belizean meals are even less expensive, and it's possible to get grilled fish at lunch for as little as B$12 ($6). The breakfasts are overpriced.

EVENING ENTERTAINMENT

THE TACKLE BOX BAR, off Barrier Reef Drive near the south end of town. No phone.
The first thing to do is drop in for beer (B$3, $1.50) or a piña colada (B$7, $3.50) here at San Pedro's most famous bar, out at the end of a short pier. Local fishermen and sailors gather here to exchange information. If you want a boat to another caye, the folks behind the bar will be able to set you up with a ride. Nautical motifs decorate the interior, and out behind the back terrace is an enclosed tank full of sharks and giant sea turtles. Don't miss it! The last time I was there, a sign had been posted to the effect that British soldiers were no longer admitted due to their unruly behavior. So don't expect any Hollywood-style brawls here.

FIDO'S BAR, Fido's Courtyard on Barrier Reef Drive. No phone.
Pronounce it "Feedo," and people will think you're a local. Fido Badillo runs a popular open-air bar that looks out over the water. Fido himself is a one-man band who performs upbeat western music, including a few songs he has written himself. "Just Another Gringo in Belize" is a favorite with crowds here.

SANDAL'S PUB, north end of Barrier Reef Drive just outside the gate to the Paradise Resort Hotel. No phone.
Loud rock music plays all day and far into the night at this classically beachy little bar. The floor is covered with sand, and there's a thatch canopy over the bar. The walls are made of skinny palm tree trunks. Be sure to read the sign out front with the bar's hours on it: "Open most days about 9 or 10, occasionally as early as 7, but sometimes as late as 12 or 1 . . ." Then push through the western-style swinging doors and order up a cold bottle of Belikin.

BIG DADDY'S, across from the Barrier Reef Hotel and behind the church. No phone.
Nowhere have I ever seen a bar or disco located so close to a church. The saints and sinners seem to be in a competition to see who can play the loudest music. The church often throws its doors open and cranks up the volume on its organ, but there always seems to be more people in the disco. The dress is casual, and the drinks are not overpriced.

EXCURSIONS

If you've been on the island for a while and want to see more of Belize contact **Amigo Travel** and **Island Rentals,** both on Barrier Reef Drive. They offer excursions to various locations—including Altun Ha, Xunantunich, Mountain Pine Ridge, and

Tikal. The popular day trip to the Mayan ruins at Altun Ha begins on the *Hustler,* a powerful little boat that will whisk you over to the mainland. You'll then take a taxi to the ruins and have lunch before returning to San Pedro for B$120 ($60) per person. Call 026-2049 or 026-2279.

3. CAYE CAULKER

Distances: 20 miles from Belize City; 10 miles from Ambergris Caye.

GETTING THERE By Air   At this time, it is not yet possible to fly to Caye Caulker, but an airstrip is under construction.

By Boat   High-speed launches leave from behind the Shell gas station on North Front Street just inland from the Swing Bridge. Several boats a day leave between 10:30 and 11am. The most reliable and best-known is the *Soledad,* skippered by Chocolate, a 60-year-old native who has been making the trip all his life. The motorboat, which seats 20 people, departs Belize City daily at 10:30am. Fare: B$12 ($6). Another reliable boat is the *Blue Wave.* If you don't go over on either of these ask around for a recommendation, inspect the boat (it should have two motors in case one fails), and don't pay until you reach your destination. A reputable skipper won't ask you to. Chocolate returns to Belize City from Caulker every morning at 6:45am from the Front Bridge. Stop by his gift shop (open in the afternoon only) at the northern end of town to reserve space.

The *Banana Boat* makes two runs a day from San Pedro on Mon, Wed, Fri, Sat, and Sun. It departs from San Pedro at 9am and 3:30pm and from Caye Caulker at 9:30am and 4pm. Duration: 30 minutes. Fare: B$20 ($10) one way, B$35 ($17.50) round trip.

ESSENTIALS Orientation   Boats dock at the Front Bridge, so named because this is the front side of the island facing the reef (east). The town extends north and south from here. As you debark, you'll be able to see across to the western side of the island and the Back Bridge/dock. Caye Caulker consists of two main sand roads, a few cross streets, and numerous paths.

Fast Facts   There are no banks on Caye Caulker. Change money and traveler's checks at your hotel. The Caye Caulker Health Center, across from the Hotel Marin, can provide first aid—open Mon–Fri 8–11:30am and 1–4:30pm. Several ladies on the island take in laundry; watch for their signs. Safety is becoming more of a concern in Caye Caulker, so don't leave anything valuable in your hotel room. The telephone office is near The Reef Hotel on a cross street—open Mon–Fri 8am–noon and 1–4pm, Sat 8am–noon. Remember to dial 0 before the phone number when calling from within Belize.

Long the secret budget beach hideaway of Belize, Caye Caulker (pop. 1,000) is on the verge of becoming another San Pedro. While I was there last, the island's residents were voting on whether to open the long-talked-about airstrip. The general consensus was a hearty affirmative. It is unfortunate for backpacking travelers that this airstrip, when completed, could spell the end of cheap lodgings on this quiet island.

This is still a great place in which to just do nothing; but if you really want to get away from things, head down the coast to Placencia. There's not much in the way of tourist amenities: some basic hotels and hostelries and a few simple restaurants and bars. However, the accommodations and restaurants have vastly improved in the past couple of years. As on Ambergris Caye, there's no real beach here, just a few docks for sunbathing and swimming. (If I didn't tell you about "the beach" called The Cut, you probably wouldn't recognize it as such.) Caye Caulker is primarily a lobster-fishing village supplying the export market. The lobster catch has been down in recent years due to overfishing, and more and more the island's residents are turning to the tourism industry to make a dollar. Its residents—a blend of Creoles, Mestizos, and a few immigrant Anglos—quietly welcome the mostly young tourists who come over from Belize City for the sun, swimming, quiet, and, most of all, the low prices.

Unfortunately, some of the tourist hustling that characterizes Belize City has crept over to Caye Caulker. Young local men will approach you constantly, trying to sell you everything from a cheap room to marijuana. Just refuse politely and go on your way. Remember: Never pay for a boat trip until the trip is completed.

WHAT TO SEE AND DO

The main activity on Caye Caulker is swimming and sunbathing at The Cut or off the docks. Currents through The Cut can be swift, and only strong swimmers or those with flippers should attempt to swim it. The water is very calm off Back Bridge, making it a good place to practice if you're an inexperienced snorkeler. Take care if you're swimming off a dock. After a swimmer was killed by a boat, a designated swimming area was set aside off the Front Bridge.

Several boats leave from the front-side docks on day-long trips to the reef. For safety's sake, the boat should be in good condition, with a working motor (even on sailboats) in case the seas become rough or in the rare event that a quick rescue is needed. Your guide should be attentive and aware of your experience or inexperience.

Ellen McRae, resident marine biologist and founder of Cari Search, Ltd. (a group dedicated to research and protection of Belize's natural environment), advises that "you'll be safe with just about any of the residents who take people out, but it's still best to find out about the recent experiences of fellow tourists on the island." If you want to know more about what you'll see at the reef, Ellen offers a Reef Ecology Tour that includes a one-hour lecture in the morning before an afternoon of guided snorkeling for B$20 ($10) with gear rental extra. She also offers three-hour bird/cayes ecology hikes for B$10 ($5). Bring binoculars if you have them. You can find Ellen at the **Galeria Hicaco** (tel. 022-2178) gift shop, near the Tropical Paradise, which features original artwork made in Belize.

Another local to look for is resident artist Philip Lewis, whose drawings of Belize and detailed map of Caulker are sold in the Galeria. If you'd like to see more than what's on display, Philip (also known by his nickname, "Karate") can usually be found eating the heavenly ice cream at the Tropical in the mornings; he'll be the one carrying the large sketchpad.

Sea-ing is Belizing (open daily from 9am–noon and 1–6pm) is another gallery specializing in underwater photography by co-owner James Beveridge, who has been photographing Belize since 1969. Besides selling photographic postcards and framed and unframed prints, the gallery offers a slide show illustrating the reefs and cayes. The program is held regularly during the busy season and during the off-season can be arranged for groups of ten or more people. It costs about B$3 ($1.50) per person. They also offer T-shirts, books about Belize, and film processing.

Right beside Sea-ing Is Belizing is **Belize Diving Services,** Caye Caulker's only full-service dive center. Open Mon–Sat from 8:30am–5pm; Sun from 10am–4pm. A two-tank dive will cost you B$80 ($40). They also offer cave diving to certified cave divers, four-day scuba-diving courses, and equipment rental.

WHERE TO STAY

Accommodations on Caye Caulker have improved in recent years, but they're still far from luxurious. In the off-season (May through August), it's possible to get substantial discounts. However, you'll have to put up with biting flies in May and mosquitoes in June, July, and August. Besides the hotels listed below, there are furnished houses for rent on Caye Caulker—just walk around, and you'll see signs for them.

DOUBLES FOR LESS THAN B$35 ($17.50)

JIMENEZ'S HUTS, Caye Caulker. Tel. 501/22-2175. 8 rms, 3 with bath.
$ Rates: B$10 ($5) single; B$15 ($7.50) double; B$30 ($15) cabaña for 1–4 people. No credit cards.

⭐ Across the island from the Tropical Paradise Hotel (below) is this very attractive little grouping of cabañas set in a sunny garden with conch shell–lined walkway. The three "huts" are peaceful and secluded, and have palm-trunk walls, thatched roofs, and little porches. Inside each contains one or two double beds, a hammock, and a very basic bathroom with cold water only. The other eight rooms are not nearly as nice, so hold out for a hut. The owner was a lobster fisherman for years until the lobster harvest began to decline.

THE ANCHORAGE, south of the Front Bridge, Caye Caulker. No phone. 4 rms., all with bath.
$ Rates: B$35 ($17.50) single/double. No credit cards.
A ten-minute walk south of the Front Bridge, The Anchorage is the sort of place tropical travelers on a very low budget dream about—white sand, coconut palms rustling in the trade winds, turquoise water, and the distant murmur of waves crashing on the barrier reef. There are four white-washed adobe huts with palm-thatch roofs, each with its own bath (cold-water showers only). American Jo Ann Wilson is the owner here.

IGNACIO'S BEACH CABAÑAS, south of Front Bridge, Caye Caulker. No phone. 9 rms., all with bath.
$ Rates: B$10.50 ($5.25) single; B$21 ($10.50) double; B$31.50 ($15.75) triple; B$3.50 ($1.75) per person to camp. No credit cards.

Ⓢ These are currently the accommodations on the island most popular with the backpack set. Located next door to The Anchorage, the cabañas here are brightly painted little wooden boxes that sit right on the sand and give the appearance of a shanty town, but the groups of young people relaxing in hammocks strung between the palm trees indicate that this is a low-budget tropical paradise. The owner, Ignacio, is one of the island's more colorful characters.

TOM'S HOTEL, south of Front Bridge. Tel. 501/22-2102. 23 rms, 3 with bath.
$ Rates: B$15 ($7.50) single; B$25 ($12.50) double without bath, B$60 ($30) double with bath. No credit cards.
The rooms here are tiny and can get hot and stuffy, but if you spend all your time snorkeling or hanging out elsewhere, you won't mind very much. It's certainly difficult to beat the prices. There are a veranda overlooking the water and a private dock for tanning. The cabañas, with private baths, are much roomier than the rooms in the main building. Consider the rooms last resorts if none of the cabañas is available.

DOUBLES FOR LESS THAN B$70 [$35]

TROPICAL PARADISE HOTEL, RESTAURANT, AND ICE CREAM PARLOUR, Caye Caulker. Tel. 501/022-2124. Fax 501/22-2225. 13 rms, 2 with A/C, all with bath.
$ Rates: B$50–B$60 ($25–$30) single; B$60–B$75 ($30–$37.50) double; B$75–B$85 ($37.50–$42.50) triple. No credit cards.

⭐ This should be your first choice for both a room and a good meal on Caye Caulker. Proprietor Ramon Reyes runs a tight ship: The rooms are very clean and paneled, with a little bit of storage space for your things and a narrow front porch for catching the breeze. The hot water is a bit finicky, however. Of the 13 rooms, 8 are cabins. These last are the most expensive and are quite a bit larger than the rooms. But the cabins aren't as breezy as the rooms at the back of the complex behind the restaurant that bears the same name. This is as good as budget accommodations get in Belize.

REEF HOTEL, north of the Front Bridge, Caye Caulker. Tel. 501/22-2196. 16 rms., all with bath.

$ Rates: B$40 ($20) single; B$50 ($25) double; B$60 ($30) triple; lower rates in May–Oct. No credit cards.

⑤ This is one of the better hotels on the island, although it's still very basic: a two-story building with 16 rooms facing the water. The rooms are quite small, but there are chairs for relaxing on the porches that run the length of the building. All the rooms have private baths with hot water, ceiling fans, double beds, and water views. The manager can be found at the bar next door.

RAINBOW HOTEL, north of Front Bridge, Caye Caulker. Tel. 501/22-2123. 16 rms., all with bath.

$ Rates: B$50 ($25) single; B$60 ($30) double; B$70 ($35) triple; lower rates in May–Oct. No credit cards.

Located next door to the Reef Hotel, the Rainbow is very similar in appearance to the Reef, both inside and out. Only a few feet from the water it has a veranda and a private dock for guests. The rooms are clean, with tiled showers, ceiling fans, and louvered windows that let in the breezes. Double and twin beds are available. It may be difficult to find the manager; sometimes there's someone around and sometimes there isn't.

WHERE TO EAT

As on Ambergris Caye, seafood is popular and plentiful all year but cheaper than in San Pedro. Do remember to abide by the seasons on lobster, conch, shrimp, and don't order turtle steaks (sea turtles are endangered). The seasons are the same for Ambergris Caye. Restaurants are not supposed to serve lobster in the off-season, when the lobsters are breeding. If it's on the menu off-season, please don't order it.

Caye Caulker has a thriving cottage industry of snack bakers. Wander the streets and you're sure to see signs offering yogurt and granola, freshly squeezed juices, hot lobster pie, sweet rolls, chocolate or cheese pie—each B$1 (50¢). Don't be bashful: Just step right up and knock on the door for a homemade treat. You won't be disappointed. (It's also a chance to get a glimpse into a few Belizean homes.) For more substantial meals, try one of the restaurants listed below.

MEALS FOR LESS THAN B$15 ($7.50)

ABERDEEN RESTAURANT, just south of the Hotel Martinez. Tel. 022-2127.
Cuisine: CHINESE.
$ Prices: B$8–B$16 ($4–$8). MC, V.
Open: Daily 8am–10pm.

The menu is Chinese, the music is reggae, the servings are generous, and the decor is sparse. You can pick from a long list of all the standards prepared with nearly every type of meat or seafood. How about sweet-and-sour conch or lobster chop suey. The most interesting dishes available are listed on the back of the menu: tempting offerings such as salty pepper shrimp and lobster with peppers and black soy beans. If you've been missing vegetables in your diet, this is the place to eat your fill.

CABANAS BAR & RESTAURANT, on the water just before The Cut. Tel. 022-2200.
Cuisine: SEAFOOD/INTERNATIONAL.
$ Prices: B$8–B$15 ($4–$7.50). No credit cards.
Open: Daily 7am–3pm and 6pm–midnight.

★ Up at the north end of the island, near The Cut, this little restaurant serves up some tasty seafood dinners. Barbecued fish and fish with mustard sauce were the day's specials when I stopped by. Originally, the restaurant was just a tiny bar in an old house, but, as it gained popularity, the owners built onto the front and expanded into a restaurant. The white tables contrast with the plain wood interior and with the colorful nautical flags that hang above the bar. Louvered windows let in the tradewinds. The menu consists primarily of fish, conch, shrimp, and lobster prepared in sweet-and-sour sauce, curry sauce, or tomato sauce. The fresh-fruit juices are a delicious accompaniment to any meal here. Great place to stop after a sunset swim at The Cut.

TROPICAL PARADISE HOTEL RESTAURANT AND ICE CREAM PARLOR, south of Front Bridge. Tel. 022-2124.
   Cuisine: INTERNATIONAL.
$ Prices: Breakfast B$3–B$7 ($1.50–$3.50); dinner B$7–B$13 ($3.50–$6.50). No credit cards.
   Open: Daily 8am–2pm and 6–9pm.

The Tropical Paradise stays packed for all three meals. It's so popular because it serves the most consistent food on the island at very good prices. Inside, it's light and breezy and has the feel of a small-town diner. Try one of the dinner specials, such as curried shrimp and lobster lasagna for B$13 ($6.50). In the afternoon and evening, everyone on the island comes for soft ice cream, which goes for B$1 (50¢) small and B$1.50 (75¢) large. Flavors change daily and include vanilla, blueberry, peach, peanut and chocolate, and Ta Mara.

HOTEL MARTINEZ'S RESTAURANT AND BAR, north of Front Bridge near the Reef Hotel. Tel. 022-2113.
   Cuisine: SEAFOOD/MEXICAN.
$ Prices: Breakfast B$4–B$5 ($2–$2.50); lunch and dinner B$7–B$12 ($3.50–$6). No credit cards.
   Open: Daily 7am–10pm.

S Martinez's serves throughout the day, and it's almost always busy with locals and tourists alike. Start your day here with lobster and eggs for B$9 ($4.50); for lunch and dinner, you have your choice of steaks, burgers, lobster, and fish. Do try a fishburger at least once while you're here. Whenever hunger strikes, you can duck in here and get a cheap fast Mexican snack for B$1 (50¢). Plus, there's always the old stand-by of rice and beans or beans and rice. Martinez's popular rum punch is sold by the bottle for B$9 ($4.50) or by the glass for B$2.50 ($1.25)—it's guaranteed to put you in a tropical frame of mind.

MEALS FOR LESS THAN B$25 ($12.50)

MARIN'S RESTAURANT, located a block west of the Tropical Paradise. Tel. 022-2104.
   Cuisine: INTERNATIONAL.
$ Prices: Complete dinner B$8–B$18 ($3.50–$9). MC.
   Open: Daily 8am–2pm and 5:30–10:30pm.

There's plenty of local atmosphere here, with soca music playing all day long. Marin's serves fresh seafood in its outdoor garden or in its mosquito-proof dining room. Try the shrimp or lobster with pineapple (Belizean style, sweet-and-sour) for B$18 ($9) or the catch of the day (steamed, fried, or baked) for B$8 ($4). If you're starving, go for the Marin's special, a platter of fried shrimp, conch, and fish.

EVENING ENTERTAINMENT

Star gaze, go for a night dive, or have a drink in one of the island's handful of bars. That's about it for nightlife on Caye Caulker.

SHOPPING

There are only a few shops on the island: a couple of general stores, a couple of gift shops, a deli, a yogurt and whole-wheat bread company, and the two galleries mentioned under "What to See and Do."

Jan's Deli is a good place to pick up bread, cheese, yogurt, drinks, and other staples. Open Monday to Saturday from 7am to 1pm and 3 to 7pm, Sunday from 8am to noon.

CHAPTER 17

ELSEWHERE IN BELIZE

1. BELMOPAN
- **FROMMER'S FAVORITE BELIZE EXPERIENCES**

2. PLACENCIA

3. SAN IGNACIO AND THE CAYO DISTRICT

4. COROZAL TOWN AND THE NORTHERN HIGHWAY

As is often the case in places blessed with beautiful islands, warm waters, and colorful coral reefs, areas away from the water can be overlooked. When you've had enough sunshine and swimming out on the cayes, spend some time exploring the rest of Belize. Once the heart of the Mayan empire, Belize has many excavations scattered throughout the country.

In Western Belize's Cayo District, a densely forested region of limestone mountains and clear-running rivers, Caracol is the largest Mayan city yet discovered. Though Caracol has not been turned into a major tourist destination like the Mayan ruins in Mexico or Guatemala, it's worth seeing for serious students of Mesoamerican cultures. The mountains here are laced with caves, several of which can be explored.

Wildlife abounds throughout Belize, though it is increasingly endangered. The Belize Zoo, near the capital city of Belmopan is dedicated to educating the public about the benefits of preserving Belize's wild heritage. South of Belmopan is the Cockscomb Basin Wildlife Preserve, world's first jaguar preserve. North of Belmopan are the Community Baboon Sanctuary (a howler monkey preserve) and the Crooked Tree Wildlife Sanctuary, another preserve that is home to many rare species of tropical birds.

If you find yourself in need of another dose of beach life, Placencia, in southern Belize, offers the best beach in the country. Miles of sand stretch northward from this tranquil little village at the tip of a long peninsula.

1. BELMOPAN

Distances: 52 miles from Belize City;
30 miles from San Ignacio; 90 miles from Placencia.

GETTING THERE   By Bus   Batty Bros., Novelos, Z-Line, and Venus all run buses to Belmopan frequently throughout the day. Duration: 1½ hours. Fare: B$2.75 ($1.38).

By Car   From Belize City, take Cemetery Road to the Western Highway.

DEPARTING   Buses run frequently to San Ignacio, Belize City, and Dangriga. From Dangriga you can get a bus to Placencia if you arrive before 3pm. It's about 1½ hours to either Belize City or San Ignacio and 3 hours to Dangriga.

ESSENTIALS   Orientation   Belmopan is a planned city with a ring road and wide deserted streets. The bus station is on the west side, and the three hotels listed

FROMMER'S FAVORITE
BELIZE EXPERIENCES

A Sailboat Trip to Hol Chan Marine Reserve The barrier reef off the coast of Belize is the second longest in the world, and the wooden sailboats that sail from Caye Caulker will take you to the protected waters of the Hol Chan Marine Reserve off Ambergris Caye. After a couple of hours of sailing, you can snorkel or scuba dive, then visit San Pedro on Ambergris Caye before sailing back to Caye Caulker.

Canoeing on the Macal River Three-foot-long iguanas bask along the rocky banks and skitter for cover as canoes float past. Women wash their laundry while standing knee-deep in the river, and children swing from ropes and splash into the water. A day spent paddling quietly along the course of the Macal and the nearby Mopan rivers is a day well spent.

A Visit to the Cockscomb Basin Wildlife Preserve This preserve was created to protect the world's largest concentration of jaguars. Trails lead through the jungle, and it's even possible to camp here.

A Day Trip to the Mountain Pine Ridge Deep in the mountains of western Belize's Cayo District is a rugged forest reserve with a waterfall called both Hidden Valley Falls and Thousand Foot Falls, as well as the Río Frio (Cold River). You'll be thankful for the cold water after a hot day of exploring the caves, waterfalls, and remote roads of the Mountain Pine Ridge.

here are on the east side. There is only one road in or out of the city. It branches off the Hummingbird (Southern) Highway 2½ miles south of the Western Highway.

Conceived as the dynamic center of a growing Belize, Belmopan (pop. 4,000) is actually a sleepy place 2½ miles in from the Western Highway. Modest government buildings are laid out according to a master plan, and small residential areas are enclosed by a ring road. Business seems limited to a gas station, a few little food shops, and three modest hostelries. The facilities here that you may find useful are a bank, post office, hospital, and microwave telephone installation.

Belmopan is a model city designed and built from scratch in the jungle at the geographical center of the country. It's still under construction, and as with all such new-founded capitals, it'll be a while before it becomes the cultural center of the country. A 20-year development plan predicts a pulsating metropolis of 30,000 before the end of the century, but there's still much to be done. It's still, hot, and quiet here, with cicadas humming constantly; women use umbrellas to protect themselves against the sun, with good reason.

The Western Highway to Belmopan (about 50 miles) is sometimes good, sometimes bad. The road to the new capital takes you into the foothills of the Maya Mountains and through farming country that's quite pretty. Onward from Belmopan, the road climbs slowly into the Maya Mountains, and the seamy, ramshackle way of life in Belize's coastal towns gives way to cooler, less humid air, a workaday farming life, and greater natural beauty. This is home to macaws, mahogany, mangoes, jaguars, and orchids.

WHAT TO SEE AND DO
IN TOWN

If you're in town on Monday, Wednesday, or Friday morning, you may be able to arrange a guided tour of the vault in the basement of the **Archeology Department** (near the bus station). Since Belize doesn't yet have a museum the many Mayan artifacts found at sites around the country are displayed here.

OUT OF TOWN

There are several possible excursions that can be made with Belmopan as a base.

The Belize Zoo

By the time you finally get around to visiting the Belize Zoo, you'll already be familiar with the zoo's most famous resident—April the tapir—because her picture appears on posters all over the country. April is just one of dozens of species of animals native to Belize that are housed in this zoo. Among the most popular are a variety of indigenous Belizean cats and other wild animals in natural surroundings. The animals here are some of the liveliest and happiest-looking that I've ever seen in a zoo. It's obvious that they're well cared for. All the exhibits have informative signs accompanying them. One such explains that parrots are noisy and like to squawk and talk—a lot—and that they live as long as 75 years.

The entrance is a mile in from the highway. If you're stopping here on your way to the border, make sure before you get off the bus that there is no sign saying the zoo is temporarily closed. Do a bit of calculating as to when the next bus will be coming by, or plan on hitching to your next destination. A new zoo is under construction, but funding (this is a private zoo) is slow. By the time you visit, the new zoo may be open; it's right on the highway in the same location.

Admission is B$10 ($5). Open daily 10am–4:30pm. At mile 28 Western Highway.

Guanacaste Park

Where the Hummingbird Highway turns off of the Western Highway, about 2½ miles north of Belmopan, is a 50-acre park that's an excellent introduction to tropical forests. Guanacaste Park is named for a huge old guanacaste tree that is found within the park. Guanacaste trees were traditionally preferred for building dugout canoes, but this particular tree, which is about 100 years old, was spared the boat-builders' ax because it has a triple trunk that makes it unacceptable for canoe building. More than 35 species of epiphytes (plants that grow on other plants), including orchids, bromeliads, ferns, mosses, lichens, and philodendrons cover its trunk and branches.

There are nearly 2 miles of trails in the park, with several benches for sitting and observing wildlife. The park is bordered on the west by Roaring Creek and on the north by the Belize River. Among the animals you might see are more than 100 species of birds, large iguanas, armadillos, kinkajous, deer, agoutis (large rodents that are a favorite game meat in Belize), and jaguarundis (small jungle cats). A map and a brochure about the park are available from the Belize Audubon Society in Belize City.

St. Herman's Cave and the Blue Hole

The Maya Mountains are primarily limestone and consequently are laced with caves. In fact, this region of Belize is known as Cave Branch because of the numerous caves. About 11 miles from Belmopan on the Hummingbird Highway, you'll come across a dirt road to the right. About half a mile down this road is the entrance to St. Herman's Cave, one of the largest and most easily accessible caves in Belize. You'll need at least two good flashlights and sturdy shoes to explore this undeveloped ½-mile long cave.

Equally fascinating is the collapsed cavern just off the Hummingbird Highway, 12½ miles from Belmopan. After locking your car and placing any valuables in the trunk, walk down the cement steps. Dense jungle surrounds a small natural pool of a deep turquoise. A limestone cliff rises up from the edge of the pool on two sides. The water flows for only about 100 feet on the surface before disappearing into a cave. This is a great place for a quick dip on a hot day because the water is refreshingly cool and clear. You can clearly see fish swimming around the edges of the Blue Hole.

WHERE TO STAY AND EAT

CIRCLE A HOTEL, 37 Half Moon Ave., Belmopan. Tel. 501/8-22296. 14 rms., all with bath.

$ Rates: B$50 ($25) single, B$60 ($30) single with A/C; B$60 ($30) double, B$70 ($35) double with A/C. MC, V.

There aren't too many reasons to come to Belmopan, unless you have business at one of the government ministries. However, if you do stay over, this is the place to check first. To reach the Circle A, take a taxi or drive around the circle road that goes left from the bus station. If you want to walk, it'll take about ten minutes along the path behind the market to the right; when the path forks, bear left and follow it to the end. A shopping center will be on your right and Half Moon Avenue will be on your left. Most of the rooms here are carpeted, and some have TVs. The restaurant next door is open from 7am to 10pm and serves Chinese food for B$7 ($3.50) to B$15 ($7.50).

BULL FROG INN, 25 Half Moon Ave., P.O. Box 28, Belmopan. Tel. 501/8-22111 or 8-23155. 13 rms., all with bath. A/C TV

$ Rates: B$63–B$90 ($31.50–$45) single; B$74–B$110 ($37–$55) double; B$130 ($65) triple. AE, MC, V.

The only other budget lodging in town is just a couple of doors down from the Circle A Hotel. The higher prices are for the new rooms, which are larger and much nicer than the old rooms. The old rooms, although small, have air conditioning, fans, TVs, and carpeting. The new rooms have more light, balconies, phones, and very nice bathrooms with tubs. There's a cool open-air restaurant attached to the hotel serving breakfast for B$8 ($4) and lunch and dinner for B$8 to B$22 ($4 to $11).

BANANA BANK RANCH, Box 48, Belmopan. Tel. 501/8-23180 or 8-22677. Fax 501/8-22366. 2 cabins, 1 rm with bath, 3 rms without bath.

$ Rates: (including three meals): B$109.25 ($54.63) single without bath, B$155.25 ($77.63) single with bath; B$172.50 ($86.25) double without bath; B$218.50 ($109.25) double with bath; B$304.75 ($152.38) triple with bath; B$345 ($172.50) quad with bath. No credit cards.

The turnoff for this fascinating lodge is at Mile 47 on the Western Highway, not far past the turnoff for Belmopan. From here it is about 1¼ miles to the ranch. Owners John and Carolyn Carr moved to Belize from the United States nearly 15 years ago. Carolyn is an artist who sells her oil paintings here in Belize, and John is a cowboy from Montana. Together, they operate one of the oldest cattle ranches in Belize and for several years have been taking in paying guests. The guest quarters are on the banks of the Belize River. Each of the two cabins comes complete with a sleeping loft, room for six people, a private bathroom, two bedrooms, queen-size beds, and plenty of space to spread out and make yourself at home. These cabins also have their own private patios overlooking the river. One room in the main house even has a waterbed. On the property you can visit a Mayan ruin and meet the Carr's pet jaguar, Tika. Horseback riding, canoeing, and even horse-drawn buggy rides can be arranged at additional cost. Meals are served in a small dining room. The house specialty is barbecued pork spare ribs, served with all the trimmings.

CAMPING

MONKEY BAY WILDLIFE SANCTUARY, Mile 32 Western Highway, P.O. Box 187, Belmopan. No phone.

About 1½ miles down a dirt road off the Western Highway, 4 miles west of the Belize Zoo, is a tranquil spot where you can park your RV or pitch a tent. There are no monkeys and no bay, but there are beautiful big trees, acres of pasture, a creek, a river nearby, and plenty of solitude. The privately owned sanctuary is only just being developed and so the facilities are primitive. Register with the caretaker, Pedro Reyes, who lives in the little house on the other side of the fence.

2. PLACENCIA

Distances: 150 miles from Belize City (120 miles by New Belize Road); 100 miles from Belmopan; 55 miles from Punta Gorda.

GETTING THERE By Plane There are six flights daily between Big Creek (across the bay from Placencia) and Belize City on Maya Airways. Fare: B$76 ($38) one way, B$141 ($70.50) round trip.

By Bus On Mon, Wed, Fri, and Sat there is bus service between Dangriga and Placencia. Buses depart Dangriga around 4pm and from Placencia at 6am. Fare: B$6 ($3). Alternatively, there are several buses daily that operate between Dangriga and Mango Creek (Z-Line and Williams Bus) and between Belize City and Mango Creek (Williams Bus Service from the Pound Yard Bridge and Z-Line from Magazine Road). Fares: from Belize City B$12 ($6), from Dangriga B$4 ($2). From Mango Creek, you must take a boat across Placencia Lagoon—see "By Boat" below for details.

By Car Take the Western Highway from Belize City. Around Mile 30, watch for the New Belize Road turnoff for Democracia and points south. This good dirt road now has a bridge where it was once necessary to ford a river, which was possible only in the dry season. The road cuts 30 miles off the drive to Placencia but bypasses Belmopan, the Blue Hole, St. Herman's Cave, and Guanacaste Park. At the end of the New Belize Road turn left onto the Hummingbird Highway. In 1½ miles, you'll come to the turnoff for the Southern Highway (Dangriga is 6 miles farther). After 22½ miles on the Southern Highway, turn left onto the road to Riversdale and Placencia. From this turnoff it's another 20 miles to Placencia. Be sure to fill your tank in Dangriga.

By Boat Outboard-powered skiffs, which can carry up to six people, can be hired for the trip across Placencia Lagoon from Big Creek or Mango Creek for B$25 ($12.50), one way.

DEPARTING The bus for Dangriga leaves Mon, Wed, Fri, and Sat at 6am from Placencia. Buses also leave from Mango Creek several times daily for Dangriga, Belize City, and Punta Gorda. There are also daily flights from Big Creek to Belize City.

ESSENTIALS Orientation There's only one road in Placencia, and it ends at the dock and gas station at the south end of town. The town's main thoroughfare is the Sidewalk, a narrow cement path that parallels the beach beginning at the Fishermen's Co-op by the dock.

Fast Facts The post office is east of the Fishermen's Co-op, behind the Firebun Bar. Open Monday to Friday from 8am to noon and 1 to 4pm, Saturday from 8am to 1pm. The village's public phone is also in the Firebun Bar.

Located at the southern tip of a long, sandy peninsula that is separated from the mainland by a narrow lagoon, Placencia is a tiny Creole village of pastel-colored houses on stilts. The town's main thoroughfare is a sidewalk, which will give you some idea of how laid-back and quiet this place is. If you're looking for lots to see and do, you're better off going to Ambergris Caye. The people here are still friendly to tourists, and you don't have the hassles that come with a stay on Caye Caulker. Best of all is that Placencia has the only "real" beach in Belize—16 miles of white sand backed with dense vegetation.

WHAT TO SEE AND DO

There isn't much to do in Placencia, which is exactly why people come here. You just can't help slowing down and relaxing. Sit back, sip a seaweed punch, and forget your cares. Nobody ever seems to get up early (except maybe the fishermen), and most people spend their days reading and eating seafood. The beach, although narrow, is the only real beach I know of in Belize. You can walk for miles and see hardly a soul. North of town a mile or two, there's good snorkeling right off the beach.

If you're serious about diving or snorkeling, you'll want to get a group together and hire a boat to take you out to the dozens of little offshore cayes. It's between 10 and 25 miles out to the reef here, so a snorkeling or dive trip is not cheap. At **Placencia Dive Shop** (Kitty's Place), north of town, scuba divers pay between B$120 and B$140 ($60 and $70) for two dives; snorkelers B$70 to B$90 ($35 to $45) for trips including equipment, food, drinks, and a guide. Bring a lot of sunscreen. More adventurous types can organize overnight boat trips to remote rivers where the wildlife is said to be spectacular. These trips are B$200 per day at Placencia Dive Shop, although less expensive day trips also are available. If you ask around town, you can probably arrange a trip out to the reef or cayes for much less than what Kitty charges. Snorkeling trips (including equipment, lunch, and drinks) can be arranged at the Firebun Bar for B$20 ($10).

Fishing around here is some of the best in Belize. A day's fishing expedition will cost B$400 ($200) for a boat. Grouper, tarpon, bonefish, and snook are the popular gamefish.

WHERE TO STAY
DOUBLES FOR LESS THAN B$35 ($17.50)

SEASPRAY, Placencia. No phone. 6 rms., 4 with bath.
$ Rates: B$21 ($10.50) double without bath, B$32 ($16) double with bath. No credit cards.
The rooms here are small and lack any semblance of style, but they're inexpensive and conveniently located in the middle of town. Fans help you stay cool at night, and, if you're traveling in a group, you might appreciate the bunkbeds. The rooms are arranged on either side of a wide hallway, which serves as the lounge and library.

Jene's Restaurant is just across the sidewalk; a little thatched-roof bar is out back by the water.

PARADISE VACATION HOTEL, Placencia. Tel. 501/6-23119. 12 rms., 4 with bath.
$ Rates: B$15 ($7.50) single without bath; B$30 ($15) double without bath; B$35 ($17.50) triple without bath; B$40 ($20) single/double/triple with bath. No credit cards.

$ Although it hardly lives up to its glorious name, the Paradise Vacation Hotel is Placencia's best and most popular true budget hotel. You'll find everyone from backpackers to vacationing lodge owners here. The ground-floor rooms have private baths and are slightly more spacious than the rooms without baths. The eight rooms on the second floor get more breezes and share two moderately clean bathrooms downstairs and at the back of the building. The calm waters of the bay lap at your doorstep and there's a pier that is great for sunning and swimming.

Tentacles restaurant next door serves good seafood and is a popular place to hang out and meet interesting people. Meals range from B$7 to B$15 ($3.50 to $7.50).

DOUBLES FOR LESS THAN B$100 ($50)

SONNY'S RESORT, Placencia. Tel. 501/6-2046, ext. 103. 11 rms., all with bath.
$ Rates: B$70 ($35) single; B$100 ($50) double; B$120 ($60) cabaña. V.
One of the older hotels in Placencia, Sonny's was started with a couple of mobile homes that had been divided into three guest rooms each. Over the years, screened porches were added to them, giving them a more permanent feel, and although they have seen better days, they still suffice. However, since the new owner, Louise Wade, took over, she has added three new cabins and plans to add more. These new cabins are spacious wooden buildings raised up on stilts. Each has a large porch and is situated to make the most of the prevailing tradewinds. They also have small refrigerators, coffeemakers, reading lamps, and high ceilings with fans.

The resort's restaurant is a casual diner-style place with a small bar where fishermen swap stories in the evening. It's open 7am to 10pm daily. Prices range from B$6 to B$12 ($3 to $6).

WORTH THE EXTRA BUCKS

RANGUANA LODGE, Placencia. Tel. 501/6-23112. 5 cabins, all with bath.
$ Rates: B$80 ($40) single; B$160 ($80) double; B$85 ($170) triple. No credit cards.

Although the five cabins here are packed together on a tiny piece of sand in the middle of town, they're still very attractive inside. The water is only a few steps away. Nearly everything in these cozy cabins is made of hardwood—walls, floors, ceilings, even the louvered windows. Each has a little refrigerator and coffeemaker, porch, tub, and table.

Just outside your door, you'll find a little thatch-roofed open-air bar where folks (both local and foreign) love to sit around all day gabbing and drinking and soaking up the sun. The Kingfisher serves as the restaurant for the Ranguana Lodge. It's a big screened-in room right on the water, where a meal will cost anywhere from B$12 to B$25 ($6 to $12.50).

WHERE TO EAT

THE GALLEY, near the police station. No phone.
Cuisine: BELIZEAN.
$ Prices: Fruit shakes B$3 ($1.50); meals B$6–B$10 ($3–$5). No credit cards.
Open: Daily 8am–9pm.

The best snacks and milk shakes in Placencia—or in all of Belize, for that matter—are to be found at a walk-up window beneath an old wooden Caribbean-style house on stilts near the south end of the Placencia sidewalk. The lady who runs The Galley takes whatever fruits are available and turns them into delicious icy shakes. Fruits with names such as craboo, mamey, and soursop are some of the more unusual flavors. For less adventurous imbibers there are mango, papaya, and melon shakes. Order a piece of casava cake too for a very filling snack or breakfast. There are even a few tables here in the sand beneath the house. You can order complete meals, such as venison, steaks, conch fritters, fish filets, and even chow mein and chop suey. The Galley epitomizes the laid-back life of Placencia. That's why it's my favorite place to eat here.

KINGFISHER RESTAURANT, behind Ranguana Lodge. No phone.
Cuisine: BELIZEAN/SEAFOOD.
$ Prices: B$8–B$25 ($4–$12.50). No credit cards.
Open: Wed–Mon 7am–11pm.

Situated on the beach, the Kingfisher is a large, open room with screen walls that let in the sea breezes. The big porch out front is a great place to relax with a drink and meet interesting people. Inside, the decor is early jungle rustic, with a jaguar skin nailed to the wall. Fish, shrimp, conch, and lobster make up the bulk of the short menu, with pork chops, fried chicken, and steaks also available. There are daily seafood specials for around B$12 ($6), which make this one of the best places to find inexpensive seafood.

JENE'S RESTAURANT, across from Seaspray Hotel. Tel. 06-23110.
Cuisine: BELIZEAN/INTERNATIONAL.
$ Prices: B$10–B$25 ($5–$12.50). No credit cards.
Open: Tues–Sun 7:30am–10pm.

Jene's is a long-time favorite in Placencia. The small dining room has hardwood paneling, floors, and ceiling. Paper money from countries all over the world adorns one wall—a testimonial to the diverse backgrounds of visitors who've discovered Placencia. Another wall features a large map of Belize. You can plan your upcoming jungle expeditions while you dine on lobster, fish filets, conch, or shrimp. All meals can be fried, boiled, or broiled and come with french fries and a vegetable. Hamburgers, fishburgers, and veggie burgers also available. Refreshing fresh juices are available daily.

TENTACLES, next door to Paradise Vacation Hotel. No phone.
    Cuisine: SEAFOOD.
$ **Prices:** B$8–B$16 ($4–$8). No credit cards.
    Open: Thurs–Tues 7:30am–10pm.

★   It's hard to beat the view from the second-floor deck of this restaurant at the very southern end of Placencia. There are more tables outside than there are inside, but no matter where you sit, you'll be among friendly locals, tourists, businesspeople, and boaters in from the sailboats moored offshore. The conversation is usually lively. You'll find all the Belizean standards on the menu. If the food isn't memorable, the setting certainly is: The mangrove swamps begin a few steps away, while several little islands dot the far horizon; sailboats rock gently at anchor while skiffs race back and forth to the mainland. It's positively bewitching when the moon sparkles on the waves.

EVENING ENTERTAINMENT

The Cozy Corner Disco is where it's happening in Placencia. Locals and tourists dance the night away at this tiny place right on the beach, behind the police station. It's open Wednesday, Friday, and Saturday.

SHOPPING

You'll see a couple of little shops around the village offering black coral jewelry for sale and prominently displaying their permits to do so. Please don't take this as a sign that it's okay to buy black coral jewelry. Black coral is an endangered organism due to over collecting, so please don't contribute to the further demise of this coral by encouraging its collection for jewelry-manufacturing purposes.

EXCURSION

THE COCKSCOMB BASIN WILDLIFE SANCTUARY

Weighing up to 200 pounds and measuring more than 6 feet from nose to tip of the tail, at twice the size of pumas, jaguars are the kings of the new-world jungles. Nocturnal predators, jaguars prefer to hunt peccaries (wild piglike animals), deer, and other small mammals. The Cockscomb Basin, a wildlife sanctuary established in 1986 as the world's first jaguar reserve, covers nearly 150 square miles of rugged forested mountains and has the greatest density of jaguars in the world. It is part of the even larger Cockscomb Basin Forest Reserve, which was created in 1984.

The forests within the preserve are home to other wild cats as well, including pumas, ocelots, and margays, all of which are very elusive, so don't get your hopes of seeing them too high. Few people do. Other mammals that you might spot if you're lucky include otters, coatimundis, kinkajous, deer, peccaries, anteaters, and armadillos.

The largest land mammal native to Central America—the tapir—is also resident. Locally known as a "mountain cow," the tapir is the national animal of Belize. A tapir can weigh up to 600 pounds and is related to the horse, although its protruding upper lip is more like an elephant's trunk. April, the Belize Zoo's tapir, appears on many wildlife protection posters, which you have probably seen in your travels around Belize.

Much more easily spotted in the dense vegetation that hems in the preserve's trails are the nearly 300 species of birds that have been identified here including the scarlet macaw, the keel-billed toucan, the king vulture, and the great curassow.

Great caution should be exercised when visiting the preserve—in addition to jaguars, which can be dangerous, there are also poisonous snakes, including the deadly fer-de-lance. Always wear shoes, preferably boots, when hiking the trails here.

Visitors' facilities include an information center, picnic area, campground, and a few primitive cabins. Drinking water is available. For more information on the preserve, contact the **Belize Audubon Society,** P.O. Box 1001, Belize City (tel. 02-77369).

---

3. SAN IGNACIO AND
THE CAYO DISTRICT

Distances: 72 miles W of Belize City; 40 miles W of Belmopan;
9 miles E of the Guatemalan border.

GETTING THERE By Bus Novelos and Batty Bros. buses leave frequently from their Collet Canal stations in Belize City. Duration: 3 hours. Fare: B$4 ($2). There's also frequent daily service from Belmopan. Duration: 1½ hours. Fare: B$3 ($1.50).

By Car Take the Western Highway from Belize City.

ESSENTIALS Orientation San Ignacio is on the banks of the Macal River, on the far side of an old metal bridge. Just across the bridge is a traffic circle. Downtown San Ignacio is to the right on Burns Avenue, and the San Ignacio Hotel is to the left on Buena Vista Road. Most of the hotels and restaurants are on or within a block of Burns Avenue.

Information See Bob at Eva's Restaurant on Burns Avenue for answers to questions about the area. He can help you arrange tours and accommodations

Fast Facts There is a drugstore downstairs from the Venus Hotel on Burns Avenue. The police emergency phone number is 2022. The telephone office is across from the Venus Hotel on Burns Avenue. Open Mon–Fri 8am–noon and 1–4pm, Sat 8am–noon.

DEPARTING Novelos and Batty Bros. operate buses to Belmopan and Belize City between 4am and 4pm. They take 2 hours and cost B$3 ($1.50) to Belmopan and B$4 ($2) to Belize City.

In the foothills of the mountains, close to the Guatemalan border, lie the twin towns of Santa Elena and San Ignacio (pop. 7,100) on either side of a beautiful calm, clear river (good for a swim). San Ignacio is the administrative center for the Cayo District, a region of cattle ranches and dense forests, of clear rivers and Mayan ruins. If you've come from Guatemala, you'll sense immediately that you are now in a Caribbean country. If you've come up from the coast, you might be surprised by how cool it can get up here in the mountains. Cayo and the cayes are worlds apart. While the cayes cater to those looking for fun in the sun, Cayo caters to those interested in nature. This area makes a good first stop in Belize; you can get in a lot of activity before heading to the beach to relax.

WHAT TO SEE AND DO

The first thing you should do is take a walk up to Linda Vista, a small gazebo perched on a hill above Santa Elena (walk up the hill on a dirt road near the Santa Elena end of the suspension bridge). From this vantage point, the towns look like picture-book scenes of tropical villages: white town hall, a bridge over the Macal River, and parrots squawking as they fly overhead in pairs. No one living here seems to have a care about the outside world.

Now that you've gotten a good view of the beautiful Macal River, you'll probably be anxious for a dip. Although you can hop in the river right beneath the bridge, there's a much better swimming hole 1½ miles away at a spot called Branch Mouth.

This is where the different-colored waters of the Macal and Mopan rivers converged. Branch Mouth is a favorite picnic spot, with shady old trees clinging to the river banks. There's even a rope swing from one of the trees. The road is dusty, so you'll be especially happy to go for a swim here.

For much of Belize's history, the rivers were the highways. The Mayans used them for trading, and British loggers used them to get at the mahogany they were seeking. If you're interested, you can explore the Cayo District's two rivers by canoe. In fact, you can paddle as far as the coast if you're so inclined. The waters in these rivers have a few riffles, but you don't need white-water experience. The trips are leisurely, with stops for swimming or land excursions. Scott Cast of **Float Belize,** P.O. Box 48, San Ignacio (tel. 092-2188), has been renting canoes here and guiding river trips for years, charging B$36 ($18) per day for a canoe, plus an additional charge for shuttling the canoe (anywhere from B$44 to B$90 [$22 to $45] depending on the number). Overnight trips and trips of up to seven days (to the coast) can be arranged.

Scott now has stiff competition from a young Belizean man named **Tony Santiago** (tel. 092-2267), who rents canoes for only B$25 ($12.50) per day. Tony charges similar shuttle fees and still comes out cheaper than Scott.

If you enjoy horseback riding, contact **Mountain Equestrian Trails,** Mile 8 Mountain Pine Ridge Road, Central Farm P.O., Cayo (tel. 092-2060). Although not cheap, they provide excellent horseback tours of the area, including visits to caves and waterfalls. A half-day trip costs B$90 ($45) per person; a full-day trip costs B$130 ($65).

WHERE TO STAY

Good accommodations in San Ignacio are scarce: There are lots of choices that are outside your budget and several that are more basic than you'll probably want, but little in between. Still, there are a few options in this beautiful neck of the Belizean woods.

DOUBLES FOR LESS THAN B$25 ($12.50)

VENUS HOTEL, 29 Burns Ave., San Ignacio, Cayo. Tel. 501/92-2186. 22 rms., 10 with bath.

$ Rates: B$22 ($11) single/double/triple without bath; B$40–B$60 ($20–$30) double with bath. AE.

The Venus Hotel, which opened in 1990, fills a gap in the San Ignacio hotel scene. Previously, there were high- and low-end hotels but nothing in the middle. Make this your first choice now. The rooms are large, clean, and bright. There are two TV lounges and a long veranda from which you can observe life in the street below. Although the cheapest rooms are quite basic (just beds), the larger rooms are quite nice, with wallpaper, attractive curtains, new vinyl floors, and ceiling fans. The only drawback here is that the showers have only cold water. The Venus is located upstairs from the Venus Store, down the street from Eva's Restaurant.

HI-ET, corner of Waight and West streets, San Ignacio, Cayo. No phone. 6 rms., none with bath.

$ Rates: B$10 ($5) single; B$20 ($10) double. No credit cards.

The water is cold and you have to share a bathroom, but the Hi-Et is family run, clean, and secure. This is the best of the backpacker-frequented hotels in San Ignacio. Unfortunately, it's almost always full.

WORTH THE EXTRA BUCKS

HOTEL SAN IGNACIO, San Ignacio, Cayo. Tel. 501/92-2034. 20 rms., all with bath.

$ Rates: B$55–B$105 ($27.50–$52.50) single; B$65–B$130 ($32.50–$65) double; B$75–B$150 ($37.50–$75) triple. AE, MC, V.

The Hotel San Ignacio is up the steep hill just past the police station, at the west end of the bridge into town. Because it's situated on Buena Vista Road, it has magnificent views of the jungle. The Hotel San Ignacio is a welcome oasis in this country of generally substandard accommodations, but it's often full by sundown. Although this hotel is a bit expensive, it's clean and comfortable.

There's a good restaurant and bar with decent food. A full breakfast costs B$7 to B$12 ($3.50 to $6). A complete dinner of chicken on a skewer, fried, or in a stew ranges from B$8 to B$14 ($4 to $7).

CAMPING

Cosmos Camping is a campground on the road leading out toward Branch Mouth and Las Casitas, where you can park your van or pitch your tent for B$10 ($5) per day. It has a cold-water shower and an outhouse, but there isn't much other than that. The river is just across a field, which makes this a rather nice spot.

JUNGLE LODGE SPLURGES

If you've made it this far, you're probably the adventurous type, and I'm sure you'd like to know about some wonderful splurges in the Cayo District. Within a few miles of San Ignacio are several jungle lodges where you can experience the peacefulness of a tropical jungle, canoe down clear rivers past 4-foot iguanas sunning themselves on the rocks, ride horses to Mayan ruins, hike jungle trails, and spot dozens of beautiful birds and, occasionally, other wild animals. I highly recommend that you stay at one of the jungle lodges listed below while you're in the area. They're all outside your budget (charging about $90 for a double per night, with three meals included), but the experience is well worth it. You can stay without taking meals, but you're a long way from the nearest restaurant. All the lodges will arrange trips to various sites in the area—such as Mountain Pine Ridge, Xunantunich, and Tikal—although you may be able to arrange the same trip yourself at a substantial savings by going into town and talking with a taxi driver. If you're lucky, you may be able to get a ride out from town with a lodge vehicle or maybe even on one of their boats. If not, you can hire a taxi, although this is quite expensive: B$50 ($25) to Chaa Creek and B$60 ($30) to duPlooy's.

DOUBLES FOR LESS THAN B$200 ($100)

LAS CASITAS, Branch Mouth, San Ignacio, Cayo. Tel. 501/92-2506. 3 cabins, none with bath.

$ Rates (not including meals): B$30 ($15) single; B$38 ($19) double. No credit cards.

The cabins here are very basic, each with screen walls, a bed, and a small sitting area, but the price and location are hard to beat. Branch Mouth is the confluence of the Mopan and Macal rivers, and to reach Las Casitas you'll need to take a boat. The best way to do this is to stop by Eva's and ask the friendly folks there to call out to Las Casitas so that a boat will be waiting for you. When your boat is arranged, head out of town on the dirt road that leads behind the soccer field. It's about 1½ miles to the point where the two rivers come together, a spot popular for picnicking and swimming. Las Casitas has an unusual lookout tower that you have to pay to climb, but the views are splendid. You can rent a hammock, a horse, or a boat here and keep yourself entertained for several days. This is the closest that you'll get to a "jungle lodge" experience if you're traveling on a tight budget.

Meals in the restaurant at Las Casitas are around B$8 ($4).

NABITUNICH, San Lorenzo Farm, c/o P.O. Benque Viejo, Cayo. Tel. 501/93-2309. 8 rms., all with bath.

$ Rates (including three meals): B$115 ($57.50) single; B$161 ($80.50) double. No credit cards.

With the rapid rise in room rates at the Cayo District's jungle lodges, Nabitunich has become the best deal around. This former farm/ranch is owned by Rudy and Margaret Juan. Rudy's family has owned the land for years, and Margaret is a nurse from England. Easy accessibility from the highway makes this my new favorite choice in the area. You can take a taxi out here (expensive) or catch a bus bound for the border and ask to be let off when you see the Nabitunich sign. The cottages are set on a gently sloping hillside with pastures all around. Down at the bottom of the hill, you'll find the Mopan River and a trail through the forest (both areas are great for birdwatching). Each cottage is different from the others—some are of white stucco and some are of stone, but all have thatched roofs. There are orchids all around the grounds; off in the distance you can see the ruins of Xunantunich. Equestrian-types can ride for hours on nearby bridle trails.

The dining room is spacious, and there's a bar on the patio of the dining hall.

DOUBLES FOR LESS THAN B$250 [$125]

MAYA MOUNTAIN LODGE, P.O. Box 46, San Ignacio, Cayo. Tel. 501/92-2164. In the U.S., toll free 800/344-MAYA. Fax 501/92-2029. 8 cottages, 6 rms., all with bath.

$ Rates (including three meals): B$180 ($90) single; B$240 ($120) double. MC, V.
Before you cross the bridge into San Ignacio, you'll see a sign to the left for this conveniently located lodge. It's about a three-quarter-mile walk from here or a five-minute taxi ride from town. The hotel offers very pleasant cottages and rooms with Guatemalan blankets, vinyl floors, and large baths. If you ask for a cottage, you'll get one with a spacious porch that contains a hammock. The small rooms are in a large old building that looks a bit like a Caribbean warehouse. Inside, you'll find bright clean rooms.

Home-style meals are served in the comfy, open-air dining room. Bart and Suzi Mickler are the friendly hosts here.

WINDY HILL COTTAGES, San Ignacio, Cayo. Tel. 501/92-2055 or 92-2017. 14 rms., all with bath.

$ Rates (including three meals): B$150 ($75) single; B$224 ($112) double; B$300 ($150) triple. AE, MC, V.
Right on the main highway heading west from San Ignacio is another easy-to-reach lodge. Set on a gently sloping grassy hill, the Windy Hill boasts a small above-ground pool and plenty of horses for riding. All the stucco-walled cottages have fabulous views over the forested mountains of western Belize. Bob and Lourdes Hales and their children run the lodge. Their son, Robert, has a small menagerie that includes a peccary, a spider monkey, and a coatimundi, among other animals.

There's a large open-air dining room with a thatched roof where delicious large meals are served.

WORTH THE EXTRA BUCKS

CHAA CREEK COTTAGES, P.O. Box 53, San Ignacio, Cayo. Tel. 501/92-2037. Fax 501/92-2501. 16 rms., all with bath.

$ Rates (including three meals): B$195.50 ($97.75) single; B$287.50 ($143.75) double. AE, MC, V.
Much loving care has gone into creating the beautiful grounds and cottages here; if you decide to spend the extra money, I'm sure you'll be glad you did. This is one of the oldest of the jungle lodges in the Cayo District and is located on the Macal River. To reach the cottages, drive 5 miles west from San Ignacio and watch for the sign on your left. It's another couple of miles down a very rough dirt road from the main highway. All of the thatched-roof cottages are artistically decorated with Guatemalan textiles and handcrafts and have private baths with hot water. There are canoes available at an additional charge, and horseback rides can always be arranged. For those seeking a real jungle experience, several-day hiking trips through the jungle can be arranged. Mick and Lucy Fleming are the engaging hosts here.

A separate bar and dining room provide plenty of space for socializing.

DUPLOOY'S, San Ignacio, Cayo. Tel. 501/92-2188. Fax 501/92-2057. 9 rms., all with bath.

$ Rates: B$184 ($92) single; B$276 ($138) double. MC, V (5% extra).

★ You'll certainly think that you're lost long before you reach this remote lodge, but keep following the rutted road. When you finally top a very steep hill and gaze down into the pastured valley below, you won't want to ever leave. The lodge is situated overlooking the Macal River, with jungle-covered limestone cliffs opposite. Jungle covers the surrounding hills. Ken and Judy duPlooy, who moved here a few years ago from South Carolina, are your hosts. Their lodge is a bit more luxurious than the others in the area; this, combined with the stunning location, make duPlooy's my favorite of Cayo's jungle lodges. The nine rooms are in three stone-and-stucco buildings with tile roofs. Each has a screened porch and a private bath. There's a beach on the river, and canoes and snorkeling and fishing equipment are available for rent. Follow the directions for Chaa Creek Cottages. DuPlooy's is a bit farther on the same dirt road, but be sure to take the right fork and follow the signs.

Breakfast is served in the rooms, and lunch and dinner are served in a small open-air restaurant overlooking the Macal River.

EL INDIO PERDIDO, Benque Viejo del Carmen, Cayo. Tel. 501/92-2188. In the U.S., tel. 408/646-1621, or toll free 800/833-9992 outside California. 11 rms., 5 with bath.

$ **Rates:** B$103.50 ($51.75) single without bath, B$115 ($57.50) single with bath; B$184 ($92) double without bath, B$207 ($103.50) double with bath. MC, V.

A jungle lodge should be an adventurous place, and reaching it should be part of the adventure. To reach El Indio Perdido (The Lost Indian), head west 2 miles from San Ignacio and watch for the signs pointing down a dirt road to the right. At the end of the road, you'll have to leave your car and take a hand-pulled ferry across the river, which is less than 100 feet wide. The lodge is run by the very entertaining Colette Gross, a Frenchwoman who has lived here for many years. Most of the rooms are in attractively decorated thatched-roof cottages, and even though half of them have private baths, the showers are cold water only. Some 75 acres of forest and pastures surround the lodge. Nine horses are available for riding. The Xunantunich ruins are only 2 miles away, so you can easily walk or ride to them.

WHERE TO EAT

EVA'S RESTAURANT & BAR, 22 Burns Ave. Tel. 092-2267.
   Cuisine: BELIZEAN/INTERNATIONAL.
$ **Prices:** B$4–B$8 ($2–$4). No credit cards.
   Open: Daily 7am–midnight.

⑤ What Mom's is to Belize City, Eva's is to San Ignacio. A postcard collection covers a few walls, the tabletops are Formica, and the conversation is lively. Although it's short on atmosphere, Eva's is long on information. Owner Bob Jones is a wealth of information about the area and acts as the local branch of the tourist board. If you want to get a group of people together to rent a taxi or canoe or to defray the costs of a tour, let Bob know—he'll try to put you in touch with other like-minded folks. Rice, beans, and chicken cost B$4 ($2); fish and fries cost B$6 ($3). There are daily specials (usually local dishes) that are always good choices.

MAXIM'S CHINESE RESTAURANT, corner of Far West and Bullet Tree roads. Tel. 092-2282.
   Cuisine: CHINESE.
$ **Prices:** B$6–B$16 ($3–$8). No credit cards.
   Open: Daily 11:30am–2:30pm and 5pm–midnight.

For delicious Chinese food, try this casual place. Various plates of fried rice range from B$5.75 ($2.90) to B$10 ($5), and sweet-and-sour dishes cost B$8 ($4) to B$10 ($5). There's also a host of vegetarian dishes. Try the Belikin Stout if you like dark beer with a bite. The owner goes into Belize City once a week to secure fish and other ingredients. (The owner will also change traveler's checks as a favor.) Take-out is also available.

SERENDIB RESTAURANT, 27 Burns Ave. Tel. 092-2302.

Cuisine: SRI LANKAN.

$ Prices: B$8–B$15 ($4–$7.50). No credit cards.

Open: Mon-Thurs 9:30am-3pm, Fri-Sat until midnight.

⭐ This pleasant little restaurant is an unexpected surprise in the tiny town of San Ignacio. Owner Hantley Pieris is from Sri Lanka and came to Belize years ago with the British army. He now runs a restaurant serving excellent curries in the style of his native country. You can get beef or chicken curry with yellow or fried rice, potatoes, and a salad for B$8.50 ($4.25). There are also sandwiches, burgers, chow mein, and fried fish on the menu for B$2 to B$9 ($1 to $4.50).

EXCURSIONS

XUNANTUNICH

Although you may not be able to pronounce it (say "Shoo-nahn-too-nitch"), you can visit it. Xunantunich is a Mayan ruin 6½ miles past San Ignacio on the road to Benque Viejo. The name translates as "maiden of the rocks." Open daily from 8am to 4pm. The admission is B$3 ($1.50).

The pyramid is still officially the highest structure in Belize, at 127 feet, despite the new glass-tower addition to the Fort George Hotel in Belize City. The panorama from the top is amazing. Don't miss it. On the east side of the pyramid, near the top, is a remarkably well-preserved stucco frieze.

Down below, under the protection of a thatched palapa in the temple forecourt, are three magnificent stelae portraying rulers of the region. Xunantunich was a thriving Mayan city about the same time as Altun Ha, in the Classic Period, about A.D. 600 to 900.

Take a bus bound for Benque Viejo and get off in San José Succotz. To reach the ruins, you must cross the Mopan River aboard a tiny hand-cranked car-ferry in the village of San José Succotz. You're bound to see colorfully dressed women washing clothes in the river as you are cranked across by the ferryman. After crossing the river, it is a short walk to the ruins. You can also take a taxi, but it's very expensive—unless you share one for B$3 ($1.50) to the border and ask the driver to drop you off at the ferry.

IX CHEL FARM AND THE PANTI MAYAN MEDICINE TRAIL

Located adjacent to Chaa Creek Cottages, Ix Chel Farm is a tropical plant research center operated by Drs. Greg Shropshire and Rosita Arvigo. Rosita studied traditional herbal medicine for five years with a local Mayan medicine man. Here on the farm she has built a trail through the forest to share with visitors the medicinal values of many of the tropical forest's plants. You'll learn about many of the fascinating plants that grow wild in the forests. If you have a group of six people, you can spend a day touring the Panti Trail with Rosita as your guide. After a natural-food vegetarian lunch and a swim in the Macal River, you'll learn about the farm and traditional healing in Belize. The price is B$70 ($35) per person. You can also simply tour the trail with Rosita as your guide or use her guidebook to the trail and read about each of the plants on your own. The charge for this is a lot less.

Contact your lodge owner or Bob at Eva's Restaurant for information on scheduling a visit.

MOUNTAIN PINE RIDGE AND CARACOL

Few people think of pine trees as being a tropical species, but you'll see plenty of them in Belize, especially in these rugged mountains. This 3,400-foot ridge is complete with Mayan reminders, a secret waterfall, wild orchids, parrots, keel-billed toucans, and other exotic flora and fauna. Mountain Pine Ridge, Hidden Valley Falls (also called Thousand Foot Falls), and the Río On and Río Frío Caves are off the Western Highway near Georgeville.

These roads are nearly impassable even in the dry season, so don't even think about attempting the trip in anything less than a four-wheel-drive vehicle, preferably a

Land Rover. All the lodges offer tours to the area, with prices ranging from B$60 to B$90 ($30 to $45) per person if you have a group of four or five people. You can arrange a trip for somewhat less if you simply hire a taxi to take you out there. Talk to Bob at Eva's Restaurant. He'll put you in touch with other people who are interested in going.

Caracol is a ruin that's believed to be the largest Mayan site. It's not really set up as a tourist sight, but if you have the interest, stamina, and vehicle to make it, you can visit. It's on the same road as Mountain Pine Ridge, several very rough miles farther south. Don't try it in the rainy season.

MOVING ON TO GUATEMALA AND TIKAL

If you stay overnight in Ix Chel on the way to Guatemala, the first bus that comes through at 8:30 or 9am will take you (for B$1, [50¢]) to Melchor de Mencos, Guatemala and connect with the 11am bus to Flores. Otherwise a shared taxi to the border will cost B$3 ($1.50). A hired taxi will cost B$25 ($12.50) to the border.

Benque Viejo, the town nearest the border, 8 miles up the road from San Ignacio, is a good place to stop for a soft drink if you've driven from Belize City. Then it's a short ride of less than a mile to the border.

If you spent the night in Benque Viejo, jump on any Novelos bus going to the border. They'll let you on for free, and they seem to make the trip hourly.

At the border the Belizean officials will ask to see your passport and will give you an exit card to fill out. If you have a car, you'll have to turn in your Temporary Entry Permit. The exit tax is B$1 (50¢) per person and B$5 ($2.50) per vehicle. As you cross the border, notice the Belizean sign that reads "Belize—Central America's newest independent country." On the Guatemalan side, in turn, there is a large map of Guatemalan territory that includes Belize. Guatemala has a long-standing claim to all of Belize, but British protection keeps the controversy to a diplomatic squabble.

The officials at the Guatemalan border station keep the place open most of the time—including weekends—but charge extra if you demand their services outside of business hours (8am to noon and 2 to 6pm Monday through Friday). In fact, they may demand a minimal amount from you even during business hours. You will have to pay $5 for your Tourist Card. Car papers cost Q20 ($4), and the fumigation of your tires, required by law, will cost Q5 ($1.25); you should be given a receipt for all this. The total for services rendered may come to Q25 ($6.25), or, if it is outside normal hours, it may be more, depending on the officials' whims that day.

A bank is in operation at the Guatemalan border station, and you should not fail to change money here, particularly if you're going straight to Tikal. At hours when the bank is closed, use one of the moneychangers who will approach you. There are no banks in Tikal, but the three lodges there will accept U.S. dollars or traveler's checks for payment. However, they will not change traveler's checks otherwise. Flores has banks, but they close by 2pm, 2:30pm on Friday. Guatemalan currency, the quetzal, is equal to about 25¢ U.S., and so if you change $50, you should receive Q200.

NOTE: If you are a citizen of the U.K., Ireland, Canada, or Australia you will need a visa to enter Guatemala. The nearest Guatemalan consulate is in Chetumal, Mexico.

Walk out of the border station toward Melchor de Mencos, and head up the main street on the right. The center of this dusty border town is up the hill, a few hundred yards from the border station. Here you'll come across a few modest hotels. Shops and a small market sell provisions in central Melchor.

Now you've got to do some planning, as getting to see Tikal can be tricky. First, find out when the next bus leaves Melchor for points west. It's a terrible, bumpy two hours at least to El Cruce (also called Ixlu), the turnoff for Tikal. You can get off here and hope for a bus coming from Flores (if it is early enough in the morning) or try hitching. El Cruce has no facilities except a gas station. The road from El Cruce to Tikal is paved (24 miles or 45 minutes), as is the portion from El Cruce to Flores; you'll look forward to it.

The journey straight to Tikal may seem chancy to you, in which case you should hop a bus from Melchor directly to Flores, three hours of bumping and wheezing away. You will have to backtrack a bit to reach Tikal. Pinita and Rosita bus lines leave Melchor for Flores at 3, 5, 8, and 11a.m., and 1 and 4p.m.; tickets cost Q6 ($1.50).

There is an alternative: if you can get together with some other Tikal travelers to split the cost, you can attempt to hire a taxi in Belize City. The cabby will take you straight to Tikal for B$400 ($200) or B$500 ($250) if you want to stay overnight. However, if you are willing to spend this much, you should just fly to Tikal from Belize City on Aerovias Airlines.

4. COROZAL TOWN AND THE NORTHERN HIGHWAY

Distances: 96 miles N of Belize City; 31 miles N of Orange Walk; 8 miles S of the Mexican border.

GETTING THERE   By Air   Maya Airways operates two flights daily from San Pedro. Duration: 20 minutes. Fare: B$54 ($27) one way, B$104 ($52) round trip.

By Bus   Both Batty Bros. and Venus bus lines run several buses daily from Belize City. Duration: 3 hours. Fare: B$6 ($3). Buses originating from Chetumal, Mexico go into town daily every hour from 4am to 6pm.

By Car   Corozal Town is the last town on the Northern Highway before you reach the Mexican border. Take Freetown Road out of Belize City to connect with the Northern Highway. If you want to visit the Altun Ha ruins, take the Old Northern Highway. The turnoff is 22 miles from Belize City, on the right. If you're driving in from Mexico, you'll reach a fork in the road 3 miles from the border; bear left to reach Corozal Town.

ESSENTIALS   The bus station is located two blocks west of the town's central park. Three of the four hotels listed here are at the south end of town where the Northern Highway runs alongside the bay.

Nine miles from the Mexican border, Corozal Town (pop. 8,700) is for many people their first glimpse of Belize. There isn't much to see or do in Corozal. It's mostly just a stopping point for weary travelers. However, it sits on the shores of the **Bay of Chetumal,** which has the most amazing turquoise-blue water. The town was settled in the mid-19th century by refugee Mestizos from Mexico, and Spanish is still the principal language spoken here. Before the 1850s, the area had been one of the last centers of the Mayan civilization. You can visit two Mayan ruins in the vicinity and also the remains of a fort on the town's central park. It was built some time after the Mexican refugees settled here.

Corozal is a pleasant town; people will probably say hello to you on the street before you say hello to them. There's a very large expatriate community and if you spend any time at all in town, you're likely to hear many personal stories of how people "left it all behind to pursue the good life" in quiet Belize.

WHAT TO SEE AND DO

If you've just come from Mexico, swim in the bay, or walk around town and marvel at the difference between Mexican culture and Belizean culture. The countries are so close and yet worlds apart. Belize is truly a Caribbean country, the frame houses built on high stilts to provide coolness, protection from floods, and to give storage room and shade for sitting. Farming and growing sugarcane are what Corozal survives on, plus perhaps a little fishing.

If you haven't yet had your fill of Mayan ruins, there are a couple to visit in the area. If you look across the water from the shore in Corozal Town, you can see **Cerros** or **Cerro Maya** on the far side of the Bay of Chetumal. It's that little bump in the forest, but up close it seems much larger. Cerros was an important coastal trading center during the Late Pre-Classic Period. Some of the remains of this city are now under the waters of the bay, but there's still a 65-foot-tall **pyramid** that you can visit. By asking around town, you should be able to find someone willing to take you across to the ruins in a boat.

Right in town is another small ruin called **Santa Rita.** Corozal Town is actually built on the ruins of Santa Rita, which was an important Late Post-Classic Mayan town and was still occupied at the time of the Spanish Conquest. The only excavated building is a small temple across the street from the Coca-Cola bottling plant. To reach it, head north past the bus station and, at the curve to the right, take the road straight ahead that leads up a hill. You'll see the building one block over to the right.

WHERE TO STAY AND EAT

Three of the listings below are at the southern end of the town. Ask the bus driver to drop you off, or take a taxi from the bus station.

DOUBLES FOR LESS THAN B$25 [$12.50]

CARIBBEAN MOTEL, Cabins and Trailer Park, south end of town on Belize Highway, Corozal Town. No phone. 6 rms., all with bath.
$ Rates: B$22 ($11) single/double. No credit cards.

On the bay, in an idyllic location shaded by lofty palms and with a swimming dock across the street, this is the traditional place to stay. Even though it has seen better days, the Caribbean is still a great deal and may provide the cheapest room with private bath that you'll find in Belize. Quaint and primitive thatched bungalows are built on traditional Mayan designs and are almost identical (from the outside) to the ones that you see all over the Yucatán.

The owner, Jo, serves up the biggest and best salads (a real treat, especially if you've been in Mexico for a while) and burgers in town, each for B$5 ($2.50). Ask anyone in town to attest to it. The restaurant is open every day except Tuesday (try to time your stay accordingly, other choices for food aren't as good) and serves all three meals. This is the place to eat.

NESTOR'S HOTEL, 123 Fifth Ave., Corozal Town. Tel. 501/4-2354. 25 rms., all with bath.
$ Rates: B$14.50 ($7.25) single; B$16.50–B$19 ($8.25–$9.50) double. No credit cards.

The cheapest prices in town are to be found here, on the corner of Fifth Avenue and Fourth Street. Jake's rooms are basic, with solar-heated showers, but the plumbing tends to act up now and then in the back rooms, but he'll fix it if you let him know. Jake's been in Belize a long time and will gladly give you a few pointers.

DOUBLES FOR LESS THAN B$50 [$25]

HOTEL MAYA, P.O. Box 112, Corozal Town. Tel. 501/4-22082. 17 rms., all with bath.
$ Rates: B$33 ($16.50) single; B$44 ($22) double; B$66 ($33) triple; B$165 ($82.50) quint. MC, V.
Located on the shore road south of town, the Maya is probably your best bet. The rooms are very clean and basic, and all have private showers with hot and cold running water. This place tends to be popular with American businesspeople who come to negotiate deals, so you may find no rooms available. Unfortunately, it can also get a little bit noisy. You can get a big breakfast for B$8.50 ($4.25), including meat, beans, orange juice, coffee, and toast, or johnny cakes. Dinner runs B$7 to B$10 ($3.50 to $5).

WORTH THE EXTRA BUCKS

TONY'S MOTEL, south end, Corozal Town. Tel. 501/4-2055. 26 rms., all with bath.

$ Rates: B$52 ($26) single; B$80 ($40) double, B$130 ($65) double with A/C; B$100 ($50) triple, B$150 ($75) triple with A/C; B$10–B$20 ($5–$10) cheaper in summer months; children under 17 free in parents' room. AE, MC, V.

The rooms here are newer and larger than those in the above hostelries, and consequently this place is popular with group tours and conferences. Tony's is on the left just past the Caribbean Motel on the shore road south of town. The grounds are nicely landscaped, with lawn chairs that overlook the ocean. There's even a little beach. The rooms come with mahogany furniture, tile floors, attractive floral-print bedspreads, and even potted plants. The rooms with air conditioning also come with cable color TVs. Although the prices in the restaurant here are high, especially if you've been traveling in Mexico, it's certainly a welcome oasis of cool air during the summer.

MOVING ON
TO ORANGE WALK AND BELIZE CITY

From Corozal Town, the Southern Highway heads south to Orange Walk and Belize City. Buses for Belize City leave regularly. There's nothing of much interest to tourists in Orange Walk. Just south from Orange Walk two roads branch off for Belize City. Just after the town of Carmelita, take the left fork, the Northern Highway. If you want to go to the Altun Ha ruins, ask around in Orange Walk to find a cross between a farm truck and a military transport going your way; they're uncomfortable but dependable.

Where to Stay

HOTEL BARONS, Belize-Corozal Road, Orange Walk. Tel. 501/32-2518 or 032-2364. 31 rms., all with bath.

$ Rates: B$42 ($21) single; B$47.25 ($23.63) double, B$84 ($42) double with A/C. No credit cards.

Spacious, clean rooms with tile floors and hot and cold water await you here, a surprisingly nice hotel on an otherwise dreary section of road, if you just can't go any farther. You'll also find a cool swimming pool with a tiled patio around it. The restaurant serves Belizean and Chinese food at reasonable prices.

TO MEXICO

From Corozal Town, it's 8 miles north to the Mexican border. If you're heading this way, be sure that you have a Mexican Tourist Card already. They don't pass them out at the border. You can get one at the Mexican Embassy in Belize City. There are several buses daily from Corozal Town to Chetumal, Mexico, beginning at 2:30pm. The fare is B$1.50 (75¢). The bus will take you right to the bus station in Chetumal after everyone has been through the border formalities.

THE METRIC SYSTEM—IN A NUTSHELL

Length

1 millimeter (mm)	=	.04 inches (*or* less than 1/16 in.)
1 centimeter (cm)	=	.39 inches (*or* just under ½ in.)
1 meter (m)	=	39 inches (*or* about 1.1 yards)
1 kilometer (km)	=	.62 miles (*or* about ⅔ of a mile)

To convert kilometers to miles, multiply the number of kilometers by .62. Also use to convert kilometers per hour (kmph) to miles per hour (m.p.h.).

To convert miles to kilometers, multiply the number of miles by 1.61. Also use to convert speeds from m.p.h. to kmph.

Capacity

1 liter (l)	=	33.92 fluid ounces	=	2.1 pints	=	1.06 quarts
	=	.26 U.S. gallons				
1 Imperial gallon	=	1.2 U.S. gallons				

To convert liters to U.S. gallons, multiply the number of liters by .26.

To convert U.S. gallons to liters, multiply the number of gallons by 3.79.

To convert Imperial gallons to U.S. gallons, multiply the number of Imperial gallons by 1.2.

To convert U.S. gallons to Imperial gallons, multiply the number of U.S. gallons by .83.

Weight

1 gram (g)	=	.035 ounces (*or* about a paperclip's weight)
1 kilogram (kg)	=	35.2 ounces = 2.2 pounds
1 metric ton	=	2,205 pounds = 1.1 short ton

To convert kilograms to pounds, multiply the number of kilograms by 2.2.

To convert pounds to kilograms, multiply the number of pounds by .45.

Area

1 hectare (ha)	=	2.47 acres		
1 square kilometer (km^2)	=	247 acres	=	.39 square miles

To convert hectares to acres, multiply the number of hectares by 2.47.

To convert acres to hectares, multiply the number of acres by .41.

To convert square kilometers to square miles, multiply the number of square kilometers by .39.

To convert square miles to square kilometers, multiply the number of square miles by 2.6.

Temperature

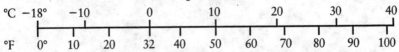

°C	−18°	−10		0		10		20		30		40
°F	0°	10	20	32	40	50	60	70	80	90	100	

To convert degrees Celsius to degrees Fahrenheit, multiply °C by 9, divide by 5, and add 32 (example: 20°C × 9/5 + 32 = 68°F).

To convert degrees Fahrenheit to degrees Celsius, subtract 32 from °F, multiply by 5, then divide by 9 (example: 85°F − 32 × 5/9 = 29.4°C).

INDEX

GENERAL INFORMATION

BELIZE

Accommodations, 266
  see also Accommodations index
Ambergris Caye, 278–85
  excursions from, 284–5
  Fast Facts, 278
  getting there, 278
  nightlife, 284
  orientation, 278
Art and architecture, 254

Belize City, 269–78
  emergencies, 273
  Fast Facts, 271, 273–4
  getting around, 271
  getting to, 269–70
  map, 272
  nightlife, 276–7
  orientation, 270–1
  safety, 273
Belmopan, 290–3
  getting to, 290
  orientation, 290–1

Caulker, Caye, 285–9
  Fast Facts, 285
  getting there, 285
  nightlife, 289
  orientation, 285
  shopping, 289
Cayes, The, 278–89
Climate, 258
Corozal Town and the Northern Highway, 305–7
Cruises and package tours, 261

Drinks, 255

Entry requirements, 256

Fast Facts, 266–7
Food, 254–5

Geography of Belize, 251–2

Holidays, 258

Maps, 262–3
  Belize City, 272
Money-saving tips, 266–7

Natural history tours, 259
Nightlife, 254

Orange Walk, 307
Orientation, 251–5

Package tours and cruises, 261
People, 254
Placencia, 294–8
  excursions from, 297–8
  getting there, 294
  nightlife, 297
  orientation, 294
  shopping, 297
Planning and preparing for your trip, 256–9
  entry requirements, 256
  health, insurance, and other concerns, 258
  holidays, 258
  money, 257
  tips for seniors, 258–9
  tips for singles, 259
  tips for students, 259
  tips for the disabled, 258
  what to pack, 258
  when to go, 258
Politics of Belize, 254

San Ignacio and the Cayo District, 298–305
  excursions from, 303–4
  getting there, 299
  orientation, 299
Saving money, 266–7
Sights and attractions:
  Frommer's favorite experiences, 291
  see also Sights & Attractions index
Sports and recreation, 254
Suggested itineraries, 261, 264–5

Tours, 259
Transportation, 265
Traveling:
  to Belize, 259–61
  to Guatemala from Belize, 304–5
  to Mexico from Corozal Town, 307

COSTA RICA

Accommodations, 26
  with kitchenettes, 27
  saving money on, 27
  See also Accommodations *index*
Addresses, locating, 25–6
Addresses, street, San José, 33–4
Adventure travel, 20–1
Air travel:
  to Costa Rica, 21
  within Costa Rica, 24, 32
  saving money on, 19, 28
Alajuela, 60
Ambulance, 29
American Express, 29, 36
Apartotels, 26
Appetizers, 11
Architectural highlights, 9–10
Art, 9

Babysitters, 36
Bargaining, 28
Bars, 56–7
Bats, 18
Beaches, 4
Beer, wine, 12–13
Boat trips and cruises:
  Cahuita, 103
  from Puntarenas, 82–3
Books about Costa Rica, 13
Bookstore, 36
Brasilito, Playa, 75
British Embassy, 29
Bucket shops, 21
Business hours, 29
Bus travel, 21
  within Costa Rica, 24
  in San José, 34

Cahuita, 102–7
Calendar of events, 17
Canadian Embassy, 29
Caribbean Coast, 5, 98–111
  Cahuita, 102–7
  Limón and Tortuguero National Park, 98–102
  what's special about, 99
Cars and driving, 22
  breakdowns, 25
  driving rules, 25
  gasoline, 25
  maps, 25
  rentals, 24–5, 28, 32
  San José, 36
Cartago, 58
Climate, 16–17
Clothing to pack, 18–19
Coffee, shopping for, 28, 54

Consulates, 29
Cost of everyday items, 16
Credit cards, 15–16, 29
Crime, 28
Cruises, 57
Cuisine, 11–12
Culture, 9–10
Currency, 15, 36
Customs, 29

Del Coco, Playa, 70–73
Dentists, 36
Desserts, 12
Dining hours and customs, 11
Disabled travelers, tips for, 19
Discounts: *see* Money-saving tips
Doctors, 36
Dominical, 97
Drinks, 12, 47
Drug laws, 29
Drugstores, 29, 36

Ecotourism and adventure travel, 20–1, 63–4
Educational/study travel, 19–20
Elderhostels, 19
Electricity, 29
Embassy and consulates, 29, 36
Emergencies, 29, 36
Entertainment, saving money on, 27
Entry requirements, 14–15
Esterillos, Playa, 88, 89
Etiquette, 29
Excursions from San José, 57–61
Eyeglasses, 36

Famous Costa Ricans, 10
Fast Facts, 29–30
Ferry, 25
Fire, 29
Fishing
  Cahuita, 103
  Pacific Coast, 82, 91
  Tamarindo Beach, 78
Flamingo, Playa, 74–7
Food, 11–12
  glossary of menu words, 111
Fruits, 12

Gambling casinos, 57
Gasoline, 25
Geography, 3–5
Golfito, 97
Grecia, 60
Guanacaste Peninsula, 5, 62

Hairdressers/barbers, 36
Handcrafts, shopping for, 54–5
Health, 18
  drinking water, 30
Health insurance, 18
Heredia, 60

Hermosa, Playa, 73–4, 89
Herradura, Playa, 89
History, 5, 8–9
Hitchhiking, 25, 29–30
Holidays, 17
Horseback riding, 57, 91
Hospitals, 37
Hostels, 19
House rentals:
    Cahuita, 105
    Manuel Antonio, 94
    Playa Flamingo and nearby beaches, 77

Insurance, 18
Interesting facts, 9
Itineraries, suggested, 22–3
    San José, 49

Jacó Beach, 85–9
Jewelry, shopping for, 28
Juan Santamaría International Airport, 32
Jungle lodges, 26
Jungle Train, 28, 61

Language, 30
Laundry/dry cleaning, 37
Liberia, 68–70
Limón, 98–101
Liquor, 12–13
Liquor laws, 30

Magazines, 30
Mail, 30
Malaria, 18
Maps, 6–7
    road, 25
    San José, 35
    where to get, 30
Markets, 28
Meals and dining customs, 11
Meat, 11
Meseta Central, 4
Money, 15–16
    changing, 29
Money-saving tips:
    accommodations, 27
    airfares, 19, 21
    meals, 27
    services and other transactions, 29
    shopping, 27–8
    sight-seeing and entertainment, 27
    transportation, 28
    $25-a-day budget, 26–7
Monteverde, 62–8
Mountains, 4–5
Movie theaters, 57
Museums of pre-Columbian artifacts, 4

Natural spectacles, 4
Nature trail, Cahuita, 103
Newspapers and magazines, 30, 37

Nightclubs, 56
Nightlife, 10, 55–7
Northwest of Costa Rica, 63–80

Osa Peninsula, 97
Ox carts, miniature, 28

Pacific Coast, 5, 81–97
    Jacó Beach, 85–9
    Puntarenas, 81–4
    Quepos and Manuel Antonio, 89–97
    what's special about, 82
Package tours, 22
Packing for your trip, 18–19
Panamá, Playa, 73
Pan de Azucar, Playa, 75–6
Parks and gardens, 4
People of Costa Rica, 10
Performing arts, 10, 55–6
Pets, 30
Photographic needs, 29, 37
Pickpockets and bag slashers, 28
Planning and preparing for your trip:
    alternative/adventure travel, 19–21
    calendar of events, 17
    entry requirements, 14–15
    getting there, 21–2
    health, 18
    holidays, 17
    insurance, 18
    money, 15–16
    packing for your trip, 18–19
    suggested itineraries, 22–3
    tips for the disabled, seniors, singles, and
        students, 19
    tourist information, 14
    transportation within Costa Rica, 24–6
    when to go, 16–17
Police, 30
Post office, 37
Potrero, Playa, 75–7
Puerto Vargas, 103
Puerto Viejo, 107–11
Puntarenas, 81–4

Quepos, 89–97

Radio and TV, 30, 37
Rainfall, 17
Recreational activities, 10
Refrescos, 47
Regions of Costa Rica, 4–5
Religious services, 37
Religious shrines, 4
Restaurants, 26
    San José, 47–8
    saving money on, 27
    sodas, 47
    see also Restaurants *index*
Restrooms, 30, 37
Retirement in Costa Rica, 19

Safety, 30, 37
Sandwiches and snacks, 11
San José, 31–61
    arriving in, 32
    budget bests, 30–1
    excursions from, 57–61
    Fast Facts, 36–7
    getting around, 34, 36
    layout of, 33–4
    map, 35
    restaurants, 47–8
    suggested itineraries, 49
    tourist information, 32–3
    walking tours, 52–3
    what's special about, 33
    worth the extra money, 32
Sarchí, 60
Seafood, 11
Senior citizens, tips for, 19
Shoe repairs, 37
Shopping, 54–5, 67
    Cahuita, 107
    Puerto Viejo, 110
    Quepos, 96–7
    saving money on, 27–8
Sights and attractions:
    Frommer's favorite experiences, 23
    saving money on sight-seeing, 27
    see also Sights & Attractions index
Single travelers, tips for, 19
Snorkeling, 103, 111
Sodas, 47
Soups, 11
Special and free events, 53
Sports and recreational activities, 53, 57–8
Street addresses, 25–6
Street food, 47–8
Students, tips for, 19
Surfing:
    Jacó Beach, 85–6
    Puerto Viejo, 108

Tamarindo, Playa, 77–80
Taxes, 30, 37
Taxis, in San José, 34
Telegrams/telexes, 37
Telephone, 29, 30, 37
    saving money on calls, 29
Temperatures, average monthly, 17
Time, 30
Tipping, 29
Tortuguero National Park, 98, 101–2
Tourist information, 14
    San José, 32–3
    for seniors, 19
Tours, organized, 53, 57–8, 107
    adventure, 20–1
    package, 22
    see also Boat trips and cruises
Train travel:
    within Costa Rica, 24

saving money on, 28
Transportation:
    within Costa Rica, 24–6
    in San José, 34, 36
    saving money on, 28
Travel agencies, 61
Traveler's checks, 15
Travel insurance, 18

United States Consulate, 29

Vaccinations, 18
Vegetables, 12

Walking, in San José, 34, 36
Walking tours, San José, 52–3
Water and soft drinks, 12, 30, 37–8
Water sports, 73
White-water rafting, 57–8

Zarcero, 60

GUATEMALA

Accommodations, 139, 152–6
    saving money on, 140
    see also Accommodations index
Addresses, locating, 138–9
Air travel:
    to Guatemala, 132–3, 137
    within Guatemala, 169
Alternative/adventure travel, 131–2
Amatitlán, Lake, 246–7
    getting to, 246–7
    orientation, 247
American Express, 142, 150
Antigua, 136, 196–210, 243
    excursions from, 209–10
    map, 199
    nightlife, 208–9
    orientation, 197
    shopping, 209
    sights and attractions, 198
    transportation to, 196–7
APEX (advance purchase excursion), 133
Architecture, 121–2
Art, 121
Atitlán, Lake, 187
Atlantic Highway, 225–42
    Chiquimula, 230, 231
    Cobán, 225–31
    Copán (Honduras), 231–3
    Esquipulas, 230, 233–5
    Lake Izabal, 237–9
    Lívingston, 239–42
    Mario Dary Rivera Biotopo, 228–9
    Puerto Barrios, 239–42
    Quiriguá, 235–7
    Río Dulce, 237–9
    Río Hondo, 230–1

what's special about, 226
Beer, 125
Boat trips and cruises:
Lake Atitlán, 195
river trips, 132, 136
Books about Guatemala, 125
Bookstore, Guatemala City, 150
Budget bests, Guatemala City, 145
Business hours, 142
Bus travel, 133, 137
Guatemala City, 146, 148, 150

Calendar of events, 129–30
Cars and driving, 133–4, 137
Guatemala City, 146–7, 150
Chichicastenango, 136, 182–6
Chiquimila, 230, 231
Ciudqad Vieja, 209
Climate, 129
Clothing to pack, 130
Cobán, 225–31
excursions from, 228–9
getting to, 225
orientation, 225
sights and attractions, 226–7
Consulates, 142–3
Copán (Honduras), 231–3
getting to, 231
sights and activities, 232–3
useful information, 231–2
Cost of everyday items, 128
Credit cards, 129, 142
Cuisine, 124
Cultural and social life, 123
Currency, 127–8
Currency exchange, 142, 151
Customs, 142

Dentists, 151
Disabled travelers, tips for, 130–1
Discount opportunities, 145
Doctors, 151
Drinking water, 125, 144
Drinks, 125
Drug laws, 142
Drugstores, 151

Educational/study travel, 131
El Petén, 211–24
Flores and Santa Elena, 211–18
Tikal, 219–24
Embassy and consulates, 142–3, 151
Emergencies, 143, 151
Entry requirements, 126–7
Esquipulas, 230, 233–5

Fast Facts, 142–4
Guatemala City, 150–2
Ferries, 138
Flores, 211–18
car rentals, 213
orientation, 213

transportation to, 211–13
Food, 124
Frommer's favorite experiences, 136
Fuentes Georgina, 182

Gasoline, 137
Geography of Guatemala, 116
Glossary of terms, 247–8
Guatemala City, 145–70
arriving in, 146
from a budget point of view, 145
getting around, 148, 150
layout of, 147–8
map, 149
neighborhoods, 148
nightlife, 168
restaurants, 156–9
sights and attractions, 159–66
telephone code, 142
tourist information, 147
what's special about, 147

Handcrafts, shopping for, Guatemala City,
166, 168
Highlands, 171–210
Antigua, 196–210
Chichicastenango, 182–6
Ciudad Vieja, 209
Panajachel, 186–96
Quetzaltenango, 175–82
San Francisco El Alto and Momostenango,
181–2
Santiago Atitlán, 195–6
what's special about, 172
Zunil and Fuentes Georgina, 182
History of Guatemala, 116–18, 121
Hitchhiking, 138, 143
Holidays, 130
Hospitals, 151
Huehuetenango, 171–5

Insect repellent, 130
Interesting facts about Guatemala, 122
Izabal, Lake 237–9

La Democracia, 245–6
Language, 143
Laundry/dry cleaning, 151
Libraries, 151
Liquor, 125
Liquor laws, 143
Literature, 122
Lívingston and Puerto Barrios, 240–1
Lost property, 151
Luggage storage, Guatemala City, 151

Magazines, 143
Mail, 143
Maps, 119–20
Guatemala City, 149; walking tour, 164,
167

Maps (cont'd)
  where to get, 138, 143
Mario Dary Rivera Biotopo, 228-9
Meals and dining customs, 124
Momostenango, 181-2
Money, 127-9, 142
Money-saving tips, 140-2

Nebaj, 186
Newspapers and magazines, 143, 151
Nightlife:
  Guatemala City, 168
  Huehuetenango, 175
  Quetzaltenango, 181
  see also specific places

Pacific Highway, 243-8
  getting to, 243
  La Democracia, 245-6
  Lake Amatitlán, 246-8
  orientation, 243
  Retalhuleu, 243-6
  what's special about, 244
Package tours, 134-5
Packing for your trip, 130
Panajachel, 186-96
Performing arts, 123-4, 168
Petén, El, 211-14
Pets, 143
Photographic needs, 142, 152
Planning and preparing for your trip, 126-44
  accommodations, 139
  alternative/adventure travel, 131-2
  calendar of events, 129-30
  climate, 129
  entry requirements, 126-7
  Fast Facts, 142-4
  getting around, 137-9
  getting there, 132-5
  information sources, 126
  money, 127-9
  money-saving tips, 140-2
  packing for your trip, 130
  restaurants, 139
  suggested itineraries, 135-7
  tips for the disabled, seniors, singles, and
    students, 130-1
Police, 143
Post offices, Guatemala City, 152
Puerto Barrios, 239-41

Quetzaltenango, 175-82, 243
Quiriguá, 235-7

Radio and TV, 143, 152
Rainfall, 129
Recreational vehicles, 138

Religion, myths, and folklore, 122-3
Religious services, 152
Restaurants, 139
  saving money in, 140
  see also Restaurants index
Restrooms, 143, 152
Retalhuleu, 243-6
Río Dulce and Lake Izabal, 237-9
Río Hondo, 230-1
River trips, 132, 136

Safety, 143-4, 152
San Francisco El Alto, 181
San Pedro Carcha, 227
Santa Cruz del Quiché, 186
Santa Elena, 211-18
  orientation, 213
  transportation to, 211-13
Santiago Atitlán, 195-6
Senior citizens, tips for, 131
Shopping, 166, 168
  Antigua, 209
  Guatemala City, 166, 168
  Highlands, 181
  Panajachel, 194
  saving money, 140-1
Single travelers, tips for, 131
Sports and recreational activities, 124
Students, tips for, 131
Suggested itineraries, 135-7

Taxes, 144
Telegrams, 152
Telephones, 144
  Guatemala City, 152
  saving money on calls, 142
Temperatures, average monthly, 129
Tikal, 219-24
Tipping, 141
Tourist information, 126
  Guatemala City, 147
Tours, organized:
  package, 134-5
  Guatemala City, 166
Transportation, 137-8
  within Guatemala, 169-70
  saving money on, 141
Traveler's checks, 128
Traveling to Guatemala, 132-5
  from Belize, 304-5

Walking, in Guatemala City, 150
Walking tours, Guatemala City, 164-7
Water, 125, 144
Wine, 125

Zunil, 182

SIGHTS & ATTRACTIONS

BELIZE

AMBERGRIS CAYE

Bottom-Time Dive Shop, 279
The Coral Beach Dive Club, 279
Hol Chan Marine Reserve, 279–80

BELIZE CITY

Altun Ha Ruins, 277

BELMOPAN

Archeology Department, 291–2
Belize Zoo, 292
The Blue Hole, 292
Guanacaste Park, 292
St. Herman's Cave, 292

CAULKER, CAYE

Belize Diving Services, 286
Galeria Hicaco, 286
Sea-ing is Belizing, 286
Sports and recreational activities, 286

COROZAL TOWN & THE NORTHERN HIGHWAY

Cerros (Cerro Maya), 305
Chetumal, Bay of, 305
Pyramid, 306
Santa Rita, 306

PLACENCIA

The Cockscomb Basin Wildlife Sanctuary, 297–8
Placencia Dive Shop, 295

SAN IGNACIO & THE CAYO DISTRICT

Boat trips, 299
Caracol, 304
Ix Chel Farm, 303
Mountain Equestrian Trails, 299
Mountain Pine Ridge, 303–4
The Panti Mayan Medicine Trail, 303

COSTA RICA

CARIBBEAN COAST

Cahuita National Park, 103
Kékoldi Indian Reservation, near Puerto Viejo, 110
Manzanillo-Gandoca Wildlife Refuge, near Puerto Viejo, 111
Tortuguero National Park, 101

GUANACASTE & THE NORTHWEST

Arenal Volcano, 67
Brasilito, Playa, 75
Flamingo, Playa, 74–7
Hermosa, Playa, 73
Hummingbird Gallery, 64
Lake Arenal, 67
Monteverde Cloud Forest Preserve, 23
Pan de Azucar, Playa, 75–6
Potrero, Playa, 75–7
Rincón de la Vieja National Park, 69
Santa Rosa National Park, 68–9
Irazú Volcano, 23, 58–9
Juan Santamaría Museum (Alajuela), 60
Jungle Train, 23, 61
Lankester Gardens (near Cartago), 58
Manzanillo, 110–11
Nuestra Señora de Los Angeles, Basilica de (Cartago), 58
Orosi Valley, 59

PACIFIC COAST

Caño Island Biological Reserve, 97
Carara Biological Reserve (Jacó Beach), 86
Corcovado National Park, 97
Guayabo, Negritos, and Pájaros Islands Biological Reserve, 82
Manuel Antonio National Park, 23, 90, 91
Poás Volcano, 23, 59–60
Punta Uva, 110

SAN JOSÉ AND ENVIRONS

Arte Costarricense, Museo de, 50, 52
Jade Marco Fidel Tristan, Museo de, 50
Nacional de Costa Rica, Museo, 49–50
Oro Banco Central, Museo de, 50
Parque Zoológico Simón Bolívar, 52
San José National Theater, 23
Serpentarium, 52

GUATEMALA

ATLANTIC HIGHWAY, THE

Boat trips and cruises (Río Dulce and Lake Izabal), 238–9

Castillo de San Felipe (Río Dulce and Lake Izabal), 238
Lanquín Caves, 229–30
Mayan ruins (Copán, Honduras), 232

GUATEMALA CITY

Arqueología Y Etnología, Museo de, 160
Artes e Industrias Populares, Museo de, 163
Capilla Yurrita, 162–3
Catedral Metropolitana, 162
Centro Cívico, 163, 165
Historia, Museo de, 163
Ixchel de Traje Indígena, Museo, 161
Kaminal Juyú, Ruins of, 162
Mapa en Relieve, 161–2
Nacional de Arte Moderna, Museo, 163
Palacio Nacional, 161
Popol Vuh, Edificio Galeria Reforma, Museo, 160–1

HIGHLANDS

Agua volcano (near Antigua), 209
Capuchinas, Convent of the (Antigua), 200
Cofradias (Chichicastenango), 184
Holy Week (Antigua), 201
Iximche, 196

Lake Atitlán, 187
market (Antigua), 201
Mercado La Democracia (Quetzaltenango), 176–7
Our Lady of Mercy, Convent and Church of (Antigua), 200
Pacaya volcano (near Antigua), 209–10
Palacio de Gobierno (Antigua), 198
Regional, Museo (Chichicastenango), 184
ruins of Zaculeu (near Huehuetenango), 173
San Francisco, Church of (Antigua), 200
Santiago, Museo de (Antigua), 198
Teatro Municipal (Quetzaltenango), 176
University of San Carlos (Antigua), 198, 200

PACIFIC HIGHWAY, THE

La Democracia Museum (La Democracia), 246

TIKAL & ENVIRONS

El Ceibal and other more remote ruins, 224
Great Plaza, 221–2
Museum at Tikal, 222
Ruins at Tikal, 220–1
Uaxactún, 223–4

ACCOMMODATIONS

BELIZE

AMBERGRIS CAYE

Barrier Reef Hotel (*), 281–2
Fido Badillo, 282
Lily's, 281
Martha's, 281
Milo's, 280
Rubie's Hotel, 280–1
San Pedrano, Hotel, 281
S&L Travel Service, Belize City, 282
Tomas Hotel, 281

BELIZE CITY

Belize Guest House (*), 274–5
El Centro, Hotel, 275–6
Fort Street Guest Restaurant & Guesthouse (*), 275
Maruba Resort, Maskall Village (*), 277–8
Mom's Triangle Inn, 275
Mopan, Hotel, 275
Seaside Guest House ($), 274

BELMOPAN

Banana Bank Ranch (*), 293
Bull Frog Inn, 293
Circle A Hotel, 293
Monkey Bay Wildlife Sanctuary (CG), 293

CAULKER, CAYE

The Anchorage, 287
Ignacio's Beach Cabañas ($), 287
Jimenez's Huts (*), 286–7
Rainbow Hotel, 288
Reef Hotel ($), 287–8
Tom's Hotel, 287
Tropical Paradise Hotel, Restaurant, and Ice Cream Parlour (*), 287

COROZAL TOWN & THE NORTHERN HIGHWAY

Barons, Hotel, Orange Walk, 306–7
Caribbean Motel, Corozal Town (*), 306
Maya, Hotel, Corozal Town ($), 306
Nestor's Hotel, Corozal Town ($), 306
Tony's Motel, Corozal Town, 306–7

PLACENCIA

Paradise Vacation Hotel ($), 295
Ranguana Lodge (*), 296
Seaspray, 295
Sonny's Resort, 295–6

SAN IGNACIO & THE CAYO DISTRICT

Chaa Creek Cottages, San Ignacio (S/JL), (S)(J), 301
Cosmos Camping (CG), 300
Duplooy's, San Ignacio (S/JL*), 301–2
El Indio Perdido, Benque Viejo del Carmen (S/JL), 302
Hi-Et, San Ignacio, 299
Las Casitas, San Ignacio (S/JL$), 300
Maya Mountain Lodge, San Ignacio (S/JL), 301
Nabitunich, Benque Viejo (S/JL*), 300–1
San Ignacio, Hotel, San Ignacio, 299–300
Venus Hotel, San Ignacio ($), 299
Windy Hill Cottages, San Ignacio (S/JL), 301

COSTA RICA

CARIBBEAN COAST

Acon, Hotel, Limón ($), 99–100
Cabinas Atlantida, Cahuita, 105
Cabinas Black Beach, Cahuita (*), 105
Cabinas Black Sands, Puerto Viejo (*), 108–9
Cabinas Chimuri, Puerto Viejo (*), 109
Cabinas Cocori, Limón, 100
Cabinas Jacaranda, Puerto Viejo ($), 109
Cabinas Palmer, Cahuita ($), 104
Cabinas Playa Negra, Puerto Viejo, 109
Cabinas Sol Y Mar, Cahuita ($), 104–5
Cabinas Vaz, Cahuita, 104
Cahuita, Hotel, Cahuita, 103–4
Chalet Hibiscus, Cahuita (*), 105
El Pizote, Puerto Viejo (S*), 109–10
Ilan-Ilan, Hotel, Limón, 101
Jungla Lodge, Limón, 101
Las Olas, Hotel, Limón ($), 100
Maritza, Hotel, Puerto Viejo, 108
Matama, Hotel, Limón (*), 100
Park Hotel, Limón, 99
Puerto Viejo, Hotel, Puerto Viejo, 108
Rio Colorado Lodge, Limón, 102
Surf Side Cabins, Cahuita, 104
Tortuga Lodge, Limón, 101–2

GUANACASTE & THE NORTHWEST

Bahia Flamingo Beach Resort, Playa Flamingo, 76–7
Belmar, Hotel, Monteverde (*), 66–7
Bramadero, Hotel, Liberia, 69
Cabinas Chale, Playa del Coco ($), 72
Cabinas El Coco, Playa del Coco, 71
Cabinas El Sueño, Tilarán, 68

KEY TO ABBREVIATIONS: CG = Camping; JL = Jungle Lodge; S = Splurge; * = Author's Favorite; $ = Super-Special Value

Cabinas Luna Tica, Playa del Coco, 71–2
Cabinas Playa Hermosa, Playa Hermosa (*), 73–4
Cabinas Zully Mar, Playa Tamarindo ($), 79
Costa Alegre, Playa Hermosa, 74
Doly, Pension, Playa Tamarindo, 78
El Iman, Santa Elena, 66
El Quetzal, Pensión, Monteverde (*), 65
El Sitio, Hotel, Liberia (*), 69
Finca Cristina, Playa Potrero ($), 76
Flor Mar, Pensión, 65
Fonda Vela, Hotel, Monteverde ($), 65–6
Heliconia, Hotel, Monteverde, 66
La Flor de Itabo, Hotel Resort, Playa del Coco (S*), 72
Las Espuelas, Hotel, Liberia, 70
La Siesta, Hotel, Liberia ($), 69
Los Corales, Playa Hermosa, 74
Montaña Monteverde, Hotel de, Monteverde (S), 66
Monteverde Inn, Pensión, Monteverde ($), 64–5
New Hotel Boyeros, Liberia, 69–70
Pozo Azul, Hotel, Playa Tamarindo, 79
Sugar Beach, Hotel, Playa Pan de Azucar (*), 76
Tamarindo Diriá, Hotel, Playa Tamarindo (*), 79
Tucan, Hotel, Santa Elena, 66

PACIFIC COAST

Apartamentos El Mar, Jacó Beach, 88
Apartotel El Colibri, Quepos (*), 94–5
Apartotel Gaviotas, Jacó Beach (S*), 87–8
Ayi Con, Hotel, Puntarenas, 83
Cabinas Alice, Jacó Beach ($), 86–7
Cabinas El Bohio, Jacó Beach, 86
Cabinas Espadilla, near Manuel Antonio, 93–4
Cabinas Las Palmas, Jacó Beach, 86
Cabinas Los Almendros, near Manuel Antonio ($), 93
Cabinas Manuel Antonio, near Manuel Antonio, 92
Cabinas Pedro Miguel, near Manuel Antonio, 92
Cabinas Vela-Bar, near Manuel Antonio, 93
Ceciliano, Hotel, Quepos ($), 91
Club-Hotel Colonial, Puntarenas ($), 84
Cocal, Hotel, Jacó Beach, 87
Costa Verde, Quepos ($), 94
Delfin, Hotel, Playa Esterillos, 88
Divisamar, Hotel, Quepos, 95
El Hicaco, Jacó Beach (CG), 87
Imperial, Hotel, Puntarenas, 83
Karahé, Quepos, 95
La Quinta, Quepos, 94
Las Brisas, Hotel, Puntarenas ($), 84
Madrigal, Jacó Beach (CG), 87
Malinche, Hotel, Quepos, 91–2
Manuel Antonio, Hotel, near Manuel Antonio ($), 92

Plinio, Hotel, between Quepos and Manuel Antonio (*), 93
Porto Bello, Hotel, Puntarenas, 84
Quepos, Hotel, Quepos ($), 92
Ramirez, Cabinas, near Manuel Antonio, 92–3
Tangerí Chalet, Jacó Beach (*), 86
Tioga, Hotel, Puntarenas (*), 83–4
Zabamar, Hotel, Jacó Beach, 87

SAN JOSÉ

Alameda, Hotel, 40
American, Pensión, 38
Amstel, Hotel (S$), 42–3
Bella Vista, Hotel, 38
Cacts, Hotel (*), 39
Castilla, Apartotel ($), 41–2
Costa Rica Inn, Pensión, 39–40
Diplomat, Hotel ($), 40–1
Don Carlos, Hotel (*), 42
Dunn Inn, Hotel, 43
Fortuna, Hotel, 40
Johnson, Hotel ($), 38–9
Petit Hotel ($), 39
Plaza, Hotel (*), 41
Ritz, Hotel (*), 39
San José, Apartotel, 42
Santo Tomas, Hotel, 43–4
Talamanca, Hotel, 40
Toruma Youth Hostel ($), 41

GUATEMALA

THE ATLANTIC HIGHWAY

Caribe, Hotel, Livingston, 241–2
Cobán Imperial, Hotel, 227
Cristo Negro, Hotel Posada del, Esquipulas, 234
Doña María, Hotel, Quiriguá, 237
Don Humberto, Hotel, Río Dulce, 239
El Atlántico, Hotel, Santa Cruz Río Hondo, 230–1
El Gran Chorti, Hotel (*), 235
El Reformador, Hotel, Puerto Barrios ($), 241
Henry Berrisford, Hotel, Puerto Barrios, 241
Hospedaje El Ranchito del Quetzal, Baja Verapaz, 229
Izabal Tropical, Hotel, Lake Izabal ($), 239
La Posada, Hotel (*), 227
Longarone, Motel, Río Hondo (*), 231
Los Angeles, Hotel, Esquipulas ($), 234
Mansión Armenia, Hotel, 227
Montaña del Quetzal, Posada, Baja Verapaz (*), 229
Montecristo, Hotel, Esquipulas, 234
Norte, Hotel del, Puerto Barrios (*), 241
Nuevo Pasabien, Hotel, Santa Cruz Teculután, 230

Payaqui, Hotel, Esquipulas, 234–5
Rabin Ajua, Hotel, 227–8
Río Dulce, Hotel, Lívingston ($), 242
Royal, Hotel, Quiriguá, 237
Santa Monica, Hotel ($), 237
Tucan Dugu, Hotel, Lívingston (*), 242

GUATEMALA CITY

Centenario, Hotel, 154
Centro, Hotel del ($), 155
Chalet Suizo (*), 153
Colonial, Hotel ($), 154
Guatemala International, Hotel, 154
Hernani, Hotel, 153
Hogar Del Turista, 153
Lessing House, Hotel ($), 153
Pan American, Hotel (*), 156
Plaza, Hotel ($/$), 155–6
Posada Belen (*), 154–5
Ritz Continental, Hotel, 156
Spring Hotel, 153
Suites Cordoba, 154
Villa Española, Hotel, 155

HIGHLANDS

Antigua, Hotel, Antigua (S), 204
Apartamentos Bugambilila, Antigua ($), 202
Atitlán, Hotel, Panajachel (S), 191–2
Aurora, Hotel, Antigua (*), 203
Auto Hotel Vasquez, Huehuetenango, 173–4
Cacique Inn, Panajachel (S), 191
Campo, Hotel del, Quetzaltenango, 178
Capri, Hotel, Quetzaltenango, 179
Casa de Santa Lucia, Antigua ($), 202
Casa Kaehler, Quetzaltenango ($), 178–9
Casa Suiza, Quetzaltenango, 177
Centroamericana Inn, Hotel, Quetzaltenango, 178
Chi-Nim-Ya, Hotel, Santiago Atitlán, 195–6
"El Descanso," Hotel, Antigua, 202
El Rosario Lodge, Antigua, 201–2
Fonda Del Sol, Hotel, Panajachel, 188
Galindo, Hotel, Panajachel ($), 189
Gran Hotel Americano, Quetzaltenango ($), 177–8
Hospedaje Cabana Country Club, Panajachel ($), 191
Hospedaje Santa Elena Annexo, Panajachel, 191
Kiktem-Ja, Hotel, Quetzaltenango (*), 177
Lago, Hotel Del, Panajachel, 192
Mary, Hotel, Huehuetenango ($), 174
Maya Kanek, Hotel, Panajachel, 188

Maya Lodge, Chichicastenango, 184–5
Mayan Inn, Chichicastenango (*), 185–6
Maya Palace, Hotel, Panajachel ($), 189
Modelo, Hotel, Quetzaltenango (*), 178
Monterrey, Hotel, Panajachel, 189
Pensión Bonifaz, Hotel, Quetzaltenango (*), 179
Pensión Chuguilá, Chichicastenango (*), 184
Pensión El Arco, Antigua, 203
Pensión Rosita, Santiago Atitlán, 195
Pino Montano, Hotel, Huehuetenango, 174
Placido, Hotel, Antigua, 203–4
Playa Linda, Hotel, Panajachel (*), 189–90
Posada de Don Rodrigo, Hotel, Antigua (S*), 204
Posada San Sebastián, Antigua ($), 203
Primavera, Hotel, Panajachel (*), 189
Ramada Antigua, Antigua (S), 204–5
Rancho Grande Inn, Panajachel (*), 190
Regis, Hotel, Panajachel (*), 190
Río Azul, Hotel, Quetzaltenango ($), 177
Santo Tomas, Hotel, Chichicastenango, 185
Sol-Mor, Hotel, Antigua (*), 202–3
Tzanjuyu, Hotel, Panajachel, 190
Vision Azul, Hotel, Panajachel (S*), 191
Zaculeu, Hotel, Huehuetenango (*), 174

THE PACIFIC HIGHWAY

Astor, Hotel, Retalhuleu ($), 244–5
"La Colonia," Hotel, Retalhuleu (*), 244
Modelo, Hotel, Retalhuleu, 245
Posada de Don Jose, Retalhuleu (*), 245
Siboney, Hotel, Retalhuleu, 244

EL PETÉN

Costa Del Sol, Santa Elena ($), 215
El Gringo Perdido, near Flores (*), 217
Maya Internacional, Hotel, Santa Elena (*), 215–6
Monja Blanca, Hotel, Santa Elena, 214
Patio-Tikal, Hotel del, Santa Elena (S*), 216
Petén, Hotel, Flores, 215
Posada El Tucan, Flores ($), 214
San Juan, Hotel, Santa Elena, 214
Savanna Hotel, Flores ($), 216
Tziquinaha, Hotel, Santa Elena (S), 216–17
Yum Kax, Hotel, Flores, 215

TIKAL

camping, 223
Jaguar Inn, 222
Jungle Lodge, 222
Tikal Inn, Hotel (*), 222–3

RESTAURANTS

BELIZE

AMBERGRIS CAYE

Coco Palms Restaurant ($; seafood/Mexican), 284
Elvi's Kitchen (*; seafood/international), 283
Lily's (seafood), 283
Marino's (seafood/Belizean), 283
Navigator (seafood/pizza), 283
The Pizza Place (pizza), 282–3
Tai-Pei Chinese Restaurant (Chinese), 282

BELIZE CITY

Dit's (cakes), 276
Macy's (*; Belizean), 276
Mom's (American/Mexican/Creole), 276
The Pizza House (pizza), 276

BELMOPAN

Banana Bank Ranch (barbecued pork spare ribs), 293
Circle A Hotel (Chinese), 293

CAULKER, CAYE

Aberdeen Restaurant (Chinese), 288
Cabanas Bar & Restaurant (*; seafood/Chinese), 288–9
Marin's Restaurant (international), 289
Martinez's Restaurant and Bar, Hotel ($; seafood/Mexican), 289
Tropical Paradise Hotel Restaurant and Ice Cream Parlour (international), 289

COROZAL TOWN & THE NORTHERN HIGHWAY

Caribbean Motel (salads/burgers), 306
Maya, Hotel, 306

PLACENCIA

The Galley ($; Belizean), 296
Jene's Restaurant (Belizean/international), 296–7
Kingfisher Restaurant (Belizean/seafood), 296
Tentacles (*; seafood), 297

SAN IGNACIO & THE CAYO DISTRICT

Eva's Restaurant & Bar (Belizean/international), 302
Maxim's Chinese Restaurant (Chinese), 302
Serendib Restaurant (*; Sri Lankan), 302–3

COSTA RICA

CARIBBEAN COAST

Cahuita National Park, Restaurant, Cahuita (seafood), 106
Edith, Restaurant, Cahuita ($; varied menu), 106
Soda Tamara, Puerto Viego (Costa Rican), 110
Tipico Cahuita, Restaurante, Cahuita (*; Costa Rican), 105–6
Vaz, Restaurant, Cahuita (local specialties), 106

GUANACASTE & THE NORTHWEST

Aqua Sport (Costa Rican), 74
El Bosque, Restaurant (Costa Rican), 67
El Oasis, Restaurant-Bar, Playa del Coco (Costa Rican), 72
El Sapo Dorado (Costa Rican), 67
El Tercer Mundo, Restaurant, Playa Tamarindo ($; Costa Rican), 80
Fiesta Del Mar, Playa Tamarindo (steak/seafood), 80
Guajira, Restaurant, Playa del Coco (Costa Rican), 72–3
Las Perlas, Restaurant, Playa Potrero (American), 77
Marie's, Playa Flamingo (*; sandwiches/lunch/Costa Rican), 77
Panaderia Johan, Playa Tamarindo (picnic fare), 80
Pókopí, Restaurante, Liberia (*; Continental/pizza), 70
Supermercado, Playa Tamarindo (picnic fare), 80

IRAZU VOLCANO

Linda Vista, Restaurant (Costa Rican), 59

PACIFIC COAST

Barba Roja, Quepos-Manuel Antonio Road (seafood/chicken/breakfast/sandwiches), 96
Club-Hotel Colonial, Puntarenas (seafood/live music), 84
El Bosque, Jacó Beach (international), 89
Isabel, Restaurant, Quepos (sandwiches/steak/breakfast), 95

KEY TO SYMBOLS: * = Author's Favorite; $ = Super-Special Value

Mariquería Los Manudos, Restaurant, Jacó Beach (international), 88–9
Mar Y Sombra, Restaurant, Quepos ($; seafood/Costa Rican), 96
Porto Bello, Puntarenas (steak), 84

SAN JOSÉ

Amstel Grill Room ($; international), 46–7
Café de Teatro Nacional (*; international), 45
Café Parisienne (*; international), 46
Campesino, Restaurante (*; Costa Rican), 44–5
Churreria Manolo (Costa Rica), 44
El Balcon de Europa (Continental), 48
Hardee's (fast food), 47
Kentucky Fried Chicken (fast food), 47
La Casa de Sandwich (sandwiches), 44
La Cocina de Leña (Costa Rican), 46
La Esmeralda (Costa Rican), 45–6
La Perla (international), 44
McDonald's (fast food), 47
Nutrisoda (vegetarian), 45
Pizza Hut (fast food), 47
Soda La Casita ($; Costa Rican), 45

GUATEMALA

THE ATLANTIC HIGHWAY

Café El Tirol (coffee/sandwiches), 228
El Ganadero (steak/Guatemalan), 228
Henry Berrisford, Hotel, Puerto Barrios (Guatemalan/Caribbean/international), 241
Izabal Tropical, Hotel, Lake Izabal (international), 239
Motel Langarone, Río Hondo (Guatemalan/American), 231
Norte, Hotel del, Puerto Barrios (seafood), 241
Semuc Champey, 229–30

GUATEMALA CITY

Altuna, Restaurant (*; Spanish), 157–8
Bologna, Restaurant (Italian), 157
Café Bohemia (pastries), 159
Cafetería El Roble (Guatemalan), 158
El Gran Pavo (Mexican), 158
Long Wah, Restaurant (Chinese), 157
Los Antojitos (*; Guatemalan), 157
McDonald's (fast food), 158
Multirestaurantes (international), 159
Pollo Campero (chicken), 158–9
Ruby, Restaurant ($; Chinese), 157

HIGHLANDS

Al Chisme, Panajachel (international), 193–4
Café Café, Antigua (Guatemalan/international), 206
Café Flor, Antigua (Mexican), 206
Cafetería El Kopetin, Quetzaltenango (*; Guatemalan/international), 180
Casablanca, Panajachel (*; international), 194
Casa de Café Ana, Antigua (Guatemalan/international), 205
Doña Luisa, Restaurant, Antigua (international), 205
Dona María Gordillo Dulces Tipicos, Antigua (sweets), 207
Ebony Restaurant (Guatemalan/international), 174–5
El Gran Sol, Restaurant, Santiago Atitlán, 196
El Patio, Panajachel (*; international/Guatemalan), 193
El Sereno, Antigua (*; international), 208
El Torito, Restaurante, Chichicastenango (steak), 186
Fonda de la Calle Real, Antigua (*; Guatemalan/international), 206
Italiano "El Capuchino", Restaurant, Antigua (Italian), 206–7
Katok, Restaurant, Antigua (*; Guatemalan/international), 207
La Estrella, Antigua (Chinese), 205
La Hamburguesa Gigante, Panajachel (burgers/Guatemalan), 192–3
La Laguna Restaurant, Panajachel ($; Guatemalan/international), 193
La Posada del Pintor and the Circus Bar, Panajachel (international), 194
Le Cenioienta Pasteles, Antigua (pastries), 207–8
Mesón Panza Verde, Restaurant, Antigua (Continental), 208
Mistral, Antigua (*; Guatemalan/international), 205–6
Pasteleria Bombonier, Quetzaltenango (sandwiches), 179–80
Pizza Ricca, Quetzaltenango (pizza), 180–1
Pizzeria Italiana Martedino, Restaurante, Antigua (Italian), 206
Pollo Frito Albumar, Quetzaltenango (Guatemalan/international), 180
Posada de Don Rodrigo, Antigua ($; Guatemalan/international), 207
Ranchón Típica Atitlán, Panajachel ($; Guatemalan), 193
Shanghai, Restaurant, Quetzaltenango (Chinese), 180
Taberna de Don Rodrigo, Quetzaltenango (sandwiches), 180
Tocoyal, Panajachel (*; Guatemalan/international), 193

THE PACIFIC HIGHWAY

Astor, Hotel, Retalhuleu (Guatemalan/steak), 244–5
"La Colonia," Hotel, Retalhuleu (steak/seafood), 244

Siboney, Hotel, Retalhuleu (steak/seafood), 244

EL PETÉN

Gran Jaguar, Restaurant, Flores (*; Guatemalan/international), 218

La Jungla, Restaurant, Flores (Guatemalan/international), 218
La Mesa de Los Mayas, Restaurant, Flores (Guatemalan/international), 218
Ventanas Del Lago, Santa Elena, 217–18

NOW, SAVE MONEY ON ALL YOUR TRAVELS!
Join Frommer's™ Dollarwise® Travel Club

Saving money while traveling is never a simple matter, which is why the **Dollarwise Travel Club** was formed 31 years ago. Developed in response to requests from Frommer's Travel Guide readers, the Club provides cost-cutting travel strategies, up-to-date travel information, and a sense of community for value-conscious travelers from all over the world.

In keeping with the money-saving concept, the annual membership fee is low —$20 for U.S. residents or $25 for residents of Canada, Mexico, and other countries—and is immediately exceeded by the value of your benefits, which include:

1. Any TWO books listed on the following pages.
2. Plus any ONE Frommer's City Guide.
3. A subscription to our quarterly newspaper, *The Dollarwise Traveler*.
4. A membership card that entitles you to purchase through the Club all Frommer's publications for 33% to 40% off their retail price.

The eight-page *Dollarwise Traveler* tells you about the latest developments in good-value travel worldwide and includes the following columns: **Hospitality Exchange** (for those offering and seeking hospitality in cities all over the world); **Share-a-Trip** (for those looking for travel companions to share costs); and **Readers Ask . . . Readers Reply** (for those with travel questions that other members can answer).

Aside from the Frommer's Guides and the Gault Millau Guides, you can also choose from our Special Editions. These include such titles as *California with Kids* (a compendium of the best of California's accommodations, restaurants, and sightseeing attractions appropriate for those traveling with toddlers through teens); *Candy Apple: New York with Kids* (a spirited guide to the Big Apple by a savvy New York grandmother that's perfect for both visitors and residents); *Caribbean Hideaways* (the 100 most romantic places to stay in the Islands, all rated on ambience, food, sports opportunities, and price); *Honeymoon Destinations* (a guide to planning and choosing just the right destination from hundreds of possibilities in the U.S., Mexico, and the Caribbean); *Marilyn Wood's Wonderful Weekends* (a selection of the best mini-vacations within a 200-mile radius of New York City, including descriptions of country inns and other accommodations, restaurants, picnic spots, sights, and activities); and *Paris Rendez-Vous* (a delightful guide to the best places to meet in Paris whether for power breakfasts or dancing till dawn).

To join this Club, simply send the appropriate membership fee with your name and address to: Frommer's Dollarwise Travel Club, 15 Columbus Circle, New York, NY 10023. Remember to specify which single city guide and which two other guides you wish to receive in your initial package of member's benefits. Or tear out the next page, check off your choices, and send the page to us with your membership fee.

FROMMER BOOKS
PRENTICE HALL PRESS
15 COLUMBUS CIRCLE
NEW YORK, NY 10023
212/373-8125

Date_____

Friends: Please send me the books checked below.

FROMMER'S™ GUIDES

(Guides to sightseeing and tourist accommodations and facilities from budget to deluxe, with emphasis on the medium-priced.)

☐ Alaska $14.95
☐ Australia $14.95
☐ Austria & Hungary $14.95
☐ Belgium, Holland & Luxembourg $14.95
☐ Bermuda & The Bahamas. $14.95
☐ Brazil $14.95
☐ Canada $14.95
☐ Caribbean. $14.95
☐ Cruises (incl. Alaska, Carib, Mex, Hawaii, Panama, Canada & US) $14.95
☐ California & Las Vegas $14.95
☐ Egypt. $14.95
☐ England & Scotland $14.95
☐ Florida $14.95
☐ France $14.95
☐ Germany $14.95
☐ Italy. $14.95
☐ Japan & Hong Kong $14.95
☐ Mid-Atlantic States $14.95
☐ New England. $14.95
☐ New Mexico (avail. June '91) $12.95
☐ New York State $14.95
☐ Northwest $15.95
☐ Portugal, Madeira & the Azores $14.95
☐ Scandinavia (avail. May '91). $15.95
☐ South Pacific. $14.95
☐ Southeast Asia $14.95
☐ Southern Atlantic States $14.95
☐ Southwest $14.95
☐ Switzerland & Liechtenstein $14.95

☐ USA $16.95

FROMMER'S $-A-DAY® GUIDES

(In-depth guides to sightseeing and low-cost tourist accommodations and facilities.)

☐ Europe on $40 a Day $15.95
☐ Australia on $40 a Day $13.95
☐ Costa Rica; Guatemala & Belize on $35 a day (avail. Mar. '91). $15.95
☐ Eastern Europe on $25 a Day $15.95
☐ England on $50 a Day. $13.95
☐ Greece on $35 a Day $13.95
☐ Hawaii on $60 a Day. $14.95
☐ India on $25 a Day $12.95
☐ Ireland on $40 a Day. $14.95
☐ Israel on $40 a Day. $13.95
☐ Mexico on $35 a Day $14.95
☐ New York on $60 a Day. $13.95
☐ New Zealand on $45 a Day $13.95
☐ Scotland & Wales on $40 a Day $13.95
☐ South America on $40 a Day $15.95
☐ Spain on $50 a Day $15.95
☐ Turkey on $30 a Day. $13.95
☐ Washington, D.C. & Historic Va. on $40 a Day. $13.95

FROMMER'S TOURING GUIDES

(Color illustrated guides that include walking tours, cultural and historic sites, and other vital travel information.)

☐ Amsterdam. $10.95
☐ Australia $10.95
☐ Brazil. $10.95
☐ Egypt. $8.95
☐ Florence. $8.95
☐ Hong Kong $10.95
☐ London $10.95
☐ New York $10.95
☐ Paris $8.95
☐ Rome. $10.95
☐ Scotland. $9.95
☐ Thailand. $10.95
☐ Turkey $10.95
☐ Venice $8.95

(TURN PAGE FOR ADDITONAL BOOKS AND ORDER FORM)

1290

FROMMER'S CITY GUIDES

(Pocket-size guides to sightseeing and tourist accommodations and facilities in all price ranges.)

☐ Amsterdam/Holland	$8.95	☐ Minneapolis/St. Paul	$8.95
☐ Athens	$8.95	☐ Montréal/Québec City	$8.95
☐ Atlanta	$8.95	☐ New Orleans	$8.95
☐ Atlantic City/Cape May	$8.95	☐ New York	$8.95
☐ Barcelona	$7.95	☐ Orlando	$8.95
☐ Belgium	$7.95	☐ Paris	$8.95
☐ Berlin (avail. Mar '91)	$8.95	☐ Philadelphia	$8.95
☐ Boston	$8.95	☐ Rio	$8.95
☐ Cancún/Cozumel/Yucatán	$8.95	☐ Rome	$8.95
☐ Chicago	$8.95	☐ Salt Lake City	$8.95
☐ Denver/Boulder/Colorado Springs	$7.95	☐ San Diego	$8.95
☐ Dublin/Ireland	$8.95	☐ San Francisco	$8.95
☐ Hawaii	$8.95	☐ Santa Fe/Taos/Albuquerque	$8.95
☐ Hong Kong	$7.95	☐ Seattle/Portland	$7.95
☐ Las Vegas	$8.95	☐ St. Louis/Kansas City (avail. May '91)	$8.95
☐ Lisbon/Madrid/Costa del Sol	$8.95	☐ Sydney	$8.95
☐ London	$8.95	☐ Tampa/St. Petersburg	$8.95
☐ Los Angeles	$8.95	☐ Tokyo	$7.95
☐ Mexico City/Acapulco	$8.95	☐ Toronto	$8.95
☐ Miami	$8.95	☐ Vancouver/Victoria	$7.95

☐ Washington, D.C. $8.95

SPECIAL EDITIONS

☐ Beat the High Cost of Travel	$6.95	☐ Motorist's Phrase Book (Fr/Ger/Sp)	$4.95
☐ Bed & Breakfast—N. America	$14.95	☐ Paris Rendez-Vous	$10.95
☐ California with Kids	$15.95	☐ Swap and Go (Home Exchanging)	$10.95
☐ Caribbean Hideaways	$14.95	☐ The Candy Apple (NY with Kids)	$12.95
☐ Honeymoon Destinations (US, Mex &		☐ Travel Diary and Record Book	$5.95
Carib)	$14.95	☐ Where to Stay USA (From $3 to $30 a	
☐ Manhattan's Outdoor Sculpture	$15.95	night)	$13.95

☐ Marilyn Wood's Wonderful Weekends (CT, DE, MA, NH, NJ, NY, PA, RI, VT) $11.95
☐ The New World of Travel (Annual sourcebook by Arthur Frommer for savvy travelers) $16.95

GAULT MILLAU

(The only guides that distinguish the truly superlative from the merely overrated.)

☐ The Best of Chicago	$15.95	☐ The Best of Los Angeles	$16.95
☐ The Best of France	$16.95	☐ The Best of New England	$15.95
☐ The Best of Hawaii	$16.95	☐ The Best of New Orleans	$16.95
☐ The Best of Hong Kong	$16.95	☐ The Best of New York	$16.95
☐ The Best of Italy	$16.95	☐ The Best of Paris	$16.95
☐ The Best of London	$16.95	☐ The Best of San Francisco	$16.95

☐ The Best of Washington, D.C. $16.95

ORDER NOW!

In U.S. include $2 shipping UPS for 1st book; $1 ea. add'l book. Outside U.S. $3 and $1, respectively.
Allow four to six weeks for delivery in U.S., longer outside U.S.

Enclosed is my check or money order for $_____

NAME _____

ADDRESS _____

CITY _____ STATE _____ ZIP _____